Computer Fundamentals

Anita Goel
Fellow
Institute of Life Long Learning (ILLL)
University of Delhi

Pearson

Original edition, entitled Computer Fundamentals, 1/e by Goel, published by Pearson Education Ltd., Copyright © 2010.

Indian Subcontinent Reprint

ISBN 978-81-317-3309-7

First Impression,2010
Forty One Impression, 2025
Forty Two Impression, 2026

Published by Pearson India Education Services Pvt. Ltd, CIN: U72200TN2005PTC057128.

Head Office: 1st Floor, Berger Tower, Plot No. C-001A/2, Sector 16B, Noida - 201 301,Uttar Pradesh, India.
Registered Office: 6th Floor, Tower A, Unit A and B International Tech Park, CapitaLand Chennai, 200 Feet Radial Road, Zamin Pallavaram, Old Pallavaram Chennai – 600117, Tamil Nadu, India
Website: in.pearson.com; Email: companysecretary.india@pearson.com

Printed in India by Pushp Print Services

Dedication

To My Parents

Urmila and Amar Chand

BRIEF CONTENTS

CONTENTS

PREFACE

Computers play a key role in our everyday lives. In addition to communication media like television, radio and newspaper, we now have another communication medium, i.e. computers. We use computers to e-mail, to chat, for the Internet browsing, for teleconferencing, for video conferencing, etc. We also use them for e-learning, e-commerce, e-banking, e-governance, e-ticketing and for many more things. And the interesting part is, while we interact with the other media like television, radio, newspaper, etc. to merely get information, the interaction in computers is two ways—we can be a creator as well as a user. We may use a computer as a medium to get more information, as a tool to perform certain activities, or as an integral part of another component.

The fundamentals of computer are the stepping stones to computer science. Nowadays, all courses, related and unrelated to computer science, require using a computer. Knowledge of the basics of computers has become a fundamental requirement, in whatever area we choose to study or follow professionally. Computer fundamentals are also an introductory course to a more advanced study of computer science.

ABOUT THE BOOK

This book is written with the aim of introducing the fundamentals of computers to the reader. Attention has been paid to include chapters that are required by the students studying different courses. The book deals with both the theoretical concepts and the practicals. The unique features of this book are as follows:

- ***Style of Writing***
  - The *language used* in the book is lucid, is easy to understand, and facilitates easy grasping of concepts.
  - The chapters have been *logically arranged* in sequence.
  - The book is written in a *reader-friendly* manner both for the students and the teachers.
  - Most of the content presented in the book is in the form of bullets, organized sequentially. This form of presentation, rather than in a paragraph form, facilitates the reader to view, understand and remember the points better.
  - The explanation is *supported by diagrams, pictures and images* wherever required.
  - Sufficient *exercises* have been included for practice in addition to the *solved examples.*
  - The questions at the end of the chapter are given section-wise. It is easier for the reader to find answers for the *section-wise questions* in a particular section rather than the whole chapter.
- ***Content of Book—Theory (Chapters 1–14)***
  - Several *latest topics* have been included in the book. Some of these topics are
    - USB, Zip disk, Flash memory
    - Wireless networking
    - Notebook, Netbook, PDA, smartphones
    - Aspect Oriented Programming (AOP)
    - Imparting education via multimedia
    - Cryptography, Digital signature, Firewall, Biometrics
    - System clock, BIOS, CMOS, SIMM & DIMM memory module
  - In the theory chapters (Chapters 1–14), the *theory is supported with the practical information* like, the name of supercomputer of India, how to create mp3 file from CD, what is a streaming video and understanding machine configuration.

- This book *does not discuss in detail the old technologies* that have become too common or are no longer used, like, about keys in a keyboard, magnetic tape, using mouse, drum printers and message switching.
- Several *colored inserts* in the book provide a colored view of the photographs.

⊙ ***Content of Book—Practical (Chapters 15–21) and Appendix***

- This book describes *MS-Office* with the latest commercially available version, version *2007*.
- This book includes description of *Windows Vista and Windows 7* in addition to the detailed description of Windows XP.
- The *solved examples* in the MS-Office chapters are described *step-wise*.
- A *long list of practical exercises* is provided at the end of each chapter.
- Some *chapters* are new to a book on computer fundamentals. These chapters are
  - Chapter 11—Information Systems
  - Chapter 12—Fundamentals of Database
  - Chapter 14—Computer Security
  - Chapter 19—MS-Access
  - Chapter 20—Network and Internet Connections
  - Chapter 21—Using LaTeX
  - Appendix D—Assembling a PC.

TARGET AUDIENCE

This book has been written keeping in mind the readers familiar and not-so familiar with computers. Several chapters have been included that cover the syllabi of different universities in India. The book is well suited for the following target audience:

⊙ *Computer science students* undergoing a course in computer science—DCA, MCA, BSc(Gen), BSc(Hons), MSc(IT), BSc(IT), BCA, DOEACC level courses.

⊙ *Engineering students* of first year—BTech, BE.

⊙ *Science students* pursuing BSc in physics, chemistry, botany, zoology and mathematics.

⊙ *Non-science students* pursuing BCom(P), BCom(Hons), BA(P), BDP, BBA, MBA, BBE

⊙ *Students enrolled in short-term courses* on *IT* in polytechnics, training institutes, Technical Institutes.

⊙ *Any learner* interested in computer science.

STRUCTURE OF THE TEXT

The book follows a structured and modular design, to facilitate the instructor in the teaching of the course and the students in the reading of the book. Figure 1 shows the design of the book. The following paragraphs present a brief review of the four units of the book.

Unit I comprises *five* chapters. This unit *introduces the reader to the computer as a machine.* Chapter 1 provides a brief introduction to computers—their evolution, types and applications. Chapter 2 discusses organization of the computer, different parts inside a computer case and their interaction. Chapter 3 provides an overview of the memory hierarchy, different kinds of memory of the computer and storage devices that are required for storing large quantities of data. The different devices that are used for providing input to the computer, and the presentation of output from the computer are discussed in Chapter 4. The computer uses the binary number system; Chapter 5 discusses binary coding schemes, logic gates, and the representation and conversion of numbers in the binary, octal and hexadecimal number system.

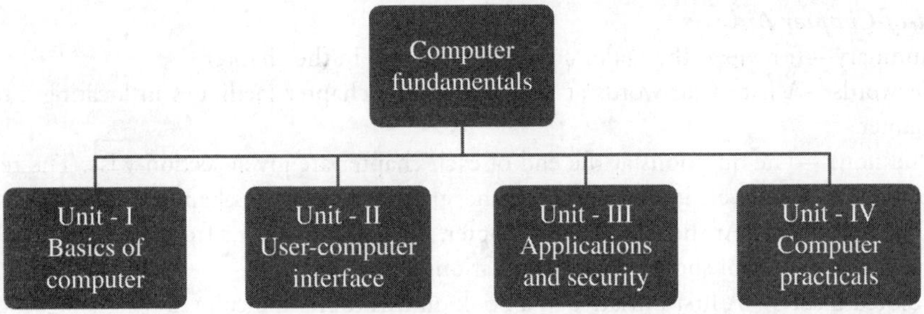

Figure 1 Modular structure of text

Unit II comprises *five* chapters. This unit *focusses on the interaction of user and computer, and the Internet.* Chapter 6 provides a description of the system software and the application software. Chapter 7 describes the operating system in detail. The writing of the programming logic and the different programming paradigms are discussed in Chapter 8. Chapters 9 and 10 relate to networking and the Internet. Chapter 9 discusses computer networks and the communication of data across the network. The Internet and its services are detailed in Chapter 10.

Unit III contains *four* chapters. This unit is *about applications and security.* Chapter 11 describes the information systems. This chapter is included bearing in mind the non-science courses. For teaching this paper in a science course, you may skip this chapter. The fundamentals of databases are discussed in Chapter 12. Chapter 13 describes the different elements of the multimedia system—text, audio, graphics, video and animation. Chapter 14 on computer security discusses the security attacks, and the way to handle them.

Unit IV consists of *seven* chapters. This unit is *designed for the computer practicals.* A detailed discussion on Windows XP is provided in Chapter 15, including a brief description about Windows Vista and Windows 7. Chapters 16 through 19 are about the four main components of MS-Office 2007, i.e. MS-Word, MS-Excel, MS-Powerpoint and MS-Access. Chapter 20 is about Network and the Internet connections. This chapter facilitates the reader in the creation and managing of computer network and the Internet connection. Chapter 21 is about using LaTeX which is used for the production of publication-quality typeset documents.

PEDAGOGICAL FEATURES

Pedagogy is the art and science of how something is taught and how students learn it. How the teaching occurs, the approach to teaching and learning, the way the content is delivered and what the students learn as a result of the process are all included in pedagogy. The following are the pedagogical features of this book:

- ***Start-of-Chapter Aids***
  - Contents—An overall view of the topics discussed in the chapter is provided, at the beginning of each chapter.
  - Why this chapter—It describes the need of including this chapter in computer fundamentals and why one should read it.
- ***In-Between Chapter Aids***
  - Visualization—"A picture is worth a thousand words" is a famous quote. This book supports the concepts with figures, diagrams and images to facilitate visualization.
  - Bulleted text—The book follows a bulleted approach of writing the text in contrast to the long paragraphs. The bulleted text approach is easier to read, understand and grasp.

⊙ ***End-of-Chapter Aids***

- Summary—It reviews the major concepts discussed in the chapter.
- Keywords—A list of keywords at the end of each chapter facilitates in locating a topic in the chapter.
- Questions—The questions at the end of each chapter are given section-wise. The reader has to search for the answers in this section, rather than the complete chapter.
- Extra questions—At the end of each chapter, the extra questions from the complete chapter are given in the form of short notes, abbreviations and differences.
- Colored inserts—A first initiative in a book on this topic, the colored inserts provide the reader with actual images in colour.

FEEDBACK

For interacting with the author, or for suggestions and comments on this book, please send your e-mails at goel.anita.book@gmail.com.

Acknowledgements

It took me almost 2 years to write this book. During my journey of book writing, I have been helped and supported by my family, friends and colleagues. I express my gratitude to one and all for their extensive support in this endeavour.

I am grateful to Dr. S. C. Gupta, Prof. S. K. Wasan and Dr. Mukul Sinha for encouraging me to write a book. I thank them for their valuable advice and for their encouragement to disseminate information. I also thank them for continually inspiring me to write a good book.

I thank Mr Neeraj Saxena, Ms Renu Saxena and Mr Rajendra for their extensive help in clicking the photographs in this book.

My special thanks go to all my students, Amit Jain in particular, who have always been eager to inform me about the expectations of the students about the book. Their suggestions and feedback have helped me to write the book in a student-friendly manner.

Thanks to Mr Sachin Saxena and the team of Pearson Education for their extensive support. The book in its present form is a result of the long discussions and the brainstorming sessions with Sachin. I am grateful to Sachin for his ideas, suggestions and excellent support provided to me during the writing of this book.

I express my regards and love to my mother Urmila, and my father Amar Chand. Being their child makes me feel special, and I thank them both for guiding me through life. Through this book, I carry forward the legacy of book writing from my maternal grandfather late Mr C. S. Jain. I express my respect and thanks to my father-in-law Gopal Krishan for his motivation and cooperation, and for taking care of matters while I was busy writing the book. My thanks are due, in memory of my mother-in-law Pushpa who has always loved and supported me.

Thanks to my loving husband, Ajay, for standing by me in the difficult times during the course of writing this book. He is a bagful of innovative ideas and has contributed creatively to the writing of this book. My special thanks to my lovely and beautiul children, Anirudh and Ashima, who brilliantly contributed towards the creation and editing of this book. They are my greatest source of inspiration and motivation.

Since this is not the first book on this topic, I thank the authors of other books on similar topic, whose books have been a source of ideas for me.

I thank the Almighty without whose grace it would have been impossible for me to accomplish this task.

Unit I BASICS OF COMPUTER

INTRODUCTION TO COMPUTER

1

Contents

- Digital and analog computers
- Characteristics of computer—Speed, accuracy, diligence, storage capability, versatility
- History of computer—Calculating machines, Napier's bones, slide rule, Pascal's adding and subtraction machine, Leibniz's multiplication and dividing machine, punch card system, Babbage's analytical engine, Hollerith's punched card tabulating machine
- Generations of computer
  - First generation (1940 to 1956): Using vacuum tubes
  - Second generation (1956 to 1963): Using transistors
  - Third generation (1964 to 1971): Using integrated circuits
  - Fourth generation (1971 to present): Using microprocessors
  - Fifth generation (present and next): Using artificial intelligence
- Classification of computer—Microcomputers (desktop computer or Personal Computer (PC), notebook computers or laptop, netbook, tablet computer, handheld computer or Personal Digital Assistant (PDA), smart phones), minicomputers, mainframe computers, supercomputers
- The computer system—Hardware, software, data, users
- The Input-process-output concept
- Components of computer hardware—Input/output unit, central processing unit, storage unit
- Application of computers—Education, entertainment, sports, advertising, medicine, science and engineering, government, home

Why this chapter

Computers are an integral part of our lives. Wherever we are—sitting in our homes, working in the office, driving on roads, sitting in a movie hall, staying in a hotel, etc.—our lives are directly or indirectly affected by the computers. In this era of information, we are dependent on the storage, flow and processing of data and information, which can only be possible with the help of computers. The purpose of this chapter is to introduce you to the "computer".

1.1 INTRODUCTION

Nowadays, computers are an integral part of our lives. They are used for the reservation of tickets for airplanes and railways, payment of telephone and electricity bills, deposit and withdrawal of money from banks, processing of business data, forecasting of weather conditions, diagnosis of diseases, searching for information on the Internet, etc. Computers are also used extensively in schools, universities, organizations, music industry, movie industry, scientific research, law firms, fashion industry, etc.

The term computer is derived from the word *compute*. The word *compute* means *to calculate*. A *computer* is an electronic machine that accepts data from the user, processes the data by performing calculations and operations on it, and generates the desired output results. Computer performs both simple and complex operations, with speed and accuracy.

This chapter discusses the history and evolution of computer, the concept of input-process-output and the characteristics of computer. This chapter also discusses the classification of digital computers based on their size and type, and the application of computer in different domain areas.

1.2 DIGITAL AND ANALOG COMPUTERS

A *digital computer* uses distinct values to represent the data internally. All information are represented using the digits 0s and 1s. The computers that we use at our homes and offices are digital computers.

Analog computer is another kind of a computer that represents data as variable across a continuous range of values. The earliest computers were analog computers. Analog computers are used for measuring of parameters that vary continuously in real time, such as temperature, pressure and voltage. Analog computers may be more flexible but generally less precise than digital computers. Slide rule is an example of an analog computer.

This book deals only with the *digital computer* and uses the term *computer* for them.

1.3 CHARACTERISTICS OF COMPUTER

Speed, accuracy, diligence, storage capability and versatility are some of the key characteristics of a computer. A brief overview of these characteristics are—

- ***Speed*** The computer can process data very fast, at the rate of millions of instructions per second. Some calculations that would have taken hours and days to complete otherwise, can be completed in a few seconds using the computer. For example, calculation and generation of salary slips of thousands of employees of an organization, weather forecasting that requires analysis of a large amount of data related to temperature, pressure and humidity of various places, etc.
- ***Accuracy*** Computer provides a high degree of accuracy. For example, the computer can accurately give the result of division of any two numbers up to 10 decimal places.
- ***Diligence*** When used for a longer period of time, the computer does not get tired or fatigued. It can perform long and complex calculations with the same speed and accuracy from the start till the end.
- ***Storage Capability*** Large volumes of data and information can be stored in the computer and also retrieved whenever required. A limited amount of data can be stored, temporarily, in the primary memory. Secondary storage devices like hard disk and compact disk can store a large amount of data permanently.
- ***Versatility*** Computer is versatile in nature. It can perform different types of tasks with the same ease. At one moment you can use the computer to prepare a letter document and in the next moment you may play music or print a document.

Computers have several limitations too. Computer can only perform tasks that it has been programmed to do. Computer cannot do any work without instructions from the user. It executes instructions as specified by the user and does not take its own decisions.

1.4 HISTORY OF COMPUTER

Until the development of the first generation computers based on vacuum tubes, there had been several developments in the computing technology related to the mechanical computing devices. The key developments that took place till the first computer was developed are as follows—

- ***Calculating Machines*** ABACUS was the first mechanical calculating device for counting of large numbers. The word ABACUS means calculating board. It consists of bars in horizontal positions on which sets of beads are inserted. The horizontal bars have 10 beads each, representing units, tens, hundreds, etc. An abacus is shown in Figure 1.1

Figure 1.1 Abacus

- ***Napier's Bones*** was a mechanical device built for the purpose of multiplication in 1617 AD. by an English mathematician John Napier.
- ***Slide Rule*** was developed by an English mathematician Edmund Gunter in the 16th century. Using the slide rule, one could perform operations like addition, subtraction, multiplication and division. It was used extensively till late 1970s. Figure 1.2 shows a slide rule.

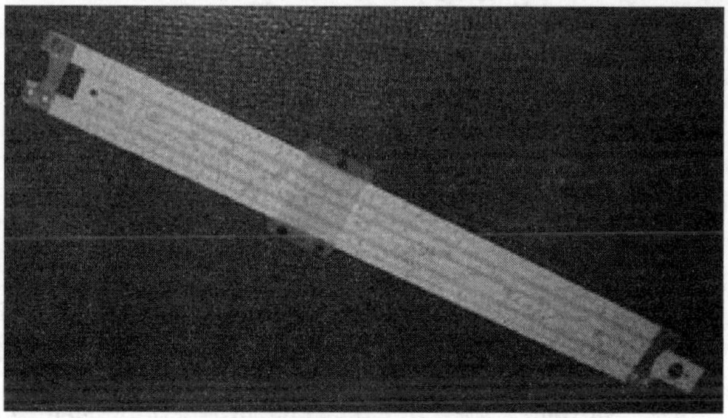

Figure 1.2 Slide rule

- ***Pascal's Adding and Subtraction Machine*** was developed by Blaise Pascal. It could add and subtract. The machine consisted of wheels, gears and cylinders.
- ***Leibniz's Multiplication and Dividing Machine*** was a mechanical device that could both multiply and divide. The German philosopher and mathematician Gottfried Leibniz built it around 1673.
- ***Punch Card System*** was developed by Jacquard to control the power loom in 1801. He invented the punched card reader that could recognize the presence of hole in the punched card as binary one and the absence of the hole as binary zero. The 0s and 1s are the basis of the modern digital computer. A punched card is shown in Figure 1.3.

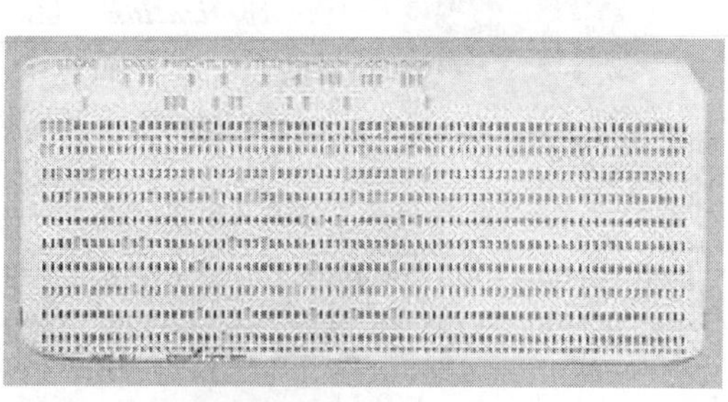

Figure 1.3 Punched card

- ⊙ ***Babbage's Analytical Engine*** An English man Charles Babbage built a mechanical machine to do complex mathematical calculations, in the year 1823. The machine was called as difference engine. Later, Charles Babbage and Lady Ada Lovelace developed a general-purpose calculating machine, the analytical engine. Charles Babbage is also called the father of computer.
- ⊙ ***Hollerith's Punched Card Tabulating Machine*** was invented by Herman Hollerith. The machine could read the information from a punched card and process it electronically.

The developments discussed above and several others not discussed here, resulted in the development of the first computer in the 1940s.

1.5 GENERATIONS OF COMPUTER

The computer has evolved from a large-sized simple calculating machine to a smaller but much more powerful machine. The evolution of computer to the current state is defined in terms of the generations of computer. Each generation of computer is designed based on a new technological development, resulting in better, cheaper and smaller computers that are more powerful, faster and efficient than their predecessors. Currently, there are five generations of computer. In the following subsections, we will discuss the generations of computer in terms of—

(i) the technology used by them (hardware and software),
(ii) computing characteristics (speed, i.e., number of instructions executed per second),
(iii) physical appearance, and
(iv) their applications.

1.5.1 First Generation (1940 to 1956): Using Vacuum Tubes

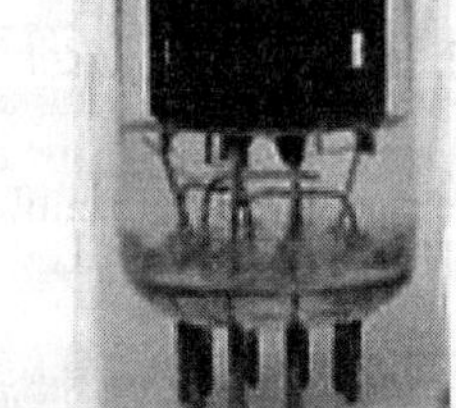

Figure 1.4 Vacuum tube

- ⊙ ***Hardware Technology*** The first generation of computers used vacuum tubes (Figure 1.4) for circuitry and magnetic drums for memory. The input to the computer was through punched cards and paper tapes. The output was displayed as printouts.
- ⊙ ***Software Technology*** The instructions were written in machine language. Machine language uses 0s and 1s for coding of the instructions. The first generation computers could solve one problem at a time.
- ⊙ ***Computing Characteristics*** The computation time was in milliseconds.
- ⊙ ***Physical Appearance*** These computers were enormous in size and required a large room for installation.
- ⊙ ***Application*** They were used for scientific applications as they were the fastest computing device of their time.
- ⊙ ***Examples*** UNIVersal Automatic Computer (UNIVAC), Electronic Numerical Integrator And Calculator (ENIAC), and Electronic Discrete Variable Automatic Computer (EDVAC).

The first generation computers used a large number of vacuum tubes and thus generated a lot of heat. They consumed a great deal of electricity and were expensive to operate. The machines were prone to frequent malfunctioning and required constant maintenance. Since first generation computers used machine language, they were difficult to program.

1.5.2 Second Generation (1956 to 1963): Using Transistors

- ***Hardware Technology*** Transistors (Figure 1.5) replaced the vacuum tubes of the first generation of computers. Transistors allowed computers to become smaller, faster, cheaper, energy efficient and reliable. The second generation computers used *magnetic core technology* for primary memory. They used magnetic tapes and magnetic disks for secondary storage. The input was still through punched cards and the output using printouts. They used the concept of a stored program, where instructions were stored in the memory of computer.

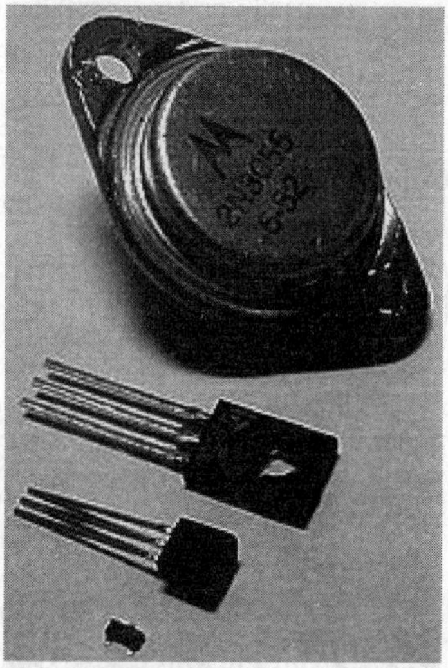

Figure 1.5 Transistors

- ***Software Technology*** The instructions were written using *assembly language*. Assembly language uses mnemonics like ADD for addition and SUB for subtraction for coding of the instructions. It is easier to write instructions in assembly language, as compared to writing instructions in machine language. High-level programming languages, such as early versions of COBOL and FORTRAN were also developed during this period.
- ***Computing Characteristics*** The computation time was in microseconds.
- ***Physical Appearance*** Transistors are smaller in size compared to vacuum tubes, thus, the size of the computer was also reduced.
- ***Application*** The cost of commercial production of these computers was very high, though less than the first generation computers. The transistors had to be assembled manually in second generation computers.
- ***Examples*** PDP-8, IBM 1401 and CDC 1604.

Second generation computers generated a lot of heat but much less than the first generation computers. They required less maintenance than the first generation computers.

1.5.3 Third Generation (1964 to 1971): Using Integrated Circuits

- ***Hardware Technology*** The third generation computers used the *Integrated Circuit (IC)* chips. Figure 1.6 shows IC chips. In an IC chip, multiple transistors are placed on a silicon chip. Silicon is a type of semiconductor. The use of IC chip increased the speed and the efficiency of computer, manifold. The keyboard and monitor were used to interact with the third generation computer, instead of the punched card and printouts.

Figure 1.6 IC chips

- ***Software Technology*** The keyboard and the monitor were interfaced through the *operating system*. Operating system allowed different applications to run at the same time. *High-level languages* were used extensively for programming, instead of machine language and assembly language.
- ***Computing Characteristics*** The computation time was in nanoseconds.
- ***Physical Appearance*** The size of these computers was quite small compared to the second generation computers.

- ⊙ ***Application*** Computers became accessible to mass audience. Computers were produced commercially, and were smaller and cheaper than their predecessors.
- ⊙ ***Examples*** IBM 370, PDP 11.

The third generation computers used less power and generated less heat than the second generation computers. The cost of the computer reduced significantly, as individual components of the computer were not required to be assembled manually. The maintenance cost of the computers was also less compared to their predecessors.

1.5.4 Fourth Generation (1971 to present): Using Microprocessors

- ⊙ ***Hardware Technology*** They use the *Large Scale Integration (LSI)* and the *Very Large Scale Integration (VLSI)* technology. Thousands of transistors are integrated on a small silicon chip using LSI technology. VLSI allows hundreds of thousands of components to be integrated in a small chip. This era is marked by the development of microprocessor. *Microprocessor* is a chip containing millions of transistors and components, and, designed using LSI and VLSI technology. A microprocessor chip is shown in Figure 1.7. This generation of computers gave rise to Personal Computer (PC). Semiconductor memory replaced the earlier magnetic core memory, resulting in fast random access to memory. Secondary storage device like magnetic disks became smaller in physical size and larger in capacity. The *linking of computers* is another key development of this era. The computers were linked to form networks that led to the emergence of the Internet. This generation also saw the development of pointing devices like mouse, and handheld devices.

Figure 1.7 Microprocessors

- ⊙ ***Software Technology*** Several new operating systems like the MS-DOS and MS-Windows developed during this time. This generation of computers supported *Graphical User Interface* (*GUI*). GUI is a user-friendly interface that allows user to interact with the computer via menus and icons. High-level programming languages are used for the writing of programs.
- ⊙ ***Computing Characteristics*** The computation time is in picoseconds.
- ⊙ ***Physical Appearance*** They are smaller than the computers of the previous generation. Some can even fit into the palm of hand.
- ⊙ ***Application*** They became widely available for commercial purposes. Personal computers became available to the home user.
- ⊙ ***Examples*** The Intel 4004 chip was the first microprocessor. The components of the computer like Central Processing Unit (CPU) and memory were located on a single chip. In 1981, IBM introduced the first computer for home use. In 1984, Apple introduced the Macintosh.

The microprocessor has resulted in the fourth generation computers being smaller and cheaper than their predecessors. The fourth generation computers are also portable and more reliable. They generate much lesser heat and require less maintenance compared to their predecessors. GUI and pointing devices facilitate easy use and learning on the computer. Networking has resulted in resource sharing and communication among different computers.

1.5.5 Fifth Generation (Present and Next): Using Artificial Intelligence

The goal of fifth generation computing is to develop computers that are capable of learning and self-organization. The fifth generation computers use *Super Large Scale Integrated (SLSI)* chips that are able to store millions of components on a single chip. These computers have large memory requirements.

This generation of computers uses *parallel processing* that allows several instructions to be executed in parallel, instead of serial execution. Parallel processing results in faster processing speed. The Intel dual-core microprocessor uses parallel processing.

The fifth generation computers are based on *Artificial Intelligence (AI)*. They try to simulate the human way of thinking and reasoning. Artificial Intelligence includes areas like Expert System (ES), Natural Language Processing (NLP), speech recognition, voice recognition, robotics, etc.

1.6 CLASSIFICATION OF COMPUTER

The digital computers that are available nowadays vary in their sizes and types. The computers are broadly classified into four categories (Figure 1.8) based on their size and type—(1) Microcomputers, (2) Minicomputers, (3) Mainframe computers, and (4) Supercomputer.

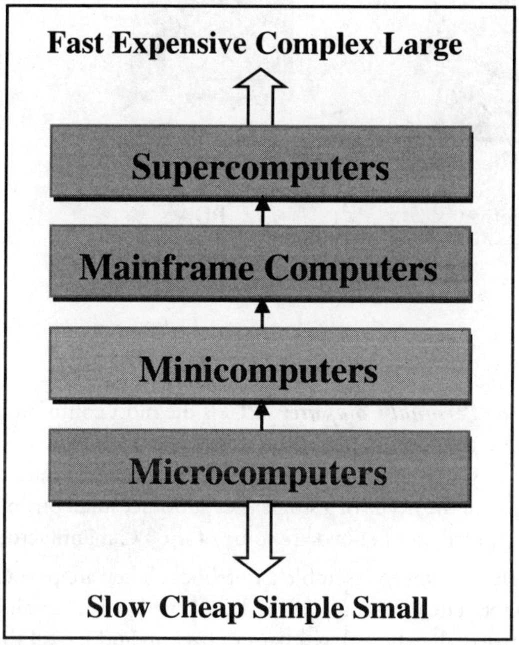

Figure 1.8 Classification of computers based on size and type

1.6.1 Microcomputers

Microcomputers are small, low-cost and single-user digital computer. They consist of CPU, input unit, output unit, storage unit and the software. Although microcomputers are stand-alone machines, they can be connected together to create a network of computers that can serve more than one user. IBM PC based on Pentium microprocessor and Apple Macintosh are some examples of microcomputers. Microcomputers include desktop computers, notebook computers or laptop, tablet computer, handheld computer, smart phones and netbook, as shown in Figure 1.9.

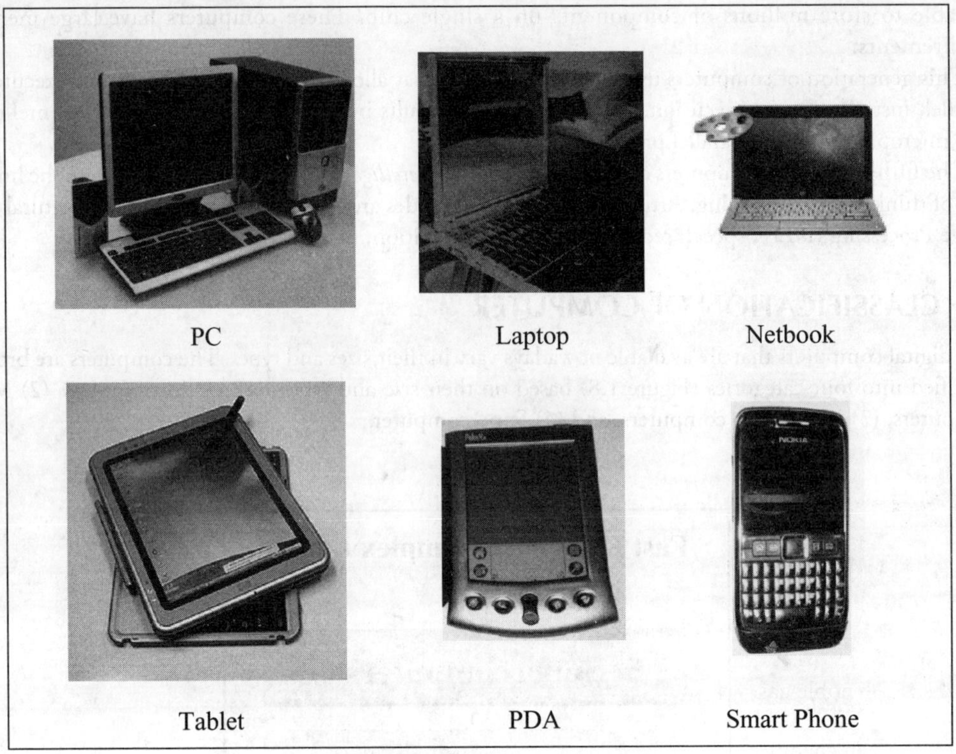

Figure 1.9 Microcomputers

- ***Desktop Computer or Personal Computer (PC)*** is the most common type of microcomputer. It is a stand-alone machine that can be placed on the desk. Externally, it consists of three units—keyboard, monitor, and a system unit containing the CPU, memory, hard disk drive, etc. It is not very expensive and is suited to the needs of a single user at home, small business units, and organizations. Apple, Microsoft, HP, Dell and Lenovo are some of the PC manufacturers.
- ***Notebook Computers or Laptop*** resemble a notebook. They are portable and have all the features of a desktop computer. The advantage of the laptop is that it is small in size (can be put inside a briefcase), can be carried anywhere, has a battery backup and has all the functionality of the desktop. Laptops can be placed on the lap while working (hence the name). Laptops are costlier than the desktop machines.
- ***Netbook*** These are smaller notebooks optimized for low weight and low cost, and are designed for accessing web-based applications. Starting with the earliest netbook in late 2007, they have gained significant popularity now. Netbooks deliver the performance needed to enjoy popular activities like streaming videos or music, emailing, web surfing or instant messaging. The word *netbook* was created as a blend of Inter*net* and note*book*.
- ***Tablet Computer*** has features of the notebook computer but it can accept input from a stylus or a pen instead of the keyboard or mouse. It is a portable computer. Tablet computer are the new kind of PCs.

- ***Handheld Computer or Personal Digital Assistant (PDA)*** is a small computer that can be held on top of the palm. It is small in size. Instead of the keyboard, PDA uses a pen or a stylus for input. PDAs do not have a disk drive. They have a limited memory and are less powerful. PDAs can be connected to the Internet via a wireless connection. Casio and Apple are some of the manufacturers of PDA. Over the last few years, PDAs have merged into mobile phones to create smart phones.
- ***Smart Phones*** are cellular phones that function both as a phone and as a small PC. They may use a stylus or a pen, or may have a small keyboard. They can be connected to the Internet wirelessly. They are used to access the electronic-mail, download music, play games, etc. Blackberry, Apple, HTC, Nokia and LG are some of the manufacturers of smart phones.

1.6.2 Minicomputers

Minicomputers (Figure 1.10) are digital computers, generally used in multi-user systems. They have high processing speed and high storage capacity than the microcomputers. Minicomputers can support 4–200 users simultaneously. The users can access the minicomputer through their PCs or terminal. They are used for real-time applications in industries, research centers, etc. PDP 11, IBM (8000 series) are some of the widely used minicomputers.

Figure 1.10 Minicomputer

1.6.3 Mainframe Computers

Mainframe computers (Figure 1.11) are multi-user, multi-programming and high performance computers. They operate at a very high speed, have very large storage capacity and can handle the workload of many users. Mainframe computers are large and powerful systems generally used in centralized databases. The user accesses the mainframe computer via a terminal that may be a dumb terminal, an intelligent terminal or a PC. A *dumb terminal* cannot store data or do processing of its own. It has the input and output device only. An *intelligent terminal* has the input and output device, can do processing, but, cannot store data of its own. The dumb and the intelligent terminal use the processing power and the storage facility of the mainframe computer. Mainframe computers are used in organizations like banks or companies, where many people require frequent access to the same data. Some examples of mainframes are CDC 6600 and IBM ES000 series.

Figure 1.11 Mainframe computer

1.6.4 Supercomputers

Supercomputers (Figure 1.12) are the fastest and the most expensive machines. They have high processing speed compared to other computers. The speed of a supercomputer is generally measured in FLOPS (FLoating point Operations Per Second). Some of the faster supercomputers can perform trillions of calculations per second. Supercomputers are built by interconnecting thousands of processors that can work in parallel.

Supercomputers are used for highly calculation-intensive tasks, such as, weather forecasting, climate research (global warming), molecular research, biological research, nuclear research and aircraft design. They are also used in major universities, military agencies and scientific research laboratories. Some examples of supercomputers are IBM Roadrunner, IBM Blue gene and Intel ASCI red. PARAM is a series of supercomputer assembled in India by C-DAC (Center for Development of Advanced Computing), in Pune. PARAM Padma is the latest machine in this series. The peak computing power of PARAM Padma is 1 Tera FLOP/FLOPS.

Figure 1.12 Supercomputer

1.7 THE COMPUTER SYSTEM

Computer is an electronic device that accepts data as input, processes the input data by performing mathematical and logical operations on it, and gives the desired output. The computer system consists of four parts—(1) Hardware, (2) Software, (3) Data, and (4) Users. The parts of computer system are shown in Figure 1.13.

Hardware consists of the mechanical parts that make up the computer as a machine. The hardware consists of physical devices of the computer. The devices are required for input, output, storage and processing of the data. Keyboard, monitor, hard disk drive, floppy disk drive, printer, processor and motherboard are some of the hardware devices.

Figure 1.13 Parts of computer system

Software is a set of instructions that tells the computer about the tasks to be performed and how these tasks are to be performed. *Program* is a set of instructions, written in a language understood by the computer, to perform a specific task. A set of programs and documents are collectively called software. The hardware of the computer system cannot perform any task on its own. The hardware needs to be instructed about the task to be performed. Software instructs the computer about the task to be performed. The hardware carries out these tasks. Different software can be loaded on the same hardware to perform different kinds of tasks.

Data are isolated values or raw facts, which by themselves have no much significance. For example, the data like *29, January*, and *1994* just represent values. The data is provided as input to the computer, which is processed to generate some meaningful information. For example, 29, January and 1994 are processed by the computer to give the date of birth of a person.

Users are people who write computer programs or interact with the computer. They are also known as *skinware, liveware, humanware or peopleware*. Programmers, data entry operators, system analyst and computer hardware engineers fall into this category.

1.7.1 The Input-Process-Output Concept

A computer is an electronic device that (1) accepts data, (2) processes data, (3) generates output, and (4) stores data. The concept of generating output information from the input data is also referred to as *input-process-output* concept.

The input-process-output concept of the computer is explained as follows—

- ***Input*** The computer accepts input data from the user via an input device like keyboard. The input data can be characters, word, text, sound, images, document, etc.
- ***Process*** The computer processes the input data. For this, it performs some actions on the data by using the instructions or program given by the user of the data. The action could be an arithmetic or logic calculation, editing, modifying a document, etc. During processing, the data, instructions and output are stored temporarily in the computer's main memory.
- ***Output*** The output is the result generated after the processing of data. The output may be in the form of text, sound, image, document, etc. The computer may display the output on a monitor, send output to the printer for printing, play the output, etc.
- ***Storage*** The input data, instructions and output are stored permanently in the secondary storage devices like disk or tape. The stored data can be retrieved later, whenever needed.

1.7.2 Components of Computer Hardware

The computer system hardware comprises of three main components —

(1) Input/Output (I/O) Unit,

(2) Central Processing Unit (CPU), and

(3) Memory Unit.

The I/O unit consists of the input unit and the output unit. CPU performs calculations and processing on the input data, to generate the output. The memory unit is used to store the data, the instructions and the output information. Figure 1.14 illustrates the typical interaction among the different components of the computer.

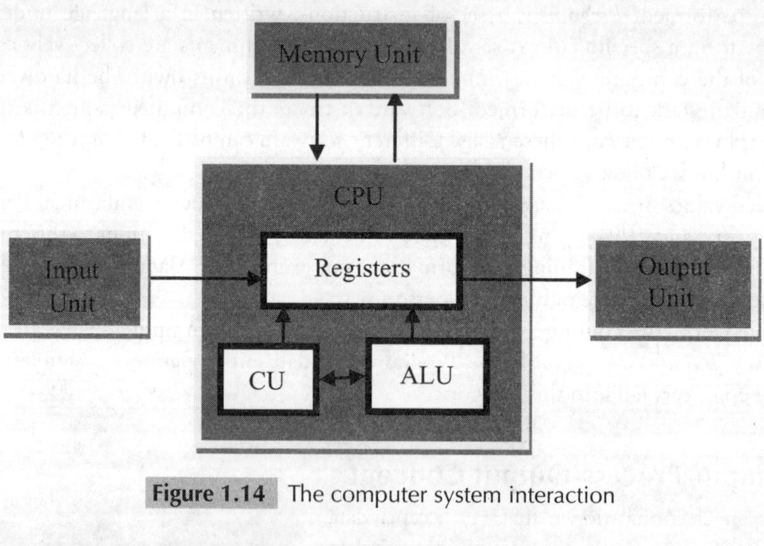

Figure 1.14 The computer system interaction

- ***Input/Output Unit*** The user interacts with the computer via the I/O unit. The Input unit accepts data from the user and the Output unit provides the processed data i.e. the information to the user.

The Input unit converts the data that it accepts from the user, into a form that is understandable by the computer. Similarly, the Output unit provides the output in a form that is understandable by the user. The input is provided to the computer using input devices like keyboard, trackball and mouse. Some of the commonly used output devices are monitor and printer.

- ***Central Processing Unit*** CPU controls, coordinates and supervises the operations of the computer. It is responsible for processing of the input data. CPU consists of Arithmetic Logic Unit (ALU) and Control Unit (CU).
    - ALU performs all the arithmetic and logic operations on the input data.
    - CU controls the overall operations of the computer i.e. it checks the sequence of execution of instructions, and, controls and coordinates the overall functioning of the units of computer.

    Additionally, CPU also has a set of *registers* for temporary storage of data, instructions, addresses and intermediate results of calculation.

- ***Memory Unit*** Memory unit stores the data, instructions, intermediate results and output, *temporarily*, during the processing of data. This memory is also called the *main memory or primary memory* of the computer. The input data that is to be processed is brought into the main memory before processing. The instructions required for processing of data and any intermediate results are also stored in the main memory. The output is stored in memory before being transferred to the output device. CPU can work with the information stored in the main memory. Another kind of storage unit is also referred to as the *secondary memory* of the computer. The data, the programs and the output are stored *permanently* in the storage unit of the computer. Magnetic disks, optical disks and magnetic tapes are examples of secondary memory.

1.8 APPLICATION OF COMPUTERS

Computers have proliferated into various areas of our lives. For a user, computer is a tool that provides the desired information, whenever needed. You may use computer to get information about the reservation of tickets (railways, airplanes and cinema halls), books in a library, medical history of a person, a place in a map, or the dictionary meaning of a word. The information may be presented to you in the form of text, images, video clips, etc.

Figure 1.15 shows some of the applications of computer. Some of the application areas of the computer are listed below—

- ***Education*** Computers are extensively used, as a tool and as an aid, for imparting education. Educators use computers to prepare notes and presentations of their lectures. Computers are used to develop computer-based training packages, to provide distance education using the e-learning software, and to conduct online examinations. Researchers use computers to get easy access to conference and journal details and to get global access to the research material.
- ***Entertainment*** Computers have had a major impact on the entertainment industry. The user can download and view movies, play games, chat, book tickets for cinema halls, use multimedia for making movies, incorporate visual and sound effects using computers, etc. The users can also listen to music, download and share music, create music using computers, etc.
- ***Sports*** A computer can be used to watch a game, view the scores, improve the game, play games (like chess, etc.) and create games. They are also used for the purposes of training players.
- ***Advertising*** Computer is a powerful advertising media. Advertisement can be displayed on different websites, electronic-mails can be sent and reviews of a product by different customers can be

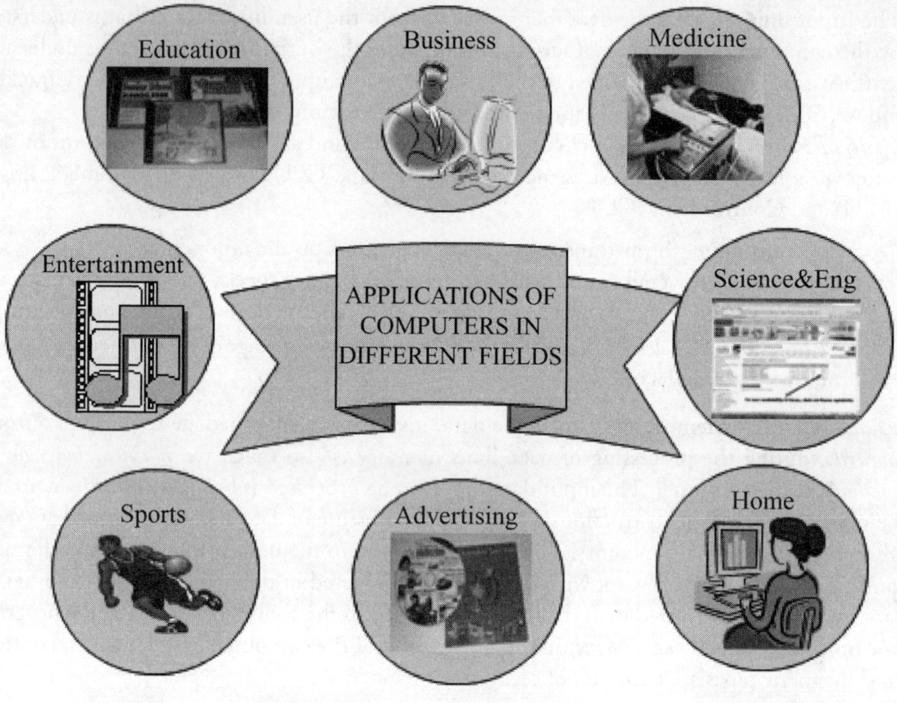

Figure 1.15 Applications of computer

posted. Computers are also used to create an advertisement using the visual and the sound effects. For the advertisers, computer is a medium via which the advertisements can be viewed globally. Web advertising has become a significant factor in the marketing plans of almost all companies. In fact, the business model of Google is mainly dependent on web advertising for generating revenues.

- ***Medicine*** Medical researchers and practitioners use computers to access information about the advances in medical research or to take opinion of doctors globally. The medical history of patients is stored in the computers. Computers are also an integral part of various kinds of sophisticated medical equipments like ultrasound machine, CAT scan machine, MRI scan machine, etc. Computers also provide assistance to the medical surgeons during critical surgery operations like laparoscopic operations, etc.
- ***Science and Engineering*** Scientists and engineers use computers for performing complex scientific calculations, for designing and making drawings (CAD/CAM applications) and also for simulating and testing the designs. Computers are used for storing the complex data, performing complex calculations and for visualizing 3-dimensional objects. Complex scientific applications like the launch of the rockets, space exploration, etc., are not possible without the computers.
- ***Government*** The government uses computers to manage its own operations and also for e-governance. The websites of the different government departments provide information to the users. Computers are used for the filing of income tax return, paying taxes, online submission of water and electricity bills, for the access of land record details, etc. The police department uses computers to search for criminals using fingerprint matching, etc.
- ***Home*** Computers have now become an integral part of home equipment. At home, people use computers to play games, to maintain the home accounts, for communicating with friends and

relatives via Internet, for paying bills, for education and learning, etc. Microprocessors are embedded in house hold utilities like, washing machines, TVs, food processors, home theatres, security devices, etc.

The list of applications of computers is so long that it is not possible to discuss all of them here. In addition to the applications of the computers discussed above, computers have also proliferated into areas like banks, investments, stock trading, accounting, ticket reservation, military operations, meteorological predictions, social networking, business organizations, police department, video conferencing, telepresence, book publishing, web newspapers, and information sharing.

SUMMARY

- *Computer* is an electronic device which accepts data as input, performs processing on the data, and gives the desired output. A computer may be *analog or digital computer*.
- Speed, accuracy, diligence, storage capability and versatility are the main *characteristics of computer.*
- The *computing devices* have evolved from simple mechanical machines, like ABACUS, Napier's bones, Slide Rule, Pascal's Adding and Subtraction Machine, Leibniz's Multiplication and Dividing Machine, Jacquard Punched Card System, Babbage's Analytical Engine and Hollerith's Tabulating Machine, to the first electronic computer.
- Charles Babbage is called the father of computer.
- The evolution of computers to their present state is divided into *five generations of computers*, based on the hardware and software they use, their physical appearance and their computing characteristics.
- *First generation computers* were vacuum tubes based machines. These were large in size, expensive to operate and instructions were written in machine language. Their computation time was in milliseconds.
- *Second generation computers* were transistor based machines. They used the stored program concept. Programs were written in assembly language. They were smaller in size, less expensive and required less maintenance than the first generation computers. The computation time was in microseconds.
- *Third generation computers* were characterized by the use of IC. They consumed less power and required low maintenance compared to their predecessors. High-level languages were used for programming. The computation time was in nanoseconds. These computers were produced commercially.
- *Fourth generation computers* used microprocessors which were designed using the LSI and VLSI technology. The computers became small, portable, reliable and cheap. The computation time is in picoseconds. They became available both to the home user and for commercial use.
- *Fifth generation computers* are capable of learning and self organization. These computers use SLSI chips and have large memory requirements. They use parallel processing and are based on AI. The fifth generation computers are still being developed.
- *Computers are broadly classified* as microcomputers, minicomputers, mainframe computers, and supercomputers, based on their sizes and types.
- *Microcomputers* are small, low-cost standalone machines. Microcomputers include desktop computers, notebook computers or laptop, netbooks, tablet computer, handheld computer and smart phones.

- *Minicomputers* are high processing speed machines having more storage capacity than the microcomputers. Minicomputers can support 4-200 users simultaneously.
- *Mainframe computers* are multi-user, multi-programming and high performance computers. They have very high speed, very large storage capacity and can handle large workloads. Mainframe computers are generally used in centralized databases.
- *Supercomputers* are the most expensive machines, having high processing speed capable of performing trillions of calculations per second. The speed of a supercomputer is measured in FLOPS. Supercomputers find applications in computing-intensive tasks.
- *Computer* is an electronic device based on the input-process-output concept. Input/Output Unit, CPU and Memory unit are the three main *components of computer.*
- *Input/Output Unit* consists of the Input unit which accepts data from the user and the Output unit that provides the processed data. *CPU* processes the input data, and, controls, coordinates and supervises the operations of the computer. CPU consists of ALU, CU and Registers. The memory unit stores programs, data and output, temporarily, during the processing. Additionally, storage unit or secondary memory is used for the storing of programs, data and output permanently.
- Computers are used in various areas of our life. Education, entertainment, sports, advertising, medicine, science and engineering, government, office and home are some of the *application areas of computers.*

KEYWORDS

QUESTIONS

Section 1.2

1. Define an analog computer and a digital computer.
2. Give an example each of analog computer and digital computer.

Section 1.3

3. List the main characteristics of the computer.
4. Describe the characteristics of the computer.
5. List three significant limitations of the computer.

Section 1.4

6. Explain briefly the developments in computer technology starting from a simple calculating machine to the first computer.
7. What is a calculating machine?
8. What is the key feature of the Jacquard's punch card?
9. Name the first calculating device for the counting of large numbers.
10. Who is called the Father of Computer?

Section 1.5.1

11. The first generation computers used ___________ for circuitry.
12. Describe the first generation computer based on the (a) Hardware (b) Software (c) Computing characteristics (d) Physical appearance, and (e) Their applications.
13. Give two examples of first generation computers.
14. List the drawbacks of the first generation computers.

Section 1.5.2

15. The second generation computers used ___________ for circuitry.
16. Describe the second generation computer based on the (a) Hardware (b) Software (c) Computing characteristics (d) Physical appearance and (e) Their applications.
17. Give two examples of second generation computers.
18. List the drawbacks of the second generation computers.

Section 1.5.3

19. The third generation computers used ___________ for circuitry.
20. Describe the third generation computer based on the (a) Hardware (b) Software (c) Computing characteristics (d) Physical appearance, and (e) Their applications.
21. Give two examples of third generation computers.
22. List the drawbacks of the third generation computers.

Section 1.5.4

23. The fourth generation computers used ___________ for circuitry.
24. Describe the fourth generation computer based on the (a) Hardware (b) Software (c) Computing characteristics (d) Physical appearance and (e) Their applications.
25. Give two examples of fourth generation computers.
26. List the drawbacks of the fourth generation computers.

Section 1.5.5

27. The fifth generation computers used ___________ for circuitry.
28. Describe the fifth generation computer based on the (a) Hardware (b) Software (c) Computing characteristics (d) Physical appearance and (e) Their applications.
29. Give two examples of fifth generation computers.
30. Compare in detail the five generations of computers based on the (a) Hardware (b) Software (c) Computing characteristics (d) Physical appearance and (e) Their applications. Also give at least one example of each generation of computer.

Section 1.6.1

31. Define microcomputer.
32. Give two examples of microcomputer.
33. List three categories of microcomputers.

Section 1.6.2

34. Define minicomputers.
35. Give two examples of minicomputer.

Section 1.6.3

36. Define mainframe computer.
37. Give two examples of mainframe computer.
38. Define a dumb terminal.
39. Define an intelligent terminal.

Section 1.6.4

40. Define a supercomputer.
41. Give two examples of supercomputer.
42. The speed of supercomputer is generally measured in ________.
43. List two uses of the supercomputer.
44. Name the supercomputer assembled in India.
45. Highlight the differences between microcomputer, minicomputer, mainframe computer and supercomputer.

Section 1.7

46. Define a computer.
47. Define (1) Program (2) Software (3) Hardware (4) ALU (5) CU (6) CPU (7) Data.
48. Differentiate between software, data and hardware.
49. List the components of computer hardware.
50. Explain in detail the components of computer hardware.
51. List the steps in the working of the computer.
52. Explain the working of the computer.
53. Explain the input-process-output cycle.

Section 1.8

54. List some areas where the computers are used.
55. Explain briefly the use of computers in the following areas—(a) Education, (b) Advertising, and (c) Government.

Extra Questions

56. Give full form of the following abbreviations

(i) CPU	(ii) I/O	(iii) ALU
(iv) CU	(v) LSI	(vi) VLSI
(vii) PC	(viii) GUI	(ix) SLSI
(x) ES	(xi) NLP	(xii) AI
(xiii) PDA	(xiv) FLOPS	(xv) UNIVAC
(xvi) ENIAC	(xvii) EDVAC	

57. Write short notes on
    (a) Components of Computer
    (b) Input-Process-Output
    (c) I/O Unit
    (d) Central Processing Unit
    (e) Storage Unit
    (f) History of Computers
    (g) First Generation Computer
    (h) Second Generation Computer
    (i) Third Generation Computer
    (j) Fourth Generation Computer
    (k) Fifth Generation Computer
    (l) Microcomputers
    (m) Minicomputers
    (n) Mainframe Computers
    (o) Supercomputer
    (p) Personal Computer (PC)
    (q) Notebook Computer
    (r) Tablet Computer
    (s) Netbook
    (t) Personal Digital Assistant (PDA)
    (u) Applications of Computer
58. Give differences between the following:
    (a) Analog and Digital Computer
    (b) Dumb Terminal and Intelligent Terminal
    (c) Microcomputer and Minicomputer
    (d) Minicomputer and Mainframe Computer
    (e) Mainframe computer and Supercomputer
    (f) First Generation Computers and Second Generation Computers
    (g) Second Generation Computers and Third Generation Computers
    (h) Third Generation Computers and Fourth Generation Computers
    (i) Fourth Generation Computers and Fifth Generation Computers
    (j) Desktop Computer and Notebook Computer

THE COMPUTER SYSTEM HARDWARE 2

Contents

Why this chapter

The computer as a machine consists of different components that interact with each other to provide the desired functionality of the computer. As a user of the computer, we need to be aware of the main components of the computer, their functions and the interconnection between the different components of the computer. This chapter describes the different hardware components of the computer.

2.1 INTRODUCTION

When we talk of computer hardware, the three related terms that require introduction are—computer architecture, computer organization and computer design. *Computer architecture* refers to the structure and behavior of the computer. It includes the specifications of the components, for example, instruction format, instruction set and techniques for addressing memory, and how they connect to the other components. Given the components, *computer organization* focuses on the organizational structure. It deals with how the hardware components operate and the way they are connected to form the computer. Given the system specifications, *computer design* focuses on the hardware to be used and the interconnection of parts. Different kinds of computer, such as a PC or a mainframe computer may have different organization; however, basic organization of the computer remains the same.

A computer consists of three main components—(1) Input/Output (I/O) Unit, (2) Central Processing Unit (CPU), and (3) Memory Unit. The computer user interacts with the computer via the I/O unit. The purpose of I/O unit is to provide data and instructions as input to the computer and to present relevant information as output from the computer. CPU controls the operations of the computer and processes the received input to generate the relevant output. The memory unit stores the instructions and the data during the input activity, to make instructions readily available to CPU during processing. It also stores the processed output. This chapter discusses the hardware components of the computer and the interaction between them.

2.2 CENTRAL PROCESSING UNIT

Central Processing Unit (CPU) or the processor is also often called the *brain of computer.* CPU (Figure 2.1) consists of Arithmetic Logic Unit (ALU) and Control Unit (CU). In addition, CPU also has a set of registers which are temporary storage areas for holding data, and instructions. *ALU* performs the arithmetic and logic operations on the data that is made available to it. *CU* is responsible for organizing the processing of data and instructions. CU controls and coordinates the activity of other units of computer. CPU uses the registers to store data, instructions during processing.

CPU executes *the stored program instructions*, i.e. instructions and data are stored in memory before execution. For processing, CPU gets data and instructions from the memory. It interprets the program instructions and performs the arithmetic and logic operations required for the processing of data. Then, it sends the processed data or result to the memory. CPU also acts as an administrator and is responsible for supervising operations of other parts of the computer.

The CPU is fabricated as a single Integrated Circuit (IC) chip, and is also known as the *microprocessor.* The microprocessor is plugged into the motherboard of the computer (*Motherboard* is a circuit board that has electronic circuit etched on it and connects the microprocessor with the other hardware components).

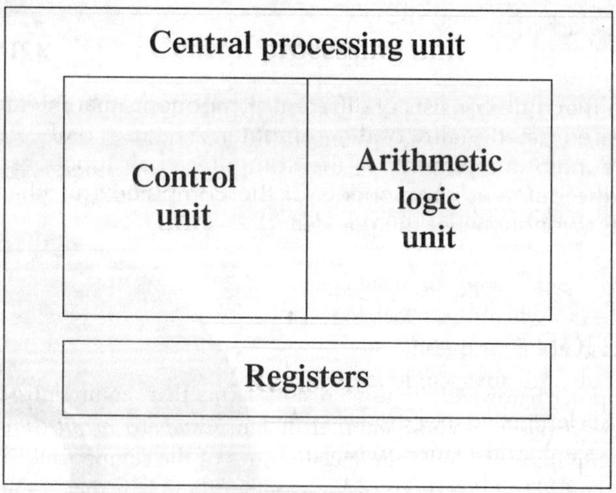

Figure 2.1 CPU

2.2.1 Arithmetic Logic Unit

- ALU consists of two units—arithmetic unit and logic unit.
- The arithmetic unit performs arithmetic operations on the data that is made available to it. Some of the arithmetic operations supported by the arithmetic unit are—addition, subtraction, multiplication and division.

- The logic unit of ALU is responsible for performing logic operations. Logic unit performs comparisons of numbers, letters and special characters. Logic operations include testing for greater than, less than or equal to condition.
- ALU performs arithmetic and logic operations, and uses *registers* to hold the data that is being processed.

2.2.2 Registers

- Registers are high-speed storage areas within the CPU, but have the least storage capacity. Registers are not referenced by their address, but are directly accessed and manipulated by the CPU during instruction execution.
- Registers store data, instructions, addresses and intermediate results of processing. Registers are often referred to as the CPU's *working memory*.
- The data and instructions that require processing must be brought in the registers of CPU before they can be processed. For example, if two numbers are to be added, both numbers are brought in the registers, added and the result is also placed in a register.
- Registers are used for different purposes, with each register serving a specific purpose. Some of the important registers in CPU (Figure 2.2) are as follows—
    - Accumulator (ACC) stores the result of arithmetic and logic operations.
    - Instruction Register (IR) contains the current instruction most recently fetched.
    - Program Counter (PC) contains the address of next instruction to be processed.
    - Memory Address Register (MAR) contains the address of next location in the memory to be accessed.
    - Memory Buffer Register (MBR) temporarily stores data from memory or the data to be sent to memory.
    - Data Register (DR) stores the operands and any other data.

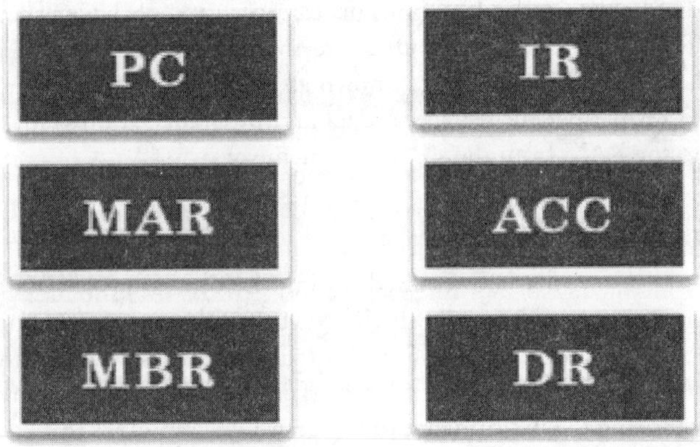

Figure 2.2 CPU registers

- The number of registers and the size of each (number of bits) register in a CPU helps to determine the power and the speed of a CPU.
- The overall number of registers can vary from about ten to many hundreds, depending on the type and complexity of the processor.
- The size of register, also called *word size*, indicates the amount of data with which the computer can work at any given time. The bigger the size, the more quickly it can process data. The size of a register

may be 8, 16, 32 or 64 bits. For example, a 32-bit CPU is one in which each register is 32 bits wide and its CPU can manipulate 32 bits of data at a time. Nowadays, PCs have 32-bit or 64-bit registers.

- 32-bit processor and 64-bit processor are the terms used to refer to the size of the registers. Other factors remaining the same, a 64-bit processor can process the data twice as fast as one with 32-bit processor.

2.2.3 Control Unit

- The control unit of a computer does not do any actual processing of data. It organizes the processing of data and instructions. It acts as a supervisor and, controls and coordinates the activity of the other units of computer.
- CU coordinates the input and output devices of a computer. It directs the computer to carry out stored program instructions by communicating with the ALU and the registers. CU uses the instructions in the Instruction Register (IR) to decide which circuit needs to be activated. It also instructs the ALU to perform the arithmetic or logic operations. When a program is run, the Program Counter (PC) register keeps track of the program instruction to be executed next.
- CU tells when to fetch the data and instructions, what to do, where to store the results, the sequencing of events during processing etc.
- CU also holds the CPU's Instruction Set, which is a list of all operations that the CPU can perform.

The function of a (CU) can be considered synonymous with that of a conductor of an orchestra. The conductor in an orchestra does not perform any work by itself but manages the orchestra and ensures that the members of orchestra work in proper coordination.

2.3 MEMORY UNIT

The memory unit consists of cache memory and primary memory. *Primary memory or main memory* of the computer is used to store the data and instructions during execution of the instructions. Random Access Memory (RAM) and Read Only Memory (ROM) are the primary memory. In addition to the main memory, there is another kind of storage device known as the secondary memory. Secondary memory is non-volatile and is used for permanent storage of data and programs. A program or data that has to be executed is brought into the RAM from the secondary memory.

2.3.1 Cache Memory

- The data and instructions that are required during the processing of data are brought from the secondary storage devices and stored in the RAM. For processing, it is required that the data and instructions are accessed from the RAM and stored in the registers. The time taken to move the data between RAM and CPU registers is large. This affects the speed of processing of computer, and results in decreasing the performance of CPU.
- Cache memory is a very high speed memory placed in between RAM and CPU. Cache memory increases the speed of processing.
- Cache memory is a storage buffer that stores the data that is used more often, temporarily, and makes them available to CPU at a fast rate. During processing, CPU first checks cache for the required data. If data is not found in cache, then it looks in the RAM for data.
- To access the cache memory, CPU does not have to use the motherboard's system bus for data transfer. (The data transfer speed slows to the motherboard's capability, when data is passed through system bus. CPU can process data at a much faster rate by avoiding the system bus.)

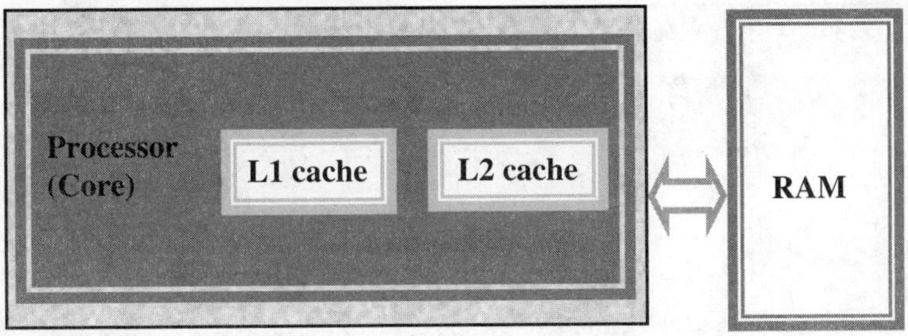

Figure 2.3 Illustration of cache memory

- Cache memory is built into the processor, and may also be located next to it on a separate chip between the CPU and RAM. Cache built into the CPU is faster than separate cache, running at the speed of the microprocessor itself. However, separate cache is roughly twice as fast as RAM.
- The CPU has a built-in *Level 1 (L1)* cache and *Level 2 (L2)* cache, as shown in Figure 2.3. In addition to the built-in L1 and L2 cache, some CPUs have a separate cache chip on the motherboard. This cache on the motherboard is called *Level 3 (L3)* cache. Nowadays, high-end processor comes with built-in L3 cache, like in Intel core i7. The L1, L2 and L3 cache store the most recently run instructions, the next ones and the possible ones, respectively. Typically, CPUs have cache size varying from 256KB (L1), 6 MB (L2), to 12MB (L3) cache.
- Cache memory is very expensive, so it is smaller in size. Generally, computers have cache memory of sizes 256 KB to 2 MB.

2.3.2 Primary Memory

- Primary memory is the main memory of computer. It is used to store data and instructions during the processing of data. Primary memory is semiconductor memory.
- Primary memory is of two kinds—Random Access Memory (RAM) and Read Only Memory (ROM).
- RAM is volatile. It stores data when the computer is on. The information stored in RAM gets erased when the computer is turned off. RAM provides *temporary storage* for data and instructions.
- ROM is non-volatile memory, but is a read only memory. The storage in ROM is permanent in nature, and is used for storing standard processing programs that permanently reside in the computer. ROM comes programmed by the manufacturer.
- RAM *stores data and instructions during the execution* of instructions. The data and instructions that require processing are brought into the RAM from the storage devices like hard disk. CPU accesses the data and the instructions from RAM, as it can access it at a *fast* speed than the storage devices connected to the input and output unit (Figure 2.4).
- The input data that is entered using the input unit is stored in RAM, to be made available during the processing of data. Similarly, the output data generated after processing is stored in RAM before being sent to the output device. Any intermediate results generated during the processing of program are stored in RAM.
- RAM provides a *limited storage capacity*, due to its *high cost*.

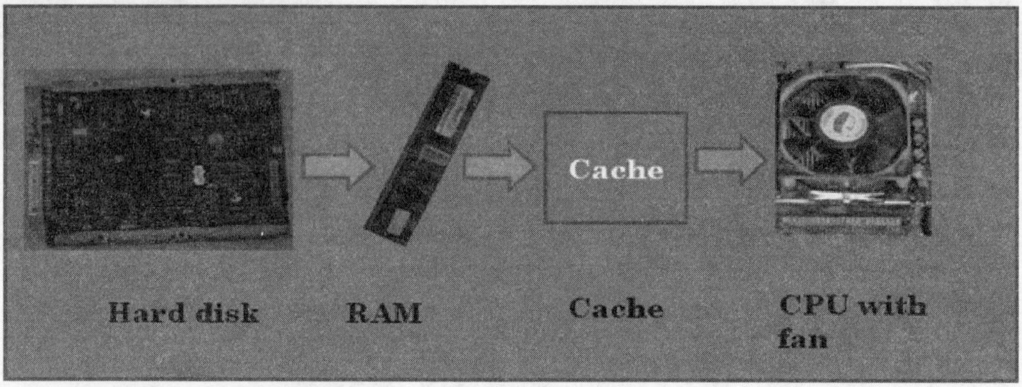

Figure 2.4 Interaction of CPU with memory

2.3.3 Secondary Memory

- The secondary memory stores data and instructions *permanently*. The information can be stored in secondary memory for a long time (years), and is generally permanent in nature unless erased by the user. It is a non-volatile memory.
- It provides *back-up storage* for data and instructions. Hard disk drive, floppy drive and optical disk drives are some examples of storage devices.
- The data and instructions that are currently not being used by CPU, but may be required later for processing, are stored in secondary memory.
- Secondary memory has a *high storage capacity* than the primary memory.
- Secondary memory is also *cheaper* than the primary memory.
- It takes *longer time to access* the data and instructions stored in secondary memory than in primary memory.

Magnetic tape drives, disk drives and optical disk drives are the different types of storage devices.

2.4 INSTRUCTION FORMAT

A computer program is a *set of instructions* that describe the steps to be performed for carrying out a computational task. The program and the data on which the program operates, are stored in main memory, waiting to be processed by the processor. This is also called the *stored program concept.*

An instruction is designed to perform a task and is an elementary operation that the processor can accomplish. An instruction is divided into groups called fields. The common fields of an instruction are—Operation (op) code and Operand code (Figure 2.5). The remainder of the instruction fields differs from one computer type to other. The *operation code* represents action that the processor must execute. It tells the processor what basic operations to perform. The *operand code* defines the parameters of the action and depends on the operation. It specifies the locations of the data or the operand on which the operation is to be performed. It can be data or a memory address.

Figure 2.5 Instruction format

ADD op code	1st operand address	2nd operand address

Figure 2.6 Instruction format for ADD command

The number of bits in an instruction varies according to the type of data (could be between 8 and 32 bits). Figure 2.6 shows the instruction format for ADD command.

2.5 INSTRUCTION SET

A processor has a set of instructions that it understands, called as instruction set. An instruction set or an instruction set architecture is a part of the computer architecture. It relates to programming, instructions, registers, addressing modes, memory architecture, etc. An *Instruction Set* is the set of all basic operations that a processor can accomplish. Examples of some instructions are shown in Figure 2.7. The instructions in the instruction set are the language that a processor understands. All programs have to communicate with the processor using these instructions. An instruction in the instruction set involves a series of logical operations (may be thousands) that are performed to complete each task. The instruction set is embedded in the processor (hard-wired), which determines the machine language for the processor. All programs written in a high-level language are compiled and translated into machine code before execution, which is understood by the processor for which the program has been coded.

LOAD R1, A

ADD R1, B

STORE R1, X

Figure 2.7 Examples of some instructions

Two processors are different if they have different instruction sets. A program run on one computer may not run on another computer having a different processor. *Two processors are compatible* if the same machine level program can run on both the processors. Therefore, the system software is developed within the processor's instruction set.

Microarchitecture is the processor design technique used for implementing the *Instruction Set.* Computers having different microarchitecture can have a common Instruction Set. Pentium and Athlon CPU chips implement the x86 instruction set, but have different internal designs.

2.6 INSTRUCTION CYCLE

The primary responsibility of a computer processor is to execute a sequential set of instructions that constitute a program. CPU executes each instruction in a series of steps, called *instruction cycle* (Figure 2.8).

- A instruction cycle involves four steps (Figure 2.9)—
  - ***Fetching*** The processor fetches the instruction from the memory. The fetched instruction is placed in the *Instruction Register. Program Counter* holds the address of next instruction to be fetched and is incremented after each fetch.
  - ***Decoding*** The instruction that is fetched is broken down into parts or decoded. The instruction is translated into commands so that they correspond to those in the CPU's instruction set. The instruction set architecture of the CPU defines the way in which an instruction is decoded.
  - ***Executing*** The decoded instruction or the command is executed. CPU performs the operation implied by the program instruction. For example, if it is an ADD instruction, addition is performed.
  - ***Storing*** CPU writes back the results of execution, to the computer's memory.

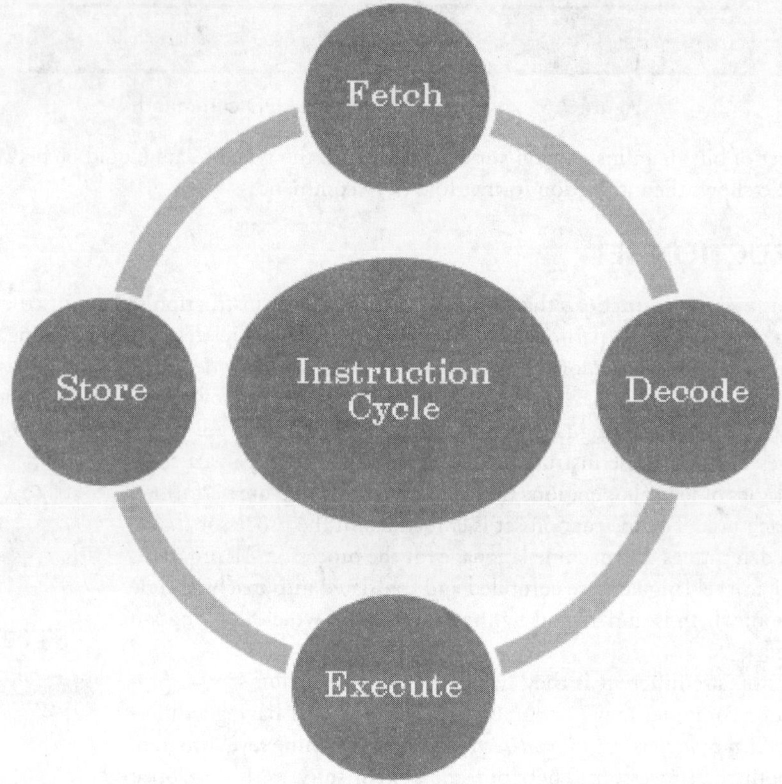

Figure 2.8 Instruction cycle

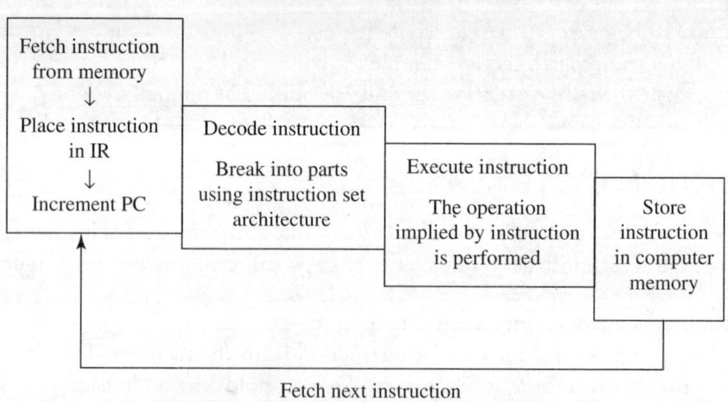

Figure 2.9 Steps in instruction cycle

- Instructions are of different categories. Some categories of instructions are—
  - Memory access or transfer of data between registers.
  - Arithmetic operations like addition and subtraction.
  - Logic operations such as AND, OR and NOT.
  - Control the sequence, conditional connections, etc.

A CPU performance is measured by the number of instructions it executes in a second, i.e., ***MIPS*** (million instructions per second), or ***BIPS*** (billion instructions per second).

2.7 MICROPROCESSOR

A processor's instruction set is a determining factor in its architecture. On the basis of the instruction set, microprocessors are classified as—Reduced Instruction Set Computer (RISC), and Complex Instruction Set Computer (CISC). The *x86* instruction set of the original Intel 8086 processor is of the CISC type. The PCs are based on the *x86* instruction set.

- ***CISC*** architecture hardwires the processor with complex instructions, which are difficult to create otherwise using basic instructions. CISC combines the different instructions into one single CPU.
    - CISC has a large instruction set that includes simple and fast instructions for performing basic tasks, as well as complex instructions that correspond to statements in the high level language.
    - An increased number of instructions (200 to 300) results in a much more complex processor, requiring millions of transistors.
    - Instructions are of variable lengths, using 8, 16 or 32 bits for storage. This results in the processor's time being spent in calculating where each instruction begins and ends.
    - With large number of application software programs being written for the processor, a new processor has to be backwards compatible to the older version of processors.
    - AMD and Cyrix are based on CISC.
- ***RISC*** has simple, single-cycle instructions, which performs only basic instructions. RISC architecture does not have hardwired advanced functions. All high-level language support is done in the software.
    - RISC has fewer instructions and requires fewer transistors, which results in the reduced manufacturing cost of processor.
    - The instruction size is fixed (32 bits). The processor need not spend time in finding out where each instruction begins and ends.
    - RISC architecture has a reduced production cost compared to CISC processors.
    - The instructions, simple in nature, are executed in just one clock cycle, which speeds up the program execution when compared to CISC processors.
    - RISC processors can handle multiple instructions simultaneously by processing them in parallel.
    - Apple Mac G3 and PowerPC are based on RISC.

Processors like Athlon XP and Pentium IV use a hybrid of both technologies.

Pipelining improves instruction execution speed by putting the execution steps into parallel. A CPU can receive a single instruction, begin executing it, and receive another instruction before it has completed the first. This allows for more instructions to be performed, about, one instruction per clock cycle.

Parallel Processing is the simultaneous execution of instructions from the same program on different processors. A program is divided into multiple processes that are handled in parallel in order to reduce execution time.

2.8 INTERCONNECTING THE UNITS OF A COMPUTER

CPU sends data, instructions and information to the components inside the computer as well as to the peripherals and devices attached to it. ***Bus*** is a set of electronic signal pathways that allows information and signals to travel between components inside or outside of a computer. The different components of computer, i.e., CPU, I/O unit, and memory unit are connected with each other by a bus. The data, instructions and the signals are carried between the different components via a bus. The features and functionality of a bus are as follows—

- A bus is a set of wires used for interconnection, where each wire can carry one bit of data.
- A bus width is defined by the number of wires in the bus.
- A computer bus can be divided into two types—Internal Bus and External Bus.
- The Internal Bus connects components inside the motherboard like, CPU and system memory. It is also called the *System Bus*. Figure 2.10 shows interaction between processor and memory.

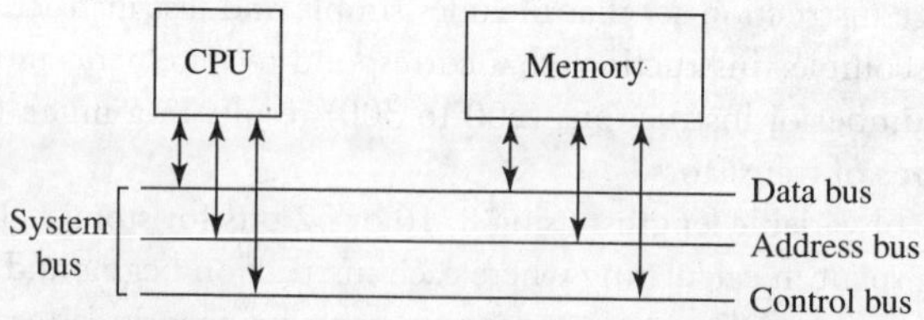

Figure 2.10 Interaction between CPU and memory

- The External Bus connects the different external devices, peripherals, expansion slots, I/O ports and drive connections to the rest of computer. The external bus allows various devices to be attached to the computer. It allows for the expansion of computer's capabilities. It is generally slower than the system bus. It is also referred to as the *Expansion Bus*.
- A system bus or expansion bus comprise of three kinds of buses - data bus, address bus and control bus.
- The interaction of CPU with memory and I/O devices involves all the three buses.
  - The command to access the memory or the I/O device is carried by the ***control bus***.
  - The address of I/O device or memory is carried by the ***address bus***.
  - The data to be transferred is carried by the ***data bus***.

Figure 2.11 shows interaction between processor, memory and the peripheral devices.

2.8.1 System Bus

The functions of data bus, address bus and control bus, in the system bus, are as follows—

- ***Data Bus*** transfers data between the CPU and memory. The bus width of a data bus affects the *speed of computer*. The size of data bus defines the size of the processor. A processor can be 8, 16, 32 or 64-bit processor. An 8-bit processor has 8 wire data bus to carry 1 byte of data. In a 16-bit processor, 16-wire bus can carry 16 bits of data, i.e., transfer 2 bytes, etc.
- ***Address Bus*** connects CPU and RAM with set of wires similar to data bus. The width of address bus

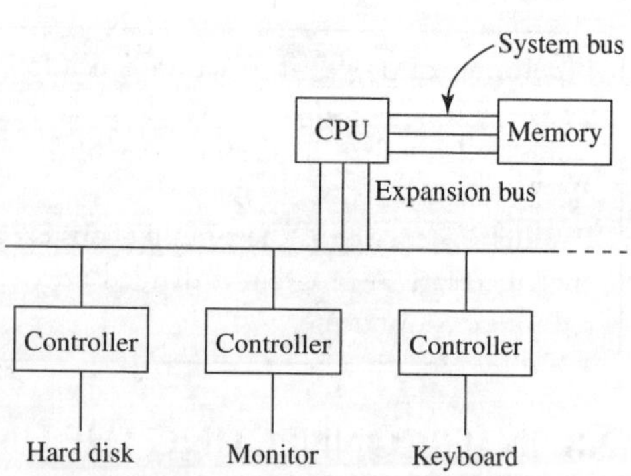

Figure 2.11 Interaction between CPU, memory and peripheral devices

determines the *maximum number of memory locations* the computer can address. Currently, Pentium Pro, II, III, IV have 36-bit address bus that can address 2^{36} bytes or 64 GB of memory.

- ***Control Bus*** specifies whether data is to be read or written to the memory, etc.

2.8.2 Expansion Bus

The functions of data bus, address bus and control bus, in the expansion bus, are as follows—

- The expansion bus connects external devices to the rest of computer. The external devices like monitor, keyboard and printer connect to ports on the back of computer. These ports are actually a part of the small circuit board or *expansion card* that fits into an *expansion slot* on the motherboard. Expansion slots are easy to recognize on the motherboard.
- Expansion slots make up a row of long plastic connectors at the back of the computer with tiny copper 'finger slots' in a narrow channel that grab the connectors on the expansion cards. The slots are attached to tiny copper pathways on the motherboard (the expansion bus), which allows the device to communicate with the rest of computer.
- ***Data Bus*** is used to transfer data between I/O devices and CPU. The exchange of data between CPU and I/O devices is according to the industry standard data buses. The most commonly used standard is Extended Industry Standard Architecture (EISA) which is a 32-bit bus architecture. Some of the common bus technologies are—
    - Peripheral Component Interconnect (PCI) bus for hard disks, sound cards, network cards and graphics cards,
    - Accelerated Graphics Port (AGP) bus for 3-D and full motion video,
    - Universal Serial Bus (USB) to connect and disconnect different devices.
- ***Address Bus*** carries the addresses of different I/O devices to be accessed like the hard disk, CD ROM, etc.
- ***Control Bus*** is used to carry read/write commands, status of I/O devices, etc.

2.8.3 External Ports

The peripheral devices interact with the CPU of the computer via the bus. The connections to the bus from the peripheral devices are made via the ports and sockets provided at the sides of the computer. The different ports and sockets facilitate the connection of different devices to the computer. Some of the standard port connections available on the outer sides of the computer are—port for mouse, keyboard, monitor, network, modem, and, audio port, serial port, parallel port and USB port. The different ports are physically identifiable by their different shapes, size of contact pins and number of pins. Figure 2.12 shows the interaction of serial and parallel port interfaces with the devices.

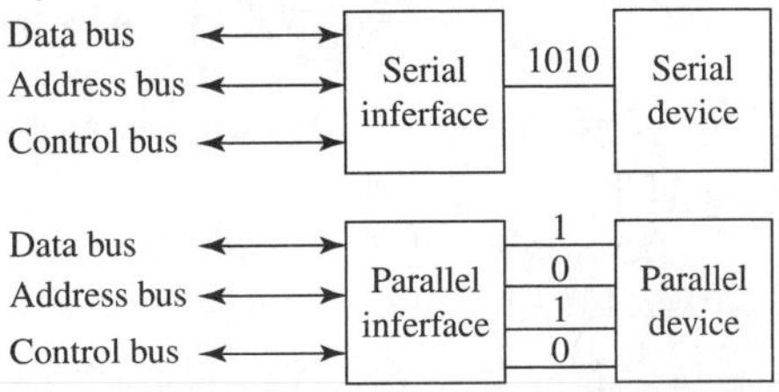

Figure 2.12 Interaction of serial and parallel port interfaces

2.9 PERFORMANCE OF A COMPUTER

There are a number of factors involved that are related to the CPU and have an effect on the overall speed and performance of the computer. Some of the factors that affect the performance of the computer include—

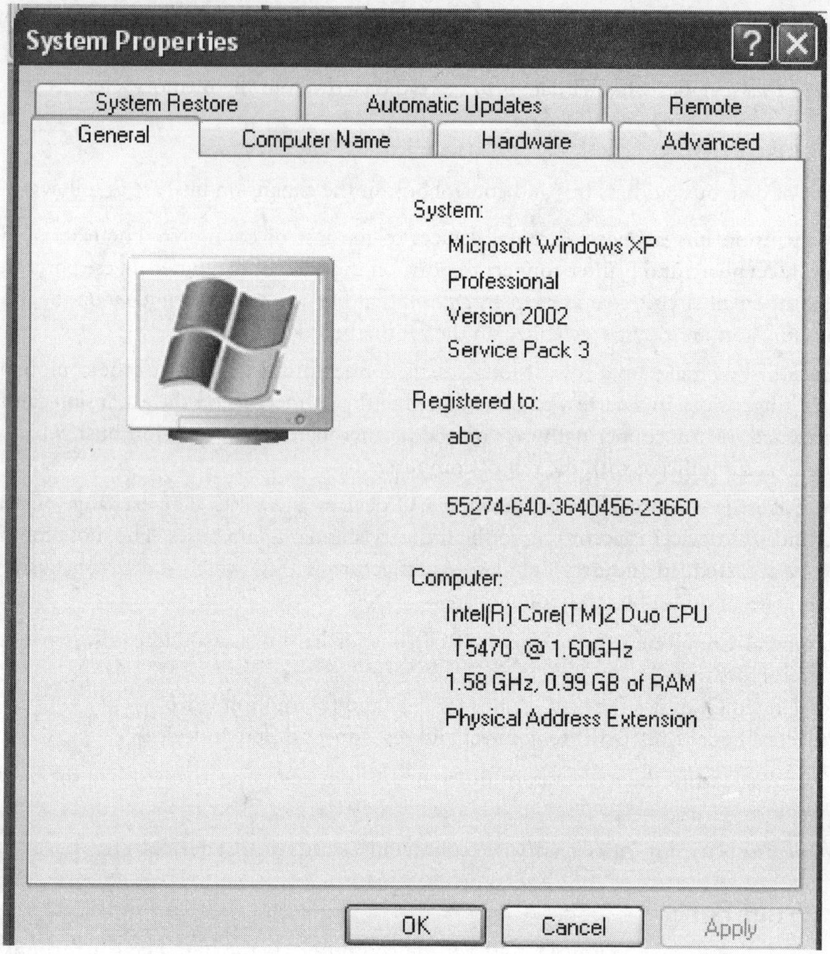

Figure 2.13 System properties in Windows XP Professional

- ***Registers*** The size of the register (word size) indicates the amount of data with which the computer can work at any given time. The bigger the size, the more quickly it can process data. A 32-bit CPU is one in which each register is 32 bits wide.
- ***RAM*** It is used to store data and instructions during execution of the instructions. Anything you do on your computer requires RAM. When the computer is switched on, the operating system, device drivers, the active files and running programs are loaded into RAM. If RAM is less, then the CPU waits each time the new information is swapped into memory from the slower devices. Larger the RAM size, the better it is. PCs nowadays usually have 1 GB to 4 GB of RAM.
- ***System Clock*** The clock speed of a CPU is defined as the frequency with which a processor executes instructions or the data is processed. Higher clock frequencies mean more clock ticks per second. The computer's operating speed is linked to the speed of the system clock. The clock frequency is measured in millions of cycles per second or megahertz (MHz) or gigahertz (GHz) which is billions of cycles per second. A CPU's performance is measured by the number of instructions it executes in a second, i.e., *MIPS* or *BIPS*. PCs nowadays come with a clock speed of more

than 1 GHz. *In Windows OS, you can select the System Properties dialog box to see the processor name and clock frequency.*

- **Bus** *Data bus* is used for transfering data between CPU and memory. The data bus width affects the speed of computer. In a 16-bit processor, 16-bit wire bus can carry 16 bits of data. The bus speed is measured in MHz. Higher the bus speed the better it is. *Address bus* connects CPU and RAM with a set of wires similar to data bus. The address bus width determines the *maximum number of memory locations* the computer can address. Pentium Pro, II, III, IV have 36-bit address bus that can address 2^{36} bytes or 64 GB of memory. PCs nowadays have a bus speed varying from 100 MHz to 400 MHz.
- ***Cache Memory*** Two of the main factors that affect a cache's performance are its size (amount of cache memory) and level L1, L2 and L3. Larger the size of cache, the better it is. PCs nowadays have a L1 cache of 256KB and L2 cache of 1MB.

Figure 2.13 shows the general information about a computer as displayed in the system properties window in Windows XP Professional.

2.10 INSIDE A COMPUTER CABINET

The computer cabinet encloses the components that are required for the running of computer. The components inside a computer cabinet include the power supply, motherboard, memory chips, expansion slots, ports and interface, processor, cables and storage devices.

2.10.1 Motherboard

The computer is built up around a *motherboard*. The motherboard is the most important component in the PC. It is a large Printed Circuit Board (PCB), having many chips, connectors and other electronics mounted on it. The motherboard is the hub, which is used to connect all the essential components of a computer. The RAM, hard drive, disk drives and optical drives are all plugged into interfaces on the motherboard. The motherboard contains the processor, memory chips, interfaces and sockets, etc.

The motherboard may be characterized by the form factor, chipset and type of processor socket used. *Form factor* refers to the motherboard's geometry, dimensions, arrangement and electrical requirements. Different standards have been developed to build motherboards, which can be used in different brands of cases. Advanced Technology Extended (ATX) is the most common design of motherboard for desktop computers. *Chipset* is a circuit, which controls the majority of resources (including the bus interface with the processor, cache memory and RAM, expansion cards, etc.) Chipset's job is to coordinate data transfers between the various components of the computer (including the processor and memory). As the chipset is integrated into the motherboard, it is important to choose a motherboard, which includes a recent chipset, in order to maximize the computer's upgradeability. The *processor socket* may be a rectangular connector into which the processor is mounted vertically (slot), or a square-shaped connector with many small connectors into which the processor is directly inserted (socket). The Basic Input Output System (BIOS) and Complementary Metal-Oxide Semiconductor (CMOS) are present on the motherboard.

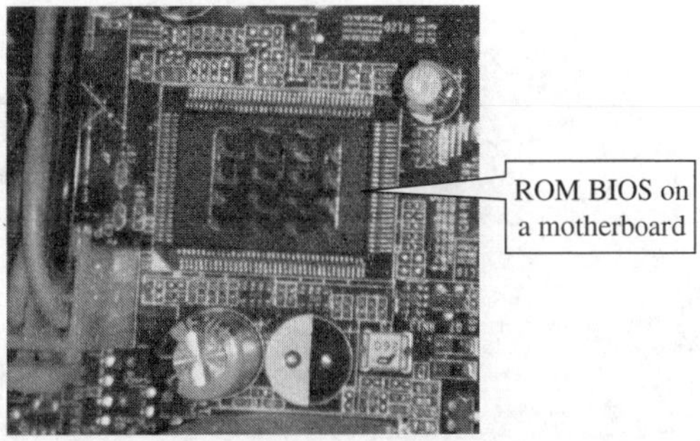

Figure 2.14 ROM BIOS

- ***BIOS*** It is the basic program used as an interface between the operating system and the motherboard. The BIOS (Figure 2.14) is stored in the ROM and cannot be rewritten. When the computer is switched on, it needs instructions to start. BIOS contain the instructions for the starting up of the computer. The BIOS runs when the computer is switched on. It performs a Power On Self Test (POST) that checks that the hardware is functioning properly and the hardware devices are present. It checks whether the operating system is present on the hard drive. BIOS invokes the bootstrap loader to load the operating system into memory. BIOS can be configured using an interface named BIOS setup, which can be accessed when the computer is booting up (*by pressing the DEL key*).

- ***CMOS Chip*** BIOS ROMs are accompanied by a smaller CMOS (CMOS is a type of memory technology) memory chip. When the computer is turned off, the power supply stops providing electricity to the motherboard. When the computer is turned on again, the system still displays the correct clock time. This is because the CMOS chip saves some system information, such as time, system date and essential system settings. CMOS is kept powered by a button battery located on the motherboard (Figure 2.15). The CMOS chip is working even when the computer power is switched off. Information of the hardware installed in the computer (such as the number of tracks or sectors on each hard drive) is stored in the CMOS chip.

Figure 2.15 Battery for CMOS chip

2.10.2 Ports and Interfaces

Motherboard has a certain number of I/O sockets that are connected to the ports and interfaces found on the rear side of a computer (Figure 2.16). You can connect external devices to the ports and interfaces, which get connected to the computer's motherboard.

- Serial Port—to connect old peripherals.
- Parallel Port—to connect old printers.

Figure 2.16 Ports on the rear side of a PC

- USB Ports—to connect newer peripherals like cameras, scanners and printers to the computer. It uses a thin wire to connect to the devices, and many devices can share that wire simultaneously.
- Firewire is another bus, used today mostly for video cameras and external hard drives.
- RJ45 connector (called LAN or Ethernet port) is used to connect the computer to a network. It corresponds to a network card integrated into the motherboard.
- VGA connector for connecting a monitor. This connector interfaces with the built-in graphics card.
- Audio plugs (line-in, line-out and microphone), for connecting sound speakers and the microphone. This connector interfaces with the built-in sound card.
- PS/2 port to connect mouse and keyboard into PC.
- SCSI port for connecting the hard disk drives and network connectors.

2.10.3 Expansion Slots

The expansion slots (Figure 2.17) are located on the motherboard. The expansion cards are inserted in the expansion slots. These cards give the computer new features or increased performance. There are several types of slots:

- ISA (Industry Standard Architecture) slot—To connect modem and input devices.
- PCI (Peripheral Component InterConnect) slot—To connect audio, video and graphics. They are much faster than ISA cards.
- AGP (Accelerated Graphic Port) slot—A fast port for a graphics card.
- PCI (Peripheral Component InterConnect) Express slot—Faster bus architecture than AGP and PCI buses.
- PC Card—It is used in laptop computers. It includes Wi-Fi card, network card and external modem.

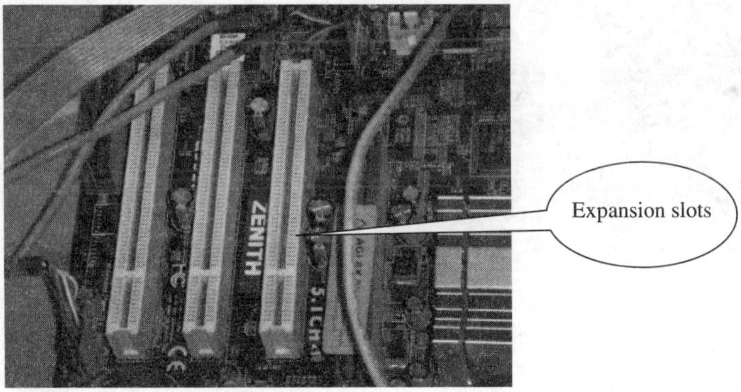

Figure 2.17 Expansion slots

2.10.4 Ribbon Cables

Ribbon cables (Figure 2.18) are flat, insulated and consist of several tiny wires moulded together that carry data to different components on the motherboard. There is a wire for each bit of the word or byte and additional wires to coordinate the activity of moving information. They also connect the floppy drives, disk drives and CD-ROM drives to the connectors in the motherboard. Nowadays, Serial Advanced Technology Attachment (SATA) cables have replaced the ribbon cables to connect the drives to the motherboard.

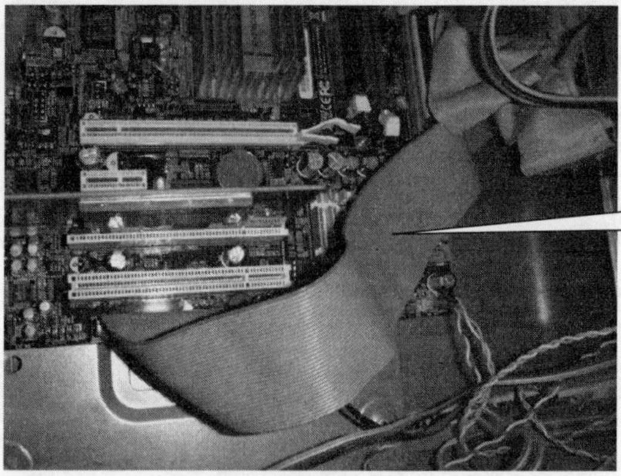

Figure 2.18 Ribbon cables inside a PC

2.10.5 Memory Chips

The RAM consists of chips on a small circuit board (Figure 2.19). Two types of memory chips—Single In-line Memory Module (SIMM) and Dual In-line Memory Module (DIMM) are used in desktop computers. The CPU can retrieve information from DIMM chip at 64 bits compared to 32 bits or 16 bits transfer with SIMM chips. DIMM chips are used in Pentium 4 onwards to increase the access speed.

Figure 2.19 RAM memory chip

2.10.6 Storage Devices

The disk drives are present inside the machine. The common disk drives in a machine are hard disk drive, floppy drive (Figure 2.20 (i & ii)) and CD drive or DVD drive. High-storage devices like hard disk, floppy disk and CDs (Figure 2.20 (iii) & (iv)) are inserted into the hard disk drive, floppy drive and CD drive, respectively. These storage devices can store large amounts of data, permanently.

2.10.7 Processor

The processor or the CPU is the main component of the computer. Select a processor based on factors like its speed, performance, reliability and motherboard support. Pentium Pro, Pentium 2 and Pentium 4 are some of the processors.

Figure 2.20 Storage devices (i) Hard disk drive, (ii) DVD drive, (iii) Floppy disk, (iv) CD

SUMMARY

- Different computers may have different organization, but the basic *organization of computer* remains the same.
- I/O Unit, CPU and Memory Unit are the *main components of computer*.
- *CPU or microprocessor* is called the brain of computer. It processes data and instructions. It also supervises the operations of the other parts of computer.
- Registers, Arithmetic Logic Unit and Control Unit are the *parts of CPU*.
- Cache memory, primary memory and secondary memory constitute the *memory unit*. Primary memory consists of RAM and ROM.
- *Registers* are low-storage capacity, high-speed storage areas within the CPU. The data, instructions, addresses and intermediate results of processing are stored in the registers by the CPU.
- *Cache memory* is a very high-speed memory placed in between RAM and CPU, to increase the processing speed. Cache memory is available in three levels - L1, L2 and L3.
- *RAM* provides temporary storage, has a limited storage capacity and is volatile memory. The access speed of RAM is faster than access speed of the storage devices like hard disk. The data and the instructions stored in the hard disk are brought into the RAM so that the CPU can access the data and the instructions and process it.
- *CU* organizes the processing of data and instructions. It acts as a supervisor and controls and coordinates the activity of other units of computer.
- *ALU* performs arithmetic operations and logic operations on the data.
- An *instruction* is an elementary operation that the processor can accomplish. The instructions in the *instruction set* are the language that a processor understands. The instruction set is embedded in the processor which determines the machine language for the processor.
- A CPU *instruction cycle* involves four steps—(1) Fetching the instructions from the memory, (2) Decoding instructions so that they correspond to those in the CPU's instruction set, (3) Executing the decoded instructions, and (4) Storing the result to the computer memory.
- *RISC and CISC* are the two kinds of microprocessors classified on the basis of instruction set. CISC has a large and complex instruction set. RISC has fewer instructions.
- The different components of computer are connected with each other by a *bus*. A computer bus is of two types—system bus and expansion bus. A system bus or expansion bus comprise of three kinds of buses—data bus, address bus and control bus.
- The *System Bus* connects the CPU, system memory, and all other components on the motherboard.
- The *Expansion Bus* connects the different external devices, peripherals, expansion slots, I/O ports and drive connections to the rest of computer.
- The *performance of computer* is affected by the size of registers, size of RAM, speed of system clock, width of bus, and size of cache memory.
- Inside a *computer cabinet*, there is a motherboard, ports and interfaces, expansion slots, ribbon cables, RAM memory chips, high storage disk drives, and, processor.

- The *motherboard* is characterized by the form factor, chipset and type of processor socket. Form factor is the motherboard's geometry, dimensions, arrangement and electrical requirements. Chipset controls the majority of resources of the computer.
- *BIOS and CMOS* are present on the motherboard. BIOS is stored in ROM and is used as an interface between the operating system and the motherboard. The time, the system date, and essential system settings are saved in CMOS memory chip present on the motherboard. When the computer power is switched off, CMOS chip remains alive powered by a button battery.
- *Ports and interfaces* are located on the sides of the computer case to which the external devices can be connected. Some of the ports and interfaces are—Serial port, Parallel port, USB port, Firewire, RJ45 connector, VGA connector, Audio plugs, PS/2 port, and SCSI port.

KEYWORDS

Accelerated Graphics Port (AGP) *29*
Address bus *28*
Arithmetic Logic Unit (ALU) *20*
Audio plugs *33*
Basic Input Output System (BIOS) *31*
Billion Instructions Per Second (BIPS) *27*
Brain of computer *20*
Bus *27*
Cache memory *31*
Central Processing Unit (CPU) *20*
Chipset *31*
Complementary Metal-Oxide Semiconductor (CMOS) *31*
Complex Instruction Set Computer (CISC) *27*
Computer architecture *19*
Computer design *19*
Computer organization *19*
Control bus *29*
Control Unit (CU) *20*
CPU performance *27*
Data bus *28*
Decoding *25*
Executing *25*
Expansion bus *28*
Expansion card *29*
Expansion slot *29*
Extended Industry Standard Architecture (EISA) *29*
Fetching *25*
Firewire *33*
Form factor *31*
Input/Output (I/O) unit *12*
Instruction format *24*
Instruction set *25*
Instruction cycle *25*
Memory Unit *22*
Microprocessor *20*
Million Instructions Per Second (MIPS) *27*
Motherboard *20*
Parallel port *32*
Peripheral Component Interconnect (PCI) *29*
Power On Self Test (POST) *32*
Primary memory *22*
PS/2 Port *33*
Random Access Memory (RAM) *22*
Read Only Memory (ROM) *22*
Reduced Instruction Set Computer (RISC) *27*
Registers *30*
Ribbon cables *33*
SCSI port *33*
Serial port *29*
Speed of computer *28*
Stored program *20*
Storing *25*
System bus *28*
System clock *30*
Universal Serial Bus (USB) *29*
Word size *21*

QUESTIONS

Section 2.1

1. Define computer architecture, computer organization and computer design.
2. Give a brief description of the working of computer.

Section 2.2

3. CPU is also often called the ________ of computer.
4. Define a microprocessor.
5. Define a motherboard.
6. The different parts of the CPU are ________, ________ and ________.
7. What is the purpose of the primary memory?
8. ________ and ________ are the primary memory.
9. List the main functions of the CPU.

Section 2.2.1–2.2.3

10. ALU consists of the ________ unit and ________ unit.
11. What are the functions of ALU?

12. ______ is also called the working memory of CPU.
13. List five important registers of the CPU. Also state the purpose of each register.
14. Why are Registers used in the CPU?
15. Define word size.
16. "This is a 64-bit processor". Explain its meaning.
17. The size of register is also the ______ size.
18. Which is faster—a 32-bit processor or a 64-bit-processor?
19. What are the functions of the control unit?

Section 2.3–2.3.3

20. Explain the need of the cache memory?
21. The ______ memory is placed between the RAM and the CPU.
22. There are _______ levels of cache memory.
23. Explain the three levels of the cache memory.
24. State three important features of the cache memory.
25. The size of the cache memory is generally in the range ________.
26. What is the purpose of RAM?
27. List the features of primary memory.
28. List the key features of secondary memory.

Section 2.4

29. Define the stored program concept.
30. Describe the format of an instruction.
31. The common fields of an instruction are ______ code and ______ code.
32. What is the function of the operand code and the operation code?

Section 2.5

33. Define an Instruction set.
34. What is the significance of the Instruction set in the CPU?
35. "Two processors are compatible". How do you deduce this statement?
36. Define microarchitecture.

Section 2.6

37. Define an instruction cycle.
38. Give a detailed working of the instruction cycle.
39. Name the four steps involved in an instruction cycle.
40. The number of instructions executed in a second by the CPU, is measured in _____.

Section 2.7

41. The microprocessors are classified as _____ and _____ on the basis of the instruction set.
42. The x86 instruction set of the original Intel 8086 processor is of the _____ type.
43. Describe the features of the CISC architecture.
44. Give two examples of the CISC processor.
45. Describe the features of the RISC architecture.
46. Give two examples of the RISC processor.
47. What is the use of parallel processing and pipelining?

Section 2.8

48. Define a bus.
49. Define a system bus.
50. Define an expansion bus.
51. Why is a bus used?
52. Define—control bus, address bus and data bus.
53. A system bus or expansion bus comprises of three kinds of buses _______, ______ and ______.
54. Name the bus connecting CPU with memory?
55. Name the bus connecting I/O devices with CPU?

Section 2.8.1

56. In a system bus, what is the significance of the control bus, address bus and data bus?
57. The ______ of data bus affects the speed of computer.
58. Name the bus whose width affects the speed of computer?
59. The __________ of address bus determines the maximum number of memory locations the computer can address.
60. Name the bus whose width determines the maximum number of memory locations the computer can address?

Section 2.8.2–2.8.3

61. What are the functions of data bus, address bus and control bus in the expansion bus?
62. Where is the expansion card fixed on the motherboard?
63. What is an expansion slot?
64. Name three common bus technologies.
65. What kind of devices is attached to the PCI bus, AGP bus and USB bus?

Section 2.9

66. List the factors that affect the performance of computer.
67. Explain in detail the factors that affect the performance of computer.
68. What is the use of the system clock?
69. The clock frequency is measured in _____.

Section 2.10–2.10.1

70. "The motherboard is characterized by the form factor, chipset and the type of processor socket used". Explain.
71. Define form factor.
72. Define chipset.
73. _____ is the most common design of the motherboard for desktop computers.
74. What is the significance of the chipset?
75. What is the function of the BIOS?
76. What is the function of the CMOS chip?
77. Explain the booting process when the computer is switched on.
78. What is POST?

Section 2.10.2–2.10.7

79. List five ports and interfaces available on the backside of the computer to connect the devices.
80. What devices are attached to—(a) Serial Port, (b) Parallel Port, (c) USB Port, (d) Firewire, (e) RJ45 connector, (f) VGA connector, (g) Audio plugs (Line-In, Line-Out and microphone), (h) PS/2 Port, and (h) SCSI Port.
81. List five expansion slots available in the computer.
82. What devices are attached to—(a) ISA slots, (b) PCI slot, (c) AGP slot, (d) PCI Express slot, and (e) PC Card.
83. What is the purpose of the Ribbon cables?
84. Two types of memory chips ______ and ______ are used in desktop computers.
85. List any three storage devices that are attached to the computer.

Extra Questions

86. Give full form of the following abbreviations

(i) IC	(ii) MIPS	(iii) EISA
(iv) PCI	(v) USB	(vi) AGP
(vii) BIPS	(viii) SIMM	(ix) DIMM
(x) GHz	(xi) MHz	(xii) PCB
(xiii) BIOS	(xiv) CMOS	(xv) POST
(xvi) ISA	(xvii) ROM	(xviii) ACC
(xix) IR	(xx) PC	(xxi) MAR
(xxii) MBR	(xxiii) DR	(xxiv) RISC
(xxv) CISC	(xxvi) ATX	(xxvii) SATA

87. Write short notes on—

(a) Working of computer	(b) Central processing unit
(c) Registers	(d) Cache memory
(e) RAM	(f) Control unit
(g) ALU	(h) Instruction format
(i) Instruction set	(j) Instruction Cycle
(k) Microprocessor	(l) System bus
(m) Expansion bus	(n) Performance of computer
(o) System clock	(p) Motherboard
(q) BIOS	(r) CMOS chip
(s) Ports and interfaces in computer	
(t) Expansion slots	(u) Main components in a computer case

88. Give differences between the following—
    (a) Registers and cache memory
    (b) Cache memory and RAM
    (c) RISC and CISC
    (d) System bus and expansion bus
    (e) Data bus, address bus and control bus

3 COMPUTER MEMORY

Contents

Why this chapter

From the moment you switch on a computer till you switch it off, computer uses its primary memory. When you request for the processing of data and instructions, the processor uses its registers, cache memory, primary memory and secondary memory. As a computer user, you need to be aware of the memory present in a computer. This chapter describes the different kind of memories, their use and the interaction between them.

3.1 INTRODUCTION

The computer's memory stores data, instructions required during the processing of data, and output results. Storage may be required for a limited period of time, instantly, or, for an extended period of time. Different types of memories, each having its own unique features, are available for use in a computer. The cache memory, registers, and RAM are fast memories and store the data and instructions temporarily during the processing of data and instructions. The secondary memory like magnetic disks and optical disks have large storage capacities and store the data and instructions permanently, but are slow memory devices. The memories are organized in the computer in a manner to achieve high levels of performance at the minimum cost.

In this chapter, we discuss different types of memories, their characteristics and their use in the computer.

3.2 MEMORY REPRESENTATION

The computer memory stores different kinds of data like input data, output data, intermediate results, etc., and the instructions. ***Binary digit or bit*** is the basic unit of memory. A *bit* is a single binary digit, i.e., 0 or 1. A bit is the smallest unit of representation of data in a computer. However, the data is handled by the computer as a combination of bits. A group of 8 bits form a **byte**. One byte is the smallest unit of data that is handled by the computer. One byte can store 2^8, i.e., 256 different combinations of bits, and thus can be used to represent 256 different symbols. In a byte, the different combinations of bits fall in the range 00000000 to 11111111. A group of bytes can be further combined to form a **word**. A word can be a group of 2, 4 or 8 bytes.

1 bit = 0 or 1
1 Byte (B) = 8 bits
1 Kilobyte (KB) = 2^{10} = 1024 bytes
1 Megabyte (MB) = 2^{20} = 1024KB
1 Gigabyte (GB) = 2^{30} = 1024 MB = 1024 *1024 KB
1 Terabyte (TB) = 2^{40}= 1024 GB = 1024 * 1024 *1024 KB

Memory is logically organized as a linear array of locations. For a processor, the range of the memory addresses is 0 to the maximum size of memory. Figure 3.1 shows the organization of a 16 MB block of memory for a processor with a 32-bit word length.

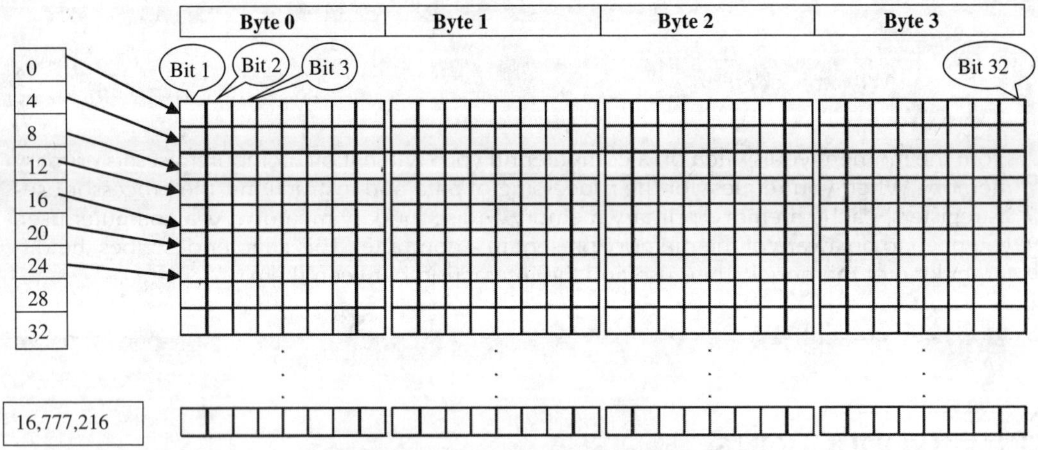

Figure 3.1 Organization of memory

3.3 MEMORY HIERARCHY

The memory is characterized on the basis of two key factors—capacity and access time. *Capacity* is the amount of information (in bits) that a memory can store. *Access time* is the time interval between the read/write request and the availability of data. The lesser the access time, the faster is the *speed of memory*. Ideally, we want the memory with *fastest speed and largest capacity*. However, the cost of fast memory is very high. The computer uses a hierarchy of memory that is organized in a manner to enable the fastest speed and largest capacity of memory. The hierarchy of the different memory types is shown in Figure 3.2.

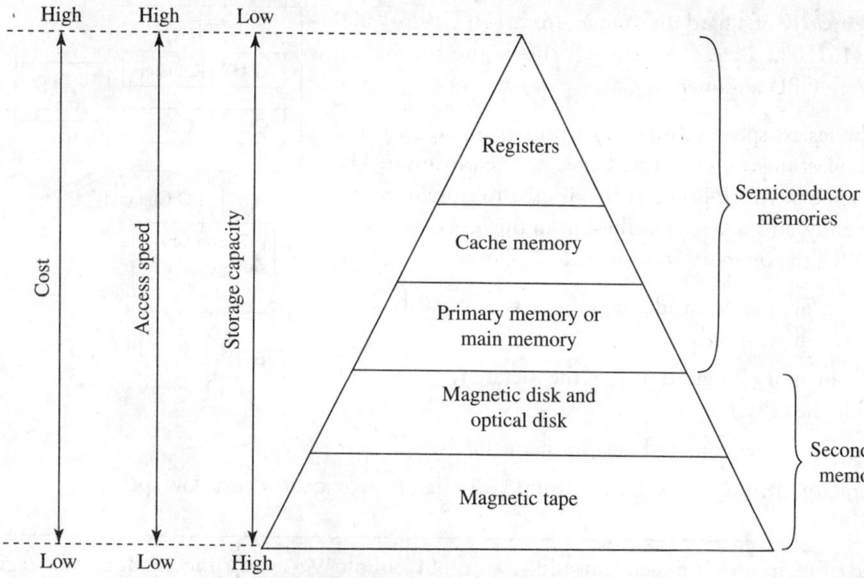

Figure 3.2 Memory hierarchy

The internal memory and external memory are the two broad categories of memory used in the computer. The internal memory consists of the CPU registers, cache memory and primary memory. The internal memory is used by the CPU to perform the computing tasks. The external memory is also called the secondary memory. The secondary memory is used to store the large amount of data and the software.

> In general, referring to the computer memory usually means the internal memory.

- ***Internal Memory***—The key features of internal memory are—(1) limited storage capacity, (2) temporary storage, (3) fast access, and (4) high cost. Registers, cache memory, and primary memory constitute the internal memory. The primary memory is further of two kinds—RAM and ROM. Registers are the fastest and the most expensive among all the memory types. The registers are located inside the CPU, and are directly accessible by the CPU. The speed of registers is between 1–2 ns (nanosecond). The sum of the size of registers is about 200B. Cache memory is next in the hierarchy and is placed between the CPU and the main memory. The speed of cache is between 2–10 ns. The cache size varies between 32 KB to 4MB. Any program or data that has to be executed must be brought into RAM from the secondary memory. Primary memory is relatively slower than the cache memory. The speed of RAM is around 60ns. The RAM size varies from 512KB to 3GB.
- ***Secondary Memory***—The key features of secondary memory storage devices are—(1) very high storage capacity, (2) permanent storage (non-volatile), unless erased by user, (3) relatively slower access, (4) stores data and instructions that are not currently being used by CPU but may be required later for processing, and (5) cheapest among all memory. The storage devices consist of two parts—drive and device. For example, magnetic tape drive and magnetic tape, magnetic disk drive and disk, and, optical disk drive and disk. The speed of magnetic disk is around 60ms.

The capacity of a hard disk ranges from 160 GB to 1,600 GB (1.6 Tera Bytes). Figure 3.3 shows the interaction between CPU and memory.

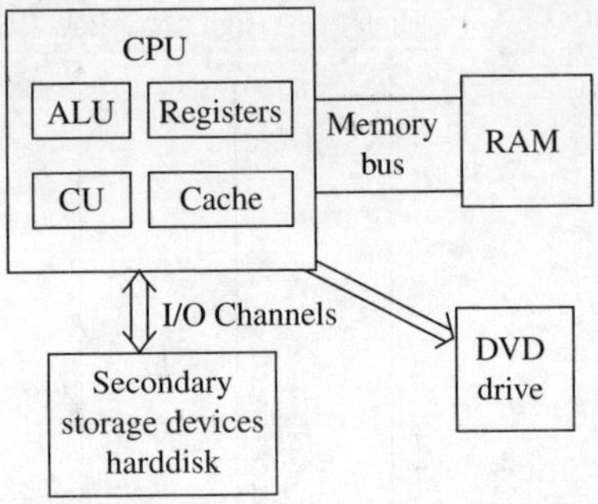

Figure 3.3 CPU and the memory

To get the fastest speed of memory with largest capacity and least cost, the fast memory is located close to the processor. The secondary memory, which is not as fast, is used to store information permanently, and is placed farthest from the processor. With respect to CPU, the memory is organized as follows—

- Registers are placed inside the CPU (small capacity, high cost, very high speed)
- Cache memory is placed next in the hierarchy (inside and outside the CPU)
- Primary memory is placed next in the hierarchy
- Secondary memory is the farthest from CPU (large capacity, low cost, low speed)

The speed of memories is dependent on the kind of technology used for the memory. The registers, cache memory and primary memory are semiconductor memories. They do not have any moving parts and are fast memories. The secondary memory is magnetic or optical memory, has moving parts and has slow speed.

3.4 CPU REGISTERS

- Registers are very high-speed storage areas located inside the CPU. After CPU gets the data and instructions from the cache or RAM, the data and instructions are moved to the registers for processing. Registers are manipulated directly by the control unit of CPU during instruction execution. That is why registers are often referred to as the CPU's *working memory*. Since CPU uses registers for the processing of data, the number of registers in a CPU and the size of each register affect the power and speed of a CPU. The more the number of registers (ten to hundreds) and bigger the size of each register (8 bits to 64 bits), the better it is.

3.5 CACHE MEMORY

- Cache memory is placed in between the CPU and the RAM. Cache memory is a fast memory, faster than RAM. When the CPU needs an instruction or data during processing, it first looks in the cache. If the information is present in cache, it is called a *cache hit*, and the data or instruction is retrieved from the cache. If the information is not present in cache, then it is called a *cache miss* and the information is then retrieved from RAM. The content of cache is decided by the cache controller (a circuit on the motherboard). The most recently accessed information or instructions help the controller to guess the RAM locations that may be accessed next. To get good system performance, the number of hits must far outnumber the misses. The two main factors that affect the performance of cache are its size and level (L1, L2 and L3).

The CPU registers and the cache memory have been discussed in detail in the previous chapter.

3.6 PRIMARY MEMORY

Primary memory is the main memory of computer. It is a chip mounted on the motherboard of computer. Primary memory is categorized into two main types-

- Random Access Memory (RAM), and
- Read Only Memory (ROM)

RAM is used for the temporary storage of input data, output data and intermediate results. The input data entered into the computer using the input device, is stored in RAM for processing. After processing, the output data is stored in RAM before being sent to the output device. Any intermediate results generated during the processing of program are also stored in RAM. Unlike RAM, the data once stored in ROM either cannot be changed or can only be changed using some special operations. Therefore, ROM is used to store the data that does not require a change. *Flash memory* is another form of rewritable read-only memory that is compact, portable, and requires little energy.

3.6.1 Random Access Memory

- RAM is used to *store data and instructions during the operation of computer.*
    - The data and instructions that need to be operated upon by CPU are first brought to RAM from the secondary storage devices like the hard disk.
    - CPU interacts with RAM to get the data and instructions for processing.
- RAM loses information when the computer is powered off. It is a *volatile memory*. When the power is turned on, again, all files that are required by the CPU are loaded from the hard disk to RAM. Since RAM is a volatile memory, any information that needs to be saved for a longer duration of time must not be stored in RAM.
- RAM provides *random access* to the stored bytes, words, or larger data units. This means that it requires same amount of time to access information from RAM, irrespective of where it is located in it.
- RAM can be *read from and written to* with the same speed.
- The *size of RAM is limited* due to its *high cost*. The size of RAM is measured in MB or GB.
- The performance of RAM is affected by—
    - Access speed (how *quickly* information can be retrieved). The speed of RAM is expressed in nanoseconds.
    - Data transfer unit size (how *much* information can be retrieved in one request).
- RAM affects the speed and power of a computer. More the RAM, the better it is. Nowadays, computers generally have 512 MB to 4 GB of RAM.
- RAM is a microchip implemented using semiconductors.
- There are two categories of RAM, depending on the technology used to construct a RAM—(1) Dynamic RAM (DRAM), and (2) Static RAM (SRAM).
- ***DRAM*** is the most common type of memory chip. DRAM is mostly used as *main memory* since it is small and cheap.
    - It uses transistors and capacitors. The transistors are arranged in a matrix of rows and columns. The capacitor holds the bit of information 0 and 1. The transistor and capacitor are paired to make a *memory cell.* The transistor acts as a switch that lets the control circuitry on the memory chip read the capacitor or change its state.

- DRAM must be refreshed continually to store information. For this, a memory controller is used. The memory controller recharges all the capacitors holding a 1 before they discharge. To do this, the memory controller reads the memory and then writes it right back.
- DRAM gets its name from the refresh operation that it requires to store the information; otherwise it will lose what it is holding. The refresh operation occurs automatically thousands of times per second. DRAM is slow because the refreshing takes time.
- Access speed of DRAM ranges from 50 to 150 ns.

⊙ ***SRAM*** chip is usually used in *cache memory* due to its high speed.

- SRAM uses multiple transistors (four to six), for each memory cell. It does not have a capacitor in each cell.
- A SRAM memory cell has more parts so it takes more space on a chip than DRAM cell.
- It does not need constant refreshing and therefore is faster than DRAM.
- SRAM is more expensive than DRAM, and it takes up more space.
- It stores information as long as it is supplied with power.
- SRAM are easier to use and very fast. The access speed of SRAM ranges from 2–10 nanosecond.

⊙ The memory chips (Figure 3.4) are available on a separate Printed Circuit Board (PCB) that is plugged into a special connector on the motherboard. Memory chips are generally available as part of a card called a *memory module*. There are generally two types of RAM modules—Single In-line Memory Module (SIMM) and Dual In-line Memory Module (DIMM).

Figure 3.4 PCB containing RAM chip of 1 GB

- SIMM modules have memory chip on one side of the PCB. SIMM modules can store 8 bits to 32 bits of data simultaneously.
- DIMM modules have memory chips on both sides of the PCB. DIMM format are 64-bit memories. Smaller modules known as Small Outline DIMM (SO DIMM) are designed for portable computers. SO DIMM modules have 32-bit memory.

3.6.2 Read Only Memory

ROM is a *non-volatile* primary memory. It does not lose its content when the power is switched off. The features of ROM are described as follows—

⊙ ROM, as the name implies, has only read capability and no write capability. After the information is stored in ROM, it is permanent and cannot be corrected.

⊙ ROM comes programmed by the manufacturer. It stores standard processing programs that permanently reside in the computer. ROM stores the data needed for the start up of the computer. The instructions that are required for initializing the devices attached to a computer are stored in ROM.

- The ROM memory chip (Figure 3.5) stores the *Basic Input Output System (BIOS)*. BIOS provides the processor with the information required to boot the system. It provides the system with the settings and resources that are available on the system. BIOS is a permanent part of the computer. It does not load from disk but instead is stored in a ROM memory chip. The program code in the BIOS differs from ordinary software since it acts as an integral part of the computer. When the computer is turned on, BIOS does the following things—

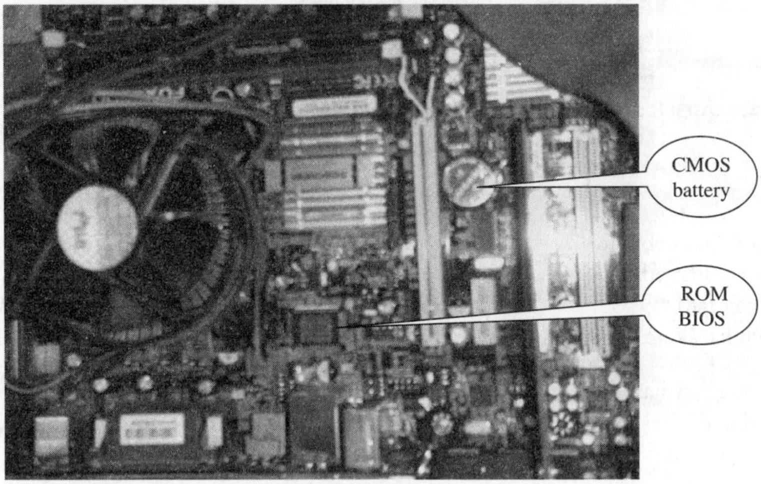

Figure 3.5 ROM BIOS and CMOS battery on a motherboard

  - *Power On Self Test (POST)* is a program that runs automatically when the system is booted. BIOS performs the power-on self-test. It checks that the major hardware components are working properly.
  - BIOS setup program, which is a built-in utility in BIOS, lets the user set the many functions that control how the computer works. BIOS displays the system settings and finds the bootable devices. It loads the interrupt handlers and device drivers. It also initializes the registers.
  - *Bootstrap Loader* is a program whose purpose is to start the computer software for operation when the power is turned on. It loads the operating system into RAM and launches it. It generally seeks the operating system on the hard disk. The bootstrap loader resides in the ROM. The BIOS initiates the bootstrap sequence.

- ROMs are of different kinds. They have evolved from the fixed read only memory to the ones that can be programmed and re-programmed. They vary in the number of re-writes and the method used for the re-writing. Programmable ROM (PROM), Erasable Programmable ROM (EPROM) and Electrically Erasable Programmable ROM (EEPROM) are some of the ROMs. All the different kinds of ROM retain their content when the power is turned off.

  - ***PROM*** can be programmed with a special tool, but after it has been programmed the contents cannot be changed. PROM memories have thousands of fuses (or diodes). High voltage (12 V) is applied to the fuses to be burnt. The burnt fuses correspond to 0 and the others to 1.
  - ***EPROM*** can be programmed in a similar way as PROM, but it can be erased by exposing it to ultra violet light and re-programmed. EPROM chips have to be removed from the computer for re-writing.

- ***EEPROM*** memories can be erased by electric charge and re-programmed. EEPROM chips do not have to be removed from the computer for re-writing.

⊙ ***Flash Memory*** is a kind of semiconductor-based non-volatile, rewritable computer memory that can be electrically erased and reprogrammed (Figure 3.6). It is a specific type of EEPROM.

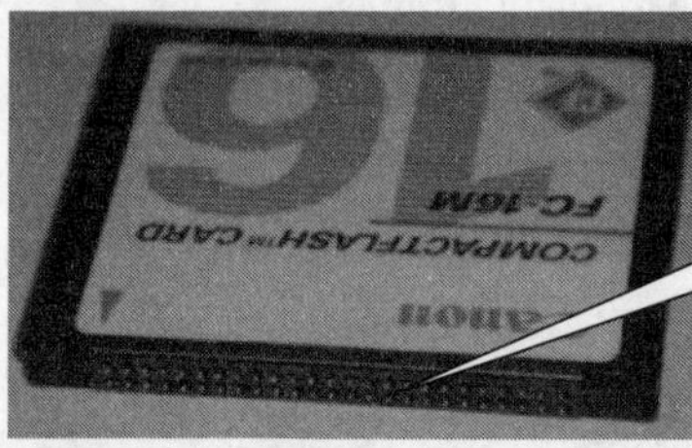

Figure 3.6 Flash memory

- It combines the features of RAM and ROM. It is a random access memory and content can be stored in it at any time. However, like ROM, the data is not lost when the machine is turned off or the electric power is cut. Flash memory stores bits of data in memory cells.
- Flash memories are high-speed memories, durable, and have low-energy consumption. Since flash memory has no moving part, it is very shock-resistant. Due to these features, flash memory is used in devices such as digital camera, mobile phone, printer, laptop computer, and record and play back sound devices, such as MP3 players.

3.7 SECONDARY MEMORY

In the previous section, we saw that RAM is expensive and has a limited storage capacity. Since it is a volatile memory, it cannot retain information after the computer is powered off. Thus, in addition to primary memory, an auxiliary or secondary memory is required by a computer. The secondary memory is also called the storage device of computer. *In this chapter, the terms secondary memory and storage device are used interchangeably.* In comparison to the primary memory, the secondary memory stores much larger amounts of data and information (for example, an entire software program) for extended periods of time. The data and instructions stored in secondary memory must be fetched into RAM before processing is done by CPU.

Magnetic tape drives, magnetic disk drives, optical disk drives and magneto-optical disk drives are the different types of storage devices.

3.8 ACCESS TYPES OF STORAGE DEVICES

The information stored in storage devices can be accessed in two ways—

(a) Sequential access

(b) Direct access

3.8.1 Sequential Access Devices

Sequential access means that computer must run through the data in sequence, starting from the beginning, in order to locate a particular piece of data. Magnetic tape is an example of sequential access device.

Let us suppose that magnetic tape consists of 80 records. To access the 25th record, the computer starts from first record, then reaches second, third etc. until it reaches the 25th record. Sequential access devices are generally slow devices.

3.8.2 Direct Access Devices

Direct access devices are the ones in which any piece of data can be retrieved in a non-sequential manner by locating it using the data's address. It accesses the data directly, from a desired location. Magnetic disks and optical disks are examples of direct access devices. There is no predefined order in which one can read and write data from a direct access device. In a magnetic disk consisting of 80 records, to access the 25th record, the computer can directly access the 25th record, without going past the first 24 records. Based on access, magnetic tapes are sequential access devices, and, magnetic disks, optical disk and magneto-optical disks are direct access devices.

3.9 MAGNETIC TAPE

Magnetic tape is a plastic tape with magnetic coating (Figure 3.7). It is a storage medium on a large open reel or in a smaller cartridge or cassette (like a music cassette). Magnetic tapes are cheaper storage media. They are durable, can be written, erased, and re-written. Magnetic tapes are sequential access devices, which mean that the tape needs to rewind or move forward to the location where the requested data is positioned in the magnetic tape. Due to their sequential nature, magnetic tapes are not suitable for data files that need to be revised or updated often. They are generally used to store back-up data that is not frequently used or to transfer data from one system to other.

Figure 3.7 A 10.5-inch reel of 9-track tape

The **working of magnetic tape** is explained as follows—

- Magnetic tape is divided horizontally into tracks (7 or 9) and vertically into frames (Figure 3.8). A frame stores one byte of data, and a track in a frame stores one bit. Data is stored in successive frames as a string with one data (byte) per frame.

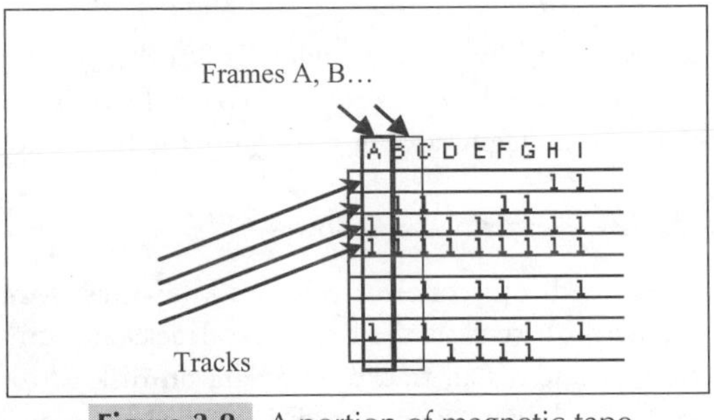

Figure 3.8 A portion of magnetic tape

- Data is recorded on tape in the form of blocks, where a block consists of a group of data also called as records. Each block is read continually. There is an *Inter-Record Gap (IRG)* between two blocks that provides time for the tape to be stopped and started between records (Figure 3.9).

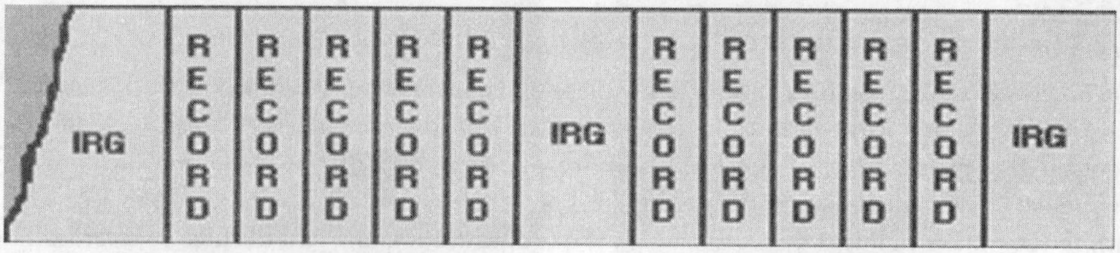

Figure 3.9 Blocking of data in a magnetic tape

- Magnetic tape is mounted on a magnetic tape drive for access. The basic ***magnetic tape drive*** mechanism consists of the supply reel, take-up reel, and the read/write head assembly. The magnetic tape moves on tape drive from the supply reel to take-up reel, with its magnetic coated side passing over the read/write head.
- Tapes are categorized based on their width - ¼ inch, ½ inch, etc.
- The storage capacity of the tape varies greatly. A 10-inch diameter reel of tape which is 2400 feet long can store up to 180 million characters.

The features of magnetic tape are—

- Inexpensive storage device
- Can store a large amount of data
- Easy to carry or transport
- Not suitable for random access data
- Slow access device
- Needs dust prevention, as dust can harm the tape
- Suitable for back-up storage or archiving

3.10 MAGNETIC DISK

Magnetic disk is a direct access secondary storage device. It is a thin plastic or metallic circular plate coated with magnetic oxide and encased in a protective cover. Data is stored on magnetic disks as magnetized spots. The presence of a magnetic spot represents the bit 1 and its absence represents the bit 0.

The working of magnetic disk is explained as follows—

- The surface of disk is divided into concentric circles known as ***tracks***. The outermost track is numbered 0 and the innermost track is the last track. Tracks are further divided into ***sectors***. A sector is a pie slice that cuts across all tracks. The data on disk is stored in sector. Sector is the smallest unit that can be read or written on a disk. A disk has eight or more sectors per track (Figure 3.10).

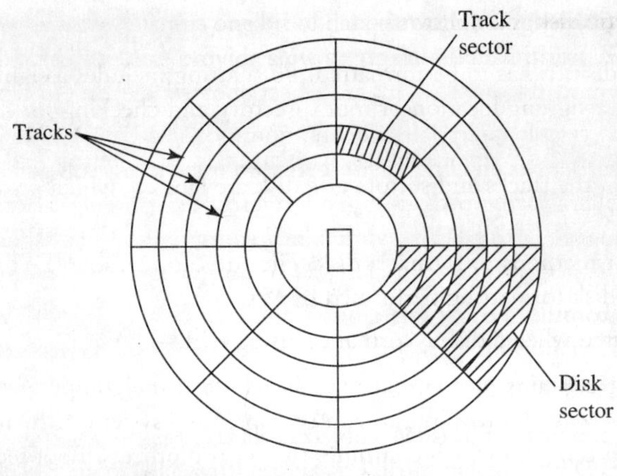

Figure 3.10 Tracks and sectors of a disk

- Magnetic disk is inserted into a magnetic disk drive for access. The drive consists of a read/write head that is attached to a disk arm, which moves the head. The disk arm can move inward and outward on the disk.
- During reading or writing to disk, the motor of disk drive moves the disk at high speed (60–150 times/sec.)
- Accessing data on the disk requires the following—
    - The read/write head is positioned to the desired track where the data is to be read from or written to. The time taken to move the read/write head to the desired track is called the ***seek time***.
    - Once the read/write head is at the right track, then the head waits for right sector to come under it (disk is moving at high speed). The time taken for desired sector of the track to come under read/write head is called the ***latency time***.
    - Once the read/write head is positioned at the right track and sector, the data has to be written to disk or read from disk. The rate at which data is written to disk or read from disk is called ***data transfer rate***.
    - The sum of seek time, latency time and time for data transfer is the ***access time*** of the disk.
- The storage capacity of disk drive is measured in gigabytes (GB).
- Large disk storage is created by stacking together multiple disks. A set of same tracks on all disks forms a ***cylinder***. Each disk has its own read/write head which work in coordination.
- A disk can also have tracks and sectors on both sides. Such a disk is called ***double-sided disk***.

The features of magnetic disk are—

- Cheap storage device
- Can store a large amount of data
- Easy to carry or transport
- Suitable for frequently read/write data
- Fast access device
- More reliable storage device
- To be prevented from dust, as the read/write head flies over the disk; any dust particle in between can corrupt the disk.

Finding data on a magnetic disk is as follows—

- In order to use a disk, it has to be formatted. Formatting includes assigning addresses to various locations on disk, assigning location of root directory and checking for defects on the surface of disk.
- During formatting, the tracks and sectors of a disk are labeled, which provides an address to each location of the disk.
- There are different methods to format a disk. File Allocation Table (FAT) is the commonly used logical format for disk formatting performed by Windows.
- Four areas are created when a disk is formatted using FAT—
    - ***Boot Sector*** It contains the program that runs when the computer is started. The program checks if the disk has files required to run the operating system. It then transfers control to an operating system program which continues the startup process. Boot sector also contains information about the disk, like number of bytes per sector and number of sectors per track. This information is required by the operating system to access the data on the disk.
    - ***File Allocation Table*** It records the location of each file and status of each sector. While reading or writing to disk, operating system checks the FAT to find free area or locate where data is stored on disk, respectively.
    - ***Root Directory*** This is the main folder of disk. It contains other folders in it, creating a hierarchical system of folders. The root directory contains information about all folders on the disk.
    - ***Data Area*** The remaining area of the disk (after boot sector, FAT, root directory) is the data area. It stores the program files and data files that are stored on the disk.
- The Windows XP and the Windows 2000 operating system use the New Technology File System (NTFS) 5 file system. The NTFS 5 file system offers better security and increased performance. It allows using of filenames that are more than eight characters long.
- Floppy disk, hard disk and zip disk are the different types of magnetic disks.

3.10.1 Floppy Disk

- Floppy disk (FD) is a flat, round, single disk made of Mylar plastic and enclosed in square plastic jacket (Figure 3.11).
- Floppy Disk Drive (FDD) is the disk drive for floppy disk.
- The floppy disk is inserted into the floppy disk drive to read or write data to it.
- Floppy disk has a write-protect slide tab that prevents a user from writing to it.
- A floppy disk may be single-sided or double-sided disk, i.e., data can be read and written on one and both sides of floppy disk, respectively.
- They are portable. They can be removed from the disk drive, carried or stored separately.
- They are small and inexpensive.
- Floppy disks are slower to access than hard disk. They have less storage capacity and are less expensive than hard disk.
- They come in two basic sizes—5-¼ inch and 3-½ inch.

Figure 3.11 Floppy disk

- The 5-¼ inch disk came around 1987. It can store 360 KB to 1.2 MB of data.
- The 3-½ inch disk has capacity of 400 KB to 1.44 MB. It usually contains 40 tracks and 18 sectors per track and can store 512 bytes per sector.

3.10.2 Hard Disk

- A hard disk (HD) consists of one or more platters divided into concentric tracks and sectors. It is mounted on a central spindle, like a stack. It can be read by a read/write head that pivots across the rotating disks. The data is stored on the platters covered with magnetic coating (Figure 3.12).

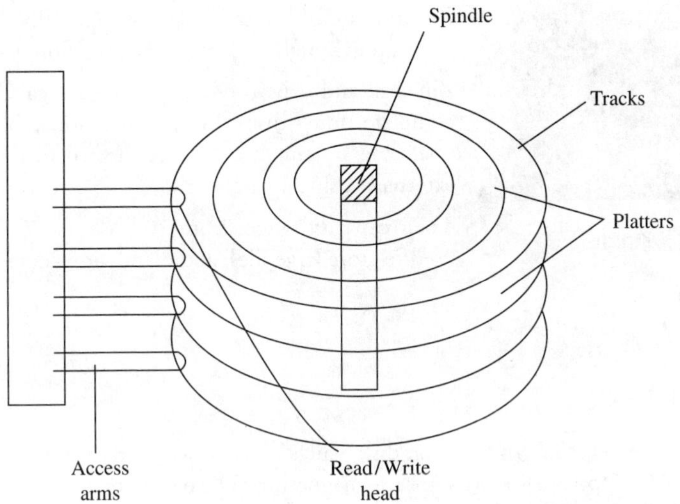

Figure 3.12 Parts of hard disk

- Hard disk is a fixed disk. The disk is not removable from the drive, unlike floppy disk.
- The hard disk and Hard Disk Drive (HDD) is a single unit.
- Hard disk can store much more data than floppy disk. The data in hard disk are packed more closely (because fast spinning uses smaller magnetic charges) and they have multiple platters, with data being stored on both sides of each platter. Large capacity hard disks may have 12 or more platters.
- Unlike floppy disk, the read/write head of hard disk does not touch the disk during accessing.
- Hard disk can spin at the speed of up to 10,000 revolutions per minute and have an access time of 9–14 ms. It stores 512 bytes per sector but the number of sectors are more per track (54 or more) than floppy disk.
- Nowadays, hard disks are available that can store up to 500 GB of data. Generally, PCs come with 160 GB hard disk.
- Hard disk is the key secondary storage device of computer. The operating system is stored on the hard disk. The performance of computer like speed of computer boot up, loading of programs to

primary memory, loading of large files like images, video, audio etc., is also dependent on the hard disk.

- Nowadays, *portable external hard disk drive* is available which can be attached to the USB drive of the computer. They come in the storage capacities of 80 GB to 500 GB.

Figure 3.13 Zip disk

3.10.3 Zip Disk

- They are high-capacity removable disk and drive.
- They have the speed and capacity of hard disk and portability of floppy disk.
- Zip disk are of the same size as floppy disk, i.e., 3-½ inch but have a much higher capacity than the floppy disk (Figure 3.13).
- Zip disk and drive were made by Iomega Corp. It comes as a complete unit—disk, drive, connection cable, power cord and operating system. It can be connected to the computer system externally using a parallel chord or SCSI cable.
- Their capacity ranges from 100 MB to 750 MB. They can be used to store large files, audio and video data.

3.11 OPTICAL DISK

Optical disk (Figure 3.14) is a flat and circular disk which is coated with reflective plastic material that can be altered by laser light. Optical disk does not use magnetism. The bits 1 and 0 are stored as spots that are relatively bright and light, respectively.

Figure 3.14 Optical disk

- An optical disk consists of a single spiral track that starts from the edge to the centre of disk. Due to its spiral shape, it can access large amount of data sequentially, for example music and video. The random access on optical disk is slower than that of magnetic disk, due to its spiral shape.
- The tracks on optical disk are further divided into sectors which are of same length. Thus, the sectors near the centre of disk wrap around the disk longer than the sectors on the edges of disk. Reading the disk thus requires spinning the disk faster when reading near the centre and slower when reading near the edge of disk. Optical disks are generally slower than hard disks. Figure 3.15 shows the tracks and sectors in a magnetic disk and optical disk.

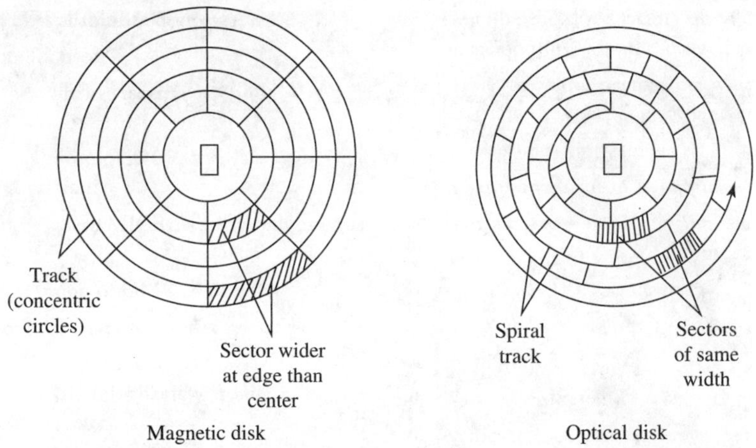

Figure 3.15 Sectors and track in magnetic disk and optical disk

- Optical disks can store large amount of data, up to 6 GB, in a small space. Commonly used optical disks store 600–700 MB of data.
- The access time for an optical disk ranges from 100 to 200 ms.
- There are two most common categories of optical disks—read-only optical disks and recordable optical disks.

3.11.1 CD-ROM

- Originally, Compact Disk (CD) was a popular medium for storing music. Now, it is used in computers to store data and is called Compact Disk-Read Only Memory (CD-ROM).
- As the name suggests, CD-ROM (Figure 3.16) is an optical disk that can only be read and not written on. CD-ROM is written on by the manufacturer of the CD-ROM using the laser light.
- A CD-ROM drive reads data from the compact disk. Data is stored as pits (depressions) and lands (flat area) on CD-ROM disk. When the laser light is focused on the disk, the pits scatter the light (interpreted as 0) and the lands reflect the light to a sensor (interpreted as 1).
- As CD-ROM is read only, no changes can be made into the data contained in it.
- Since there is no head touching the disk, but a laser light, CD-ROM does not get worn out easily.
- The storage density of CD-ROM is very high and cost is low as compared to floppy disk and hard disk.
- Access time of CD-ROM is less. CD-ROM drives can read data at 150Kbps. They come in multiples of this speed like—2x, 4x, 52x, 75x, etc.
- It is a commonly used medium for distributing software and large data.

3.11.2 DVD-ROM

- Digital Video Disk-Read Only Memory (DVD-ROM) is an optical storage device used to store digital video or computer data (Figure 3.17).
- DVDs look like CDs, in shape and physical size.

Figure 3.16 CD-ROM

Figure 3.17 DVDs

- It improves on CD technology.
- It is a high-density medium with increased track and bit density.
- DVD-ROM uses both sides of the disk and special data compression technologies. The tracks for storing data are extremely small.
- A full-length movie can be stored on a single disk.

- Each side of DVD-ROM can store 4.7 GB of data, so a single DVD can store 9.4 GB of data.
- New DVD-ROMs use layers of data track, to double its capacity. Such dual layer disks can store 17 GB of data.

3.11.3 Recordable Optical Disk

In addition to the read only CDs and DVDs, recordable optical disks (Figure 3.18) are also available. Users can record music, video, audio and data on it. The recordable optical disks are—

- ***Compact Disk-Recordable (CD-R)*** is a Write Once-Read Many (WORM) disk. A CD-R disk allows the user to write data permanently on to the disk. Once the data is written, it cannot be erased. CD-R disk uses a laser that burns pits into the disk surface. It looks like a CD disk externally. To write to a CD-R disk, a device named CD-Writer or CD-burner is required. A CD-R disk can store 700 MB of data that can run for 80 minutes. CD-R is used to create music CDs in home computers, back up data from other storage devices, archives of large data, etc.
- ***Compact Disk-ReWritable (CD-RW)*** allows data to be written, erased and re-written on. The capacity of CD-RW is same as a CD. They generally do not play on all CD-ROM drives.
- ***Digital Video Disk-Recordable (DVD-R)*** allows recording of data on a DVD. A DVD writer device is required to write the data to DVD. The data once written on a DVD cannot be erased or changed.

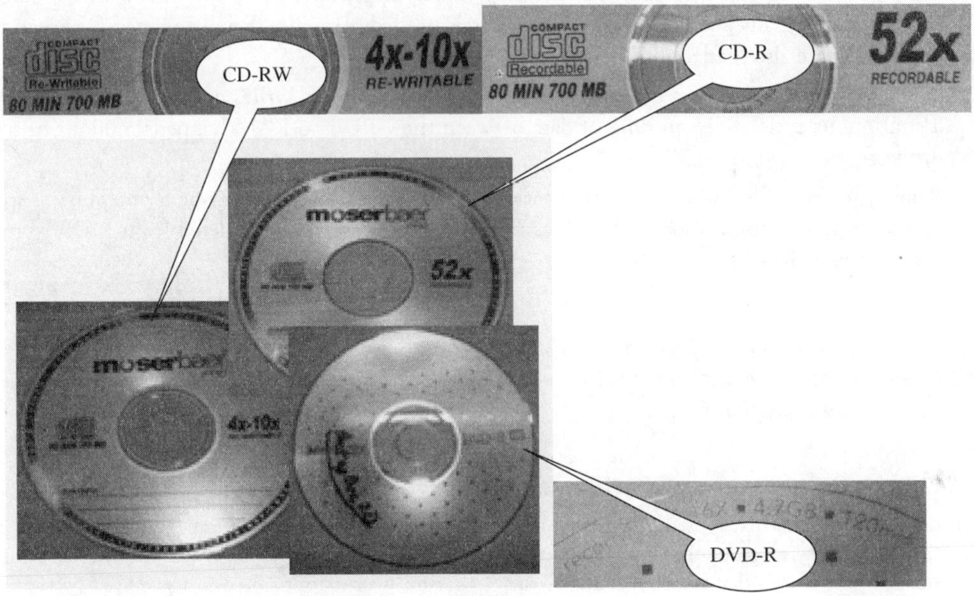

Figure 3.18 CD-R, CD-RW and DVD-R

3.12 MAGNETO-OPTICAL DISK

- Magneto-optical disks use laser beam to read data and magnetic field to write data to disk.
- These are optical disks where data can be written, erased and re-written.

- They are expensive and outdated. They were used during the mid 1990s. They have now been replaced by CD-RW and DVD-R.

3.13 USING THE COMPUTER MEMORY

The computer starts using the memory from the moment the computer is switched on, till the time it is switched off. The list of steps that the computer performs from the time it is switched on are—

- Turn the computer on.
- The computer loads data from ROM. It makes sure that all the major components of the computer are functioning properly.
- The computer loads the BIOS from ROM. The BIOS provides the most basic information about storage devices, boot sequence, security, plug and play capability and other items.
- The computer loads the OS from the hard drive into the system's RAM. CPU has immediate access to the OS as the critical parts of the OS are maintained in RAM as long as the computer is on. This enhances the performance and functionality of the overall system.
- Now the system is ready for use.
- When you load or open an application it is loaded in the RAM. Since the CPU looks for information in the RAM, any data and instructions that are required for processing (read, write or update) is brought into RAM. To conserve RAM usage, many applications load only the essential parts of the program initially and then load other pieces as needed. Any files that are opened for use in that application are also loaded into RAM.
- The CPU requests the data it needs from RAM, processes it and writes new data back to RAM in a continuous cycle. The shuffling of data between the CPU and RAM happens millions of times every second.
- When you save a file and close the application, the file is written to the secondary memory as specified by you. The application and any accompanying files usually get deleted from RAM to make space for new data.
- If the files are not saved to a storage device before being closed, they are lost.

Sometimes, when you write a program and the power goes off, your program is lost if you have not saved it. This is because your program was in the RAM and was not saved on the secondary memory; the content of the RAM gets erased when the power is switched off.

SUMMARY

- *Bit* is the smallest unit that is used to represent data in a computer. *Byte* is a group of 8 bits. One byte is the smallest unit of data that can be handled by the computer.
- *Memory is characterized* on the basis of its capacity and access time. The computer organizes its memory hierarchically so as to give the fastest speed and largest capacity of memory.
- *Memory* is fundamentally of two types—Internal memory and External memory.
- *Internal memory* has limited storage capacity, provides temporary storage, has fast access, the data and instructions stored in it are used by the CPU during execution, and is more expensive than secondary memory. Registers, cache memory, and primary memory constitute the internal memory. RAM and ROM are the two kinds of primary memory.
- *External memory or Secondary memory* have very high storage capacity, are non-volatile unless erased by

user, have slow access, store the data and instructions that are not currently being used by CPU, and are cheapest among all memory. Magnetic disk and optical disk are storage devices.

- *Organization of memory* with respect to the CPU, is as follows—registers are placed inside CPU, cache memory is placed inside CPU, primary memory is placed next in the hierarchy, and secondary memory is the farthest from CPU.
- *Registers* are very high-speed storage areas located inside the CPU. Registers are manipulated directly by the control unit of CPU during instruction execution.
- *Cache*, the fast memory, is placed between the CPU and the RAM. The contents from the RAM are stored in the cache.
- *RAM* stores data and instructions during the operation of computer. RAM is a random access volatile memory having limited size due to its high cost. RAM affects the speed and power of computer.
- *RAM memory chips* are of two types—DRAM and SRAM. DRAM is used as main memory as it is small and cheap. SRAM chip is used in cache memory due to its high speed.
- *ROM* is a non-volatile primary memory which stores the data needed for the start up of computer. Instructions to initialize different devices attached to computer and the bootstrap loader are stored in ROM. PROM, EPROM and EEPROM are some of the ROMs.
- *Flash memory* is a kind of semiconductor-based non-volatile, rewritable computer memory. It is used in digital camera, mobile phone, printer, laptop computer, and MP3 players.
- *Magnetic tapes* are inexpensive, can store a large amount of data, are easy to transport, are slow access device, and are suitable for back-up storage.
- *Magnetic disks* are cheap storage device, can store a large amount of data, are easy to carry, are suitable for frequently read/write data and are fast access device. Access time of disk is the sum of seek time, latency time and time for data transfer.
- *Floppy disk* is a flat, round, single disk enclosed in a jacket. It is portable, small, inexpensive and slower to access than hard disk. It comes in two basic sizes—5-¼ inch and 3-½ inch.
- *Hard disk* is a fixed disk and can store much more data than floppy disk. Hard disk is the key secondary storage device of computer.
- *Zip disk* have the speed and capacity of hard disk and portability of floppy disk.
- *Optical disk* consists of a single spiral track that starts from the edge to the centre of disk. It can store large amount of data in small space.
- *CD-ROM* is an optical disk that can only be read and not written on. It has high-storage density and is a low-cost device compared to floppy disk and hard disk.
- *DVD-ROM* is a high-density optical storage device which stores data on both sides of the disk. It is used to store a full-length movie.
- *Recordable optical disks* are CD-R, CD-RW and DVD-R.
- *Computer uses its memory* from the time you switch on the computer till you switch it off.

KEYWORDS

Access time *40*
Basic Input Output System (BIOS) *45*
Bit *40*
Boot sector *50*
Bootstrap loader *45*
Byte *40*
Cache Hit *42*
Cache memory *42*
Cache Miss *42*
Compact Disk (CD) *53*
Compact Disk - Read Only Memory (CD-ROM) *53*
Compact Disk-Recordable (CD-R) *55*
Compact Disk-ReWritable (CD-RW) *55*
Complementary Metal-Oxide Semiconductor (CMOS) *45*
Data Transfer Rate *49*
Digital Video Disk-Read Only Memory (DVD-ROM) *53*
Digital Video Disk-Recordable (DVD-R) *55*
Direct Access *46*
Dual Inline Memory Module (DIMM) *44*
Dynamic RAM (DRAM) *43*
Electrically Erasable Programmable ROM (EEPROM) *45*
Erasable Programmable ROM (EPROM) *45*
File Allocation Table (FAT) *50*

QUESTIONS

Section 3.1–3.2

1. ______ is the basic unit of memory.
2. What is the unit of memory representation in a computer?
3. A bit is a single binary digit ____ or ___.
4. Define a bit.
5. Define a byte.
6. Define a word.
7. What is the significance of a byte?
8. One byte can store _____ different combination of bits.
9. 1 Byte = ____bits
10. 1 Kilobyte (KB) = _____ bytes
11. 1 Megabyte (MB) = ______KB
12. 1 Gigabyte (GB) = _____ MB = _____ KB
13. 1 Terabyte (TB) = _____ GB = ______ KB

Section 3.3

14. What are the two key factors that characterize the memory?
15. Define (1) Capacity of memory, (2) Access time of memory.
16. The memory is fundamentally divided into two types ______ and _____.
17. List the key features of the internal memory.
18. List the key features of the main memory.
19. The registers are located inside the _____.
20. Which is the fastest memory?
21. Arrange the memories in increasing order of speed—Register, RAM, Hard Disk Drive, Magnetic Tape, Cache Memory
22. Give the approximate speed and size of the Registers, Cache memory, RAM and Magnetic disk.
23. Show the memory hierarchy.
24. List the different memories available in the computer in order of their hierarchy with respect to the CPU.
25. Why is primary memory faster than the secondary memory?

Section 3.4–3.5

26. Define a cache hit and cache miss.
27. What is the purpose of the Registers?
28. What is the purpose of the cache memory?

Section 3.6–3.6.1

29. ______ and _____ are the two main types of primary memory.
30. What is the unit to measure the size of RAM?
31. List the characteristic features of the RAM.
32. What is the meaning of volatile memory? Also give an example of volatile memory.

33. "The performance of RAM is affected by the access speed and the data transfer unit size". Explain.
34. Name the two categories of RAM chips.
35. _____ memory chip is used for main memory and _____ memory chip is used for cache memory.
36. List the features of the DRAM memory chip.
37. Explain the working of the DRAM memory chip.
38. List the features of the SRAM memory chip.
39. Which is faster—SRAM or DRAM?
40. Define a memory module.
41. _____ and ______ are the two types of RAM modules.
42. What is the difference between the SIMM and DIMM memory modules?

Section 3.6.2

43. What are the functions of Bootstrap loader, POST and CMOS chip?
44. What is a bootstrap loader?
45. List the different kinds of ROM memory.
46. How are these different—PROM, EPROM and EEPROM?
47. What is a flash memory?
48. What are the features of flash memory?

Section 3.7–3.8.2

49. What do you mean by sequential access?
50. What is the meaning of direct access?
51. Give an example of sequential access device and direct access device.

Section 3.9

52. Explain briefly the working of magnetic tape.
53. What is the significance of track and frame in a magnetic tape?
54. What is the purpose of Inter-Record Gap in a magnetic tape?
55. Data is stored on tape in the form of ______.
56. How does a magnetic tape drive work?
57. List the features of a magnetic tape.

Section 3.10

58. Explain briefly the working of magnetic disk.
59. What is the significance of track and sector in a magnetic disk?
60. Define (i) seek time, (ii) latency time, (iii) data transfer rate, and (iv) access time of the magnetic disk.
61. How is the access time of disk calculated? Explain in detail?
62. List the features of the magnetic disk.
63. What is the need of formatting the disk?
64. Name the four areas that are created when the disk is formatted using FAT.
65. Define (i) Boot sector, and (ii) File Allocation Table.
66. How do you find data on a magnetic disk?
67. What is the need of the root directory in a magnetic disk?
68. Name two types of magnetic disk.

Section 3.10.1–3.10.3

69. List the key features of the floppy disk.
70. Floppy disk comes in two basic sizes_______inch and _____inch.
71. List the key features of the hard disk.
72. List the key features of the zip disk.
73. What are the approximate storage capacity ranges of the floppy disk, hard disk and zip disk?
74. Zip disk has the capacity of ________ disk and portability of ________ disk.

Section 3.11–3.13

75. List the key features of the optical disk.
76. Why is optical disk generally slower than hard disk?
77. List the key features of CD-ROM.
78. List the key features of DVD-ROM.
79. What are the approximate storage capacity ranges of CD-ROM and DVD-ROM?
80. ____, ______ and ______ are recordable optical disks.
81. What is a WORM disk?
82. Write two features each of CD-R, CD-RW and DVD-R.
83. What are magneto-optical disk?
84. List the steps the computer performs when it is switched on till from the time it is ready for use.
85. When you write a program and the electricity goes off, your program is lost if you have not saved it. Why?

Extra Questions

86. Give full form of the following abbreviations

(i) RAM	(ii) ROM
(iii) CD-ROM	(iv) SRAM
(v) DRAM	(vi) PROM
(vii) EPROM	(viii) EEPROM

(ix) FAT (x) FDD
(xi) HDD (xii) ZD
(xiii) CD-ROM (xiv) WORM
(xv) CD-R (xvi) CD-RW
(xvii) DVD-R (xviii) bit
(xix) KB (xx) MB
(xxi) GB (xxii) TB
(xxiii) ns (xxiv) SIMM
(xxv) DIMM (xxvi) SO DIMM
(xxvii) BIOS (xxviii) CMOS
(xxix) POST (xxx) IRG
(xxxi) NTFS (xxxii) DVD-ROM

87. Write short notes on:
(a) Memory representation (b) Memory hierarchy
(c) Internal Memory (d) Primary Memory
(e) Secondary memory (f) Registers
(g) Cache memory (h) RAM
(i) Memory chips (j) Memory modules
(k) ROM (l) Flash memory
(m) Access types of storage devices (n) Working of mag netic tape
(o) Working of magnetic disk (p) Finding data on magnetic disk
(q) Floppy disk (r) Hard disk
(s) Zip disk (t) Optical disk
(u) CD-ROM (v) DVD-ROM
(w) Recordable optical disk (x) Computer start-up process

88. Give differences between the following:
(a) Bit and Byte
(b) Primary memory and Secondary memory
(c) RAM and ROM
(d) DRAM and SRAM
(e) SIMM and DIMM
(f) PROM, EPROM and EEPROM
(g) Sequential access devices and Direct access devices
(h) Floppy disk and hard disk
(i) CD-ROM and DVD-ROM
(j) CD-R, CD-W and DVD-R

INPUT AND OUTPUT DEVICES

4

Contents

- Input-output unit—Input unit, output unit
- Input devices—Human data entry devices, source data entry devices
- Human data entry devices
  - Keyboard
  - Pointing devices—Mouse, trackball, joystick, digitizing tablet
  - Pick devices—Light pen, touch screen
- Source data entry devices
  - Audio input device (microphone, sound card, speech recognition)
  - Video input device (video camera, digital camera)
  - Optical input devices—Scanner (hand held, flat bed), OCR, MICR, OMR, barcode reader
- Output devices—Hard copy devices, soft copy devices
- Hard copy devices
  - Printer—Impact printers (dot matrix, daisy wheel, drum), non-impact printers (ink-jet, laser)
  - Plotter—Drum plotter, flatbed plotter
  - Computer output on microfilm (microfiche)
- Soft copy devices—Monitor, visual display terminal, video output, audio response (speakers, headphone)
- I/O port—Parallel port, serial port, USB port, firewire port
- Working of I/O system—I/O devices, device controller, device driver

Why this chapter

What is the use of computer for us? We may want to process data, write project reports, listen to sound recordings, watch a movie and do many more things. But to do any of these things, we should be able to provide the data to computer and also get the output from it. The input devices and output devices are used this purpose. The aim of this chapter is to introduce the different kinds of input and output devices.

4.1 INTRODUCTION

A computer interacts with the external environment via the input-output (I/O) devices attached to it. Input device is used for providing data and instructions to the computer. After processing the input data, computer provides output to the user via the output device. The I/O devices that are attached, externally, to the computer machine are also called *peripheral devices*. Different kinds of input and output devices are used for different kinds of input and output requirements. In this chapter, we shall discuss different kinds of input devices and output devices.

4.2 INPUT-OUTPUT UNIT

An I/O unit is a component of computer. The I/O unit is composed of two parts—input unit and output unit. The input unit is responsible for providing input to the computer and the output unit is for receiving output from the computer.

4.2.1 Input Unit

- The input unit gets the data and programs from various input devices and makes them available for processing to other units of the computer.
- The input data is provided through input devices, such as—keyboard, mouse, trackball and joystick. Input data can also be provided by scanning images, voice recording, video recording, etc.
- Irrespective of the kind of input data provided to a computer, all input devices must translate the input data into a form that is understandable by the computer, i.e., in machine readable form. The transformation of the input data to machine readable form is done by the *input interface* of input device.

In brief, the input unit accepts input data from the user via input device, transforms the input data in computer acceptable form using input interface for the input device and provides the transformed input data for processing.

4.2.2 Output Unit

- The output unit gets the processed data from computer and sends it to output devices to make them available to the user of computer.
- The output data is provided through output devices like display screen, printer, plotter and speaker.
- The processed data sent to the output device is in a machine understandable form. This processed data is converted to human readable form by the *output interface* of output device.

In brief, the output unit accepts output data from computer via output device, transforms the output information to human readable form using the output interface of output device and provides the transformed output to user.

In addition to input devices and output devices, some devices function as both input and output devices. The I/O devices provide the input to computer as well as get output from computer. The I/O devices are used by both the input unit and the output unit. Hard disk drive, floppy disk drive, optical disk drives are examples of I/O devices. Table 4.1 lists the different I/O devices.

Input Devices	Keyboard, Mouse, Digitizing Tablet, Track Ball, Joystick, TouchScreen, Light Pen, Speech Recognition System, Digital camera, Scanner, Magnetic Ink Character Recognition (MICR), Optical Character Recognition (OCR), Optical Mark Recognition (OMR), Barcode Reader
Output Devices	Monitor, Visual Display Terminal, Printer, Plotter, Computer Output on Microfilm (COM), Video Output System, Audio Response System
Input-Output Devices	Hard disk drive, Floppy disk drive, USB drive, CD drive, DVD drive

Table 4.1 *I/O devices*

4.3 INPUT DEVICES

Input devices allow users and other applications to input data into the computer, for processing. The data input to a computer can be in the form of text, audio, video, etc. Figure 4.1 shows some users working in an office. The data is entered manually by the user or with minimal user intervention. Input devices are classified as follows—

Figure 4.1 Users working on computers in an office

- Human data entry devices
  - Keyboard
  - Pointing devices—mouse, trackball, joystick, digitizing tablet
  - Pick devices—light pen, touch screen
- Source data entry devices
  - Audio input—speech recognition
  - Video input—digital camera
  - Scanner—hand-held scanner, flat-bed scanner
  - Optical Scanner—OCR, OMR, MICR, barcode reader

The input is provided to the computer using an input device, and must be translated to a form that the computer can understand. The translation is done by the input interface of the input device.

In addition to the above devices, the input to a computer can also be provided from a storage device on the computer, another computer, or another piece of equipment, such as a musical instrument, thermometer or sensors.

4.4 HUMAN DATA ENTRY DEVICES

Input devices that require data to be entered manually to the computer are identified as human data entry devices. The data may be entered by typing or keying in, or by pointing a device to a particular location.

4.4.1 Keyboard

Features Keyboard is a common input device. It is provided along with the computer, and is easy to use. It is used for entering the text data. For inputting the data, the user types the data using the keyboard. When the data is being typed, the display monitor displays the typed data. Cursor is a vertical line, an underscore, blinking line, etc. Cursor moves with each typed character. The position of cursor indicates the location on monitor where the typed-in character will be displayed. A keyboard is shown in Figure 4.2.

Description The design of a keyboard is similar to a standard typewriter. The modern keyboards are QWERTY keyboard (Q, W, E, R, T, Y are the sequence of keys in top row of letters). Standard keyboard contains 101 keys which are arranged in the same order as a typewriter. The keyboard has five sections (1) Typing keys (1, 2, 3…, A, B, C…), (2) Numeric keypad (numeric keys on right side), (3) Function keys (F1, F2… on top side), (4) Control keys (cursor keys, ctrl, alt…), and (5) Special-purpose keys (Enter, shift, spacebar…). Some keyboards have 110 keys, where the extra keys are designed to work with the Windows operating system.

Working When a key is pressed, keyboard interacts with a keyboard controller and keyboard buffer. The keyboard controller stores the code of pressed key in keyboard buffer and informs the computer software that an action has happened on the keyboard. The computer software checks and reads the keyboard buffer and passes the code of pressed character to the system software. Due to a time gap between pressing of a key on keyboard and reading by the system software, keyboard buffer is designed to store many keystrokes together.

Figure 4.2 Keyboard

4.4.2 Pointing Devices

Pointing devices are used for providing the input to computer by moving the device to point to a location on computer monitor. The input data is not typed; instead, the data is entered by moving the pointing device. The cursor on the computer monitor moves with the moving pointing device. Operations like move, click and drag can be performed using the pointing devices. Mouse, trackball, joystick and digitizing tablet are some of the common pointing devices.

4.4.2.1 Mouse

Features It is the most common pointing input device. The data is entered by pointing the mouse to a location on the computer screen. The mouse may also be used to position the cursor on screen, move an object by dragging, or select an object by clicking. The key benefit of using a mouse is that the cursor moves with the mouse. So, the cursor can be positioned at any location on the screen by simply moving the mouse. Moreover, it provides an easy way to select and choose commands from menus, dialog boxes, icons, etc. Mouse is used extensively, while working with graphics elements such as line, curve, shapes, etc.

Description Mouse is a small hand-held device having two or three buttons on its upper side. In addition to the buttons, mouse also has a small wheel between the buttons. Figure 4.3 (i) shows a mouse. The wheel of the mouse is used for the up and down movement, for example, scrolling a long document. A mouse is classified as physical mouse or optical mouse.

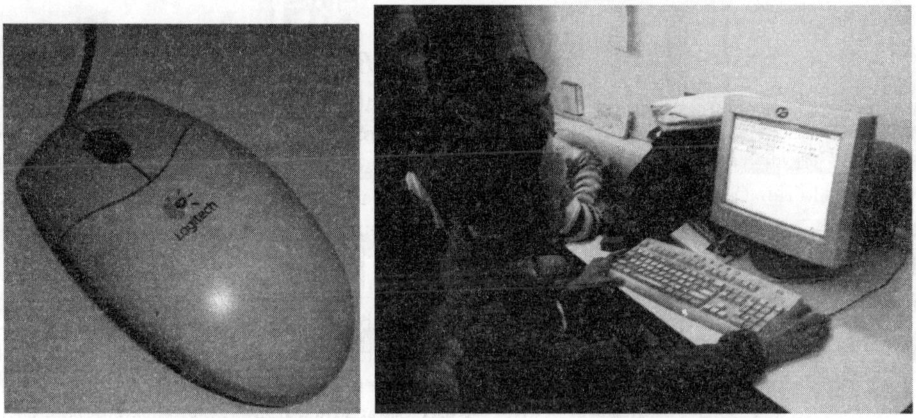

Figure 4.3 (i) Mouse, (ii) A user working with a mouse

Physical Mouse has a rubber ball on the bottom side that protrudes when the mouse is moved. It requires a smooth, dust free surface, such as a mouse pad, on which it is rolled.

Optical Mouse uses a Light Emitting Diode (LED) and a sensor to detect the movement of mouse. Optical mouse requires an opaque flat surface underneath it. Optical mouse was introduced by Microsoft in 1999. Optical mouse is better than physical mouse as there is no moving part that can cause wear and tear, and dirt cannot get inside it. A user is working with an optical mouse in Figure 4.3 (ii).

Working In a ***physical mouse***, rollers and sensors are used to sense the direction and rate of movement of mouse. When the ball of mouse moves, the rollers sense the horizontal and vertical movement and sensors sense the speed of movement. This information is passed to computer via the mouse chord. When an *optical mouse* is moved, a beam of light is reflected from its underside. These pulses of light determine the direction and rate of movement. This information is sent to computer via the mouse chord.

Using the mouse The mouse can be used in five different ways, as follows—

- ***Pointing*** points to a location or object on the computer screen. Moving the mouse by hand moves the cursor on computer screen. The cursor moves in the direction in which the mouse moves.
- ***Left Click or Click*** means pressing the left button of mouse and releasing it. Clicking is used to select a button, command or icon on the screen.
- ***Right Click*** involves pressing the right button on mouse and releasing it. Right click displays a menu that contains options like cut, copy, paste, font, paragraph, etc. for the item on which the mouse is pointing.
- ***Double Click*** means pressing the left button of mouse twice successively, without moving the mouse, and then releasing the mouse. It is used to start a program or open a folder.
- ***Drag and Drop*** drags an object and drops it at another location. Drag means pointing mouse to an object on screen, pressing the left button of mouse, keeping it pressed and moving the mouse to point to a new location. The object gets dragged to the new location along with the mouse. When the left button of mouse is released, the object gets dropped at the new location. Drag and drop is used for moving folders, files and icons to new locations on the screen.

4.4.2.2 TrackBall

Figure 4.4 Trackball

Features Trackball is a device that is a variant of the mouse but has the functionality of mouse. It is easy to use and takes less space than a mouse. Trackball is generally built in laptops since there is no space for the mouse to move on the lap. Trackballs come in various sizes—small and big.

Description Trackball looks like an upside-down mouse. Instead of moving the whole device to move the cursor on computer screen, trackball requires the ball to be rotated manually with a finger. The trackball device remains stationary. The cursor on the computer screen moves in the direction in which the ball is moved. The buttons on trackball are used in the same way as mouse buttons. A trackball is shown in Figure 4.4.

Working Trackball works in the same way as a physical mouse.

4.4.2.3 Joystick

Features Joystick (Figure 4.5) is a device which is commonly used for playing video games. Joystick is mainly used to control the speed of the cursor and is thus popular in games involving speed like racing and flying games. The direction of push of the stick and the amount of deflection determines the change in position and the change in speed, respectively.

Description It is a stick with its base attached to a flexible rubber sheath inside a plastic cover. The plastic cover contains the circuit that detects the movement of stick and sends the information to computer. The position of the stick movement is given by the x and y coordinates of the stick.

Figure 4.5 Joystick

4.4.2.4 Digitizing Tablet

Features It is an input device used primarily to input drawings, sketches, etc. Digitizing tablet is used for Computer Aided Design (CAD) for the design of buildings, automotive designs, and designing of maps, etc. Figure 4.6 shows a digitizing tablet.

Description Digitizing tablet consists of two parts—electronic tablet and pen. The electronic tablet is a flat bed tablet. The pen looks like a ball pen but has an electronic head. The pen in moved on the tablet. Each position on the tablet corresponds to a fixed position on the screen. Drawings can be made on the tablet using a pen, and is provided as input to computer, where, a location on the tablet corresponds to a specific location on the screen.

Figure 4.6 Digitizing tablet

Working The tablet contains circuit that can detect the movement of pen on the tablet, convert the movements into digital signals and send the digital signal to the computer.

4.4.3 Pick Devices

Pick devices are used for providing input to the computer by pointing to a location on the computer monitor. The input data is not typed; the data is entered by pointing the pick device directly on the computer screen. Light pen and touch screen are some common pick devices.

Figure 4.7 Using a light pen

4.4.3.1 *Light Pen*

Features It is a light sensitive pen-like input device and is used to select objects directly on the computer screen. It is used for making drawing, graphics and for menu selection. Figures and drawings can be made by moving the pen on computer screen.

Description and Working The pen contains a photocell in a small tube. When the pen is moved on the screen, light from the screen at the location of pen causes the photocell to respond. The electric response is transmitted to the computer that can identify the position on screen at which the light pen is pointing. Figure 4.7 shows a user using a light pen on the screen.

4.4.3.2 *Touch Screen*

Features It is an input device that accepts input when the user places a fingertip on the computer screen. The computer selects the option from the menu of screen to which the finger points. Touch screen are

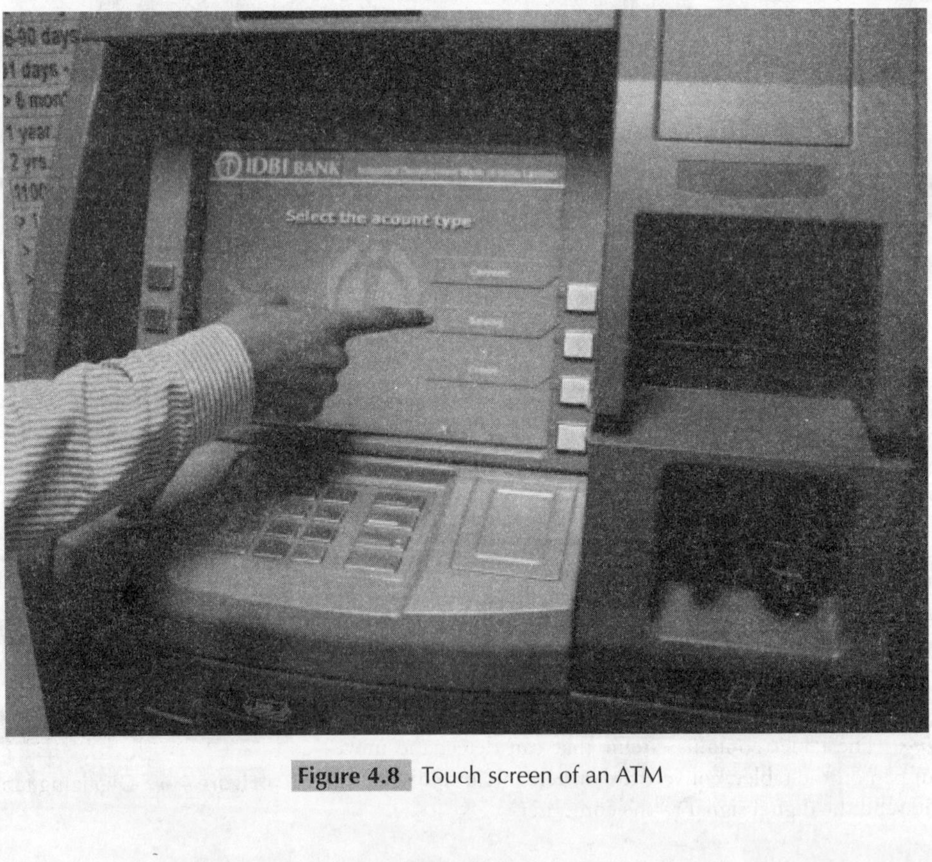

Figure 4.8 Touch screen of an ATM

generally used in applications like Automated Teller Machine (ATM), public information computers like hospitals, airline reservation, railway reservation, supermarkets, etc. (Figure 4.8).

Description Touch screen consists of a clear glass panel that is placed over the view area of computer screen. In addition to the glass panel with sensors, it has a device driver, and a controller that translates the information captured by the glass panel sensors to a form that the computer can understand.

Working Touch screens have an infrared beam that criss-cross the surface of screen. When a fingertip is touched on the screen, the beam is broken, and the location is recorded. Some touch screens have ultrasonic acoustic waves that cross the surface of screen. When a fingertip is touched on the screen, the wave is interrupted, and the location is recorded. The recorded location is sent to the computer via the controller of touch screen, in a form that the computer can understand.

4.5 SOURCE DATA ENTRY DEVICES

Source data entry devices are used for audio input, video input and to enter the source document directly to the computer. Source data entry devices do not require data to be typed-in, keyed-in or pointed to a particular location.

4.5.1 Audio Input Device

Audio input can be provided to the computer using human voice or speech. Audio input to the computer can be used for different purposes. It can be used for making telephone calls, for audio and video conferencing over Internet, to record voice, to create audio files and embed these files to be sent over e-mail, or, to translate spoken words into text, etc.

Audio input devices like a *microphone* is used to input a person's voice into the computer. A *sound card* (Figure 4.9 (i)) translates analog audio signals from microphone into digital codes that the computer can store and process. Sound card also translates back the digital sound into analog signals that can be sent to the speakers. Translating spoken words into text is also known as *speech recognition or voice recognition.* The audio input along with the software for voice recognition forms the speech recognition system or voice recognition system.

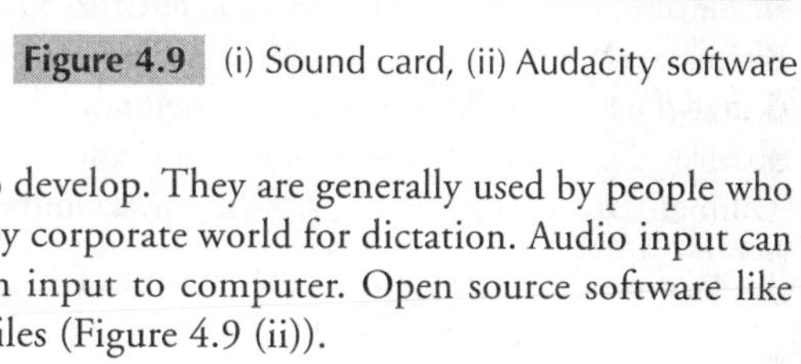

Figure 4.9 (i) Sound card, (ii) Audacity software

The computer can be operated using voice commands. The user can dictate the commands to the computer, instead of typing them. The computer has to be trained to recognize the voice of user using the speech patterns and pronunciation of words. The system thus adapts to the voice of user. Speech recognition systems are costly and difficult to develop. They are generally used by people who have difficulty in typing, people with disabilities or by corporate world for dictation. Audio input can be recorded on an mp3 recorder and provided as an input to computer. Open source software like Audacity is used for recording and editing of audio files (Figure 4.9 (ii)).

4.5.2 Video Input Device

Video input is provided to the computer using *video camera and digital camera* (Figure 4.10). Video camera can capture full motion video images. The images are digitized and can be compressed and stored in the computer disk. Webcam is a common video camera device. It is placed on the computer above the screen to capture the images of the user who is working on the computer. A video capture card allows the user to connect video devices like camcorders to the computer.

Figure 4.10 Video input devices

Digital camera works like video camera but can capture still images. The digital camera digitizes images, compresses them and stores them on a memory card like flash memory. The information from the digital camera can be brought into the computer and stored. The video files can be edited using software like VLC media player. Computer vision is an area of computer science that deals with images. Computer vision has applications in areas like robotics and industrial processing.

4.5.3 Optical Input Devices

Optical input devices allow computers to use light as a source of input. Scanner is an example of optical input device. Other common optical input devices are magnetic ink character reader used for Magnetic Ink Character Recognition (MICR), optical mark reader used for Optical Mark Recognition (OMR), optical character reader for Optical Character Recognition (OCR) and Barcode Reader.

4.5.3.1 Scanner

Scanner is an input device that accepts paper document as an input. Scanner is used to input data directly into the computer from the source document without copying and typing the data. The input data to be scanned can be a picture, a text or a mark on a paper. It is an optical input device and uses light as an input source to convert an image into an electronic form that can be stored on the computer. Scanner accepts the source paper document, scans the document and translates it into a bitmap image to be stored on the computer. The denser the bitmap, the higher is the resolution of the image. The quality of scan increases with the increase in resolution. Scanners come with utility software that allow the stored scanned documents to be edited, manipulated and printed. Hand-held scanner and flat-bed scanner are the two common types of scanners.

- ***Hand-held Scanners*** are portable and are placed over the document to be scanned. They consist of light emitting diodes. The scanned documents are converted and stored as an image in the computer memory. Hand-held scanners have to be moved at a constant speed over the document to be scanned, to get good quality scans. They are preferably used for low volume of documents, small pictures or photos. They are difficult to use if there is a need to scan a full page document. Some of the documents that are primarily scanned using hand-held scanners are price tags, label and ISBN number on books.
- ***Flat-bed Scanners*** provide high quality scan in a single pass. It is a box shaped machine similar to a photocopy machine and has a glass top and a lid that covers the glass (Figure 4.11). The

Figure 4.11 Flat bed scanner

document to be scanned is placed on the glass top, which activates the light beam beneath the glass top and starts the scan from left to right. They are largely used to scan full page documents.

4.5.3.2 Optical Character Recognition (OCR)

OCR is a technique for the scanning of a printed page, translating it, and then using the OCR software to recognize the image as ASCII text that is editable. OCR uses optical character reader for recognition. The optical character reader stores the scanned image as bitmap image which is a grid of dots. Thus, you cannot edit the text that has been scanned. To edit the scanned text, you need OCR software. The OCR software translates the array of dots into text that the computer can interpret as words and letters. To recognize the words and letters of text, the OCR software compares the pattern on the scanned image with the patterns stored inside the computer. The text files generated via OCR can be stored in different formats. Figure 4.12 shows the working of the OCR system.

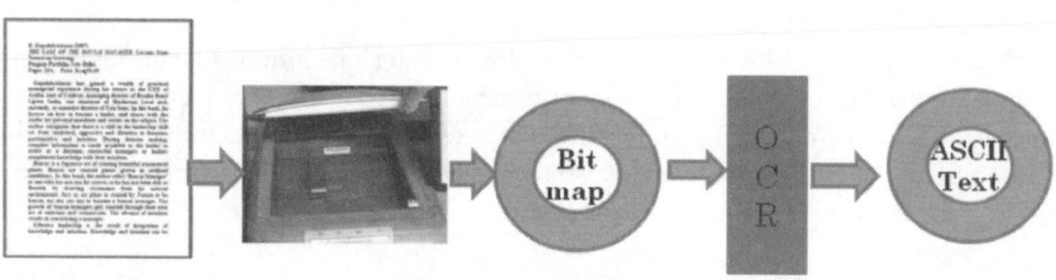

Figure 4.12 OCR system

4.5.3.3 *Magnetic Ink Character Recognition (MICR)*

MICR is used in banks to process large volumes of cheques (Figure 4.13). It is used for recognizing the magnetic encoding numbers printed at the bottom of a cheque. The numbers on the cheque are human readable, and are printed using an ink which contains iron particles. These numbers are magnetized. MICR uses magnetic ink character reader for character recognition. When a cheque is passed through Magnetic Ink Character Reader, the magnetic field causes the read head to recognize the characters or numbers of cheque. The readers are generally used in banks to process the cheques. The numbers in the bottom of the cheque include the bank number, branch number and cheque number. The reading speed of MICR is faster than OCR.

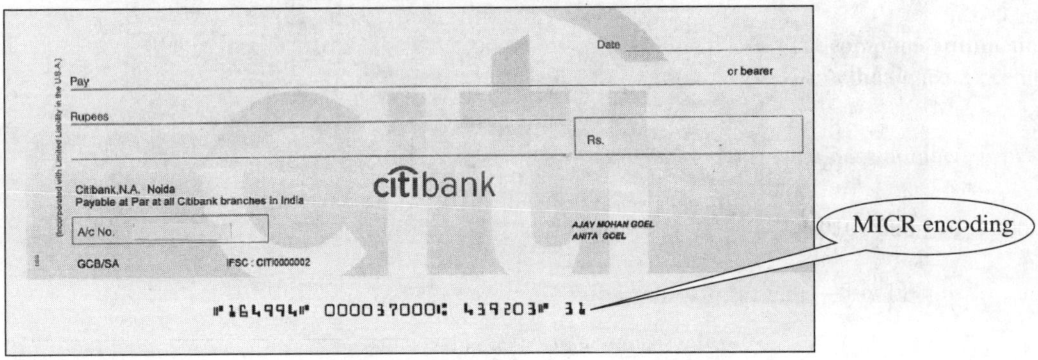

Figure 4.13 MICR encoded cheque

4.5.3.4 *Optical Mark Recognition (OMR)*

OMR is used to detect marks on a paper. The marks are recognized by their darkness. OMR uses an optical mark reader to read the marks. The OMR reader scans the forms, detects the mark that is positioned correctly on the paper and is darker than the surrounding paper, and passes this information to the computer for processing by application software. For this, it uses a beam of light that is reflected on the paper with marks, to capture presence and absence of marks. The optical mark reader detects the presence of mark by measuring the reflected light. The pattern of marks is interpreted and stored in the computer.

OMR is widely used to read answers of objective type tests, where the student marks an answer by darkening a particular circle using a pencil. OMR is also used to read forms, questionnaires, order forms, etc. Figure 4.14 shows a marked OMR answer sheet.

4.5.3.5 *Barcode Reader*

Barcodes are adjacent vertical lines of different width that are machine readable. Goods available at supermarkets, books, etc. use barcode for identification. Barcodes are read using reflective light by barcode readers. This information is input to the computer which interprets the code using the spacing and thickness of bars. Hand-held barcode readers are generally used in departmental stores to read the labels, and in libraries to read labels on books. Figure 4.15 (i) shows a barcode printed at the back of a book.

Barcode readers (Figure 4.15 (ii)) are fast and accurate. They enable faster service to the customer and are also used to determine the items being sold, number of each item sold or to retrieve the price of item.

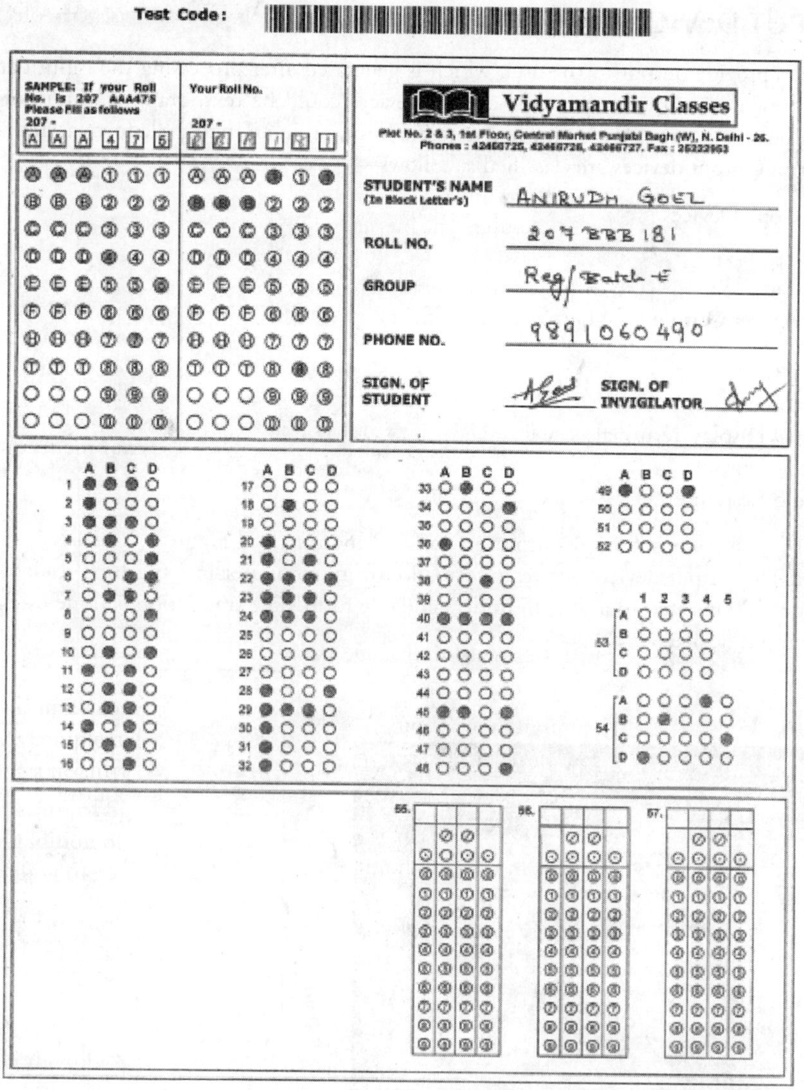

Figure 4.14 OMR answer sheet

Figure 4.15 (i) Barcode of a book, (ii) Barcode reader

4.6 OUTPUT DEVICES

Output devices provide output to the user, which is generated after processing the input data. The processed data, presented to the user via the output devices could be text, graphics, audio or video. The output could be on a paper or on a film in a tangible form, or, in an intangible form as audio, video and electronic form. Output devices are classified as follows—

- Hard Copy Devices
  - Printer
  - Plotter
  - Computer Output on Microfilm (microfiche)
- Soft Copy Devices
  - Monitor
  - Visual Display Terminal
  - Video Output
  - Audio Response

Figure 4.16 (i) shows a soft copy output on an LCD monitor and Figure 4.16 (ii) is a hard copy output on paper. The output device receives information from computer in a machine readable form. The received output is translated to a human understandable form. The translation is done using the output interface of output device.

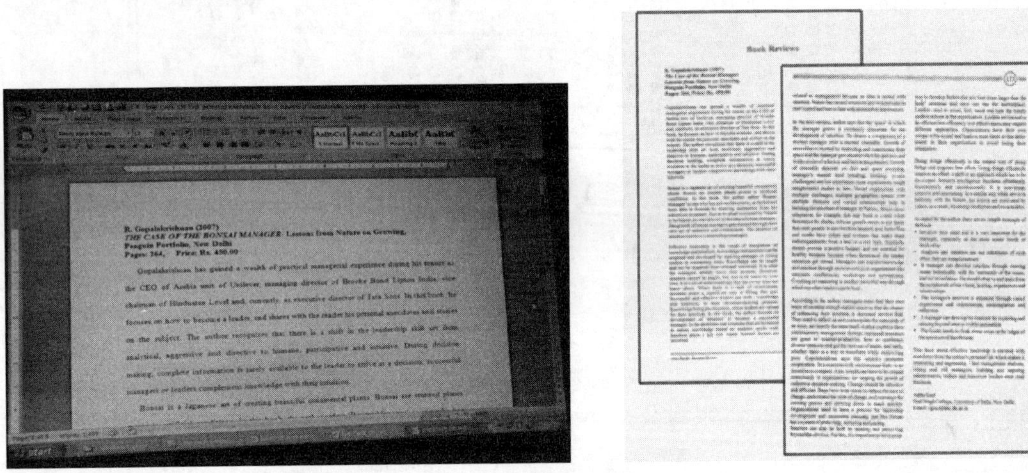

Figure 4.16 (i) Soft copy output, (ii) Hard copy output

4.6.1 Hard Copy Devices

The output obtained in a tangible form on a paper or any surface is called hard copy output. The hard copy can be stored permanently and is portable. The hard copy output can be read or used without a computer. The devices that generate hard copy output are called hard copy devices. Printer, plotter and microfiche are common hard copy output devices.

4.6.1.1 Printer

A printer prints the output information from the computer onto a paper. Printers are generally used to print textual information, but nowadays printers also print graphical information. The print quality (sharpness and clarity of print) of the printer is determined by the resolution of the printer. Resolution is measured in dots per inch (dpi). Printers with a high resolution (more dpi) provide better quality output. Different kinds of printers are available for different types of applications. Printers are classified into two categories—impact printer and non-impact printer.

Impact printers use the typewriter approach of physically striking a typeface against the paper and inked ribbon. Impact printers can print a character or an entire line at a time. Impact printers are low-cost printers useful for bulk printing. Dot matrix printers, daisy wheel printers and drum printers are examples of impact printers.

- ***Dot Matrix Printers*** (Figure 4.17) print one character at a time. The speed of dot matrix printer lies between 200 and 600 characters per second (cps) and their resolution ranges from 72 to 360 dpi. Dot matrix printers normally come in two sizes—80 column printer and 132 column printer. Dot matrix printers can print alphanumeric characters, special characters, charts and graphs. They can print only in black and white. Some dot matrix printers can print in both directions - left to right and right to left. Dot matrix printers are commonly used for printing in applications like payroll and accounting.

Figure 4.17 Dot matrix printer

- ***Daisy Wheel Printers*** (Figure 4.18) print one character at a time. They produce letter quality document which is better than a document printed by a dot matrix printer. The speed of daisy wheel printers is about 100 cps. The print head of the printer is like a daisy flower, hence the name. These printers are slow, can only print text (not graphics), and are costly in comparison to dot matrix printers. Daisy wheel printers are used where high quality printing is needed and no graphics is needed.

Figure 4.18 Daisy wheel for printers

- ***Drum Printers*** are line printers. They are expensive and faster than character printers but produce a low quality output. They can print 200–2500 lines per minute. Drum printers are generally used for voluminous print outputs.

Non-Impact Printers do not hit or impact a ribbon to print. They use electro-static chemicals and ink-jet technologies. Non-impact printers are faster and quieter than impact printers. They produce high quality output and can be used for printing text and graphics both in black and white, and color. Ink-jet printers and laser printers are non-impact printers.

- ***Ink-jet Printers*** spray ink drops directly on the paper like a jet (Figure 4.19 (i)). Their resolution is more than 500 dpi. They produce high quality graphics and text. Ink-jet printers are commonly found in homes and offices.
- ***Laser Printers*** (Figure 4.19 (ii)) provide highest quality of text and graphics printing. Laser printers process and store the entire page before printing and are also known as *page printers.* The laser printer can print 5-24 pages of text per minute and their resolution ranges from 400 to

Figure 4.19 (i) Inkjet printer, (ii) Laser printer

1200 dpi. They are faster and expensive than impact printers. Laser printers are used in applications requiring high quality voluminous printing.

4.6.1.2 Plotter

A plotter (Figure 4.20) is used for vector graphics output to draw graphs, maps, blueprints of ships, buildings, etc. Plotters use pens of different colors (cyan, magenta, yellow and black) for drawing. Plotters draw continuous and accurate lines, in contrast to printers where a line is drawn as closely spaced dots. Plotter is a slow output device and is expensive. Plotters are of two kinds—drum plotter and flatbed plotter. In a *drum plotter*, pens mounted on the carriage are stationary and move only horizontally; for vertical movement, the drum on which the paper is fixed moves clockwise and anti-clockwise. In a *flatbed plotter*, the paper is fixed on a flat bed. The paper is stationary and the pens mounted on the carriage move horizontally and vertically to draw lines. Plotters are mainly used for drawings in AUTOCAD (computer assisted drafting), Computer Aided Design (CAD) and Computer Aided Manufacturing (CAM) applications.

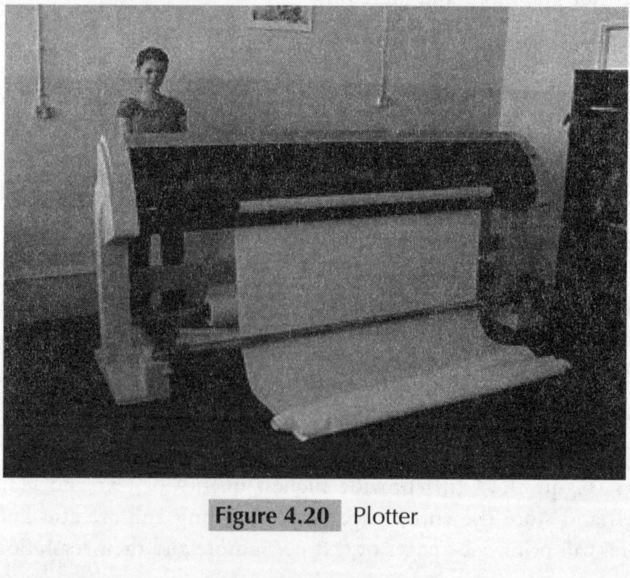

Figure 4.20 Plotter

4.6.1.3 *Computer Output on Microfilm*

A microfilm (Figure 4.21) is in a fiche or roll format, and is used to record computer output directly from the computer tape or cartridge. Computer Output on Microfilm (COM) is a high speed and low cost process. It can produce data in microfilm form at a much faster speed from that of a paper printer. The standard roll film is 16 mm wide with a film image that is 1/24 of the original document. The copy of the image on microfilm retains its original clarity. Microfilm can be indexed to facilitate retrieving information from it. For reading images stored on microfilm, a microfilm reader is used. A screen is used for viewing the enlarged images. COM is suited for storing large amounts of data for manuals and archive records for long periods of time that have to be referenced occasionally. COM is used for storing output in banking and insurance applications, medical X rays, etc.

Figure 4.21 Microfilm

4.6.2 Soft Copy Devices

The output obtained in an intangible form on a visual display, audio unit or video unit is called soft copy output. The soft copy allows corrections to be made, can be stored, and, can be sent via e-mail to other users. The soft copy output requires a computer to be read or used. The devices that generate soft copy output are called soft copy devices. Visual output devices like computer monitor, visual display terminal, video system and audio response system are common soft copy output devices.

4.6.2.1 *Monitor*

Monitor is a common output device. The monitor is provided along with the computer, to view the displayed output. A monitor is of two kinds - monochrome display monitor and color display monitor. A monochrome display monitor uses only one color to display text and color display monitor can display 256 colors at one time. The number of colors displayed by a color monitor varies with the kind of color adapter attached to it—CGA, EGA, VGA, XGA and SVGA. The CGA monitor supports four colors and SVGA supports around 16,000,000 colors. Monitors are available in various sizes like 14, 15, 17, 19 and 21 inches.

An image on the monitor is created by a configuration of dots, also known as *pixels*. The clarity of image on the computer screen depends on three factors—

(1) ***Resolution of Screen***—the number of pixels in horizontal and vertical direction. More the number of pixels, the sharper is the image. The common resolution of computer screen is 800x600 and 1024x768,

(2) ***Dot Pitch***—the diagonal distance between two colored pixels on a display screen, and

(3) ***Refresh Rate***—the number of times per second the pixels are recharged so that their glow remains bright.

Monitors may be *Cathode Ray Tube (CRT)* monitors (Figure 4.22) that look like a television or *Liquid Crystal Display (LCD)* monitors (Figure 4.23, Figure 4.24) that have a high resolution, flat screen, flat panel display. Nowadays, LCD monitors are generally used.

4.6.2.2 *Visual Display Terminal*

A monitor and keyboard together are known as *Visual Display Terminal (VDT)*. A keyboard is used to input data and monitor is used to display the output from the computer. The monitor is connected to the computer by a cable. Terminals are categorized as dumb, smart and intelligent terminals. The dumb terminals do not have processing and programming capabilities. Smart terminals have built-in processing capability but do not have its own storage capacity. Intelligent terminals have both built-in processing and storage capacity.

Figure 4.22 CRT monitor

4.6.2.3 Video Output

Screen image projector or data projector (Figure 4.25 (i)) is an output device that displays information from the computer onto a large white screen. The projector is mainly used to display visual output to a large gathering of people required for the purposes of teaching, training, meetings, conference presentations, etc. (Figure 4.25 (ii)).

4.6.2.4 Audio Response

A complete sound system consists of sound card, microphone, speaker and the appropriate software. In addition to recording and playing the sound, the software allows editing of sound, like cutting, copy, amplification and creation of vibrant sound effects.

Audio response provides audio output from the computer. Audio output device like *speakers, headset or headphone* (Figure 4.26) is used for audio output sound from computer. The signals are sent to the speakers via the sound card that translates the digital sound back into analog signals. The audio response from the computer may be generated by synthesizing the input human speech to give audio output, or may be a result of a set of rules that are used to create artificial speech.

Audio output is commonly used for customer service in airlines, banks, etc. It is also used in video conferences, surveys, etc. Audio response is used by visually impaired to read information from the screen. For speech impaired people, audio response helps them to communicate with other people.

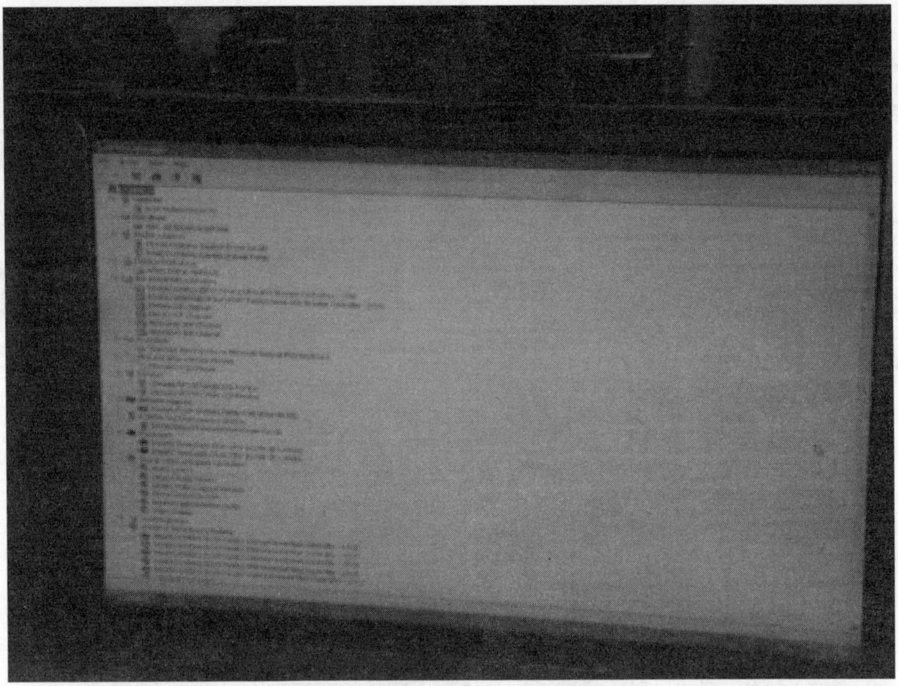

Figure 4.23 LCD monitor

Figure 4.24 A user viewing the output on a LCD monitor

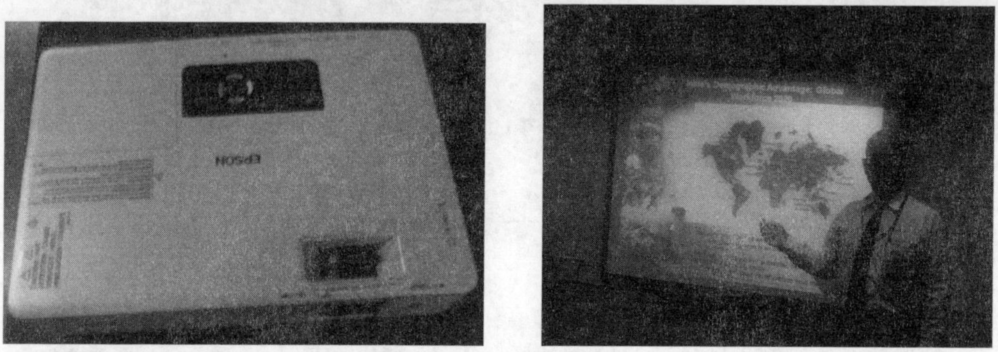

Figure 4.25 (i) LCD projector, (ii) A presentation in progress using LCD projector

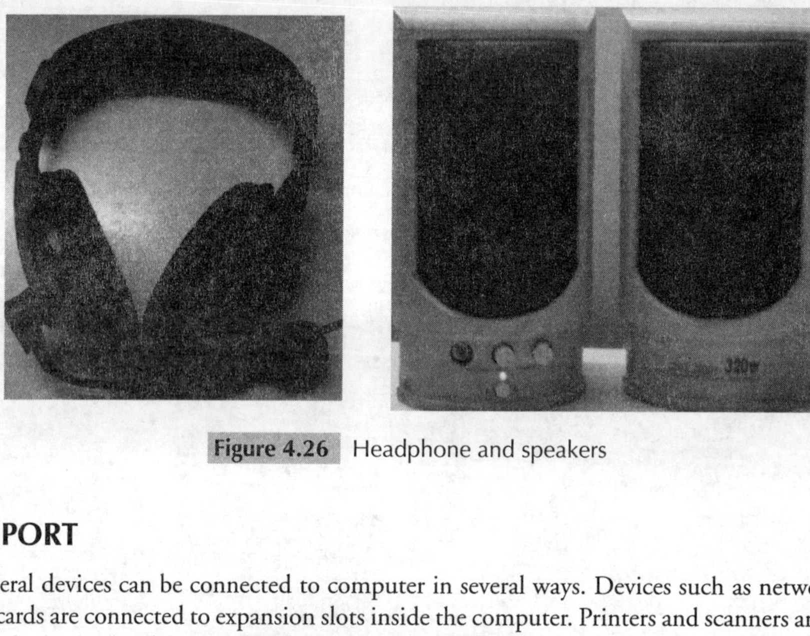

Figure 4.26 Headphone and speakers

4.7 I/O PORT

The peripheral devices can be connected to computer in several ways. Devices such as network adapters and sound cards are connected to expansion slots inside the computer. Printers and scanners are connected to ports on the backside of the computer. Also in a portable computer, the PC Card connects to the PC Card slot on it.

The I/O ports are the external interfaces that are used to connect input and output devices like printer, modem and joystick to the computer. The I/O devices are connected to the computer via the serial and parallel ports, Universal Serial Bus (USB) port, Firewire port, etc. (Figure 4.27).

- ***Parallel Port*** A parallel port is an interface for connecting eight or more data wires. The data flows through the eight wires simultaneously. They can transmit eight bits of data in parallel. As a result, parallel ports provide high speed data transmission. Parallel port is used to connect printer to the computer.

- ***Serial Port*** A serial port transmits one bit of data through a single wire. Since data is transmitted serially as single bits, serial ports provide slow speed data transmission. Serial port is used to connect external modems, plotters, barcode reader , etc.
- ***USB Port*** Nowadays, USB is a common and popular external port available with computers. Normally, two to four USB ports are provided on a PC. USB allows different devices to be connected to the computer without requiring re-boot of the computer. USB also has the plug and play feature which allows devices ready to be run simply by plugging them to the USB port. A single USB port can support connection of up to 127 devices.
- ***Firewire (IEEE 1394)*** It is used to connect audio and video multimedia devices like video camera. It is an expensive technology and is used for large data movement. Hard disk drive and new DVD drives connect through firewire. It has data transfer rate of up to 400 MB/sec.

In addition to the above ports, other ports also exist like Musical Instrument Digital Interface (MIDI) port to connect musical instruments like synthesizers and drum machines, PC expansion boards, and PC card and many more.

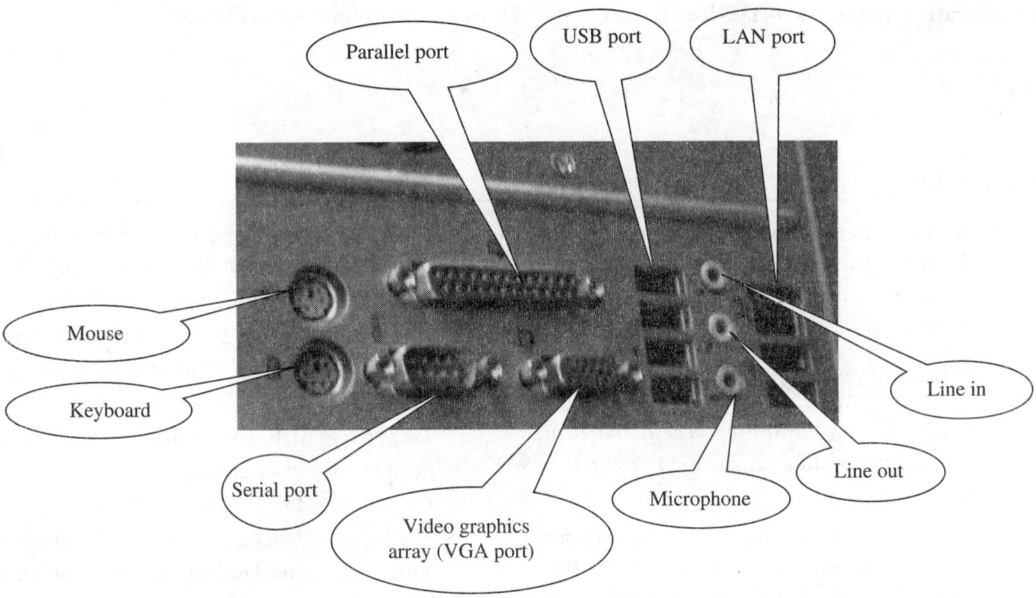

Figure 4.27 Backside of computer cabinet with different ports

4.8 WORKING OF I/O SYSTEM

The working of I/O system combines I/O hardware and I/O software. The I/O hardware includes ports, buses and device controllers for different devices, and I/O devices. The I/O software is the device driver software that may be embedded with operating system or comes with each device. The working of I/O system is described as follows—

- ***I/O Devices*** are attached to computer via the *ports* of computer. There are many standard ports available on the backside of the computer case like serial port and parallel port. If one or more devices use a common set of wires, it is called a bus. For example, PCI bus, PCI Express bus, etc.
- ***Device Controller*** operates on a bus, a port or a device. It controls the signals on the wires of port or bus. The controllers have one or more registers for data and control signals. Controller may be simple like a serial port controller for a serial port, or, complex like a SCSI controller. Some devices have their own built-in controllers.
- ***Device Driver*** is software via which the operating system communicates with the device controllers. Each device has its own device driver, and a device controller which is specific to the device. The device drivers hide the differences among the different device controller and present a uniform interface to the operating system.
- Application programs use an I/O device by issuing commands and exchanging data with the device driver. The device driver provides correct commands to the controller, interprets the controller register, and transfers data to and from device controller registers as required for the correct device operation.

Operating system ------ Device Drivers -------- Device Controllers ------- Devices

SUMMARY

- A user interacts with the computer via *Input-Output (I/O) devices*. The *peripheral devices* are attached externally to the computer machine.
- *Input unit* accepts input data from the user via input device, transforms the input data in computer acceptable form and provides the transformed input data for processing.
- *Output unit* accepts output data from computer via output device, transforms the output information to human readable form and provides the transformed output to user.
- Some devices are both *input and output devices*. Hard disk drive, floppy disk drive, optical disk drives are examples of input-output devices.
- *Keyboard* is used to enter text data. Standard keyboard contains 101 keys to 110 keys.
- *Mouse* is a small hand-held pointing input device used to enter data by pointing to a location on the computer monitor screen.
- *Trackball* looks like an upside-down mouse and requires the ball to be rotated manually with a finger.
- *Joystick* is a stick with its base attached to a flexible rubber sheath inside a plastic cover. It is used for playing video games.
- *Digitizing tablet* has a flat bed tablet, and a pen with an electronic head which is moved on the tablet. Digitizing tablet is used for computer aided design of buildings, maps, etc.
- *Light pen* contains a photocell in a small tube and is used to select objects directly on the computer screen.
- *Touch screen* is a clear glass panel that is placed over the view area of the computer screen. The user uses the fingertip on the computer screen to select an option. It is used in ATMs.

- *Audio input devices* use a microphone to input a person's voice, a sound card to translate analog audio signals from microphone into digital codes and speech recognition to translate spoken words into text.
- *Video input* is provided using video camera and digital camera. Computer vision is an area of computer science that deals with images.
- *Scanner* is used to input data directly into the computer from the source document without copying and typing the data. A scanner can be a hand-held scanner or flat bed scanner.
- *OCR* is a technique for the scanning of a printed page, translating it, and then using the OCR software to recognize the image as ASCII text that is editable.
- *MICR* is used in banks to process large volumes of cheques. It is used to recognize the magnetic encoding numbers printed at the bottom of a cheque.
- *OMR* uses an optical mark reader to detect marks on a paper. OMR is widely used to read answers of objective type tests, questionnaires, etc.
- *Barcodes* are adjacent vertical lines of different width that are machine readable. Barcode reader reads the barcode. They are used to read labels in departmental stores and in libraries.
- *Printer* prints the output onto a paper. *Plotter* is used for drawing maps, blueprints of ships, buildings, etc.
- *Impact printers* are those in which the typeface strikes against the paper. Dot matrix printers, daisy wheel printers and drum printers are examples of impact printers.
- *Non-Impact printers* do not hit or impact a ribbon to print. Ink-jet printers and laser printers are non-impact printers.
- *COM* is a high-speed and low-cost process to record computer output directly from the computer tape on a microfilm. It is used to store manuals and for archiving of records.
- *Monitor* is attached to the computer on which the output is displayed. The clarity of image on the computer screen depends on the resolution of screen, the dot pitch, and the refresh rate.
- *Screen image projectors* display information from the computer onto a large white screen.
- *Audio output device* like speakers, headset or headphone are used to output sound from the computer system.
- *I/O ports* connect the I/O devices to the computer. Serial and parallel ports, USB port and Firewire are some of the commonly used I/O ports.
- *I/O system* uses the I/O hardware (buses, ports, *device controllers* and I/O devices) and the I/O software (*device drivers*) for its working.

KEYWORDS

Audio Response System *77*
Barcode Reader *72*
Bus *80*
Characters per Second (cps) *75*
Computer Output on Microfilm (COM) *77*
Daisy wheel Printer *75*
Device Controller *82*
Device Driver *82*
Digital Camera *69*
Digitizing Tablet *67*
Dot matrix Printer 75
dots per inch (dpi) 75
Double Click *66*
Drag and Drop *66*
Drum Plotter *76*
Drum Printer *75*
Firewire Port *80*
Flatbed Plotter *61*
Flat-bed Scanner *70*
Hand-held Scanner *70*
Hard Copy Devices *74*
Headphone *78*
Impact Printer *75*
Ink-jet Printer *75*
Input Device *63*
Input Interface *62*

QUESTIONS

Section 4.1–4.2

1. Define peripheral devices.
2. Explain in detail the input unit of computer.
3. What is the purpose of input interface?
4. Explain in detail the output unit of computer.
5. What is the purpose of output interface?
6. Name three input-output devices.

Section 4.3–4.4.1

7. Show the classification of input devices.
8. Describe the features of keyboard.
9. Give a description of keyboard.
10. What is a cursor?
11. Explain the working of a keyboard
12. Name the different sections of a keyboard.

Section 4.4–4.4.2.4

13. Name three pointing devices.
14. Describe the features of mouse.
15. Give a description of mouse.
16. Explain the working of a physical mouse and optical mouse.
17. Describe a physical mouse.
18. Give description of an optical mouse.
19. What is right click, left click and double click when you use a mouse?
20. What is the purpose of drag and drop when you use a mouse?
21. Describe the features of trackball.
22. What is a trackball?
23. In which areas is joystick mostly used?
24. Give a brief description of joystick along with its features.
25. Name an application of digitizing tablet.
26. Describe a digitizing tablet.

Section 4.4.3–4.5.3.5

27. Name an application where a light pen is used.
28. Describe a touch screen. Give its features and explain its working.
29. Name some applications where you use a touch screen.
30. Explain the working of audio input devices.
31. Why is a sound card used?
32. Define speech recognition.
33. ______ and ______ are examples of video input devices.
34. Name an application where computer vision is used.

35. Name three optical scanner devices.
36. Why is a scanner used?
37. Describe hand-held scanners and flat-bed scanners.
38. What is the purpose of OCR software in optical character recognition?
39. An application where MICR is commonly used is ______.
40. Name an application of OMR.
41. How does optical character reader recognize characters?
42. How does magnetic ink character reader recognize the magnetic characters?
43. How does optical mark reader recognize marks?
44. What is the use of barcode reader?

Section 4.6–4.6.1.1

45. Dot Matrix printers come in two sizes—______ column printer and ______column printer.
46. The sharpness and clarity of print of the printer is determined by the _______ of printer.
47. Resolution of printer is measured in _______.
48. Describe a dot-matrix printer.
49. Describe a daisywheel printer.
50. Dot matrix and daisy wheel printers are character printer but drum printer is a _______ printer and laser printer is a _______ printer.
51. Describe non-impact printers.

Section 4.6.1.2–4.6.2.4

52. What is the use of a plotter?
53. Plotters are of two kinds—_______plotter and _______plotter.
54. Name two applications where plotters are used.
55. Define a microfilm.
56. When do we use a microfilm?
57. Give a description of the monitor.
58. Define the resolution of the screen.
59. Define the refresh rate of the screen.
60. Define the dot pitch of the screen.
61. The common resolution of computer screen is _______ and _______.
62. Describe the three factors on which the clarity of image on the computer screen depends.
63. Name the three factors on which the clarity of image on the computer screen depends.
64. Name some color adapters.
65. What is a visual display terminal?
66. Why are screen image projectors used?
67. Describe how the audio response system works.
68. Name two applications of audio response system.

Section 4.7–4.8

69. Name the different types of I/O ports.
70. Name at least one device each that can be connected to the serial port, parallel port, USB port, MIDI port and firewire.
71. Explain the working of the I/O system.
72. What is the purpose of ports, buses and controllers in the I/O system?
73. What is a device driver?
74. What is the use of device driver?
75. Is device controller a hardware or software?
76. Is device driver a hardware or software?

Extra Questions

77. Give full form of the following abbreviations

(i) I/O	(ii) LED	(iii) CAD
(iv) ATM	(v) MICR	(vi) OMR
(vii) OCR	(viii) dpi	(ix) cps
(x) CAM	(xi) COM	(xii) CRT
(xiii) LCD	(xiv) VDT	(xv) USB
(xvi) MIDI		

78. Write short notes on

(a) Input-iutput unit	(b) Input Unit
(c) Output unit	(d) Keyboard
(e) Mouse	(f) Trackball
(g) Joystick	(h) Digitizing tablet
(i) Light pen	(j) Touch screen
(k) Input devices	(l) Audio input device
(m) Video input device	(n) Optical input devices
(o) Scanner	(p) MICR
(q) OMR	(r) OCR
(s) Printer	(t) Impact printers

(u) Non-impact printers
(v) Plotter
(w) Computer output on microfilm
(x) Monitor
(y) Visual display terminal
(z) Video output
(aa) Audio response
(bb) I/O ports
(cc) Working of the I/O system

79. Give differences between the following
(a) Input unit and output unit
(b) Physical mouse and Optical mouse
(c) Pointing devices and Pick devices
(d) Hand-held scanners and Flat-bed scanners
(e) Impact printers and Non-Impact printers
(f) Dot matrix printers and Daisy wheel printers
(g) Ink-jet printers and Laser printers

5 DATA REPRESENTATION

Contents

- Number system
  - Decimal number system
  - Binary number system
  - Octal number system
  - Hexadecimal number system
- Conversion from decimal to binary, octal, hexadecimal
  - Converting decimal *integer* to binary, octal, hexadecimal
  - Converting decimal *fraction* to binary, octal, hexadecimal
  - Converting decimal *integer.fraction* to binary, octal, hexadecimal
- Conversion of binary, octal, hexadecimal to decimal
- Conversion of binary to octal, hexadecimal
- Conversion of octal, hexadecimal to binary
- Binary arithmetic—Binary addition, binary subtraction
- Signed and unsigned numbers—Complement of binary numbers
- Binary data representation—Fixed point number representation, floating point number representation
- Binary coding schemes—EBCDIC, ASCII, unicode
- Logic gates

Why this chapter

We use computer to process the data and get the desired output. The data input can be in the form of alphabets, digits, symbols, audio, video, magnetic cards, finger prints, etc. Since computer can only understand 0 and 1, the data must be represented in the computer in 0s and 1s. The purpose of this chapter is to introduce you to the data representation in computer.

5.1 INTRODUCTION

The data stored in the computer may be of different kinds, as follows—

- Numeric data (0, 1, 2, …, 9)
- Alphabetic data (A, B, C, …, Z)
- Alphanumeric data—Combination of any of the symbols—(A, B, C… Z), (0, 1… 9), or special characters (+,–, Blank), etc.

All kinds of data, be it alphabets, numbers, symbols, sound data or video data, is represented in terms of 0s and 1s, in the computer. Each symbol is represented as a unique combination of 0s and 1s.

This chapter discusses the number systems that are commonly used in the computer. The number systems discussed in this chapter are—(1) Decimal number system, (2) Binary number system, (3) Octal number system, and (4) Hexadecimal number system. The number conversions described in this chapter are—

- Decimal (Integer, Fraction, Integer.Fraction) to Binary, Octal, Hexadecimal
- Binary, Octal, Hexadecimal (Integer, Fraction, Integer.Fraction) to Decimal
- Binary to Octal, Hexadecimal
- Octal, Hexadecimal to Binary

The chapter also discusses the binary arithmetic operations and the representation of signed and unsigned numbers in the computer. The representation of numbers using binary coding schemes and the logic gates used for the manipulation of data are also discussed.

5.2 NUMBER SYSTEM

A number system in *base r or radix r* uses unique symbols for *r* digits. One or more digits are combined to get a number. The *base* of the number decides the valid digits that are used to make a number. In a number, the *position* of digit starts from the right-hand side of the number. The rightmost digit has position 0, the next digit on its left has position 1, and so on. The digits of a number have two kinds of values—

- Face value, and
- Position value.

The **face value** of a digit is the digit located at that position. For example, in decimal number 52, face value at position 0 is 2 and face value at position 1 is 5.

The **position value** of a digit is ($base^{position}$). For example, in decimal number 52, the position value of digit 2 is 10^0 and the position value of digit 5 is 10^1. Decimal numbers have a base of 10.

The **number** is calculated as the sum of, face value * $base^{position}$, of each of the digits. For decimal number 52, the number is $5*10^1 + 2*10^0 = 50 + 2 = 52$

In computers, we are concerned with four kinds of number systems, as follows—

- Decimal Number System —Base 10
- Binary Number System —Base 2
- Octal Number System —Base 8
- Hexadecimal Number System—Base 16

The numbers given as input to computer and the numbers given as output from the computer, are generally in decimal number system, and are most easily understood by humans. However, computer understands the binary number system, i.e., numbers in terms of 0s and 1s. The binary data is also represented, internally, as octal numbers and hexadecimal numbers due to their ease of use.

A number in a particular base is written as $(number)_{base\ of\ number.}$ For example, $(23)_{10}$ means that the number 23 is a decimal number, and $(345)_8$ shows that 345 is an octal number.

5.2.1 Decimal Number System

- It consists of 10 digits—0, 1, 2, 3, 4, 5, 6, 7, 8 and 9.
- All numbers in this number system are represented as combination of digits 0–9. For example, 34, 5965 and 867321.

- The position value and quantity of a digit at different positions in a number are as follows—

Position:	3	2	1	0	.	–1	–2	–3
Position Value:	10^3	10^2	10^1	10^0		10^{-1}	10^{-2}	10^{-3}
Quantity:	1000	100	10	1		1/10	1/100	1/1000

5.2.2 Binary Number System

- The binary number system consists of two digits—0 and 1.
- All binary numbers are formed using combination of 0 and 1. For example, 1001, 11000011 and 10110101.
- The position value and quantity of a digit at different positions in a number are as follows—

Position:	3	2	1	0	.	–1	–2	–3
Position Value:	2^3	2^2	2^1	2^0		2^{-1}	2^{-2}	2^{-3}
Quantity:	8	4	2	1		1/2	1/4	1/8

5.2.3 Octal Number System

- The octal number system consists of eight digits—0 to 7.
- All octal numbers are represented using these eight digits. For example, 273, 103, 2375, etc.
- The position value and quantity of a digit at different positions in a number are as follows—

Position:	3	2	1	0	.	–1	–2	–3
Position Value:	8^3	8^2	8^1	8^0		8^{-1}	8^{-2}	8^{-3}
Quantity:	512	64	8	1		1/8	1/64	1/512

5.2.4 Hexadecimal Number System

- The hexadecimal number system consists of sixteen digits—0 to 9, A, B, C, D, E, F, where (A is for 10, B is for 11, C-12, D-13, E-14, F-15).
- All hexadecimal numbers are represented using these 16 digits. For example, 3FA, 87B, 113, etc.
- The position value and quantity of a digit at different positions in a number are as follows—

Position:	3	2	1	0	.	–1	–2	–3
Position Value:	16^3	16^2	16^1	16^0		16^{-1}	16^{-2}	16^{-3}
Quantity:	4096	256	16	1		1/16	1/256	1/4096

Table 5.1 summarizes the base, digits and largest digit for the above discussed number systems. Table 5.2 shows the binary, octal and hexadecimal equivalents of the decimal numbers 0–16.

	Base	Digits	Largest Digit
Decimal	10	0–9	9
Binary	2	0,1	1
Octal	8	0–7	7
Hexadecimal	16	0–9, A, B, C, D, E, F	F (15)

Table 5.1 *Summary of number system*

Decimal	Binary	Octal	Hexadecimal
0	0000	000	0
1	0001	001	1
2	0010	002	2
3	0011	003	3
4	0100	004	4
5	0101	005	5
6	0110	006	6
7	0111	007	7
8	1000	010	8
9	1001	011	9
10	1010	012	A
11	1011	013	B
12	1100	014	C
13	1101	015	D
14	1110	016	E
15	1111	017	F
16	10000	020	10

Table 5.2 *Decimal, binary, octal and hexadecimal equivalents*

5.3 CONVERSION FROM DECIMAL TO BINARY, OCTAL, HEXADECIMAL

A decimal number has two parts—integer part and fraction part. For example, in the decimal number 23.0786, 23 is the integer part and .0786 is the fraction part. The method used for the conversion of the integer part of a decimal number is different from the one used for the fraction part. In the following sub-sections, we shall discuss the conversion of decimal integer, decimal fraction and decimal integer.fraction number into binary, octal and hexadecimal number.

5.3.1 Converting Decimal *Integer* to Binary, Octal, Hexadecimal

A decimal integer is converted to any other base, by using the division operation.
To convert a decimal integer to—

- binary-divide by 2,
- octal-divide by 8, and,
- hexadecimal-divide by 16.

Let us now understand this conversion with the help of some examples.

Example 1: **Convert 25 from Base 10 to Base 2.**

1. Make a table as shown below. Write the number in centre and *toBase* on the left side.

to Base	Number (Quotient)	Remainder
2	25	

2. Divide the number with *toBase.* After each division, write the remainder on right-side column and quotient in the next line in the middle column. Continue dividing till the quotient is 0.

to Base	Number (Quotient)	Remainder
2	25	
2	12	1
2	6	0
2	3	0
2	1	1
	0	1

3. Write the digits in *remainder column* starting from *downwards to upwards,*

to Base	Number (Quotient)	Remainder
2	25	
2	12	1
2	6	0
2	3	0
2	1	1
	0	1

The binary equivalent of number $(25)_{10}$ is $(11001)_2$

The steps shown above are followed to convert a decimal integer to a number in any other base.

Example 2: **Convert 23 from Base 10 to Base 2, 8, 16.**

to Base	Number (Quotient)	Remainder
2	23	
2	11	1
2	5	1
2	2	1
2	1	0
	0	1

The binary equivalent of $(23)_{10}$ is $(10111)_2$

to Base	Number (Quotient)	Remainder
8	23	
8	2	7
	0	2

The octal equivalent of $(23)_{10}$ is $(27)_8$

to Base	Number (Quotient)	Remainder
16	23	
16	1	7
	0	1

The hexadecimal equivalent of $(23)_{10}$ is $(17)_{16}$

Example 3: **Convert 147 from Base 10 to Base 2, 8 and 16.**

to Base	Number (Quotient)	Remainder
2	147	
2	73	1
2	36	1
2	18	0
2	9	0
2	4	1
2	2	0
2	1	0
	0	1

The binary equivalent of $(147)_{10}$ is $(10010011)_2$

to Base	Number (Quotient)	Remainder
8	147	
8	18	3
8	2	2
	0	2

The octal equivalent of $(147)_{10}$ is $(223)_8$

to Base	Number (Quotient)	Remainder
16	147	
16	9	3
	0	9

The hexadecimal equivalent of $(147)_{10}$ is $(93)_{16}$

Example 4: **Convert 94 from Base 10 to Base 2, 8 and 16.**

to Base	Number (Quotient)	Remainder
2	94	
2	47	0
2	23	1
2	11	1
2	5	1
2	2	1
2	1	0
	0	1

The binary equivalent of $(94)_{10}$ is $(1011110)_2$

to Base	Number (Quotient)	Remainder
8	94	
8	11	6
8	1	3
	0	1

The octal equivalent of $(94)_{10}$ is $(136)_8$

to Base	Number (Quotient)	Remainder
16	94	
16	5	14
	0	5

The number 14 in hexadecimal is E.

The hexadecimal equivalent of $(94)_{10}$ is $(5E)_{16}$

5.3.2 Converting Decimal *Fraction* to Binary, Octal, Hexadecimal

A fractional number is a number less than 1. It may be .5, .00453, .564, etc. We use the multiplication operation to convert decimal fraction to any other base.
To convert a decimal fraction to—

- binary-multiply by 2,
- octal-multiply by 8, and,
- hexadecimal-multiply by 16.

Steps for conversion of a decimal fraction to any other base are—

(1) Multiply the fractional number with the *toBase*, to get a resulting number.

(2) The resulting number has two parts, non-fractional part and fractional part.

(3) Record the non-fractional part of the resulting number.

(4) Repeat the above steps at least four times.

(5) Write the digits in the non-fractional part starting from *upwards to downwards.*

Example 5: Convert 0.2345 from Base 10 to Base 2.

0.2345
x 2
0.4690

.4690
x 2
0.9380

.9380
x 2
1.8760

.8760
x 2
1.7520

.7520
x 2
1.5040

.5040
x 2
1.0080

The binary equivalent of $(0.2345)_{10}$ is $(0.001111)_2$

Example 5a: Convert 0.865 fromBase 10 to Base 2, 8 and 16.

0.865
x 2
1.730
x 2
1.460
x 2
0.920
x 2
1.840
x 2
1.680
x 2
1.360

The binary equivalent of $(.865)_{10}$ is $(.110111)_2$

0.865
x 8
6.920
x 8
7.360
x 8
2.880
x 8
7.040

The octal equivalent of $(0.865)_{10}$ is $(.6727)_8$

0.865
x 16
5190
865 x
13.840
x 16
5040
840 x
13.440
x 16
2640
440 x
7.040

The number 13 in hexadecimal is D.

The hexadecimal equivalent of $(0.865)_{10}$ is $(.DD7)_{16}$

5.3.3 Converting Decimal *Integer.Fraction* to Binary, Octal, Hexadecimal

A decimal *integer.fraction* number has both integer part and fraction part. The steps for conversion of a decimal *integer.fraction* to any other base are—

(1) Convert decimal integer part to the desired base following the steps shown in section 5.3.1.

(2) Convert decimal fraction part to the desired base following the steps shown in section 5.3.2.

(3) The integer and fraction part in the desired base is combined to get *integer.fraction.*

Example 6: **Convert 34.4674 from Base 10 to Base 2.**

to Base	Number (Quotient)	Remainder
2	34	
2	17	**0**
2	8	**1**
2	4	**0**
2	2	**0**
2	1	**0**
	0	**1**

The binary equivalent of $(34)_{10}$ is $(100010)_2$

0.4674
x 2
0.9348
x 2
1.8696
x 2
1.7392
x 2
1.4784
x 2
0.9568
x 2
1.936

The binary equivalent of $(0.4674)_{10}$ is $(.011101)_2$

The binary equivalent of $(34.4674)_{10}$ is $(100010.011101)_2$

Example 7: **Convert 34.4674 from Base 10 to Base 8.**

to Base	Number (Quotient)	Remainder
8	34	
8	4	**2**
	0	**4**

The octal equivalent of $(34)_{10}$ is $(42)_8$

0.4674
x 8
3.7392
x 8
5.9136
x 8
7.3088
x 8
2.4704

The octal equivalent of $(0.4674)_{10}$ is $(.3572)_8$

The octal equivalent of $(34.4674)_{10}$ is $(42.3572)_8$

Example 8: **Convert 34.4674 from Base 10 to Base 16.**

to Base	Number (Quotient)	Remainder
16	34	
16	2	**2**
	0	**2**

The hexadecimal equivalent of $(34)_{10}$ is $(22)_{16}$

```
  0.4674
    x 16
  28044
  4674x
  9.4784
    x 16
  28704
  4784x
  7.6544
    x 16
  39264
  6544x
 10.4704
    x 16
  28224
  4904x
  7.5264
```

The hexadecimal equivalent of $(0.4674)_{10}$ is $(.97A7)_{16}$

The hexadecimal equivalent of $(34.4674)_{10}$ is $(22.97A7)_{16}$

5.4 CONVERSION OF BINARY, OCTAL, HEXADECIMAL TO DECIMAL

A binary, octal or hexadecimal number has two parts—integer part and fraction part. For example, a binary number could be 10011, 0.011001 or 10011.0111. The numbers 45, .362 or 245.362 are octal numbers. A hexadecimal number could be A2, .4C2 or A1.34.

The method used for the conversion of integer part and fraction part of binary, octal or hexadecimal number to decimal number is the same; multiplication operation is used for the conversion. The conversion mechanism uses the face value and position value of digits. The steps for conversion are as follows—

(1) Find the sum of the ***Face Value*** * ***(fromBase)***^{position} for each digit in the number.

   (a) *In a non-fractional number, the rightmost digit has position 0 and the position increases as we go towards the left.*

   (b) *In a fractional number, the first digit to the left of decimal point has position 0 and the position increases as we go towards the left. The first digit to the right of the decimal point has position –1 and it decreases as we go towards the right (–2, –3, etc.)*

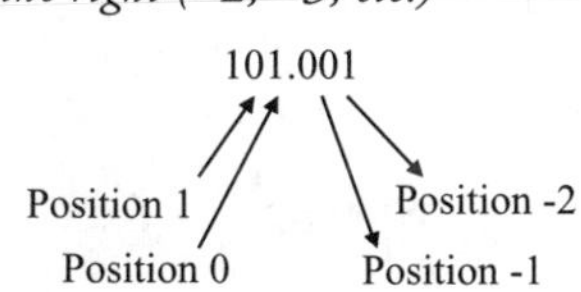

Example 9: **Convert 1011 from Base 2 to Base 10.**
Convert 62 from Base 8 to Base 10.
Convert C15 from Base 16 to Base 10.

1011 fromBase 2 toBase 10 $1011 = 1*2^3 + 0*2^2 + 1*2^1 + 1*2^0$ $= 1*8 + 0*4 + 1*2 + 1*1$ $= 8 + 0 + 2 + 1$ $= 11$ The decimal equivalent of $(1011)_2$ is 11.	62 fromBase 8 toBase 10 $62 = 6*8^1 + 2*8^0$ $= 6*8 + 2*1$ $= 48 + 2$ $= 50$ The decimal equivalent of $(62)_8$ is 50.	C15 fromBase 16 toBase 10 $C15 = C*16^2 + 1*16^1 + 5*16^0$ $= 12*256 + 1*16 + 5*1$ $= 3072 + 16 + 5$ $= 3093$ The decimal equivalent of $(C15)_{16}$ is 3093

Example 10: **Convert .1101 from Base 2 to Base 10.**
Convert .345 from Base 8 to Base 10.
Convert .15 from Base 16 to Base 10.

.1101 fromBase 2 toBase 10 $.1101 = 1*2^{-1} + 1*2^{-2} + 0*2^{-3} + 1*2^{-4}$ $= 1/2 + 1/4 + 0 + 1/16$ $= 13/16$ $= .8125$ The decimal equivalent of $(.1101)_2$ is .8125	.345 fromBase 8 toBase 10 $.345 = 3*8^{-1} + 4*8^{-2} + 5*8^{-3}$ $= 3/8 + 4/64 + 5/512$ $= 229/512$ $= .447$ The decimal equivalent of $(.345)_8$ is .447	.15 fromBase 16 toBase 10 $.15 = 1*16^{-1} + 5*16^{-2}$ $= 1/16 + 5/256$ $= 21/256$ $= .082$ The decimal equivalent of $(.15)_{16}$ is .082

Example 11: **Convert 1011.1001 from Base 2 to Base 10.**
Convert 24.36 from Base 8 to Base 10.
Convert 4D.21 from Base 16 to Base 10.

1011.1001 fromBase 2 toBase 10 $1011.1001 = 1*2^3 + 0*2^2 + 1*2^1 + 1*2^0 + 1*2^{-1} + 0*2^{-2} + 0*2^{-3} + 1*2^{-4}$ $= 8 + 0 + 2 + 1 + 1/2 + 0 + 0 + 1/16$ $= 11 + 9/16$ $= 11.5625$ The decimal equivalent of $(1011.1001)_2$ is 11.5625	24.36 fromBase 8 toBase 10 $24.36 = 2*8^1 + 4*8^0 + 3*8^{-1} + 6*8^{-2}$ $= 16 + 4 + 3/8 + 6/64$ $= 20 + 30/64$ $= 20.4687$ The decimal equivalent of $(24.36)_8$ is 20.4687	4D.21 fromBase 16 toBase 10 $4D.21 = 4*16^1 + D*16^0 + 2*16^{-1} + 1*16^{-2}$ $= 64 + 13 + 2/16 + 1/256$ $= 77 + 33/256$ $= 77.1289$ The decimal equivalent of $(4D.21)_{16}$ is 77.1289

5.5 CONVERSION OF BINARY TO OCTAL, HEXADECIMAL

A binary number can be converted into octal or hexadecimal number using a shortcut method. The shortcut method is based on the following information—

- An octal digit from 0 to 7 can be represented as a combination of 3 bits, since $2^3 = 8$.
- A hexadecimal digit from 0 to 15 can be represented as a combination of 4 bits, since $2^4 = 16$.

The Steps for Binary to Octal Conversion are—

(1) Partition the binary number in groups of three bits, starting from the right-most side.

(2) For each group of three bits, find its octal number.

(3) The result is the number formed by the combination of the octal numbers.

The Steps for Binary to Hexadecimal Conversion are—

(1) Partition the binary number in groups of four bits, starting from the right-most side.

(2) For each group of four bits, find its hexadecimal number.

(3) The result is the number formed by the combination of the hexadecimal numbers.

Example 12: Convert the binary number 1110101100110 to octal.

Given binary number 1110101100110

1. Partition binary number in groups of three bits, starting from the right-most side.

   1 110 101 100 110

2. For each group find its octal number.

   1 110 101 100 110

   1 6 5 4 6

3. The octal number is 16546.

Example 13: Convert the binary number 1110101100110 to hexadecimal

Given binary number 1110101100110

1. Partition binary number in groups of four bits, starting from the right-most side.

   1 1101 0110 0110

2. For each group find its hexadecimal number.

   1 1101 0110 0110

   1 D 6 6

3. The hexadecimal number is 1D66.

5.6 CONVERSION OF OCTAL, HEXADECIMAL TO BINARY

The conversion of a number from octal and hexadecimal to binary uses the inverse of the steps defined for the conversion of binary to octal and hexadecimal.

The Steps for Octal to Binary Conversion are—

(1) Convert each octal number into a three-digit binary number.

(2) The result is the number formed by the combination of all the bits.

The Steps for Hexadecimal to Binary Conversion are—

(1) Convert each hexadecimal number into a four-digit binary number.

(2) The result is the number formed by the combination of all the bits.

Example 14: Convert the hexadecimal number 2BA3 to binary.

(1) Given number is 2BA3

(2) Convert each hexadecimal digit into four digit binary number.

2	B	A	3
0010	1011	1010	0011

(3) Combine all the bits to get the result 0010101110100011.

Example 15: Convert the octal number 473 to binary.

(1) Given number is 473

(2) Convert each octal digit into three digit binary number.

4	7	3
100	111	011

(3) Combine all the bits to get the result 100111011.

5.7 BINARY ARITHMETIC

The arithmetic operations—addition, subtraction, multiplication and division, performed on the binary numbers is called *binary arithmetic*. In computer, the basic arithmetic operations performed on the binary numbers is—

- Binary addition, and
- Binary subtraction.

In the following subsections, we discuss the binary addition and the binary subtraction operations.

5.7.1 Binary Addition

Binary addition involves addition of two or more binary numbers. The *binary addition rules* are used while performing the binary addition. Table 5.3 shows the binary addition rules.

Input 1	Input 2		Sum	Carry
0	0	→	0	No carry
0	1	→	1	No carry
1	0	→	1	No carry
1	1	→	0	1

Table 5.3 *Binary addition rules*

Binary addition of three inputs follows the rule shown in Table 5.4.

Input 1	Input 2	Input 3		Sum	Carry
0	0	0	→	0	No Carry
0	0	1	→	1	No Carry
0	1	0	→	1	No Carry
0	1	1	→	0	1
1	0	0	→	1	No Carry
1	0	1	→	0	1
1	1	0	→	0	1
1	1	1	→	1	1

Table 5.4 *Binary addition of three inputs*

Addition of the binary numbers involves the following steps—

(1) Start addition by adding the bits in unit column (the right-most column). Use the rules of binary addition.

(2) The result of adding bits of a column is a *sum* with or without a *carry*.

(3) Write the *sum* in the result of that column.

(4) If a *carry* is present, the *carry* is carried-over to the addition of the next left column.

(5) Repeat steps 2–4 for each column, i.e., the tens column, hundreds column and so on.

Let us now understand binary addition with the help of some examples.

Example 1: **Add 10 and 01. Verify the answer with the help of decimal addition.**

When we add 0 and 1 in the unit column, sum is 1 and there is no carry. The sum 1 is written in the unit column of the result. In the tens column, we add 1 and 0 to get the sum 1. There is no carry. The sum 1 is written in the tens column of the result.

Binary Addition	Decimal Addition
1 0 + 0 1 **Result** 1 1	2 + 1 3
$11_2 = 3_{10}$	

Example 2: **Add 01 and 11. Verify the answer with the help of decimal addition.**

When we add 1 and 1 in the unit column, sum is 0 and carry is 1. The sum 0 is written in the unit column of the result. The carry is carried-over to the next column, i.e., the tens column. In the tens column, we add 0, 1 and the carried-over 1, to get sum 0 and carry 1. The sum 0 is written in the tens column of the result. The carry 1 is carried-over to the hundreds column. In the hundreds column, the result is 1.

Binary Addition	Decimal Addition
1 1 ← Carry 0 1 + 1 1 **Result** 1 0 0	1 + 3 4
$100_2 = 4_{10}$	

Example 3: **Add 11 and 11. Verify the answer with the help of decimal addition.**

Binary Addition	Decimal Addition
1 1 ← Carry 1 1 + 1 1 Result 1 1 0	3 + 3 6
$110_2 = 6_{10}$	

Example 4: **. Add 1001 and 1111. Verify the answer with the help of decimal addition.**

Binary Addition	Decimal Addition
1 1 1 1 ← Carry 1 0 0 1 + 1 1 1 1 1 1 0 0 0	9 + 1 5 2 4
$11000_2 = 24_{10}$	

Example 5: **Add 10111, 11000 and 111. Verify the answer with the help of decimal addition.**

Binary Addition	Decimal Addition
1 1 1 1 1 ← Carry 1 0 1 1 1 + 1 1 0 0 0 1 1 1 1 1 0 1 1 0	2 3 + 2 4 7 5 4
$110110_2 = 54_{10}$	

5.7.2 Binary Subtraction

Binary subtraction involves subtracting of two binary numbers. The *binary subtraction rules* are used while performing the binary subtraction. The binary subtraction rules are shown in Table 5.5, where "Input 2" is subtracted from "Input 1."

Input 1	Input 2		Difference	Borrow
0	0	→	0	No borrow
0	1	→	1	1
1	0	→	1	No borrow
1	1	→	0	No borrow

Table 5.5 *Binary subtraction rules*

The steps for performing subtraction of the binary numbers are as follows—

(1) Start subtraction by subtracting the bit in the lower row from the upper row, in the unit column.

(2) Use the binary subtraction rules. If the bit in the upper row is less than lower row, *borrow* 1 from the upper row of the next column (on the left side). The result of subtracting two bits is the *difference*.

(3) Write the *difference* in the result of that column.

(4) Repeat steps 2 and 3 for each column, i.e., the tens column, hundreds column and so on.

Let us now understand binary subtraction with the help of some examples.

Example 1: **Subtract 01 from 11. Verify the answer with the help of decimal subtraction.**

When we subtract 1 from 1 in the unit column, the difference is 0. Write the difference in the unit column of the result. In the tens column, subtract 0 from 1 to get the difference 1. Write the difference in the tens column of the result.

Binary Subtraction	Decimal Subtraction
1 1 – 0 1 Result 1 0	3 – 1 2
$10_2 = 2_{10}$	

Example 2: **Subtract 01 from 10. Verify the answer with the help of decimal subtraction.**

When we subtract 1 from 0 in the unit column, we have to borrow 1 from the left column since 0 is less than 1. After borrowing from the left column, 0 in the unit column becomes 10, and, 1 in the left column becomes 0. We perform 10–1 to get the difference 1. We write the difference in the unit column of the result. In the tens column, subtract 0 from 0 to get the difference 0. We write the difference 0 in the tens column of the result.

Binary Subtraction	Decimal Subtraction
0 10 ~~1~~ 0 – 0 1 0 1	2 – 1 1
$01_2 = 1_{10}$	

Example 3: **Subtract 0111 from 1110. Verify the answer with the help of decimal subtraction.**

When we do 0–1 in the unit column, we have to borrow 1 from the left column since 0 is less than 1. After borrowing from the left column, 0 in the unit column becomes 10, and, 1 in the left column becomes 0. We perform 10–1 to get the difference 1. We write the difference in the unit column of the result. In the tens column, when we do 0–1, we again borrow 1 from the left column. We perform 10–1 to get the difference 1. We write the difference in the tens column of the result. In the hundreds column, when we do 0–1, we again borrow 1 from the left column. We perform 10–1 to get the difference 1. We write the difference in the hundreds column of the result. In the thousands column, 0–0 is 0. We write the difference 0 in the thousands column of the result.

Binary Subtraction	Decimal Subtraction
0 10 0 10 } Borrow 0 10 ~~1~~ ~~1~~ ~~1~~ 0 – 0 1 1 1 0 1 1 1	1 4 – 0 7 7
$0111_2 = 7_{10}$	

Example 4: **Subtract 100110 from 110001. Verify the answer with the help of decimal subtraction.**

Binary Subtraction	Decimal Subtraction
1 1 ~~10~~ ~~10~~ 10 Borrow 1 ~~1~~ 0 0 0 1 1 0 0 1 1 0 0 0 1 0 1 1	4 9 − 3 8 1 1
$001011_2 = 11_{10}$	

5.8 SIGNED AND UNSIGNED NUMBERS

A binary number may be positive or negative. Generally, we use the symbol "+" and "–" to represent positive and negative numbers, respectively. The sign of a binary number has to be represented using 0 and 1, in the computer. An *n-bit signed binary number* consists of two parts—sign bit and magnitude. The left most bit, also called the Most Significant Bit (MSB) is the *sign bit*. The remaining $n-1$ bits denote the *magnitude* of the number.

In signed binary numbers, the sign bit is 0 for a positive number and 1 for a negative number. For example, 01100011 is a positive number since its sign bit is 0, and, 11001011 is a negative number since its sign bit is 1. An 8-bit *signed number* can represent data in the range –128 to +127 (-2^7 to $+2^7-1$). The left-most bit is the sign bit.

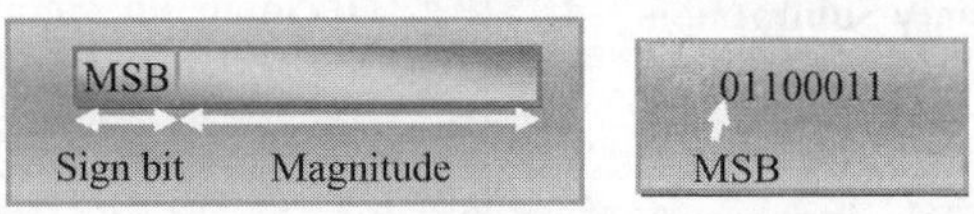

In an *n-bit unsigned binary number*, the magnitude of the number *n* is stored in *n* bits. An 8-bit *unsigned number* can represent data in the range 0 to 255 ($2^8 = 256$).

5.8.1 Complement of Binary Numbers

Complements are used in computer for the simplification of the subtraction operation. For any number in base *r*, there exist two complements—(1) *r's* complement and (2) *r*–1*'s* complement.

Number System	Base	Complements possible
Binary	2	1's complement and 2's complement
Octal	8	7's complement and 8's complement
Decimal	10	9's complement and 10's complement
Hexadecimal	16	15's complement and 16's complement

Let us now see how to find the complement of a binary number. There are two types of complements for the binary number system—1's complement and 2's complement.

- ***1's Complement of Binary Number*** is computed by changing the bits 1 to 0 and the bits 0 to 1. For example,

  1's complement of 101 is 010
  1's complement of 1011 is 0100
  1's complement of 1101100 is 0010011

- ***2's Complement of Binary Number*** is computed by adding 1 to the 1's complement of the binary number. For example,

  2's complement of 101 is 010 + 1 = 011
  2's complement of 1011 is 0100 + 1 = 0101
  2's complement of 1101100 is 0010011 + 1 = 0010100

> The rule to find the complement of any number N in base r having n digits is
> $(r - 1)$'s complement—$(r^n - 1) - N$
> $(r$'s$)$ complement—$(r^n - 1) - N + 1 = (r^n - N)$

5.9 BINARY DATA REPRESENTATION

A binary number may also have a binary point, in addition to the sign. The binary point is used for representing fractions, integers and integer-fraction numbers. *Registers* are high-speed storage areas within the Central Processing Unit (CPU) of the computer. All data are brought into a register before it can be processed. For example, if two numbers are to be added, both the numbers are brought in registers, added, and the result is also placed in a register. There are two ways of representing the position of the binary point in the register—fixed point number representation and floating point number representation.

The *fixed point number representation* assumes that the binary point is fixed at one position either at the extreme left to make the number a fraction, or at the extreme right to make the number an integer. In both cases, the binary point is not stored in the register, but the number is treated as a fraction or integer. For example, if the binary point is assumed to be at extreme left, the number 1100 is actually treated as 0.1100.

The *floating point number representation* uses two registers. The first register stores the number without the binary point. The second register stores a number that indicates the position of the binary point in the first register.

We shall now discuss representation of data in the fixed point number representation and floating point number representation.

5.9.1 Fixed Point Number Representation

The integer binary signed number is represented as follows—

- For a positive integer binary number, the sign bit is 0 and the magnitude is a positive binary number.
- For a negative integer binary number, the sign bit is 1. The magnitude is represented in any one of the three ways—

  - ***Signed Magnitude Representation***—The magnitude is the positive binary number itself.
  - ***Signed 1's Complement Representation***—The magnitude is the 1's complement of the positive binary number.
  - ***Signed 2's Complement Representation***—The magnitude is the 2's complement of the positive binary number.

Table 5.6 shows the representation of the signed number 18.

+18	0 0010010		Sign bit is 0. 0010010 is binary equivalent of +18
−18	Signed magnitude representation	1 0010010	Sign bit is 1. 0010010 is binary equivalent of +18
	Signed 1's complement representation	1 1101101	Sign bit is 1. 1101101 is 1's complement of +18
	Signed 2's complement representation	1 1101110	Sign bit is 1. 1101110 is 2's complement of +18

Table 5.6 *Fixed point representation of the signed number 18*

Signed magnitude and signed 1's complement representation are seldom used in computer arithmetic.

Let us now perform arithmetic operations on the signed binary numbers. We use the signed 2's complement representation to represent the negative numbers.

- ***Addition of Signed Binary Numbers***—The addition of any two signed binary numbers is performed as follows—
    - Represent the positive number in binary form.(For example, +5 is 0000 0101 and +10 is 0000 1010)
    - Represent the negative number in 2's complement form. (For example, −5 is 1111 1011 and −10 is 1111 0110)
    - Add the bits of the two signed binary numbers.
    - Ignore any carry out from the sign bit position.

Please note that the negative output is automatically in the 2's complement form.

We get the decimal equivalent of the negative output number, by finding its 2's complement, and attaching a negative sign to the obtained result.

Let us understand the addition of two signed binary numbers with the help of some examples.

Example 1: **Add +5 and +10.**

+5 in binary form, i.e., 0000 0101. +10 in binary form, i.e., 0000 1010.

Binary Addition	Decimal Addition
0 0 0 0 0 1 0 1	+ 5
0 0 0 0 1 0 1 0	+ 1 0
0 0 0 0 1 1 1 1	+ 1 5
The result is 0000 1111_2 i.e, $+15_{10}$	

Example 2: **Add −5 and +10.**

−5 in 2's complement form is 1111 1011. +10 in binary form is 0000 1010.

Binary Addition	Decimal Addition
1 1 1 1 1 0 1 1	− 5
0 0 0 0 1 0 1 0	+ 1 0
0 0 0 0 0 1 0 1	+ 5
The result is 0000 0101_2, i.e., $+5_{10}$	

Example 3: **Add +5 and –10.**

+5 in binary form is 0000 0101. –10 in 2's complement form is 1111 0110.

Binary Addition	Decimal Addition
0 0 0 0 0 1 0 1	+ 5
1 1 1 1 0 1 1 0	– 1 0
1 1 1 1 1 0 1 1	– 5
The result is 1111 1011_2, i.e., -5_{10}	

The result is in 2's complement form. To find its decimal equivalent—

Find the 2's complement of 1111 1011, i.e., 0000 0100 + 1 = 0000 0101. This is binary equivalent of +5. Attaching a negative sign to the obtained result gives us –5.

Example 4: **Add –5 and –10.**

–5 in 2's complement form is 1111 1011. –10 in 2's complement form is 1111 0110.

Binary Addition	Decimal Addition
1 1 1 1 1 0 1 1	– 5
1 1 1 1 0 1 1 0	– 1 0
1 1 1 1 0 0 0 1	– 1 5
The result is 1111 0001_2, i.e., -15_{10}	

The result is in 2's complement form. To find its decimal equivalent—

Find the 2's complement of 1111 0001, i.e., 0000 1110 + 1 = 0000 1111. This is binary equivalent of +15. Attaching a negative sign to the obtained result gives us –15.

- **Subtraction of Signed Binary Numbers**—The subtraction of signed binary numbers is changed to the addition of two signed numbers. For this, the sign of the second number is changed before performing the addition operation.

(–A) – (+B) = (–A) + (–B) (+B in subtraction is changed to –B in addition)
(+A) – (+B) = (+A) + (–B) (+B in subtraction is changed to –B in addition)
(–A) – (–B) = (–A) + (+B) (–B in subtraction is changed to +B in addition)
(+A) – (–B) = (+A) + (+B) (–B in subtraction is changed to +B in addition)

We see that the subtraction of signed binary numbers is performed using the addition operation.

The hardware logic for the fixed point number representation is simple, when we use 2's complement for addition and subtraction of the signed binary numbers. When two large numbers having the same sign are added, then an overflow may occur, which has to be handled.

5.9.2 Floating Point Number Representation

The floating point representation of a number has two parts—mantissa and exponent. The mantissa is a signed fixed point number. The exponent shows the position of the binary point in the mantissa.

For example, the binary number +11001.11 with an 8-bit mantissa and 6-bit exponent is represented as follows—

- Mantissa is 01100111. The left most 0 indicates that the number is positive.
- Exponent is 000101. This is the binary equivalent of decimal number + 5.
- The floating point number is Mantissa × $2^{exponent}$, i.e., + (.1100111) × 2^{+5}.

The arithmetic operation with the floating point numbers is complicated, and uses complex hardware as compared to the fixed point representation. However, floating point calculations are required in scientific calculations, so, computers have a built-in hardware for performing floating point arithmetic operations.

5.10 BINARY CODING SCHEMES

The alphabetic data, numeric data, alphanumeric data, symbols, sound data and video data, are represented as combination of bits in the computer. The bits are grouped in a fixed size, such as 8 bits, 6 bits or 4 bits. A code is made by combining bits of definite size. *Binary Coding schemes* represent the data such as alphabets, digits 0–9, and symbols in a standard code. A combination of bits represents a unique symbol in the data. The standard code enables any programmer to use the same combination of bits to represent a symbol in the data.

The binary coding schemes that are most commonly used are—

- Extended Binary Coded Decimal Interchange Code (EBCDIC),
- American Standard Code for Information Interchange (ASCII), and
- Unicode

In the following subsections, we discuss the EBCDIC, ASCII and Unicode coding schemes.

5.10.1 EBCDIC

- The Extended Binary Coded Decimal Interchange Code (EBCDIC) uses 8 bits (4 bits for zone, 4 bits for digit) to represent a symbol in the data.
- EBCDIC allows $2^8 = 256$ combinations of bits.
- 256 unique symbols are represented using EBCDIC code. It represents decimal numbers (0–9), lower case letters (a–z), uppercase letters (A–Z), Special characters, and Control characters (printable and non-printable, e.g., for cursor movement, printer vertical spacing, etc.).
- EBCDIC codes are mainly used in the mainframe computers.

5.10.2 ASCII

- The American Standard Code for Information Interchange (ASCII) is widely used in computers of all types.
- ASCII codes are of two types—ASCII-7 and ASCII-8.
- ***ASCII-7*** is a 7-bit standard ASCII code. In ASCII-7, the first 3 bits are the zone bits and the next 4 bits are for the digits. ASCII-7 allows $2^7 = 128$ combinations. 128 unique symbols are represented using ASCII-7. ASCII-7 has been modified by IBM to ASCII-8.
- ***ASCII-8*** is an extended version of ASCII-7. ASCII-8 is an 8-bit code having 4 bits for zone and 4 bits for the digit. ASCII-8 allows $2^8 = 256$ combinations. ASCII-8 represents 256 unique symbols. ASCII is used widely to represent data in computers.
- The ASCII-8 code represents 256 symbols.
  - Codes 0 to 31 represent control characters (non-printable), because they are used for actions like, Carriage return (CR), Bell (BEL), etc.
  - Codes 48 to 57 stand for numeric 0–9.
  - Codes 65 to 90 stand for uppercase letters A–Z.
  - Codes 97 to 122 stand for lowercase letters a–z.
  - Codes 128 to 255 are the extended ASCII codes.

5.10.3 Unicode

- Unicode is a universal character encoding standard for the representation of text which includes letters, numbers and symbols in multi-lingual environments. The Unicode Consortium based in California developed the Unicode standard.
- Unicode uses 32 bits to represent a symbol in the data.
- Unicode allows 2^{32} = 4164895296 (~ 4 billion) combinations.
- Unicode can uniquely represent any character or symbol present in any language like Chinese, Japanese, etc. In addition to the letters; mathematical and scientific symbols are also represented in Unicode codes.
- An advantage of Unicode is that it is compatible with the ASCII-8 codes. The first 256 codes in Unicode are identical to the ASCII-8 codes.
- Unicode is implemented by different *character encodings*. UTF-8 is the most commonly used encoding scheme. UTF stands for Unicode Transformation Format. UTF-8 uses 8 bits to 32 bits per code.

If you wish to see the Unicode character encoding in MS-Word 2007, do as follows—

<Insert> <Symbol>. A Symbol dialog box will appear which displays the symbols, and the character codes in a coding scheme, as shown in Figure 5.1.

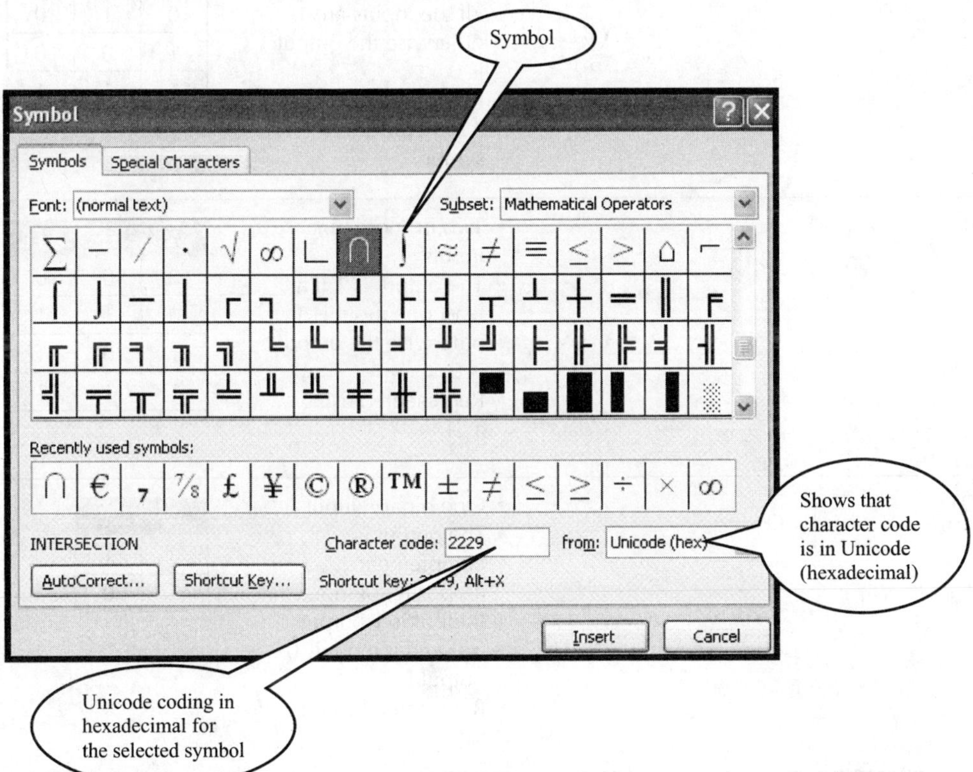

Figure 5.1 Unicode coding

5.11 LOGIC GATES

The information is represented in the computer in binary form. Binary information is represented using signals in two states *off* or *on* which correspond to 0 or 1, respectively. The manipulation of the binary information is done using logic gates. *Logic gates* are the hardware electronic circuits which operate on the input signals to produce the output signals. Each logic gate has a unique symbol and its operation is described using algebraic expression. For each gate, the *truth table* shows the output that will be outputted for the different possible combinations of the input signal. The AND, OR and NOT are the basic logic gates. Some of the basic combination of gates that are widely used are—NAND, NOR, XOR and XNOR.

Table 5.7 shows the different logic gates, their symbols, their algebraic function and the truth table for each logic gate. The comments list the features of each logic gate.

<table>
<tr><th>Operation</th><th>Symbol</th><th>Algebraic Function</th><th>Comments</th><th>Truth Table</th></tr>
<tr><td>AND</td><td>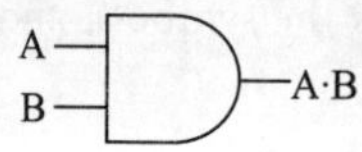
</td><td>X = A.B or
X = AB</td><td>• Two or more binary inputs
• The output is 1 if all the inputs are 1, otherwise the output is 0.
• Represented using a multiplication symbol "."</td><td><table><tr><th>A</th><th>B</th><th>A.B</th></tr><tr><td>0</td><td>0</td><td>0</td></tr><tr><td>0</td><td>1</td><td>0</td></tr><tr><td>1</td><td>0</td><td>0</td></tr><tr><td>1</td><td>1</td><td>1</td></tr></table></td></tr>
<tr><td>OR</td><td>
</td><td>X = A + B</td><td>• Two or more binary inputs
• The output is 1 if at least one input is 1, otherwise the output is 0.
• Represented using a "+"</td><td><table><tr><th>A</th><th>B</th><th>A+B</th></tr><tr><td>0</td><td>0</td><td>0</td></tr><tr><td>0</td><td>1</td><td>1</td></tr><tr><td>1</td><td>0</td><td>1</td></tr><tr><td>1</td><td>1</td><td>1</td></tr></table></td></tr>
<tr><td>NOT</td><td>
</td><td>A = A′</td><td>• One binary input
• The output is complement (opposite) of input. If input is 1 output is 0 and if input is 0 output is 1.
• Represented using a " ′ "</td><td><table><tr><th>A</th><th>A′</th></tr><tr><td>0</td><td>1</td></tr><tr><td>1</td><td>0</td></tr></table></td></tr>
</table>

(Continued)

<table>
<tr><th>Operation</th><th>Symbol</th><th>Algebraic Function</th><th>Comments</th><th>Truth Table</th></tr>
<tr><td>NAND</td><td>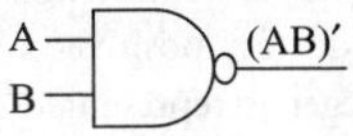
</td><td>X = (AB)′</td><td>• Two or more binary inputs
• NAND is complement of AND</td><td><table><tr><th>A</th><th>B</th><th>(A.B)′</th></tr><tr><td>0</td><td>0</td><td>1</td></tr><tr><td>0</td><td>1</td><td>1</td></tr><tr><td>1</td><td>0</td><td>1</td></tr><tr><td>1</td><td>1</td><td>0</td></tr></table></td></tr>
<tr><td>NOR</td><td>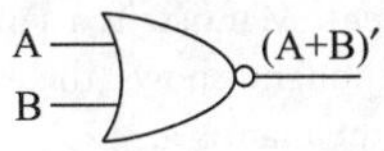
</td><td>X = (A + B)′</td><td>• Two or more binary inputs
• NOR is complement of OR.</td><td><table><tr><th>A</th><th>B</th><th>(A+B)′</th></tr><tr><td>0</td><td>0</td><td>1</td></tr><tr><td>0</td><td>1</td><td>0</td></tr><tr><td>1</td><td>0</td><td>0</td></tr><tr><td>1</td><td>1</td><td>0</td></tr></table></td></tr>
<tr><td>XOR</td><td>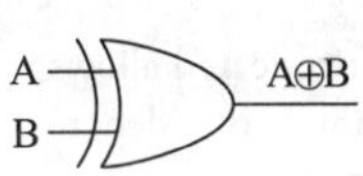
</td><td>X = (A ⊕ B)</td><td>• Two or more binary inputs
• The output is 1 if the odd number of inputs is 1.
• Represented using a " ⊕ "</td><td><table><tr><th>A</th><th>B</th><th>(A⊕ B)</th></tr><tr><td>0</td><td>0</td><td>0</td></tr><tr><td>0</td><td>1</td><td>1</td></tr><tr><td>1</td><td>0</td><td>1</td></tr><tr><td>1</td><td>1</td><td>0</td></tr></table></td></tr>
<tr><td>XNOR</td><td>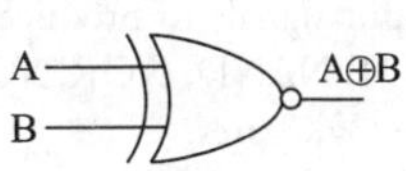
</td><td>X = (A ⊕ B)′</td><td>• Two or more binary inputs
• XNOR is complement of XOR.</td><td><table><tr><th>A</th><th>B</th><th>(A⊕B)′</th></tr><tr><td>0</td><td>0</td><td>1</td></tr><tr><td>0</td><td>1</td><td>0</td></tr><tr><td>1</td><td>0</td><td>0</td></tr><tr><td>1</td><td>1</td><td>1</td></tr></table></td></tr>
</table>

Table 5.7 *Logic gates*

SUMMARY

- *Face value* of a digit is the digit located at that place. The *position value* of digit is ($base^{position}$). The number is the sum of (face value * $base^{position}$) of all the digits.
- In computer science, decimal *number system* (base 10), binary number system (base 2), octal number system (base 8), and hexadecimal number system (base 16) concern us.
- *Decimal number system* has 10 digits—0 to 9, the maximum digit being 9.
- *Binary number system* has two digits—0 and 1.
- *Octal number system* consists of eight digits—0 to 7, the maximum digit being 7.
- *Hexadecimal number system* has sixteen digits—0 to 9, A, B, C, D, E, F, where (A is for 10, B is for 11, C—12, D—13, E—14, F—15). The maximum digit is F, i.e., 15.
- *Conversion of octal or hexadecimal number to binary* or vice-versa uses the shortcut method. Three and four bits of a binary number correspond to an octal digit and hexadecimal digit, respectively.
- *Binary arithmetic operations* are the binary addition, subtraction, multiplication and division operations performed on the binary numbers.
- For any number in base *r*, there is *r's complement and r–1's complement.* For example, binary numbers can be represented in 1's complement and 2's complement.
- *Sign bit* is the most significant bit. The sign bit is 1 and 0 for a positive number and negative number, respectively.
- *Position of binary point* in a binary number is represented using Fixed Point Number Representation and Floating Point Number Representation.
- In *fixed point representation*, the positive integer binary number is represented with sign bit 0 and magnitude as positive binary number. The negative integer is represented in signed magnitude representation, signed 1's complement representation and signed 2's complement representation.
- *Addition of two signed binary numbers* requires the positive number to be represented as binary number and negative number to be represented in 2's complement form.
- *Floating point representation* has two parts—Mantissa and Exponent. Mantissa is a signed fixed point number and exponent shows the position of the binary point in the mantissa.
- *Binary Coding schemes* represent data in a binary form in the computer. ASCII, EBCDIC, and Unicode are the most commonly used binary coding scheme.
- *EBCDIC* is a 8-bit code with 256 different representations of characters. It is mainly used in mainframe computers.
- *ASCII-8* is a 8-bit code and allows 256 characters to be represented. ASCII is widely to represent data in computers, internally.
- *Unicode* is a universal character encoding standard for the representation of text in multi-lingual environments. UTF-8 is the most commonly used encoding.
- *Logic gate* is the hardware electronic circuit that operates on input signals to produce output signal. AND, OR, NOT, NAND, NOR, XOR and XNOR are some of the logic gates.

KEYWORDS

Face Value 95
Fixed Point Number Representation 103
Floating Point Number Representation 105
Fraction 92
Hexadecimal Number 89
Integer 90
Logic Gates 108
Mantissa 105
Most Significant Bit (MSB) 102
NAND Gate 108
NOR Gate 108
NOT Gate 108
Number 88
Number System 88
Numeric Data 87
Octal Number 89
OR Gate 108
Position 88
Position Value 88
r–1's Complement 102
r's Complement 102
Signed 1's Complement Representation 103
Signed 2's Complement Representation 103
Signed Magnitude Representation 103
Signed Number 102
Truth Table 108
Unicode 107
Unicode Transformation Format (UTF) 107
Unsigned Number 102
UTF-8 107
XNOR Gate 108
XOR Gate 108
Zone Bits 106

QUESTIONS

Section 5.2–5.3.3

1. What is the significance of the base of number?
2. Explain the significance of the face value and position value of a number. Give an example.
3. What is the position value of a digit?
4. The decimal number system is in base _____.
5. The binary number system is in base _____.
6. The octal number system is in base _____.
7. The hexadecimal number system is in base _____.
8. Give the valid digits in the number systems—(a) decimal, (b) binary, (c) octal, and (d) hexadecimal.
9. Write the largest digit in the number systems—(a) decimal, (b) binary, (c) octal, and (d) hexadecimal.
10. How many valid digits are there in the number systems—(a) decimal, (b) binary, (c) octal, and (d) hexadecimal?
11. Show the octal, binary and hexadecimal equivalent of the decimal number 11.
12. Convert the following decimal numbers into binary, octal and hexadecimal.

    (i) 24 (ii) 47 (iii) 675 (iv) 89
    (v) 34.24 (vi) 150.64 (vii) .98 (viii) .29
    (ix) 24.14 (x) 16.1 (xi) 22.33

Section 5.4

13. Convert the following binary numbers into decimal numbers.

    (i) 110000111 (ii) 110011
    (iii) 1001111 (iv) 11000001
    (v) 1100110.1110 (vi) 11110.0000
    (vii) 01001.0101 (viii) 1010.10101
    (ix) 11000011.111 (x) 11001.1101
    (xi) 100.111 (xii) 101.0111

14. Convert the following octal numbers into decimal numbers.

    (i) 234 (ii) 36 (iii) 456 (iv) 217
    (v) 25.33 (vi) 65.34 (vii) 34.56 (viii) 267.12

15. Convert the following hexadecimal numbers into decimal numbers.

    (i) E16 (ii) 389 (iii) 2AB (iv) FF
    (v) E4.16 (vi) 2A.1B (vii) 23.89
    (viii) AC.BD

Section 5.5

16. Convert the following binary into octal.

    (i) 1100011 (ii) 110011001100
    (iii) 100111100 (iv) 110000011
    (v) 110011011 (vi) 1111000
    (vii) 0010101 (viii) 101010101

17. Convert the following binary into hexadecimal.

    (i) 11000011111 (ii) 110011001 1
    (iii) 100111100 (iv) 1100000100
    (v) 11001101110 (vi) 111100000
    (vii) 010010101 (viii) 101010101

Section 5.6

18. Convert the following octal into binary
    (i) 25 (ii) 65 (iii) 34 (iv) 267
    (v) 45 (vi) 71 (vii) 150 (viii) 111
19. Convert the following hexadecimal into binary.
    (i) A1 (ii) 2AB (iii) 239 (iv) CCD
    (v) 45C (vi) 71D (vii) 150 (viii) AAA

Section 5.7

20. Perform binary addition on the following binary numbers.
    (i) 111100, 011011 (ii) 1001, 1111
    (iii) 0110, 1100 (iv) 1100, 1010
21. Perform binary subtraction on the following binary numbers.
    (i) 111000, 011010 (ii) 1111, 1001
    (iii) 0110, 0010 (iv) 1100, 1010

Section 5.7.1

22. Find 1's complement of the following binary numbers.
    (i) 11000011111 (ii) 1100110011
    (iii) 100111100 (iv) 1100000100
23. Find 2's complement of the following binary numbers.
    (i) 11000011111 (ii) 1100110011
    (iii) 100111100 (iv) 1100000100
24. What is the relation between the 1's complement and 2's complement of a binary number?

Section 5.8–5.8.2

25. In addition to the digits, a number may contain a ___ and ______.
26. What is a sign bit?
27. Which bit is considered as a sign bit when representing a number?
28. What is the value of sign bit for a positive number?
29. What is the value of sign bit for a negative number?
30. What is the range of data that can be represented using an 8-bit signed number?
31. What is the range of data that can be represented using an 8-bit unsigned number?
32. ______ representation and ________ representation are the two ways of representing the position of the binary point in the register.
33. Represent the following as 8-bit numbers in (a) Signed Magnitude representation, (b) Signed 1's complement representation, and (c) Signed 2's complement representation
    (i) –22 (ii) –55 (iii) –34 (iv) –67
34. Represent the following as 8-bit numbers in Fixed Point number representation.
    (i) +22 (ii) +55 (iii) +34 (iv) +67
35. Perform binary addition of the following numbers.
    (i) (+7) + (–9) (ii) (+3) + (+15)
    (iii) (–12) + (+15) (iv) (–14) + (+25)
    (v) (–7) + (–7) (vi) (–9) + (–23)
    (vii) (–2) + (+4) (viii) (+34) + (–2)
36. Perform binary subtraction of the following numbers
    (i) (+7) – (–19) (ii) (+13) – (+15)
    (iii) (–12) – (+15) (iv) (–14) – (+25)
    (v) (–7) – (–7) (vi) (–9) – (–23)
    (vii) (–2) – (+4) (viii) (+34) – (–2)
37. Represent the following binary numbers in Floating Point number representation.
    (i) 1100.011 (ii) 110.001
    (iii) 11.110 (iv) 1010.011

Section 5.9

38. Why are binary coding schemes needed?
39. List any four commonly used binary coding schemes.
40. What number of bits is used to represent the following codes—(a) EBCDIC, (b) ASCII-7, and (c) ASCII-8?
41. How many characters can be represented in the following codes—(a) EBCDIC, (b) ASCII-7, and (c) ASCII-8?
42. How is Unicode different from the other Binary coding schemes? (Hint: multilingual, no. of characters)
43. What is UTF-8 character encoding?

Section 5.10

44. Name the basic logic gates.
45. Draw the symbols of the following logic gates—(a) AND, (b) OR, (c) NOT, (d) NAND, (e) NOR, (f) XOR, and (g) XNOR.
46. Write the truth table of the following logic gates—(a) AND, (b) OR, (c) NOT, (d) NAND, (e) NOR, (f) XOR, and (g) XNOR.

47. Write the algebraic function of the following logic gates- (a) AND, (b) OR, (c) NOT, (d) NAND, (e) NOR, (f) XOR, and (g) XNOR.

Extra Questions

48. Give full form of the following abbreviations
    (i) EBCDIC (ii) MSB
    (iii) UTF (iv) ASCII
49. Write short notes on
    (a) Decimal Number System
    (b) Binary Number System
    (c) Octal Number System
    (d) Hexadecimal Number System
    (e) Binary arithmetic operations
    (f) 1's complement of Binary number
    (g) 2's complement of Binary number
    (h) Fixed Point Number Representation
    (i) Floating Point Number Representation
    (j) Addition of signed binary numbers
    (k) Subtraction of signed binary numbers
    (l) Binary Coding schemes
    (m) Logic Gates
    (n) ASCII coding scheme
    (o) EBCDIC coding scheme
    (p) Unicode character encoding
50. Give differences between the following
    (a) 1's complement and 2's complement of Binary number
    (b) ASCII coding scheme and EBCDIC coding scheme
    (c) Decimal Number System and Binary Number System
    (d) Octal Number System and Hexadecimal Number System
    (e) Fixed Point Number Representation and Floating Point Number Representation

ANSWERS

12. (i) $(24)_{10} = (11000)_2 = (30)_8 = (18)_{16}$
    (ii) $(47)_{10} = (101111)_2$, $(57)_8 = (2F)_{16}$
    (iii) $(675)_{10} = (1010100011)_2 = (1243)_8 = (2A3)_{16}$
    (iv) $(89)_{10} = (10110001)_2 = (131)_8 = (59)_{16}$
    (v) $(34.24)_{10} = (100010.00111)_2 = (42.1727)_8 = (22.3D70)_{16}$
    (vi) $(150.64)_{10} = (10010110.1010)_2 = (226.5075)_8 = (96.A70A)_{16}$
    (vii) $(.98)_{10} = (.1111)_2 = (.7656)_8 = (FAE1)_{16}$
    (viii) $(.29)_{10} = (.0100)_2 = (.2243)_8 = (.4A3D)_{16}$
    (ix) $(24.14)_{10} = (11000.0010)_2 = (30.1075)_8 = (18.23D)_{16}$
    (x) $(16.1)_{10} = (10000.0001)_2 = (20.063)_8 = (10.199)_{16}$
    (xi) $(22.33)_{10} = (10110.0101)_2 = (26.250)_8 = (16.547)_{16}$
    (xii) $(24.14)_{10} = (11000.0010)_2 = (30.1075)_8 = (18.23D)_{16}$
13. (i) $(110000111)_2 = (391)_{10}$
    (ii) $(110011)_2 = (51)_{10}$
    (iii) $(1001111)_2 = (79)_{10}$
    (iv) $(11000001)_2 = (193)_{10}$
    (v) $(1100110.1110)_2 = (102.087)_{10}$
    (vi) $(11110.0000)_2 = (30.0)_{10}$
    (vii) $(01001.0101)_2 = (9.312)_{10}$
    (viii) $(1010.10101)_2 = (10.65)_{10}$
    (ix) $(11000011.111)_2 = (195.875)_{10}$
    (x) $(11001.1101)_2 = (25.8125)_{10}$
    (xi) $(100.111)_2 = (4.875)_{10}$
    (xii) $(101.0111)_2 = (5.4375)_{10}$
14. (i) $(234)_8 = (156)_{10}$
    (ii) $(36)_8 = (30)_{10}$
    (iii) $(456)_8 = (302)_{10}$
    (iv) $(217)_8 = (143)_{10}$
    (v) $(25.33)_8 = (21.4218)_{10}$
    (vi) $(65.34)_8 = (53.4375)_{10}$
    (vii) $(34.56)_8 = (28.7187)_{10}$
    (viii) $(267.12)_8 = (183.1562)_{10}$
15. (i) $(E16)_{16} = (3606)_{10}$
    (ii) $(389)_{16} = (905)_{10}$
    (iii) $(2AB)_{16} = (683)_{10}$
    (iv) $(FF)_{16} = (255)_{10}$
    (v) $(E4.16)_{16} = (228.0859)_{10}$
    (vi) $(2A.1B)_{16} = (42.1054)_{10}$
    (vii) $(23.89)_{16} = (35.5351)_{10}$
    (viii) $(AC.BD)_{16} = (172.7382)_{10}$

16. (i) $(1100011)_2 = (143)_8$
(ii) $(110011001100)_2 = (6314)_8$
(iii) $(100111100)_2 = (474)_8$
(iv) $(110000011)_2 = (603)_8$
(v) $(110011011)_2 = (633)_8$
(vi) $(1111000)_2 = (170)_8$
(vii) $(0010101)_2 = (025)_8$
(viii) $(101010101)_2 = (525)_8$

17. (i) $(11000011111)_2 = (61F)_{16}$
(ii) $(1100110011)_2 = (333)_{16}$
(iii) $(100111100)_2 = (13C)_{16}$
(iv) $(1100000100)_2 = (304)_{16}$
(v) $(11001101110)_2 = (66E)_{16}$
(vi) $(111100000)_2 = (1E0)_{16}$
(vii) $(010010101)_2 = (095)_{16}$
(viii) $(101010101)_2 = (155)_{16}$

18. (i) $(25)_8 = (010101)_2$
(ii) $(65)_8 = (110101)_2$
(iii) $(34)_8 = (011100)_2$
(iv) $(267)_8 = (010110111)_2$
(v) $(45)_8 = (100101)_2$
(vi) $(71)_8 = (111001)_2$
(vii) $(150)_8 = (001101000)_2$
(viii) $(111)_8 = (001001001)_2$

19. (i) $(A1)_{16} = (10100001)_2$
(ii) $(2AB)_{16} = (001010101011)_2$
(iii) $(239)_{16} = (001000111001)_2$
(iv) $(CCD)_{16} = (110011001101)_2$
(v) $(45C)_{16} = (010001011100)_2$
(vi) $(71D)_{16} = (011100011101)_2$
(vii) $(150)_{16} = (000101010000)_2$
(viii) $(AAA)_{16} = (101010101010)_2$

20. (i) 1919111 (ii) 11000
(iii) 10010 (iv) 10110

21. (i) 11110 (ii) 0110
(iii) 0100 (iv) 0010

22. (i) 00111100000 (ii) 001001100
(iii) 011000011 (iv) 0011111011

23 (i) 00111100001 (ii) 001001101
(iii) 011000100 (iv) 0011111100

33(a) (i) 10010110 (ii) 10110111
(iii) 10100010 (iv) 11000011

33(b) (i) 01101001 (ii) 01001000
(iii) 01011101 (iv) 00111100

33(c) (i) 01101010 (ii) 01001001
(iii) 01011110 (iv) 00111101

34. (i) 00010110 (ii) 00110111
(iii) 00100010 (iv) 01000011

35. (i) $-2 = (11111110)_2$ (ii) $+18 = (00010010)_2$
(iii) $+3 = (00000011)_2$ (iv) $+11 = (00001011)_2$
(v) $-14 = (11110010)_2$ (vi) $-32 = (11100000)_2$
(vii) $+2 = (00000010)_2$ (viii) $+32 = (00100000)_2$

36. (i) $+26 = (00011010)_2$ (ii) $-2 = (11111110)_2$
(iii) $-27 = (11100101)_2$ (iv) $-39 = (11011001)_2$
(v) $0 = (00000000)_2$ (vi) $+14 = (00001110)_2$
(vii) $-6 = (11111010)_2$ (viii) $+36 = (00100100)_2$

37. (i) $.1100011x2^{+4}$ (ii) $.110001x2^{+3}$
(iii) $.11110x2^{+2}$ (iv) $.1010011x2^{+4}$

Unit II USER-COMPUTER INTERFACE

INTERACTION OF USER AND COMPUTER 6

Contents

- Types of software—System software, and application software
- System software
  - For management and functionality of computer—Operating system, device drivers, and system utilities
  - For development of application software—Programming languages, translator software, loader, and linker
- Operating system
- Device drivers
- System utility software—Anti-virus, data compression, cryptographic, disk compression, disk partitioning, disk cleaner, backup, system profiling, and network manager
- Programming language—Machine language, assembly language, high-level language, and different generations of programming languages
- Translator software—Assembler, compiler, and interpreter
- Linker, and loader software
- Application software—Word processing software, image processing software, accounting software, spreadsheet software, presentation software, CAD/CAM software, and web browser software

Why this chapter

The computer, as a machine, can do nothing for you without the software. Software is required for the functioning of computer. Software programs instruct computer about the actions to be performed, so as to get the desired output. The purpose of this chapter is to introduce you to the different categories of software.

6.1 INTRODUCTION

A computer system consists of hardware and software. The computer hardware cannot perform any task on its own. It needs to be instructed about the tasks to be performed. Software is a set of programs that instructs the computer about the tasks to be performed. Software tells the computer how the tasks are to be performed; hardware carries out these tasks. Different sets of software can be loaded on the same hardware to perform different kinds of tasks. For example, a user can use the same computer hardware for writing a report or for running a payroll program. The components like monitor, keyboard, processor, and mouse, constitute the hardware (Figure 6.1). In this chapter, we will discuss the different categories of computer software.

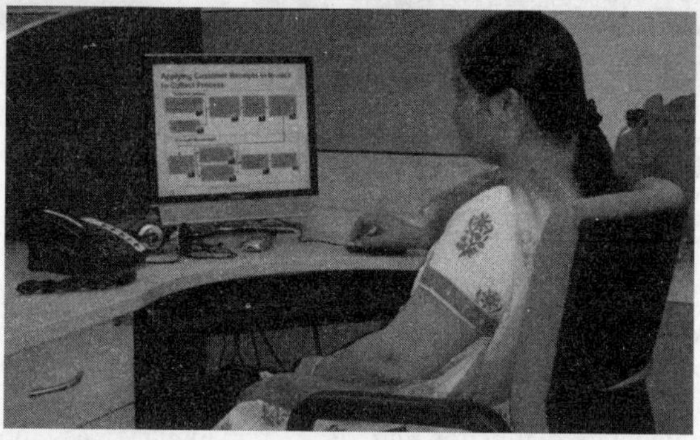

Figure 6.1 Making diagrams using hardware and software

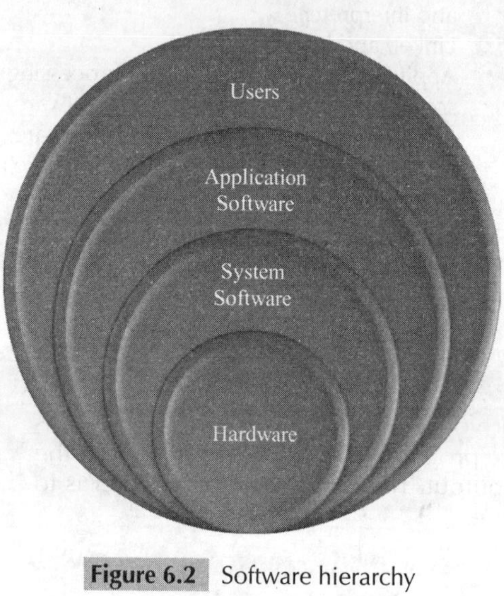

Figure 6.2 Software hierarchy

6.2 TYPES OF SOFTWARE

Software can be broadly classified in two categories:

(1) System Software, and

(2) Application Software.

System software provides the basic functions that are performed by the computer. It is necessary for the functioning of a computer. Application software is used by the users to perform specific tasks. The user may choose the appropriate application software, for performing a specific task, which provides the desired functionality. The system software interacts with hardware at one end and with application software at the other end. The application software interacts with the system software and the users of computer. Figure 6.2 shows the hierarchy of software, hardware and users.

6.3 SYSTEM SOFTWARE

System software provides basic functionality to the computer. System software is required for the working of computer itself. The user of computer does not need to be aware about the functioning of system software, while using the computer. For example, when you buy a computer, the system software would also include different device drivers. When you request for using any of the devices, the corresponding device driver software interacts with the hardware device to perform the specified request. If the appropriate device driver for any device, say a particular model of a printer, is installed on the computer, the user does not need to know about the device driver, while printing on this printer.

The *purposes of the system software* are:

- To provide basic functionality to computer,
- To control computer hardware, and
- To act as an interface between *user, application software* and *computer hardware.*

On the basis of their functionality, system software may be broadly divided into two categories (Figure 6.3) as follows—

- System software for the *management and functionality of computer* relates to the functioning of different components of the computer, like, processor, input and output devices etc. System software is required for managing the operations performed by the components of computer and the devices attached to the computer. It provides support for various services, as requested by the application software. Operating system, device drivers, and system utilities constitute the system software for management of computer and its resources.
- System software for the *development of application software* provides services required for the development and execution of application software. System software provides the software tools required for the development of application software. The programming language software, translator software, loader, and linker are also categorized as system software, and are required for the application software development.

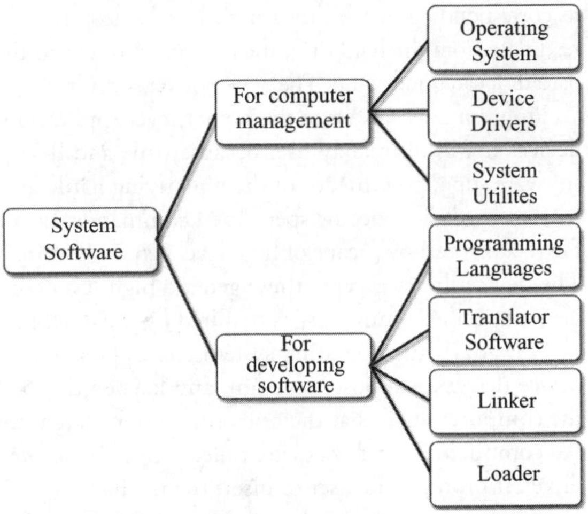

Figure 6.3 System software

6.3.1 Operating System

Operating System (OS) is an important part of a computer. OS intermediates between the user of a computer and the computer hardware. Different kinds of application software use specific hardware resources of a computer like CPU, I/O devices and memory, as needed by the application software. OS controls and coordinates the use of hardware among the different application software and the users. It provides an interface that is convenient for the user to use, and facilitates efficient operations of the computer system resources. The key functions of OS are—

- It provides an environment in which users and application software can do work.
- It manages different resources of the computer like the CPU time, memory space, file storage, I/O devices etc. During the use of computer by other programs or users, operating system manages various resources and allocates them whenever required, efficiently.
- It controls the execution of different programs to prevent occurrence of error.
- It provides a convenient interface to the user in the form of commands and graphical interface, which facilitates the use of computer.

Some available operating systems are Microsoft Disk Operating System (MS-DOS), Windows 7, Windows XP, Linux, UNIX, and Mac OS X Snow Leopard.

6.3.2 Device Driver

A device driver acts as a translator between the hardware and the software that uses the devices. In other words, it intermediates between the device and the software, in order to use the device.

Some devices that are commonly connected to the computer are—keyboard, mouse, hard disk, printer, speakers, microphone, joystick, webcam, scanner, digital camera, and monitor. For proper working of a device, its corresponding device driver must be installed on the computer. For example, when we give a command to read data from the hard disk, the command is sent to the hard disk driver and is translated to a form that the hard disk can understand. The device driver software is typically supplied by the respective device manufacturers.

Programmers can write the higher-level application code independently of whatever specific hardware devices it will ultimately use, because code and device can interface in a standard way, regardless of the software superstructure, or of the underlying hardware. Each version of a device, such as a printer, requires its own hardware-specific specialized commands. In contrast, most applications instruct devices (such as a file to a printer) by means of high level generic commands for the device, such as PRINTLN (print a line). The device-driver accepts these generic high-level commands and breaks them into a series of low-level, device-specific commands, as required by the device being driven.

Nowadays, the operating system comes preloaded with some commonly used device drivers, like the device driver for mouse, webcam, and keyboard. The device drivers of these devices are pre-installed on the computer, such that the operating system can automatically detect the device when it is connected to the computer. Such devices are called *plug and play devices*. In case the computer does not find the device driver, it prompts the user to insert the media (like a CD which contains the corresponding device driver) provided along with the device. Most device manufacturers, host the device drivers for their devices on their companies' websites; users can download the relevant driver and install it on their computer.

- Each device has its own device driver (Figure 6.4).
- Whenever a new device is connected to a computer, its device driver has to be loaded in the computer's memory, to enable use of the device. When you buy a new printer, you get the device driver CD with it. You must install the device driver on your computer, to use the new printer. Each printer comes with its own device driver. If you replace your old printer with a new model, you need to install the device driver for the new printer.
- Device drivers can be *character* or *block device* drivers. Character device drivers are for character based devices like keyboard, which transfer data character by character. Block device driver are for devices that transfer data as a block, like in hard disk.

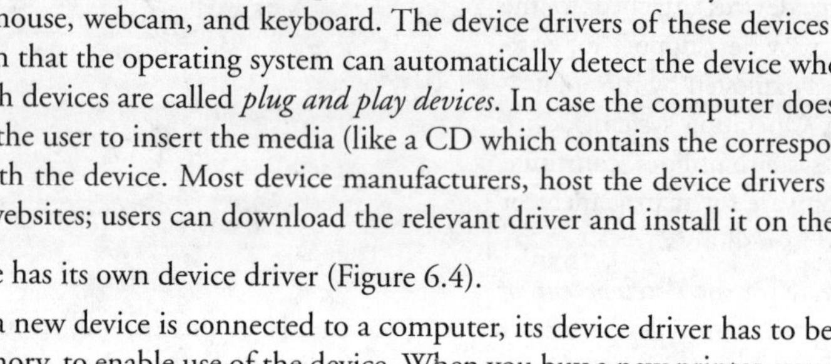

Figure 6.4 Device driver (i) CD of a printer (ii) Sony audio recorder

6.3.3 System Utilities

System utility software is required for the maintenance of computer. System utilities are used for supporting and enhancing the programs and the data in computer. Some system utilities may come embedded with OS and others may be added later on. Some examples of system utilities are:

- *Anti-virus* utility to scan computer for viruses (Figure 6.5).
- *Data Compression* utility to compress the files.

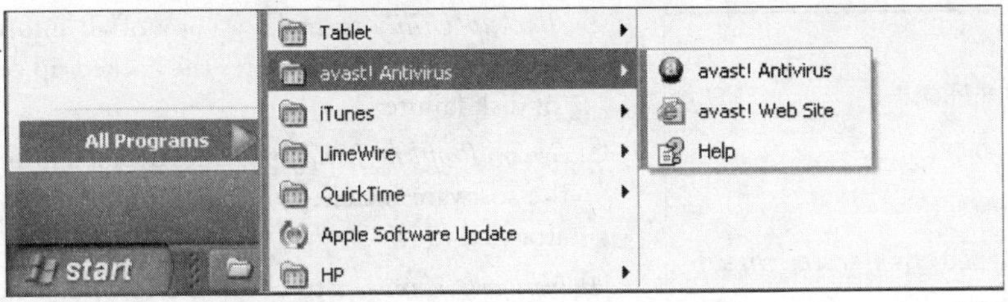

Figure 6.5 Antivirus software on a computer

- *Cryptographic* utility to encrypt and decrypt files.
- *Disk Compression* utility to compress contents of a disk for increasing the capacity of a disk.
- *Disk Partitioning* to divide a single drive into multiple logical drives. Each drive is then treated as an individual drive and has its own file system. Figure 6.6 shows a hard disk with three partitions.
- *Disk Cleaners* to find files that have not been used for a long time. It helps the user to decide what to delete when the hard disk is full.

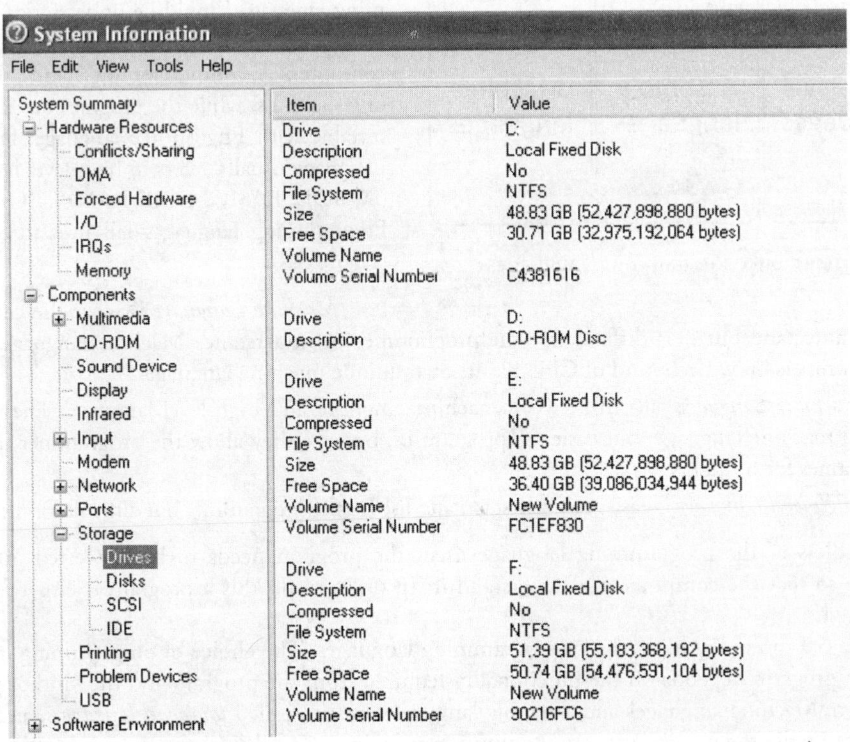

Figure 6.6 A hard disk having three partitions—C, E, and F

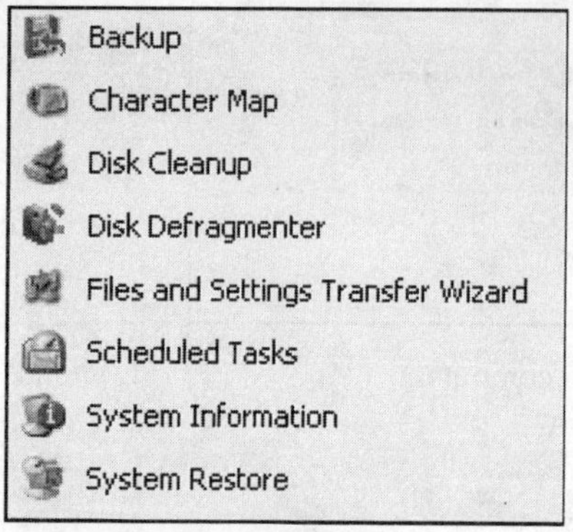

Figure 6.7 Some system tools in Windows XP

- *Backup Utility* to make a copy of all information stored on the disk. It also restores the backed up contents in case of disk failure.
- *System Profiling Utility* provides detailed information about the software installed on the computer and the hardware attached to it.
- *Network Managers* to check the computer network and to log events.

The system utilities on a computer working on Windows XP OS can be viewed by clicking <Start><All Programs><Accessories><System Tools>. Figure 6.7 shows system tools in Windows XP.

6.3.4 Programming Languages

A Programming Language consists of a set of vocabulary and grammatical rules, to express the computations and tasks that the computer has to perform. Programming languages are used to write a program, which controls the behavior of computer, codify the algorithms precisely, or enables the human-computer interface. Each language has a unique set of keywords (words that it understands) and a special syntax for organizing program instructions. The programming language should be understood, both by the programmer (who is writing the program) and the computer. A computer understands the language of 0's and 1's, while the programmer is more comfortable with English-like language. Programming Language usually refers to high-level languages like COBOL, BASIC, FORTRAN, C, C++, Java etc. Programming languages fall into three categories (Figure 6.8):

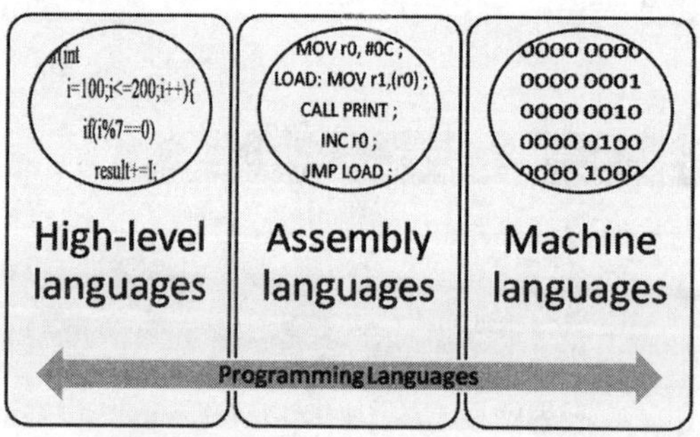

Figure 6.8 Programming languages

- *Machine Language* is what the computer can understand but it is difficult for the programmer to understand. Machine languages consist of numbers only. Each kind of CPU has its own unique machine language.
- *Assembly Language* falls in between machine language and high-level language. They are similar to machine language, but easier to program in, because they allow the programmer to substitute names for numbers.
- *High-level Language* is easier to understand and use for the programmer but difficult for the computer.

Regardless of the programming language used, the program needs to be converted into machine language so that the computer can understand it. In order to do this a program is either compiled or interpreted.

Figure 6.9 shows the hierarchy of programming languages. The choice of programming language for writing a program depends on the functionality required from the program and the kind of program to be written. Machine languages and assembly languages are also called *low-level languages*, and are generally used to write the system software. Application software is usually written in *high-level languages*. The program written in a programming language is also called the *source code*.

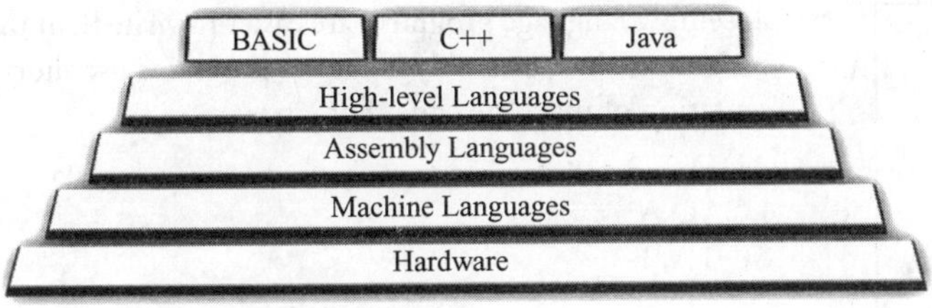

Figure 6.9 A program in machine language

6.3.4.1 *Machine Language*

A program written in machine language is a collection of binary digits or bits that the computer reads and interprets. It is a system of instructions and data executed directly by a computer's CPU. It is also referred to as machine code or object code. It is written as strings of 0's and 1's, as shown in Figure 6.10. Some of the features of a program written in machine language are as follows:

```
00000000101000010000000000011000
00000000100011100001100000100001
10001100011000100000000000000000
10001100111100100000000000000100
10101100111100100000000000000000
10101100011000100000000000000100
00000011111000000000000000001000
```

Figure 6.10 Machine language code

- The computer can understand the programs written in machine language directly. No translation of the program is needed.
- Program written in machine language can be executed very fast (Since no translation is required).
- Machine language is defined by the hardware of a computer. It depends on the type of the processor or processor family that the computer uses, and is thus machine-dependent. A machine-level program written on one computer may not work on another computer with a different processor.
- Computers may also differ in other details, such as memory arrangement, operating systems, and peripheral devices; because a program normally relies on such factors, different computer may not run the same machine language program, even when the same type of processor is used.
- Most machine-level instructions have one or more *opcode* fields which specify the basic instruction type (such as arithmetic, logical, jump, etc), the actual operation (such as add or compare), and some other fields.
- It is difficult to write a program in machine language as it has to be written in binary code. For e.g., 00010001 11001001. Such programs are also difficult to modify.
- Since writing programs in machine language is very difficult, programs are hardly written in machine language.

6.3.4.2 *Assembly Language*

A program written in assembly language uses symbolic representation of machine codes needed to program a particular processor (CPU) or processor family. This representation is usually defined by the CPU manufacturer, and is based on abbreviations (called mnemonics) that help the programmer remember individual instructions, registers, etc. Small, English-like representation is used to write the program in assembly language, as shown in Figure 6.11. Some of the features of a program written in assembly language are as follows:

```
MOV   B, A
MVI   C, 06H
LXI   H, XX50H
ADD   M
JNC   NXTITM
INR   B
INX   H
DCR   C
JNZ   NXTBIT
```

Figure 6.11 Assembly language code

- Assembly language programs are easier to write than the machine language programs, since assembly language programs use short, English-like representation of machine code. For e.g.:

  ADD 2, 3
  LOAD A
  SUB A, B
- The program written in assembly language is the source code, which has to be converted into machine code, also called object code, using translator software, namely, assembler.
- Each line of the assembly language program is converted into one or more lines of machine code. Hence assembly language programs are also machine-dependent.
- Although assembly language programs use symbolic representation, they are still difficult to write.
- Assembly language programs are generally written where the efficiency and the speed of program are the critical issues, i.e. programs requiring high speed and efficiency.

6.3.4.3 High-level Language

A program in a high-level language is written in English-like language. Such languages hide the details of CPU operations and are easily portable across computers. A high-level language isolates the execution semantics of computer architecture from the specification of the program, making the process of developing a program simpler and more understandable with respect to assembly and machine level languages. Some of the features of a program written in high-level language are as follows:

- Programs are easier to write, read or understand in high-level languages than in machine language or assembly language. For example, a program written in C++ is easier to understand than a machine language program (Figure 6.12).
- Programs written in high-level languages is the source code which is converted into the object code (machine code) using translator software like interpreter or compiler.
- A line of code in high-level program may correspond to more than one line of machine code.
- Programs written in high-level languages are easily portable from one computer to another.

6.3.4.4 Different Generations of Programming Languages

In addition to the categorization of programming languages into machine language, assembly language, and high-level language, programming languages are also classified in terms of generations in which they have evolved. Table 6.1 shows the classification of programming languages based on generations.

6.3.5 Translator Software

Translator software is used to convert a program written in high-level language and assembly language to a form that the computer can understand. Translator software converts a program written in assembly

```
/* PROGRAM NO:1
A menu driven program to perform the following:
a. Calculate the n th term of fibonnaci series
b. Calculate the n the prime number
c. Calculate the sum of digits of a number
d. Reverse a number                          */

#include<iostream.h>
#include<process.h>
#include<conio.h>
class menu
{ int n,i;
public:
  void get_data();
  void fibo();
  void prime();
  void sum();
  void reverse();
} f;
void menu::get_data()
{ cout << "\n Enter the value of n: ";
  cin>> n; }
void menu::sum()
{ int rem,sum=0,t=n;
  while(n>0)
  { rem = n % 10;     n = n /10;     sum += rem; }
  cout << " Sum of digits of " << t << ": " << sum;
}
void menu::reverse()
{ int mod,rev=0,t1=n;
  while(n>0)
  { mod = n % 10;     n  = n / 10;     rev = rev *
10 + mod;  }
  cout << " Reverse of the number " << t1 << " is "
<< rev;
}
void menu::fibo()
{ int f1=0,f2=1,f;
  cout << f1 << "\t" << f2 << "\t";
  for(i=3;i<=n;i++)
  { f = f1 + f2;
    f1 = f2;     f2 = f;
    cout << f << "\t";
  }}
void menu::prime()  // to display n th prime number
{ int p=2, k=2, h=0;
  while(k < 1000)
  { p = 2;
    while(p<=k)
    { if (k%p==0)
           break;  p++;     }
    if(p == k)
    { h++;
          if(h == n)
            cout <<" " << n << " th prime number is:
" << p;    }
    k++;    }}
void main()
{ int ch,ch1;
 do
 { clrscr();
   cout << "\t\t***** M E N U *****";
   cout << "\n 1. Fibonnaci Series";
   cout << "\n 2. Nth Prime number";
   cout << "\n 3. Sum of digits";
   cout << "\n 4. Reverse of a number";
   cout << "\n 5. Exit";
   cout << "\n Enter your choice: ";
   cin >> ch;
   switch(ch)
   {case 1: f.get_data();
              f.fibo();          break;
    case 2: f.get_data();
              f.prime();         break;
    case 3: f.get_data();
              f.sum();           break;
    case 4: f.get_data();
              f.reverse();       break;
    case 5 exit(0);              break;
    default:cout << "\n Sorry";
   }
   cout << "\n\n Do you wish to continue ? Press 5
to exit: ";
   cin >> ch1;
 }while(ch1 != 5);
 getch();
}
```

Figure 6.12 A C++ program

First Generation	Machine language
Second Generation	Assembly language
Third Generation	C, COBOL, Fortran, Pascal, C++, Java, ActiveX (Microsoft) etc.
Fourth Generation	.NET (VB.NET, C#.NET etc.) Scripting language (Javascript, Microsoft Frontpage etc.)
Fifth Generation	LISP, Prolog

Table 6.1 *Generations of programming languages*

Figure 6.13 Translator software

language, and high-level language to a machine-level language program (Figure 6.13). The translated program is called the *object code*. There are three different kind of translator software:

- Assembler,
- Compiler, and
- Interpreter.

Assembler converts a program written in assembly language to machine language. Compiler and interpreter convert a program written in high-level language to machine language. Let's now discuss, briefly, the different kinds of translator software.

6.3.5.1 Assembler

Assembly language is also referred to as a symbolic representation of the machine code. Assembler is a software that converts a program written in assembly language into machine code (Figure 6.14). There is usually a one-to-one correspondence between simple assembly statements and machine language instructions. The machine language is dependent on the processor architecture, though computers are generally able to carry out the same functionality in different ways. Thus the corresponding assembly language programs also differ for different computer architectures.

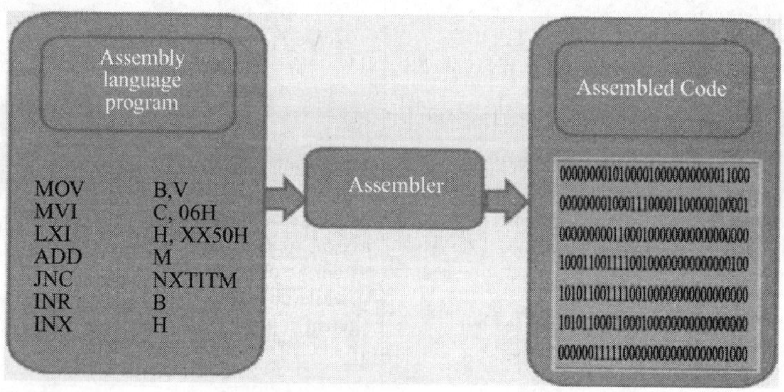

Figure 6.14 Assembler

6.3.5.2 Compiler

A program written in a high-level language has to be converted to a language that the computer can understand, i.e. *binary form*. Compiler is the software that translates the program written in a high-level language to machine language. The program written in high-level language is referred to as the *source code* and compiled program is referred as the *object code*. The object code is the *executable code*, which can run as a stand-alone code. It does not require the compiler to be present during execution. Each programming language has its own compiler. Some languages that use a compiler are C++, COBOL, Pascal, and FORTRAN. In some languages, compilation using the compiler and linking using the linker are required for creating the executable object code.

The compilation process generally involves two parts—breaking down the source code into small pieces and creating an intermediate representation, and, constructing the object code for the intermediate representation. The compiler also reports syntax errors, if any, in the source code.

6.3.5.3 Interpreter

The purpose of interpreter is similar to that of a compiler. The interpreter is used to convert the high-level language program into computer-understandable form. However, the interpreter functions in a different way than a compiler. Interpreter performs line-by-line execution of the source code during program execution. Interpreter reads the source code line-by-line, converts it into machine understandable form, executes the line, and then proceeds to the next line. Some languages that use an interpreter are BASIC and Python.

Difference Between a Compiler and An Interpreter: Compiler and Interpreter are used to convert a program written in high-level language to machine language; however, they work differently. The key differences between a compiler and an interpreter are as follows:

- Interpreter looks at a source code line-by-line. Compiler looks at the entire source code.
- Interpreter converts a line into machine executable form, executes the line, and proceeds with the next line. Compiler converts the entire source code into object-code and creates the object code. The object code is then executed by the user.
- For a given source code, once it is compiled, the object code is created. This object code can be executed multiple number of times by the user. However, interpreter executes line-by-line, so executing the program using an interpreter means that during each execution, the source code is first interpreted and then executed.
- During execution of an object code, the compiler is not required. However, for interpretation, both interpreter and the source code is required during execution (because source code is interpreted during execution).
- Since interpreter interprets line-by-line, the interpreted code runs slower than the compiled code.

6.3.6 Linker

Linker is a program that links several object modules and libraries to a single executable program. A source code of a program is often very large consisting of several hundred or more lines. The source code may also include reference to libraries. All these independent modules may not be stored in a single object file. The code is broken down into many independent modules for easy debugging and maintenance. Before execution of the program, these modules and the required libraries are linked together using the *linker* software. The compiled and the linked program are called the *executable code*.

6.3.7 Loader

The *loader* software is used to load and re-locate the executable program in the main memory. Software has to be loaded into the main memory during execution. Loader assigns storage space to the program in the main memory for execution. Figure 6.15 shows the working of a Java Runtime Environment (JRE). The java source file *Sample.java* is compiled and converted into a set of bytecodes and are stored in *Sample.class* file. At runtime, the class loader loads the bytecodes from the hard disk, checks it, and runs it in an interpreter. The interpreter executes the bytecode and makes calls to the underlying hardware.

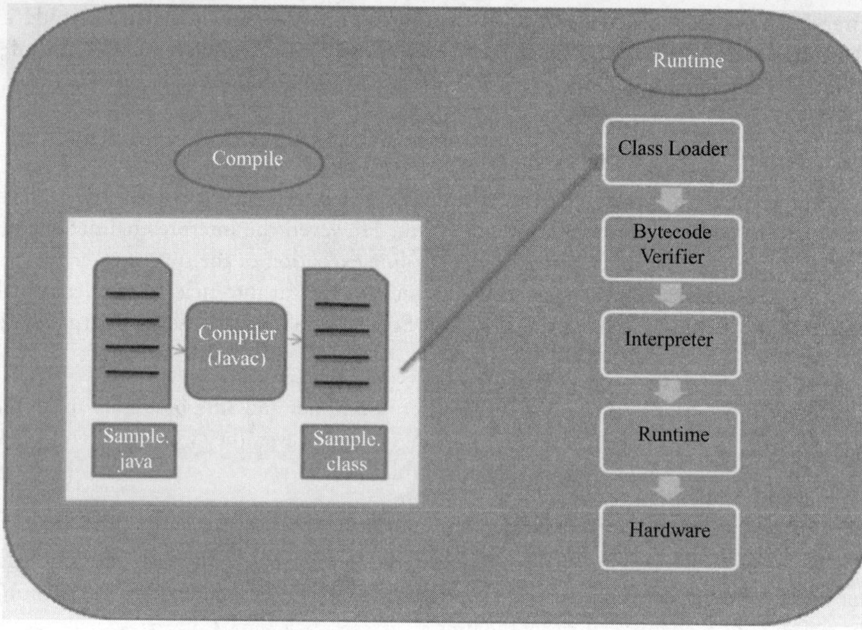

Figure 6.15 Working of java runtime environment

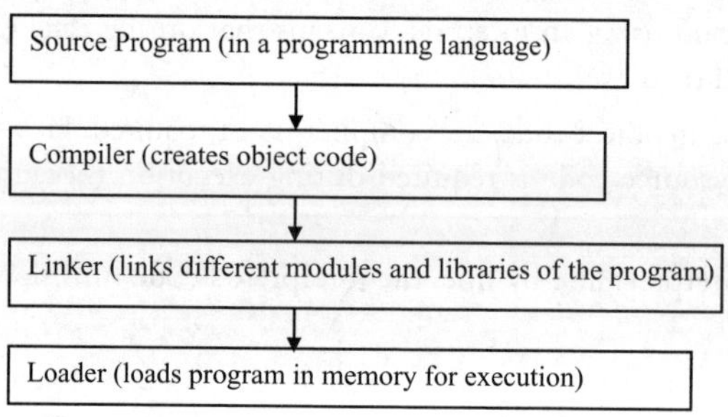

Figure 6.16 Hierarchy of program execution

The hierarchy of program execution from writing the program to its execution is shown in Figure 6.16.

6.4 APPLICATION SOFTWARE

The software that a user uses for accomplishing a specific task is the *application software*. Application software may be a single program or a set of programs. A set of programs that are written for a specific purpose and provide the required functionality is called *software package*. Application software is written for different kinds of applications—graphics, word processors, media players, database applications, telecommunication, accounting purposes etc.

Some examples of application software packages (Figure 6.17) are as follows:

- *Word Processing Software:* For writing letter, reports, documents etc. (e.g. MS-WORD).
- *Image Processing Software:* For assisting in drawing and manipulating graphics (e.g. Adobe Photoshop).
- *Accounting Software*: For assisting in accounting information, salary, tax returns (Tally software).

Figure 6.17 Some application software

- *Spreadsheet Software:* Used for creating budget, tables etc. (e.g. MS-Excel).
- *Presentation Software:* To make presentations, slide shows (e.g. MS-PowerPoint)
- *Suite of Software having Word Processor, Spreadsheet and Presentation Software:* Some examples are MS-Office, Google Docs, Sun Openoffice, Apple iWork.
- *CAD/CAM Software:* To assist in architectural design. (e.g. AutoCAD, Autodesk)
- *Geographic Information Systems:* It captures, stores, analyzes, manages, and presents data, images and maps that are linked to different locations. (e.g. ArcGIS)
- *Web Browser Software:* To access the World Wide Web to search documents, sounds, images etc. (e.g. Internet Explorer, Netscape Communicator, Chrome).

6.5 SOFTWARE ACQUISITION

Different kinds of software are made available for use to users in different ways. The user may have to purchase the software, can download for free from the Internet, or can get it bundled along with the hardware. Nowadays with the advent of Cloud computing, many application software are also available on the cloud for use through the Internet, e.g. Google Docs. The different ways in which the software are made available to users are:

- **Retail Software** is off-the-shelf software sold in retail stores. It comes with printed manuals and installation instructions. For example, Microsoft Windows operating system.
- **OEM Software** stands for "Original Equipment Manufacturer" software. It refers to software which is sold, and bundled with hardware. Microsoft sells its operating system as OEM software to hardware dealers. OEM software is sold at reduced price, without the manuals, packaging and installation instructions. For example, Dell computers are sold with the "Windows 7" OS pre-loaded on them.
- **Demo Software** is designed to demonstrate what a purchased version of the software is capable of doing and provides a restricted set of features. To use the software, the user must buy a fully-functional version.
- **Shareware** is a program that the user is allowed to try for free, for a specified period of time, as defined in the license. It is downloadable from the Internet. When the trial period ends, the software must be purchased or uninstalled.

- **Freeware** is software that is free for personal use. It is downloadable from the Internet. The commercial use of this software may require a paid license. The author of the freeware software is the owner of the software, though others may use it for free. The users abide by the license terms, where the user cannot make changes to it, or sell it to someone else.
- **Public Domain Software** is free software. Unlike freeware, public domain software does not have a copyright owner or license restrictions. The source code is publicly available for anyone to use. Public domain software can be modified by the user.
- **Open-Source Software** is software whose source code is available and can be customized and altered within the specified guidelines laid down by the creator. Unlike public domain software, open-source software has restrictions on their use and modification, redistribution limitations, and copyrights. Linux, Apache, Firefox, OpenOffice are some examples of open-source software.

SUMMARY

- *Software* can be classified into two categories—System Software, and Application Software.
- *System software* provides basic functionality to the computer, controls computer hardware, and acts as an interface between user and computer hardware. System software may be used for the management of the computer, and, for the development of application software.
- *Operating System (OS)* intermediates between user of computer and computer hardware. It manages resources of the computer system, controls execution of programs, and provides a convenient interface to the user for use of the computer.
- MS-DOS, Windows XP, Windows 7, UNIX and Mac OS X, are some examples of OS.
- *Device driver* intermediates between the device and the software that uses the device. Each device has its own device driver, which must be installed on the computer for the proper working of device. Device drivers can be *character* or *block* device drivers.
- For *plug and play devices,* the device drivers come preloaded with the operating system.
- *System utility software* is required for maintenance of the computer. Anti-virus, data compression, disk partitioning, backup, system profiling are some system utilities.
- *Programming languages* include a set of commands that the user follows to write a program.
- *Machine language* is defined by the hardware of the computer. A program written in machine language is very fast, machine-dependent, and is difficult to write.
- *Assembly language* uses symbolic representation of machine code. An assembly language program is easier to write than the machine language program but is still machine dependent.
- A program written in a *high-level language* is English-like. High-level language programs are easier to write and are easily portable from one computer to another.
- The programming languages are classified into five *generation of languages.*
- *Translator software* is used to convert a program written in high-level language and assembly language to a form that the computer can understand. Assembler, compiler, and interpreter are the three kinds of translator software.
- *Assembler* converts a program written in assembly language into machine code.
- *Compiler* translates the program written in a high-level language to machine language. The high-level language program is the source code, and compiled program is the object code.
- *Interpreter* converts the high-level language program into machine code, but performs line-by-line execution of the source code, during the program execution.
- *Linker* links several object modules and libraries to a single executable program.
- *Loader* loads and re-locates the executable program in the main memory.
- *Application software* is a single program or a set of programs that perform a specific task. Word processing software, image processing software, geographical information systems, accounting software, spreadsheet, presentation software, and web browser software are examples of application software.
- *Software acquisition* may require the user to purchase the software like retail software, or use free software like freeware, public-domain software, and open-source software.

KEYWORDS

Accounting software *126*
Anti-virus utility *118*
Application software *116*
Assembler *124*
Assembly language *121*
Backup *120*
Block device driver *118*
CAD/CAM software *127*
Character device driver *118*
Compiler *124*
Cryptographic utility *119*
Data compression utility *118*
Demo software *127*
Device driver *117*
Disk cleaners *119*
Disk compression *119*
Disk partitioning *119*
Executable code *124*
Freeware *128*
Generations of Programming languages *122*
High-level language *120*
Image processing software *126*
Interpreter *125*
Linker *125*
Loader *125*
Low-level language *120*
Machine language *120*
Network managers *120*
Object code *124*
OEM software *127*
Open-source software *128*
Operating system *117*
Plug and play devices *118*
Presentation Software *127*
Program *115*
Programming languages *120*
Public domain software *128*
Retail software *127*
Shareware *127*
Software *116*
Software package *126*
Source code *120*
Spreadsheet software *127*
System profiling *120*
System software *116*
System utility *118*
Translator software *122*
Web browser software *127*
Word processing software *126*

QUESTIONS

Section 6.1–6.3

1. _____ and _____ are the two main categories of software.
2. What is the purpose of system software?
3. What is system software?
4. Give two examples of system software.
5. Describe the two categories of system software.

Section 6.3.1–6.3.3

6. What is the need of an operating system?
7. Describe the functions of an operating system.
8. "OS controls and coordinates the use of hardware among the different application software and the users". Explain.
9. Name any three operating systems.
10. Define a device driver.
11. What are plug and play devices?
12. Give an example of a plug and play device.
13. Where is the device driver of the plug and play device located on the computer?
14. What is the purpose of a device driver?
15. What are character device driver and block device driver?
16. Give an example of a character device driver.
17. Give an example of a block device driver.
18. What are the uses of system utilities?
19. List any five system utilities and also list the purpose of each.
20. Explain the purpose of the following system utilities in one line—(i) Anti-virus, (ii) Data compression, (iii) Cryptographic, (iv) Disk compression, (v) Disk partitioning, (vi) Disk cleaners, (vii) Backup utility, (viii) System Profiling utility, (ix) Network managers.

Section 6.3.4–6.3.4.4

21. Why are programming languages used?
22. What is the need for programming languages?
23. Name the three categories of programming languages.
24. What are low-level languages?
25. Define source code?
26. Define object code?
27. Machine language is hardware dependent—True or False.
28. List the key features of machine language.
29. List the key features of assembly language.
30. List the key features of high-level languages.

31. Why is it difficult to write a program in machine language?
32. State three features of the program written in machine language?
33. Why is it easier to write a program in high-level language than the assembly language?
34. Classify the programming languages based on their generations?
35. COBOL and C are _____ generation languages.
36. Name two high-level languages.

Section 6.3.5–6.3.7

37. What is the purpose of an assembler?
38. What is an executable code?
39. What is the purpose of a compiler?
40. How does an interpreter work?
41. Name two high-level languages that use compiler for translation.
42. Name two high-level languages that use interpreter for translation.
43. What is the purpose of linker?
44. What is the purpose of loader?
45. Draw the cycle from the writing of the program in a high-level language to its execution.

Section 6.4

46. Define a software package.
47. What is the use of application software?
48. Explain the purpose of the following application software in one line—(i) Word processing software, (ii) Image processing software, (iii) Accounting software, (iv)Spreadsheet software, (v) Presentation software, (vi) Web browser software, and (vii) Geographical Information Systems.
49. Give an example each of the following application software—(i) Word processing software, (ii) Image processing software, (iii) Accounting software, (iv) Spreadsheet software, (v) Presentation software, (vi) Web browser software, and (vii) Geographical Information Systems.
50. What are the different ways of acquiring software?

Extra Questions

51. Give full form of the following abbreviations
    (i) OS (ii) MS-DOS
52. Write short notes on:
    (a) System software (b) Operating System
    (c) Device driver (d) System utilities
    (e) Programming Language
    (f) Machine language (g) Assembly language
    (h) High-level languages
    (i) Generation of Programming Languages
    (j) Translator software (k) Assembler
    (l) Compiler (m) Interpreter
    (n) Linker and Loader
    (o) Application Software
53. Give differences between the following:
    (a) System Software and Application Software
    (b) Machine language and Assembly language
    (c) Assembly language and High-level languages
    (d) Assembler and Compiler
    (e) Compiler and Interpreter
    (f) Linker and Loader

OPERATING SYSTEM 7

Contents

- Objectives of OS
- Types of OS—Single user and single task, single user and multitasking, multiuser, multiprocessing, real time, embedded OS
- Functions of OS—Process management, memory management, file management, device management, protection and security, user interface
- Process management
    - Process—Process states (new, ready, running, waiting, terminated)
    - CPU scheduling—Scheduler, scheduling algorithms (FCFS, SJF, RR)
    - Process synchronization—Concurrent processes, race condition
    - Deadlock—Deadlock conditions, deadlock prevention, deadlock avoidance
- Memory management
    - Memory allocation—Multiple partition allocation, paging
    - Virtual memory—Demand paging
- File management—Files, directory structure
- Device management—Device drivers, I/O scheduling, buffering, spooling
- Protection and security
- User interface—CLI, GUI
- Examples of operating systems—MS-DOS, Windows family of OS, Linux

Why this chapter

Any computer system you use has an operating system. The user interacts with the machine via the operating system. A software on the machine interacts with the hardware via the operating system. Operating system intermediates between the hardware and the user. The purpose of this chapter is to introduce you to the Operating System.

7.1 INTRODUCTION

The computer system comprises of a functional set of hardware, software, user and data. Hardware consists of the components of computer like memory, processor, storage devices, and Input/Output devices. The software may be of different kinds—application software and system software. A computer system may be a single stand-alone system or may consist of several interconnected systems. The user uses the application software to perform various tasks, for example, the user uses word processing software for document preparation. While using the application software, the user uses the storage of a computer—to store a document on the hard disk, to execute a command on the CPU, to retrieve a document from a peripheral device or to print document on printer. For using the hardware, there is a need for software that interacts with both the hardware and the application software. Operating

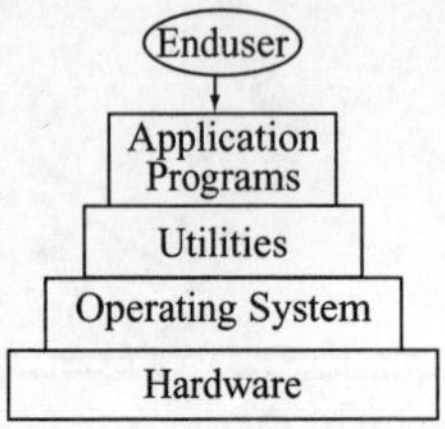

Figure 7.1 View of components of computer system

system (OS) is the software that provides an interface between the computer hardware, and the application programs or users (Figure 7.1).

In this chapter, we discuss about the components of operating system, the different types of operating system and the functions of operating system. A brief description of some operating systems is also given.

7.2 OBJECTIVES OF OPERATING SYSTEM

Operating system is system software that controls and coordinates the use of hardware among the different application software and users. OS intermediates between the user of computer and the computer hardware. The user gives a command and the OS translates the command into a form that the machine can understand and execute. OS has two main objectives—(1) to make the computer system convenient and easy to use, for the user, and—(2) to use the computer hardware in an efficient way, by handling the details of the operations of the hardware.

- OS hides the working of the hardware from the user and makes it *convenient for the user* to use the machine. The application program used by the user requires the use of the hardware during processing. Some examples are—display of application's user interface, loading a program into memory, using I/O devices, allocating CPU to different processes during execution, and store or load data from hard disk. When using the machine, the user gives the command to perform the required actions to the OS and the OS handles all the operational steps. The user is not bothered about how these actions will be performed. This is the job of OS. OS provides an interface to the application programs to interact with the hardware. The user need not get into the details of this interaction.
- At the other end, the different resources of computer hardware have to be managed and controlled. This includes managing the communication between different devices, controlling the sequence and execution of processes, allocating space on hard disk, providing error handling procedures etc. OS supervises and manages the hardware of the computer.

Some of the commonly used operating systems are Microsoft Disk Operating System (MS-DOS), Windows 7, Windows XP, Linux, UNIX, and Mac OS X Snow Leopard.

7.3 TYPES OF OS

OS are classified into different types depending on their capability of processing—(1) Single user, (2) Multiuser, (3) Multitasking, (4) Multiprocessing, (5) Real time, and (6) Embedded.

- **Single User and Single Task OS** is for use by a single user for a standalone single computer for performing a single task (Figure 7.2). Operating system for Personal Computers (PC) are single-user OS. For example, if the user is editing a document, then a document cannot be printed on the printer simultaneously. Single user OS are simple operating system designed to manage one task at a time. MS-DOS is an example of single user OS.

Figure 7.2 A single user performing a single task

- **Single User and Multitasking OS** allows execution of more than one task or process concurrently. For this, the processor time is divided amongst different tasks. This division of time is also called *time sharing*. The processor switches rapidly between processes. For example, the user can listen to music on the computer while writing an article using a word processor software. The user can switch between the applications and also transfer data between them (Figure 7.3). Windows 95 and all later versions of Windows are examples of multitasking OS.

Figure 7.3 A single user performing multitasking (issuing print command and making drawings)

- **Multiuser OS** is used in computer networks that allow same data and applications to be accessed by multiple users at the same time (Figure 7.4). The users can also communicate with each other. Linux, UNIX, and Windows 7 are examples of multiuser OS.
- **Multiprocessing OS** have two or more processors for a single running process. Processing takes place in parallel and is also called *parallel processing*. Each processor works on different parts of the same task, or, on two or more different tasks. Since execution takes place in parallel, they are used for high speed execution, and to increase the power of computer. Linux, UNIX and Windows 7 are examples of multiprocessing OS.

Figure 7.4 Multiple users working on connected computers

- **Real Time OS** are designed to respond to an event within a predetermined time. These operating systems are used to control processes. Processing is done within a time constraint. OS monitors the events that affect the execution of process and respond accordingly. They are used to respond to queries in areas like medical imaging system, industrial control systems etc. LynxOS is an example of real time OS.
- **Embedded OS** is embedded in a device in the *ROM*. They are specific to a device and are less resource intensive. They are used in appliances like microwaves, washing machines, traffic control systems etc.

7.4 FUNCTIONS OF OS

Operating system is a large and complex software consisting of several components. Each component of the operating system has its own set of defined inputs and outputs. Different components of OS perform specific tasks to provide the overall functionality of the operating system (Figure 7.5). Main functions of the operating system are as follows:

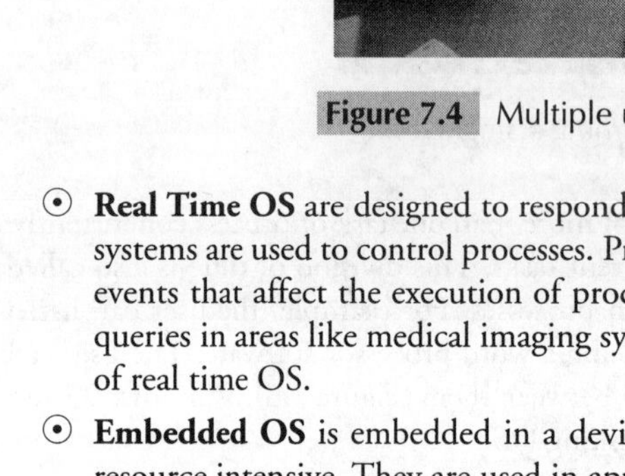

Figure 7.5 Functions of OS

- **Process Management**—The process management activities handled by the OS are—(1) control access to shared resources like file, memory, I/O and CPU, (2) control execution of applications, (3) create, execute and delete a process (system process or user process), (4) cancel or resume a process (5) schedule a process, and (6) synchronization, communication and deadlock handling for processes.
- **Memory Management**—The activities of memory management handled by OS are—(1) allocate memory, (2) free memory, (3) re-allocate memory to a program when a used block is freed, and (4) keep track of memory usage.

- **File Management**—The file management tasks include—(1) create and delete both files and directories, (2) provide access to files, (3) allocate space for files, (4) keep back-up of files, and (5) secure files.
- **Device Management**—The device management tasks handled by OS are—(1) open, close and write device drivers, and (2) communicate, control and monitor the device driver.
- **Protection and Security**—OS protects the resources of system. User authentication, file attributes like read, write, encryption, and back-up of data are used by OS to provide basic protection.
- **User Interface or Command Interpreter**—Operating system provides an interface between the computer user and the computer hardware. The user interface is a set of commands or a graphical user interface via which the user interacts with the applications and the hardware.

7.5 PROCESS MANAGEMENT

- A *process* is a program in a state of execution. It is a unit of work for the operating system. A process can be created, executed, and stopped. In contrast, a program is always static and does not have any state. A program may have two or more processes running. A process and a program are, thus, two different entities.
- To accomplish a task, a process needs to have access to different system resources like I/O devices, CPU, memory etc. The process management function of an operating system handles allocation of resources to the processes in an efficient manner. The allocation of resources required by a process is made during process creation and process execution.
- A process changes its state as it is executed. The various states that a process changes during execution are as follows (Figure 7.6):

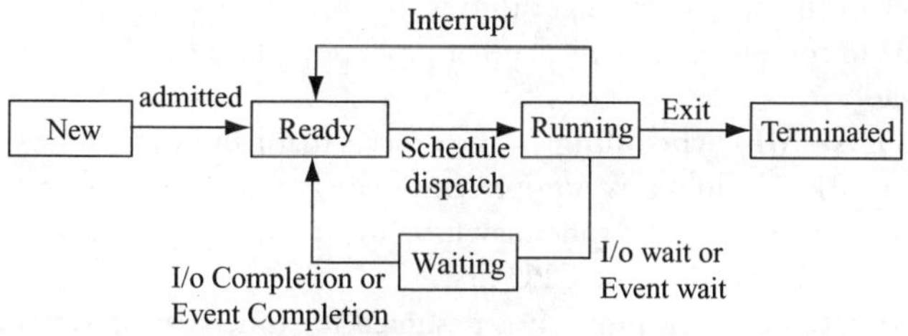

Figure 7.6 Process states

  - New—process is in a new state when it is created,
  - Ready—process is in ready state when it is waiting for a processor,
  - Running—process is in running state if processor is executing the process,
  - Waiting—process is in waiting state when it waits for some event to happen (I/O etc), and
  - Terminated—process that has finished execution is in terminated state.
- A system consists of collection of processes—(1) system process that execute system code, and (2) user process that execute user code. OS mainly handles the execution of user code, though it may also handle various system processes.

The concurrent execution of the process requires process synchronization and CPU scheduling. The CPU scheduling, process synchronization, communication, and deadlock situations are described in the following subsections.

7.5.1 CPU Scheduling

- CPU or processor is one of the primary computer resources. All computer resources like I/O, memory, and CPU are scheduled for use.
- CPU scheduling is important for the operating system. In a multiprogramming and time sharing system, the processor executes multiple processes by switching the CPU among the processes, so that no user has to wait for long for a program to execute. To enable running of several concurrent processes, the processor time has to be distributed amongst all the processes efficiently.
- *Scheduler* is a component of the operating system that is responsible for scheduling transition of processes. At any one time, only one process can be in running state and the rest are in ready or waiting state. The scheduler assigns the processor to different processes in a manner so that no one process is kept waiting for long.
- Scheduling can be non-pre-emptive scheduling or pre-emptive scheduling. In *non-pre-emptive scheduling*, the processor executes a process till termination without any interruption. Hence the system resources are not used efficiently. In *pre-emptive scheduling*, a running process may be interrupted by another process that needs to execute. Pre-emption allows the operating system to interrupt the executing task and handle any important task that requires immediate action. In pre-emptive scheduling, the system resources are used efficiently.
- There are many different *CPU scheduling algorithms* that are used to schedule the processes. Some of the common CPU scheduling algorithms are as follows—
  - **First Come First Served (FCFS) Scheduling**: As the name says, the process that requests for the CPU first, gets the CPU first. A queue is maintained for the processes requesting the CPU. The process first in the queue is allocated the CPU first. FCFS scheduling is non-pre-emptive. The drawback of this scheduling algorithm is that the process that is assigned to the CPU may take long time to complete, keeping all other processes waiting in the queue, even if they require less CPU time.
  - **Shortest Job First (SJF) Scheduling**: The process that requires the least CPU time is allocated the CPU first. SJF scheduling is non-pre-emptive. The drawback of this scheduling is that a process that requires more CPU time may have to wait for long time, since processes requiring less CPU time will be assigned the CPU first.
  - **Round Robin (RR) Scheduling**: It is designed for time-sharing systems. RR scheduling is pre-emptive. In this scheduling, a small quantum of time (10–100 ms) is defined, and each process in the queue is assigned the CPU for this quantum of time circularly. New processes are added at the tail of the queue and the process that has finished execution is removed from the queue. RR scheduling overcomes the disadvantage of FCFS and SJF scheduling. A process does not have to wait for long, if it is not the first one in the queue, or, if it requires CPU for a long period of time.

Figure 7.7 shows the ready queue—P#1 with CPU time requirement of 5 units, P#2 with 7 units and P#3 with 4 units, are scheduled, using the different CPU scheduling algorithms.

7.5.2 Process Synchronization

- In a computer, multiple processes are executing at the same time. The processes that share the resources have to communicate with one another to prevent a situation where one process disrupts another process.

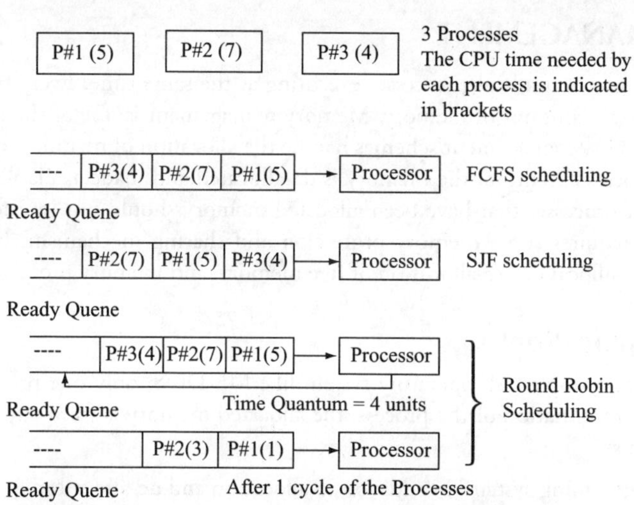

Figure 7.7 Illustrating CPU scheduling algorithms with an example

- When two or more processes execute at the same time, independent of each other, they are called *concurrent processes.*
- A situation where multiple processes access and manipulate the same data concurrently, in which the final result depends on the order of process execution, is called a *race condition*. To handle such situations, synchronization and coordination of the processes is required.

7.5.3 Deadlock

- In a multiprogramming environment, multiple processes may try to access a resource. A deadlock is a situation when a process waits endlessly for a resource and the requested resource is being used by another process that is waiting for some other resource (Figure 7.8).
- A *deadlock* arises when the four necessary conditions hold true simultaneously in a system. These conditions are as follows:
  - **Mutual Exclusion**—Only one process at a time can use the resource. Any other process requesting the resource has to wait until the resource is released.
  - **No Pre-emption**—A process releases the resource by itself. A process cannot remove the resource from another process.
  - **Hold and Wait**—A process holds a resource while requesting another resource, which may be currently held by another process.
  - **Circular Wait**—In this situation, a process P1 waits for a resource held by another process P2, and the process P2 waits for a resource held by process P1.

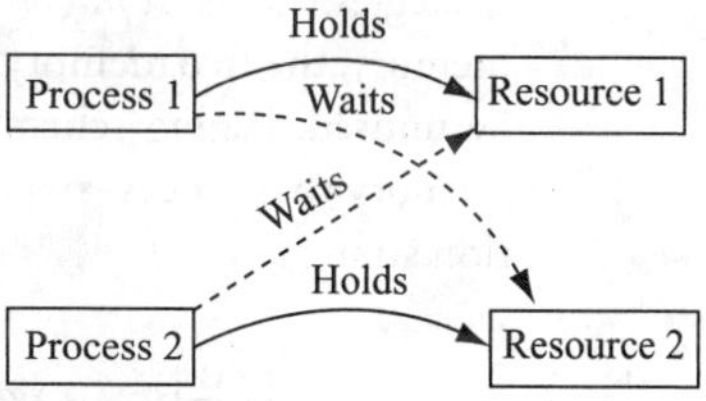

Figure 7.8 Deadlock

- Deadlock handling can be done by deadlock avoidance and deadlock prevention.
  - **Deadlock Prevention** is a set of method that ensures that at least one of the above four necessary conditions required for deadlock, does not hold true.
  - **Deadlock Avoidance** requires that the operating system be given information in advance regarding the resources a process will request and use. This information is used by the operating system to schedule the allocation of resources so that no process waits for a resource.

7.6 MEMORY MANAGEMENT

In a computer, there may be multiple processes executing at the same time. Every process that needs to execute, requires a certain amount of memory. Memory management is one of the tasks handled by the operating system. Memory management schemes handle the allocation of memory to different processes. On completion of process execution, the memory is de-allocated and made available to another process. Additionally, different processes that have been allocated memory should not interfere into each other's memory space. This requires some memory protection and sharing mechanism. Now we will discuss memory allocation, de-allocation, re-allocation of free memory, and memory protection and sharing.

7.6.1 Memory Allocation

- In single-user and single-task operating system like MS-DOS, only one process can execute at a time. After the termination of the process, the allocated memory is freed and is made available to any other process.
- In a multiprogramming system, in addition to allocation and de-allocation of memory, more tasks are involved like keeping track of processes allocated to the memory, memory protection and sharing etc.
- There are different memory allocation schemes to allocate memory to the processes that reside in memory at the same time. The different memory allocation schemes are as follows:
  - **Multiple Partition Allocation**—The operating system keeps track of blocks of memory which are free and those which are unavailable. The single block of available memory is called a *hole*. When a process requires memory, a *hole* large enough for the process is allocated. As different processes release the memory, the released block of memory is placed in the set of holes. During allocation of memory, the set of holes is searched to determine which hole is to be allocated. For this, three *hole allocation strategies* are used—(1) first-fit (allocate the first hole that is big enough for the process, (2) best-fit (allocate the smallest hole that is big enough for the process, and (3) worst-fit (allocate the largest available hole). Memory allocated using any of these strategies results in *fragmentation*. When the processes are allocated memory and removed from memory, the free memory is broken into small pieces. These small pieces of fragmented memory lie unused. Paging scheme is used to overcome fragmentation. Figure 7.9 shows allocation of memory to a process requiring 8 KB of memory, using the first fit, best fit, and worst fit allocation strategies.

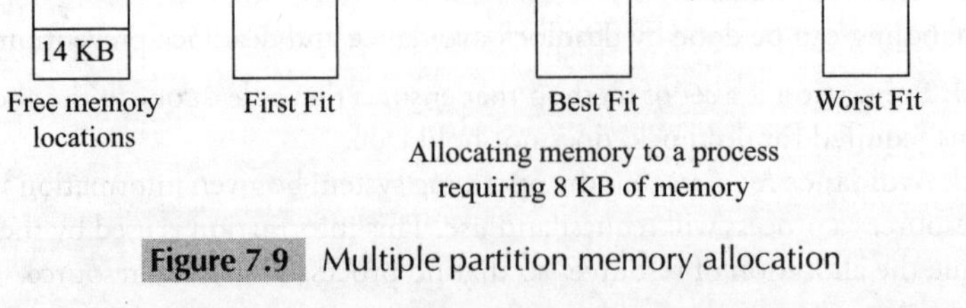

Figure 7.9 Multiple partition memory allocation

- **Paging**—In paging, the physical memory is broken into fixed size blocks called *frames*. This is the primary memory allocated to the process. The logical memory is broken into blocks of the same size called *pages*. Generally pages are of sizes varying from 1 KB to 8 KB. When a process is executed, its pages are loaded into the frames.
  An address generated by CPU has two parts—page number and page offset. A *page table* is maintained by the operating system that maps the page number to the frame number. The page number is used to index the page table and get the frame number. The page offset is added to the page frame number to get the physical memory address (Figure 7.10).

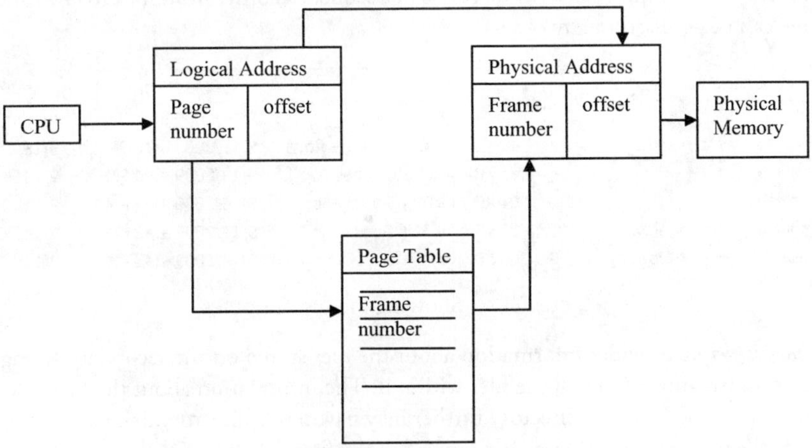

Figure 7.10 Paging

Paging handles the problem of fragmentation. The frames need not be contiguous and can reside anywhere in the memory. A process can be allocated memory from holes created by fragmentation, which may be anywhere in the memory.

7.6.2 Virtual Memory

- In the memory management schemes discussed in the previous section, the whole process is kept in memory before the execution starts. However, for some applications, large memory is required to run the applications, and the whole program cannot be loaded into the memory.
- *Virtual memory* allows the execution of those processes that are not completely in memory.
- Virtual memory is commonly implemented by *demand paging*. Demand paging is similar to paging with swapping. *Swapping* is transferring of block of data from the on-line secondary storage like hard disk to the memory and vice versa.
- In demand paging, the processes reside in the on-line secondary memory. When a process executes and a page is required, that page is swapped-in into the memory (Figure 7.11). This allows execution of large-sized programs without loading them completely into the memory.

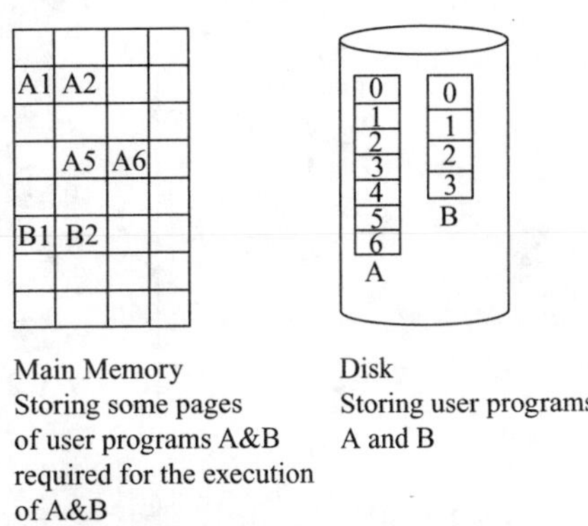

Main Memory
Storing some pages
of user programs A&B
required for the execution
of A&B

Disk
Storing user programs
A and B

Figure 7.11 Virtual memory

7.7 FILE MANAGEMENT

- The file management function of the operating system involves handling the file system which consists of two parts—a set of files, and a directory structure.
- *File* is a collection of related information, has a name, and is stored on a secondary storage. It is the smallest named unit that can be written to a secondary storage device. Data cannot be stored on the secondary storage if it is not in the form of a file. A file has attributes like its name, location, size, type, time, and date of creation etc. (Figure 7.12). The information stored in a file can be accessed in different ways—*sequential access* (access is in a sequential order from start to end) and *direct access* (the file can be accessed in any order).

Name	Size	Type	Date Modified	Date Created
Administration		File Folder	9/17/2009 5:30 AM	9/16/2009 4:49 PM
Animation Requirement	43 KB	Microsoft Office Po...	9/19/2009 5:15 PM	9/19/2009 5:15 PM
arithmetic	41 KB	Adobe Acrobat Doc...	9/14/2009 4:44 PM	9/14/2009 4:44 PM
Binary Arithmetic	21 KB	MHTML Document	9/14/2009 4:43 PM	9/14/2009 4:43 PM
Binary Arithmetic -- Technical ...	28 KB	MHTML Document	9/14/2009 4:42 PM	9/14/2009 4:42 PM
Binary numeral system - Wikip...	365 KB	MHTML Document	9/14/2009 4:43 PM	9/14/2009 4:42 PM

Figure 7.12 Showing the file attributes

- *Directory structure* provides information about the files stored on the secondary storage. Directory contains information about all the files within it. The information about the files is kept as entries in the directory of device. A directory further may have a sub-directory defined within it. Directory contains the name, location, size, and type of all the files defined on the device. The *tree-structured directory* (Figure 7.13) is the commonly used directory structure.

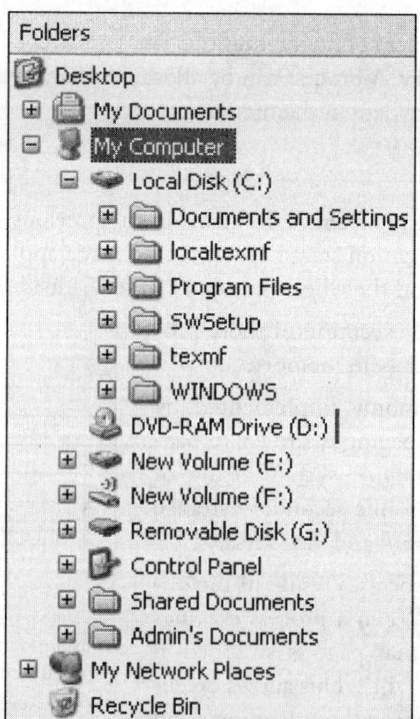

Figure 7.13 Tree-structured directory in Windows XP

- The operating system manages the storage media like disk and implements the abstract concept of the file. *System calls* are the interface between the process and operating system. Operating system provides system calls for creating, reading, writing, deleting, repositioning, and truncating a file. Some of the operations that can be performed on a directory are—search for a file, create, delete and rename a file, list a directory, and traverse the file system within the directory. The user simply uses the system calls like "dir", "list" to perform operation on a file or directory, without going into the details of its working.

7.8 DEVICE MANAGEMENT

- Several peripheral devices like mouse, hard disk, printer, plotter etc. are connected to the computer. The peripheral devices have varying characteristics like character or block device, sequential or random access device, and dedicated or shared device.
- OS manages and controls the devices attached to the computer. OS provides appropriate functionality to the application programs for controlling different aspects of the devices. Figure 7.14 shows the device manager and system properties in Windows XP Professional.
- OS handles the devices by combining both hardware and software techniques. The I/O hardware includes the ports, buses, and device controllers for the devices. The OS communicates with the I/O hardware via the *device driver* software. The device driver software comes along with each device.
- A device communicates with the computer hardware via a *port* (for example, a serial port or a parallel port). *Bus* is a common set of wires used by one or more devices. The computer uses different kinds of buses like PCI bus for connecting processor or memory to the fast devices, expansion bus to connect to slow I/O devices and SCSI bus to connect disks. A device controller operates a port, bus, and a device. Device controller is just like a bridge between the device and the operating system. The device controller receives the data from a connected device, stores it temporarily, and then communicates the data to the device's device driver. Device driver is the software with which the device controller communicates with the operating system (Figure 7.15).

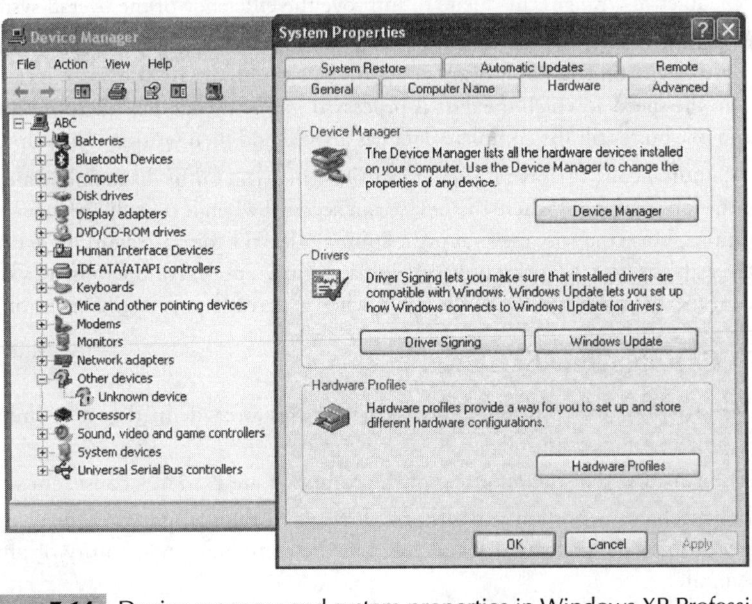

Figure 7.14 Device manager and system properties in Windows XP Professional

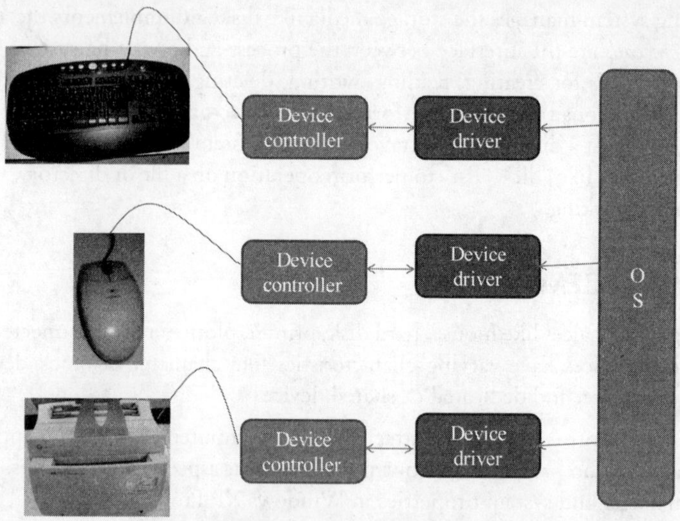

Figure 7.15 Devices interacting with OS

- Operating system enables handling of the different I/O devices in a uniform way. The complexity of handling the different devices is abstracted and hidden in the device drivers of the devices. The device drivers hide the differences among the different device controllers and present a uniform interface to the operating system.
- In addition to managing the peripheral devices, OS also provides various services related to I/O like I/O scheduling, buffering, spooling, and error handling.
- *Scheduling of I/O requests* involves ordering the requests to improve performance of the system and provide fair access to all processes. For this, a queue of request is maintained for each device. The I/O scheduler re-arranges the queue to improve the efficiency of the overall system.
- *Buffer* is a memory area that stores the data, while it is being transferred between two devices or between a device and an application. The speed at which the I/O device can transfer data is different from the speed at which the data is processed. *Buffering* handles the speed mismatch by storing the data in a buffer till the complete data has arrived and then writing it in a single write operation.
- *Spool* (Simultaneous Peripheral Operation On-Line) is a buffer in memory area or disk. *Spooling* stores the jobs in a spool where the device can access it when it is ready. Spooling is commonly used for printers. Users may give several print commands, and continue working with other operations. However, the printer can print only one job at a time. The rest of the jobs are stored in the spool in a queue, and the printer accesses the spool when it is ready to print the next job.

7.9 PROTECTION AND SECURITY

- The access of programs, processes, and users, to the resources defined by the computer are controlled by the protection mechanism.
- Protection ensures that the resources of the computer are used in a consistent way.
- Security mechanism prevents unauthorized access to the computer. Security concerns include—security of software, security of data stored in the computer, and security of physical resources of the computer.

- In a personal computer, security can be ensured using—(1) user accounts—individual accounts for each user, (2) user authentication—using password protection (Figure 7.16), (3) access rights—define rights for access of different kind of information for different people, (4) data encryption—store data in computer in encrypted form, and (5) data backup—storing data on a peripheral device other than the hard disk. In a networked environment, only trusted computers should be able to share data. Some of the common security threats occur due to hacking, viruses etc.

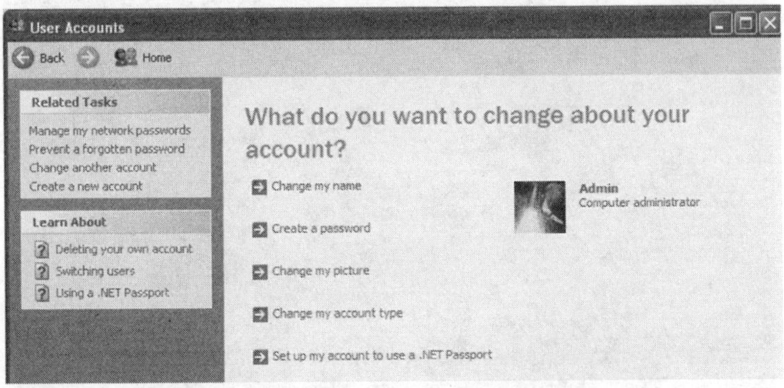

Figure 7.16 Create password and manage user account in Windows XP Professional

7.10 USER INTERFACE

- The primary goal of operating system is to make the computer convenient for use by its user. It should allow users to easily access and communicate with the applications and the hardware.
- The users can interact with the computer by using mainly two kinds of interfaces—(1) Command Line Interface (CLI), and (2) Graphical User Interface (GUI).
- CLI requires the user to interact with operating system in the form of text keyed in from the keyboard. In this, the user has to learn and remember the different commands required for copying, deleting, opening a file or folder etc. (Figure 7.17). MS-DOS and Linux shell are examples of command line mode of interfaces.

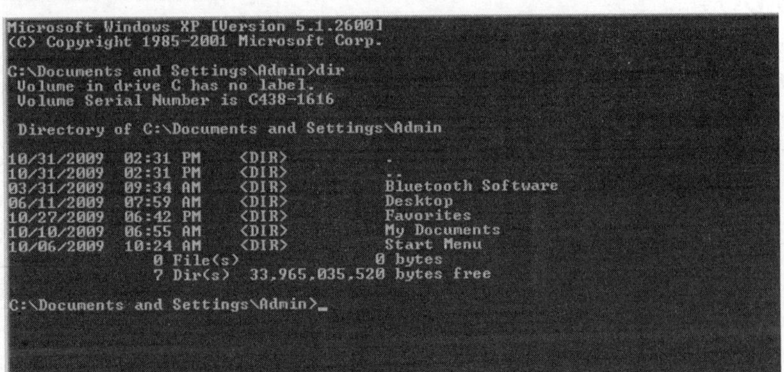

Figure 7.17 Command line interface

- GUI use graphics to display the various commands. The interface consists of icons, menus, windows, and pointers. The user need not learn the commands, instead, the user can give instructions by moving the pointer on the screen using a mouse and pressing the mouse button (Figure 7.18). "Windows 7" and "Mac OS 10" are examples of graphical mode of interface. GUI interface for the Linux OS also exist like the GNU Object Model Environment (GNOME).

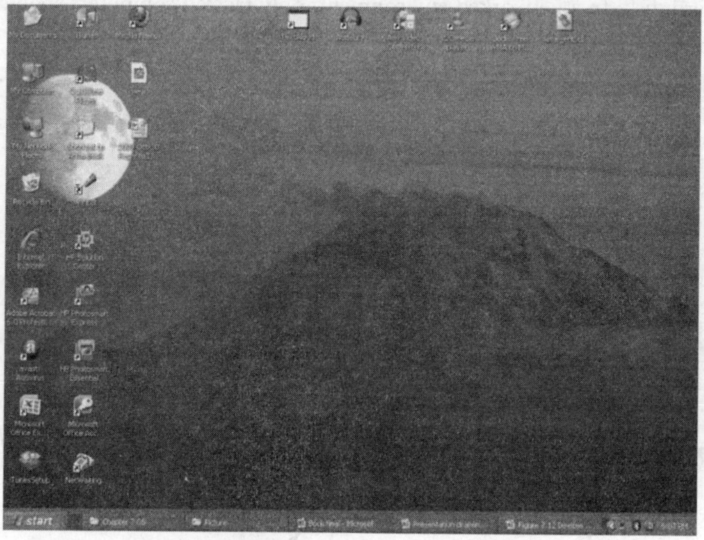

Figure 7.18 Graphical user interface

7.11 EXAMPLES OF OPERATING SYSTEMS

MS-DOS, Windows family of operating systems, Unix OS, Linux OS, and Mac OS X are some examples of commonly used OSs. Each operating system has specific characteristics. Here, we will discuss the features of MS-DOS, Windows family of operating systems and Linux operating system.

7.11.1 MS-DOS

- MS-DOS was the first widely-installed operating system for PCs in 1980s.
- MS-DOS is easy to load and install. It neither requires much memory for the operating system, nor a very powerful computer to run on.
- MS-DOS is a command line user interface operating system. This means that the user has to type single line commands through the command interface. So, user has to remember the different commands and their syntax.
- It is a single-user and single-tasking operating system for the PC. Only one user can use it and only one task can be executed, at a given point of time. Also, it does not have a built-in support for networking.
- MS-DOS is a 16-bit OS, meaning thereby that it can send or receive 16 bits of data at a time and can process 16 bits of data. It is not able to take the advantage of 32-bit processors.
- To use MS-DOS, user must know where the programs and data are stored and how to interact with it. In the MS-DOS command mode, *command.com* routine interprets the typed in command from the keyboard.

To get the window of the command prompt  in the Windows environment

- <Start> <Run> Type "*cmd*" <Enter>, or
- <Start> <All programs> <Accessories> <Command Prompt>

cmd.exe or command prompt is the command line interpreter on the current Windows-based OS. It is similar to command.com in MS-DOS. cmd.exe is a Windows program that acts as a DOS-like command line interpreter.

7.11.2 Windows Family of OS

- Windows is a personal computer operating system from Microsoft.
- The Windows family of OS which is currently in use includes the Windows 9x family (Windows 95, Windows 98 and Windows 2000), Windows XP, Windows Vista, and Windows 7 operating systems.
- Windows family of OS is GUI-based operating system. Since GUI interfaces are easy to use and are user-friendly, these have become very popular.
- Windows support multi-tasking. It means Windows OS allows simultaneous execution of multiple tasks (Figure 7.19).
- Windows contains built-in networking, which allows users to share files and applications with each other, if their PCs are connected to a network.
- Windows 7 comes in six different editions, Starter, Home Basic, Home Premium, Professional, Enterprise and Ultimate.
- With each new version of the Windows OS, the user interface undergoes some changes and the user has to learn to use the new interface. This becomes troublesome for the user.

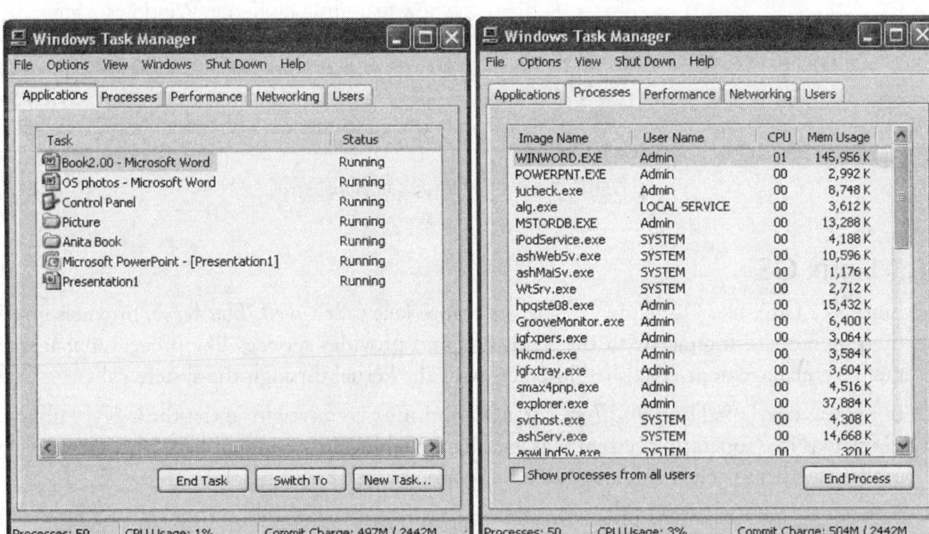

Figure 7.19 Windows task manager

7.11.2.1 Brief History of Windows OS

The Windows OS has evolved from the Windows 1.0 in the 1985 to the Windows 7 in 2009. In this span of 24 years, several versions of the Windows OS have been released. Table 7.1 gives an overview of the history of the Windows OS, along with their significance.

Year	Windows OS Released	Comments
1985	Windows 1.0	It was not successful
1990	Windows 3.0	The first commercially successful version of Windows. It is an upgrade to the interface over Windows 1 and 2
1993	Windows NT 3.1	The first Microsoft OS not based in DOS. Separate versions of NT with their DOS counterparts are released
1995	Windows 95	The first native 32 bit OS. Microsoft plans to merge the NT and DOS platforms but are unsuccessful due to backward compatibility issues and lack of hardware support of NT.
1998	Windows 98	Microsoft integrates its web browser in the GUI and file manager. Hackers can use the Internet to infiltrate a computer or network.
2000	Windows 2000	As with Windows 95, Microsoft planned Windows 2000 to merge the NT and DOS based OS's but was unsuccessful
2001	Windows XP	Windows XP successfully merges the compatibility found in Windows 98 with the stability found in Windows NT/2000. It provides enhanced stability over Windows 98.
2005	Windows XP Professional x64 Edition	OS was slow to take off due to the dearth of 64-bit software and drivers
2008	Windows Vista	First 3D operating system
2009	Windows 7	Some of the new features included in Windows 7 are advancements in touch, speech, and handwriting recognition, support for virtual hard disks, support for additional file formats, improved performance on multi-core processors, improved boot performance, and kernel improvements.

Table 7.1 *Windows OS overview*

7.11.3 Linux OS

- Linux is a Unix-like OS. Unix OS has a user interface called *shell*. The *kernel* provides interface for the programs to interact with the hardware, and provides services like process management and memory management. The shell interacts with the kernel through the system calls.
- Linux was developed by *Linus Torvalds* in 1992. Linux is copyright under the GNU Public License. Linux is a "free" operating system that is easily available. Since Linux follows the open development model, it is being constantly upgraded by programmers across the globe.
- Some organizations offer Linux with add-on features and capabilities. Red Hat, Mandrake, Debian and Novell are the popular vendors of Linux OS.
- Tux, the Linux penguin is the official mascot of Linux.

- Linux is a command line user interface OS. Linux has GUI interfaces called desktop environments like GNOME and K Desktop Environment (KDE). The GUI interface is convenient for the user to use.
- Linux is a 32-bit, multi-tasking OS. It supports multiple users and multiple processors.
- Linux is a reliable and secure OS, and is available almost for free. So, Linux is fast becoming very popular and powerful OS.
- Linux OS is easily available, such as Redhat Linux ver. 9, and, Debian's—Ubuntu, Kubuntu, and Edubuntu.

SUMMARY

- *Operating system* intermediates between the computer hardware and the computer user.
- The *objective of OS* is to make the computer system convenient for the user to use, and to use the computer hardware efficiently.
- *Types of OS*—Single user and single task OS is for use by a single user for a single task. Multitasking OS allow execution of more than one task concurrently. Multiuser OS allows concurrent access of same data and applications by multiple users. Multiprocessing OS have two or more processors for a single running process, which execute in parallel. Real time OS respond to an event within a predetermined time. Embedded OS is embedded in appliances like microwaves and washing machines.
- *Functions of OS* are process management, memory management, file management, device management, protection and security, and user interface.
- *Process management* includes handling the scheduling of processes, process synchronization and communication, and deadlock situations.
- A *process* is a program in a state of execution. During execution, a process can be in a new, ready, running, waiting or terminated state.
- *CPU scheduler* assigns the processor to different processes so that no process is kept waiting for long. Scheduling can be non-pre-emptive scheduling and pre-emptive scheduling.
- FCFS, SJF and RR are *CPU scheduling algorithms.* In FCFS, process that requests for CPU first gets the CPU first. In SJF, process that requires least CPU time, is allocated the CPU first. In RR scheduling, each process in the queue gets CPU for a quantum of time circularly.
- *Process synchronization* is required when multiple processes access and manipulate the same data, concurrently.
- A *deadlock* arises when the four necessary conditions—mutual exclusion, no preemption, hold and wait, and circular wait, hold true simultaneously in a system.
- *Memory management* includes memory allocation, de-allocation, re-allocation of free block, and memory protection and sharing.
- *Virtual memory* is implemented by demand paging, which is paging with swapping.
- The *file manager* handles the file system consisting of a set of files and a directory structure. OS provides system calls for performing operations on the file.
- OS handles the *devices* using a combination of hardware and software techniques. The I/O hardware includes the ports, buses and device controllers for the devices. OS interacts with I/O hardware via the device driver software of the device.
- *Spooling* stores the jobs in a spool (a buffer in memory area or disk) where the device can access it when it is ready.
- *Protection* ensures that the resources of computer are used in a consistent way. *Security* mechanism prevents unauthorized access to a system.
- CLI and GUI are the two kinds of *user interfaces.*
- MS-DOS, Windows XP, UNIX, Linux, and Mac OS X are some *examples* of OSs.

KEYWORDS

Device driver *141*
Device Management *135*
Directory structure *140*
Embedded OS *134*
File *140*
File Management *135*
First Come First Served (FCFS) *136*
Fragmentation *138*
Frames *139*
Graphical User Interface (GUI) *143*
Hole *138*
I/O scheduling *142*
Linux *146*
Mac OS X *132*
Memory allocation *138*
Memory Management *134*
MicroSoft Disk Operating System (MS-DOS) *132*
Multiple Partition Allocation *138*
Multiprocessing *133*
Multitasking *133*
Multiuser *133*
Non-pre-emptive scheduling *136*
Operating System (OS) *132*
Pages *139*
Page table *139*
Paging *139*
Parallel processing *133*
Pre-emptive scheduling *136*
Process *135*
Process Management *134*
Process states *135*
Process Synchronization *136*
Protection and Security *135*
Race condition *137*
Real time OS *134*
Round Robin (RR) *136*
Scheduler *136*
Scheduling algorithms *136*
Shortest Job First (SJF) *136*
Single Task OS *132*
Single user *132*
Spooling *142*
Swapping *139*
System calls *141*
Time sharing *133*
Tree-structured directory *140*
UNIX *132*
User Interface *135*
Virtual memory *139*
Window XP *132*

QUESTIONS

Section 7.1–7.3

1. Explain the objective of OS.
2. "OS makes it convenient for the user to use the machine". Explain.
3. "OS supervises and manages the hardware of the computer". Explain.
4. Name any three operating systems.
5. Classify the OS into different types based on their processing capability.
6. What is Single user and Single Task OS?
7. What is Single user and Multitasking OS?
8. What is time sharing?
9. What is a Multiuser OS?
10. What is a Multiprocessing OS.
11. Define parallel processing.
12. What is the purpose of Real time OS?
13. What is the purpose of Embedded OS?
14. Give an example each of the following types of OS (i) Single user and Single Task, (ii) Single user and Multitasking, (iii) Multiuser, (iv) Multiprocessing, and (v) Real time.

Section 7.4

15. List the main function of the OS.
16. Describe in detail the main functions of the OS.
17. List the activities handled by each of the following functions of the OS (i) Process Management, (ii) Memory Management, (iii) File Management, (iv) Device Management, (v) Protection and Security, and (vi) User Interface.

Section 7.5–7.5.4

18. Define a process.
19. List the various states for a process in execution.
20. Why is CPU scheduling needed?
21. Define scheduler.
22. Define pre-emptive scheduling and non-pre-emptive scheduling.
23. List the CPU scheduling algorithms.
24. Explain the working of (i) FCFS, (ii) SJF, and (iii) RR scheduling algorithms.
25. What is the drawback of FCFS algorithm?
26. What is the drawback of SJF algorithm?
27. How does RR algorithm overcome the drawback of FCFS and SJF?
28. Define concurrent processes.
29. When does a race condition occur?
30. Define a deadlock.
31. List the necessary conditions for a deadlock.
32. Deadlock can be handled by deadlock ______ and deadlock ______.

33. What is deadlock avoidance?
34. What is deadlock prevention?
35. Explain the following in context of the deadlock: (i) Mutual Exclusion, (ii) No preemption, (iii) Hold and Wait, and (iv) Circular wait.

Section 7.6 – 7.6.2

36. What is the need of memory management?
37. Describe the multiple partition allocation memory management scheme.
38. Define a hole.
39. _____, ______ and ______ are the three hole allocation strategies.
40. Explain the three hole allocation strategies.
41. Define memory fragmentation.
42. How is memory fragmentation handled?
43. Describe the paging memory management scheme.
44. What is the use of a page table?
45. "Paging handles the problem of fragmentation". Explain.
46. Describe demand paging in brief.
47. Define swapping.

Section 7.7–7.8

48. Describe a file.
49. What is the purpose of directory structure?
50. Define a system call.
51. ________is a commonly used structure for the directory.
52. What is the need of device management?
53. What is the purpose of a device driver?
54. Define buffering.
55. Why is buffering needed?
56. Define spooling.
57. Name a spooled device.
58. What is the purpose of spooling?

Section 7.9

59. How is protection different from security?
60. Name few techniques used for ensuring security of a stand-alone computer.
61. List the two kinds of user interfaces.
62. Give one example each of OS using CLI and GUI interfaces.
63. What do you mean by a CLI interface?
64. What do you mean by a GUI interface?
65. Write short note on MS-DOS, Windows family of OS, and Linux OS.
66. Describe briefly, the history of the Windows OS.

Extra Questions

67. Give full form of the following abbreviations:
    (i) MS-DOS (ii) FCFS
    (iii) SJF (iv) RR
    (v) CLI (vi) GUI
    (vii) GNOME (viii) KDE
    (ix) SPOOL
68. Write short notes on:
    (a) Objectives of OS
    (b) Types of OS
    (c) Functions of OS
    (d) Process Management
    (e) Process
    (f) CPU Scheduling
    (g) Scheduling algorithms
    (h) Process Synchronization
    (i) Deadlock
    (j) Memory Management
    (k) Memory allocation
    (l) Memory Fragmentation
    (m) Paging
    (n) Demand paging
    (o) File Management
    (p) Device Management
    (q) Device drivers
    (r) Protection and Security
    (s) User Interface
    (t) MS-DOS
    (u) Windows family of OS
    (v) Linux OS
69. Give differences between the following:
    (a) Multitasking and Multiprocessing
    (b) Program and Process
    (c) Pre-emptive scheduling and Non-pre-emptive scheduling
    (d) FCFS and SJF
    (e) RR and FCFS
    (f) Best-fit and worst-fit memory allocation
    (g) CLI and GUI

COMPUTER PROGRAMMING FUNDAMENTALS

8

Contents

- Program development life cycle—Problem analysis, program design, program development, program documentation and maintenance
- Algorithm
- Control structures—Sequential, selection (branch or conditional), iterative (loop)
- Flowchart—Flowchart symbols, preparing a flowchart
- Pseudo code—Preparing a pseudo code
- Difference between algorithm, flowchart and pseudo code
- Programming paradigms
  - Structured programming—Procedural programming, modular programming
  - Object-oriented programming—Class, object, abstraction, encapsulation, inheritance, polymorphism (static binding, dynamic binding)
  - Aspect-oriented programming—Crosscutting concerns, aspect
- Characteristics of a good program

Why this chapter

A program is a set of instructions written for performing a specific task. However, writing a good program is not a straightforward task. For writing a program, we have to follow the program development life cycle which includes choosing a programming paradigm, and selecting a computer programming language in which to write the program. With practice, you can easily acquire the skill of program writing. The purpose of this chapter is to introduce you to the fundamentals of Computer Programming.

8.1 INTRODUCTION

Computer is an electronic device that accepts data, processes it, and generates the relevant output. It can perform both simple and complex tasks with very high speed and accuracy. However, a computer cannot perform any task—simple or complex, of its own. Computers need to be instructed about "how" the task is to be performed. The set of instructions that instruct the computer about the way the task is to be performed is called a *program*. A program is required for processing all kind of tasks—simple tasks like addition of two numbers, and complex tasks like gaming etc.

In this chapter, we will discuss the steps that are followed while writing a computer program. A brief description of different programming constructs is also presented. We will also discuss the characteristics of a good program.

8.2 PROGRAM DEVELOPMENT LIFE CYCLE

As stated earlier, a program is needed to instruct the computer about the way a task is to be performed. The instructions in a program have three essential parts:

(1) Instructions to accept the input data that needs to be processed,

(2) Instructions that will act upon the input data and process it, and

(3) Instructions to provide the output to user

The instructions in a program are defined in a specific sequence. Writing a computer program is not a straightforward task. A person who writes the program (computer programmer) has to follow the Program Development Life Cycle.

Let's now discuss the steps that are followed by the programmer for writing a program:

- **Problem Analysis**—The programmer first understands the problem to be solved. The programmer determines the various ways in which the problem can be solved, and decides upon a single solution which will be followed to solve the problem.
- **Program Design**—The selected solution is represented in a form, so that it can be coded. This requires three steps—
    - An *algorithm* is written, which is an English-like explanation of the solution.
    - A *flowchart* is drawn, which is a diagrammatic representation of the solution. The solution is represented diagrammatically, for easy understanding and clarity.
    - A *pseudo code* is written for the selected solution. Pseudo code uses the structured programming constructs. The pseudo code becomes an input to the next phase.
- **Program Development**
    - The computer programming languages are of different kinds—low-level languages, and high-level languages like C, C++ and Java. The pseudo code is coded using a *suitable* programming language.
    - The coded pseudo code or program is compiled for any syntax errors. *Syntax errors* arise due to the incorrect use of programming language or due to the grammatical errors with respect to the programming language used. During compilation, the syntax errors, if any, are removed.
    - The successfully compiled program is now ready for execution.
    - The executed program generates the output result, which may be correct or incorrect. The program is tested with various inputs, to see that it generates the desired results. If incorrect results are displayed, then the program has *semantic error* (logical error). The semantic errors are removed from the program to get the correct results.
    - The successfully tested program is ready for use and is installed on the user's machine.
- **Program Documentation and Maintenance**—The program is properly documented, so that later on, anyone can use it and understand its working. Any changes made to the program, after installation, forms part of the maintenance of program. The program may require updating, fixing of errors etc. during the maintenance phase.

Table 8.1 summarises the steps of the program development cycle.

Program Analysis	• Understand the problem • Have multiple solutions • Select a solution
Program Design	• Write Algorithm • Write Flowchart • Write Pseudo code
Program Development	• Choose a programming language • Write the program by converting the pseudo code, and then using the programming language. • Compile the program and remove syntax errors, if any • Execute the program. • Test the program. Check the output results with different inputs. If the output is incorrect, modify the program to get correct results. • Install the tested program on the user's computer.
Program Documentation and maintenance	• Document the program, for later use. • Maintain the program for updating, removing errors, changing requirements etc.

Table 8.1 *Program development life cycle*

8.3 ALGORITHM

Algorithm is an ordered sequence of finite, well defined, unambiguous instructions for completing a task. Algorithm is an English-like representation of the logic which is used to solve the problem. It is a step-by-step procedure for solving a task or a problem. The steps must be ordered, unambiguous and finite in number.

For accomplishing a particular task, different algorithms can be written. The different algorithms differ in their requirements of time and space. The programmer selects the best-suited algorithm for the given task to be solved.

Let's now look at two simple algorithms to find the greatest among three numbers, as follows:

Algorithm to find the greatest among three numbers—

ALGORITHM 1.

Step 1: Start
Step 2: Read the three numbers A, B, C
Step 3: Compare A and B. If A is greater perform step 4 else perform step 5.
Step 4: Compare A and C. If A is greater, output "A is greatest" else output "C is greatest". Perform step 6.
Step 5: Compare B and C. If B is greater, output "B is greatest" else output "C is greatest".
Step 6: Stop

ALGORITHM 2.

Step 7: Start
Step 8: Read the three numbers A, B, C
Step 9: Compare A and B. If A is greater, store A in MAX, else store B in MAX.

Step 10: Compare MAX and C. If MAX is greater, output "MAX is greatest" else output "C is greatest".

Step 11: Stop

Both the algorithms accomplish the same goal, but in different ways. The programmer selects the algorithm based on the advantages and disadvantages of each algorithm. For example, the first algorithm has more number of comparisons, whereas in the second algorithm an additional variable MAX is required.

8.4 CONTROL STRUCTURES

The logic of a program may not always be a linear sequence of statements to be executed in that order. The logic of the program may require execution of a statement based on a decision. It may repetitively execute a set of statements unless some condition is met. *Control structures* specify the statements to be executed and the order of execution of statements.

Flowchart and Pseudo code use control structures for representation. There are three kinds of control structures:

- Sequential—instructions are executed in linear order
- Selection (branch or conditional)—it asks a true/false question and then selects the next instruction based on the answer
- Iterative (loop)—it repeats the execution of a block of instructions.

The flowchart and the pseudo code control structures are explained in their respective sections.

8.5 FLOWCHART

A *flowchart* is a diagrammatic representation of the logic for solving a task. A flowchart is drawn using boxes of different shapes with lines connecting them to show the flow of control. The purpose of drawing a flowchart is to make the logic of the program clearer in a visual form. There is a famous saying "A photograph is equivalent to thousand words". The same can be said of flowchart. The logic of the program is communicated in a much better way using a flowchart. Since flowchart is a diagrammatic representation, it forms a common medium of communication.

8.5.1 Flowchart Symbols

A flowchart is drawn using different kinds of symbols. A symbol used in a flowchart is for a specific purpose. Figure 8.1 shows the different symbols of the flowchart along with their names. The flowchart symbols are available in most word processors including MS-WORD, facilitating the programmer to draw a flowchart on the computer using the word processor.

A single line description of the flowchart symbols is given in Table 8.2.

8.5.2 Preparing a Flowchart

A flowchart may be simple or complex. The most common symbols that are used to draw a flowchart are—Process, Decision, Data, Terminator, Connector and Flow lines. While drawing a flowchart, some rules need to be followed—(1) A flowchart should have a start and end, (2) The direction of flow in a flowchart must be from top to bottom and left to right, and (3) The relevant symbols must be used while drawing a flowchart. While preparing the flowchart, the sequence, selection or iterative structures may be used wherever required. Figure 8.2 shows the sequence, selection and iteration structures.

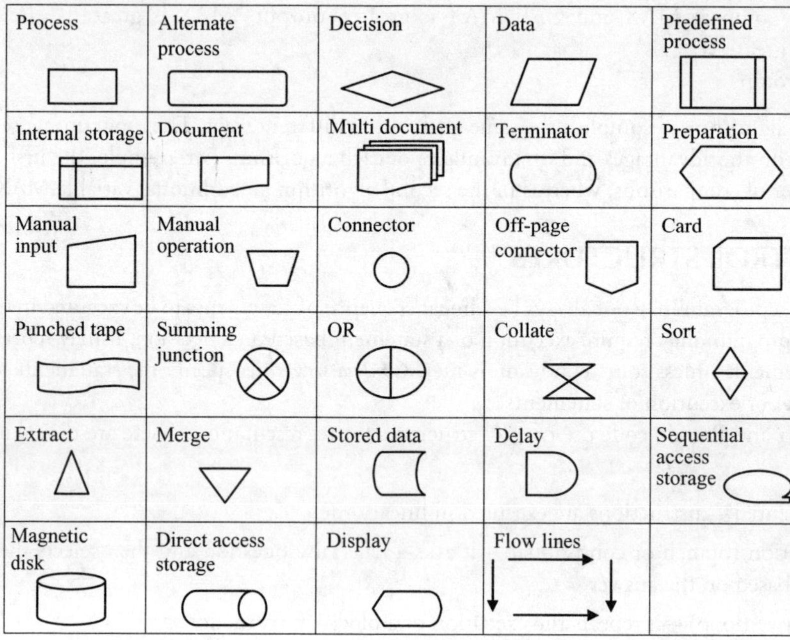

Figure 8.1 Flowchart symbols (available for use in MS-WORD)

Process—operation or action step
Alternate Process—alternate to normal process
Document—a document
Multi document—more than one document
Preparation—set-up process
Punched Tape—I/O from punched tape
Collate—organize in a format
Merge—merge in a predefined order
Sort—sort in some order
Display—display output
Predefined process—process previously specified
Internal Storage—stored in memory
Termination—start or stop point
Delay—wait

Decision—decision or a branch
Data—I/O to or from a process
Manual Input—Data entry from a form
Manual Operation—operation to be done manually
Connector—join flow lines
Off page connector—continue on another page
Summing Junction—Logical AND
OR—Logical OR
Sequential Access storage—stored on magnetic tape
Stored Data—general data storage
Magnetic Disk—I/O from magnetic disk
Direct access storage—storing on hard disk
Flow lines—indicates direction of flow
Extract—split process
Card—I/O from a punched card

Table 8. 2 *Description of flowchart symbols*

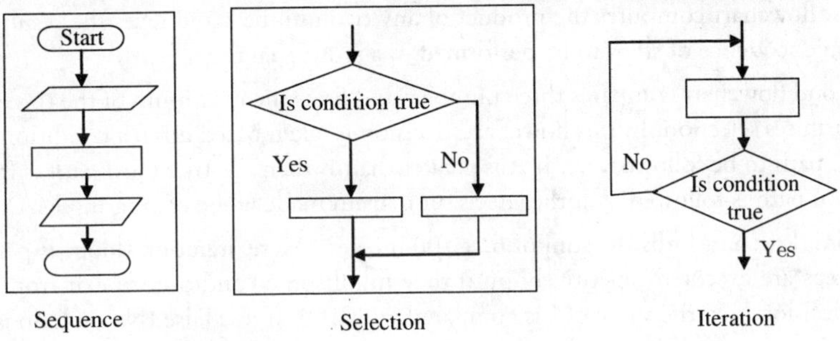

Figure 8.2 Control structures in flowchart

We see that in a sequence, the steps are executed in linear order one after the other. In a selection operation, the step to be executed next is based on a decision taken. If the condition is true (yes) a different path is followed than if the condition evaluates to false (no). In case of iterative operation, a condition is checked. Based upon the result of this conditional check, true or false, different paths are followed. Either the next step in the sequence is executed or the control goes back to one of the already executed steps to make a loop.

Here, we will illustrate the method to draw flowchart, by discussing three different examples. To draw the flowcharts, relevant boxes are used and are connected via flow lines. The flowchart for the examples is shown in Figure 8.3.

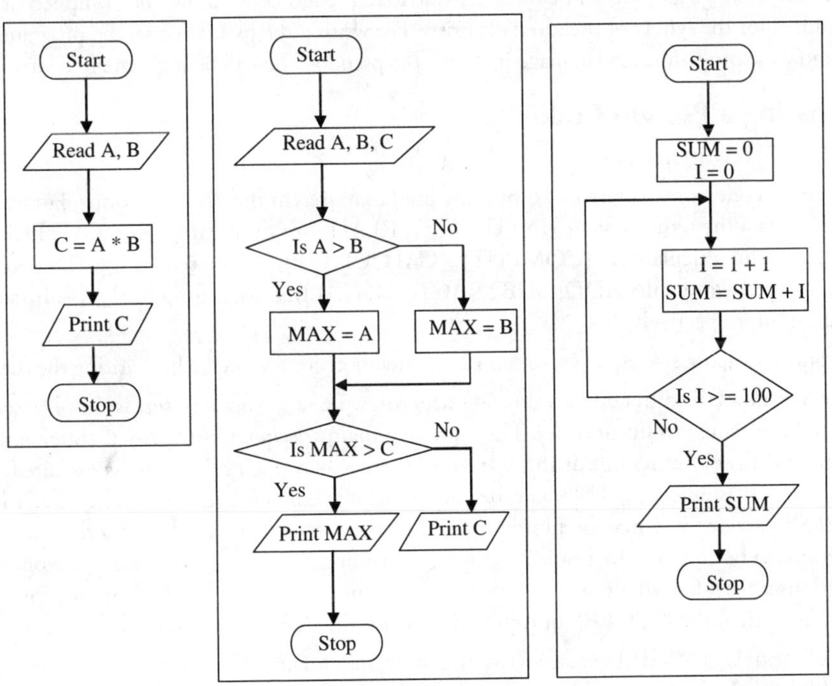

Figure 8.3 Examples of flowchart

- The first flowchart computes the product of any two numbers and gives the result. The flowchart is a simple sequence of steps to be performed in a sequential order.
- The second flowchart compares three numbers and finds the maximum of the three numbers. This flowchart uses selection. In this flowchart, decision is taken based upon a condition, which decides the next path to be followed, i.e. If A is greater than B then the true (Yes) path is followed else the false (No) path is followed. Another decision is again made while comparing MAX with C.
- The third flowchart finds the sum of first 100 integers. Here, iteration (loop) is performed so that some steps are executed repetitively until they fulfill some condition to exit from the repetition. In the decision box, the value of I is compared with 100. If it is false (No), a loop is created which breaks when the condition becomes true (Yes).

Flowcharts have their own benefits; however, they have some limitations too. A complex and long flowchart may run into multiple pages, which becomes difficult to understand and follow. Moreover, updating a flowchart with the changing requirements is a challenging job.

8.6 PSEUDO CODE

Pseudo code consists of short, readable and formally-styled English language used for explaining an algorithm. Pseudo code does not include details like variable declarations, subroutines etc. Pseudo code is a short-hand way of describing a computer program. Using pseudo code, it is easier for a programmer or a non-programmer to understand the general working of the program, since it is not based on any programming language. It is used to give a sketch of the structure of the program, before the actual coding. It uses the structured constructs of the programming language but is not machine-readable. Pseudo code cannot be compiled or executed. Thus, no standard for the syntax of pseudo code exists. For writing the pseudo code, the programmer is not required to know the programming language in which the pseudo code will be implemented later.

8.6.1 Preparing a Pseudo Code

- Pseudo code is written using structured English.
- In a pseudo code, some terms are commonly used to represent the various actions. For example, for inputting data the terms may be (INPUT, GET, READ), for outputting data (OUTPUT, PRINT, DISPLAY), for calculations (COMPUTE, CALCULATE), for incrementing (INCREMENT), in addition to words like ADD, SUBTRACT, INITIALIZE used for addition, subtraction, and initialization, respectively.
- The control structures—sequence, selection, and iteration are also used while writing the pseudo code.
- Figure 8.4 shows the different pseudo code structures. The *sequence structure* is simply a sequence of steps to be executed in linear order. There are two main *selection constructs*—if-statement and case statement. In the *if-statement*, if the condition is true then the THEN part is executed otherwise the ELSE part is executed. There can be variations of the if-statement also, like there may not be any ELSE part or there may be nested ifs. The *case statement* is used where there are a number of conditions to be checked. In a case statement, depending on the value of the expression, one of the conditions is true, for which the corresponding statements are executed. If no match for the expression occurs, then the OTHERS option which is also the default option, is executed.
- WHILE and DO-WHILE are the two iterative statements. The WHILE loop and the DO-WHILE loop, both execute while the condition is true. However, in a WHILE loop the condition is checked at the start of the loop, whereas, in a DO-WHILE loop the condition is checked at the end of the loop. So the DO-WHILE loop executes at least once even if the condition is false when the loop is entered.

```
Step 1

Step 2

Step 3
:
:
:
```

Sequence

```
IF (condition) THEN
    Statement(s) 1
ELSE
    Statement(s) 2
ENDIF
```

```
IF (condition) THEN
    Statement(s) 1
ENDIF
```

```
CASE expression of
Condition1 : statement1
Condition2 : statement2
:
condition : statement N
OTHERS: default statement(s)
```

Selection

```
WHILE (condition)
    Statement 1
    Statement 2
    :
    :
END
```

```
DO
    Statement 1
    Statement 2
    :
    :
WHILE (condition)
```

Iteration

Figure 8.4 Control structures for pseudo code

In Figure 8.5, the pseudo code is written for the same three tasks for which the flowchart was shown in the previous section. The three tasks are—(i) compute the product of any two numbers, (ii) find the maximum of any three numbers, and (iii) find the sum of first 100 integers.

```
READ values of A and B
COMPUTE C by multiplying A with B
PRINT the result C
STOP
```

(i) Find product of any two numbers

```
READ values of A, B, C
IF A is greater than B THEN
    ASSIGN A to MAX
ELSE
    ASSIGN B to MAX
IF MAX is greater than C THEN
    PRINT MAX is greatest
ELSE
    PRINT C is greatest
STOP
```

(ii) Find maximum of any three numbers

```
INITIALIZE SUM to zero
INIT IALIZE I to zero
DO WHILE (I less than 100)
    INCREMENT I
    ADD I to SUM and store in SUM
PRINT SUM
STOP
```

(iii) Find sum of first 100 integers

Figure 8.5 Examples of pseudo code

A pseudo code is easily translated into a programming language. But, as there are no defined standards for writing a pseudo code, programmers may use their own style for writing the pseudo code, which can be easily understood. Generally, programmers prefer to write pseudo code instead of flowcharts.

Difference between Algorithm, Flowchart, and Pseudo Code: An algorithm is a sequence of instructions used to solve a particular problem. Flowchart and Pseudo code are tools to document and represent the algorithm. In other words, an algorithm can be represented using a flowchart or a pseudo code. Flowchart is a graphical representation of the algorithm. Pseudo code is a readable, formally styled English like language representation of the algorithm. Both flowchart and pseudo code use structured constructs of the programming language for representation. The user does not require the knowledge of a programming language to write or understand a flowchart or a pseudo code.

8.7 PROGRAMMING PARADIGMS

The word "paradigm" means an example that serves as a pattern or a model. Programming paradigms are the different patterns and models for writing a program. The programming paradigms may differ in terms of the basic idea which relates to the program computation. Broadly, programming paradigms can be classified as follows:

(1) Structured Programming,
(2) Object-Oriented Programming (OOP), and
(3) Aspect-Oriented Programming (AOP). AOP is a new programming paradigm.

Earlier, the unstructured style of programming was used, where all actions of a small and simple program were defined within a single program only. It is difficult to write and understand a long and complex program using unstructured programming. The unstructured style of programming is not followed nowadays.

8.7.1 Structured Programming

- Structured programming involves building of programs using small modules. The modules are easy to read and write.
- In structured programming, the problem to be solved is broken down into small tasks that can be written independently. Once written, the small tasks are combined together to form the complete task.
- Structured programming can be performed in two ways—*Procedural Programming* and *Modular Programming* (Figure 8.6).
- **Procedural Programming** requires a given task to be divided into smaller procedures, functions or subroutines. A procedural program is largely a single file consisting of many procedures and functions and a function named *main* (). A procedure or function performs a specific task. The function *main* () integrates the procedures and functions by making calls to them, in an order that implements the functionality of the program. When a procedure or function is called, the execution control jumps to the called procedure or function, the procedure or function is executed, and after execution the control comes back to the calling procedure or function.
- **Modular Programming** requires breaking down of a program into a group of files, where each file consists of a program that can be executed independently. In a modular program, the problem is divided into different independent but related tasks. For each identified task, a separate program (module) is written, which is a program file that can be executed independently. The different files of the program are integrated using a *main program file*. The main program file invokes the other files in an order that fulfills the functionality of the problem.

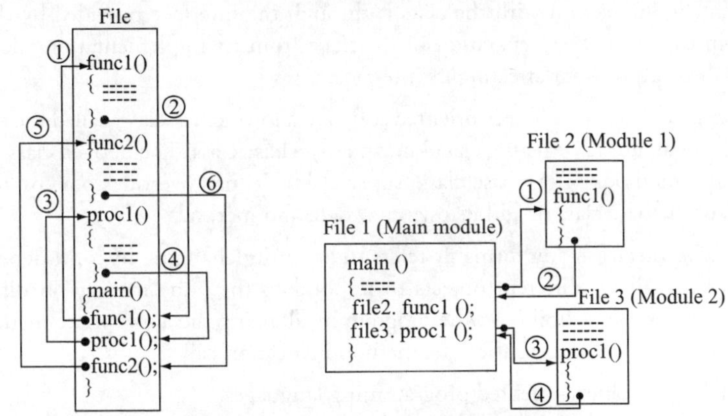

(i) Procedural programming (ii) Modular programming

Figure 8.6 Structured programming

- In structured programming, the approach to develop the software is process-centric or procedural. The software is divided into procedures or modules, based on the overall functionality of the software. As a result, the procedures and modules become tightly interwoven and interdependent. Thus, they are not re-usable.
- *C, COBOL* and *Pascal* are examples of structured programming languages.

8.7.2 Object-Oriented Programming (OOP)

OOP focuses on developing the software based on their component objects. The components interact with each other to provide the functionality of the software. Object-oriented programming differs from procedural programming. In OOP the software is broken into components not based on their functionality, but based on the components or parts of the software. Each component consists of data and the methods that operate on the data. The components are complete by themselves and are re-usable. The terms that are commonly associated with object-oriented programming are as follows:

- *Class* is the basic building block in object-oriented programming. A class consists of data attributes and methods that operate on the data defined in the class.
- *Object* is a runtime instance of the class. An object has a state, defined behavior and a unique identity. The state of the object is represented by the data defined in the class. The methods defined in the class represent object behavior. A class is a template for a set of objects that share common data attributes and common behavior.
- *Abstraction, Encapsulation, Inheritance and Polymorphism* are the unique features of object-oriented software.
- *Abstraction* allows dealing with the complexity of the object. Abstraction allows picking out the relevant details of the object, and ignoring the non-essential details. Encapsulation is a way of implementing abstraction.
- *Encapsulation* means information hiding. The encapsulation feature of object-oriented software hides the data defined in the class. Encapsulation separates implementation of the class from its

interface. The interaction with the class is through the interface provided by the set of methods defined in the class. This separation of interface from its implementation allows changes to be made in the class without affecting its interface.

- The *Inheritance* feature of object-oriented software allows a new class, called the derived class, to be derived from an already existing class known as the base class. The derived class (subclass) inherits all data and methods of the base class (super class). It may override some or all of the data and methods of the base class or add its own new data and methods.
- *Polymorphism* means, many forms. It refers to an entity changing its form depending on the circumstances. It allows different objects to respond to the same message in different ways. This feature increases the flexibility of the program by allowing the appropriate method to be invoked depending on the object executing the method invocation call.
- *C++* and *Java* are object-oriented programming languages.

8.7.3 Aspect-Oriented Programming (AOP)

Aspect-oriented programming is a new programming paradigm that handles the crosscutting concerns of the software. The *crosscutting concerns* are the global concerns like logging, authentication, security, performance, etc., that do not fit into a single module or related modules. In OOP, the business logic or *core concern* is encapsulated in well-defined classes. However, the code for implementing crosscutting concerns is intertwined with a number of related classes or modules and gets scattered in the different classes of the software.

AOP is a new paradigm that focuses on the issue of handling crosscutting concerns at the programming language level. It helps the programmer in cleanly separating the core concerns and the crosscutting concerns of the software. AOP introduces a new modular unit called "aspect" that encapsulates the functionality of the crosscutting concerns. Aspects of a system are independent elements that can be changed, inserted or removed at compile time, and even reused without affecting the rest of system. Aspects are similar to the classes of object oriented programs; however, they implement the crosscutting concerns. At compilation time, the classes of object oriented programs and the aspects are combined into a final executable form using an "aspect weaver".

- *AspectJ and AspectC* are examples of aspect-oriented programming languages.

After having selected a suitable programming paradigm for the program to be written, the coding of the logic of a program has to be done in a computer programming language. For the purposes of coding, the programmer checks the requirements and suitability of the task, and selects from among the programming languages available for the selected programming paradigm.

Characteristics of a Good Program: A program written using any of the programming language must have certain characteristics, which makes it a good program. Some of the key characteristics of a good program are as follows:

- The program should be well-written so that it is easily readable and structured.
- The program should not have hard-coded input values. This implies that it should not be written to work for a particular input value, but must be a general program (also called generic program) that accepts input from the user.
- The program should also be well-documented so that later the author or any other programmer can understand the program.
- Since new and better operating systems keep coming up, a program must be designed to be portable, i.e. with minimum dependence on a particular operating system.

A program comprising of the above features is generally characterized as a good program.

SUMMARY

- *Program* is a set of instructions that instruct the computer about the way a task is to be performed.
- *Program development life cycle* consists of—analyze problem to select a solution, write algorithm, draw flowchart and write pseudo code for the selected solution, write program code in a programming language, remove syntax and semantic errors, and install successfully tested program. Also, document the program to make program maintenance easy.
- *Algorithm* is an ordered sequence of finite, well-defined, unambiguous instructions for completing a task.
- *Control structures* specify the statements that are to be executed and the order of the statements that have to be executed. Sequential, selection, and iteration are three kinds of control structures.
- *Flowchart* is a diagrammatic representation of the logic for solving a task. Flowchart is a tool to document and represent the algorithm. Flowchart is drawn using the flowchart symbols.
- *Pseudo code* consists of short, readable and formally-styled English language which is used to explain and represent an algorithm. There is no standard syntax for writing the pseudo code, though some terms are commonly used in a pseudo code.
- A pseudo code is easily translated into a *programming language*.
- In *structured programming*, the given problem is broken down into smaller tasks based on their functionality. The individual tasks can be written independently, and later combined together to form the complete task. A structured program can be procedural or modular.
- A *procedural program* is largely a single file consisting of many procedures and functions.
- A *modular program* is a group of files, where each file consists of a program that can be executed independently.
- In *OOP*, software is broken into components based on the components of the software. *Class* is the basic building block. *Object* is a runtime instance of class. Abstraction, encapsulation, inheritance, and polymorphism are the unique features of object-oriented software.
- *AOP* is a new paradigm that focuses on the handling of crosscutting concerns like logging, authentication, security, and performance, at the programming language level. The crosscutting concerns are defined in a new modularization unit called aspect.
- A *good program* is readable, structured, generic, well-documented and portable.

KEYWORDS

Abstraction *159*
Algorithm *151*
Aspect *160*
Aspect-Oriented Programming (AOP) *158*
Class *159*
Control structures *153*
Crosscutting concerns *160*
DO-WHILE statement *156*
Dynamic binding *159*
Encapsulation *159*
Flowchart *153*
Flowchart Symbols *153*
If-Then statement *156*
Inheritance *159*
Iteration *153*
Modular Programming *158*
Object *159*
Object-Oriented Programming (OOP) *158*
Polymorphism *159*
Problem Analysis *151*
Procedural Programming *158*
Program *150*
Program Design *151*
Program Development *151*
Program Development Life Cycle *151*
Program Documentation *151*
Program Maintenance *150*
Programming paradigm *158*
Pseudo code *151*
Selection construct *156*
Semantic error *151*
Sequential structure *152*
Static binding *159*
Structured Programming *158*
Syntax error *151*
WHILE statement *156*

QUESTIONS

Section 8.1–8.2

1. Define a program.
2. Explain the program development life cycle in detail.
3. What is the difference between syntax error and semantic error?
4. Define syntax error.
5. Define semantic error.
6. What is the purpose of program maintenance?

Section 8.3–8.4

7. Define algorithm.
8. What are control structures?
9. Name the three kinds of control structures.
10. State the purpose of each of the control structures: (i) Sequence, (ii) Selection, and (iii) Iteration.

Section 8.5

11. Define flowchart.
12. Draw the flowchart symbol for the following—(i) Process, (ii) Decision, (iii) Document, (iv) Connector, and (v) Magnetic Disk.
13. State the meaning of the following flowchart symbols—(i) Process, (ii) Decision, (iii) Document, (iv) Connector, (v) Magnetic Disk, and (vi) Flow lines.
14. Draw the control structures (Sequence, Selection and Iteration) for the flowchart.

Section 8.6–8.7.3

15. Define pseudo code.
16. Write the pseudo code control structures (sequence, selection, and iteration).
17. What is the difference between WHILE and DO-WHILE statements?
18. Name the different programming paradigms.
19. What is modular programming?
20. What is procedural programming?
21. Name two procedural programming languages.
22. What are the key features of OOP?
23. Define: (i) class, (ii) object, (iii) abstraction, (iv) encapsulation, (v) inheritance, and (vi) polymorphism.
24. How is static binding different from dynamic binding in OOP?
25. Name two object-oriented programming languages.
26. How is AOP different from OOP?
27. Define an aspect.
28. Name two aspect-oriented programming languages.
29. Explain the characteristics of a good program.

Programming Exercise

30. Write the algorithm, draw a flowchart, and write pseudo code for the following:
    (a) To find the sum of square root of any three numbers.
    (b) To find the sum of first 100 integers.
    (c) To find the sum of all even numbers till 100.
    (d) To find the sum of all odd numbers till 100.
    (e) To find the sum of any five integers.
    (f) To find the factorial of a number n. *Hint:* $n! = n(n-1)(n-2)....3.2.1$
    (g) To find the first n numbers in a Fibonacci series. *Hint:* $f(0) = 0, f(1) = 1, f(n) = f(n-1) + f(n-2)$
    (h) To find the sum of digits of a number. (For example, for number 345 find 3+4+5)
    (i) To check whether a number is prime or not.
    (j) To convert the temperature from Fahrenheit to Celsius. *Hint:* C= (5/9)*(F-32)

Extra Questions

31. Give full form for the following abbreviations:
    (i) AOP (ii) OOP
32. Write short notes on:
    (a) Program Development Life Cycle
    (b) Algorithm
    (c) Control structures
    (d) Flowchart
    (e) Pseudo code
    (f) Structured programming
    (g) Object-Oriented Programming
    (h) Aspect-Oriented Programming
    (i) Characteristics of a good program
33. Give differences between the following:
    (a) Flowchart and Pseudo code
    (b) Algorithm, Flowchart and Pseudo code
    (c) Modular Programming and Procedural Programming
    (d) Selection and Iteration
    (e) OOP and AOP

DATA COMMUNICATION AND COMPUTER NETWORK

9

Contents

- Importance of networking—Resource sharing, information sharing, as a communication medium, back-up and support
- Data transmission media—Twisted pair, coaxial cable, optical fiber, RF transmission, microwave transmission, satellite transmission
- Data transmission across media
  - Transmission modes—Simplex, half-duplex, full-duplex
  - Transmission speed—Bandwidth, throughput, attenuation, distortion
  - Fundamentals of transmission—Electromagnetic waves, signals
    - Analog and digital signals
    - Modulation and demodulation—Amplitude, frequency, phase shift
    - Multiplexing—FDM, WDM
    - Asynchronous and synchronous transmission
- Data transmission and data networking
  - Switching—Circuit switching, message switching, packet switching
- Computer network
  - Network types—LAN, MAN, WAN
  - Network topologies—Bus, ring, star
  - Communication protocol—The seven layers of OSI model
  - Network devices—NIC, repeater, bridge, hub, switch, router, gateway
- Wireless networking—Bluetooth technology, wireless LAN, wireless WAN

Why this chapter

As opposed to a stand-alone computer, connected computers facilitate exchange of information. To connect the computers, you need a data transmission media and understand how data gets transmitted across the media. You can create a network of different types of computers across a room, building, city, state or the world. The purpose of this chapter is to introduce you to the data communication and the computer network.

9.1 INTRODUCTION

The communication process involves—sender of information, receiver of information, language used for communication, and medium used to establish the communication. Communication between computers also follows a similar process.

This chapter discusses the data communication and the computer networks. The section on data communication discusses the media used for transmission of data, how data can be transferred across the communication media and the relationship between data transmission and data networking. The section on computer network discusses different network types, network topologies, communication protocol and network communicating devices. A brief explanation of wireless networks is also provided.

9.2 IMPORTANCE OF NETWORKING

Networking of computers provides a communication link between the users, and provides access to information. Networking of computers has several uses, described as follows:

- **Resource Sharing**—In an organization, resources such as printers, fax machines and scanners are generally not required by each person at all times. Moreover, for small organizations it may not be feasible to provide such resources to each individual. Such resources can be made available to different users of the organization on the network. It results in availability of the resource to different users regardless of the physical location of the resource or the user, enhances optimal use of the resource, leads to easy maintenance, and saves cost too (Figure 9.1).

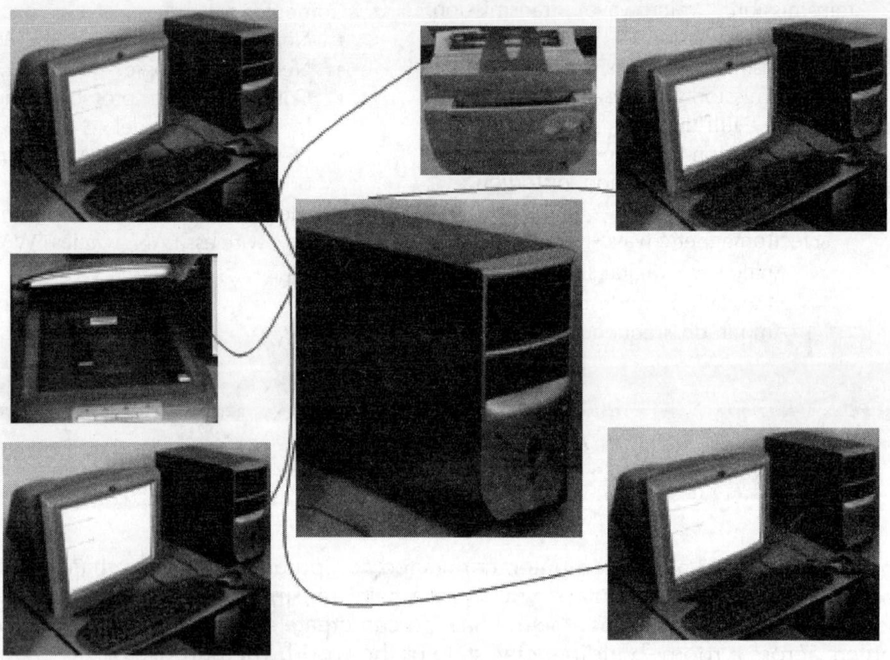

Figure 9.1 A network of computers, printer and scanner

- **Sharing of Information**—In addition to the sharing of physical resources, networking facilitates sharing of information. Information stored on networked computers located at same or different physical locations, becomes accessible to the computers connected to the network.
- **As a Communication Medium**—Networking helps in sending and receiving of electronic-mail (e-mail) messages from anywhere in the world. Data in the form of text, audio, video and pictures can be sent via e-mail. This allows the users to communicate online in a faster and cost effective manner. Video conferencing is another form of communication made possible via networking. People in distant locations can hold a meeting, and they can hear and see each other simultaneously.

- **For Back-up and Support**—Networked computers can be used to take back-up of critical data. In situations where there is a requirement of always-on computer, another computer on the network can take over in case of failure of one computer.

9.3 DATA TRANSMISSION MEDIA

The data is sent from one computer to another over a transmission medium. The transmission media can be grouped into guided media, and unguided media.

In a *guided media,* the data signals are sent along a specific path, through a wire or a cable. Copper wire and optical fibers are the most commonly used guided media. Copper wire transmits data as electric signals. Copper wires offer low resistance to current signal, facilitating signals to travel longer distances. To minimize the effect of external disturbance on the copper wire, two types of wiring is used—(1) Twisted Pair, and (2) Coaxial Pair. Optical fibers transmit data as light signals.

In the *unguided media,* the data signals are not bounded by a fixed channel to follow. The data signals are transmitted by air. Radio, microwave, and satellite transmissions fall into this category.

Now let's discuss both the guided and the unguided data transmission media.

9.3.1 Twisted Pair

- A twisted pair cable consists of four pairs of copper wires coated with an insulating material like plastic or Teflon, twisted together. The twisting of wires reduces electromagnetic interference from external sources.
- Twisted pair cabling is often used in data networks for short and medium length connections because of its relatively lower costs compared to optical fiber and coaxial cable.
- Twisted pair is of two kinds—Shielded Twisted Pair (STP), and Unshielded Twisted Pair (UTP).
- *STP* cable has an extra layer of metal foil between the twisted pair of copper wires and the outer covering. The metal foil covering provides additional protection from external disturbances. However, the covering increases the resistance to the signal and thus decreases the length of the cable. STP is costly and is generally used in networks where cables pass closer to devices that cause external disturbances.
- *UTP* is the most commonly used medium for transmission over short distances up to 100m. Out of the four pairs of wires in a UTP cable, only two pairs are used for communication. Figure 9.2 shows the cross-section of STP and UTP cables.
- UTP cables are defined in different categories. The commonly used UTP cable is the *Cat-5 cable* which is used with fast Ethernet.

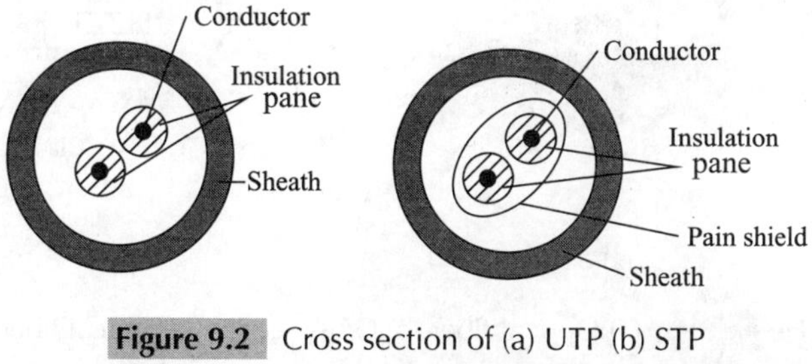

Figure 9.2 Cross section of (a) UTP (b) STP

9.3.2 Coaxial Cable

- A coaxial cable (Figure 9.3) has a single inner conductor that transmits electric signals; the outer conductor acts as a ground. The two conductors are separated by insulation. The inner conductor, insulator, and the outer conductor are wrapped in a sheath of Teflon or PVC.

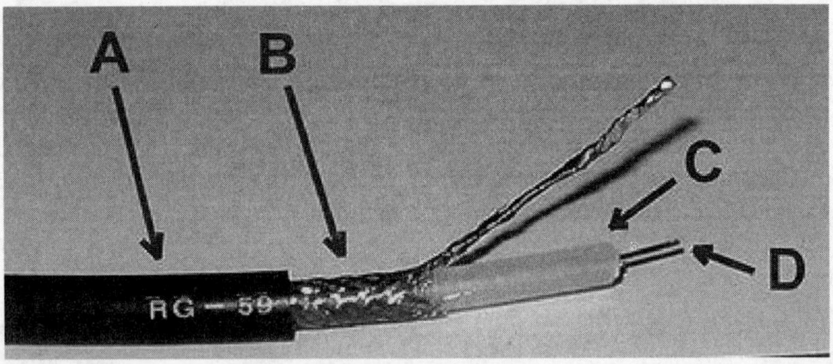

Figure 9.3 Coaxial cable (A: outer plastic sheath, B: woven copper shield, C: inner dielectric insulator, D: copper core)

- The copper wire is used for both inner and outer conductor. The signal is transmitted over the surface of the inner conductor.
- In an ideal coaxial cable the electromagnetic field carrying the signal exists only in the space between the inner and outer conductors. This allows coaxial cable runs to be installed next to metal objects such as gutters without the power losses that occur in other transmission lines, and provides protection of the signal from external electromagnetic interference.
- A thicker coaxial cable can transmit more data than a thinner one.
- The commonly used coaxial cable is *10 base 2* that transmits over a distance of 185 m, and *10 base 5* that transmits over a distance of 500 m.

9.3.3 Optical Fiber

- Optical fibers are being used for transmission of information over large distances more cost-effectively than the copper wire connection. Communication systems are now unthinkable without fiber optics.
- Optical fiber transmits data as light signals instead of electric signals.
- An optical fiber cable (Figure 9.4) consists of (1) core—optical fiber conductor (glass) that transmits light, (2) cladding—an optical material that surrounds the core to prevent any light from escaping the core, and (3) jacket—outer covering made of plastic to protect the fiber from damage.

(a)

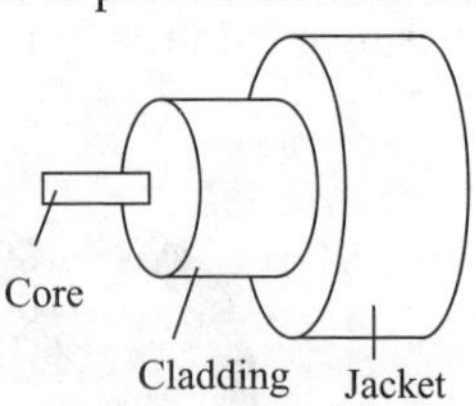

(b)

Figure 9.4 (a) Optical fiber (b) Cross section of optical fiber

- Modern optical fiber cables can contain up to a thousand fibers in a single cable, so the performance of optical networks easily accommodate large demands for bandwidth on a point-to-point basis.
- Optical fibers come in two types: (a) Single-mode fibers, and (b) Multi-mode fibers
  - Single-mode fibers have small cores (about 3.5×10^{-4} inches or 9 microns in diameter) and transmit infrared laser light (wavelength = 1,300 to 1,550 nanometers).
  - Multi-mode fibers have larger cores (about 2.5×10^{-3} inches or 62.5 microns in diameter) and transmit infrared light (wavelength = 850 to 1,300 nm) from Light Emitting Diodes (LEDs).
- The *Advantages of Optical Fibers* over wires are:
  - Optical fibers do not cause electrical interference in other cables, since they use light signals.
  - Due to much lower attenuation and interference, optical fiber has large advantages over existing copper wire in long-distance and high-demand applications.
  - A fiber can carry a pulse of light much farther than a copper wire carrying a signal.
  - Optical fiber can carry more information than a wire (light can encode more information than electrical signal).
  - A single optical fiber is required for light to travel from one computer to another (two wires are required for electric connection).
  - Because signals in optical fibers degrade less, lower-power transmitters can be used instead of the high-voltage electrical transmitters needed for copper wires. Again, this saves your provider and you, money.
  - No amplification of the optical signal is needed over distances of hundreds of kilometers. This has greatly reduced the cost of optical networking, particularly over undersea spans where the cost reliability of amplifiers is one of the key factors determining the performance of the whole cable system.
  - Optical fibers are ideally suited for carrying digital information, which is especially useful in computer networks.
  - They are highly secure as they cannot be tapped and for lack of signal radiation.
- The *Disadvantages of Optical Fiber* are:
  - Installing an optical fiber requires special equipment.
  - If a fiber breaks, finding the broken location is difficult.
  - Repairing a broken optical fiber is difficult and requires special equipment.
  - Due to its high installation costs, they are economical when the bandwidth utilization is high.

9.3.4 Radio Transmission

The electromagnetic radio waves that operate at the radio frequency are also used to transmit computer data. This transmission is also known as Radio Frequency (RF) transmission (Figure 9.5). The computers using RF transmission do not require a direct physical connection like wires or cable. Each computer attaches to an antenna that can both send and receive radio transmission.

Figure 9.5 Radio transmission

9.3.5 Microwave Transmission

Microwave transmission (Figure 9.6) refers to the technique of transmitting information over a microwave link. Microwaves have a higher frequency than radio waves. Microwave transmission can be aimed at a single direction, instead of broadcasting in all directions (like in radio waves). Microwaves can carry more information than radio waves but cannot penetrate metals. Microwaves are used where there is a clear path between the transmitter and the receiver.

Figure 9.6 Microwave transmission

Microwave transmission has the advantage of not requiring access to all contiguous land along the path of the system, since it does not need cables. They suffer from the disadvantages: a) needing expensive towers and repeaters, and b) are subject to interference from passing airplanes and rain. Because microwave systems are line-of-sight media, radio towers must be spaced approximately every 42 km along the route.

9.3.6 Satellite Transmission

The communication across longer distances can be provided by combining radio frequency transmission with satellites. Geosynchronous satellites are placed in an orbit synchronized with the rotation of the earth at a distance of 36,000 km above the surface of the earth. Geosynchronous satellites appear to be stationary when viewed from the earth. The satellite consists of transponder that can receive RF signals and transmit them back to the ground at a different angle. A ground station on one side of the ocean transmits signal to the satellite which in turn sends the signal to the ground station on the other side of the ocean (Figure 9.7).

9.4 DATA TRANSMISSION ACROSS MEDIA

Transmitting data across media implies sending bits through the transmission medium. Physically, the data is sent as electric signals, radio waves or as light signals. Let's now discuss the use of electric current to transfer digital information. For this, the bits are encoded and sent as characters.

9.4.1 Transmission Modes

The direction in which data can be transmitted between any two linked devices is of three types—(1) Simplex, (2) Half-duplex, and (3) Full-duplex, or duplex. *Simplex transmission* is uni-directional data

Figure 9.7 Satellite transmission

transmission. Of the two linked devices, only one of them can send data and the other one can only receive data. *Half-duplex transmission* is bi-directional data transmission, but the linked devices cannot send and receive at the same time. When one device is sending data the other can only receive. *Full-duplex transmission* is bi-directional and the linked devices can send and receive data simultaneously. The linked devices can send data and at the same time receive data. Figure 9.8 shows the different kinds of transmission modes used for interaction.

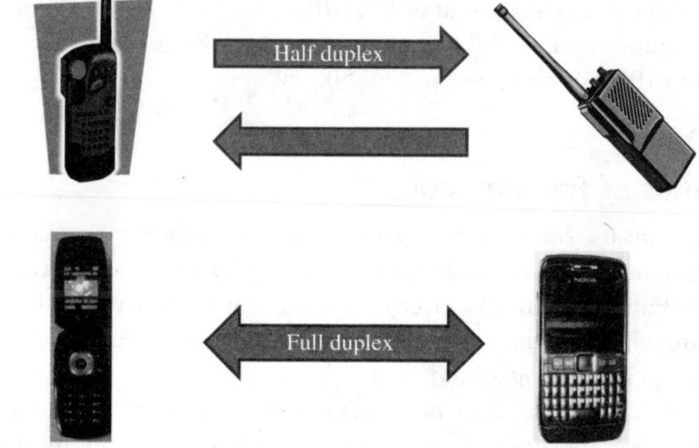

Figure 9.8 Transmission modes

9.4.2 Transmission Speed

- When the signals are transmitted between two computers, two factors need to be considered—(1) Bandwidth, and (2) Distance.
- *Bandwidth* is the amount of data that can be transferred through the underlying hardware i.e. the communication medium, in a fixed amount of time. Bandwidth is measured in *cycles per second (cps)* or *Hertz (Hz)*. The bandwidth of the transmission medium determines the data transfer rate.
- *Throughput* is the amount of data that is actually transmitted between the two computers. Throughput is specified in *bits per second (bps)*. The throughput capability of the communication medium is also called *bandwidth*. The bandwidth of the communication medium is the upper bound on the throughput, because data cannot be sent at a rate more than the throughput of the communication medium.
- Higher throughput is achieved by using a large part of the electromagnetic spectrum (large bandwidth). Technology that uses large part of the electromagnetic spectrum to achieve higher throughput is known as *broadband technology*. The technology that uses small part of the electromagnetic spectrum is known as *baseband technology*.
- Throughput is affected by the *distance* between the connected computers or devices. Even if a transmission medium is designed for a specific bandwidth, the throughput is affected by the distance of communication.
- The bandwidth of transmission medium is limited by the distance over which the medium needs to transmit the signal. The bandwidth decreases with the increase in the distance between the connected devices. When a signal has to travel long distance, the signal strength decreases; the signal strength is utilized to overcome the resistance offered by the connecting medium (cable or wire). The gradual deterioration of signal strength across long distances is called *attenuation*.
- Moreover, with increasing distance the external disturbance increases, which causes the signal to deteriorate and results in less amount of data to be transferred. The degradation of signal due to internal or external disturbances is called *distortion*.
- The bandwidth and distance of the transmission medium is selected so that it offers minimum attenuation and minimum distortion.
- The *cat-5* UTP cable has a throughput of 100 Mbps over a distance of 100m. The *10 base 2* coaxial cable has a throughput up to 10Mbps over a distance of 185 m. The *10 base 5* coaxial cable has a throughput up to 10Mbps over a distance of 500 m.

9.4.3 Fundamentals of Transmission

Telecommunication systems use *electromagnetic waves* to transfer information. Electromagnetic waves can travel through transmission media like copper wires, fiber optics or as radio waves. They can also travel in vacuum. Wireless communication uses electromagnetic waves for transmission of information. The transmission media through which the waves propagate are not perfect. As a result, the waves propagated via the transmission media get *attenuated* and *distorted.*

The information to be transmitted does not always exist in a form that is compatible with the transmission medium. Waves that are compatible with the transmission medium must be generated to carry information. A *signal* is a wave that is suitable for carrying information over a transmission medium. Signals can be electric signals, light signals, electromagnetic signals or radio signals. Electric signals are used to carry information through copper wires, light signals for fiber optic cables, and radio signals for carrying information in free space. Electrical signals have limited bandwidth and cannot be used in long distance communication. They need to be amplified or regenerated. Light signals have a high bandwidth and are suited for long distance communication.

9.4.3.1 Analog and Digital Signals

- Information carrying signals are of two types—(a) analog signal, and (b) digital signal (Figure 9.9).
- *Analog Signal:* An analog signal is a wave that continuously changes its information carrying properties over time. The wave may vary in amplitude or frequency in response to changes in sound, light, heat, position, or pressure etc. For example a telephone voice signal is analog. The intensity of the voice causes electric current variations. At the receiving end, the signal is reproduced in the same proportion.
- *Digital Signal:* A digital signal is a wave that takes limited number of values at discrete intervals of time. Digital signals are non-continuous, they change in individual steps. They consist of pulses or digits with discrete levels or values. The value of each pulse is constant, but there is an abrupt change from one digit to the next. Digital signals have two amplitude levels called *nodes*. The value of which are specified as one of two possibilities such as 1 or 0, HIGH or LOW, TRUE or FALSE, and so on.

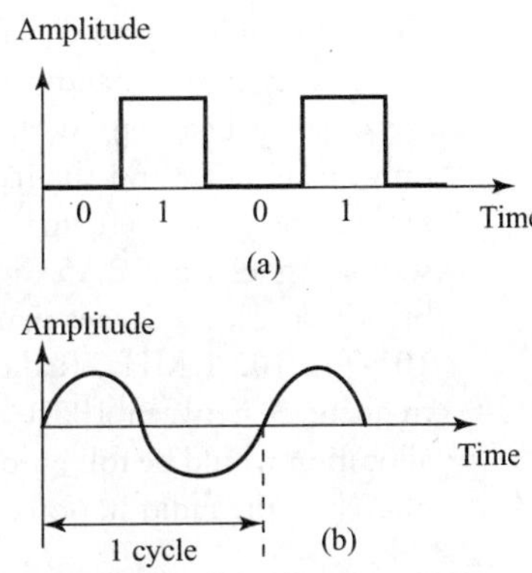

Figure 9.9 (a) Digital signal
(b) Analog signal

- Analog and digital signals are compared on the basis of—(1) impact of noise, (2) loss of information, and (3) introduction of error.
- Analog signal has the potential for an infinite amount of signal resolution. Another advantage with analog signals is that they can be processed more easily than their digital equivalent. The primary disadvantage of the analog signals is the noise. The effects of noise create signal loss and distortion, which is impossible to recover, since amplifying the signal to recover attenuated parts of the signal, also amplifies the noise. Even if the resolution of an analog signal is higher than a comparable digital signal, the difference can be overshadowed by the noise in the signal. In digital systems, degradation can not only be detected, but corrected as well.
- *Amplifier* is any device or a circuit that changes, usually increases, the amplitude of an analog signal.
- *Repeater* is an electronic device that receives a signal and retransmits it at a higher level and/or higher power, so that the signal can cover longer distances. With physical media like Ethernet or Wi-Fi, data transmissions can only span a limited distance before the quality of the signal degrades. Repeaters attempt to preserve signal integrity and extend the distance over which data can safely travel. Actual network devices that serve as repeaters usually have some other name. Active hubs, for example, are repeaters. Active hubs are sometimes also called "multiport repeaters," but more commonly they are just "hubs."

9.4.3.2 Modulation and Demodulation

- *Modulation:* Signals consist of two components—the *information signal* and the *carrier signal.* The transmission of any signal over some communication medium usually involves *modulation* of a carrier. Prior to their transmission the information signal and the carrier signal are combined and the process of combining these two signals is called *modulation.* Characteristics of the carrier signal are varied in proportion to the amplitude of the information-carrying signal. Modulation results in the transfer of the signal information to higher frequency carrier signal. In simple English terms, the information signal sits on top of the carrier signal and rides on it from the receiver to the transmitter.
- *Need for Modulation:* Let's understand the need for modulation by using a simple example. Stereophonic radio signal consist of frequency ranges from 30 Hz (Hertz) to 15 KHz (Kilo Hertz). Hence they need a bandwidth of 15 KHz. If ten different radio stations start transmitting their voice signals between 30 Hz and 15 KHz frequencies, then a combination of these signals would only create noise and the receiver would not be able to discriminate between the signals of each radio station. To overcome this, usually the FM broadcast band, used for broadcasting FM radio stations, goes from 87.5 to 108.0 MHz (Mega Hertz). For example a radio channel-1 may be broadcast using a carrier signal of 102 MHz and would typically use band of frequencies between 101.9 to 102.1 MHz. Radio channel-2 using a carrier signal of 102.2 MHz would use band of frequencies between 102.1 and 102.3 MHz. Similarly for other channels, the same method of allocation would be followed. This eliminates the problem of discrimination and decoding signals of each of the radio stations at the receiving end.

There are three primary reasons which necessitate modulation:

(a) To make efficient use of the lines or media used for communication

(b) To make radio communications feasible: The lower the frequency of signal, the larger is the size of the antenna needed for transmission and reception. A signal of 10 KHz would require an antenna whose dimensions are in the range of a few kilometers.

(c) To simplify signal processing: It is simpler to design electronic systems for narrow frequency bands.

- At the sending side (transmitter), the signal is superimposed on the carrier wave, which results in a modulated carrier wave. The modulated carrier wave is transmitted. At the receiving end, the receiver is configured to recognize the carrier that the sender is using. The receiver detects the modulation of the carrier wave and reconstructs the data signal.
- The process of segregating the data signal and the carrier signal from the modulated carrier wave is called *demodulation.* At the receiving end, the carrier wave is discarded after the data signal has been reconstructed.
- Modulation technique did not originate for data communication for computers, but has long been used for radio, television, and telephone communication. For long distance transmission, computer networks use modulation, whether the signals are transmitted over wires, optical fibers, microwave or radio frequency.
- Modulation is of three kinds, which are defined as follows:
  - *Amplitude Modulation*—The amplitude of the carrier wave is modified in proportion to the data signal. The frequency and phase of the carrier signal remains unchanged.

- *Frequency Modulation*—The frequency of the carrier signal is modified in proportion to the data signal. The amplitude and phase of the carrier signal remains unchanged.
- *Phase Shift Modulation*—The phase of the carrier signal is modified in proportion to the data signal. The amplitude and frequency of the carrier signal remains unchanged.

⊙ For computer networks, generally phase shift modulation is used. Figure 9.10 shows the different kinds of modulation of a carrier wave with signal.

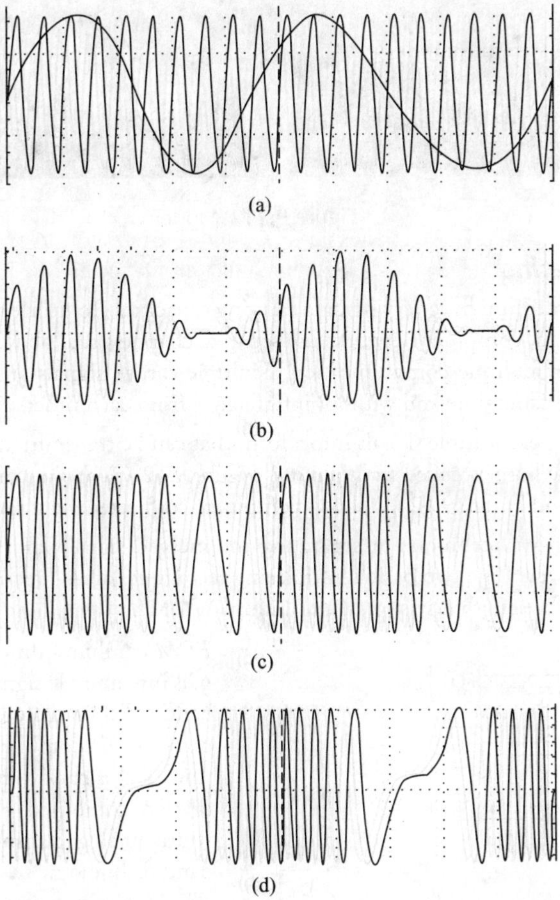

Figure 9.10 (a) Carrier wave with signal (b) Amplitude modulation (c) Frequency modulation (d) Wavelength modulation

⊙ *Modem* (Figure 9.11) is a device that has both a **mo**dulator and a **dem**odulator. Modulator accepts data signals from the computer and modulates the carrier wave accordingly. Demodulator accepts modulated carrier wave and regenerates the original data signal from it. During data communication, modem is attached to the computer, both at the sender and the receiver side. Modems are used with all transmission media like RF modem for RF transmission and optical modem for transmission through fiber optics.

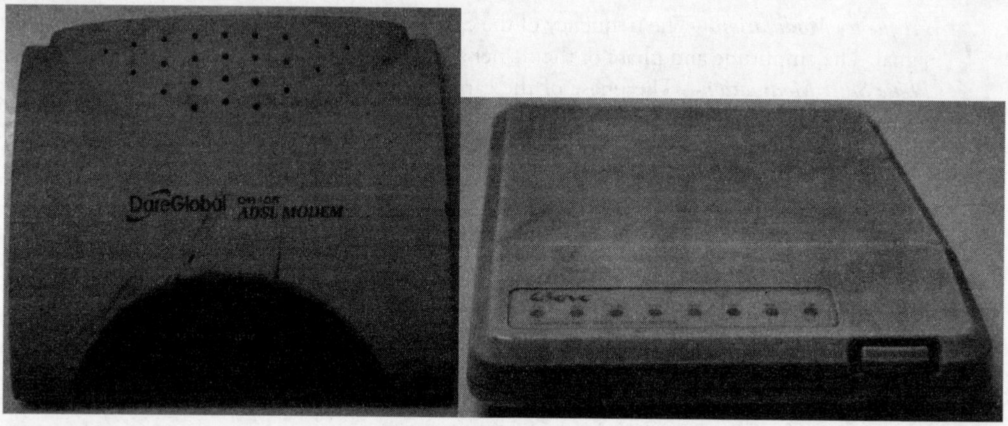

Figure 9.11 Modems

9.4.3.3 Multiplexing

- Transmission medium have varying data carrying capacities. To utilize the full capacity of the transmission medium, computer networks use separate channels that allow sharing of a single physical connection for multiple communication. Multiple carrier signals are transmitted over the same medium at the same time and without interference from each other.
- The combining of multiple signals into a form that can be transmitted over a single link of a communication medium is called *multiplexing*. Figure 9.12 (a) shows computers connected without multiplexing and Figure 9.12 (b) shows computers connected via a multiplexer.
- *Demultiplexing* is a technique of separating the merged signals and sending them to the corresponding receivers. The two basic multiplexing techniques are—Frequency Division Multiplexing (FDM) and Wavelength Division Multiplexing (WDM).

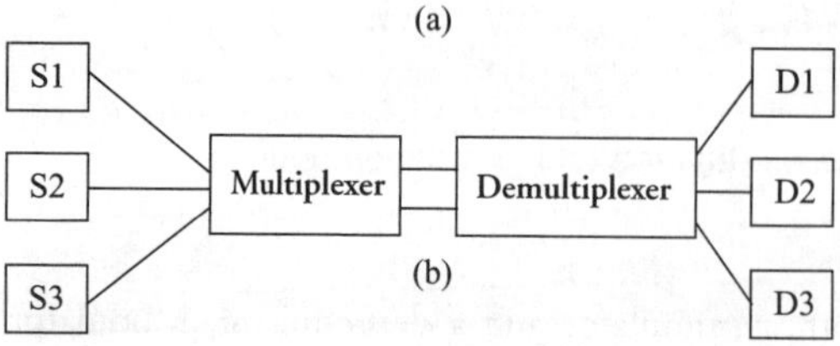

Figure 9.12 (a) No multiplexing (b) Multiplexing

- *FDM* combines different carrier frequencies signals into a single signal of higher bandwidth. The bandwidth of the communication medium link carrying the combined signal is greater than the sum of the bandwidth of the individual signals that are combined. FDM is used for high bandwidth analog transmission systems like broadband technology.
- *WDM* is similar to FDM except that FDM involves electromagnetic spectrum below light and WDM involves light signals. WDM uses very high frequencies. WDM combines different light signals coming from different sources into a larger band light signal across a single optical fiber. It also enables bi-directional communications over one strand of fiber.

9.4.3.4 Asynchronous and Synchronous Transmission

- One major difficulty in data transmission is that of synchronising the receiver with the sender. Whenever an electronic device transmits digital (and sometimes analog) data to another electronic device,

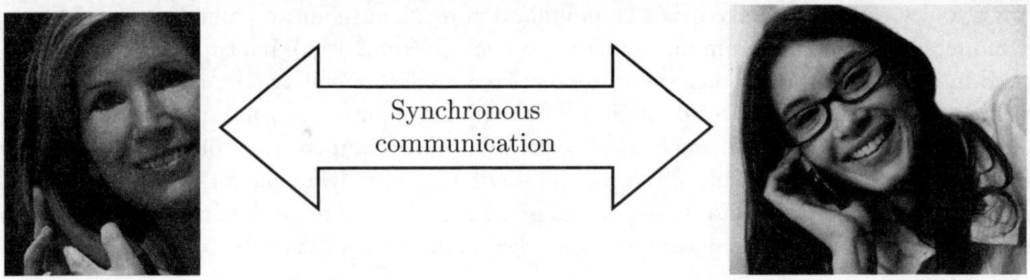

Figure 9.13 Synchronous communication

there must be a certain rhythm established between the two devices, i.e., the receiving device must have some way of knowing, within the context of the fluctuating signal that it is receiving, where each unit of data begins, and ends. The signal must be synchronized in a way that the receiver can distinguish the bits and bytes as the transmitter intends them to be distinguished. Two approaches exist to address the problem of synchronisation—synchronous transmission, and asynchronous transmission.

- *Synchronous communication* is the characteristic of a communication system in which the sender must coordinate (i.e. synchronize) with the receiver before sending data (Figure 9.13). The network is designed to move the data at the precise rate, which is not affected by the increase or decrease in network traffic. Voice system network use the synchronous transmission.
- *Asynchronous communication* is a characteristic of a communication system in which the sender and receiver do not coordinate before the transmission of data (Figure 9.14). The receiver must be prepared to accept data at any time. The sender can wait when no data is available and send when data is available for sending. Most of the data networks use asynchronous transmission. E.g.: RS-232 based serial devices use asynchronous communication.

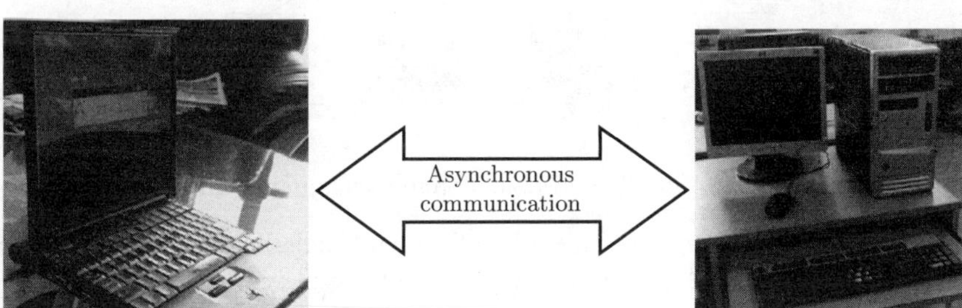

Figure 9.14 Asynchronous communication

9.5 DATA TRANSMISSION AND DATA NETWORKING

Data transmission at physical level involves the hardware required for handling individual bits and encoding bits in signals. The details of the underlying hardware are generally handled by the engineers who design the hardware.

Any two devices directly linked via a communication medium (point to point communication) can send and receive data, to and from each other respectively (Figure 9.15 a). If a large number of computers need to interact with each other, point to point communication will require direct link between all the computers. This is not a practical solution. The communication circuits and the associated hardware required for communication (like modem) are expensive. Moreover, there may not be a need to transmit data all the time, which will result in the communication medium lying idle for most of the time. For long distance communication, instead of point to point connection, a network of nodes is used as a communication medium. The different computers attached to the network share the communication facility.

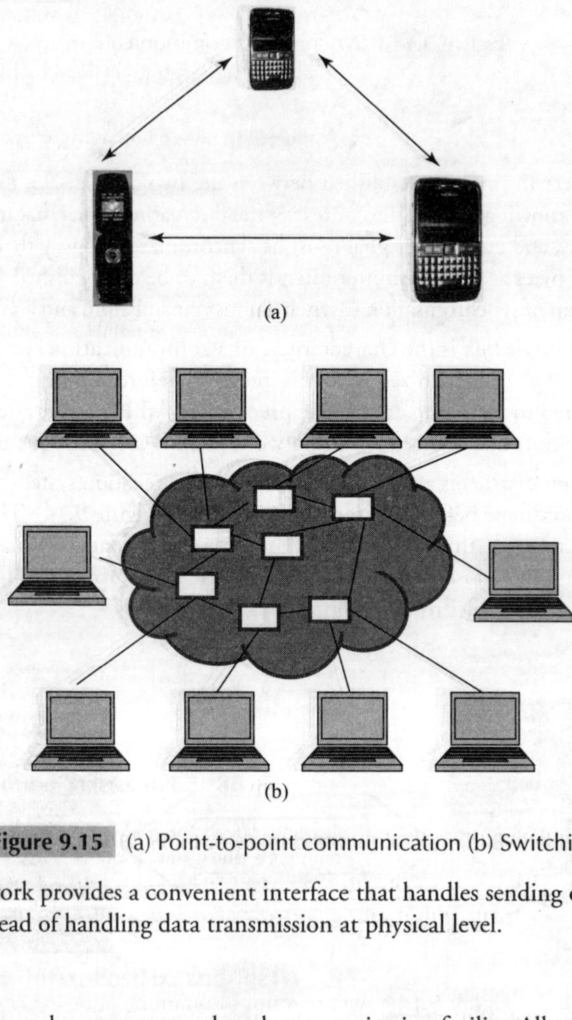

Figure 9.15 (a) Point-to-point communication (b) Switching

The computer network provides a convenient interface that handles sending of multiple bytes of data across the network instead of handling data transmission at physical level.

9.5.1 Switching

A network cannot allow or deny access to a shared communication facility. All computers attached to the network can use it to send and receive data. Networks allow sharing of communication medium using *switching* (Figure 9.15 b). Switching routes the traffic (data traffic) on the network. It sets up temporary connections between the network nodes to facilitate sending of data. Switching allows different users, fair access to the shared communication medium. There are three kinds of switching techniques—(1) Packet switching, (2) Circuit switching, and (3) Message switching. Computer networks generally use packet switching, occasionally use circuit switching but do not use message switching.

9.5.1.1 Circuit Switching

Circuit switching (Figure 9.16) sets up end-to-end communication path between the source and the destination, before the data can be sent. The path gets reserved during the duration of the connection. Circuit switching is commonly used in the telephone communication network.

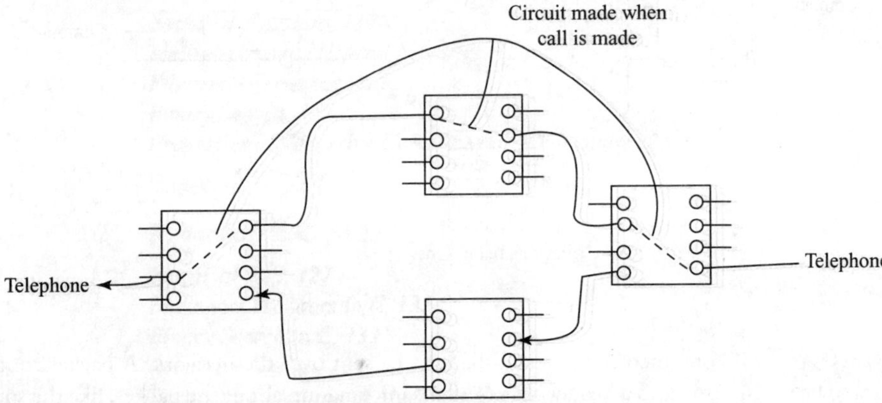

Figure 9.16 Circuit switching

9.5.1.2 Message Switching

Message switching (Figure 9.17) does not establish a physical path in advance, between the sender and the receiver. It uses the 'store and forward' mechanism. In this mechanism, the network nodes have large memory storage. The message is received from the sender and stored in the network node, and when it finds a free route, it forwards the message to the next node till it reaches the destination. Message switching requires large data storage capacity and incurs delay in storing and forwarding of message. Message switching may block the network nodes for a long time. They are thus not suitable for interactive communication. Message switching is no more used in computer networks.

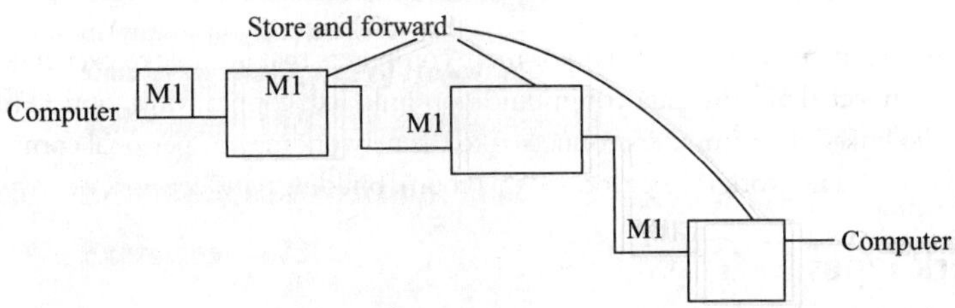

Figure 9.17 Message switching

9.5.1.3 Packet Switching

- Like message switching, packet switching does not establish a physical path between the sender and the receiver, in advance. Packet switching (Figure 9.18) also uses the 'store and forward' mechanism. However, instead of a complete message, packets are sent over the network. Packet switching splits a message into small "packets" of defined size to be sent over the network. Each packet is numbered.

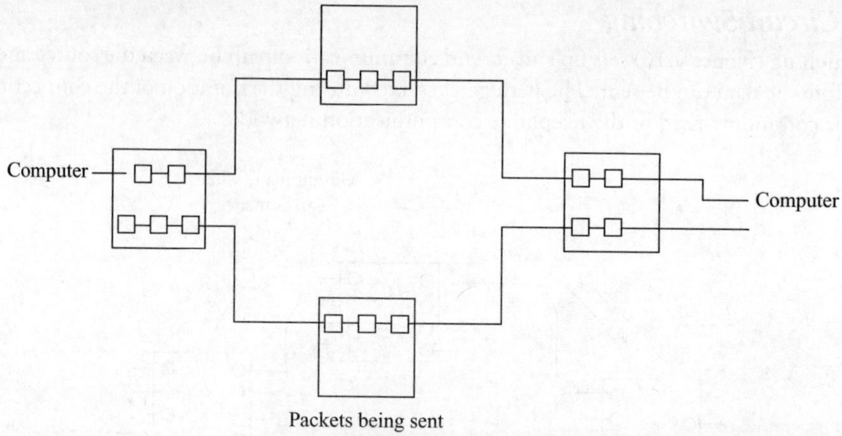

Figure 9.18 Packet switching

- A *packet* is a self-contained part of data that can be sent over the network. A packet contains the data to be transmitted and a header that contains information about the packet, like the source and destination addresses, size of packet, error checking bytes etc.
- Since the path through which the packets travel is not reserved, the packets may travel through different paths in the network and may not reach the destination in order. At the destination, the received packets are reassembled (according to the packet number), and the complete message is constructed.
- Packet switching is suited for interactive traffic. Packet switching limits the size of the packet and does not block a network node for a long time. Moreover, a node can transmit a packet before the arrival of another full packet, thus reducing the delay.
- Packet switching does not require dedicated communication link, and shares the underlying resources. Packet switching is commonly used for computer networks, including the Internet.

9.6 COMPUTER NETWORK

A *computer network* is an interconnection of two or more computers that are able to exchange information. The computers may be connected via any data communication link, like copper wires, optical fibers, communication satellites, or radio links. The computers connected to the network may be personal computers or large main frames. The computers in a network may be located in a room, building, city, country, or anywhere in the world.

9.6.1 Network Types

Computer network is broadly classified into three types—(1) Local Area Network (LAN), (2) Metropolitan Area Network (MAN), and (3) Wide Area Network (WAN). The different network types are distinguished from each other based on the following characteristics:

- Size of the network
- Transmission Technology
- Networking Topology

The *size of network* refers to the area over which the network is spread. *Transmission technology* refers to the transmission media used to connect computers on the network and the transmission protocols used for connecting. *Network topology* refers to the arrangement of computers on the network or the shape of the network. The following subsections discuss the three types of networks and their characteristics.

9.6.1.1 Local Area Network

LAN (Figure 9.19) is a computer network widely used for local communication. LAN connects computers in a small area like a room, building, office or a campus spread up to a few kilometers. They are privately owned networks, with a purpose to share resources and to exchange information.

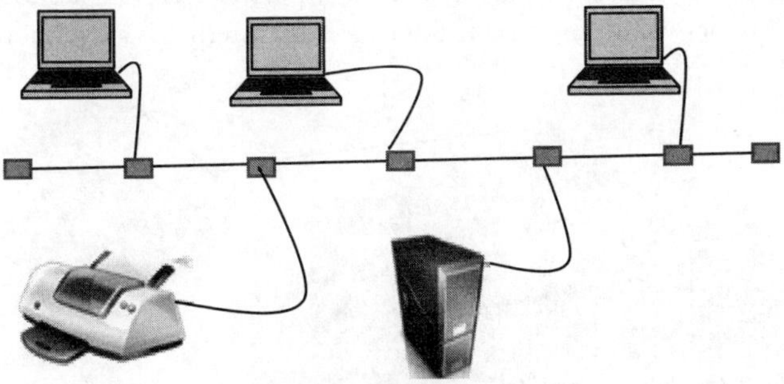

Figure 9.19 LAN

The computers in a LAN are generally connected using cables. LAN is different from other types of network since they share the network. The different computers connected to a LAN take turns to send data packets over the cables connecting them. This requires coordination of the use of the network. Some of the transmission protocols used in LAN are Ethernet, Token bus, and FDDI ring.

Star, Bus, and Ring are some of the common LAN networking topologies. LAN runs at a speed of 10 Mbps to 100 Mbps and has low delays. A LAN based on WiFi wireless network technology is called *Wireless Local Area Network (WLAN).*

9.6.1.2 Metropolitan Area Network

MAN (Figure 9.20) is a computer network spread over a city. Cable television network is an example of MAN. The computers in a MAN are connected using coaxial cables or fiber optic cables. MAN also connects several LAN spread over a city.

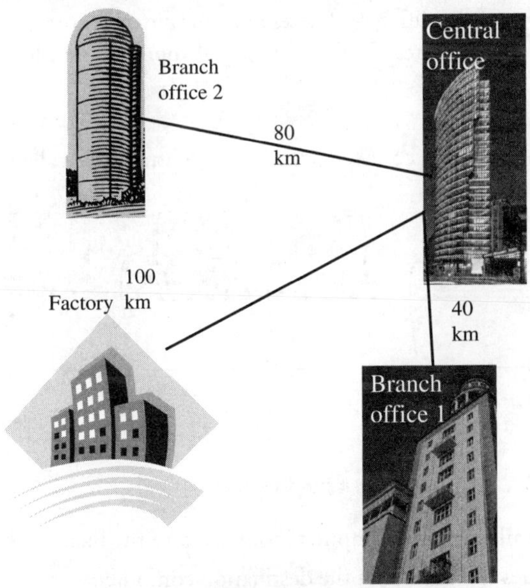

Figure 9.20 MAN

9.6.1.3 Wide Area Network

WAN is a network that connects computers over long distances like cities, countries, continents, or worldwide (Figure 9.21). WAN uses public, leased, or private communication links to spread over long distances. WAN uses telephone lines, satellite link, and radio link to connect. The need to be able to connect any number of computers at any number of sites, results in WAN technologies to be different from the LAN technologies. WAN network must be able to grow itself. Internet is a common example of WAN.

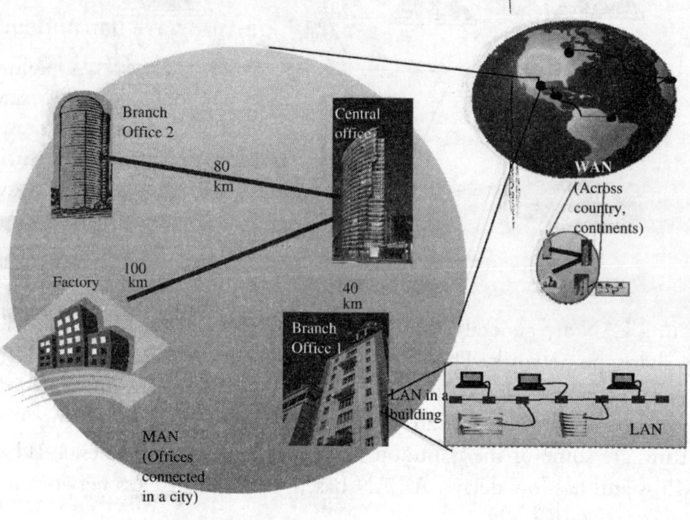

Figure 9.21 LAN, MAN and WAN

9.6.2 LAN Topologies

There are different types of network topologies that are used in a network. The network topologies differ in the structure or the layout of the different devices and computers connected to the network. The three topologies commonly used in LAN are—Bus topology, Star topology, and Ring topology.

9.6.2.1 Bus Topology

- All devices on the network are connected through a central cable called a Bus (Figure 9.22).

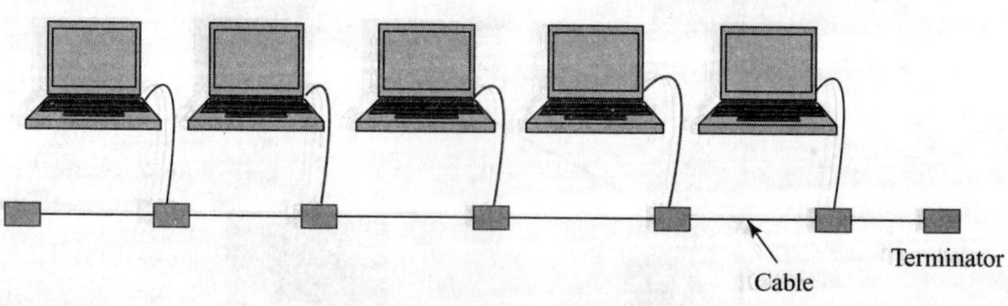

Figure 9.22 Bus topology

- The data signal is available to all computers connected to the bus.
- The data signal carries the address of the destination computer.

- Each computer on the network checks the destination address as the data signal travels through the bus. The computer whose address matches makes a copy of the signal and converts it into data. The data signal on the bus does not get destroyed and still transmits along the bus, and is finally absorbed by the terminator attached to the end of the network.
- It is good for connecting 15–20 computers.
- A single coaxial cable is generally used in bus topology, to which the computers or devices are connected.
- Ethernet is a commonly used protocol in networks connected by bus topology.

9.6.2.2 Ring Topology

- All devices in the network are connected in the form of a ring.
- Each device has a receiver and transmitter to receive the data signals and to send them to the next computer, respectively.
- Ring network does not have terminated ends, thus data signals travel in a circle.
- Ring topology (Figure 9.23) uses token passing method to provide access to the devices in the network.
- The computers or devices are connected to the ring using twisted pair cables, coaxial cables or optic fibers.
- The protocols used to implement ring topology are Token Ring and Fiber Distributed Data Interface (FDDI).

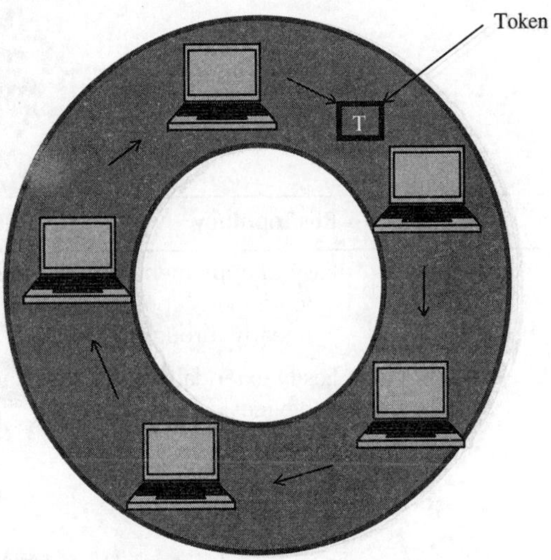

Figure 9.23 Ring topology

9.6.2.3 Star Topology

- All devices are connected through a central link forming a star-like structure.
- The central link is a hub or switch. The computers are connected to the hub or switch using twisted pair cables, coaxial cables or optic fibers.
- Star topology (Figure 9.24) is the most popular topology to connect computer and devices in network.
- The data signal is transmitted from the source computer to the destination computer via the hub or switch.
- The common protocols used in star topology are Ethernet, Token Ring, and LocalTalk.

In addition to the bus, ring, and star topologies, there are complex topologies like the tree topology, and the mesh topology used for networking in LAN. Table 9.1 lists the advantages and disadvantages of the different LAN network topologies.

9.6.3 Communication Protocol

Data networks are a combination of software and hardware components. The hardware includes transmission media, devices, and transmission equipments. The software allows the hardware to interact with one

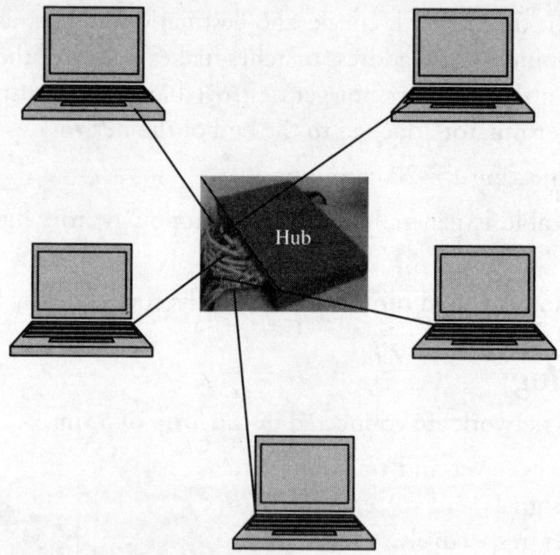

Figure 9.24 Star topology

	Bus Topology	Ring Topology	Star Topology
Advantages	Easy to implement (computers connected linearly through cable) Easily extendable (new devices can be easily added) Not very expensive	All computers in the ring have equal access to the ring Each computer in the ring gets an opportunity to transmit data.	Failure of a device attached to the network does not halt the complete network;only that device is down. Easily extendable—by attaching a new device to the hub or switch. No disturbance when a new device is added or removed. Easy to troubleshoot the network.
Disadvantages	If the cable gets damaged, the whole network collapses A computer can transmit data only if network is not being utilized Network slows down if additional computers are connected to the network.	Adding or removing devices is difficult and affects the complete network Failure in a node or the cable breaks down the ring and thus the network. The length of the ring and the number of nodes are limited	It is costly, since each device on the network is attached by a single cable to the central link. Failure of the hub or switch breaks the complete network.

Table 9.1 *Advantages and disadvantages of network topologies*

another and provide access to the network. The application programs that use the network do not interact with the hardware directly. The application programs interact with the protocol software, which follows the rules of the protocol while communicating. *Protocol* is a network term used to indicate the set of rules used by a network for communication.

All the computers connected to the network use the protocol software. The network communication protocol is organized as a stack of layers with one layer built upon the other. Each layer has a specific function and interacts with the layers above and below it. The outgoing data from a computer connected to the network passes down through each layer and the incoming data passes up through each layer. The corresponding layers on the different machines are called *peers*. The peers interact with each other using the protocol.

The International Standards Organization (ISO) has developed a seven-layer reference model for data networks, known as Open System Interconnection (OSI) model. The OSI model specifies the functions of each layer. It does not specify how the protocol needs to be implemented. It is independent of the underlying architecture of the system and is thus an open system. The seven layers of the OSI model are—(1) Physical layer, (2) Data link layer, (3) Network layer, (4) Transport layer, (5) Session layer, (6) Presentation layer, and (7) Application layer. The functions of the different layers (Figure 9.25) are as follows:

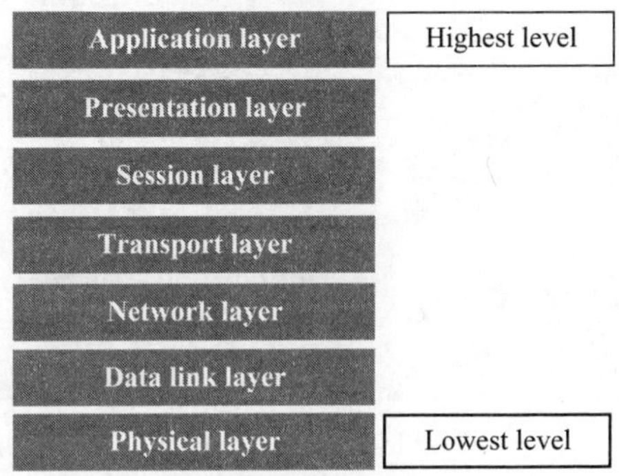

Figure 9.25 OSI model

- **Physical Layer**—This layer specifies the basic network hardware. Some of the characteristics defined in the specification are—interface between transmission media and device, encoding of bits, bit rate, error detection parameters, network topology, and the mode of transmission (duplex, half-duplex or simplex).
- **Data Link Layer**—This layer specifies the functions required for node-to-node transmission without errors. It specifies the organization of data into frames, error detection in frames during transmission, and how to transmit frames over a network.
- **Network Layer**—The network layer specifies the assignment of addresses (address structure, length of address etc.) to the packets and forwarding of packets to the destination i.e. routing.
- **Transport Layer**—It specifies the details to handle reliable transfer of data. It handles end-to-end error control and flow control, breaking up data into frames and reassembling the frames.
- **Session Layer**—The session layer maintains a session between the communicating devices. It includes specifications for password and authentication, and maintaining synchronization between the sender and the receiver.
- **Presentation Layer**—This layer specifies the presentation and representation of data. Its functions include translation of the representation of the data into an identifiable format at the receiver end, encryption, and decryption of data etc.
- **Application Layer**—This layer specifies how an application uses a network. It deals with the services attached to the data. It contains the protocols used by users like HTTP, protocol for file transfer and electronic mail.

Each layer at the sender's side transforms the data according to the function it handles. For this it attaches headers to the data. At the receiver's side, the corresponding layer applies the inverse of the transformation that has been applied at the source (Figure 9.26). As an example, if the Data link layer at the sender's side adds an error detection code to the frame, then at the receiver's side, the Data link layer verifies the error detection code and removes it from the frame before passing it to the next higher level, i.e. the Network layer.

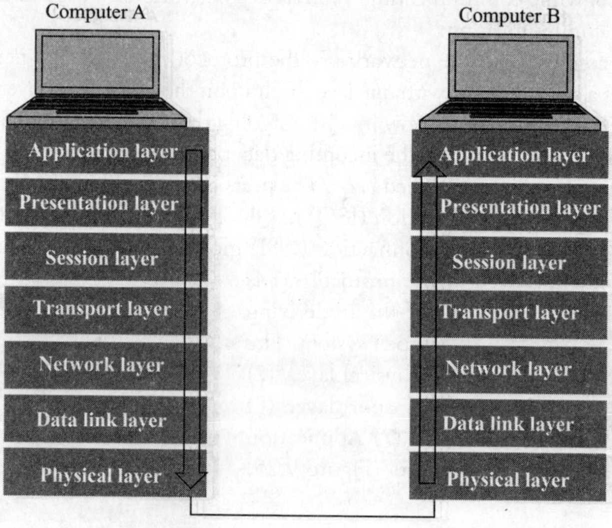

Figure 9.26 Data transfer in OSI model

The 7-layer ISO reference model forms a framework for communication between the devices attached to the network. For different networks, the number of layers and their functions may vary. For example, the TCP/IP Internet protocol is organized into five layers. The X.25 Wide Area Network protocol (the first public data network) provides connectivity to Public Switched Telephone Network (PSTN) network and has three layers.

9.6.4 Network Devices

The cables are used to transmit data in the form of signals from one computer to another. But cables cannot transmit signals beyond a particular distance. Moreover there is a need to connect multiple computers and devices. A *concentrator* is a device having two or more ports to which the computers and other devices can be connected. A concentrator has two main functions—(1) it amplifies the signal to restore the original strength of the signal, and (2) it provides an interface to connect multiple computers and devices in a network. Repeater, hub, switch, bridge, and gateway are examples of network connecting devices.

Two or more LANs using different protocols may not be able to communicate with the computers attached to their network. For example, a LAN connected using Ethernet may not be able to communicate with a LAN connected using Token Ring. Bridge, Router, and Gateway are devices used to interconnect LANs.

9.6.4.1 Network Interface Card

- A Network Interface Card (NIC) is a hardware device through which the computer connects to a network.
- NIC is an expansion card (Figure 9.27), it can be either ISA or PCI, or can be on-board integrated on a chipset. NIC has an appropriate connector to connect the cable to it. NIC for different LAN are different (NIC for token ring is different from NIC for Ethernet).

Figure 9.27 NIC card

- NIC work at both the data link layer and physical layer of the OSI reference model.
- At the data link layer, NIC converts the data packets into data frames, adds the Media ACcess address (MAC address) to data frames. At the physical layer, it converts the data into signals and transmits it across the communication medium. The MAC address is a globally unique hardware number present on the NIC and is specified by the NIC manufacturer.
- NIC depends upon the configuration of the computer, unlike hub or switches that perform independently.

9.6.4.2 Repeater

- Repeaters (Figure 9.28) are used to extend LAN. It has only two ports and can connect only two segments of a network. Multiple repeaters can be used to connect more segments. (Segment is a logical section of the same network).

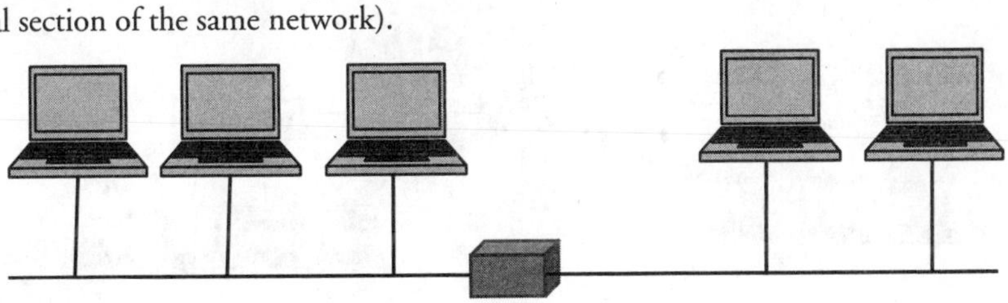

Figure 9.28 Repeater

- Repeaters operate at the Physical layer of OSI reference model.
- They are useful when computers in a network are located far away from each other.

- Repeaters amplify the signal so that the signal is as strong as the original signal. They can thus extend the reach of a network.
- Repeaters cannot be used if multiple computers need to be interconnected or multiple segments need to be interconnected.
- Repeaters cannot identify complete frames. Thus, in addition to the valid transmissions from one segment to another, repeater also propagates any electrical interference occurring on a segment to other segment.

9.6.4.3 *Hub*

- It is like a repeater with multiple ports. But, hub does not amplify the incoming signal.
- Hub (Figure 9.29) operates at the Physical layer of OSI reference model, hence treats data as a signal.

Figure 9.29 Hub

- Hubs are used to connect multiple segments of the same network.
- Hubs are also used to connect computers to network that use Star topology.
- The port on the hubs can also be used to connect another hub, switch, bridge or router.
- Hubs increase the network traffic because they broadcast data to all the devices connected to all the ports of the hub.
- It is preferable to use a hub in a small LAN having about 8-10 computers connected to it.

9.6.4.4 *Bridge*

- Bridge (Figure 9.30) is used to connect two LAN segments like a repeater; it forwards complete and correct frames to the other segment. It does not forward any electrical interference signals to the other segment.

Figure 9.30 Bridge

- Bridge forwards a copy of the frame to the other segment, only if necessary. If a frame is meant for a computer on the same segment, then bridge does not forward a copy of the frame to other segment.

- Bridge connects networks that use different protocol at the Data Link Layer. The frame format of data in the two networks is different. The bridge converts the frame format before transmitting data from one network to another, with translation software included in the bridge.
- A bridge is also used to divide a network into separate broadcast domains to reduce network traffic while maintaining connectivity between the computers.

9.6.4.5 Switch

- Like hub, switch also connects multiple computers in a network or different segments of the same network. A hub simulates a single segment that is shared by all computers attached to it (hub transmits the data to all computers attached to it). In a hub, at most two computers can interact with each other at a given point of time. However, in a switch each computer attached to a switch has a simulated LAN segment.
- Switches (Figure 9.31) work at the Data Link Layer of the OSI reference model. Hence, switches consider data as frames and not as signals.

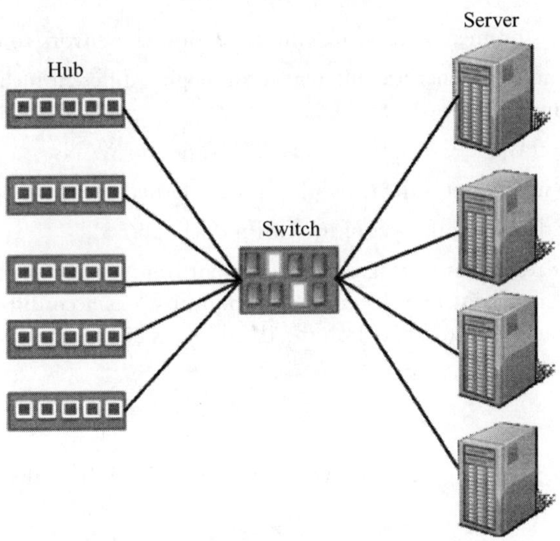

Figure 9.31 Switch

- A data frame contains the MAC address of the destination computer. A switch receives a signal as a data frame from a source computer on a port, checks the MAC address of the frame, forwards the frame to the port connected to the destination computer having the same MAC addresses, reconverts the frame back into signal and sends to the destination computer. (*Switching* is a technique that reads the MAC address of the data frame and forwards the data to the appropriate port). Switches, thus, regenerate the signals.
- Since a switch does not broadcast data, but sends the data from the source computer to the destination computer, a half of the computers attached to the switch can send data at the same time.
- Switch is also referred to as a multi-port bridge. In general, bridges are used to extend the distance of the network, and switches are primarily used for their filtering capabilities to create a multiple and smaller virtual LAN (a LAN segment can be connected to each port of the switch) from a single large LAN.

9.6.4.6 Router

- Router (Figure 9.32) is used to connect heterogeneous networks.

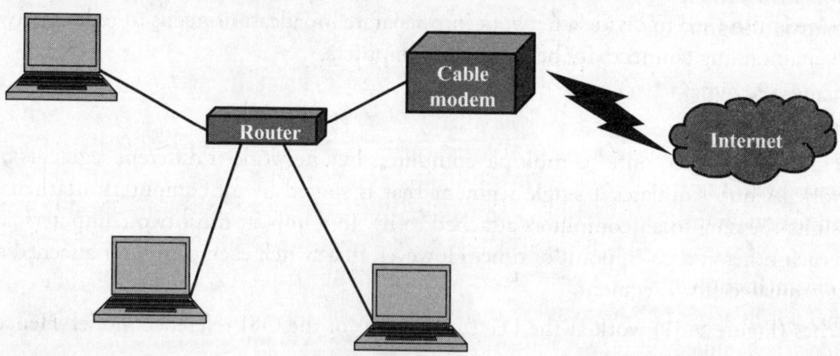

Figure 9.32 Router

- A router has a processor, memory, and I/O interface for each network to which it connects.
- A router connects networks that use different technologies, different media, and physical addressing schemes or frame formats.
- A router can connect two LANs, a LAN and a WAN, or two WANs.
- A router is used to interconnect the networks in the Internet.
- Router operates at the Network layer of the OSI model (layer 3).
- Physically, a router resembles a bridge, but is different from a bridge. A router determines which way is the shortest or fastest in a network, and routes packets accordingly. Since it works at the Network layer, it moves packets based on the IP addresses etc. In contrast, a bridge connects two LANs almost permanently.

9.6.4.7 Gateway

- *Gateway* (Figure 9.33) is a generic term used to represent devices that connect two dissimilar networks.

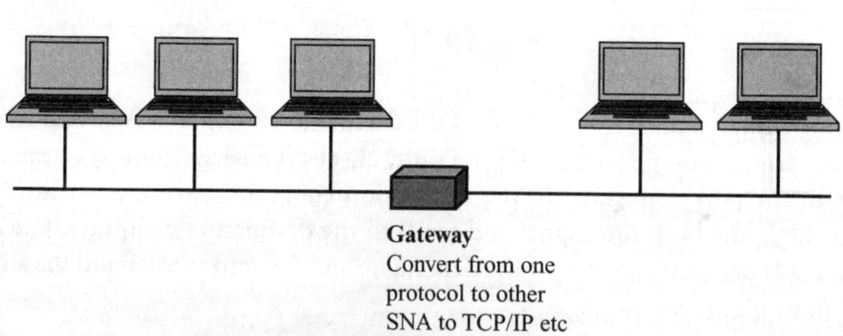

Figure 9.33 Gateway

- A gateway at the transport layer converts protocols among communications networks. It can accept a packet formatted for one protocol and convert it to a packet formatted for another protocol, before forwarding it. An application gateway can translate messages from one format to the other.

- A gateway can be implemented in hardware, software, or in both hardware and software. Generally, gateway is implemented by software installed within a router.

The network connecting devices—repeater and hub operate at the physical layer, bridge and switch operate at the data link layer, and the router operates at the network layer of the OSI model.

9.7 WIRELESS NETWORKING

Wireless technology, as the name suggests, is used to establish a wire-free connection or communication between two or more devices. In contrast to the wired technology where data is encoded as electric current and signals travel through wires, in wireless technology data is encoded on electromagnetic waves that travel through air. The wireless technology is used for broadcasting in radio and television communication, for communication using mobile phones and pagers, for connecting components of computers using Bluetooth technology, for Internet connection using Wi-Fi, Wireless LAN, PDA, and in remote controls for television, doors etc.

- Wireless network is a computer network connected wirelessly. The communication is done through a wireless media like radio waves, infrared or Bluetooth.
- The wireless networks have two main components—the wireless access points that include the transmitter along with the area it can cover, and the wireless clients like mobile handsets, laptops with Ethernet cards etc.
- The access point receives data frames from the computers attached to it wirelessly, checks the frames, and transmits them to their destination. The coverage area of a transmitter depends on the output power of the transmitter, its location, and the frequency used to transmit the data. Higher frequencies require a clear line of sight as compared to lower frequencies.
- The speed of wireless connection is determined by the distance of the wireless client device from the access point, the obstruction-free path (walls, trees etc.), interference, and the number of users using the network at a given time.
- Wireless networks can be divided into three categories based on their use:
    - *Bluetooth technology* to connect the different components of the computer in a room, a small office or home.
    - *Wireless LAN* is used to connect computers and devices wirelessly in a LAN, for example, different computers or devices in an office or campus.
    - *Wireless WAN* is used to connect wide area systems, for example access to Internet via mobile devices like cell phone, PDAs and laptops.

9.7.1 Bluetooth Technology

The different components of the computer like the keyboard, printer, monitor etc., are connected to the computer case via wires. Bluetooth technology (Figure 9.34) is used to connect the different components wirelessly. A printer placed in a room may be connected to a computer placed in a different room using Bluetooth technology. Using Bluetooth does away with the wires required to connect the components to the computer and allows portability of components within a small area lying within the Bluetooth range.

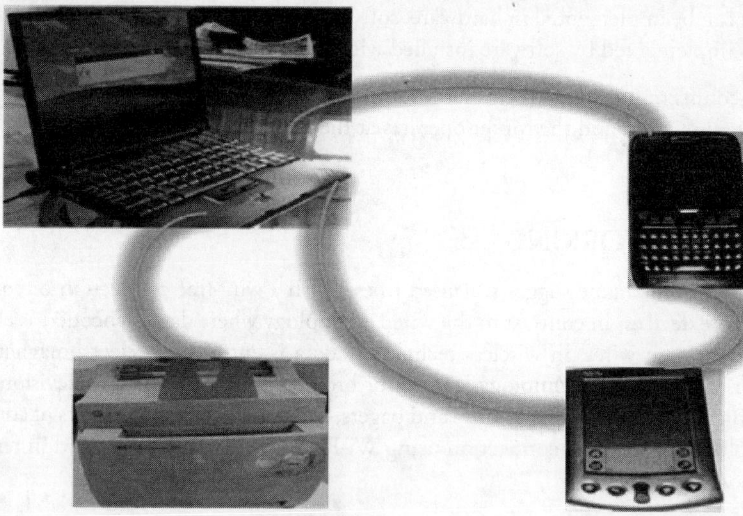

Figure 9.34 Bluetooth

9.7.2 Wireless LAN

Wireless LAN (Figure 9.35) has some benefits over the wired LANs. In wireless LAN, there is flexibility to move the computers and devices within the network. It can connect computers where cabling is not possible. It is easy to expand by using an access point. Since no physical medium is required, wireless LANs are easy to install. Since data is transmitted using radio or infrared waves, there is no attenuation or distortion of the signal due to electromagnetic interference. Wireless LANs are used at home to connect devices on different floors or to set up a home network (Figure 9.36), to provide connectivity in public places like airports, railway stations, college campus, and hotels etc., where traveling users can access the network. Wireless LANs can also be connected to a WAN thus providing access to Internet to the user. IEEE 802.11 is a standard for wireless LAN.

Figure 9.35 (a) Wireless ethernet bridge (b) Wireless antenna in a desktop

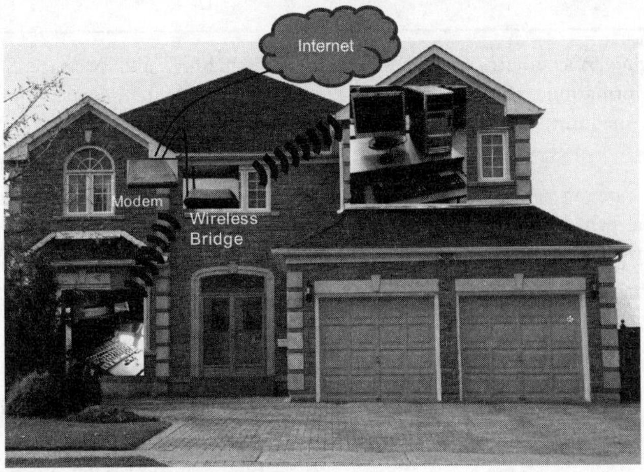

Figure 9.36 Computers at different floors in a house connected by wireless LAN

9.7.3 Wireless WAN

The radio network used for cellular telephone is an example of wireless WAN (Figure 9.37). Wireless WANs allow the users to access the Internet via their mobile devices. This provides flexibility to the user to access the Internet from any location where wireless connectivity exists.

Figure 9.37 Wireless WAN

Almost all wireless networks are connected to the wired network at the back-end to provide access to Internet. Wireless networks also offer many challenges, like, the compatibility among different standards promoted by different companies, congested networks in case of low bandwidth, the high infrastructure and service cost, data security, battery storage capability of wireless device, and health risk.

SUMMARY

- *Networking of computers* facilitates resource sharing, sharing of information, and, can be used as a communication medium, and for backup and support.
- The *transmission of data* can be via guided media like twisted pair, coaxial pair, optical fibers or as radio transmission, microwave transmission, and satellite transmission.
- A *twisted pair cable* consists of four pairs of twisted copper wires. STP and UTP are the two kinds of twisted pair.
- *Coaxial cable* has an inner conductor that transmits electric signals and an outer conductor as a ground. *Optical fibers* transmit data over large distances. They use light signals.
- Simplex, half-duplex and full-duplex are three *modes of data transmission*. Simplex is uni-directional, half-duplex is bi-directional but one device sends data and other receives it, and, full-duplex is bi-directional and both the devices can send and receive data at the same time.
- *Bandwidth* is the amount of data that can be transferred through the communication medium, in a fixed amount of time. Bandwidth is measured in Hz.
- *Throughput* is the amount of data that is actually transmitted between two computers. It is specified in bps. Throughput is affected by the distance between the connected computers.
- *Analog and digital signals* are the two types of signals that are used for carrying information over a transmission medium.
- *Modulation* is the superimposing of signal carrying data onto the carrier wave. *Demodulation* is segregation of data signal and carrier signal from the modulated carrier wave.
- *Modem* is a device that has both a modulator and a demodulator.
- The combining of multiple signals so that they can be transmitted over a single link of communication medium is called *multiplexing*.
- *Switching* allows different users fair access to the computer network. Packet Switching, Circuit Switching, and Message Switching are the three kinds of switching techniques.
- In *Packet Switching*, the message is broken into small packets and sent over the network. At destination, the received packets are reassembled and the complete message is constructed.
- *Computer Network* is interconnection of two or more computers that can exchange data.
- LAN, MAN, and WAN are the *network types* classified on the basis of the size of network, the transmission technology, and the network topology.
- Bus, Star, and Ring are the three common *LAN topologies*.
- The computers are connected to network via protocol software. *OSI model* is a seven-layer reference model for data networks.
- *Network connecting devices* are required to amplify the signal to restore the original strength of signal, and to provide an interface to connect multiple computers in a network. Repeater, hub, switch, bridge, router, and gateway are network connecting devices.
- *Repeaters* have two ports and can connect two segments of a LAN. Repeaters amplify the signal so that the signal is as strong as the original signal.
- *Bridge* connects two LAN segments and forwards correct frames to the other segment.
- *Hub* is like a repeater with multiple ports. Hub does not amplify the incoming signal.
- In a *switch,* each computer attached to it is a simulated LAN segment.
- *Router* connects networks that use different technologies, different media, and physical addressing schemes or frame formats.
- *Gateway* is a generic term used to represent devices that connect two dissimilar networks.
- *Wireless network* is a computer network connected wirelessly. Bluetooth, wireless LAN, and wireless WAN are the three categories of wireless networks.

KEYWORDS

10 base 2 *170*
10 base 5 *170*
Amplitude Modulation *172*
Analog signal *171*
Asynchronous communication *175*
Attenuation *170*
Bandwidth *170*
Baseband technology *170*
bits per second (bps) *170*
Bluetooth technology *189*
Bridge *186*
Broadband technology *170*
Bus topology *180*
Cat-5 cable *165*
Circuit switching *177*
Coaxial Pair *165*
Computer network *178*
Concentrator *184*
Copper wire *165*
cycles per second (cps) *170*
Data Transmission Media *165*
Demodulation *172*
Demultiplexing *174*
Digital signal *171*
Distortion *170*
Electric signal *171*
Electromagnetic signal *171*
Frequency Division Multiplexing (FDM) *174*
Frequency Modulation *173*
Full-duplex transmission *169*
Gateway *188*
Geosynchronous satellites *168*
Guided media *165*
Half-duplex transmission *169*
Hertz (Hz) *170*
Hub *186*
LAN Topologies *180*
Light signal *165*
Local Area Network (LAN) *178*
Message switching *177*
Metropolitan Area Network (MAN) *178*
Microwave Transmission *168*
Modem *173*
Modulation *172*
Multiplexing *174*
Networking *164*
Network Interface Card (NIC) *184*
Optical fibers *167*
OSI model *183*
Packet *178*
Packet switching *177*
Phase shift Modulation *173*
Radio Frequency (RF) transmission *167*
Radio signal *171*
Repeater *185*
Ring topology *181*
Router *188*
Satellite Transmission *168*
Shielded Twisted Pair (STP) *165*
Signal *171*
Simplex transmission *168*
Star topology *181*
Switch *187*
Synchronous communication *175*
Throughput *170*
Twisted Pair *165*
Unshielded Twisted Pair (UTP) *165*
Wavelength Division Multiplexing (WDM) *174*
Wide Area Network (WAN) *178*
Wireless LAN *189*
Wireless Networking *189*
Wireless WAN *189*

QUESTIONS

Section 9.1–9.3.6

1. Explain the importance of networking.
2. "Networking allows sharing of information and resources". Explain.
3. What do you mean by guided and unguided transmission media?
4. Name two guided transmission media.
5. Name an unguided transmission media.
6. Optical wire is a guided media. True or False.
7. _____ and ______ are the two kinds of twisted pair.
8. Cat-5 cable is a _____ twisted pair.
9. How is coaxial cable different from a twisted pair cable?
10. What are the features of a twisted pair cable?
11. What are the features of a coaxial cable?
12. List the advantages and disadvantages of optical wire over a copper wire.
13. Optical fiber transmits data as _____signals.
14. Coaxial cables transmit data as ______ signals.
15. What are the features of an optical fiber?
16. Describe the following unguided transmission media—(i) RF transmission, (2) Microwave transmission, and (iii) Satellite transmission.
17. What are geosynchronous satellites?

Section 9.4–9.4.2

18. Define: (1) Simplex transmission, (2) Half-duplex transmission, and (3) Full-duplex transmission.

19. Define bandwidth.
20. Define throughput.
21. What is the unit of measuring bandwidth?
22. What is the unit of measuring throughput?
23. What do you mean by broadband technology?
24. "The bandwidth or the throughput is affected by the distance between the connected computers". Explain
25. Define attenuation.
26. Define distortion.

Section 9.4.3–9.4.3.4

27. Define a signal.
28. Which is better to use for data transmission—analog signal or digital signal? Why.
29. What is a carrier wave?
30. Why is modulation needed?
31. Explain modulation and demodulation.
32. What is the purpose of a modem?
33. Name the three kinds of modulation.
34. Define multiplexing and demultiplexing.
35. ______ and _____ are the basic multiplexing techniques.
36. What is the difference between the FDM and WDM multiplexing techniques?
37. Define synchronous and asynchronous transmission.
38. Give an example each of synchronous and asynchronous transmission.

Section 9.5

39. Name the three kinds of switching techniques.
40. Describe briefly the circuit switching and message switching techniques.
41. Define a packet.
42. Which switching technique is most commonly used in computer networks? Why?
43. Explain the working of the packet switching technique.

Section 9.6–9.6.3

44. Define computer network.
45. Name the three types of networks classified on the basis of their size.
46. What do you mean by transmission technology?
47. What do you mean by network topology?
48. Describe briefly the LAN, MAN, and WAN transmission technologies.
49. Name three LAN topologies.
50. List the features of the following LAN topologies—(i) Bus, (ii) Star, and (iii) Ring.
51. Name the protocol(s) used to implement bus, ring and star technologies.
52. List the advantages and disadvantages of each of the LAN technology—Bus, Star, and Ring.
53. What is the need of communication protocol?
54. List the seven layers of the OSI model protocol, in order.
55. How does the OSI seven layer protocol work?
56. Describe briefly the function of each layer of the OSI model.

Section 9.6.4–9.6.4.7

57. Define a concentrator.
58. Name three network connecting devices.
59. What is the purpose of the Network Interface Card?
60. Describe the features of —(i) repeater, (ii) hub, (iii) switch, (iv) bridge, (v) router, and (vi) gateway.
61. Name a device used for connecting two LANs.
62. Name a device used for connecting computers in a LAN.
63. Name a device for connecting two WANs.
64. What is the purpose of a gateway?
65. Name a connecting device, each, that works at (i) physical layer, (ii) data link layer, and (iii) network layer.

Section 9.7

66. How is wireless networking different from wired networking.
67. Explain briefly how the wireless network works.
68. What is the use of Bluetooth technology?
69. _____ is a standard for wireless LAN.
70. What is the use of wireless LAN and wireless WAN.

Extra Questions

71. Give full form of the following abbreviations:

(i) STP	(ii) UTP	(iii) RF
(iv) Hz	(v) bps	(vi) cps
(vii) FDM	(viii) WDM	(ix) LAN

(x) MAN (xi) WAN (xii) ISO
(xiii) OSI (xiv) NIC (xv) MAC
(xvi) PSTN (xv) FDDI

72. Write short notes on:
(a) Importance of Networking
(b) Data transmission guided media
(c) Data transmission unguided media
(d) Twisted Pair
(e) Coaxial cable
(f) Optical Fiber
(g) Modulation and Demodulation
(h) Multiplexing
(i) Packet switching
(j) Network Types
(k) LAN topology
(l) Bus topology
(m) Ring topology
(n) Star topology
(o) OSI model
(p) NIC
(q) Hub
(r) Repeater
(s) Bridge
(t) Switch
(u) Router
(v) Wireless networking

73. Give differences between the following:
(a) Guided media and Unguided media
(b) STP and UTP
(c) Optical fibers and copper wires
(d) Bandwidth and Throughput
(e) Modulation and Demodulation
(f) Multiplexing and Demultiplexing
(g) Asynchronous and Synchronous Transmission
(h) Message switching and Packet switching
(i) Bus, Ring and Star LAN topologies
(j) Repeater and Bridge
(k) Hub and Switch
(l) Router and Bridge

THE INTERNET AND INTERNET SERVICES 10

Contents

- History of Internet—TCP/IP, Internet applications, WWW, browser
- Internetworking protocol—TCP/IP
- Internet architecture—Client, local ISP, regional ISP, backbone
- Managing the Internet—ISOC, IAB, IETF, IESG, IRTF, IANA, InterNIC, W3C
- Connecting to Internet
- Internet connections—Dial-up access, leased line, ISDN, DSL, cable modem
- Internet address
- Internet services
    - WWW—Web browser, URL, Internet search engines, WWW development languages
    - Electronic mail—E-mail address, e-mail message format, e-mail services (application based e-mail, webmail), how email works (client-server model)
    - File transfer protocol—How FTP works (client-server model)
    - Terminal network
    - News
    - Internet relay chat
- Uses of Internet

Why this chapter

Every one of you has heard of the Internet and most of you would have used it. You connect to the Internet, maybe, from your home, school, college, or a cyber café. Once connected, you may browse the WWW, use the e-mail facility or chat with a friend. Internet is considered as an important part of the using of the computer. The purpose of this chapter is to introduce you to the basics of the Internet and the services provided by the Internet.

10.1 INTRODUCTION

In the previous chapter, we discussed about the computer networks. The computers interconnected by LAN, MAN, and WAN are able to exchange information, within their networks, i.e. a computer connected to one network is able to exchange information with another computer connected to the same network. However, a computer connected to a particular network may need to interact with a computer connected to a different network.

Internet is defined as an interconnection of networks. Internet allows computers on different kinds of networks to interact with each other. Any two computers, often having different software and hardware, can exchange information over the Internet, as long as they obey the technical rules of Internet communication. The exchange of information may be among connected computers located anywhere, like military and research institutions, different kinds of organizations, banks, educational institutions (elementary schools, high schools, colleges), public libraries, commercial sectors etc.

This chapter discusses the history of Internet, the Internet protocol, the Internet architecture and connecting to the Internet. It also discusses the addressing on Internet and some of the services provided by the Internet.

10.2 HISTORY OF INTERNET

Internet has evolved from a research prototype project to a full-grown commercial computer communication system. The growth of Internet can be discussed in three steps, as follows:

- Internetworking Protocol—Transmission Control Protocol/Internet Protocol (TCP/IP) in 1970s
- Usenet groups and Electronic mail in 1980s
- World Wide Web in 1990s

The networking of computers has its origin at the US Department of Defense Advanced Research Projects Agency (DARPA).

- During 1970's DARPA developed the ARPANET as a WAN to connect different computers and later to connect computers on different networks (Internetworking). Internetworking became the focus of research at ARPA and led to the emergence of Internet. During their research, DARPA set up design goals for themselves, which included—(1) the ability to interconnect different types of network, (2) to connect through alternate paths if some path gets destroyed, and (3) to support applications of various types like audio, video, text etc.
- Based on the design goals, a protocol named *Transmission Control Protocol/Internet Protocol (TCP/IP)* was developed for computer communication (*Protocol* is a network term used to indicate the set of rules used by a network for communication). TCP/IP has become the protocol for Internet.
- In late 1970s, the US National Science Foundation (NSF) designed a successor to ARPANET, called NSFNET, which was open for use to all university research groups, libraries and museums. This allowed scientists across the country to share data and interact with each other for their research projects. Internet grew exponentially when ARPANET was interconnected with NSFNET.
- In 1980s, many Internet applications like electronic mail, newsgroups, file transfer facility and remote login were developed. The *Electronic mail* facility allowed users to compose, send, and receive messages. Users having common interests could exchange messages using forums like *Newsgroups*. The *Telnet* command allowed users to login to a remote computer. The *File Transfer Protocol* program was used to copy files from one computer to another on the Internet.
- In the early 1990s, a new application World Wide Web (WWW) changed the way in which Internet was used. *WWW* is a system of creating, organizing, and linking documents, and was created by British scientist Tim Berners Lee. A protocol based on hypertext was developed that allowed the documents and content on WWW to be connected via hyperlink.
- In 1993, Marc Andreessen at the University of Illinois developed the *Mosaic browser.* The WWW along with the browser made it possible to set up number of web pages that may consist of text, pictures or sound, and with link to other pages.

Internet and WWW which are interconnection of networks, and interconnection of documents and resources, respectively, has wired the whole world together.

10.3 INTERNETWORKING PROTOCOL

- TCP/IP is the communication protocol for the Internet.
- The TCP/IP protocol has two parts: TCP and IP.
- Transmission Control Protocol (*TCP*) provides reliable transport service, i.e. it ensures that messages sent from sender to receiver are properly routed and arrive intact at the destination.
- TCP converts messages into a set of packets at the source, which are then reassembled back into messages at the destination. For this, TCP operates with the *packet switching* technique, which is described as follows:
  - The message is divided into small packets.
  - Each packet contains address, sequencing information, and error control information.
  - The address is used to route the packet to its destination.
  - Since multiple users can send or receive information over the same communication line, the packets can arrive out of order at the destination. The sequencing information in the packet is used to reassemble the packets in order, at their destination.
  - The error control information is used to check that the packet arrived at the destination is the same as that sent from the source (i.e. has not got corrupted)
- Internet Protocol (*IP*) allows different computers to communicate by creating a network of networks.
- IP handles the dispatch of packets over the network.
- It handles the addressing of packets, and ensures that a packet reaches its destination traveling through multiple networks with multiple standards.

The computers connected to Internet may be personal computers or mainframes; the computers could have a slow or fast CPU, small or large memory, connected to different networks having slow or fast speed. TCP/IP protocol makes it possible for any pair of computers connected to Internet to communicate, despite their hardware differences.

10.4 THE INTERNET ARCHITECTURE

Internet is a network of interconnected networks and is designed to operate without a central control. If a portion of the network fails, connection is made through alternative paths available. The architecture of Internet is hierarchical in nature. A brief description of the architecture of Internet is as follows:

- **Client** (user of computer) at home or in a LAN network is at the lowest level in hierarchy.
- Local **Internet Service Provider (ISP)** is at the next higher level.
  - An *ISP* is an organization that has its own computers connected to the Internet and provides facility to individual users to connect to Internet through their computers.
  - Local ISP is the local telephone company located in the telephone switching office, where the telephone of client terminates. Examples of local ISP in India are Bharat Sanchar Nigam Ltd. (BSNL), Mahanagar Telephone Nigam Ltd. (MTNL), and Airtel.
  - The client calls local ISP using a modem or Network Interface Card.
- **Regional ISP** is next in the hierarchy. The local ISP is connected to regional ISP.
  - A *router* is a special hardware system consisting of a processor, memory, and an I/O interface, used for the purpose of interconnecting networks. A router can interconnect networks having different technologies, different media, and physical addressing schemes or frame formats.

- The regional ISP connects the local ISP's located in various cities via routers.
- If the packet received by regional ISP is for a client connected to this regional ISP, then the packet is delivered; otherwise, packet is sent to the regional ISP's backbone.

⊙ **Backbone** is at top of the hierarchy.

- Backbone operators are large corporations like AT&T which have their own server farms connected to the backbone. There are many backbones existing in the world.
- The backbone networks are connected to Regional ISP's with a large number of routers through high speed fiber-optics.
- Network Access Point (NAP) connects different backbones, so that packets travel across different backbones.
- If a packet at the backbone is for a regional ISP connected to this backbone, the packet is sent to the closest router to be routed to local ISP and then to its destination; otherwise, packet is sent to other backbone via NAP. The packet traverses different backbones until it reaches the backbone of regional ISP for which it is destined.

The Internet hierarchy is shown in Figure 10.1.

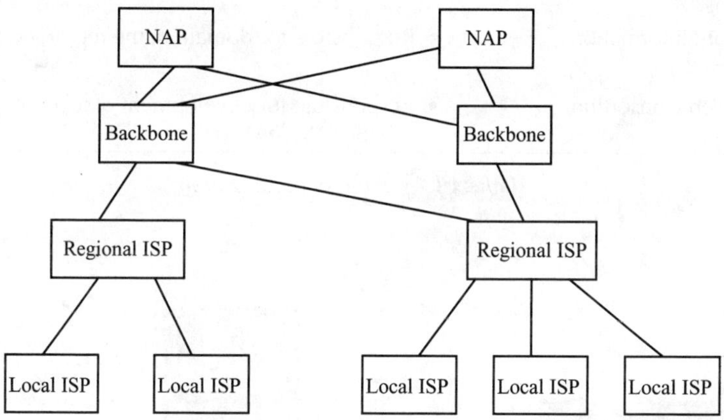

Figure 10.1 Internet hierarchy

10.5 MANAGING THE INTERNET

Internet is not controlled by any one person or an organization. A number of organizations manage the Internet. Some of the governing bodies of the Internet and their functions are shown in Table 10.1.

10.6 CONNECTING TO INTERNET

To be able to connect your computer to the Internet, you require—(1) a TCP/IP enabled computer, (2) web browser software, (3) an account with an ISP, (4) a telephone line, and (5) a modem or Network Interface Card (NIC) to connect the telephone line to the computer (Figure 10.2).

A *modem* is a device that connects a computer to Internet. A *Network Interface Card or NIC* is a device that is required to connect a computer to Internet via a LAN or high-speed Internet connection like cable modem or Digital Subscriber Line (DSL). A *web browser* is a software that allows the user to view information on WWW. WWW is a large-scale, on-line repository of information that the users search using the web browser. Internet Explorer and Netscape Navigator are examples of web browser.

Governing Bodies of Internet	Functions
Internet Society (ISOC)	• Provides information about Internet • Responsible for development of standards and protocols related to Internet
Internet Architecture Board (IAB)	• Advisory group of ISOC • Responsible for development of Internet architecture
Internet Engineering Task Force (IETF)	• Community of network designers, operators, vendors, and researchers • Responsible for evolution of Internet • Open to all individuals
Internet Engineering Steering Group (IESG)	• Reviews standards developed by IETF
Internet Research Task Force (IRTF)	• Focuses on research towards the future of Internet (Internet protocol, architecture etc.)
Internet Assigned Number Authority (IANA)	• Allots IP address to organizations and individuals
Internet Network Information Center (InterNIC)	• Responsible for domain name registration
World Wide Web Consortium (W3C)	• Responsible for development of technologies for World Wide Web

Table 10.1 *Internet organizations*

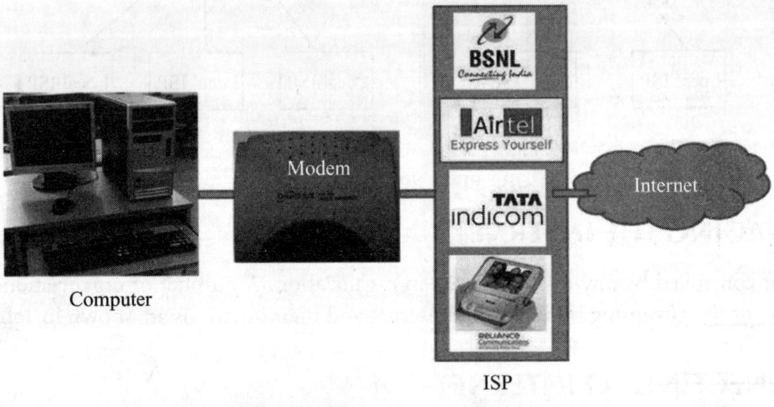

Figure 10.2 Connecting to Internet

10.7 INTERNET CONNECTIONS

The ISPs provide Internet connections of different types. Bandwidth and cost are the two factors that help you (the user) in deciding which Internet connection to use. *Bandwidth* is the amount of data that can be transferred through a communication medium in a fixed amount of time. The speed of Internet access depends on the bandwidth. The speed of Internet access increases with the increase in bandwidth. ISPs offer low speed Internet connection like Dial-up connection, and high-speed Internet connection called broadband connection. Broadband are the services with more bandwidth than standard telephone service. DSL, Cable modem, and Integrated Services Digital Network are some of the existing broadband connections, each, having a different bandwidth and cost. Let's now discuss about some of the Internet connections that are nowadays available for Internet access.

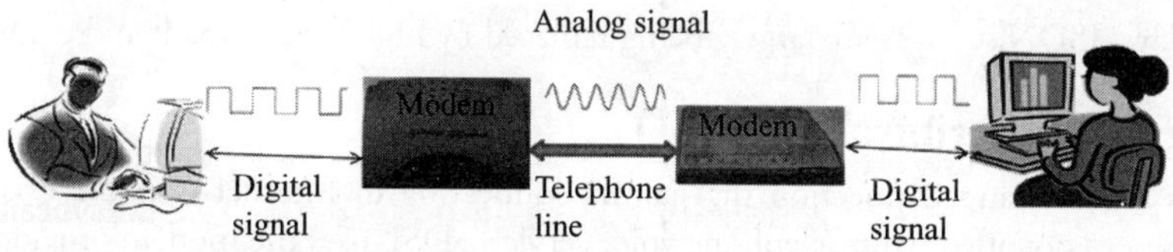

Figure 10.3 Communication via telephone line

10.7.1 Dial-up Access

- Dial-up access is a method of connecting to the Internet using an existing telephone line (Figure 10.3). When your computer is connected to the Internet, you cannot receive voice telephone calls on this telephone line during that time.
- In Dial-up access, you are assigned an account on the server of ISP along with some storage space on the disk of server. For example *agoel@vsnl.com* is an account with an ISP named VSNL. You are also assigned a user-id and password.
- You connect to Internet by dialing-up one of the computers of ISP. For this, you use a telephone number provided by ISP and connect via a 56 Kbps modem. The computer that dials-up is the *client or remote machine,* and the computer of ISP is the *server or host.*
- The client enters the user-id and password, and gets connected to the Internet via the ISP.

10.7.2 Leased Line

- Leased line is a dedicated phone line that connects a computer (also known as gateway) to Internet, using special kind of modems. At the other end, the gateway is connected to a large number of computers, which access the Internet via the gateway.
- The gateway forms a domain on Internet, e.g. *niit.com,* which is used to provide connection to the other computers on the Internet to connect to it.
- Leased lines provide reliable and high-speed Internet access.
- The entire bandwidth of leased line is reserved for the traffic between gateway and Internet.
- Leased lines are generally used by large organizations and universities that have their own internal network, and have large number of users.
- The leased lines are on-line, twenty-four hours a day and seven days a week. The leased lines are normally provided on a yearly contract basis. The charges for the leased line are fixed based on many criteria like the bandwidth, number of users etc. The fixed charges do not vary with the actual usage of Internet.

10.7.3 Integrated Services Digital Network (ISDN)

- ISDN is a digital telephone service that can transmit voice, data and control information over an existing single telephone line.
- Internet access is faster using ISDN than Dial-up access.
- ISDN is commonly used for business purposes. You are able to connect a computer, a fax machine or a telephone to a single ISDN line, and also use them simultaneously.
- ISDN is costlier than Dial-up connection. It requires a special phone service and modem.
- Nowadays, ISDN services are largely being replaced by high speed broadband connection.

10.7.4 Digital Subscriber Line (DSL)

- DSL is a broadband connection that allows connecting to Internet over the existing telephone lines. It does not affect your telephone voice services. DSL uses the modem provided by ISP.
- The data transmission speed of DSL ranges from 128Kbps to 8.448 Mbps.
- Originally, telephone lines were designed for carrying human voice and the whole system worked according to this requirement. All frequencies less than 300 Hz and above 3.4kHz were attenuated, since 300Hz to 3.4kHz is the range for human speech to be clearly audible. When using DSL, a different kind of switch is used that does not filter the frequencies, thus making entire frequency available. DSL uses frequency beyond 3.4 kHz for Internet access.
- Asymmetric DSL (ADSL), a variant of DSL, provides high-speed delivery of download data (from Internet to user), than that for upload (from user to Internet), since most users download much more than they upload. Figure 10.4 shows an ADSL modem
- The bandwidth of connecting wire is divided into three bands—(1) 0-25kHz for regular telephone, (2) 25kHz-200kHz for user to Internet (upload), and (3) 250kHz-1MHz for Internet to the user (download). The available bandwidth for each direction for Internet is divided into channels of 4 kHz.
- DSL is almost ten times faster than Dial-up access and is an always-on connection.

Figure 10.4 An ADSL modem

10.7.5 Cable Modem

- The user can connect to the Internet via a cable modem through cable television. The cable modem provides two connections—one for television and other for computer.
- The cable modem sends and receives data through the coaxial cable which connects the cable modem to the cable service provider. Coaxial cables allow transmission of Internet data, audio, and video, and control over its several channels simultaneously. The user can access the Internet and watch television at the same time.
- Like DSL, cable modem provides high-speed Internet connection. However, while using cable modem, the bandwidth is shared by many users. If many users access the Internet simultaneously then the available bandwidth for each of the user reduces.

The type of Internet connection is chosen depending upon the end user's needs and the availability of a connection. Nowadays, in cities, broadband connection is becoming more popular as it is almost ten times faster than dial-up access. For commercial purposes, leased lines and ISDN are the preferred choices. In some areas, broadband connection using a cable modem is widely used.

10.8 INTERNET ADDRESS

A computer connected to the Internet must have a unique address in order to communicate across the Internet. *Internet Protocol (IP) address* is assigned uniquely to every computer connected to the Internet. IP address is provided by the ISP whose services you use to connect your computer to the Internet. IP address is a string of numbers consisting of four parts, where each part is a number between 0 and 255. An IP address looks like 201.54.122.107. Since IP addresses are numeric, it is difficult to remember everyone's IP address. So, instead of numeric IP address, domain name is used.

Domain name is a text name (string of words) corresponding to the numeric IP address of a computer on the Internet. Domain names are used for the convenience of the user. A domain name combines a group of hosts on the Internet (e.g. Yahoo, Google, MSN etc.), and a top level domain. Some examples of top-level domain are as follows:

com—for commercial organizations,

edu—for educational institutions,

net—for gateways and administrative hosts,

org—for non-profit organizations,

co—for companies, and

ac—for academics

Some examples of domain name are *google.com, isoc.org, center.edu and vsnl.net.*

Additionally, top-level domain is also provided based on the two-letter Internet country code. For example, *in* for India, *uk* for United Kingdom, *au* for Australia etc. Example of such domain names are *du.ac.in, ibm.co.in* etc.

In order to translate numeric IP address that identifies a computer on the Internet to a domain name that is convenient for the user to remember, a mapping is needed between the IP addresses and domain names. *Domain Name System (DNS) server* is a computer having a database that stores the IP addresses and their domain names. Whenever a user uses the domain name, DNS translates it into its corresponding IP address, to access the computer on Internet. For example, DNS translates *google.com* to the IP address of the computer that houses Google.

10.9 INTERNET SERVICES

Internet is a huge de-centralized network that connects computers. Every computer connected to the Internet has a unique address, which helps to identify the computer on the Internet uniquely. Over the years, Internet has grown as the biggest network for communication and provides several services to its users. Each service has its own features and uses. Some of the important services provided by Internet are—World Wide Web, electronic mail, news, chat, and discussion groups.

10.9.1 World Wide Web (WWW)

WWW (also called as *Web*) is a large scale, online store of information. It is a system of creating, organizing, and linking of documents. Information is stored on WWW as a collection of documents that are interconnected with each other via links. The interconnected documents may be located on one or more than one computer, worldwide, thus, the name *world wide web.* The features of WWW and terms linked to WWW are given below—

- The documents on web are created in ***hypertext format.*** Hypertext facilitates linking of documents.
- The language used to create a hypertext format document is ***HyperText Markup Language (HTML).*** HTML allows the designer of the document to include text, pictures, video, images, sound, graphics, movies etc., and also to link contents on the same document or different documents using a ***hyperlink.***
- The hypertext format document is transferred on the Web using ***HyperText Transfer Protocol*** *(HTTP).*
- A single hypertext document is called a ***Web page*** (Figure 10.5).
- A group of related web pages is called a ***Web site.*** A web site displays related information on a specific topic (Figure 10.6).

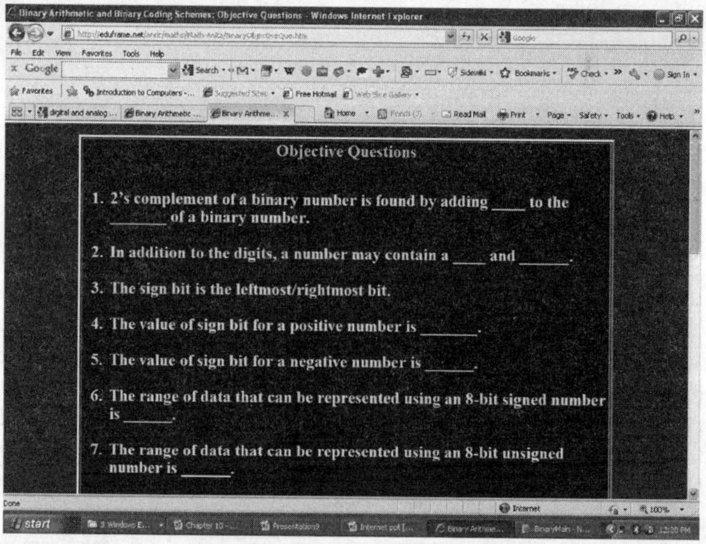

Figure 10.5 A web page

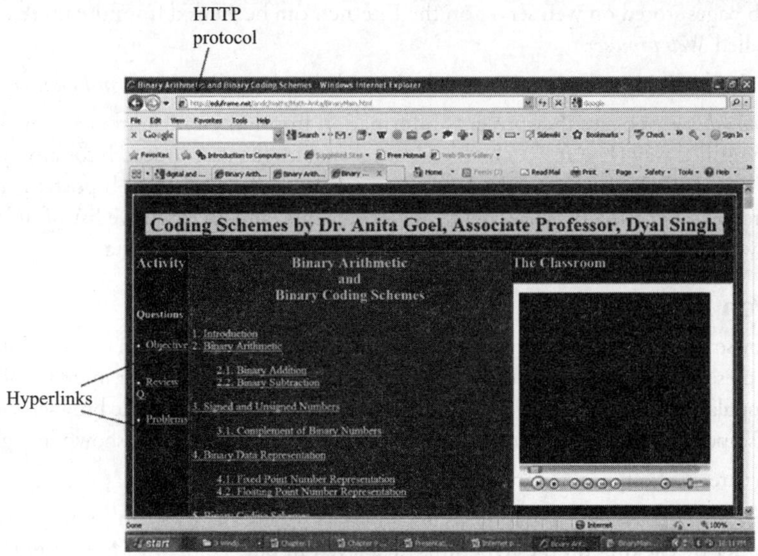

Figure 10.6 A web site

- The first web page or main page of a website is called *Home page.*
- The web pages are stored on the Internet on the *Web Server.* Web servers are host computers that can store thousands of web pages.
- The process of storing a web page on a web server is called *uploading.*
- The process of retrieving a web page from a web server onto the user's computer is *downloading.*

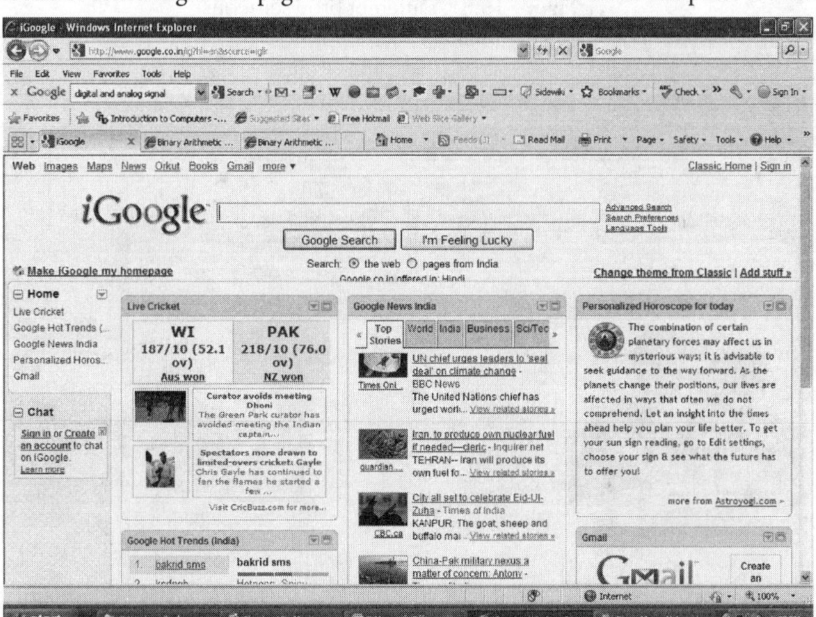

Figure 10.7 Web portal (http://www.google.co.in)

- The web pages stored on web server on the Internet, can be viewed from the user's computer using a tool called *Web browser.*
- Every web page is identified on Internet by its address, also called *Uniform Resource Locator (URL).*
- A *web portal* is a web site that presents information from different sources and makes them available in a unified way (Figure 10.7). A web portal enables the user to search for any type of information from a single location, i.e. the home page of the web portal. A web portal generally consists of a search engine, e-mail service, news, advertisements, and an extensive list of links to other sites etc. www.msn.com and www.google.co.in (*igoogle*) are popular web portals.

10.9.1.1 Web Browser

- Web Browser (or browser) is a software program that extracts information on user request from the Internet and presents it as a web page to the user. It is also referred to as the user interface of the web. Some of the popular web browsers are—Internet Explorer from Microsoft, Mosaic browser, Google's chrome, and Netscape Navigator from Netscape Inc. Some of the browser icons are shown in Figure 10.8.
- Browsers are of two types—graphical browser and text-based browser.
- *Graphical browsers* provide a graphical user interface where the user can jump from one web page to the other by clicking on the hyperlink (displayed in blue color with underline) on a web page. Internet Explorer, Chrome and Mosaic are examples of graphical browsers. (Figure 10.9)

Figure 10.8 Different browser icons

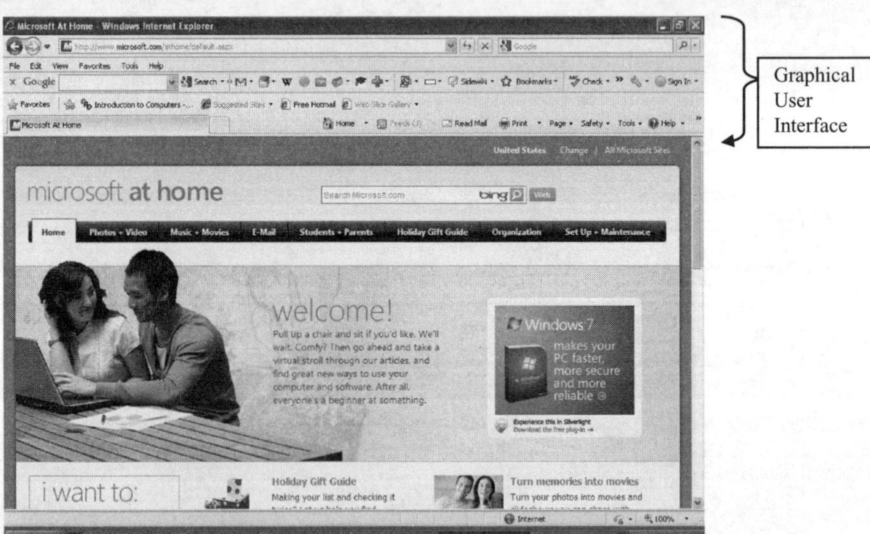

Figure 10.9 A GUI browser (Internet explorer)

- *Text browsers* are used on computers that do not support graphics. Lynx is a text browser.
- The process of using browser to view information on the Internet is known as *Browsing or Surfing.* During browsing, the user can navigate from one web page to another using URLs, hyperlinks, browser navigation tools like forward and back button, bookmarks etc.

10.9.1.2 Uniform Resource Locator (URL)

A web page on the Internet is uniquely identified by its address, called URL. URL is the address on the Internet at which the web page resides (Figure 10.10). The user uses this address to get a web page from the Internet. The general form of URL is

protocol://address/path

where,

- protocol defines the method used to access the web page, e.g., http, ftp, news etc.
- address is the Internet address of the server where the web page resides. It contains the service (e.g. www) and the domain name (e.g. google.com), and
- path is the location of web page on the server.

To access documents on WWW, the HTTP protocol is used. An example of a URL is,

http://www.dsc.com/mainpage

where, *http* is the protocol, *www.dsc.com* is the address, and *mainpage* is the path.

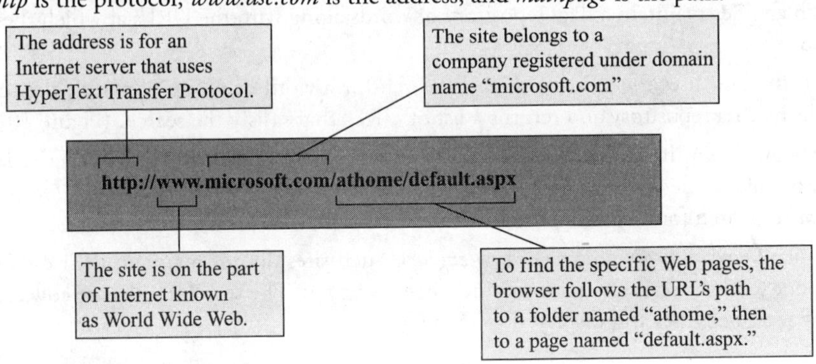

Figure 10.10 An URL

10.9.1.3 Internet Search Engines

One of the most exciting things a user can do on the Internet is to search for information from multiple sources. There are hundreds of millions of web pages available, containing information on a wide variety of topics. There is no single catalog maintained (similar to a library) that lists all the web pages and their information. The user needs to search the Internet to find the information relevant to his/her requirement. *Internet Search engines* or *Search engines* are specific web sites that help the users to find information stored on the Internet. Search engines (Figure 10.11(a)) search the Internet based on some important words (keywords) or combinations of words. Some of the common and well-known search engines are *www.google.com, www.lycos.com* and *www.yahoo.com.*

Using the Search Engine: The user uses the search engine as follows:

- Enter the address of search engine, for example *www.google.com*
- Enter the word, or combinations of words, or symbols with words, based on which the Internet is to be searched. Some options for searching are shown in Table 10.2.

Word	Search Data	What to Search	Example
Single word	Enter word	To search information about cricket	cricket
Combination of words	AND, +	To search two or more words. For e.g. Ashima, Goel	Ashima + Goel
	OR	To search either or both words. For e.g. Ashima or Goel	Ashima OR Goel
	NOT, –	To search for first word but not the second. For e.g. All Ashima's but not Goel's	Ashima – Goel
Symbols	""	To search for exact phrase. For e.g. Ashima Goel	"Ashima Goel"
	*	To search for word with all its forms For e.g. Ashita, Ashiwani, Ashiwari, Ashibhuti	Ashi*

Table 10.2 *Search engine options*

Working of Search Engine: The search engines work as follows:

- Search engines maintain a data repository of words along with the URL's at which these words are found.
- When the user uses the search engine to search for a word or group of words, the search engine checks its data repository and returns a list of URLs that satisfy the search. (Figure 10.11(b))
- To narrow down the scope of search, the search engines also provide different criteria for search. For example, some of the search criteria provided by Google search engine are *Images, News, and Scholar* to search for images, news, and published papers, respectively.
- Sites like *www.msn.com* are *metasearch engines.* Such sites do not maintain their own data repository, but send the search request to other search engines. The search results are collected from different search engines and displayed to the user.

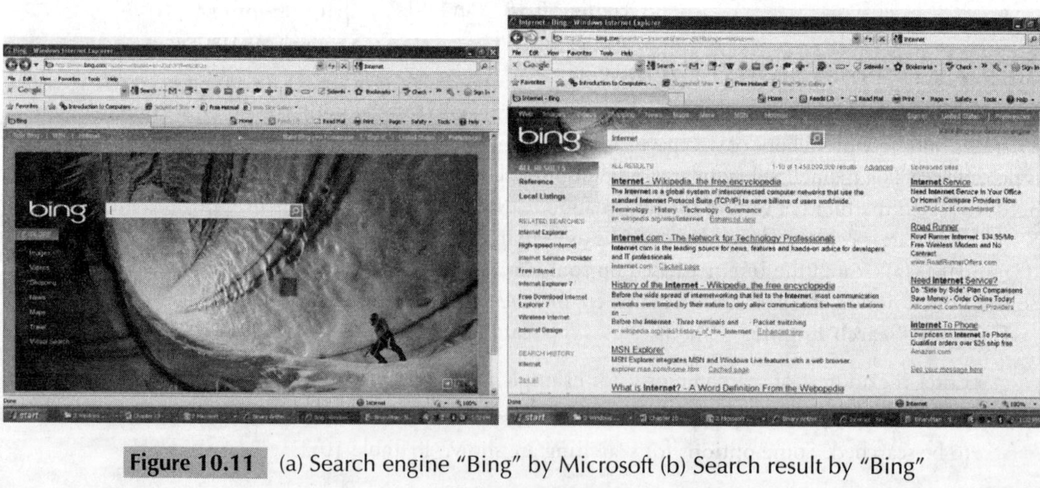

Figure 10.11 (a) Search engine "Bing" by Microsoft (b) Search result by "Bing"

10.9.1.4 WWW Development Languages

The web pages or web sites are written using web development languages. Generally, web development languages are required for developing the layout of the web site in a Graphical User Interface (GUI) based web editor, and to add interactivity to the web sites—at client side and at server side.

- HTML, Dynamic HTML (DHTML), and eXtensible Markup Language (XML) are some of the programming languages used to design and develop the web pages. You can also use software like Dreamweaver, Microsoft Front page, or your common word processor, which have the ability to save your document as a web page, for designing and development of the web pages.
  - HTML is a descriptive language that uses tags or element to convert text into hypertext. HTML allows embedding of text, images, sound, graphics etc., and, also hyperlinks, to link to other web pages. HTML can include or load scripts written in languages such as Javascript.
  - DHTML is a collection of technologies that allows creation of dynamic web pages. In a dynamic web page, the structure, style, and content of the page loaded on the browser can be changed without having to request a new page from the browser. DHTML uses static markup language like HTML, cascading style sheets, scripting languages like Javascript, and Document Object Model (DOM).
  - XML resembles HTML. However, XML allows the author to define unlimited number of tags. XML provides greater flexibility to the author, and has several advantages over HTML.
- In *client side interactivity,* the changes in the code for user interaction happen on the computer of the client side only. For example, if you are viewing a book store website, then as you move the cursor on a book, you can see a blurb showing the details of the book; this is implemented for client side.
  - Scripting languages are used for client side programming.
  - *Javascript, Java applets, and VBscript* by Microsoft (works only in Internet Explorer), are some client side scripting languages. Nowadays *AJAX,* a combination of XML and Javascript is also being used.
  - The client side script may not be allowed to access the client computer beyond the browser application, due to security reasons. ActiveX controls can be used to overcome this restriction. (ActiveX controls may harm your computer). (Figure 10.12)
  - Javascript code is included in the HTML code and is executed when you download the web page.

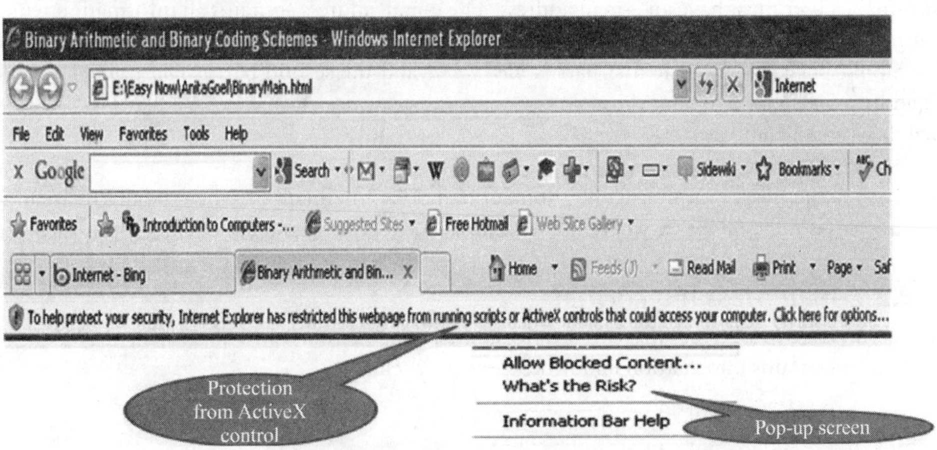

Figure 10.12 ActiveX controls blocked

- The *server side interactivity* involves the server that is hosting the web site. Here, one may need to access the database or some other content stored on the server. For example, from the book store web site you decide to purchase a book. This may require filling in a form to check the availability of the book and completing the payment transaction; this requires server side programming.
    - Practical Extraction and Reporting Language (Perl), Hypertext Preprocessor (PHP), server side VBscript, Java Server Pages (JSP), Active Server Pages (ASP), and Ruby on Rails are some server side programming languages.
    - The Common Gateway Interface (CGI) allows scripting languages to control the web servers. Scripting languages that make use of CGI include Perl, ASP, and PHP.

10.9.2 Electronic Mail

Electronic mail (E-mail) is an electronic message transmitted over a network from one user to another. E-mail is a text-based mail consisting of lines of text, and can include attachments such as audio messages, pictures and documents. The features of e-mail are as follows:

- E-mail can be sent to one person or more than one person at the same time.
- Communicating via e-mail does not require physical presence of the recipient. The recipient can open the e-mail at his/her convenience.
- Since messages are transmitted electronically, e-mail is a fast way to communicate with the people in your office or to people located in a distant country, as compared to postal system.
- E-mail messages can be sent at any time of the day.
- A copy of e-mail message that the sender has sent is available on the sender's computer for later reference.
- In addition to sending messages, e-mail is an ideal method for sending documents already on the computer, as attachments.
- E-mail has features of the regular postal service. The sender of e-mail gets the e-mail address of the recipient, composes the message and sends it. The recipient of e-mail can read the mail, forward it or reply back. The recipient can also store the e-mail or delete it.

10.9.2.1 E-mail Address

To use e-mail, a user must have an e-mail address. The e-mail address contains all information required to send or receive a message from anywhere in the world. An e-mail address consists of two parts separated by @ symbol (spelled as *at*)—the first part is *user_name* and the second part is *host computer name.* The e-mail address may look like

abcdgoel@gmail.com

where, *abcdgoel* is the *user_name,*

gmail.com is the host computer name (domain name) i.e. the mailbox where finally the mail will be delivered. *gmail* is the mail server where the mailbox "abcdgoel" exists.

10.9.2.2 E-mail Message Format

The e-mail message consists of two parts-header and body.

The header contains information about the message, such as—

- From—Sender's e-mail address.
- To—Recipient's e-mail address.
- Date—When the e-mail was sent.

- Subject—The topic of the message.
- Cc—Addresses where carbon copies of the same e-mail will be sent. The recipients of e-mail can see all e-mail addresses to which the copies have been sent.
- Bcc—Addresses where Blind carbon copies (Bcc) of the same e-mail will be sent. The recipients of e-mail do not know that the same e-mail has been sent to other e-mail addresses.
- The size of e-mail.

The body contains the text of the message and any attachments to be sent. Figure 10.13 shows the "compose mail" on gmail.com to create a new e-mail message.

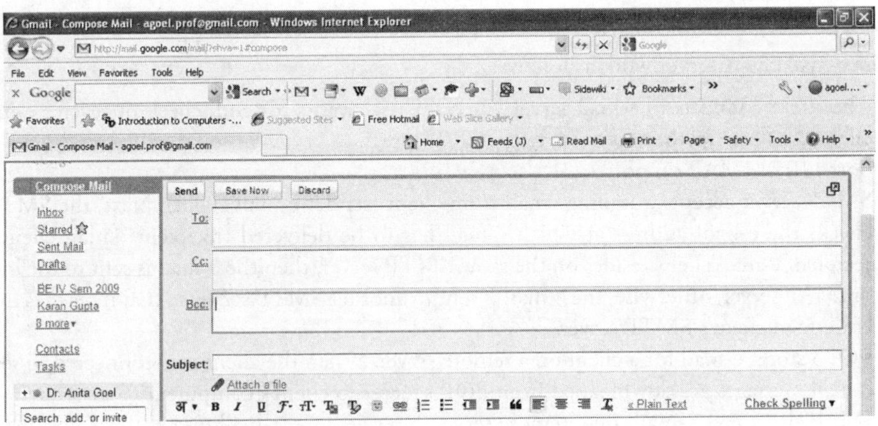

Figure 10.13 The "compose mail" screen on gmail

10.9.2.3 E-mail Services

There are two kinds of e-mail services—Application-based e-mail, and Web-based e-mail.

- *Application-based e-mail* is installed onto the user's computer. The mail is stored on the user's computer. For using an application based e-mail, the user uses a program such as Microsoft Outlook, Outlook Express etc. The user must have an e-mail account on the Internet mail server with a domain name (e.g. vsnl.com), which is provided by the ISP whose services the user is using to connect to the Internet. The user also has an e-mail address (create e-mail address by adding your *username* to e-mail server's domain name. E.g. *aagoel@vsnl.com*), which identifies the user uniquely on the e-mail server.
- *Web-based e-mail or Webmail* appears in a web browser's window. A web-based e-mail can be accessed by the user from any Internet-connected computer anywhere in the world. Web-based e-mail is not stored on the user's computer. Many free web-based e-mail services are available. *Hotmail, yahoo, and gmail* provide free e-mail accounts. An example of web-based e-mail address is *ashima1234@gmail.com.*

10.9.2.4 How E-mail Works

- The e-mail works on the client-server model.
- *E-mail clients* are the users who wish to use the e-mail facility. The basic functionality of the client includes—create new e-mail, display and store received e-mails, address list of contacts etc. Both, the sender of e-mail and the recipient of e-mail are e-mail clients.

- *E-mail server* is a combination of processes running on a server with a large storage capacity—a list of users and rules, and the capability to receive, send, and store emails and attachments. These servers are designed to operate without constant user intervention.
- The e-mail client interacts with the e-mail server to send or receive e-mail. Most email servers provide email services by running two separate processes on the same machine-Post Office Protocol 3 (POP3) and Simple Mail Transfer Protocol (SMTP). Some e-mail servers also run another process on the machine—Internet Message Access Protocol (IMAP).
- *SMTP* is used to send e-mail from the client to server and from one server to another server.
- *POP3* is used by client for application based e-mail to access mail from the server.
- *IMAP* is used by client for web-based e-mail to access mail on server.
- The e-mail client-server work as follows:
    - The client connects to e-mail server when the user wants to send, check or receive e-mail. The client connects to the server on two TCP/IP ports—(1) SMTP on port 25, and (2) POP3 on port 110 or IMAP on port 143.
    - SMTP server accepts outgoing email from client (sender e-mail client). Next, the SMTP server checks the e-mail address at which e-mail has to be delivered (recipient e-mail client). If the recipient e-mail client resides on the same SMTP server, then the e-mail is sent to the local POP or IMAP server, otherwise, the e-mail is sent to another SMTP server so that it reaches the recipient e-mail client's SMTP server.
    - POP3 stores e-mail for a client on a remote server. When the client gets connected to server, the e-mail messages are downloaded from POP3 server to client's computer.
    - IMAP also stores e-mails on a remote server. However, the e-mail messages are not downloaded to the client's computer. The user manipulates the e-mail messages directly on the e-mail server.
    - The POP3/IMAP and SMTP are linked by an internal mail delivery mechanism that moves mail between the POP3/IMAP and SMTP servers.

Figure 10.14 shows the interaction between e-mail client-server.

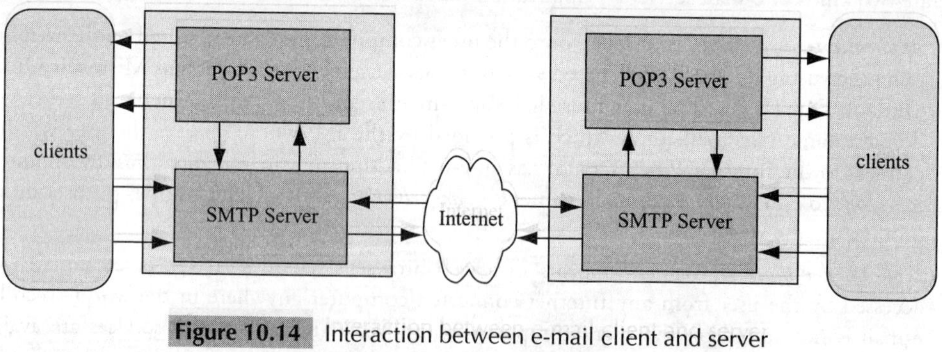

Figure 10.14 Interaction between e-mail client and server

10.9.3 File Transfer Protocol (FTP)

FTP is an Internet tool used for copying files from one computer to another. It gives access to directories or folders on remote computers, and allows software, data and text files to be transferred between different kinds of computers. Using a FTP program or a web browser, the user can log onto an FTP host computer over Internet and copy files onto their own computer. The goals of FTP are as follows:

- FTP promotes sharing of files, articles, and other types of data.
- FTP encourages indirect use of remote computers.

- Heterogeneous systems use different operating systems, character sets, directory structures, file structures, and formats. FTP shields users from these variations and transfers data reliably and efficiently.
- Universities and software companies use FTP host computers to provide visitors with access to data.

10.9.3.1 How FTP Works

FTP works on the client-server model (Figure 10.15). *FTP client* is a program running on the user's computer that enables the user to talk to, and get files from remote computers. *FTP server* is the remote computer or the *host computer* from which files are accessed by the FTP client.

The FTP client-server works as follows:

- The FTP client gives the ftp command with the address of FTP server, using a URL. For example, ftp://ftp.cs.vu.nl.
- When the FTP client gets connected to FTP server, the user enters the User Login and password. A user can login to a FTP server even if they don't have an account on the FTP server. For this, the user uses the anonymous login, where the User Login is *anonymous* and password is the e-mail address of the FTP client.
- FTP server verifies the User Login and password to allow the FTP client to access its files.
- FTP client looks in the directory for files in the FTP server.
- FTP client gets the requested file(s) and quits.

Some of the commands used for ftp are *get filename* (retrieve file from server), *mget filename* (Retrieve multiple files from server), *put filename* (copy local file to server), *mput filename* (copy multiple local files to server) and *ls* (list files in current remote directory located on the server).

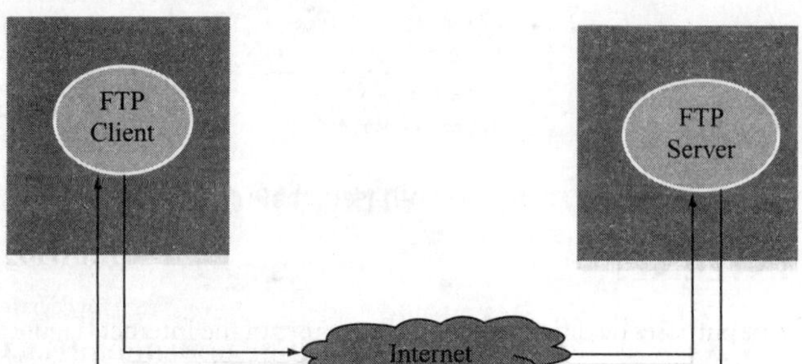

Figure 10.15 FTP

10.9.4 Terminal Network (Telnet)

Telnet uses the telecommunication network facility that allows a computer to access the contents of another computer (also called host computer). A telnet program allows the user to access or edit files, or, issue or execute commands on the host computer. Telnet is different from FTP. While FTP allows transfer of files from the host computer, Telnet allows access to the computing facility of the host computer but does not allow transfer of files. Telnet is widely used by libraries, to allow visitors to look up information, find articles, to access the computer of your office from home, etc. To start telnet, the user gives a command to log to the host computer, for example *telnet foo.cs.wisc.edu.*

10.9.5 News

News includes tens of thousands of newsgroups. Each newsgroup is focused to a specific topic for discussion. People who are interested in the topic, post their articles or views on it for others to read. People can read articles and also respond to articles. The name of the newsgroup suggests the specific topic handled by it. For example, prefix of *comp* indicates that the newsgroup is about computers, and *soc* indicates a newsgroup about social issues and socializing. To participate in a newsgroup, newsreader software like Microsoft Outlook Express is needed. Newsreader software allows the user to read articles that have been posted on a newsgroup.

10.9.6 Internet Relay Chat (IRC)

IRC allows users to communicate in real time by typing text in a special window. This means that other users with whom you chat are present online on their computers. It is an instant sending and receiving of message, unlike e-mail where the receiver may not be on-line when the e-mail message is sent. There are several IRC channels, where each is a discussion room for a user group or for discussion on a subject. A message sent by a user to IRC channel is received by all the users who have joined the channel.

Many chat rooms are set up in Web sites, enabling visitors to chat directly in their browser window, without running special chat software. This is also called *web-based chat* (Figure 10.16).

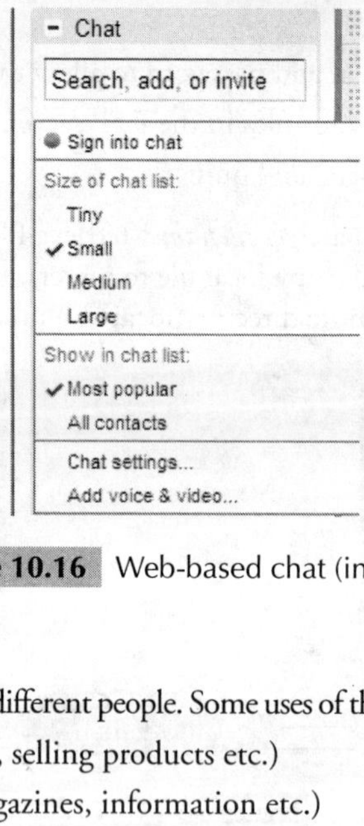

Figure 10.16 Web-based chat (in gmail)

10.10 USES OF INTERNET

Internet is used for different purposes by different people. Some uses of the Internet (Figure 10.17) are listed below:

- E-Commerce (auction, buying, selling products etc.)
- Research (on-line journals, magazines, information etc.)
- Education (e-learning courses, virtual classroom, distance learning)
- E-Governance (online filing of application (Income Tax), on-line application forms etc.)
- On-line ticket booking (airplane tickets, rail tickets, cinema hall tickets etc.)
- On-line payments (credit card payments etc.)
- Video conferencing
- Exchange of views, music, files, mails, folders, data, information etc.
- Outsourcing jobs (work flow software)
- Social networking (sites like *facebook, linkedin, twitter, orkut*)
- E-Telephony (sites like *skype*)

Figure 10.17 Uses of Internet

SUMMARY

- *Internet* is a network of interconnected networks.
- Internet has *evolved* from a research prototype project which started at the US department of Defense Advanced Research Projects Agency.
- TCP/IP is the communication *protocol for the Internet.*
- *TCP* is responsible for providing reliable transport service. TCP uses packet switching technique that converts a message into a set of packets at the source, which are re-assembled back into the message at destination.
- *IP* handles addressing of packets and ensures that the packets reach their destination.
- *Internet architecture* is hierarchical in nature. It includes the client, local ISP, regional ISP, and the backbone.
- A number of *Internet organizations* manage the Internet. Internet is not controlled centrally.
- *Internet connections* like Dial-up access, leased line, ISDN, DSL and cable modem are used by the user to connect to the Internet.
- *IP address* is a unique address for every computer connected to the Internet. IP addresses are numeric and difficult to remember.
- *Domain names* are text-based string corresponding to numeric IP addresses.
- *Internet services* include the WWW, e-mail, telnet, news, ftp, IRC etc.
- *WWW* is a system of creating, organizing and linking of documents. It is large scale collection of documents located worldwide. Hence the name World Wide Web.
- *Hypertext format* is used to create documents on the web. *HTML* is the language used to create a hypertext format document. *HTTP* protocol transfers hypertext document on the web.
- *Web browser* is a tool used by user to view web documents on the Internet. Using web browser to view information on the Internet is known as *browsing or surfing.*
- *URL* is address on the Internet at which the web page resides. URL uniquely identifies a web page on the Internet.
- *Internet search engines* are web sites used for searching specific documents on the web.
- *Web development languages* like HTML, DHTML and XML are used to design and develop the web pages. Scripting languages like *Javascript, Java applets and VBscript* are used for client side programming. Perl, PHP, server side VBscript, JSP, ASP, and Ruby on Rails are some server side programming languages.
- *E-mail* is an electronic message transmitted over a network from one user to another. The e-mail message consists of the e-mail header and the e-mail body. E-mail header contains information about the message. E-mail body contains message text and attachment to be sent.
- *FTP* is used for copying files from one computer to another. FTP works on the client-server model. FTP client runs on the user's computer and enables the

user to get files from remote computers. FTP server is the remote computer from which files are accessed by FTP client.

- *Telnet* allows access to the computing facility of the host computer. The user can access files, edit files or execute commands of another computer over the Internet.
- *Newsgroups* focus on specific topics for discussion.
- *IRC* allows users to chat on-line by typing messages in a special window. Unlike e-mail, it is an instant send and receiving of message.
- *Internet* is used for various purposes like e-commerce, research, e-governance, education, and social networking.

KEYWORDS

QUESTIONS

Section 10.1–10.3

1. Define: (1) Internet, (2) Protocol, and (3) WWW.
2. Describe the history of the Internet.
3. ______ is the protocol for the Internet.
4. Name the scientist who created WWW.
5. The Mosaic browser was developed by ______.
6. Name the first web browser.
7. What is the difference between the Internet and WWW? Explain in one or two sentences.
8. Name the two parts of the Internet protocol.

9. What is the function of TCP in the TCP/IP protocol?
10. What is the function of IP in TCP/IP protocol?
11. Name the technique used by TCP to send messages over the Internet?
12. Describe the packet switching technique?
13. What is the purpose of sequencing information in a packet sent by TCP over the Internet?
14. What is the purpose of error control information in a packet sent by TCP over the Internet?

Section 10.4–10.6

15. Give a brief description of the architecture of the Internet.
16. Define a router.
17. What is the purpose of Network Access Point (NAP)?
18. Who is the owner of the Internet?
19. Name some organizations that manage the Internet.
20. ______ is the organization responsible for domain name registration.
21. Name the governing body of the Internet that is responsible for development of technologies for WWW?
22. What are the basic requirements to connect to the Internet?
23. Define: (1) Modem, and (2) NIC.

Section 10.7

24. Define bandwidth.
25. Name two high speed Internet connections.
26. How does a Dial-up access method for the Internet connection work?
27. List the features of the Dial-up access method for the Internet connection.
28. What kind of users should preferably use the leased line Internet connection?
29. What is the purpose of the gateway in the leased line Internet connection?
30. How does a leased line Internet connection work?
31. List the features of the leased line Internet connection.
32. List the features of the ISDN Internet connection.
33. How does a DSL Internet connection work?
34. Define ADSL.
35. What is the difference between DSL and ADSL?
36. Which is faster—DSL or Dial-up access?
37. List the features of the cable modem Internet connection.
38. Name two broadband Internet connections.
39. How is the cable modem different from DSL connection?

Section 10.8

40. What is the need of the IP address?
41. What does an IP address look like? Give an example.
42. What is the range of numbers used to write an IP address?
43. What is the need of a domain name?
44. Name five top-level domains.
45. Give two examples of domain names.
46. What is the purpose of the DNS server?
47. Explain the parts of the following domain names:
    (a) yahoo.com (b) du.ac.in (du-delhi university)

Section 10.9–10.9.1

48. Name any five services provided by the Internet.
49. What is the significance of the name World Wide Web?
50. Name the format used to create document on the web.
51. Name the language used to create a hypertext document.
52. What is the use of hyperlink?
53. Name the protocol used to transfer web pages on the Internet.
54. How is uploading different from downloading?
55. Differentiate between homepage and web page.
56. What is the function of web server?
57. What is the use of web browser?
58. How is a web portal different from a web site?
59. What is a web portal?

Section 10.9.1.1–10.9.1.4

60. Define—web browser.
61. Name two web browsers.
62. What is the difference between graphical web browser and text-based browser?
63. Give one example each of graphical web browser and text-based browser.
64. Define browsing.
65. What is the purpose of URL?
66. Explain the syntax of URL?

67. Explain the parts of the following URL:http://www.niit.com/mainpage
68. How is URL different from domain name?
69. Why is there a need of Internet search engine?
70. Give examples of two Internet search engines.
71. How is a search engine different from a metasearch engine?
72. What will be searched if the following strings are entered while searching on Internet Search Engine?
    (a) software engineering
    (b) "software engineering"
    (c) soft*
    (d) software + engineering
    (e) software or engineering
73. Name two programming languages used to design and develop the web pages.
74. Write a short note on DHTML.
75. Why are scripting languages needed during the web development?
76. Name two programming languages, each, used for implementing client side and server side interactivity.

Section 10.9.2

77. List four features of e-mail?
78. Explain the syntax of e-mail address with example.
79. What is the difference between Cc and Bcc in an e-mail header?
80. Differentiate between application based e-mail and web based e-mail?
81. Explain the working of e-mail.
82. What information is stored in the e-mail header?
83. Name the TCP/IP port numbers at which computers connect to the following servers: (i) SMTP, (ii) POP3, and (iii) IMAP
84. What is the significance of the SMTP, POP3, and IMAP servers in context of the e-mail?

Section 10.9.3

85. When do you use FTP?
86. List the goals of FTP.
87. Explain the working of the FTP client-server.
88. When is anonymous login used in FTP?
89. What is the purpose of the following commands in FTP: (i) get filename, (ii) mget filename, (iii) put filename, and (iv) mput filename?
90. What is the use of telnet?
91. How is FTP different from telnet?
92. What is the purpose of news service on the Internet?
93. What is the use of IRC?
94. How is chat different from e-mail?
95. List some uses of the Internet.

Extra Questions

96. Give full form of the following abbreviations:
    (i) DARPA (ii) TCP/IP (iii) NSF
    (iv) WWW (v) ISP (vi) NAP
    (vii) ISOC (viii) IAB (ix) IETF
    (x) IESG (xi) IRTF (xii) IANA
    (xiii) InterNIC (xiv) W3C (xv) NIC
    (xvi) DSL (xv) ISDN (xvi) ADSL
    (xvii) DNS (xviii) HTML (xix) HTTP
    (xx) URL (xxi) GUI (xxii) DHTML
    (xxiii) XML (xxiv) DOM (xxv) Perl
    (xxvi) PHP (xxvii) JSP (xxviii) ASP
    (xxix) CGI (xxx) E-mail (xxxi) POP3
    (xxxii) SMTP (xxxiii) IMAP (xxxiv) FTP
    (xxxv) Telnet (xxxvi) IRC
97. Write short notes on:
    (a) History of Internet (b) TCP/IP
    (c) Internet Architecture (d) Internet Connections
    (e) DSL (f) Domain name
    (g) WWW (h) Web Browser
    (i) URL (j) Internet Search Engines
    (k) WWW Development Languages (l) E-mail
    (m) Working of e-mail (n) FTP
    (o) Telnet (p) Uses of Internet
98. Give differences between the following:
    (a) Web site and Web portal
    (b) Graphical browser and Text-based browser
    (c) Application based e-mail and Web based e-mail
    (d) Telnet and FTP
    (e) E-mail and Chat
    (f) DSL and Cable modem

Unit III APPLICATIONS AND SECURITY

INFORMATION SYSTEMS

11

Contents

Why this chapter

In this era of Information age, it is difficult for an organization to handle all its operations manually and that too effectively and efficiently. Organizations use Information Systems which encompasses the hardware, software, databases, telecommunications, people, and procedures for the collection, manipulation, storage, flow and processing of data into information. The purpose of this chapter is to introduce you to "Information Systems".

11.1 INTRODUCTION

In the previous chapters, the focus was on learning about parts of the computer, networking of computers and, the Internet. In this chapter, the focus is on the use of the computer and the telecommunication technology to generate information for businesses and organizations. *Information system* is an organized combination of people, hardware, software, communication network, and data resources that perform collection of data, process it and transform it to provide information, in an organization. The information required from the information systems at different levels of the organization hierarchy is different in nature, like operational information, management information, or information that supports the decision making process. Information systems are vital for the functioning of businesses and organizations.

This chapter discusses about the information systems, and their categorization to provide support at different levels of the organization.

11.2 DATA, INFORMATION AND KNOWLEDGE

Let's understand the distinction between data, information, and knowledge (Figure 11.1).

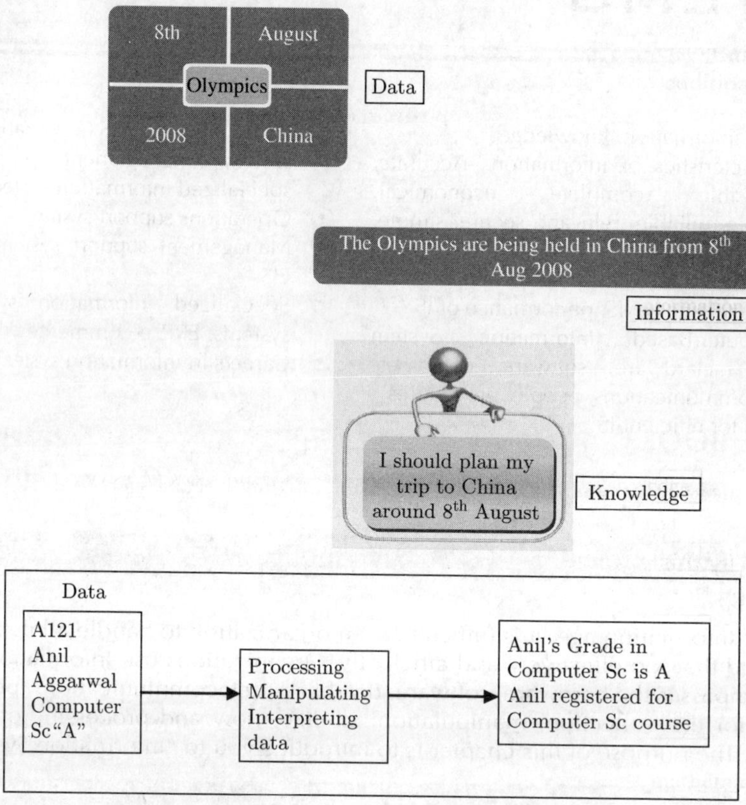

Figure 11.1 Data, information, and knowledge

- **Data** are raw facts. Data is isolated values which by themselves do not have much significance. Data may be numbers, letters or characters, image represented as graphic images and pictures, audio or video. It represents something in the real world. Data forms the raw material for the production of information. Data is not organized and does not convey a meaning. For example, the data elements like '8th', 'Aug', '2008', 'China', and 'Olympics' just represent values.
- **Information** is processed, manipulated, and interpreted data. It is the collection of data organized in such a way that they have value beyond the data itself. Information is created by defining and organizing relationships among data. For example, 'The Olympics are being held in China from 8th Aug 2008'. The processed data gives us information which can be used for different purposes.
- **Knowledge** is an inference or conclusion drawn from the information. For example, a person from India who wishes to go to China can use the information 'The Olympics are being held in China from 8th Aug 2008' to enhance his knowledge so that this person can plan his trip to China accordingly.

11.3 CHARACTERISTICS OF INFORMATION

Information that is meaningful for the people and the organization must have certain characteristics. The characteristics of the information are listed as follows—

- *Accurate:* Information must not contain any errors. It must be accurate.
- *Accessible*: Authorized users should be able to access the information whenever required.
- *Complete*: Information must contain all important and related data.
- *Economical*: Information should be economical to produce both in terms of time and cost.
- *Format*: Information should be available in the desired format.
- *Flexible*: Information should be flexible enough to be used for different purposes.
- *Reliable*: Information is dependable and is generated using correct data.
- *Relevant*: Information must be relevant so that it can be used by the organization.
- *Secure*: Unauthorized users should not be able to access the information. Access is allowed only to authorized individuals.
- *Simple*: Information must be easily understandable and usable. Complex information is difficult to use and may not serve its purpose.
- *Timely*: Information must be available when it is needed. Late or outdated information is of no use.
- *Verifiable*: There should be a means to cross check the available information.

The information having the above characteristics is valuable and is used by the organization for achieving its goals. The organization may use the information for different purposes like decision making, managing the organization etc.

11.4 INFORMATION SYSTEM (IS)

- A *system* is a set of components that work together to achieve a common goal. A system accepts input, processes it, and produces an output (Figure 11.2). A system is composed of one or more subsystems. A system may be a closed system or an open system. A closed system is a stand-alone system that does not interact with other systems. An open system interacts with other systems.

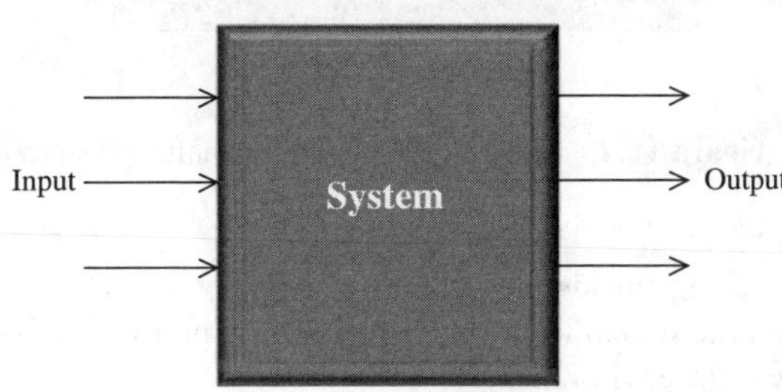

Figure 11.2 A system

- *Information System* (IS) is a set of inter-related components that (1) collect data, (2) manipulate data, (3) disseminate data and information, and (4) provide feedback to meet an objective. An information system uses resources like people, hardware, software, data, and networks to perform input, processing, output, storage, and control activities. Some examples of IS are ATMs, railway reservation system, and movie ticket reservation systems.

Components of Information System: An IS consists of four main components—Input, Process, Output, and Feedback (Figure 11.3). Input is the activity of gathering and capturing raw data. A process converts or transforms data into useful output. During processing, the input data is manipulated into information using mathematical, statistical, and other tools. Output is the generation and presentation of useful information, usually in the form of documents and reports. Feedback is an output that is used to make changes to the input, or the processing activities.

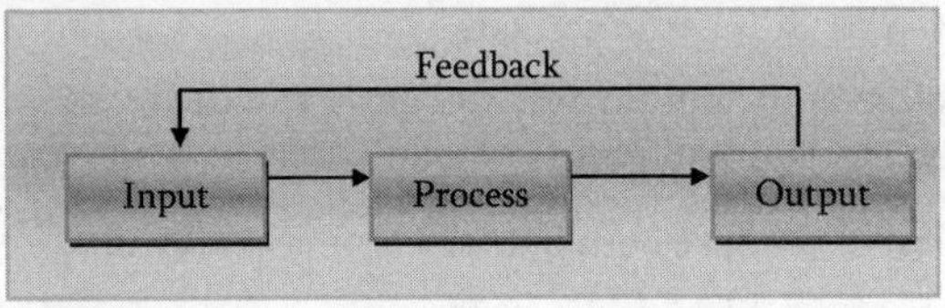

Figure 11.3 Components of information system

- Information systems are needed both by the people and the business organizations. People need information system for entertainment and enlightenment. Organizations require information systems to support decision making, coordination, problem solving and control. Information systems may also help to analyze problems, and to create new products.
- **Characteristics of IS:** Like any other system, ISs have seven characteristics (Figure 11.4)—

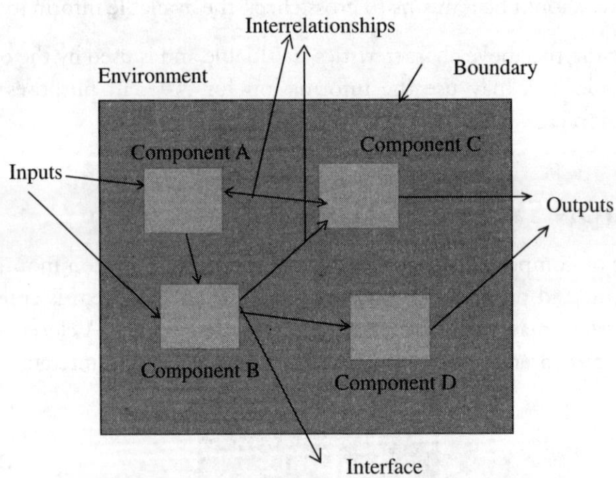

Figure 11.4 Characteristics of information system

- *Environment* is anything outside the system.
- *Boundary* separates the system from environment. Any part within boundary is the system and outside boundary is the environment.
- *Input* is the data from environment to the system. The system uses the input.
- *Output* is the information from the system to the environment. The system uses input to generate output.
- *Components* are the subparts of the system.
- *Interrelationships* are the associations between components of a system.
- *Interface* is a mechanism for interaction between different components of the system.

- The *performance* of Information System is measured by its efficiency and effectiveness. Efficiency is a measure of what is produced divided by what is consumed. Effectiveness is the extent to which a system attains its goals.
- The role of the Information System is expanding and evolving continuously. In 1950s–1960s, the focus was on data processing. Management reporting and decision support was provided during 1960s–1970s and 1970s–1980s, respectively. 1980–1990s saw it being also used for strategic and end user support. Lately in 1990s–2000s, there is a shift towards global internet-working.
- An information system can be manual and computerized.

Here, we shall focus on the computerized information system or the Computer-based Information System.

11.5 COMPUTER-BASED INFORMATION SYSTEM (CBIS)

Computer-Based Information System (CBIS) use computer and telecommunication technology for the generation of information. CBIS uses hardware, software, databases, telecommunications, people, and procedures for the collection, manipulation, storage, and processing of data into information. They take raw data as input, process it, and produce information as output.

The components of a CBIS (Figure 11.5) include the following:

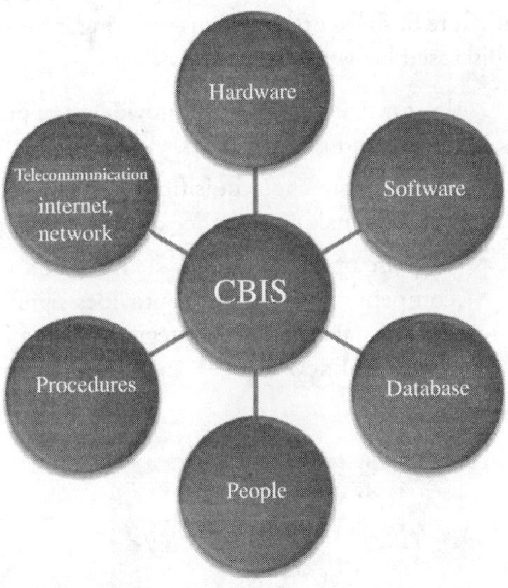

Figure 11.5 Computer-based information system

- Hardware—computer devices like keyboard, monitor, processor, and printer, used for performing the input, processing, and output activities.
- Software—computer programs that govern the operation of the computer.
- Database—an organized collection of data, consisting of two or more related data files.
- People—those who work with the CBIS. People are the most important element in most CBIS.
- Procedures—strategies, policies, methods, and rules for using the CBIS.
- Telecommunication, Network, and Internet—Telecommunication and network is used for connecting the computers and computer devices in a building, city, country, or across the world to enable electronic communication. Internet is the world's largest computer network, which is an interconnection of networks. World Wide Web (WWW) is a system with universally accepted standards for storing, retrieving, formatting, and displaying information in a networked environment. The Internet and WWW have had a tremendous impact on the role IS play in organizations. They are responsible for the increased connectivity and collaboration within and outside the organization. They have helped in transforming the structure of an organization, scope of operations, reporting and control mechanisms, work practices, and services.

IS or CBIS is transforming the way businesses are done nowadays. Communication tools like cell phones, e-mail, online conferencing, and international teleconferencing over the Internet have all become essential tools of a business. E-commerce, e-banking, e-governance, e-learning, Internet advertising, and social media marketing have all seen an increasing usage.

In this chapter, when we refer to Information Systems, we are talking about the Computer-Based Information System.

Information Technology (IT) is distinct from Information System (IS). Information Technology is used to build Information Systems. IT constitutes the hardware, software, databases, networks, and other related components. IS could be a Payroll system, Inventory system, Marketing system, or a Sales system.

11.6 NEED FOR EFFICIENT INFORMATION SYSTEM

In today's world, information systems are indispensable to businesses, industries, and organizations, to meet the future challenges. Organizations need ISs to meet the information needs of its employees. More and more business organizations are using information systems to improve the way they conduct business, as discussed below:

- IS, for many businesses, provide an opportunity to do business in a new way and thus gain huge profits and market shares.
- ISs facilitate the acquisition, transformation, and distribution of information. ISs can improve decision making, enhance organizational performance, and help increase profitability.
- The use of information systems to add value to the organization can also give an organization a competitive advantage. It provides significant, long-term benefit to a company over its competition. ISs are used for strategic planning in a competitive world. It allows changing the structure, creating of new services, and improving upon the existing services.
- Damaged or lost data can cause disruptions in normal business activities leading to financial losses, law suits, etc. ISs help an organization to better manage and secure its critical data.
- ISs also improve integration and the work processes.
- "It is a Flat World", as said by Thomas Friedman (Figure 11.6). More and more companies rely on virtual structures and outsourcing, resulting in businesses to operate around the globe. Operating in a global society poses several challenges to the organizations. Different countries have different standards, policies, and laws. Of course, there are language barriers too. Managing and controlling operations of an organization located in different countries becomes almost impossible without the support of an efficient IS.

Figure 11.6 The book "The World Is Flat"

For an organization, ISs impact the way business is carried out. Organizations need to have an efficient IS to improve and manage their function, performance, and productivity. Briefly summarized, ISs are important for business today due to the need for operational excellence, new products, services and business models, improved decision making, competitive advantage, and the most important—survival.

11.7 CATEGORIES OF INFORMATION SYSTEM

An organization structure can be shown as a pyramid which is divided both horizontally and vertically. Vertically, the divisions represent the different functional areas of the organization, like sales, marketing, accounting, human resource, and manufacturing. Horizontally, the divisions are made according to the operational level of the organization, hierarchically from the base of the pyramid to the top, i.e. operations at low level, middle level, and top level (Figure 11.7). Information systems provide support at all the levels of the organization and in the different functional areas.

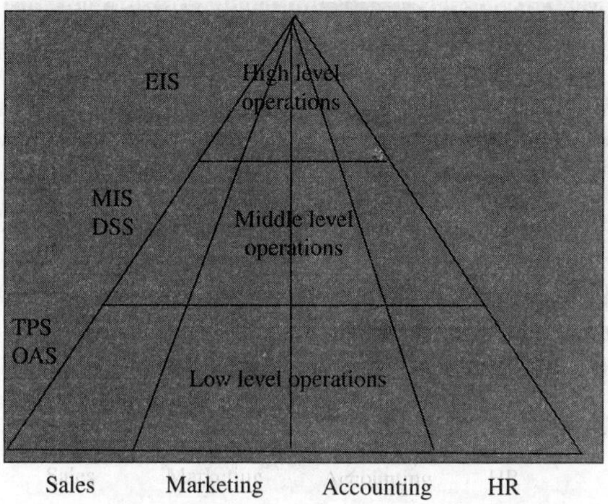

Figure 11.7 Information system categories

Major application categories of the information systems on the basis of the support provided by them at the different levels of the operations hierarchy are as follows:

- **Operations Support System** processes data generated by business operations, and is required for the low-level operations. The categories of operations support system are:
  - Transaction Processing System (TPS), and
  - Office Automation System (OAS).
- **Management Support System** provides information and support needed for decision making by the managers at middle level and top level of the organization. Major categories of management support systems are:
  - Management Information System (MIS),
  - Decision Support System (DSS), and
  - Executive Information System (EIS).

In addition to the above information systems, there is specialized information systems like—

- Expert Systems,
- Enterprise Resource Planning (ERP), and
- Electronic commerce (E-commerce) system.

11.8 OPERATIONS SUPPORT SYSTEM

The operations support system provides information about the day-to-day activities of the organization. They support the operations of the organization, by keeping track of the resources and the transactions. For example, in a banking operation, the operations support system are used to keep track of current balance of the customer; in a manufacturing unit, it helps to keep track of the inventory of the items; and, in a sales unit, it keeps track of the number of units of each item sold. Thus, transaction processing is the main function of the operations support system.

11.8.1 Transaction Processing System (TPS)

- Transaction is a basic level of activity that is performed during the business operations. It is the business-related exchange of payments to employees, sales to customers, and payments to suppliers. Examples of transactions are—withdrawal of money from bank, booking ticket for an airline, selling of goods to the customer etc.
- TPS is an organized collection of people, procedures, software, databases, and devices used for recording the business transactions. TPSs are essential parts of any business organization.
- TPSs are used for routine, repetitive, and ordinary business transactions, and transactions that are critical to the daily function of the business (Figure 11.8). TPS records the business transactions and generates the documents related to the transaction. For example, daily routine transactions for sales orders from customers, bank deposits and bank withdrawals.

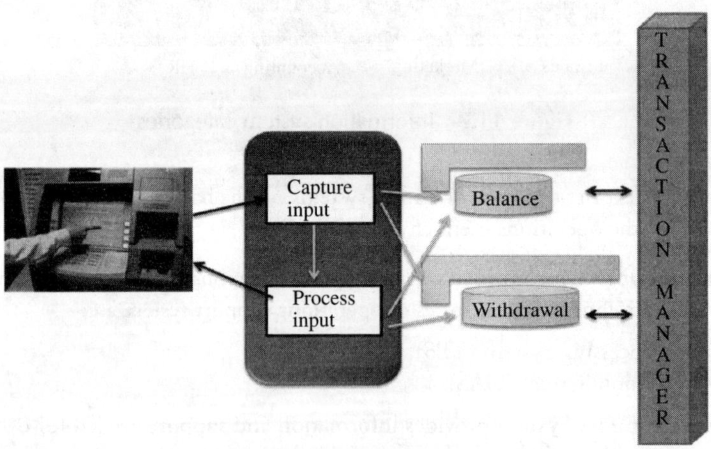

Figure 11.8 Transaction processing

- TPS automates handling of the data for the business activities and transactions.
- The goal of TPS is to increase transaction processing speed, enhance productivity, and simplify the processes.
- TPS gathers all the input necessary for other types of systems. It provides the basic input to the company's database. A transaction generates data, which is recorded by the transaction processing system. This data forms the input for the generation of the other information systems, like MIS,

DSS and EIS. For example, based on the daily transactions, a monthly sales report for middle management and marketing information for senior managers is generated.

- In an organization, there are different functional areas like manufacturing, human resource, accounts, finance, administration, sales, and marketing. The TPS information systems are developed for and used by people in the different functional areas. Examples of TPS are Payroll TPS, Sales TPS, and Marketing TPS.

11.8.2 Office Automation System (OAS)

- OAS supports automation of the tasks in an office. It supports general office work for handling and managing documents. It facilitates communication, both within the office, and, between the office and its environment. It provides support for the traditional office operations like managing the documents, sending messages for interaction, arranging and conducting meetings, scheduling of the projects etc (Figure 11.9).

Figure 11.9 Some parts of office automation system

- OAS allows use of text processing systems like word processors and desktop publishing system, to enable the creation of professional documents with graphics and special layout features.
- Spreadsheets, presentation packages like PowerPoint, personal database systems, and, note-taking systems like appointment book, notepad and calendar, are parts of an OAS.
- OAS includes the communication systems required for transmitting the messages, documents, images, video or voice. For this, it uses the network and the Internet. It incorporates the e-mail facility, voice mail, teleconferencing capabilities, accessing web sites etc. Figure 11.10 shows an automated office.

Figure 11.10 An automated office

11.9 MANAGEMENT SUPPORT SYSTEM

The purpose of the management support system is to assist the managers at different levels in an organization, in the controlling and the management of the business. Management support systems provide different kinds of reports, such as summary report, sales report, and customer balance report. They also assist the managers in the decision making process by generating projected reports like projected sales report etc. Management support systems also provide information to the executives related to the overall operations of the organization, the overall growth, profits, its performance etc. Moreover, for any of the reports, it also provides a detailed report specifying its internal details, if required.

11.9.1 Management Information System (MIS)

- MIS is a collection of people, procedures, software, databases, and devices that provides information to managers and decision makers.
- MIS provides information to the managers to help them make informed decisions. MIS supports the managers in the decision making process and enhances their productivity and performance (Figure 11.11). For example, MIS may generate information related to the sales of a product in a month and the inventory status during that month. It can also monitor the performance and maintain coordination between the different functional areas, like purchase and accounts payable, in an organization.
- MIS works with the transaction processing system. MIS uses the data generated from TPS as input, and converts them into meaningful aggregate form.
- MIS generates different kinds of reports like summary report, exception report, and detailed report. Summaries are for the high-level management and give statistical information to the managers. Exception reports provide information about the activities that are different from the normal functioning. Detailed reports generally provide operational level reports.

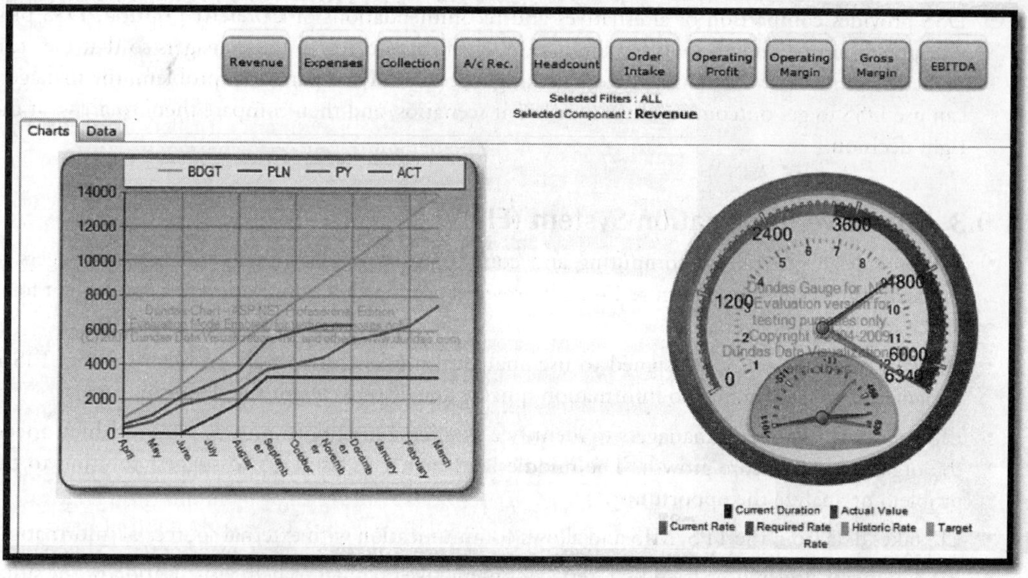

Figure 11.11 A MIS dashboard for senior management

- The different kinds of MIS reports are either scheduled to be generated at fixed intervals of time, may be event-driven and generated when an event occurs, or may be generated in an ad-hoc manner, for a particular query. Scheduled reports are periodic reports that are generated weekly, monthly, or quarterly. Ad-hoc reports are generated on-demand, whenever information is required by the managers.
- MIS can also generate customized reports, where managers can select from different data, sorting options, and display choices.
- The focus of MIS is operational efficiency. The reports generated by the MIS helps the managers in controlling the operations of the organization and in the decision making process.

11.9.2 Decision Support System (DSS)

- DSS is a collection of people, procedures, software, databases, and devices that supports problem-specific decision making.
- DSS support the middle level managers in the decision making process. They supplement the decision making power of the manager with the information technology.
- DSS facilitate decision making by applying mathematical or logical models and interactions to solve problems. For examples, a large number of mathematical and logical calculations are required to be performed on data which may be more than million in number, in order to generate information that helps in the decision making process.
- DSSs are user-friendly and highly interactive.
- DSS focuses on the decision-making effectiveness.
- DSS use data from the TPS and MIS, and, also any new data from external sources, such as current share prices or prices of competitors.

- DSS provides comparison of alternatives and recommendations of a preferred option. DSS provide powerful models and tools for simulation, optimization etc. to the managers so that they can evaluate from several alternatives before making a decision. For a particular problem, the managers can use DSS to get outcome of several different scenarios, and then compare them to arrive at the right decision.

11.9.3 Executive Information System (EIS)

- EIS provides a generalized computing and communication environment to senior managers to support strategic decisions (Figure 11.2). It provides summarized information in a convenient form to the top level managers.
- Unlike DSS, they are not designed to use analytical models for specific problem solving. EIS is designed to facilitate access to information quickly and effectively, for the senior managers.
- EIS is used by the senior managers to identify a problem, an opportunity, or a trend which affects the organization's future growth. The middle level managers use DSS to suggest solution to the problem or analyze the opportunity.
- EIS takes data from the TPS, MIS and allows communication with external sources of information.
- EIS has menu-driven user-friendly interfaces, interactive graphics to help visualization of the situation, and telecommunication links to connect to the external information, if required.

Figure 11.12 Presenting information using EIS

11.10 SPECIALIZED INFORMATION SYSTEM

Specialized information systems are both for organizational and individual use. The specialized systems help organizations and individuals achieve their goals.

11.10.1 Expert Systems

- *Artificial Intelligence (AI)* system is the people, procedures, hardware, software, data, and knowledge needed to develop computer that display the characteristics of intelligence. For certain types of well-defined problems, AI systems can replicate the human decision making. AI systems mimic the functions of the human brain.

- Expert system is an applied area of AI. An *expert system* is a knowledge-based system having two main components—knowledge base and inference engine. It uses the *knowledge base* to store relevant information, data, rules, cases, and relationships, and, the *inference engine* gets information and relationships from the knowledge base, and, provides answers and predictions the way a human expert does.
- Expert systems are used in areas where there is a need to capture and preserve irreplaceable human expertise, provide expertise that is expensive or rare, and to provide expertise needed for training and development to share the wisdom of human experts with a large number of people.
- The expert systems are used to explore new business possibilities, increase overall profitability, and reduce costs.
- Expert systems are used to provide information for problems related to classification, diagnosis, process control, scheduling and planning etc. They are used in products like antilock braking system, television, plant layout and manufacturing, credit granting and loan analysis, and stock picking.

11.10.2 Enterprise Resource Planning (ERP)

- ERP system is a computer software system that manages and coordinates all the resources, information, and functions of a business from shared data stores.
- ERP systems are integrated programs that manage all business operations. For example, they coordinate the planning, inventory control, production, and ordering.
- ERP systems integrate functions such as human resources, supply chain management, customer relations management, financial, manufacturing functions, and warehouse management functions.
- Since ERP systems are integrated systems, they help to streamline different processes and workflows, allow data to be easily shared across various departments in an organization, improve the efficiency and productivity levels, and improves customer service.
- SAP is an example of ERP system. SAP stands for Systems, Applications and Products.

11.10.3 Electronic-Commerce (E-Commerce)

- E-commerce involves any business transaction executed electronically between parties. It uses Internet and Web for doing the business. It uses services like e-mail, workflow software tools, Intranet, and, the e-payment services.
- E-commerce involves buying and selling of products and services, electronically. Figure 11.13 shows a snapshot of an e–commerce website made by students.
- The parties involved in e-commerce may be of the following kinds:
    - Companies and Companies (B2B). A data processing company handling data services for a company.
    - Companies and Consumers (B2C).
    - Consumers and Consumers (C2C). A customer selling goods to another customer, like in *e-bay.com.*
    - Business and the public sector, and, consumers and the public sector.
- E-commerce web sites are like on-line market places where you can sell and buy items, and facilitate it by advertising your product, establishing newsgroups and blogs, posting job-oriented resumes etc.
- The on-line shopping is a fast growing segment as consumers are becoming more confident to use it, with the widespread use of the Internet.

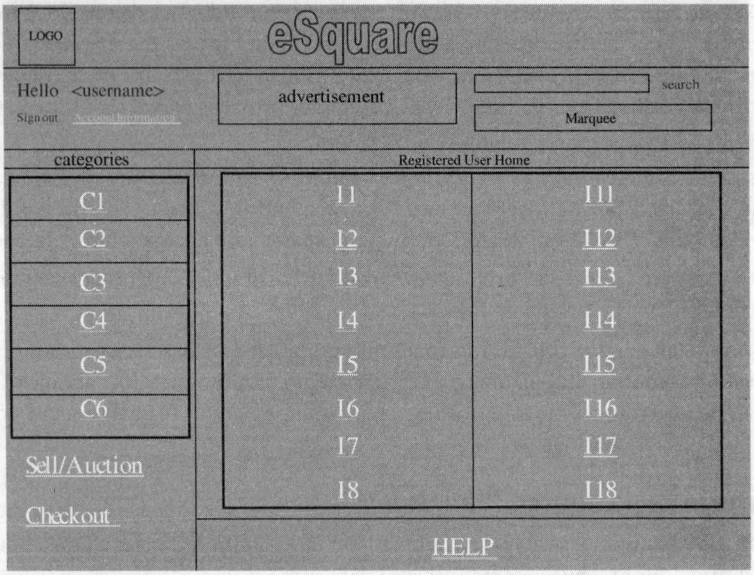

Figure 11.13 An e-commerce web site prepared by students

11.11 CAREERS IN INFORMATION SYSTEMS

Generally, all mid-size and large organizations have an Information System department that controls, coordinates and manages the information system of the organization. In the IS department, the different career opportunities that are generally available are as follows:

- *Chief Information Officer (CIO)* is the overall head of the IS department and is responsible for helping the organization to achieve its goals with the use of the IS tools and personnel.
- *LAN Administrators* are responsible for the setting up and managing of network hardware, software, and security processes.
- *System and Network Operators* focus on the efficiency of information and make sure IS works efficiently. They are involved with the start, stop, and maintenance of the hardware.
- *System Analysts and Programmers* focus on development projects and ongoing maintenance of the IS. They review, identify the needs, and develop the programs.
- *Network / Communications Analysts*
- *Software Engineers / Application Analysts*
- *Database Administrators*
- *Network / Systems Administrators*
- *Application Designers*
- *Management Analysts*
- *Business Systems Analyst / Designers*
- *Information Systems Auditors*
- *Database Architects*
- *ERP Analysts*
- *Web Content Designers / Specialists*

SUMMARY

- *Data* are raw facts like numbers, letters or characters, image, picture, sound or tune. Data forms the raw material for the production of information.
- *Information* is processed, manipulated, and interpreted data.
- *Knowledge* is an inference or conclusion drawn from the information.
- Accuracy, accessibility, completeness, economy, flexibility, reliability, relevance, security, simplicity, timeliness, and verifiability are the *characteristics of information.*
- A *system* is a set of components that work together to achieve a common goal. A system accepts input, processes it, and produces an output.
- *Information system* (IS) is an organized combination of people, hardware, software, communication network, and data resources that perform collection of data, process it and transform it to provide information, in an organization.
- Input, Process, Output, and Feedback are the four main *components of IS*.
- *ISs* have seven *characteristics* - Environment, Boundary, Input, Output, Components, Interrelationship, and Interface.
- *Computer-based information systems* use hardware, software, database, telecommunication, people, and procedures for the collection, manipulation, storage, and processing of data into information.
- Organizations need *IS* for operational excellence, new products, services and business models, improved decision making, competitive advantage, and survival.
- TPS and OAS provide support for the *low-level operations* in an organization.
- MIS, DSS and EIS provide information and support needed for decision making by the managers at *middle and top levels* of the organization.
- Expert systems, ERP and e-commerce are the *specialized information systems.*
- *TPS* records the business transactions and generates the documents related to the transaction. TPS provides the basic input to the other type of information systems.
- *OAS* provides support for traditional office operations. Text processing system, spreadsheet, presentation packages, note-taking system and communication system are part of OAS.
- *MIS* supports the managers in the decision making process and enhances their productivity and performance. MIS generates reports that are either scheduled to be generated at fixed intervals of time, may be event-driven, or generated in an ad-hoc manner.
- *DSS* support the middle level managers in the decision making process. DSS provide models and tools for the comparison of alternatives and recommendation of preferred option.
- *EIS* is used by the senior managers to support strategic decisions, like identify a problem, an opportunity, or a trend which affects the organization's future growth.
- *Expert system* is a knowledge-based system that uses the knowledge base to store information, data, rules, and relationships, and, the *inference engine* to get information from the knowledge base and provides answers the way a human expert does.
- *ERP systems* are integrated systems that help to streamline different processes and workflows, and allow data to be easily shared across various departments in an organization.
- *E-commerce* involves buying and selling of products and services, electronically.
- CIO, LAN administrators, system operators, system analyst and programmers, and web and database administrators are some of the roles available in the *IS department*

KEYWORDS

QUESTIONS

Section 11.2–11.4

1. Define: (1) Data (2) Information, and (3) Knowledge.
2. Explain the difference between data, information and knowledge with an example.
3. List the characteristics of the information.
4. Explain the characteristic features of information in detail.
5. Define a system.
6. Define an Information System.
7. List the components of an Information System.
8. Explain the components of an Information System.
9. List the characteristics of an Information System.
10. Explain the characteristics of an Information System.
11. What do you mean by the performance of the information system?
12. Define the efficiency of the information system.
13. Define the effectiveness of the information system.

Section 11.5–11.6

14. List the components of a CBIS.
15. Explain the components of a CBIS in detail.
16. What are the significances of telecommunication, network and Internet in the IS?
17. What is the need for an efficient information system?
18. How does use of information system provide a competitive advantage to an organization?
19. How does information system help the organizations having operations in different countries?

Section 11.7–11.8.2

20. List the different categories of information system.
21. List an IS, each, for low level, middle level and top level management in an organization.
22. What is a TPS?
23. List the features of a TPS.
24. What is an office automation system?
25. List the features of an office automation system.
26. Name three tools used for the automation of the tasks in an office automation system.

Section 11.9

27. What is a MIS?
28. List the features of a MIS.
29. Name the different kinds of reports generated in MIS.
30. Define summary report, exception report and detailed report generated in MIS.
31. What are scheduled reports?
32. What are ad-hoc reports?
33. What is a DSS?
34. List the features of a DSS.

35. How does DSS facilitate the decision making process.
36. What is an EIS?
37. List the features of an EIS.

Section 11.10

38. Define an Artificial Intelligence (AI) system.
39. Define an expert system.
40. What is the relation between AI systems and expert systems?
41. Name three applications of the expert system.
42. What is an ERP?
43. List the features of an ERP.
44. What is e-commerce?
45. List the features of e-commerce system.
46. What is on-line shopping?

Section 11.11

47. List the different career opportunities in information systems.
48. What is the role of CIO in information system?
49. What is the role of LAN administrators in information system?
50. What are the roles of system and network operators in information system?
51. What are the roles of system analysts and programmers in information system?

Extra Questions

52. Give full form of the following abbreviations:
    (i) IS (ii) CBIS (iii) IT
    (iv) TPS (v) OAS (vi) MIS
    (vii) DSS (viii) EIS (ix) ERP
    (x) E-commerce (xi) AI (xii) CIO
    (xiii) SAP
53. Write short notes on:
    (a) Characteristics of information
    (b) Components of IS
    (c) Characteristics of IS
    (d) Components of CBIS
    (e) Careers in Information Systems
    (f) Transaction Processing System (TPS)
    (g) Management Information System (MIS)
    (h) Office Automation System (OAS)
    (i) Decision Support System (DSS)
    (j) Executive Information System (EIS)
    (k) Expert System
    (l) Enterprise Resource Planning (ERP)
    (m) E-commerce system
54. Give differences between the following:
    (a) Data, Information and Knowledge
    (b) Operations Support System and Management Support System
    (c) Transaction Processing System and Management Information System
    (d) Decision Support System and Executive Information System

FUNDAMENTALS OF DATABASE

12

Contents

- ⊙ Database
  - File-oriented approach and database approach
  - Characteristics of database approach
  - Data models, schemas and instances
  - Conceptual data model—Entity, attribute, relationship, and E-R model
  - Representation data model—Hierarchical, network, relational data model
  - Low level, or physical data model
- ⊙ Database system
  - Components of database system—Users, software, hardware, and data
  - Architecture of database system—Internal level, conceptual level, and external level
- ⊙ Database management system
  - Data independence—Logical data independence, physical data independence
  - Data dictionary, Database Administrator (DBA)
  - Database languages—DDL, and DML
- ⊙ Database system architectures—Centralized DBMS architecture, client-server architecture, and distributed database
- ⊙ Database applications

Why this chapter

Computerized applications developed for personal use, for organizations and for enterprises, access, manipulate and manage the data. The data is stored in a database for easy access and retrieval. It is essential to have an understanding of the concepts of the database system to be able to manipulate the database and manage it properly. The purpose of this chapter is to introduce you to the fundamentals of the Databases.

12.1 INTRODUCTION

Databases and database systems are essential parts of our life. We have been interacting with non-computerized databases since long time, remember, looking for a word in a dictionary or finding the telephone number of your friend from a telephone directory. Computerized databases use computer to store, manipulate, and manage the database. In our daily lives we interact with the computerized databases when we go for the reservation of railway tickets and movie tickets, for the searching of a book in a library, to get the salary details, to get the balance of our account while using an ATM, to get the rate list while purchasing items from a cash and carry store and, this list can run into several pages. Lately, databases (Figure 12.1) are also used to store highly data intensive items like photographs (http://flickr.com), video clippings (http://YouTube.com), and images (http: //images. google.co.in).

This chapter discusses the database approach and its advantage over the traditional file-based approach. The chapter describes the components of the database system and the various data models. A brief description of the architecture of the database system is also given. In the end, the chapter highlights the different types of database architecture and the database applications.

Figure 12.1 Databases

12.2 DATABASE

Database is a repository or collection of logically related, and similar data. Database stores similar kind of data that is organized in a manner that the information can be derived from it, modified, data added, or deleted to it, and used when needed. Some examples of databases in real life situations are: dictionary—a database of words organized alphabetically along with their meaning, telephone directory—a database of telephone numbers and addresses organized by the last name of people, railway timetable—a database of trains organized by train names, and, companies listed on Stock Exchange organized by names alphabetically.

A ***database*** is defined as—(1) a collection, or repository of data, (2) having an organized structure, and (3) for a specific purpose. A database stores information, which is useful to an organization. It contains data based on the kind of application for which it is required. For example, an airline database may contain data about the airplane, the routes, airline reservation, airline schedules etc.; a college database may contain data about the students, faculty, administrative staff, courses, results etc.; a database for manufacturing application may contain data about the production, inventory, supply chain, orders, sales etc.; and a student database may contain data about students, like student names, student course etc.

12.2.1 File-Oriented Approach and Database Approach

In the early days, data was stored in files. For an application, multiple files are required to be created. Each file stores and maintains its own related data. For example, a student information system would include files like student profile, student course, student result, student fees etc. The application is built on top of the file system. However, there are many drawbacks of using the file system, as discussed below–

- *Data redundancy* means storing the same data at multiple locations. In an application, a file may have fields that are common to more than one file. The data for these common fields is thus replicated in all the files having these fields. This results in data redundancy, as more than one file has the same data values stored in them. For example, *student_name* and *student_course* may be stored in two files—"student profile" and "student fees".
- *Data inconsistency* means having different data values for the common fields in different files. During the updating process, the common fields may not get updated in all the files. This may result in different data values for the common fields in different files. For example, a student having different home address in two different files. Data redundancy provides opportunity for data inconsistency. Figure 12.2 shows data redundancy, and data inconsistency in two files.

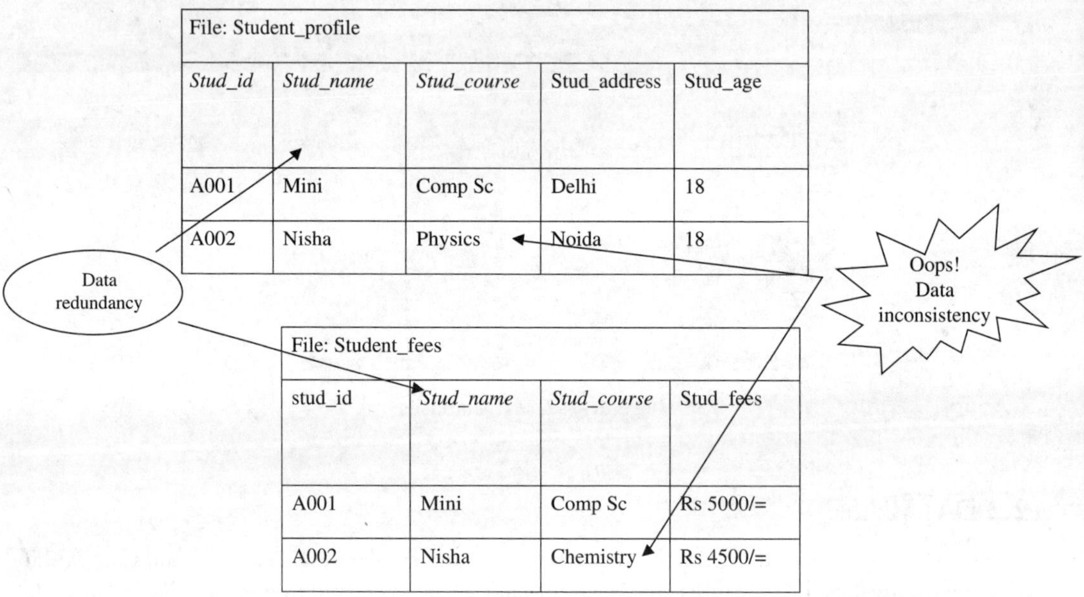

Figure 12.2 Data inconsistency and data redundancy

- The files in which the data is stored can have *different file formats*. This results in difficulty in accessing the data from the files since different methods are required for accessing the data from the files having different formats.
- In a file system, the *constraints of the system* (for example, student age > 17) become part of the program code. Adding new constraints or changing an existing one becomes difficult.
- The files can be accessed concurrently by multiple users. *Uncontrolled concurrent access* may lead to inconsistency and security problems. For example, two users may try to update the data in a file at the same time.

Database approach provides solutions for handling the problems of the file system approach. The emergence of database approach has resulted in a paradigm shift, from each application defining and maintaining its own data (file-oriented approach)—to the data being defined and administered centrally (database approach). In the database approach, data is defined and stored centrally.

12.2.2 Characteristics of Database Approach

The main characteristics of the database approach are defined as follows:

- **Data Redundancy is Minimized:** Database system keeps data at one place in the database. The data is integrated into a single, logical structure. Different applications refer to the data from the centrally controlled location. The storage of the data, centrally, minimizes data redundancy.
- **Data Inconsistency is Reduced:** Minimizing data redundancy using database system reduces data inconsistency too. Updating of data values becomes simple and there is no disagreement in the stored values. E.g. students' home addresses are stored at a single location and get updated centrally.
- **Data is Shared:** Data sharing means sharing the same data among more than one user. Each user has access to the same data, though they may use it for different purposes. The database is designed to support shared data. Authorized users are permitted to use the data from the database. Users are provided with views of the data to facilitate its use. E.g. the students' home addresses stored in the database which is shared by student profile system and library system.
- **Data Independence:** It is the separation of data description (metadata) from the application programs that use the data. In the database approach, data descriptions are stored in a central location called the *data dictionary*. This property allows an organization's data to change and evolve (within limits) without changing the application programs that process the data.
- **Data Integrity is Maintained:** Stored data is changed frequently for variety of reasons such as adding new data item types, and changing the data formats. The integrity and consistency of the database are protected using constraints on values that data items can have. Data constraint definitions are maintained in the data dictionary.
- **Data Security is Improved:** The database is a valuable resource that needs protection. The database is kept secure by limiting access to the database by authorized personnel. Authorized users are generally restricted to the particular data they can access, and whether they can update it or not. Access is often controlled by passwords.
- **Backup and Recovery Support:** Backup and recovery are supported by the software that logs changes to the database. This support helps in recovering the current state of the database in case of system failure.
- **Standards are Enforced:** Since the data is stored centrally, it is easy to enforce standards on the database. Standards could include the naming conventions, and standard for updating, accessing and protecting data. Tools are available for developing and enforcing standards.
- **Application Development Time is Reduced:** The database approach greatly reduces the cost and time for developing new business applications. Programmer can focus on specific functions required for the new application, without having to worry about design, or low-level implementation details; as related data have already been designed and implemented. Tools for the generation of forms and reports are also available.

In addition to the advantages highlighted above, there are several other implications of using the database approach like provision of multiple-user interfaces, representation of complex relationships, concurrent data access etc.

There are, however, some disadvantages of database systems over the file-based systems. The database systems are more vulnerable than file-based systems because of the centralized nature of a large integrated database. If a failure occurs, the recovery process is more complex and sometimes may result in lost transactions.

12.2.3 Data Models, Schema and Instances

The information stored inside a database is represented using *data modeling.* The data model describes the structure of the database. A *data model* consists of components for describing the data, the relationships among them, and the semantics of data and the constraints that hold data. Many data models exist based on the way they describe the structure of database. The data models are generally divided into three categories as follows:

- High level or conceptual Data Model,
- Representation or implementation Data Model, and
- Low level or physical Data Model

Schema is the logical structure of the database. A schema contains information about the descriptions of the database like the names of the record type, the data items within a record type, and constraints. A schema does not show the data in the database. The database schema does not change frequently.

Instances are the actual data contained in the database at a particular point of time. The content of the database may change from time to time.

12.2.4 High-Level or Conceptual Data Model

The conceptual data model is a description of the data requirements of the user. This model is not concerned with the implementation details. It ensures that all the functional and data requirements of the users are specified, conceptually. The conceptual model is defined using terms like (1) Entity, (2) Attribute, and (3) Relationship. The Entity-Relationship model (E-R model) is an example of conceptual data model. The following subsections, briefly describe these terms and the E-R model.

12.2.4.1 Entity

An entity is the basic unit for modeling. It is a real-world object that exists physically or conceptually. An entity that exists physically is a tangible object like student, employee, room, machine, part or supplier. An object that exists conceptually is a non-tangible object like an event or job title. For e.g. student information system may consist of entities like *student_profile, marks* and *course.* A set of entities of the same type having same properties, or attributes is defined as an *entity set.* For example, a set of all persons who are students of the university can be defined as an entity set *student.* Likewise, the entity set *course* may represent a set of all courses offered by a University. An entity set is usually referred to by the same name as an entity. For example, *Student* is an entity set of *all student entities* in the database. Diagrammatically, an entity is represented using a *rectangle.* Figure 12.3 shows the entities for a database created in MS-Access 2007.

12.2.4.2 Attribute

An *attribute* describes some property or characteristics of the entity. For e.g. *student name, student address,* and *student age* are attributes of the entity *student_profile.* An attribute ensures that similar information is stored about each entity in an entity set, in the database. However, each attribute of an entity may have its own value. The set of permitted values for an attribute is called the *domain* of the attribute. For example, the domain of the attribute *student name* is text string, or, the domain of *student age* is a positive integer ranging between 18 and 65. Diagrammatically, an attribute is represented as an *ellipse* connected to the entity with a line. Figure 12.3 shows the attributes for the entity "Employee" in MS-Access 2007.

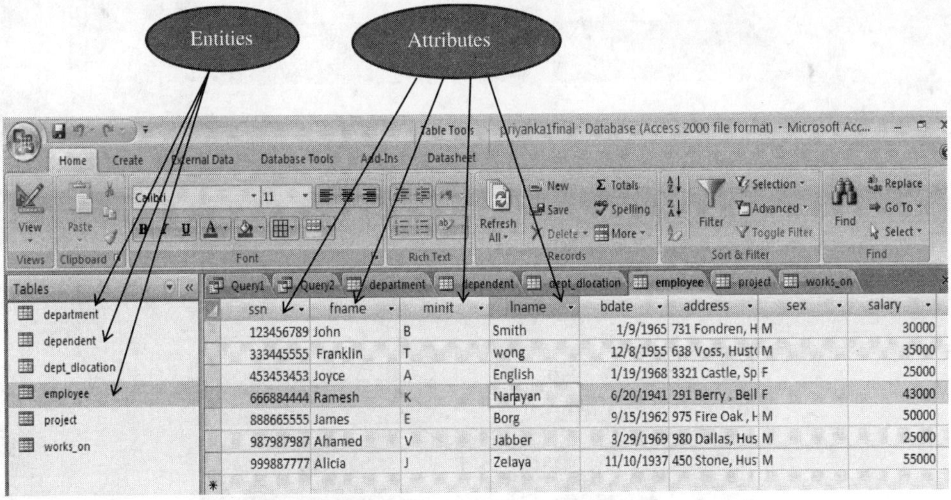

Figure 12.3 Entities and attributes

12.2.4.3 Relationship

An association or link between two entities is represented using a *relationship*. A set of relationships of the same type form a *relationship set*. For e.g. “student enrolls in course” is a relationship set between the entities student and course. *Cardinality ratio* is the number of entities to which another entity gets associated in a relationship set. The cardinality ratio of a relationship set is any one of the four kinds—(1) One-to-One, (2) One-to-Many, (3) Many-to-One, and (4) Many-to-Many. In two entity sets A and B, the different cardinality ratio imply the following:

- One-to-One: An entity in A is associated with at most one entity in B and vice versa.
- One-to-Many: An entity in A is associated with any number of entities in B, but an entity in B is associated with at most one entity in A.
- Many-to-One: An entity in A is associated with at most one entity in B, but an entity in B is associated with any number of entities in A.
- Many-to-Many: An entity in A is associated with any number of entities in B and vice versa.

Diagrammatically, a relationship is represented using a *diamond* connected to the entity by a line. Figure 12.4 shows the different kinds of relationships.

12.2.4.4 Entity-Relationship (E-R) Model

E-R model is a model of the real world. E-R model represents the entities contained in the database. The entities are further described in the database using attributes. The relation between the entities is shown using the relationships. The model also shows the cardinality constraints to which the database must adhere to. The E-R model is represented diagrammatically using an *E-R diagram*. Figure 12.5 shows a simple E-R diagram. The diagram shows two entities—*Student* and *Course*. The *Stud_Name* and *Stud_RollNo* are the attributes of the entity Student. The *Course_Id* and *Course_Name* are the attributes of the entity Course. The *Admission* relationship associates the student with the course. Database design in E-R model is converted to design in the *Representation Model* which is used for storage and processing.

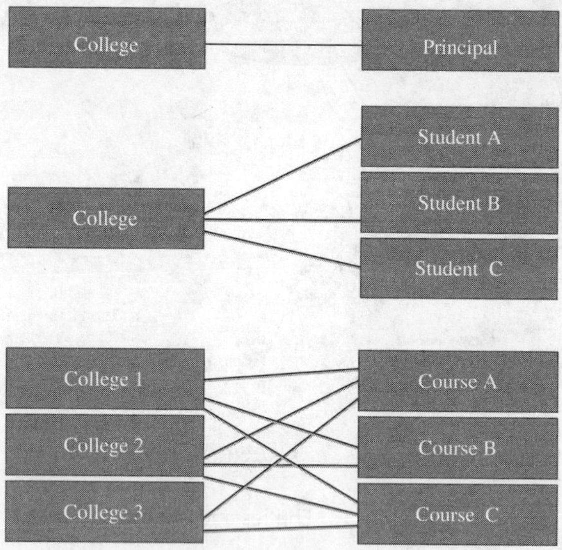

Figure 12.4 Relationships (a) One-to-one (b) One-to-many (c) Many-to-many

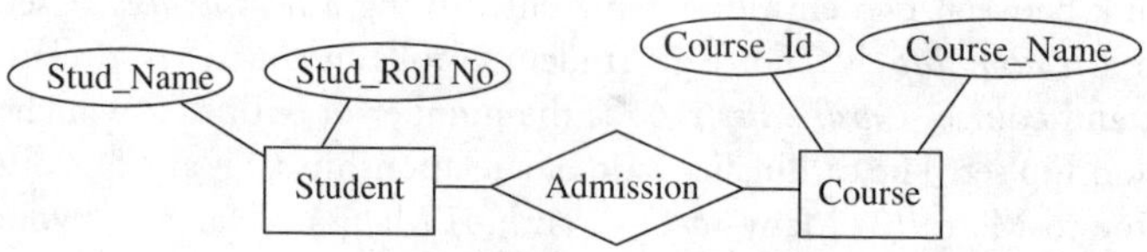

Figure 12.5 E-R diagram

> Object-Oriented (OO) database model use object-oriented programming. The object data model defines a database in terms of objects, classes, and methods. It is beneficial in web applications, and in specialized application areas like multimedia, manufacturing system, and engineering design, and for the storing of multimedia objects.

12.2.5 Representation or Implementation Data Model

The *Conceptual Data Model* is transformed into the *Representation Data Model.* Representation data model uses concepts that are understood by the end-user and are also close to the way the data is organized in the computer. These models hide the details of data storage. The data models are broadly classified as traditional data models that include—(1) hierarchical, (2) relational, and (3) network data models. Object-relational data model is an emerging data model.

12.2.5.1 Relational Database Model

The *Relational Database Model* was proposed in 1970 by E. F. Codd. The first commercial system based on the relational model became available in early eighties. Relational database model is the most common type of database model. Table, record, field, key, and data values are the terms associated with a relational model. The data elements are stored in different tables made up of rows and columns. The data in different tables are related through the use of common data elements. We briefly define the terms as follows—

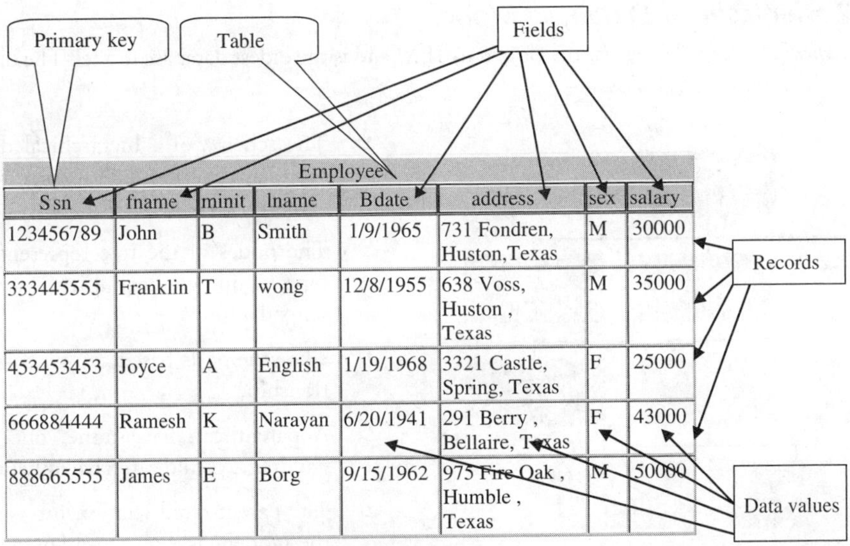

Employee							
Ssn	fname	minit	lname	Bdate	address	sex	salary
123456789	John	B	Smith	1/9/1965	731 Fondren, Huston,Texas	M	30000
333445555	Franklin	T	wong	12/8/1955	638 Voss, Huston , Texas	M	35000
453453453	Joyce	A	English	1/19/1968	3321 Castle, Spring, Texas	F	25000
666884444	Ramesh	K	Narayan	6/20/1941	291 Berry , Bellaire, Texas	F	43000
888665555	James	E	Borg	9/15/1962	975 Fire Oak , Humble , Texas	M	50000

Figure 12.6 Table "Employee"

- **Data Values** Data values are the raw data represented in numeric, character, alphanumeric, or alphabetic form. Examples of data values are 'Abhinav Bindra', '26', 'shooting', "Chandigarh" etc.
- **Field or Column** Data values or data is stored in a database as fields. For an item or object, a field holds the information of it. For example, individual fields or columns are *name, age, address, hobby* etc. for an object 'student profile'.
- **Record or Row** A group of data for related field is called a *record*. For example, for object 'student profile', the related fields are (name, age, address, and hobby). The data about the student #1 ('Abhinav Bindra', 26, 'Chandigarh', and 'Shooting') is one record.
- **Table** A collection of logically related records form a *table*. A table for an object has rows and columns. The table is organized as a set of columns, and can have any number of rows. For example a table for student profile can have four columns namely, *name, age, address, and hobby*, and have records or rows having data of 30 students.
- **Key** A *key* is an identifier in a table that uniquely identifies a row in a table. The key identifier can be the value of a single column or of multiple columns. A key is generally also referred to as the *primary key* of the table. The primary key is a unique identifier for the table. The column or combinations of columns that form the primary key have unique values. At any time, no two rows in the table can have same values for the primary key. For example, in a student table, each student has a unique *student_rollno*, which forms the primary key.

In its simplest form, a database may contain a single table stored as a file. In more complex databases, a collection of related tables may be stored together. For example, a student database may contain a table for student profile, student result, student courses etc. Figure 12.6 shows a table "Employee", with fields, records, data values & primary key.

Several commercial products like DB2, ORACLE, SQL Server, SYBASE, and INFORMIX are relational databases. The Relational Data Model is extended to include the object database concepts thus forming the *Object-Relational Data Model.*

12.2.5.2 Hierarchical Database Model

The *Hierarchical Database Model* was developed by IBM and is the oldest database model. The hierarchical database model is defined as follows—

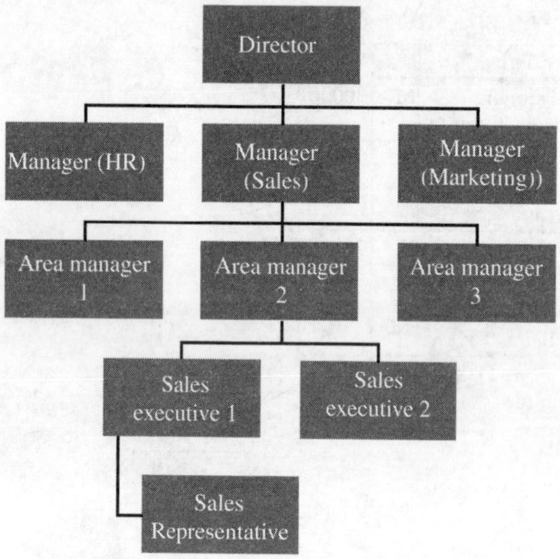

Figure 12.7 Hierarchical database model

- The schema of a hierarchical database is represented using a *tree-structure diagram* (Figure 12.7).
- The nodes of the tree represent a record type. A line connecting two nodes represents the link.
- The schema is based on *parent-child* relationship.
- A parent can have none, one, or more children. A child can have only one parent.
- The parent-child relationship is suited for the modeling of one-to-many relationship between two entities.
- It is difficult to implement a many-to-many relationship using hierarchical database model.
- Some of the hierarchical database implementations are the IMS system from IBM and System 2000 from MRI systems.

12.2.5.3 Network Database Model

The *Network Database Model* was formalized by DataBase Task Group (DBTG) group of Conference on Data Systems Languages (CODASYL) in the late 1960s. The Network Database Model is defined as follows:

- The schema of the network database model is represented using a *data-structure* diagram.
- The boxes represent the record type and the lines represent the links (Figure 12.8).
- The schema is based on *owner-member* relationship.
- The entity type is represented using record type and relationship between entities is represented using set type.
- A set type can have more than one record type as a member but only record type is allowed to be the owner in a set type.
- The owner-member relationship is suited to represent one-to-many relationships. The one-to-many relationship is converted into a set of one-to-one relationships.
- The network model handles many-to-many relationship by converting it into two or more one-to-many relationships.
- Some of the network database implementations are IDMS, DMS 1100 and IMAGE.

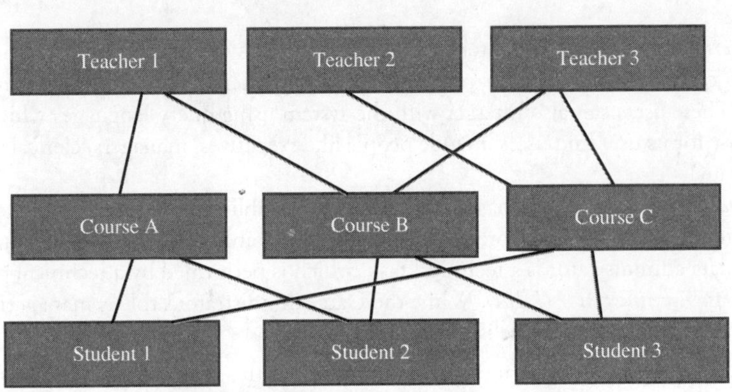

Figure 12.8 Network database model

The hierarchical model is simple to construct. However, the network model is able to handle complex relationships easily. Both hierarchical and network models are also called *legacy models* as most current systems support the *Relational Model.*

12.2.6 Low-Level or Physical Data Model

The *Physical Data Model* describes the internal storage structures, the access mechanism, and the organization of database files. Physical level describes how a record (e.g., customer) is stored. Sequential files, direct files, and indexed sequential files are the different types of file organizations at the physical level.

12.3 DATABASE SYSTEM

A bank, hospital, college, university, manufacturer, government are some examples of organizations or enterprises that are established for specific purposes. All organizations or enterprises have some basic common functions. They need to collect and store data, process data, and disseminate data for their various functions depending on the kind of organization. Some of the common functions include payroll, sales report etc.

A *database system* integrates the collection, storage, and dissemination of data required for the different operations of an organization, under a single administration. A *database system* is a computerized record keeping system. The purpose of the database system is to maintain the data and to make the information available on demand.

12.3.1 Components of Database System

A database system has four main components—(1) Users, (2) Hardware, (3) Software, and (4) Data.

- **Users** *Users* are the people who interact with the database system. The users of a database system are segregated into three categories based on the way they interact with the system— (1) Application Programmers, (2) End Users, and (3) Data Administrators.
  - *Application programmers* develop application programs that manipulate the database. The developed application programs operate on the data for its insertion, deletion and retrieval. Programs are also written for interacting with the system through calls, accessing of specialized database applications, creating form requests etc.

- *End users* are the people who interact with the database system to get information from the database to carry out their business responsibility. They interact with the system through *menus* or *forms*. These users can also interact with the system using query languages which requires some expertise for its use. End users include people like executives, managers, clerical staff, bank teller, and so on.
- *Data administrator* is the manager responsible for establishing policies for the maintenance and handling of data once it is stored. The creation of database and the implementation of policies of the data administrator is a technical task, which is performed by a technical person called the *Data Base Administrator (DBA)*. While the Data administrator's role is managerial in nature, the DataBase Administrator's role is technical in nature.

⊙ **Software** In a database system, software lies between the stored data and the users of data. The database software can be broadly classified into three types—(1) DataBase Management System (DBMS), (2) Application software, and (3) User Interface.

- *DBMS* handles requests from the users to access the database for addition, deletion, or retrieval of data. Software components required to design the DBMS are also included here. Some software components are the automated tools like Computer-Aided Software Engineering (CASE) tools for the designing of databases and application programs, software utilities, and report writers.
- *Application software* uses DBMS facilities to manipulate the database to achieve a specific business function, such as, providing reports that can be used by users. Application software is generally written in a programming language like C, or it may be written in a language supported by the DBMS.
- *User interface* of the database system constitutes the menus and the screens that the user uses to interact with the application programs and the DBMS.

⊙ **Hardware** *Hardware* is the physical device on which the database system resides. The hardware required for the database system is the computer or a group of connected computers. Hardware also includes devices like magnetic disk drives, I/O device controllers, printers, tape drives, connecting cables and other auxiliary hardware.

⊙ **Data** Data is raw numbers, characters, or facts represented by values. The data can be numeric data, non-numeric data, images or pictures. Some examples of data are 23, 45, "Divya", "Computer", "India". The data in a database system is integrated and shared.

- *Integrated data* implies that several distinct data files are unified in a manner that redundancy among these data files is wholly or partially eliminated. For example, a database may contain files for STUDENT_PROFILE having student roll no., student name, address, course enrolled etc., and MARKS file having the marks of students in various subjects. To prepare the report card, there is a need to get the complete student profile along with the marks obtained in each subject. For this, the complete profile of the student need not be stored in MARKS file as the information can be retrieved by referring to STUDENT_PROFILE file.
- *Shared data* implies that the data stored in the database can be shared among multiple users, such that each user has access to the same data, which the user can use for different purposes. For example, data for *course enrolled* in STUDENT_PROFILE file is shared by the NCC department and the Library department—both use the same data for different purposes.

12.3.2 Architecture of Database System

The *architecture* of a database system provides a general framework for database systems. Different database systems, small or big, may not support all aspects of the architecture; however, different systems can be matched to the framework. The architecture for database system is proposed by ANSI/SPARC study group and is called ANSI/SPARC architecture. The purpose of the architecture is to make databases more independent of the application that is using the database. Schema contains information about the description of the database.

The ANSI/SPARC architecture is divided into three levels (Figure 12.9), as follows:

- **Internal (Physical) Level** has an internal schema. The internal schema describes the physical storage structure of the database. It is concerned about how data is stored physically. It does not deal with the physical storage in terms of blocks, neither pages nor the device. Rather, it describes the organization of files, the access path to the database etc. The physical data model is used to describe the physical schema.
- **Conceptual Level** has a conceptual schema. The conceptual schema describes the structure of whole database for the users. It describes the entities in the database, their relationships, and constraints. The representation or implementation data model is used to describe the conceptual schema. Conceptual schema also uses the conceptual data model.
- **External Level or View Level** provides a user's and application's view of the data. It includes one or more external schema. For a particular user, the external schema describes the structure of the database relevant to it, and hides rest of the information. It uses the data model at the conceptual level.

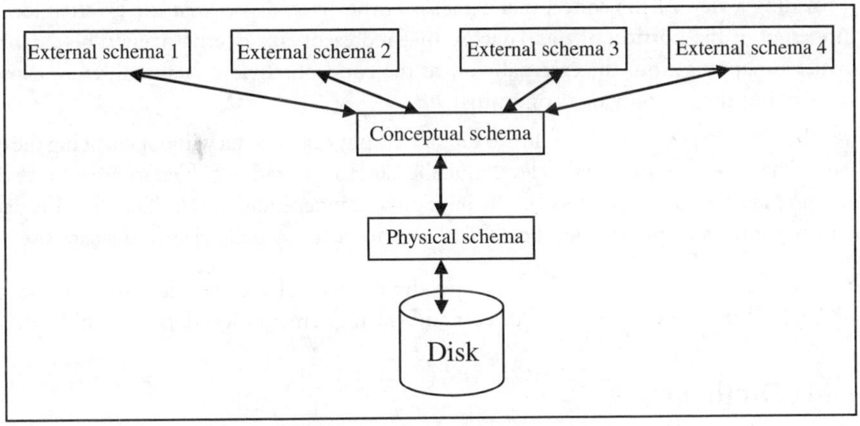

Figure 12.9 Three schema architecture

12.4 DATABASE MANAGEMENT SYSTEM

The interrelated set of data that forms the database needs to be stored and managed, so that the database can be accessed for the retrieval of data, and for insertion, deletion, or updating of data. *DBMS* is a software system for creating, organizing and managing the database. DBMS handles all access to the database and manages the database. Managing the database implies that it provides a convenient environment to the user to perform operations on the database for creation, insertion, deletion, updating, and retrieval of data. DBMS defines the scope of the use of database. This keeps data secure from unauthorized access. The functionality of DBMS includes—(1) the database that contains interrelated data, and (2) a set of programs to access the data. The DBMS implements the three schema architecture—internal schema at internal level, conceptual schema at conceptual level, and external schema at external level. The different DBMSs may not provide a clean distinction between the three levels, but generally they follow the three schema architecture.

Mapping is a term used for transforming requests and the results between different levels of the DBMS architecture. In a DBMS, the user interacts with the DBMS through the external view, and the data in the DBMS is stored at the physical level. Any request from the user, would require that the DBMS access the data and then present it to the user as specified in the external schema. This requires transforming the request from one level to the other, or mapping.

Some of the common commercial DBMSs are—Oracle Database, IBMs DB2, Microsoft's SQL Server and Microsoft Access. MySQL is a popular open source DBMS.

12.4.1 Data Independence

Data independence is defined as the ability to change a schema at one level without affecting the schema at another level. The mapping from the external level to conceptual level and from the conceptual level to the physical level provides two types of data independence—Logical Data Independence and Physical Data Independence.

- *Logical Data Independence* is the ability to modify the conceptual schema without resulting in a change in the external schema. The changes made to the conceptual schema may be like adding a record, adding a data item, updating constraints etc. The logical data independence is facilitated by providing a view of the conceptual database at the external level. At the external level, the user is interested in the portion of the database that represents its external view. The database system provides a mapping from the external view to the conceptual view. Many different external views may exist, but there is only one conceptual view.
- *Physical Data Independence* is the ability to modify the physical schema without changing the conceptual schema. The changes at the physical level could be like reorganization of files, improved access methods, change in physical storage devices etc. The physical data independence is facilitated by the database system by providing a mapping from the physical view to the conceptual view of the database.

The concept of data independence is similar to the concept of abstract data types in programming languages, where the interface is presented to user and the implementation details are hidden.

12.4.2 Data Dictionary

Data dictionary stores the data about the actual data stored in the database. Data dictionary contains metadata, i.e. data about the data. Metadata is the data that describe the properties or characteristics of other data. Some of these properties include data definitions, data structures and rules or constraints, the data item, the data type, length, minimum and maximum allowable values (where required) and a brief description of each data item. Metadata allow database designers and users to understand what data exist and what the data mean. Data dictionary keeps track of the following:

(1) *Definitions* of all data items in the database—It includes the elementary-level data items (fields), group and record-level data structures, and files or relational tables.

(2) *Relationships* that exists between various data structures,

(3) *Indexes* that are used to access data quickly, and

(4) *Screen and report format definitions* that may be used by various application programs.

12.4.3 Database Administrator (DBA)

DBA is a person or a group of persons who have centralized control of the database. DBA coordinates all activities of the database system. DBA has a good understanding of the database and of the needs and resources of the organization where it is installed. The DBA is responsible for creating, modifying and maintaining the three levels of DBMS architecture.

The functions of DBA include—(1) defining of schema, (2) defining of storage structure and access method, (3) modification of schema and physical organization, (4) granting user authority to access the database, and (5) acting in liaison with users, monitoring performance, and responding to changes in requirements.

12.4.4 Database Languages

In a DBMS, there is a need to specify the conceptual schema and the external schema. Once the schema is defined and data is filled in the schema, there is a need to manipulate the data, i.e. insertion, deletion, and modification of the data. For all these purposes, DBMS provides a set of languages—Data Definition Language (DDL), and Data Manipulation Language (DML). DDL is used by database designers for defining the database schema. DML is used for the manipulation of data. *Structured Query Language (SQL)* is a relational database language that represents a combination of both DDL and DML.

12.4.4.1 Data Definition Language (DDL)

DDL is a specification notation for defining the database schema. For example, a DDL command in SQL is as follows—

```
create table student (
    stud_rollno char(10),
    stud_name char(20),
    stud_age integer)
```

The *create table* command creates a table named student having three fields—*stud_rollno* of type character and size 10, *stud_name* of type character and size 20, and *stud_age* of type integer.

The DBMS has a DDL compiler which processes the DDL statements and generates a set of tables which are then stored in a data dictionary.

12.4.4.2 Data Manipulation Language (DML)

DML is a query language for accessing and manipulating the data stored in database. Data Manipulation Languages are of two main types—procedural, and non-procedural language. In a procedural language, user specifies both the data that is required and how to retrieve that data. The procedural language is embedded into a general-purpose programming language. However, in a non-procedural language, user specifies only what data is required without specifying how to retrieve the data. *SQL* is the *most widely used non-procedural query language.* For example, the SQL query to find name of the student having roll no A121, in the table *student* is—

```
select student.stud_name
    from student
    where student.stud_rollno = 'A121'
```

The DML commands (Figure 12.10) when used in a standalone interactive manner is called the *query language.*

```
SELECT fname, lname, mgrstartdate
FROM department, employee
WHERE mgrssn=ssn;

SELECT DISTINCT fname, lname
FROM employee, works_on
WHERE pno in(select pno
from works_on,employee
where fname='john' and lname='smith' and
   essn=ssn;)
```

Figure 12.10 DML commands

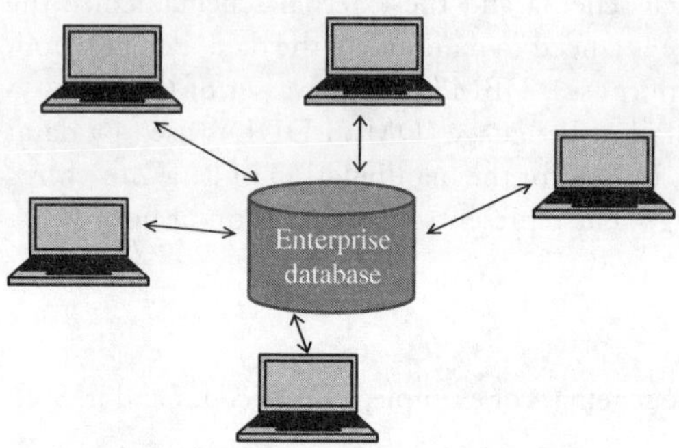

Figure 12.11 Centralized database

12.5 DATABASE SYSTEM ARCHITECTURES

The computers has evolved from big mainframe computers to small desktop personal computers. The advances in computer and its architecture have also resulted in the advances in databases and its architecture. Here, we discuss the architecture of databases of three kinds—Centralized DBMS Architecture, Client-Server Architecture, and Distributed Databases.

12.5.1 Centralized DBMS Architecture

- Centralized databases are the traditional database systems where all database functionality, data, application program and user interface processing are located on one machine. Access to the database from remote locations is via the communication links (Figure 12.11).
- In the early systems, the mainframe computers provided all the functionality required by the users of computer. The users interacted with the mainframe computers via dumb terminals. All processing was performed on the mainframe computer. The DBMS was centralized, and stored on the mainframes. The dumb terminals had only the display facility.
- The centralized database is easy to manage and administer.
- Common examples of centralized databases are personal database, and central computer database.

12.5.2 Client-Server Architecture

- The growth of Personal Computer (PC) has resulted in PCs replacing the dumb terminals. PCs are powerful and fast machines that can handle the user interface functionality.
- Client-Server systems involve a *client* machine and a *server* machine. Clients are PCs or workstations that have user interface capability and functionality for local processing. Servers are powerful computers that can manage the files (file servers), printer (printer servers), or, e-mails (e-mail servers). The client is connected to the server via a communication link. The client interacts with the server when it requires access to any additional functionality that does not exist in its own machine. Client provides interfaces to access and utilize the server resources.
- The Client-Server architecture has three components—the user interface programs, the application programs that contain the application logic, and the DBMS that stores the data. The request made by the user interface program is processed using the application logic which then accesses the database to retrieve the data.
- The DBMS architecture on the Client-Server systems are of two kinds—two-tier Client-Server architecture and three-tier Client-Server architecture.
- In *two-tier Client-Server architecture*, the user interface programs and the application programs run on the client side. An Application Program Interface (API) allows client side programs, to call the

DBMS which is at the server side. The client programs use Open Data Base Connectivity (ODBC) or Java Data Base Connectivity (JDBC) interfaces to communicate with the database.

- The *three-tier Client-Server architecture* is commonly used for web applications. In addition to the client and the database servers, it has an intermediate layer or middleware called Application Server or Web Server. The web server stores the application or business logic part of the application. The client stores the user interface. The DBMS is stored at the server side. The web server interacts with client at one end, and with the server for the DBMS at the other end. The web server acts like a pipe for receiving the client request, processing it and accessing the data from the DBMS server, and sending it back to the client. Figure 12.12 shows the two-tier and three-tier Client-Server architecture.

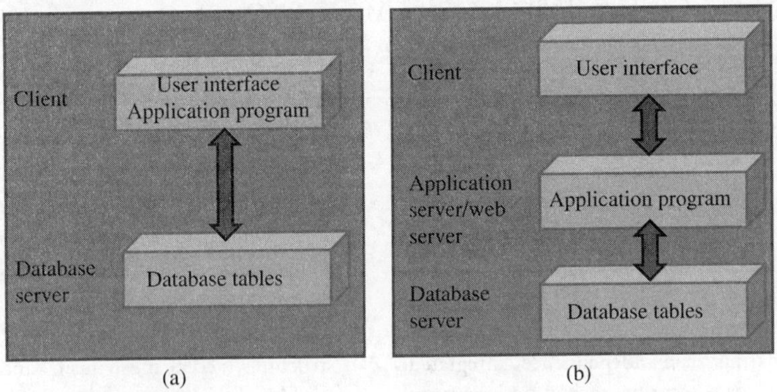

Figure 12.12 Client-server architecture (a) 2-Tier (b) 3-Tier

12.5.3 Distributed Databases

- A *distributed database* is one with decentralized functionality of the DBMS. It is distributed among a number of computers (Figure 12.13).
- The computers that store the components of database are physically placed at different geographical locations; however, all the components are logically related.
- Access to the distributed databases is from remote locations via the communication links.

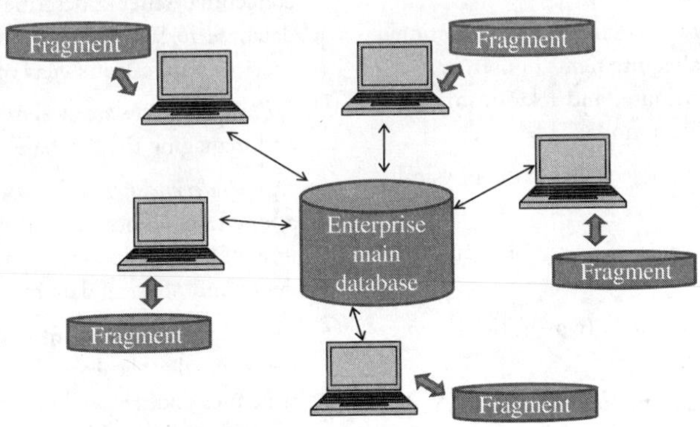

Figure 12.13 Distributed databases

12.6 DATABASE APPLICATIONS

Databases range from those designed for a single user with a desktop computer to those on mainframe computers with thousands of users. The database applications can be for different purposes like—(1)

personal databases that support one user with a stand-alone personal computer, (2) *workgroup databases* for a small team of people (less than 25) who work in collaboration on a project, (3) *departmental databases* designed to support the various functions and activities of a department (a functional unit of an organization), and (4) *enterprise databases* to support organization-wide operations and decision making. Data warehouse is an enterprise database.

The DBMS commonly provides tools to the application programmer for application development. Some of the tools provided by DBMS include tools for screen, menu, and report generation, application generators, compilers, and data and view definition facilities. Modern database systems provide language components that are much more powerful than those of traditional languages. For example, Developer 2000/PowerBuilder for Oracle, and Visual Basic for Microsoft SQL server.

SUMMARY

- *Database* is a repository or collection of logically related and similar data.
- The *file-oriented* approach has several drawbacks. *Database* approach provides solutions for handling the problems of the file system approach.
- The *characteristics of database* approach include—minimized data redundancy, reduced data inconsistency, data sharing, data independence, integrated data, improved data security, backup and recovery support, standards enforcement, and reduction in application development time.
- A *data model* describes the structure of database. *Schema* contains information about the description of database. *Instances* are the actual data contained in database.
- Conceptual Data Model, Representation Data Model and Physical Data Model are the three *types of data models.*
- *Conceptual Data Model* defines the functional requirements and data requirements of user, conceptually, using entity, attribute, and relationship. *E-R model* is a conceptual data model.
- An *entity* is a real-world object that exists physically or conceptually.
- An *attribute* describes some property, or characteristics of the entity.
- An association or link between two entities is represented using a *relationship.*
- Hierarchical, relational, and network data models are the three *representation data models.*
- Table, row, column, key and data values are the terms associated with a *relational model.* A table is made up of rows and columns. A *key* uniquely identifies a row in a table.
- The schema of a *hierarchical database* model is represented using a tree-structure diagram. The schema is based on parent-child relationship.
- The schema of *network database model* is represented using a data-structure diagram. The schema is based on owner-member relationship.
- The *physical data model* describes internal storage structures, access mechanism, and organization of the files of database.
- A *database system* integrates collection, storage and dissemination of data required for the different operations of an organization.
- Users, Hardware, Software, and Data are the four main *components of a database system.*
- The *architecture of database system* is ANSI/SPARC architecture, divided into three levels—internal schema describes the physical storage structure, conceptual schema describes the structure of whole database for users, and external schema provides a user's or application's view of the data.
- *DBMS* is a software system for creating, organizing and managing the database.
- *Data independence* is the ability to change a schema at one level without affecting the schema at another level. Data independence is logical data independence and physical data independence
- *Data dictionary* keeps track of the definitions of data items in the database, relationships between data structures, indexes used to access data, and, screen and report format definitions.
- DBMS provides a set of *languages*—DDL, and DML. DDL is used to define the database schema. DML is a query language for accessing and manipulating data stored in the database.

- *SQL* is a relational database language that represents a combination of both DDL and DML.
- The *architecture of databases* is of three kinds—Centralized DBMS architecture, Client-Server architecture and Distributed Databases.
- The *three-tier Client-Server architecture* is commonly used for web applications. The client stores the user interface. The web server stores the business logic part of the application. The DBMS is at the server side.
- The *database applications* are for different purposes like personal databases, workgroup databases, departmental databases, and enterprise databases.

KEYWORDS

QUESTIONS

Section 12.2–12.2.2

1. Define: (1) Database, (2) Data redundancy, (3) Data consistency, and (4) Data Sharing.
2. List the differences between file-oriented approach and database approach.
3. List the characteristics of the database approach.
4. Explain the characteristics of database approach.
5. "Data redundancy provides opportunity for data inconsistency". Explain.

Section 12.2.3–12.2.4.4

6. Define: (1) Data model, (2) Schema, (3) Instance, (4) Entity, (5) Attribute, (6) Domain of attribute, and (7) Cardinality Ratio.
7. How are entity and attribute related?
8. Explain the different kinds of cardinality ratios.
9. Name the symbols used to represent (1) entity, (2) attribute, and (3) relationship in an E-R diagram.
10. Give an example of conceptual data model.
11. What is an E-R diagram?

Section 12.2.5–12.2.5.1

12. Name the different types of representation data models.
13. Who proposed the Relational Data Model?
14. How are the terms table, record, field, key, and data values related?
15. What is the purpose of the key in relational data model?
16. Name two commercial relational databases.
17. What is a primary key?
18. Define the terms: (1) table, (2) record, (3) field, (4) key, and (5) data values.

Section 12.2.5.2–12.2.6

19. Describe the features of Hierarchical Data Model.
20. The schema of a hierarchical database is represented using a ________diagram.
21. The schema of hierarchical database is based on ________ relationship.
22. Name one commercial hierarchical database.
23. The hierarchical database model was developed by _______.
24. The schema of network database model is represented using a ________ diagram.
25. The schema of network database is based on ___________ relationship
26. Describe the features of Network Data Model.
27. Name one commercial network database.
28. What is the purpose of Physical Data Model?

Section 12.3–12.3.2

29. Define a database system.
30. List the components of database system.
31. Explain in detail the components of database system.
32. Explain the role of different categories of users in a database system.
33. What is the purpose of application software and user interface software in the database system?
34. "The data in a database system is integrated and shared". Explain.
35. Name the three levels of ANSI/SPARC architecture.
36. What is the purpose of internal level, conceptual level and external level in the ANSI/SPARC architecture?
37. Explain the three schema architecture of database system in detail.

Section 12.4–12.4.4.2

38. Define: (1) DBMS, (2) Mapping, and (3) Data independence.
39. What is the need of mapping in a DBMS?
40. Name two commercial DBMS software.
41. What is logical data independence?
42. What is physical data independence?
43. Define a data dictionary.
44. Explain the function of data dictionary.
45. What are the functions of DBA?
46. What is the need of database languages?
47. DBMS provides two database languages _____ and _____.
48. What is the use of DDL?
49. What is the use of DML language?
50. What is a Structured Query Language?

Section 12.5

51. What is a centralized DBMS architecture?
52. Explain the client-server architecture.
53. How is the two-tier client-server architecture different from the three-tier client-server architecture?
54. What are distributed databases?
55. Name some database applications.

Extra Questions

56. Give full form of the following abbreviations:

(i) DBMS	(ii) DBA
(iii) E-R Model	(iv) DDL
(v) DML	(vi) SQL
(vii) ODBC	(viii) JDBC
(ix) CODASYL	(x) DBTG
(xi) CASE	

57. Write short notes on:

(a) Database System	(b) DBMS
(c) Components of database system	(d) Data Model
(e) Schema	(f) Data dictionary
(g) Conceptual data model	(h) Entity
(i) Attribute	(j) Key
(k) E-R model	(l) Hierarchical model
(m) Database Applications	(n) Network model

(o) Relational model

(p) Database Architecture

(q) Data independence

(r) Client-Server Architecture

(s) Database Administrator

(t) Database Languages

58. Give differences between the following:

(a) Logical Data Independence and Physical Data Independence

(b) DDL and DML

(c) Centralized databases and Distributed databases

(d) Internal Level and Conceptual Level

(e) Hierarchical, Network and Relational data models

(f) Conceptual data model and Representation data model

(g) File-Oriented Approach and Database Approach

(h) 2-Tier and 3-Tier Client-Server architecture

13 MULTIMEDIA

Contents

- Multimedia: definition—Mass media and multimedia
- Characteristics of multimedia system—Computer, integration of elements, digital format, interactive
- Elements of multimedia
  - Text—Text font, text effects, text animation, text on the Internet
  - Graphics—Image resolution, image color, image file size, image compression, image capture, bitmap graphics, vector graphics
  - Audio—Properties of sound, digital audio, sound hardware, sound sampling, sound digitization, music and speech, audio file formats, audio editors, sound compression, selecting a quality audio, audio from a CD to web
  - Video—Analog and digital video, video editing, digitizing analog video, video compression, video file formats, video on Internet
  - Animation—Process of animation, creation of animation, hardware and software for animation, animation file formats
- Multimedia system—Desirable features of multimedia system
- Multimedia applications—Education, entertainment, training, business, virtual reality

Why this chapter

Listening to music (CD player, iPod or mp3 player), watching movies (CD, Internet), loading photographs from digital camera to the computer, loading the video clip to the computer, watching animation movies, and playing computer games are some of the multimedia applications. You are using multimedia, quite often, almost every day. The purpose of this chapter is to introduce you to the Multimedia and its elements, and the multimedia applications.

13.1 INTRODUCTION

Newspaper and television are the common medium of mass communication. However, they differ in the way they present information to the user. The information in a newspaper is presented as a combination of text, image, and graphics. This has a different impact on the user than the information presented on the television as a combination of image, photo, video, sound and music. Similarly, talking over a telephone (using sound) has a different impact on the user, than, talking using the Internet telephone with a web camera (sound and photo) attached to it. In other words, the same information when presented using different media has a different impact on the user. Or, we can say that the media used for presenting the information affects the way the user perceives and understands the information. *Multimedia* is a combination of graphics, audio, text, animation, and video using the computer.

In this chapter, we will study the different elements of multimedia like sound, graphics, text, and animation, in detail. This chapter also describes the hardware requirements for the multimedia systems like input and output devices, and the storage requirements. It also discusses the software tools required for drawing images, creating videos, introducing sound effects, and for the compression of multimedia files. Finally, the chapter discusses the penetration of multimedia in our lives, in diverse areas like education, business, training, and entertainment.

13.2 MULTIMEDIA: DEFINITION

Newspaper, radio, television and films are some of the earliest and traditional means of mass communication that use *mass media*. Newspapers use text, image and graphics, and, television uses text, image, graphics, and sound (Figure 13.1). In these traditional means of communication, the communication is one-way—from the media to the mass users. The user simply reads the newspaper, listens to the radio, and watches the television and films, and, cannot in any way manipulate the media. Mass media is used by the user in a sequence, linearly. For example, a text book consists of a sequence of combination of text, graphics, and images. The text book is meant to be read linearly from the start to the end. With mass media, the user is in a passive state (receiving whatever is communicated).

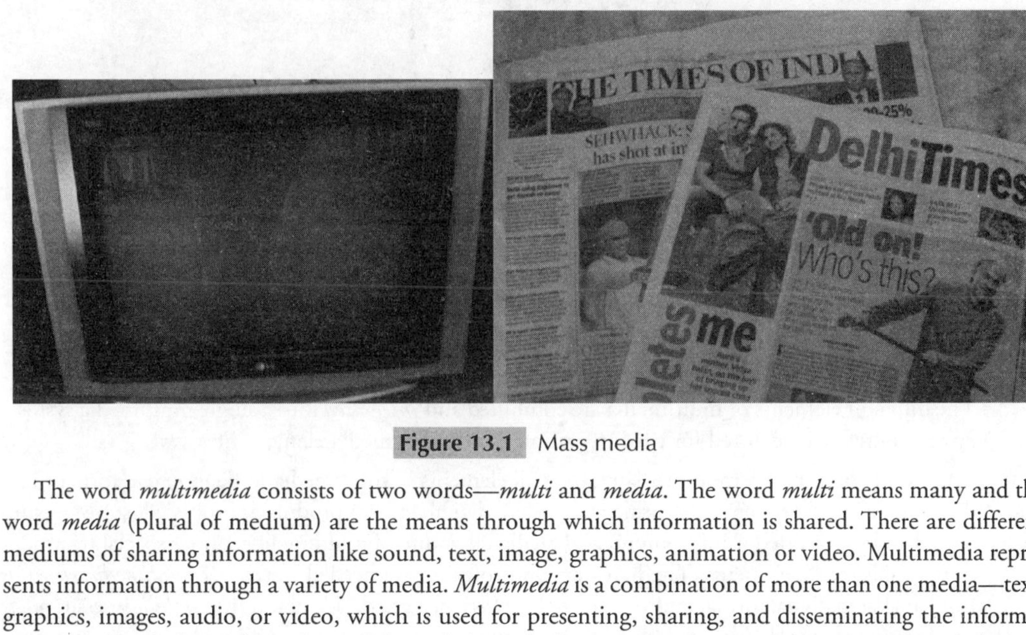

Figure 13.1 Mass media

The word *multimedia* consists of two words—*multi* and *media*. The word *multi* means many and the word *media* (plural of medium) are the means through which information is shared. There are different mediums of sharing information like sound, text, image, graphics, animation or video. Multimedia represents information through a variety of media. *Multimedia* is a combination of more than one media—text, graphics, images, audio, or video, which is used for presenting, sharing, and disseminating the information (Figure 13.2). Multimedia is delivered through the computer and microprocessor-based devices, thereby introducing the elements of interactivity, which differentiates it from the traditional forms of media (also called mass media). *Multimedia* or *Interactive multimedia* allows the user and the multimedia application to respond to each other. The user is able to control the elements of the multimedia application in terms of what elements will be delivered and when. Since multimedia systems are integrated with computers, they are also referred to as the *digital multimedia system*.

13.3 CHARACTERISTICS OF MULTIMEDIA SYSTEM

A multimedia system has four basic characteristics:

- *Computer* is an intrinsic part of the multimedia system. As a result, multimedia has become interactive. In multimedia, computer allows the user to interact with the media and thus manipulate it

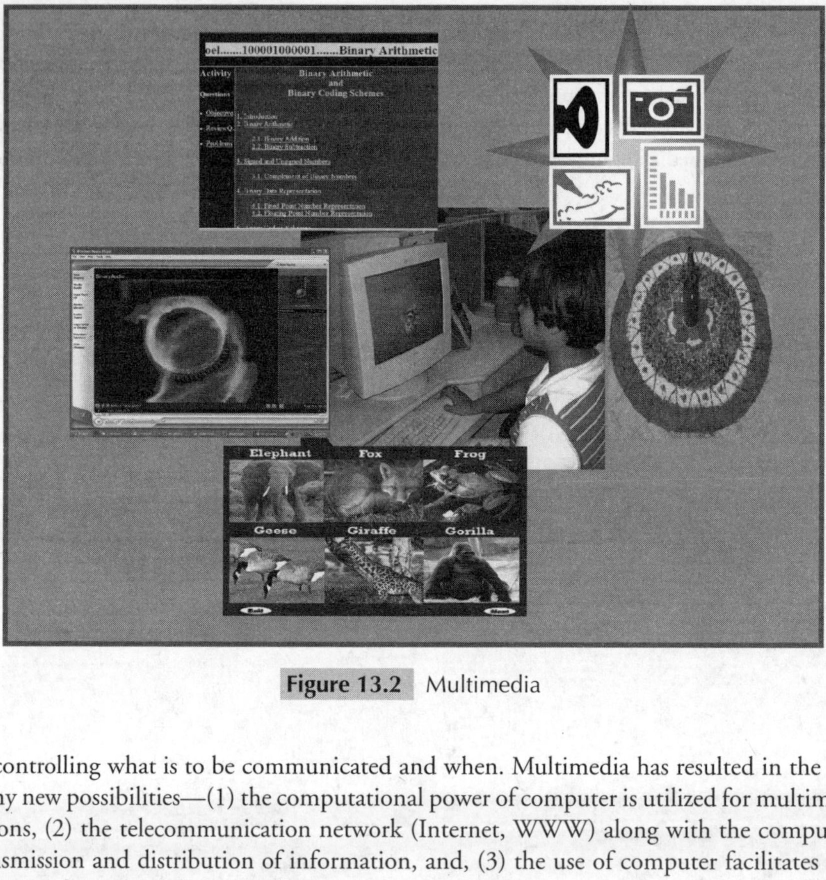

Figure 13.2 Multimedia

by controlling what is to be communicated and when. Multimedia has resulted in the creation of many new possibilities—(1) the computational power of computer is utilized for multimedia applications, (2) the telecommunication network (Internet, WWW) along with the computer enables transmission and distribution of information, and, (3) the use of computer facilitates design and creation of a variety of new applications.

- The different elements of multimedia are combined and *integrated* into a single multimedia system. Special software is required for the integration of different media element files.
- The use of computer in multimedia requires all elements of multimedia to be in *digital* format. In a digital multimedia system, the media streams are digital and are produced, processed, stored, represented and transmitted using computers. The digital nature of multimedia requires special treatment of the multimedia elements. The hardware and software are needed to *convert multimedia elements* from analog to digital format and vice versa. There is a need to decide about the *resolution* versus *quality* of output required, during storing of data in the computer. Storing multimedia files on computer hard disk takes large amount of disk space, so *compression technologies* and *file formats* for storing the different media elements is required. Moreover, special programs are required to *play* the compressed files. Similarly, special software is required to *edit* the different media element files, and to combine and integrate the different elements of the multimedia into a single multimedia system.
- Multimedia system is *interactive*. The user is active and can manipulate whatever is being communicated. Multimedia allows two-way communication. The user can use devices like keyboard, trackball or joystick to interact with the multimedia system. Interactive multimedia is non-linear. The user is able to follow the links and jump from one part of the document to the other. *Hypermedia* enables a user to gain or provide access to text, audio and video, and computer graphics using links in a non-linear way, using computers. World Wide Web (WWW) is an example of hypermedia application. The user is able to respond and control what to see or hear and when to do it.

13.4 ELEMENTS OF MULTIMEDIA

A multimedia system consists of several elements like—text, graphics, sound, video, and animation. The data streams of these different elements of the multimedia system are of two kinds—time-dependent, and time-independent. Media like text, graphics, and image are time-independent. The information is not dependent on the timing of the data stream when using these media. However, media like audio, video, and animation are time-dependent. In time-dependent media, the data streams must appear at regular time intervals for the purposes of continuity.

The different media elements are described briefly in the following subsections.

13.4.1 Text

- Text is an important element of multimedia. The purpose of using text is to write titles, to define menus, to navigate, and to write the content.
- The text in multimedia is different from the traditional text written using paper and pen. Multimedia text is combined with other elements like graphics and pictures to deliver a powerful effect. Multimedia text can be written in a way that the user needs to jump back and forth, written in multiple channels like pictures, sound, animation, and colored text.
- The text must be short and relevant wherever used. Text is often mixed with art resulting in a much greater impact on the user. Text can also be animated. Text has evolved from being displayed in one size and one color under MS-DOS, to being specified using fonts and color on a color monitor having Windows, to the vector-based text by Adobe which uses graphics-based fonts and creates images.
- *Text Font*—The text can be written in different *fonts*: (Figure 13.3) A font is composed of three things—typeface, style and size. Arial, Courier, Times are typefaces. Bold and italics are styles. Size is the length of the character (from top to bottom). *Arial 11-point italic* is a font.
- *Text effects* allow special effects to be added to text fonts by adding depth and visual impact (2D and 3D effects). Text effects can be created using MS-Word's WordArt (Figure 13.4). In WordArt, text is treated as a drawing object, i.e. text can be manipulated like an object. WordArt provides special effects to the text like, depth, direction, shape, color, and texture. Figure 13.5 shows the same text with different text effects.
- *Text animation* can be used to make the text move, change or flash. MS-WORD and MS-PowerPoint can be used for text animation.

Figure 13.3 Using different text fonts

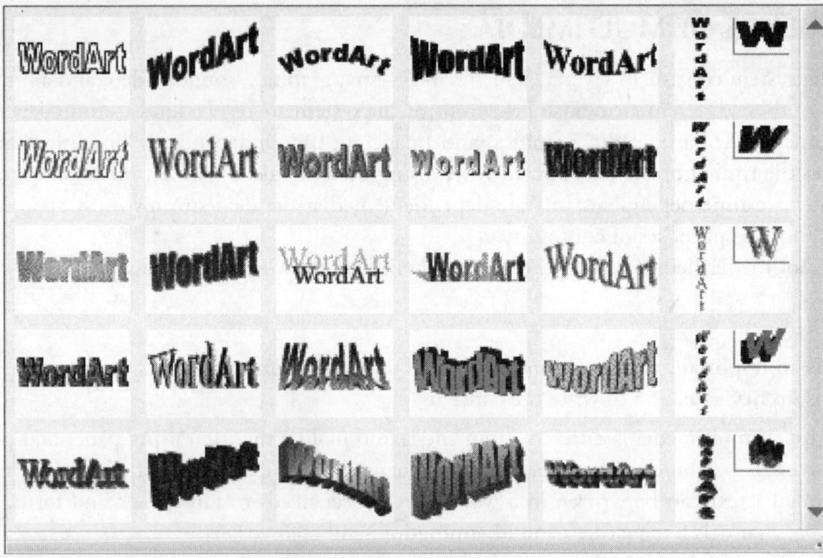

Figure 13.4 WordArt in MS-Word 2007

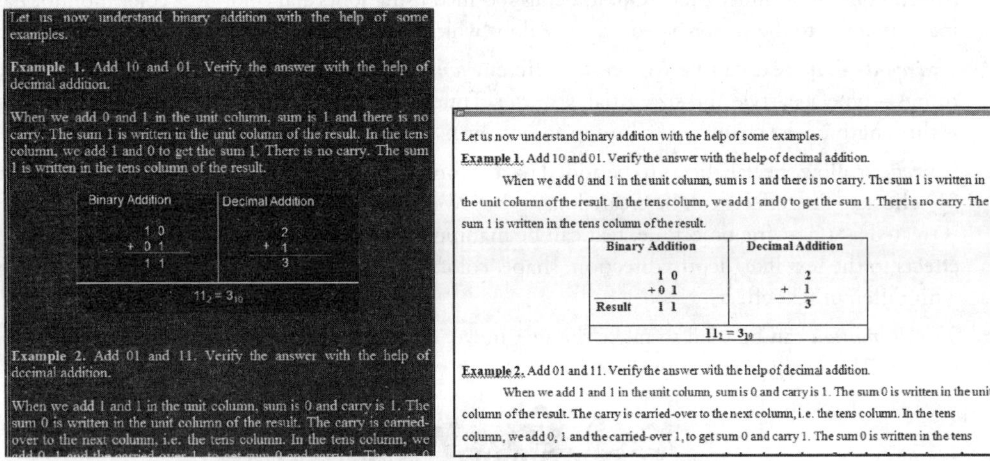

Let us now understand binary addition with the help of some examples.

Example 1. Add 10 and 01. Verify the answer with the help of decimal addition.

When we add 0 and 1 in the unit column, sum is 1 and there is no carry. The sum 1 is written in the unit column of the result. In the tens column, we add 1 and 0 to get the sum 1. There is no carry. The sum 1 is written in the tens column of the result.

Binary Addition	Decimal Addition
1 0 + 0 1 1 1	2 + 1 3
$11_2 = 3_{10}$	

Example 2. Add 01 and 11. Verify the answer with the help of decimal addition.

When we add 1 and 1 in the unit column, sum is 0 and carry is 1. The sum 0 is written in the unit column of the result. The carry is carried-over to the next column, i.e. the tens column. In the tens column, we

Let us now understand binary addition with the help of some examples.

Example 1. Add 10 and 01. Verify the answer with the help of decimal addition.

When we add 0 and 1 in the unit column, sum is 1 and there is no carry. The sum 1 is written in the unit column of the result. In the tens column, we add 1 and 0 to get the sum 1. There is no carry. The sum 1 is written in the tens column of the result.

	Binary Addition	Decimal Addition
	1 0 + 0 1	2 + 1
Result	1 1	3
$11_2 = 3_{10}$		

Example 2. Add 01 and 11. Verify the answer with the help of decimal addition.

When we add 1 and 1 in the unit column, sum is 0 and carry is 1. The sum 0 is written in the unit column of the result. The carry is carried-over to the next column, i.e. the tens column. In the tens column, we add 0, 1 and the carried-over 1, to get sum 0 and carry 1. The sum 0 is written in the tens

Figure 13.5 Text with different font colour, text effects etc.

- *Text on the Internet* can be represented as hypertext. A *hypertext* uses documents to be connected via hyperlink. Using hypertext, different documents can be linked and different parts of the same document can be linked. Hyperlinks allow the user to navigate the document in a non-linear way. Using of hyperlink results in the breakdown of the information into small parts (Figure 13.6).

13.4.2 Graphics

Communication via pictures is easier to understand. Graphics is the most important element of multimedia. Multimedia presentations are predominantly graphics-based. Graphics elements in a multimedia system are images that could be still pictures (like photographs) converted to digital format with the help of scanners, or pictures generated on the computer. They may be 2-dimensional such as photographs, or, 3-dimensional such as objects around us. They may be either static graphic elements or animated. In computer graphics, an image is always a digital image.

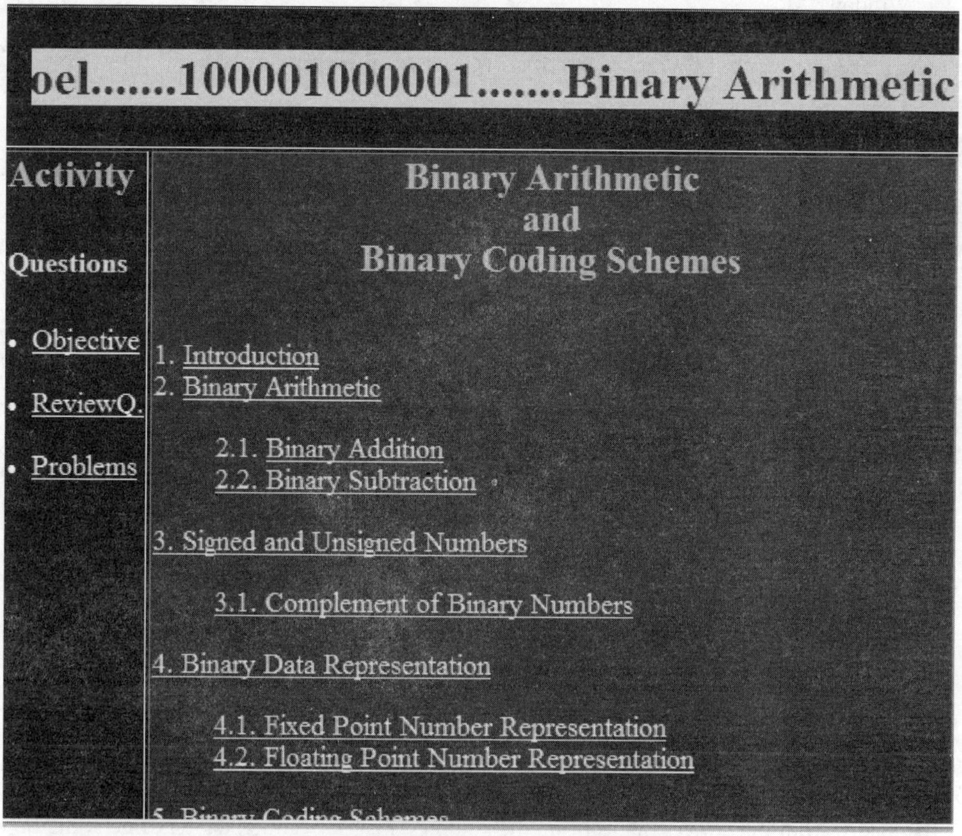

Figure 13.6 Text hyperlinks

- **Image Resolution:** The *resolution* of an image is the number of pixels in the digital image relative to the physical size of the original material. Resolution is measured in dpi (dots per inch) and is applied to the image and also to the input and output devices used to scan or print the image. Resolution of monitor is generally, 72 pixels/inch. Higher the resolution, better is the picture.
- **Image Color:** There are two image color models—Red, Green, and Blue (RGB) model, and, Hue, Saturation, and Lightness (HSL) model. The three colors—red, green, and blue—give us quite a large spectrum by just adding colors. In HSL, the classification of the color circle rests upon three attributes of colors, called Hue, Brightness, and Saturation.
- **Image File Size:** The image that has been created has to be stored on the computer. The size of a digital graphic is the size of the graphics file on the computer. The size of graphic files is dependent on three things—(i) *Dimension of the graphics* is the physical size (maximum height and width in pixels), (ii) *Bit-depth* is the amount of color information stored in each pixel, and (iii) the *compression* used to store the image. The quality and size of the graphics file is dependent on the amount of compression used.
- **Image Compression:** Usage of compression technologies is important, especially, for graphics used on the Internet, since download time goes up drastically with increasing file size. While the image is compressed, the quality of the image must not suffer. Two image compression algorithms are widely used on the Internet—Joint Photographic Experts Group (JPEG) and Graphical Interchange Format (GIF).

- **JPEG** compression works well with 24-bit color images (true color). It is suited for images that contain many colors (such as photographs). Figure 13.7 shows files stored with type .jpeg in Windows XP.

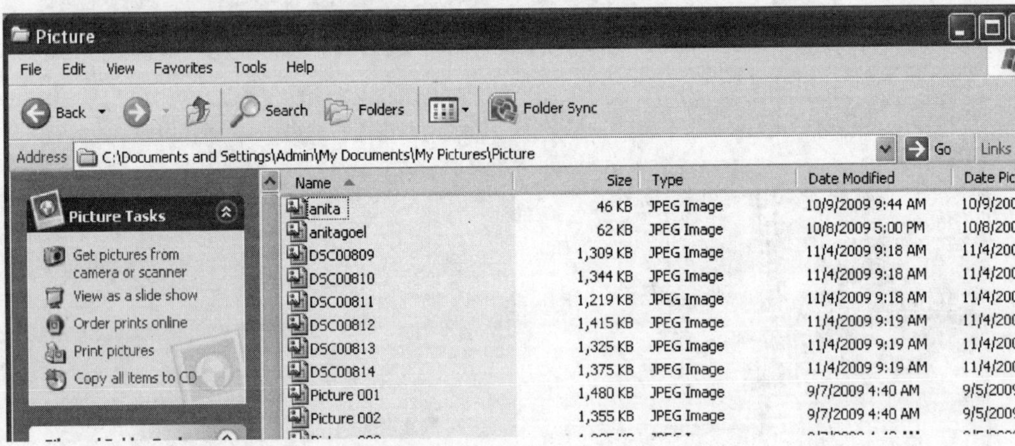

Figure 13.7 Pictures stored as jpeg

- **GIF** supports 8 bits of color information (Grayscale, Color map). GIF compression is suited to images such as line drawings, for images containing text, and cartoons containing at most 256 colors. It is preferred for vector graphics over the Internet.
- *jpg* (for JPEG) and *.gif* (for GIF) are the most common file formats in use on the web. A relatively new file format—portable network graphic (.png), improves upon some of *.gif* features. Web browsers require plug-ins for *.png*.

⊙ **Image Capture:** The graphic images on the computer can either be created using editors or can be loaded from the devices that capture the graphics images. Scanner, digital camera, digital video camera, and clip art are devices used for loading images on to the computer. Scanner looks like a photocopy machine and is used to copy an image to the computer. It converts an analog picture into digital format. Digital camera stores digitized images and digital video camera stores digitized images with motion, on the computer. Clip art are built-in collection of pictures on many word processors (Figure 13.8).

There are two types of digital graphics—bitmap graphics and vector graphics.

13.4.2.1 Bitmap Graphics

⊙ In bitmap graphics, computer programs store pictures as pixel maps (*bit-maps or raster images*). The monitor is divided into a grid of *pixels* (short form of picture elements). Screen area of 800 × 600 pixels is common on Windows platform. Each pixel contains value representing a particular color. When a picture is sent to the screen, a graphics driver converts the picture data to pixel values on the display.

⊙ *Bitmap editors* allow creating and editing graphics as bitmaps. For example, to retouch a photograph, just scan it and use bitmap editor to edit it (Figure 13.9). The paint programs and photo-editing programs are bitmap-based programs. Some of the commonly used bitmap editors are Lview Pro, GIF 89a, Paint Shop Pro, Adobe Photoshop, Fractal Design Painter, Flash, Corel Draw, Corel Photo Paint, and 3D Studio. Figure 13.10 shows an image to be edited in Adobe Photoshop.

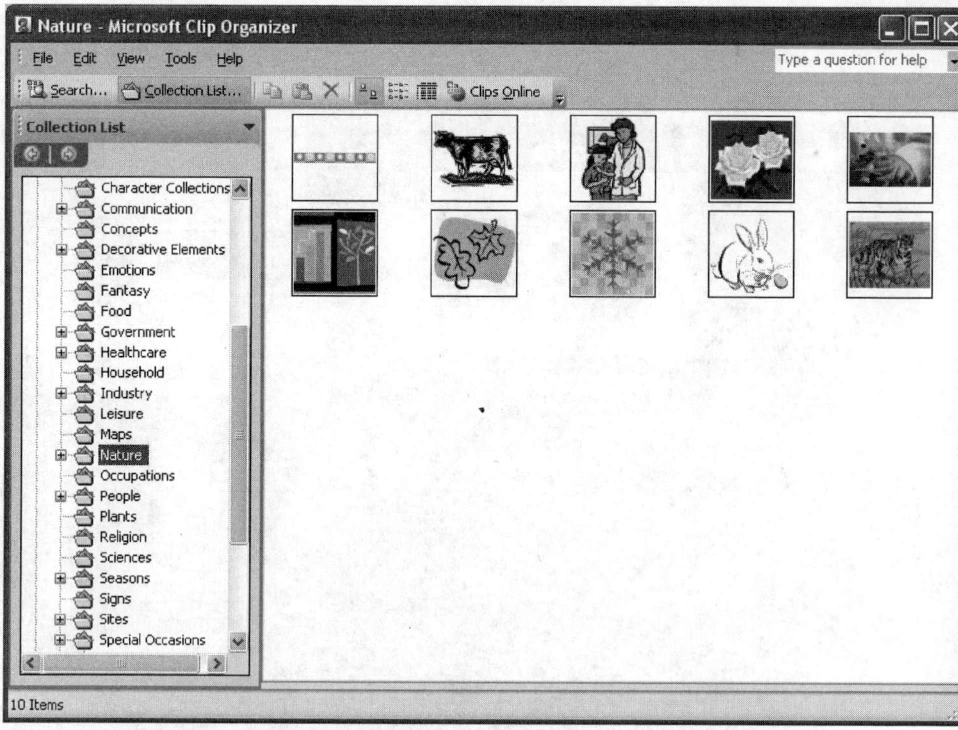

Figure 13.8 Clip art in MS-Word 2007

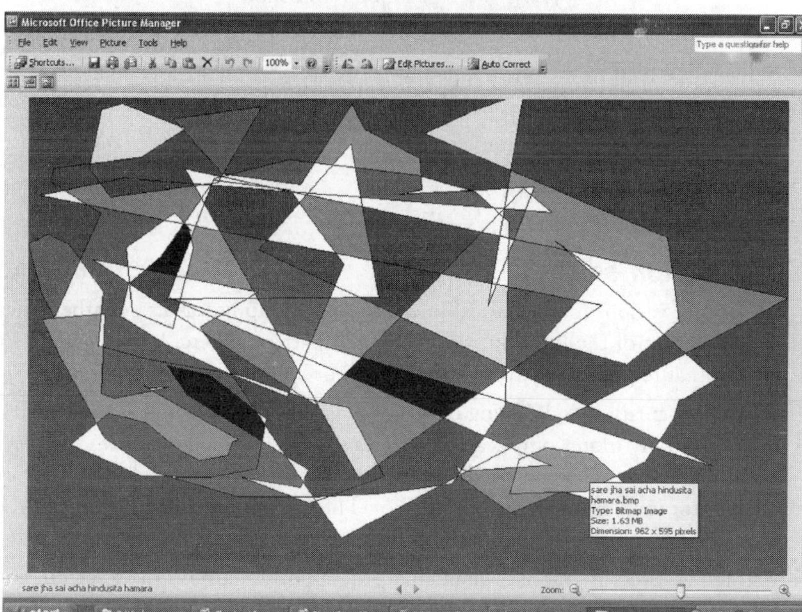

Figure 13.9 A bitmap image

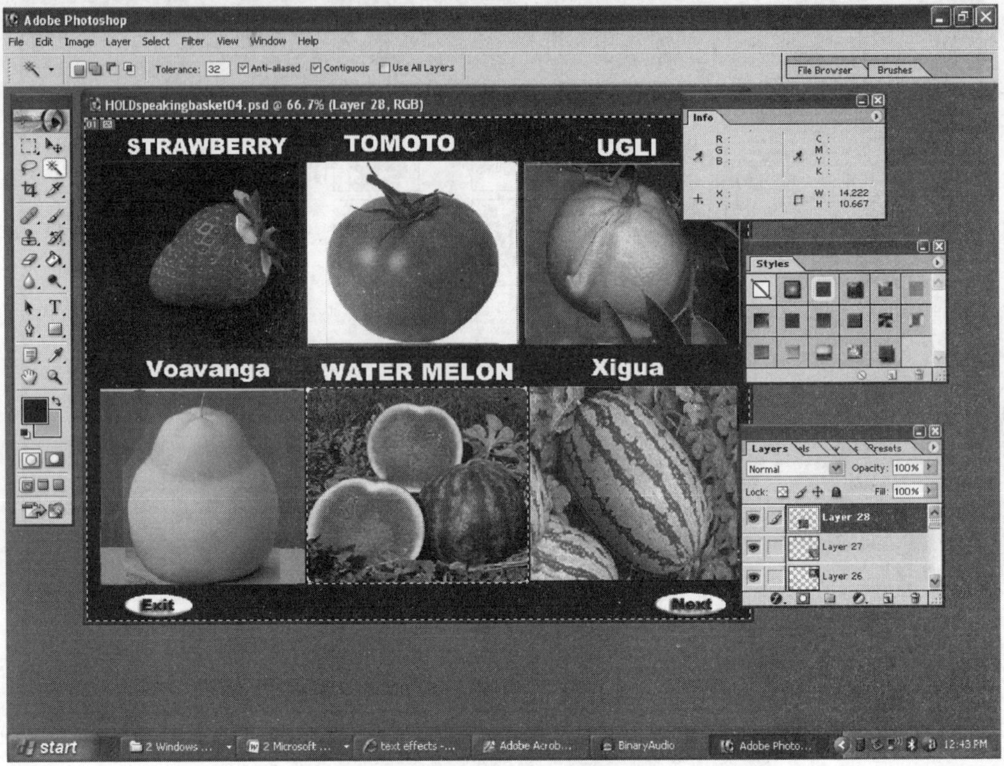

Figure 13.10 Adobe Photoshop

- A bitmap image is stored in the bit-mapped (or raster image) file format. Scanners, digital camera and digital video camera store images as bitmap images.
- Some formats for storing bitmap graphics files are GIF, JPEG, BitMaP (BMP), PostScript (PS), IRIS, and Tagged Image File Format (TIFF).

13.4.2.2 Vector Graphics

- *Vector graphics* uses various mathematical tracks to create graphics. It uses mathematical equations for the representation of the location, size, color fill, pattern fill etc. Vector graphics is suited for graphic images that require frequent re-sizing (small or enlarge), and repositioning.
- *Vector editors* allow creation and editing of vector graphics. Vector editor is used to draw cartoons, and to create or modify more complicated graphics such as photographs. For example, a geometric figure (straight line or circle) can be drawn on the monitor by using a mathematical equation. Adobe® Illustrator is an example of vector editor. The Computer Aided Design (CAD) programs, 3-dimensional modeling and animation programs are vector-based programs.
- A picture stored as a vector graphic, when enlarged, appears sharp on the screen in comparison to an enlarged picture using bitmap. This is because in vector graphics the re-sizing requires using different values in the mathematical equation representing the graphics. Clip art image can be stored both as bitmap and vector graphics.

13.4.3 Audio

Sound consists of all possible sounds which may or may not be audible to humans. Audio consists of the sounds humans can hear. For example, the sound emitted by the dog-whistle is heard by dogs but not by humans. The presence of sound enhances the effect of a graphic presentation, video or animation. In a multimedia project, sound can be used in two ways. It can be used to provide audio content in a multimedia system such as, narration for a clip playing on the screen; audio sound tracks in movies; short instructions; or, music to communicate as in a song. Sound can also be used in the background and for sound effects.

- Sound is produced through vibrations and pressure variations in the air. The vibrations generate a waveform repeated at regular intervals (periods).
- **Properties of Sound**
  - *Amplitude* measures the relative loudness or volume of the sound. It is measured in decibels.
  - *Frequency* or *pitch* is the vibrations per second. If an object vibrates rapidly, it creates a high-pitched sound. A low-pitch sound is produced by an object that vibrates slowly. The unit of frequency is hertz (Hz). The human ear can hear frequencies in the range of 20Hz to 20 kHz.
  - *Bandwidth* is the difference between the highest and the lowest frequency contained in a sound signal. A signal with frequency range of 200 Hz to 3,200 Hz, has a bandwidth of 3,000 Hz (= 3,200–200).
- **Digital Audio**—Audio is analog in nature and is a continuous waveform. Also, acoustic instruments produce analog sounds. A computer needs to transfer the analog sound waves into its digital representation consisting of discrete numbers. Representation of a waveform in a digital way is made by an Analog-to-Digital Converter (ADC). The reverse process is called Digital-to-Analog Conversion (DAC).
- **Sound Hardware**—Microphone and Speakers are the devices connected to the ADC and DAC, respectively. A microphone converts the sound waves into electrical signals. This signal is amplified, filtered, and sent to ADC. This information is then retrieved and edited using a computer. To convert this data into sound waves, the audio data is sent to the speakers via a DAC and a reconstruction filter. This produces the analog sound waves that human beings can hear.
- **Sound Sampling**—is a process that converts the analog signal into a digital format. *Sound sampling* transfers a continuous sound wave into discrete numbers. The rate at which the continuous waveform is sampled is called the *sampling rate.* The rate varies from 5,000–90,000 samples/second. Sampling rate is an important factor in determining how accurately the digitized sound represents the original analog sound. E.g. CD (Compact Disk) sampling rate is 44.1 kHz (44,100 samples/sec) and telephone quality audio is sampled at 8 kHz.
- **Sound Digitization**—is the process of assigning a discrete value to each of the sampled values. It is performed by an ADC. Recording at high sampling rates produces a more accurate capture of the high-frequency content of the sound. Along with the sampling rate, the *resolution* determines the accuracy with which the sound is digitized. The increase in the number of bits in a recording makes the sound playback increasingly realistic. Sound formats are standard in most audio editing software. Sampling rates of 8, 11, 22, and 44 kHz are normally used. There is no loss of quality when reproducing digital audio.
- **Music and Speech**—Digital audio (music and speech) can be *created* or *synthesized* using the computer. Synthesized sounds are a set of instructions to the hardware audio device on how and when to produce sound.

- Musical Instrument Digital Interface (**MIDI**) format is the most widely used digital format for generating synthesized sound. In MIDI, the actual data is not recorded. MIDI works by recording the keys depressed, time when the key was depressed, duration for which the key was depressed, and how hard the key was struck. Almost all software that support audio can play MIDI files.
- **Speech** is the natural form of human communication. Speech is time-bound, dynamic, and transient. Distortion and noise are some of the speech effects.

⊙ **Audio File Formats**—The audio is stored on the computer as an audio file. Some commonly used audio file formats are—Resource Interleave File Format (RIFF) saved with extension (.wav), Motion Picture Experts Group (MPEG) as (mpg, mp2, mp3), or MIDI as (.mid, midi).

Figure 13.11 An audio editor software

⊙ **Audio Editors**—Audio editors are used to *record* or *manipulate audio files*. The editors require a sound card to be installed on the computer. The editors allow the user to perform functions like copy and paste, and, concatenate, append, or mix two or more audio files. Sound effects can be incorporated in audio files using audio editors. Some common audio editing software for Windows are—Cool Edit, Sound Forge XP, Audacity, and Wave Flow. Figure 13.11 shows the icon of Audacity audio editor.

⊙ **Audio Compression**—Compression is used to reduce the physical size of data so that it occupies less storage space and memory. Compressed audio files are easier and faster to transfer (small size), and also reduces bandwidth utilization thus providing good sound quality. Since applications exchange audio data using networks, standards like International Consultative Committee for Telephone and Telegraph (CCITT), International Standard Organization (ISO), and MPEG are used to achieve the compatibility. The most commonly used compression scheme for audio is MPEG. *MPEG* audio coding can compress the original audio on a CD by a factor of 12 without losing the sound quality. Audio files are often encoded in Mp3 (compression ratio is 1:10-1:12) as it is the most preferred format for PC and Internet applications.

⊙ **Selecting a Quality Audio**—The choice of sampling rate and compression for an audio depends upon its use. Sound that is to be embedded on a web page and downloaded over the Internet uses a low or medium sampling rate with compression. For recording a song on a CD, the highest sampling rate of 44.1 kHz is used. Figure 13.12 and Figure 13.13 shows an audio file in windows Media players and Audacity, respectively.

13.4.3.1 Audio from a CD to Web

The conversion of audio from a CD onto the web is done in two steps—CD Ripping and MPS Encoding.

⊙ **CD Ripping**—is a process of converting audio CD into *.wav* format. It uses a program known as the CD Ripper or Grabber. A grabber reads the digital data directly from the CD and stores it as a *.wav* file on the hard disk. The *.wav* file produced by CD ripper contains exactly the same information that is on the CD, without any loss of quality. The *.wav* file is huge (10 MB per minute of sound), and is difficult to store and transfer.

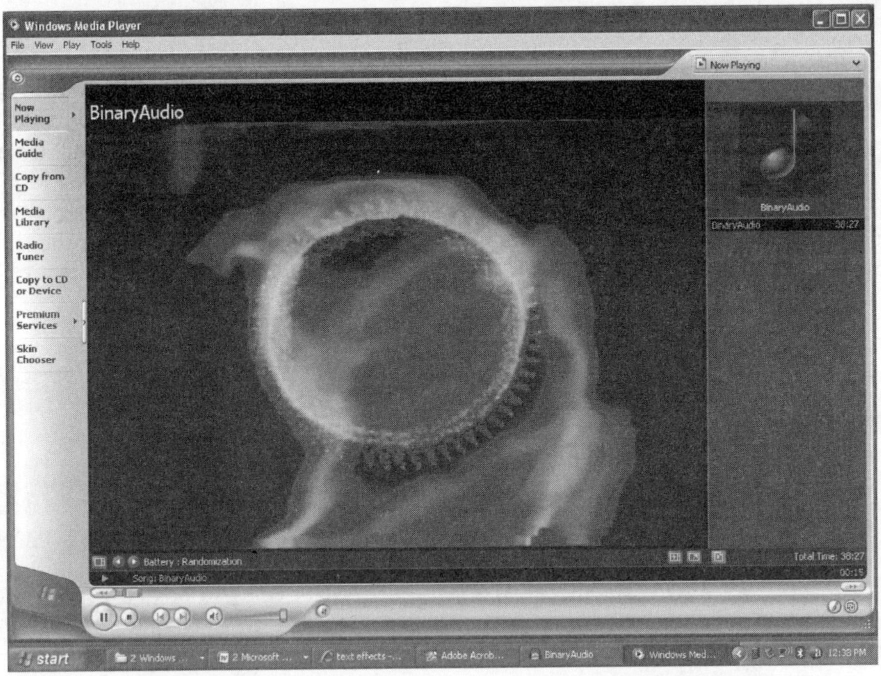

Figure 13.12 An audio file playing on Windows media player

Figure 13.13 An audio file open in audacity audio editor

Figure 13.14 Audio software to convert to mp3 file

⊙ **MPS Encoding**—is the process of converting a wave file into Mp3 format. The size of the MPS file is about 12 times smaller than that of the wave file, while the quality of MPS file is almost same as the original file. MPS encoding removes frequencies that cannot be heard by the human ear (< 20 Hz and > 20 kHz) from the wave file. Sounds masked by other sounds are also removed by MPS conversion. Common MPS encoders are CODEC (user has to pay for it), and mpegEnc v0.07 and MPlifier vO.52 (freely available). Figure 13.14 shows the lame audio software icon.

To play Mp3 music—

⊙ Get an MPS player (Winamp—Free download from www.mpS.com)

⊙ Get music—from the Web, or create MPS file from CD music. To create MPS file, convert CD music to MPS format.

- Use CD ripper software, (WinDacS2—Free download) to convert the analog signal from audio CD to a digital file. It will create *.wav* file from CD music.
- Convert the created *.wav* file to MPS using an encoder v0.06 by SoloH. It takes one hour to do one song.

13.4.4 Video

Video is another element of multimedia. Video and audio are closely related, and together they are the most effective means of communication that can be a part of the multimedia system (Figure 13.15). Digital video is used in making of movies, gaming, and IT industry. The Digital Video Disk (DVD) makes it possible to distribute large videos in a compact form.

Figure 13.15 A video film

- **Analog and Digital Video**—Digital video allows random access within a movie; cut, paste, or edit video; and addition of special effects. It is easy to duplicate digital video without loss of quality. Digital video also allows for interactivity. The video seen on TV, cable TV, or VCR is broadcast in analog format.
- **Video Editing**—Digital video is easy to edit. Editing involves removing frames, inserting frames, mixing audio with video, creating special effects on video, superimposing clips, adjusting transparency, and adjusting volume of audio (Figure 13.16). Some of the software packages that support editing are Adobe Premiere, Adobe AfterEffects CS4 and Strata Avid Video.

Figure 13.16 Video software

- **Digitizing Analog Video**—The process of digitizing analog video is called *video capture.* Video is captured using plug-in cards called *video capture cards.* A video capture card accepts a video input from an input device such as a VCR or a video camera. The audio is sampled through a separate cable which attaches to the sound card. The software with the video card synchronizes the two channels of audio and video. With the software that comes with the video card, the video capture process is started. Digital cameras can directly store full-motion video in digital formats that can be copied onto a computer's hard disk.
- **Video Compression**—Digital video files are extremely large files that take a large amount of disk space, and require high data transfer rates from hard disk to screen. Compression restructures the data to reduce the size of the file. A compressed video file is decompressed when it is played. Several compression/decompression (codec) algorithms are available for compressing digital videos. Codecs may be asymmetric or symmetric; software-based, hardware-based, or both. A symmetric codec takes almost the same time to compress and decompress data. An asymmetric codec takes longer to encode video than it does to decode. Microsoft Video 1, Cinepak and Intel Indeo Video Raw are some of the Window-based codecs. Motion JPEG (MJPEG), MPEG-1, MPEG-2 are examples of the hardware-based codecs.
- **Video File Formats**—The digital video is saved on the disk in a video file format. The *AVI* format is used for the PC, and *Quicktime* format is used for Macintosh. The AVI format is used to play video in the Windows environment. It supports 256 colors to millions of colors, sound from 5 kHz Mono to CD quality stereo sound, and, can deliver video at rates ranging from 0.03 MB/sec to 0.3 MB/sec. Quicktime is similar to the AVI format, and can be viewed on almost every platform available. Figure 13.17 shows a snapshot of Windows Movie Maker.

13.4.4.1 Video on Internet

A video captured in real time from a live source is broadcasted using live camera web site. It takes video input from a video camera and compresses it to a size that can be delivered over the Internet. Streaming video and surround video are the technology that makes video on the Internet possible.

- **Streaming Video**—allows transmitting of real time video via the Internet, enabling a user to watch the video as it downloads. The video file takes a few seconds to load before starting the image. If the transmission slows down, the reserve of video available to the user's computer memory is used for uninterrupted viewing. VDOLive, RealVideo, Web Theater, and Stream Works are some of the streaming video products. Figure 13.18 shows a popular video streaming site.

Figure 13.17 Windows movie maker

Figure 13.18 Streaming video (http://www.youtube.com/)

- **Surround Video**—allows the user to turn the image around in a Web page and interact with it from every angle. This is used for displaying products allowing the user to zoom in to any point and click on URL links.

13.4.5 Animation

Animation is creating of an illusion of movement from a series of still drawings (Figure 13.19). To create a feeling of motion of an image (still drawing), the image is projected on the screen as frames. Generally, 30 frames per second are used to make the object appear to be in smooth motion on the screen.

Figure 13.19 Animation

- **Process of Animation**—requires four steps—(1) Story board layout defines the outline of the action and the motion sequence as a set of basic events, (2) Definition of objects defines the movement for each object, (3) Key frame specifications gives the detailed drawing of the scene of animation at a particular time, and (4) Generation of in-between frames defines the number of intermediate frames between key frames.
- **Creation of Animation**—Creation and usage of animation using the computer includes processes like looping, morphing, and rendering, which are briefly discussed below:
  - **Looping** is the process of playing the animation continuously. It is used if the animation requires a basic few frames to be created. For example, a hop by a rabbit in 2–3 frames when put in a loop appears as if the rabbit is walking a long distance.
  - **Morphing** means changing of shape. Morphing is the transformation of one image to another. Morphing requires two elements—the shape to be changed and the shape after change. Morphing is used to make the object appear as if it is physically changing its shape. Morphing is used to make an object appear to move, run, dance, expand, contract etc, giving a smooth transformation of the image from one state to another. Morphing with lines, and Point morphing are some processes of morphing.
  - **Rendering** is the process to create an image from a data file. An animation requires about 30 renderings per second. Generally, a whole scene cannot be drawn by the 3-D graphics program inclusive of colors, shading etc. So, what is done is—a rough representation of the position of the object at each point in motion is provided to the rendering package. The rendering package generates the 30 frames required for the rendering which will result in the real motion of the object and thus animation. The rendering time is an important consideration in all 3-D animation.
- **Hardware and Software for Animation**—The hardware platforms used for animation are—SGI, PC, Macintosh, and Amiga. The SGI platform is used to broadcast quality computer animation productions. PCs use 3D Studio and Animator Studio applications for making animations. Some

of the most popular software packages used for animation are—3D Studio Max, Light Wave 3D, Adobe Photoshop, Adobe Premiere, and Animator Studio.

- **Animation File Formats**—Animation can be in any of the following formats—Flic format (FLI/FLC), MPEG (.mpg), and Quicktime Movie (QT/MooV). Flic format is used by 3D Studio and DOS-based graphics software packages. MPEG format is used on the Internet since it allows for a much faster file transfer because of its reduced file size. The file size is 40 times smaller than a Flic format file. The Quicktime Movie format is the standard Macintosh animation format, which allows for compression and can contain audio tracks.

13.5 MULTIMEDIA SYSTEM

The multimedia system includes the hardware and software components that are required to be used for multimedia. The hardware and software components required for a multimedia system are as follows:

- **Input Devices**—Keyboard and OCR for text; Digital cameras, Scanners and CD-ROM for graphics, MIDI keyboards, CD-ROM and microphones for sound; Video cameras, CD-ROM and frame grabbers for video; Mice, trackballs, joy sticks, virtual reality gloves and wands for spatial data; and mouse, touch screen, trackball, tablet, voice recognition system, infrared remotes, magnetic card encoder and reader, 3D input devices, and virtual reality devices.
- **Output Devices**—CD-quality speakers, Hi-resolution monitors, color printers, specialised helmets, and immersive devices displays for virtual reality, and video devices.
- **Storage Devices**—Hard disks, CD-ROM drive, Zip drive, DVD drive.
- **Communication Network**—Ethernet, Token Ring, FDDI, ATM, Intranets, and Internets.
- **Communication Devices**—Modem, Network Interface Card.
- **Computer System**—Multimedia Desktop machine, Workstation, MPEG/VIDEO hardware
- **Software**—Some of the familiar tools for multimedia software are—Word Processor (MS-WORD, WordPerfect), Spreadsheet (MS-Excel), Database (Q+E Database/VB), and, Presentation Tools (MS-PowerPoint). Some of the software tools used for different elements of multimedia are as follows—
  - Music Sequencing and Notation—Cakewalk, Cubase, Macromedia Sound Edit
  - Digital Audio—Cool Edit, Sound Forge, Pro Tools, Audacity
  - Image Editing—Adobe Illustrator, Adobe Photoshop, Macromedia Fireworks
  - Video Editing—Adobe Premiere, Windows Movie Maker, iMovie
  - Animation—3D Studio Max, Maya
- **Multimedia Authoring Tools** are programs that help the user in writing multimedia applications. A multimedia authoring tool enables the user to create a multimedia application by linking together objects, such as text, illustration, or music, to present a mixture of textual, graphical, and audio data. These tools are used to make videos, user interfaces, animations, screen savers, games, presentations, and for interactive training and simulations. Macromedia Flash and Macromedia Director are examples of multimedia authoring tools.

13.5.1 Desirable Features of Multimedia System

The hardware and software components used for a multimedia system have a minimum configuration to be used for multimedia. A multimedia system should have the following desirable features:

- Very high processing power—more than 500 MHz of processing speed.
- Large storage units (50 GB or more) and large memory (512 MB or more).
- Multimedia Capable File System to deliver real-time media e.g. video/audio streaming.
- File Formats that allow for compression/decompression in real-time.
- Efficient and fast I/O to allow for real-time recording and playback of data.
- Special operating system that supports direct transfer to disk, real-time scheduling, fast interrupt processing, and I/O streaming.
- Network Support for Internet.
- Software Tools to handle and deliver media, and, design and develop applications.

13.6 MULTIMEDIA APPLICATIONS

Multimedia applications have found their way into different arenas of our life. We are interacting with multimedia applications in the area of education and entertainment that includes sports, laser shows, video games, or animation movies. Multimedia applications have found their way in business—may it be for advertising, marketing, video meetings, result presentations or customer feedbacks. Nowadays, training is also imparted using multimedia applications like simulations and 3D designs. Entertainment parks like Disneyland use virtual reality and multimedia, innovatively design, create, and improve; their games and rides. The following subsections discuss the impact of multimedia applications in different areas of our life.

13.6.1 In Education

Using multimedia for education encompasses the use of video clips, speech and sound, music, animations, and graphics. The use of these multimedia elements impacts the whole learning process and pedagogy. It is always better to visually observe and hear about a topic than only reading it from a book.

- **For Students and Teachers**—The students are able to actually view the things being taught using graphics, animation or video clips. This brings them more nearer to the topic being taught and has much more impact on the student than only reading from the book. It also helps bridge the gap between theory and lab work. The teachers use multimedia as a tool for delivering more effective lectures (Figure 13.20). They supplement their lectures with PowerPoint presentations, drawings, graphics and 3D graphics. They also use virtual laboratories and simulations to support their lectures, share same physical resource across multiple locations, and reduce capital and operational expenditure.
- **Imparting Education**—Multimedia has resulted in spreading education to far-off places where students cannot physically go and attend classes. Moreover, a lecture by a teacher cannot be repeated or replayed unless recorded. Multimedia has enabled such recordings on the computer so that the student can view them again and again whenever required. The large diversity of students, who are slow learners, is helped by it. The use of multimedia for imparting education is available in the following forms:
    - **Self-learning CD-ROMs**—One can commonly find in the market, self-learning modules on CD-ROMs for various subjects and for different classes. These modules use graphics, video, and speech, and include training for the subject inclusive of tests and question paper along with evaluation (Figure 13.21).

Figure 13.20 A teacher using presentation for teaching

Figure 13.21 Self-learning CD-ROMs

- **E-learning Programs**—The universities imparting distance education like IGNOU, have started using e-learning software to impart lectures to the students. E-learning programs are now also being offered by the IITs for the students not physically present at IIT (Figure 13.22). It is popularly referred to as "You can still be in IIT, even if you are not physically at IIT". E-learning programs require the students to get registered for the program online. The registered student is provided with a username and password, which he uses to log on to the e-learning module to access the lectures, notes and tests based on them. These also enable Just-in-Time training on a specific topic for a person.

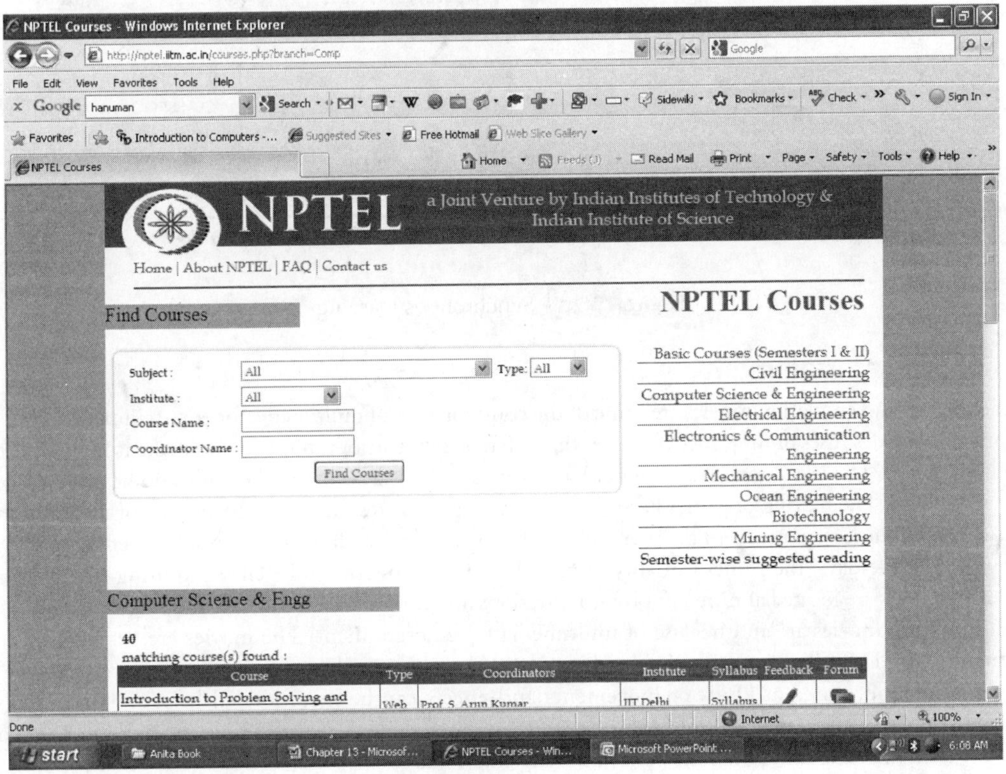

Figure 13.22 E-learning

- **Synchronous Learning Technology**—This is an initiative for imparting education using satellite communication. In this learning technology, the students are required to attend classes at various computer based learning centers at a fixed time. It is online video lectures, where the instructor delivers the lecture physically at that time at one of the centers, which is being broadcasted and delivered to the students at the computer based learning centers. It incorporates Full-motion video, duplex audio, and two-way Video /Audio/Data interaction creating classroom-like engagement. The students can listen to the instructor, see him/her on their computer screens and respond and interact with the instructor. NIIT Imperia uses this technology for delivering executive management programs (Figure 13.23).

The use of multimedia in education has made education to be more widely available, effective and entertaining.

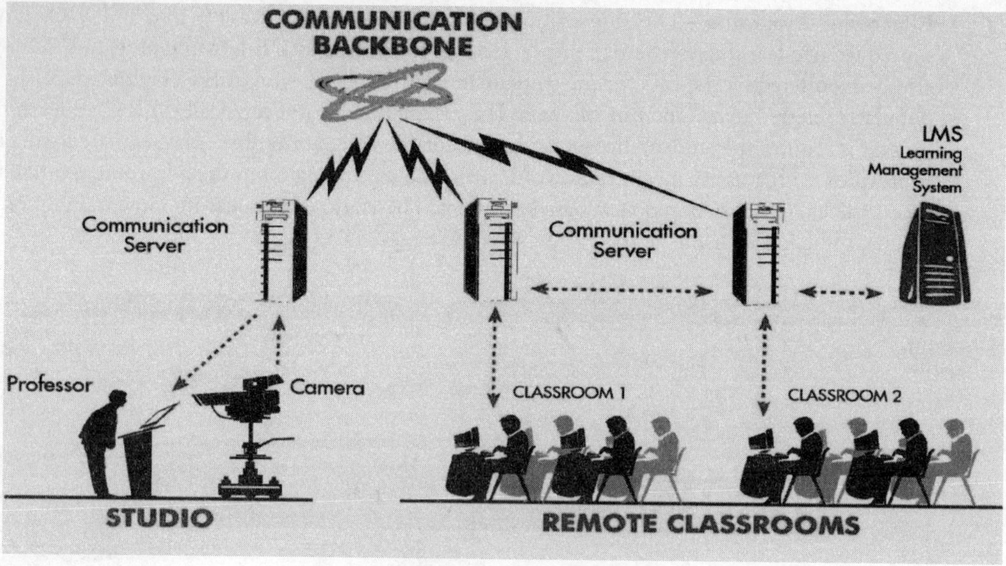

Figure 13.23 Synchronous learning

13.6.2 In Entertainment

Video games and animation movies are some of the common uses of multimedia for entertainment. Gaming is one of the oldest uses of multimedia. It uses the different elements of multimedia to make it more realistic and interactive. The users (especially children) are captivated by the beauty of the game and heavily engaged in using them. The playing of games has its own advantages as it results in the sharpening of mental faculties (requires quick response from the user), allows mixing pleasure with work, and results in enjoyment and relaxation. Nowadays, the games can also be played across the Internet (like chess requiring two players), where the users are located at different physical locations and can interact with each other over a game.

Animation movies are another use of multimedia for entertainment. The movies are generated using animation, and usually sound is provided by a well-known personality. Since the movies are generated using animation, different kinds of movements and effects can be incorporated into it. They are also cheaper than the actual movies. Some of the recent animated movies (Figure 13.24) are—Hanuman (you can see hanuman engulfing the sun, walk in the sky, make a dive etc, which are easy to show using animation than with real characters), Road Side Romeo (sound by Saif Ali Khan, Kareena Kapoor and others), Toy Story 2 (Disney/Pixar), My Friend Ganesha, Bal Ganesha etc.

Figure 13.24 Animation movies

13.6.3 In Training

Training is an important ingredient in any organization. Imparting training to employees requires significant amount of effort and resources. There are only a few people in an organization who have training skills and knowledge, to train others. Earlier, training the employees in an organization would require the training team to travel to the location of training, incur expenses (lodging, boarding, traveling etc.), and train the people and move on to next location.

With the advent of multimedia in training, software is developed which can be stored on the CD, delivered over web and used by the employees for training. On-line training and simulation are some other methods which use multimedia for training. In many safety-critical organizations, first the training is provided using simulated software without touching the actual unit. NASA uses simulation to train the astronauts, Maruti in India have car driving centers which trains the aspirant drivers using both simulation-based training and actual car driving (Figure 13.25). Simulation is also used for the training of pilots of airplane, fighter planes and ships. *Second Life* software is being used to make a candidate familiar with the inside look and feel of an organization before he/she appears for the interview.

Figure 13.25 Maruti driving school simulator

13.6.4 In Business

Multimedia is crucial for the success of business organizations. In government and non-government organizations, no meeting is complete without PowerPoint presentations and reports generated along with graphs and images. Moreover, businesses use multimedia to further their products and to enlighten people about their products. A CD giving details of the product is used. Car manufacturers, white-good manufacturers like television, microwave, refrigerators and washing machines, cell phone manufacturers etc., rely heavily on multimedia to display their product, market them, and to enhance sales of their product (Figure 13.26). Multimedia is also used by business organizations to train their people, for marketing and advertising, for creating visual and sound effects that are appealing to people, and thus making their product more saleable. Since the information inclusive of all sound and visual effects can be stored on a CD and distributed, it is considered as an inexpensive means of advertising and business promotion.

Figure 13.26 Multimedia in business

13.6.5 Virtual Reality

Virtual Reality is created using multimedia. Virtual reality is a special environment that is created using multimedia, where the users feel as if they are in a three-dimensional world. It gives the feeling to the users as if they are participating in the scenario. Virtual reality (Figure 13.27) uses a head-mounted display which consists of two display screens, and, data gloves that are used to record the hand movements. The head-mounted display and the gloves are connected to a computer which has the software for virtual reality installed into it. When the user enters into virtual reality, the position of the head of the user, eyes, and hand movement is used to decide the response; the next view is presented accordingly by the virtual reality software.

- Virtual reality system enables one or more users to move and react in a computer-simulated environment. Virtual reality systems can reshape the interface between people and information technology by offering new ways to communicate information, visualize processes, and express ideas creatively. When a user becomes fully immersed in an artificial, three-dimensional world that is completely generated by a computer, it is called *immersive virtual reality*.
- The interface devices for a virtual reality system are—(1) Head-mounted display (HMD)—Screens directed at each eye; position tracker, (2) CAVE—Provides illusion of immersion through projection of stereo images on floors and walls, and (3) Haptic interface - Relays sense of touch and other physical sensations.
- There are different forms of Virtual Reality—Immersive virtual reality, Mouse-controlled navigation through a three-dimensional environment on a graphics monitor, stereo viewing from the monitor via stereo glasses, stereo projection systems, and telepresence systems.
- Some examples of Virtual Reality applications are:
  - Experimental "gesture technology": may have military applications
  - Medicine: anxiety disorders, pain reduction
  - Education and training: anatomy, history, military training
  - Real estate marketing and tourism: virtual walkthroughs
  - Entertainment: CGI movies and games

Figure 13.27 Virtual reality

Late Prof. Randy Pausch of *Carnegie Mellon University* worked in the area of virtual reality and has developed software named "Alice" which is used to make virtual reality software. This software is freely downloadable. His book "*The Last Lecture*" (Figure 13.28) mentions the use of virtual reality by Disneyland for their entertainment park (to show Aladdin flying on a carpet etc.).

Figure 13.28 The book "The Last Lecture"

In addition to above applications of multimedia, we can see multimedia pervading into our everyday lives. Kiosks at hotels, railway stations, bus stops are self-help multimedia information centers that provide the users with the necessary information. Multimedia is also used in sports for training purposes and for analyzing the game. Some of the common use of multimedia we mostly see while viewing a cricket match is—viewing if a leg bye was correct or not, whether a player is run out or not, or, at what angle the ball was thrown. In the Hindi film "Chak De India", the trainer "Shahrukh Khan" uses multimedia to train the hockey players about the placement of the players, their moves etc.

SUMMARY

- Television, radio, newspaper are common examples of *mass media.*
- *Multimedia* is a combination of more than one media—text, graphics, images, audio, or video, which is used for presenting and sharing the information.
- *Multimedia is different* from mass media. Multimedia is delivered through the computer and introduces the element of interactivity.
- Text, graphics, video, audio, and animation are the different *elements of multimedia.*
- Integrated, digital, interactive and computers are the four main *characteristics of a multimedia system.* Computers are an intrinsic part of multimedia system. Multimedia is digital since it uses the computer. The elements of the multimedia are integrated to present a single interface to the user. Multimedia is interactive and thus non-linear.
- *Text* is used for writing titles, to define menus, to write the content, and to navigate. Text in multimedia has features like—text font, text effect, and text color. *Text* can also be *animated.* Text can be represented as *hypertext on the Internet.* The documents linked via hyperlinks allow non-linear access.
- *Graphics* can be 2D graphics such as photographs or 3D graphics such as objects we see.
- Bitmap graphics and Vector graphics are the two *types of digital graphics.*
- *Bitmap graphics* uses pixel information to generate the graphics.
- *Vector graphics* uses mathematical equations to represent the location, color, size, and color of the graphics.
- JPEG and GIF are the two widely-used *graphics image compression* algorithms.
- *Sound* is a key element of multimedia. To store the sound on the computer it has to be converted into digital form and the sound from the computer is converted into analog form to be sent to the speakers.
- *Digitization and sampling of sound* is required to store the analog sound in digital format.
- The digitized sound can be edited using *audio editors.*
- Sound can also be *synthesized* using the computer in MIDI format.
- The audio files need to be compressed to be stored on the disk and to be transmitted through the Internet. MPEG is a popular algorithm for *audio compression.*
- CD ripping and MPS encoding is used to store *audio from CD to web.*
- *Digital video* can be easily stored on DVDs. The process of digitizing analog video is called *video capture.*
- Streaming video and surround video make the *video available on the Internet.*
- *Animation* creates an illusion of movement from a series of still images.
- Looping, morphing and rendering are the processes for *creating animation.*
- I/O devices, storage devices, communication network, computer and software tools are the hardware and software components required for a *multimedia system.*
- A *multimedia system has features* like high processing power, large storage units, fast and efficient I/O, and, multimedia capable file system, and file formats.
- *Multimedia* is being widely used in *areas* like education, entertainment, business, and training.
- Multimedia has made *virtual reality* a possibility. Virtual reality uses multimedia to create an environment where the user feels in a 3D world.

KEYWORDS

QUESTIONS

Section 13.2

1. List the differences between mass media and multimedia.
2. Define: (1) multimedia (2) interactive multimedia.
3. List the elements of multimedia.

Section 13.3

4. What is the impact of computer on multimedia?
5. Describe the characteristics of multimedia system.
6. "The digital nature of multimedia requires special treatment of multimedia elements". Explain.
7. Give an example of hypermedia application.
8. Name some devices used to interact with multimedia.
9. Define hypermedia.

Section 13.4.1

10. Give two examples of time-dependent multimedia system.
11. Give two examples of time-independent multimedia system.
12. What is the purpose of using text in multimedia?
13. What is text font? Give an example.
14. Explain the meaning of the text font—"Times New Roman 11-point italic".
15. Give two examples of typeface.
16. What is the purpose of using text effects?
17. Name software used for creating text effects.
18. Name software used for creating text animation.
19. What is the use of representing text as hypertext on the Internet?

Section 13.4.2

20. What is the use of graphics element in multimedia system?
21. ________ and _______ are two types of digital graphics.
22. In what situations it is best to use bitmap graphics and vector graphics.
23. Define resolution of an image.
24. Unit of measuring resolution of an image is ________.
25. Resolution of monitor is measured in ____________.
26. Higher the resolution, the better it is (True/False).
27. Give an example of bitmap editor.
28. Give an example of vector graphics editor.
29. List the three factors on which the size of graphics file is dependent.
30. List two formats for storing bitmap graphics file.
31. Why is image compression needed?
32. The two widely-used image compression algorithms are ____ and _____.
33. List two formats used for image file format on the web.
34. Name three devices used for loading images on the computer.

35. Explain in one sentence what they do—scanner, digital camera, and clip art.

Section 13.4.3

36. State the difference between audio and sound.
37. Explain the properties of sound.
38. Define the following—(1) Amplitude, (2) Frequency or Pitch, and (3) Bandwidth.
39. What is the unit of frequency?
40. What is the range of the frequency of sound that the human ear can hear?
41. What is the use of DAC and ADC?
42. What is the purpose of microphone?
43. Define sound sampling.
44. Define sampling rate.
45. The CD sampling rate is ______.
46. Explain the purpose of audio editors.
47. Name two audio editing software for Windows.
48. __________ is the most widely-used format for generation of synthesized sound.
49. Explain MIDI format.
50. Name two audio file formats.
51. ___________ is an uncompressed audio file format.
52. Why is compression of sound needed?
53. Name two common compression schemes for audio.
54. Describe the process for converting audio from CD to web.

Section 13.4.4

55. Name two video editing software.
56. Define video capture. Describe the process of video capture.
57. Why is compression of video needed?
58. Name some codec algorithm for video.
59. The digital video is stored on a disk on a PC as _________ format.
60. The digital video is stored on a disk on a Macintosh as _____________ format.
61. _______ and ___________ technology makes video on the Internet possible.
62. What is a streaming video technology?
63. What do you mean by surround video technology?

Section 13.4.5

64. Explain the four steps that are required to be followed during the process of animation.
65. What is the purpose of morphing?
66. Explain the process of rendering.
67. An animation requires about _____ renderings per second.
68. List two software packages used for animation.
69. The file formats to store animation are ______, ________ and ____________.

Section 13.5

70. List the hardware and software requirements of a multimedia system.
71. What is the purpose of multimedia authoring tools?
72. Name two multimedia authoring tools.
73. List the desirable features of multimedia system.

Section 13.6

74. Describe the impact of multimedia on (1) Education (2) Entertainment (3) Business, and (4) Training.
75. Explain the use of multimedia in imparting education using (1) Self learning CDROMs, (2) E-learning program, and (3) Synchronous learning technology.
76. What is virtual reality?
77. Give an example of the use of virtual reality.
78. Give two examples for each, of the use of multimedia in (1) Education, (2) Entertainment, (3) Business, (4) Training, and (5) Virtual Reality.

Extra Questions

79. Give full form of the following abbreviations:

(i) Pixel	(ii) dpi	(iii) RGB
(iv) HSL	(v) GIF	(vi) BMP
(vii) PS	(viii) JPEG	(ix) TIFF
(x) ADC	(xi) DAC	(xii) MIDI
(xiii) RIFF	(xiv) MPEG	(xv) CCITT
(xvi) ISO	(xvii) HMD	

80. Write short notes on:

(a) Bitmap graphics
(b) Vector graphics
(c) Text
(d) Image compression
(e) Image File Size
(f) Sound sampling
(g) Sound digitization
(h) Sound compression
(i) Video on Internet
(j) Audio from a CD to Web
(k) Video Compression
(l) Animation Creation
(m) Multimedia system

(n) Multimedia authoring tools
(o) Multimedia in Education
(p) Multimedia in Training
(q) Multimedia in Business
(r) Multimedia in Entertainment
(s) Virtual Reality

81. Give differences between the following:
    (a) Mass media and Multimedia
    (b) Bitmap graphics and Vector graphics
    (c) Bitmap editor and Vector graphics editor
    (d) JPEG and GIF image compression
    (e) Streaming video and Surround video

COMPUTER SECURITY 14

Contents

Why this chapter

Individual users, organizations, and enterprises use the computers for keeping their data that is critical to their business and personal use. Also, they use the network (Internet) for the transmission of data. Since data is critical to the owner, there is a need to keep the computers storing the data and the network (Internet) over which the data is transmitted, secure. You should be aware of—from whom to secure your data, and also about the security mechanisms to ensure security. Computer security includes security of, both, the computer and the Internet. The purpose of this chapter is to introduce you to "Computer Security".

14.1 INTRODUCTION

We all like to be secure in our home, office, locality, city, country, and in this world. We use different mechanisms to ensure our security. Inside our homes, we keep our valuables safely locked in a cupboard that is accessible by the elders of the house; we keep the gates of our house bolted and even have an intrusion-detection system installed. We have high walls and gates surrounding our locality and also a watchman who guards the open gates. We have police for our security within a city and armed forces for the country. We take all these measures to make ourselves and our valuables, resources, possessions secure.

The widespread use of computers has resulted in the emergence of a new area for security—security of computer. Computer security is needed to protect the computing system and to protect the data that they store and access. Transmission of data using network (Internet) and communication links has necessitated the need to protect the data during transmission over the network. Here, we use the term computer security to refer to both the computer security and the network security.

Computer security focuses on the security attacks, security mechanisms and security services.

- *Security attacks* are the reasons for breach of security. Security attacks comprise of all actions that breaches the computer security.
- *Security mechanisms* are the tools that include the algorithms, protocols or devices, that are designed to detect, prevent, or recover from a security attack.
- *Security services* are the services that are provided by a system for a specific kind of protection to the system resources.

The purpose of computer security is to provide reliable security services in the environments suffering security attacks, by using security mechanisms. The security services use one or more security mechanism(s).

This chapter discusses the different security threats and security attacks from malicious software and hackers. The chapter highlights the security services. The security mechanisms like cryptography, digital signatures, and firewalls are discussed in detail. The need for security awareness and the security policy in an organization is also emphasized.

14.2 SECURITY THREAT AND SECURITY ATTACK

A *threat* is a potential violation of security and causes harm. A threat can be a malicious program, a natural disaster or a thief. *Vulnerability* is a weakness of system that is left unprotected. Systems that are vulnerable are exposed to threats. Threat is a possible danger that might exploit vulnerability; the actions that cause it to occur are the security attacks. For example, if we leave the house lock open—it is vulnerable to theft; an intruder in our locality (might exploit the open lock)—is a security threat; the intruder comes to know of the open lock and gets inside the house—This is a security attack.

A security attack may be a passive attack or an active attack.

- The aim of a *passive attack* is to get information from the system but it does not affect the system resources. Passive attacks are similar to eavesdropping (Figure 14.1). Passive attacks may analyze the traffic to find the nature of communication that is taking place, or, release the contents of the message to a person other than the intended receiver of the message. Passive attacks are difficult to detect because they do not involve any alteration of the data. Thus, the emphasis in dealing with passive attacks is on prevention rather than detection.

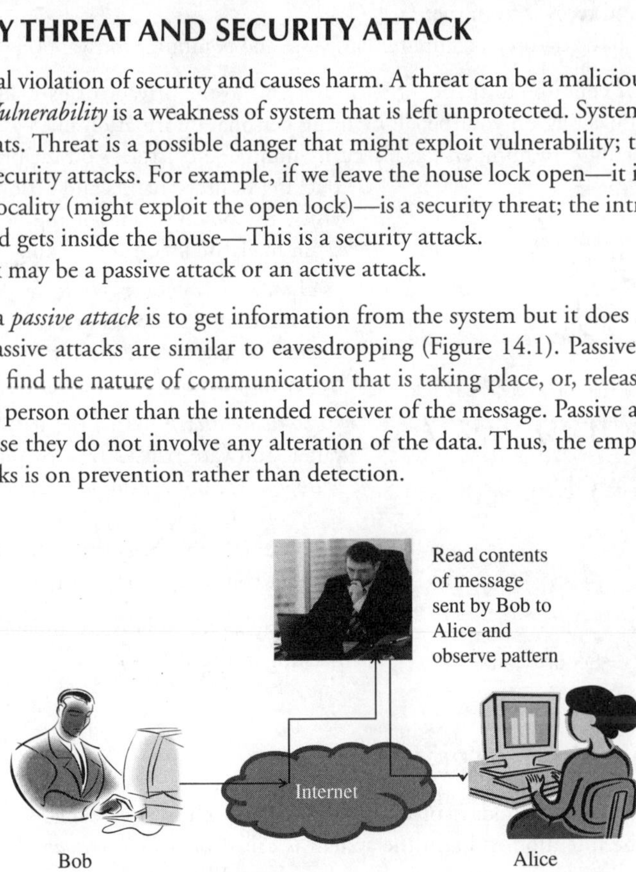

Figure 14.1 Passive attack

Figure 14.2 Active attack (masquerade)

- An *active attack* tries to alter the system resources or affect its operations. Active attack may modify the data or create a false data (Figure 14.2). An active attack may be a masquerade (an entity pretends to be someone else), replay (capture events and replay them), modification of messages, and denial of service. Active attacks are difficult to prevent. However, an attempt is made to detect an active attack and recover from them.

Security attacks can be on users, computer hardware and computer software (Figure 14.3).

- *Attacks on users* could be to the identity of user and to the privacy of user. Identity attacks result in someone else acting on your behalf by using personal information like password, PIN number in an ATM, credit card number, social security number etc. Attacks on the privacy of user involve tracking of users' habits and actions—the website user visits, the buying habit of the user etc. Cookies and spam mails are used for attacking the privacy of users.

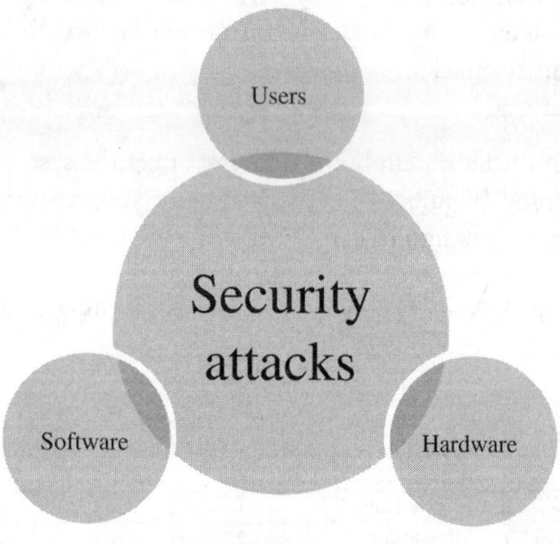

Figure 14.3 Security attacks

- *Attacks on computer hardware* could be due to a natural calamity like floods or earthquakes; due to power related problems like power fluctuations etc.; or by destructive actions of a burglar.
- *Software attacks* harm the data stored in the computer. Software attacks may be due to malicious software, or, due to hacking. *Malicious software or malware* is a software code included into the system with a purpose to harm the system. *Hacking* is intruding into another computer or network to perform an illegal act.

This chapter will discuss the malicious software and hacking in detail.

14.3 MALICIOUS SOFTWARE

Malicious users use different methods to break into the systems. The software that is intentionally included into a system with the intention to harm the system is called *malicious software*. Viruses, Trojan horse, and Worms are examples of malicious programs. Javascripts and Java applets written with the purpose of attacking, are also malicious programs.

14.3.1 Virus

Virus is a software program that is destructive in nature. Virus programs have the following properties:

- It can attach itself to other healthy programs.
- It can replicate itself and thus can spread across a network.
- It is difficult to trace a virus after it has spread across a network.
- Viruses harm the computer in many ways—
    - corrupt or delete data or files on the computer,
    - change the functionality of software applications,
    - use e-mail program to spread itself to other computers,
    - erase everything on the hard disk, or,
    - degrade performance of the system by utilizing resources such as memory or disk space.
- Virus infects an executable file or program. The virus executes when a program infected with virus is executed or you start a computer from a disk that has infected system files.
- Once a virus is active, it loads into the computer's memory and may save itself to the hard drive or copies itself to applications or system files on the disk.
- However, viruses cannot infect write protected disks or infect written documents. Viruses do not infect an already compressed file. Viruses also do not infect computer hardware; they only infect software.
- Viruses are most easily spread by attachments in e-mail messages. Viruses also spread through download on the Internet.

Some examples of viruses are—"Melissa" and "I Love You".

14.3.2 Worms

Worm is self-replicating software that uses network and security holes to replicate itself. A copy of the worm scans the network for another machine that has a specific security hole. It copies itself to the new machine using the security hole, and then starts replicating from there, as well. A worm is however different from a virus. A worm does not modify a program like a virus, however, it replicates so much that it consumes the resources of the computer and makes it slow. Some examples of worms are—"Code Red" and "Nimda".

14.3.3 Trojan Horse

Trojan horse is destructive programs that masquerade as useful programs. The name "Trojan horse" is given because of the Greek soldiers who reached the city of Troy by hiding themselves inside a large wooden horse (Figure 14.4). The people of the city of Troy themselves pulled the horse inside their city, unaware of the fact that the Greek soldiers were hiding inside the horse. Similarly, users install Trojan horses thinking that it will serve a useful purpose such as a game or provide entertainment. However, Trojan horses contain programs that corrupt the data or damage the files. Trojan horses can corrupt software applications. They can also damage files and can contain viruses that destroy and corrupt data and programs. Trojan horse does not replicate themselves like viruses.

Figure 14.4 Trojan horse

14.3.4 Javascripts, Java Applets and ActiveX Controls

Applets (Java programs), and ActiveX controls are used with Microsoft technology, which can be inserted in a Web page and are downloaded on the client browser for execution. Applets and ActiveX controls are generally used to provide added functionality such as sound and animation. However, these programs when designed with a malicious intention can be disastrous for the client machine. Java Applets have strong security checks that define what an applet can do and what it cannot. ActiveX controls do not have such security checks. Normally, ActiveX controls must be kept disabled while working on the Internet (Figure 14.5).

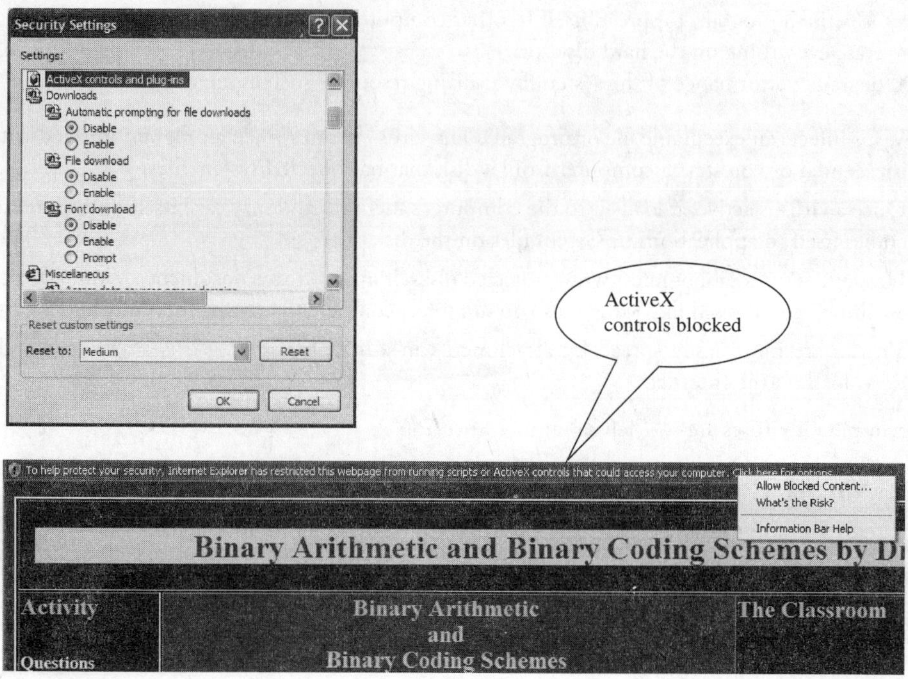

Figure 14.5 (a) Making security settings in Windows XP (b) ActiveX control popup in Internet

Javascript is a scripting language generally nested within HTML code. The client-side scripts on a HTML page execute inside the Web browser on the client computer. Javascript codes can be used to transfer files, send e-mails and write to local files. If used with a maligned intention, the scripts can be dangerous for the client machine.

14.4 HACKING

Hacking is the act of intruding into someone else's computer or network. A hacker is someone who does hacking. Hacking may result in a *Denial of Service (DoS) attack*. The DoS attack prevents authorized users from accessing the resources of the computer. It aims at making the computer resource unusable or unavailable to its intended users. It targets the computer and its network connections, to prevent the user from accessing email, web sites, online accounts (banking, etc.), or other services that rely on the affected computer. In a DoS attack, the services of the entire network, an Internet site or service, may be suppressed or disabled. The affected machine is flooded with spurious requests and messages so as to overload the network. As a result, the affected machine cannot process the valid requests. This is a denial of service to the valid users. Generally, the targets of such attacks are the sites hosted on high-profile web servers such as banks and credit card payment gateways.

Packet sniffing, E-mail hacking and Password cracking are used to get the username and password of the system to gain unauthorized access to the system. These methods gather the information when the data is being transmitted over the network.

14.4.1 Packet Sniffing

The data and the address information are sent as packets over the Internet. The packets may contain data like a user name and password, e-mail messages, files etc. Packet sniffing programs are used to intercept the packets while they are being transmitted from source to destination. Once intercepted, the data in the packets is captured and recorded. Generally, packet sniffers are interested in packets carrying the username and password. Packet sniffing attacks normally go undetected. Ethereal and Zx Sniffer are some freeware packet sniffers. Telnet, FTP, SMTP are some services that are commonly sniffed.

14.4.2 Password Cracking

Cracking of password is used by hackers to gain access to systems. The password is generally stored in the system in an encrypted form. Utilities like Password cracker is used to crack the encrypted passwords. Password cracker is an application that tries to obtain a password by repeatedly generating and comparing encrypted passwords or by authenticating multiple times to an authentication source.

14.4.3 E-mail Hacking

The e-mail transmitted over the network contains the e-mail header and the content. If this header and the content are sent without encryption, the hackers may read or alter the messages in transit. Hackers may also change the header to modify the sender's name or redirect the messages to some other user. Hackers use *packet replay* to retransmit message packets over a network. Packet replay may cause serious security threats to programs that require authentication sequences. A hacker may replay the packets containing authentication data to gain access to the resources of a computer.

14.5 SECURITY SERVICES

The security services provide specific kind of protection to system resources. Security services ensure Confidentiality, Integrity, Authentication, and Non-Repudiation of data or message stored on the computer, or when transmitted over the network. Additionally, it provides assurance for access control and availability of resources to its authorized users.

- **Confidentiality**—The confidentiality aspect specifies availability of information to only authorized users. In other words, it is the protection of data from unauthorized disclosure. It requires ensuring the privacy of data stored on a server or transmitted via a network, from being intercepted or stolen by unauthorized users. Data encryption stores or transmits data, in a form that unauthorized users cannot understand. Data encryption is used for ensuring confidentiality.
- **Integrity**—It assures that the received data is exactly as sent by the sender, i.e. the data has not been modified, duplicated, reordered, inserted or deleted before reaching the intended recipient. The data received is the one actually sent and is not modified in transit.

- **Authentication**—Authentication is the process of ensuring and confirming the identity of the user before revealing any information to the user. Authentication provides confidence in the identity of the user or the entity connected. It also assures that the source of the received data is as claimed. Authentication is facilitated by the use of username and password, smart cards, biometric methods like retina scanning and fingerprints.
- **Non-Repudiation** prevents either sender or receiver from denying a transmitted message. For a message that is transmitted, proofs are available that the message was sent by the alleged sender and the message was received by the intended recipient. For example, if a sender places an order for a certain product to be purchased in a particular quantity, the receiver knows that it came from a specified sender. Non-repudiation deals with signatures.
- **Access Control**—It is the prevention of unauthorized use of a resource. This specifies the users who can have access to the resource, and what are the users permitted to do once access is allowed.
- **Availability**—It assures that the data and resources requested by authorized users are available to them when requested.

14.6 SECURITY MECHANISMS

Security mechanisms deal with prevention, detection, and recovery from a security attack. Prevention involves mechanisms to prevent the computer from being damaged. Detection requires mechanisms that allow detection of when, how, and by whom an attacked occurred. Recovery involves mechanism to stop the attack, assess the damage done, and then repair the damage.

Security mechanisms are built using personnel and technology.

- Personnel are used to frame security policy and procedures, and for training and awareness.
- Security mechanisms use technologies like cryptography, digital signature, firewall, user identification and authentication, and other measures like intrusion detection, virus protection, and, data and information backup, as countermeasures for security attack.

14.7 CRYPTOGRAPHY

Cryptography is the science of writing information in a "hidden" or "secret" form and is an ancient art. Cryptography is necessary when communicating data over any network, particularly the Internet. It protects the data in transit and also the data stored on the disk. Some terms commonly used in cryptography are:

- *Plaintext* is the original message that is an input, i.e. unencrypted data.
- *Cipher and Code*—Cipher is a bit-by-bit or character-by-character transformation without regard to the meaning of the message. Code replaces one word with another word or symbol. Codes are not used any more.
- *Cipher text*—It is the coded message or the encrypted data.
- *Encryption*—It is the process of converting plaintext to cipher text, using an encryption algorithm.
- *Decryption*—It is the reverse of encryption, i.e. converting cipher text to plaintext, using a decryption algorithm.

Cryptography uses different schemes for the encryption of data. These schemes constitute a pair of algorithms which creates the encryption and decryption, and a key.

Key is a secret parameter (string of bits) for a specific message exchange context. Keys are important, as algorithms without keys are not useful. The encrypted data cannot be accessed without the appropriate key. The size of key is also important. The larger the key, the harder it is to crack a block of encrypted data. The algorithms differ based on the number of keys that are used for encryption and decryption. The three cryptographic schemes are as follows:

- Secret Key Cryptography (SKC): Uses a single key for both encryption and decryption,
- Public Key Cryptography (PKC): Uses one key for encryption and another for decryption,
- Hash Functions: Uses a mathematical transformation to irreversibly encrypt information.

In all these schemes, algorithms encrypt the plaintext into cipher text, which in turn is decrypted into plaintext.

14.7.1 Secret Key Cryptography

- Secret key cryptography uses a single key for both encryption and decryption. The sender uses the key to encrypt the plaintext and sends the cipher text to the receiver. The receiver applies the same key to decrypt the message and recover the plaintext (Figure 14.6). Since a single key is used for encryption and decryption, secret key cryptography is also called *symmetric encryption.*

Figure 14.6 Secret key cryptography (uses a single key for both encryption and decryption)

- Secret key cryptography scheme are generally categorized as *stream ciphers or block ciphers.*
- *Stream ciphers* operate on a single bit (byte or computer word) at a time and implement some form of feedback mechanism so that the key is constantly changing.
- *Block cipher* encrypts one block of data at a time using the same key on each block. In general, the same plaintext block will always encrypt to the same cipher text when using a same key in a block cipher.
- Secret key cryptography requires that the key must be known to both the sender and the receiver. The drawback of using this approach is the distribution of the key. Any person who has the key can use it to decrypt a message. So, the key must be sent securely to the receiver, which is a problem if the receiver and the sender are at different physical locations.
- Data Encryption Standard (DES) and Advanced Encryption Standard (AES) are some of the secret key cryptography algorithms that are in use nowadays.

14.7.2 Public-Key Cryptography

- Public-key cryptography facilitates secure communication over a non-secure communication channel without having to share a secret key.
- Public-key cryptography uses two keys—one public key and one private key.
- The public key can be shared freely and may be known publicly.
- The private key is never revealed to anyone and is kept secret.
- The two keys are mathematically related although knowledge of one key does not allow someone to easily determine the other key.

Figure 14.7 Public key cryptography (uses two keys—one for encryption and other for decryption)

- The plaintext can be encrypted using the public key and decrypted with the private key and conversely the plaintext can be encrypted with the private key and decrypted with the public key. Both keys are required for the process to work (Figure 14.7). Because a pair of keys is required for encryption and decryption; public-key cryptography is also called *asymmetric encryption.*
- Rivest, Shamir, Adleman (RSA) is the first and the most common public-key cryptography algorithm in use today. It is used in several software products for key exchange, digital signatures, or encryption of small blocks of data. The Digital Signature Algorithm (DSA) is used to provide digital signature capability for the authentication of messages.

14.7.3 Hash Functions

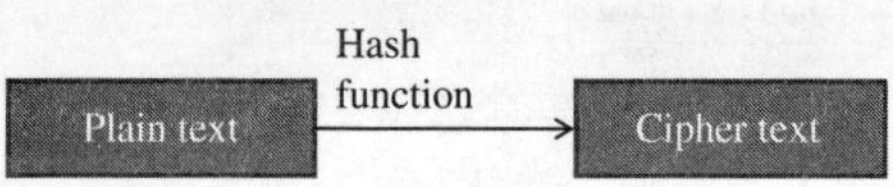

Figure 14.8 Hash function (have no key since plain text is not recoverable from cipher text)

- Hash functions are one-way encryption algorithms that, in some sense, use no key. This scheme computes a fixed-length hash value based upon the plaintext. Once a hash function is used, it is difficult to recover the contents or length of the plaintext (Figure 14.8).
- Hash functions are generally used to ensure that the file has not been altered by an intruder or virus. Any change made to the contents of a message will result in the receiver calculating a different hash value than the one placed in the transmission by the sender.
- Hash functions are commonly employed by many operating systems to encrypt passwords. Message Digest (MD) algorithm and Secure Hash Algorithm (SHA) are some of the common used hash algorithms.

The different cryptographic schemes are often used in combination for a secure transmission. Cryptography is used in applications like, security of ATM cards, computer passwords, and electronic commerce. Cryptography is used to protect data from theft or alteration, and also for user authentication.

Certification Authorities (CA) are necessary for widespread use of cryptography for e-commerce applications. CAs are trusted third parties that issue digital certificates for use by other parties. A CA issues digital certificates which contains a public key, a name, an expiration date, the name of authority that issued the certificate, a serial number, any policies describing how the certificate was issued, how the certificate may be used, the digital signature of the certificate issuer, and any other information.

14.8 DIGITAL SIGNATURE

A signature on a legal, financial or any other document authenticates the document. A photocopy of that document does not count. For computerized documents, the conditions that a signed document must hold are—(1) The receiver is able to verify the sender (as claimed), (2) The sender cannot later repudiate the contents of the message, (3) The receiver cannot concoct the message himself. A digital signature is used to sign a computerized document. The properties of a digital signature are same as that of ordinary signature on a paper. Digital signatures are easy for a user to produce, but difficult for anyone else to forge. Digital signatures can be permanently tied to the content of the message being signed and then cannot be moved from one document to another, as such an attempt will be detectable.

Digital signature scheme is a type of asymmetric cryptography. Digital signatures use the public-key cryptography, which employs two keys—private key and public key. The digital signature scheme typically consists of three algorithms:

- *Key generation algorithm* —The algorithm outputs private key and a corresponding public key.
- *Signing algorithm*—It takes, message + private key, as input, and, outputs a digital signature.
- *Signature verifying algorithm*—It takes, message + public key + digital signature, as input, and, accepts or rejects digital signature.

The use of digital signatures typically consists of two processes—Digital signature creation and Digital signature verification (Figure 14.9). Two methods are commonly used for creation and verification of the digital signatures.

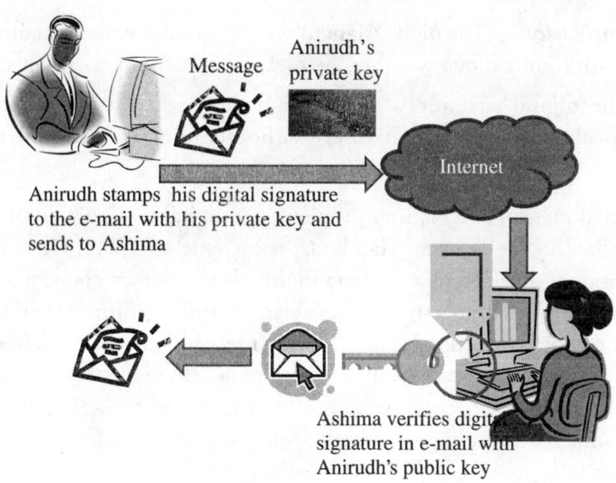

Figure 14.9 Digital signature

- In the First Method, the signer has a private key and a public key. For a message to be sent, the signer generates the digital signature by using the private key to encrypt the message. The digital signature along with the message is sent to the receiver. The receiver uses the public key (known to the receiver) to verify the digital signature. This method is used to verify the digital signature. Even if many people may know the public key of a given signer and use it to verify that signer's signature, they cannot generate the signer's private key and use it to forge digital signatures.
- In the Second Method, a hash function is used for digital signature. It works as follows:

  - *Digital signature creation*
    - The signer has a private key and a public key.
    - For a message to be sent, a hash function in the signer's software computes an "original hash result" unique to the "original message".
    - The signer uses signing algorithm to generate a unique digital signature. "original hash result" + signer's private key = digital signature.

- The generated digital signature is attached to its "original message" and transmitted with it.
- *Digital signature verification* uses digital signature, "received message" and signer's public key.
  - A "new hash result" of the "received message" is computed using the same hash function used for the creation of the digital signature.
  - The verification software verifies two things—whether the digital signature was created using the signer's private key and, whether the "received message" is unaltered. For this, the signer's public key verifies the digital signature (signer's public key can only verify a digital signature created with the signer's private key). Once the key is verified, the "original hash result" of the digital signature is available. It compares "original hash result" with the "new hash result". When the verification software verifies both the steps as "true"; it verifies the received message.

The digital signature accomplish the effects desired of a signature for many legal purposes:

- ***Signer Authentication***: The digital signature cannot be forged, unless the signer loses control of the private key.
- ***Message Authentication***: The digital signature verification reveals any tampering, since the comparison of the hash results shows whether the message is the same as when signed.
- ***Efficiency***: The digital signatures yield a high degree of assurance (as compared to paper methods like checking specimen signatures) without adding much to the resources required for processing.

The likelihood of malfunction or a security problem in a digital signature cryptosystem, designed and implemented as prescribed in the industry standards, is extremely remote. Digital signatures have been accepted in several national and international standards developed in cooperation with and accepted by many corporations, banks, and government agencies. In India "Information Technology Act 2000" provides legal recognition for transactions carried out by means of electronic data interchange and other means of electronic communication, commonly referred to as "electronic commerce", which involves the use of alternatives to paper based methods of communication and storage of information, to facilitate electronic filing of documents with the government agencies.

14.9 FIREWALL

A firewall is a security mechanism to protect a local network from the threats it may face while interacting with other networks (Internet). A firewall can be a hardware component, a software component, or a combination of both. It prevents computers in one network domain from communicating directly with other network domains. All communication takes place through the firewall, which examines all incoming data before allowing it to enter the local network (Figure 14.10).

Functions of Firewall—The main purpose of firewall is to protect computers of an organization (local network) from unauthorized access. Some of the basic functions of firewall are:

- Firewalls provide security by examining the incoming data packets and allowing them to enter the local network only if the conditions are met (Figure 14.11).
- Firewalls provide user authentication by verifying the username and password. This ensures that only authorized users have access to the local network.
- Firewalls can be used for hiding the structure and contents of a local network from external users. Network Address Translation (NAT) conceals the internal network addresses and replaces all the IP addresses of the local network with one or more public IP addresses.

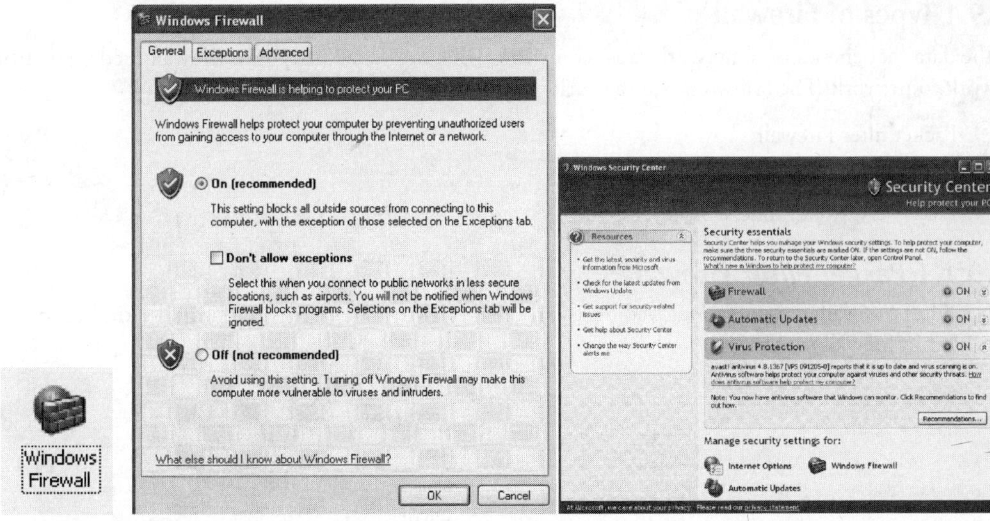

Figure 14.10 (a) Windows firewall icon in control panel (b) Windows firewall setting (c) Security center

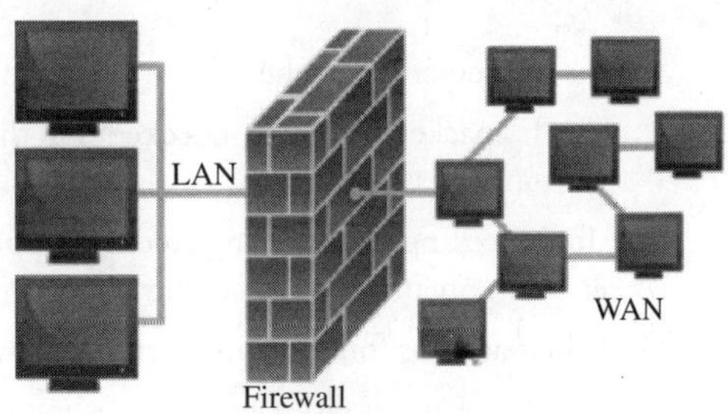

Figure 14.11 Firewall

The local network uses a single network interface to interact with the server. Local network clients use IP addresses that are not attached to any computer. When a client sends a packet to the Internet, the masquerading server replaces the IP address of the packet with its own IP address: When a packet is received by local network, the server replaces the IP address of the packet with the masqueraded address and sends the packet to the respective client.

Working of Firewall—The working of firewall is based on a filtering mechanism. The filtering mechanism keeps track of source address of data, destination address of data and contents of data. The filtering mechanism allows information to be passed to the Internet from a local network without any authentication. It makes sure that the downloading of information from the Internet to a local network happens based only on a request by an authorized user.

Firewall Related Terminology:

- ***Gateway***—The computer that helps to establish a connection between two networks is called gateway. A firewall gateway is used for exchanging information between a local network and the Internet.
- ***Proxy Server***—A proxy server masks the local network's IP address with the proxy server IP address, thus concealing the identity of local network from the external network. Web proxy and application-level gateway are some examples of proxy servers. A firewall can be deployed with the proxy for protecting the local network from external network.
- ***Screening Routers***—They are special types of router with filters, which are used along with the various firewalls. Screening routers check the incoming and outgoing traffic based on the IP address, and ports.

14.9.1 Types of Firewall

All the data that enter a local network must come through a firewall. The type of firewall used varies from network to network. The following are the various types of firewalls generally used:

- Packet filter Firewall
- Circuit Filter Firewall
- Proxy server or Application-level Gateway

14.9.1.1 Packet Filter Firewall

Packet Filter Firewall is usually deployed on the routers (Figure 14.12). It is the simplest kind of mechanism used in firewall protection.

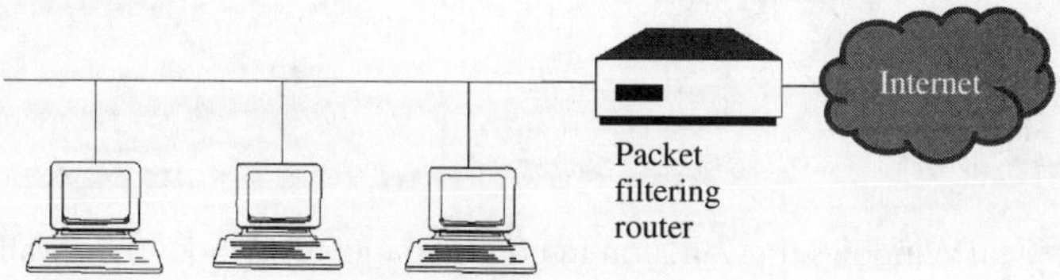

Figure 14.12 Packet filtering

- It is implemented at the network level to check incoming and outgoing packets.
- The IP packet header is checked for the source and the destination IP addresses and the port combinations.
- After checking, the filtering rules are applied to the data packets for filtering. The filtering rules are set by an organization based on its security policies.
- If the packet is found valid, then it is allowed to enter or exit the local network.
- Packet filtering is fast, easy to use, simple and cost effective.
- A majority of routers in the market provide packet filtering capability. It is used in small and medium businesses.
- Packet filter firewall does not provide a complete solution.

14.9.1.2 Circuit Filter Firewall

Circuit filter firewalls provide more protection than packet filter firewalls. Circuit filter firewall is also known as a "stateful inspection" firewall.

- It prevents transfer of suspected packets by checking them at the network layer.
- It checks for all the connections made to the local network, in contrast, to the packet filter firewall which makes a filtering decision based on individual packets.
- It takes its decision by checking all the packets that are passed through the network layer and using this information to generate a decision table. The circuit level filter uses these decisions tables to keep track of the connections that go through the firewall.
- For example, when an application that uses TCP creates a session with the remote host, the TCP port number for the remote application is less than 1024 and the TCP port number for the local client is between 1024 and 65535. A packet filter firewall will allow any packet which has a port

number within the range 1024 and 65535. However, the circuit filter firewall creates a directory of all outbound TCP connections. An incoming packet is allowed if its profile matches with an entry in the directory for the TCP port numbers.

14.9.1.3 Application-Level Gateway

An application-level gateway or a proxy server protects all the client applications running on a local network from the Internet by using the firewall itself as the gateway (Figure 14.13).

- A proxy server creates a virtual connection between the source and the destination hosts.
- A proxy firewall operates on the application layer. The proxy ensures that a direct connection from an external computer to local network never takes place.
- The proxy automatically segregates all the packets depending upon the protocols used for them. A proxy server must support various protocols. It checks each application or service, like Telnet or e-mail, when they are passed through it.
- A proxy server is easy to implement on a local network.
- Application level gateways or proxy server tend to be more secure than packet filters. Instead of checking the TCP and IP combinations that are to be allowed, it checks the allowable applications.

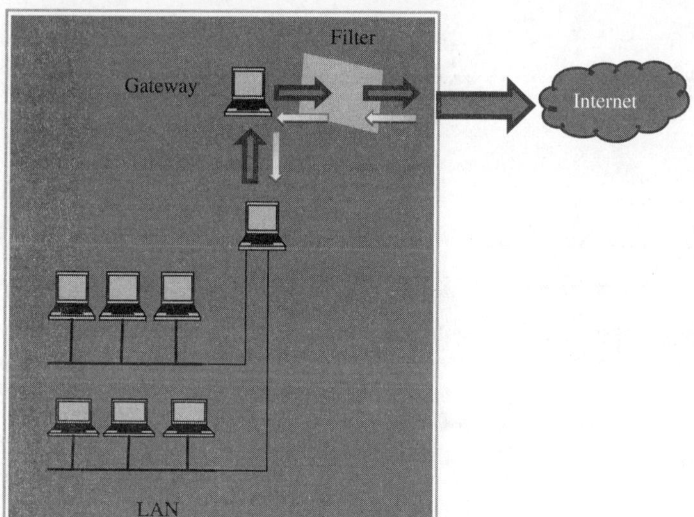

Figure 14.13 Application-level gateway

14.10 USERS IDENTIFICATION AND AUTHENTICATION

Identification is the process whereby a system recognizes a valid user's identity. *Authentication* is the process of verifying the claimed identity of a user. For example, a system uses user-password for identification. The user enters his password for identification. Authentication is the system which verifies that the password is correct, and thus the user is a valid user. Before granting access to a system, the user's identity needs to be authenticated. If users are not properly authenticated then the system is potentially vulnerable to access by unauthorized users. If strong identification and authentication mechanisms are used, then the risk that unauthorized users will gain access to a system is significantly decreased. Authentication is done using one or more combinations of—what you have (like smartcards), what you know (Password), and what you are (Biometrics like Fingerprints, retina scans).

We will now briefly discuss the following authentication mechanisms:

- User name and password
- Smart Card
- Biometrics—Fingerprints, Iris/retina scan

Once the user is authenticated, the access controls for the user are also defined. Access controls is what the user can access once he is authenticated.

14.10.1 User Name and Password

The combination of username and password is the most common method of user identification and authentication. The systems that use password authentication first require the user to have a username and a password. Next time, when the user uses the system, user enters their username and password. The system checks the username and password by comparing it to the stored password for that username. If it matches, the user is authenticated and is granted access to the system (Figure 14.14).

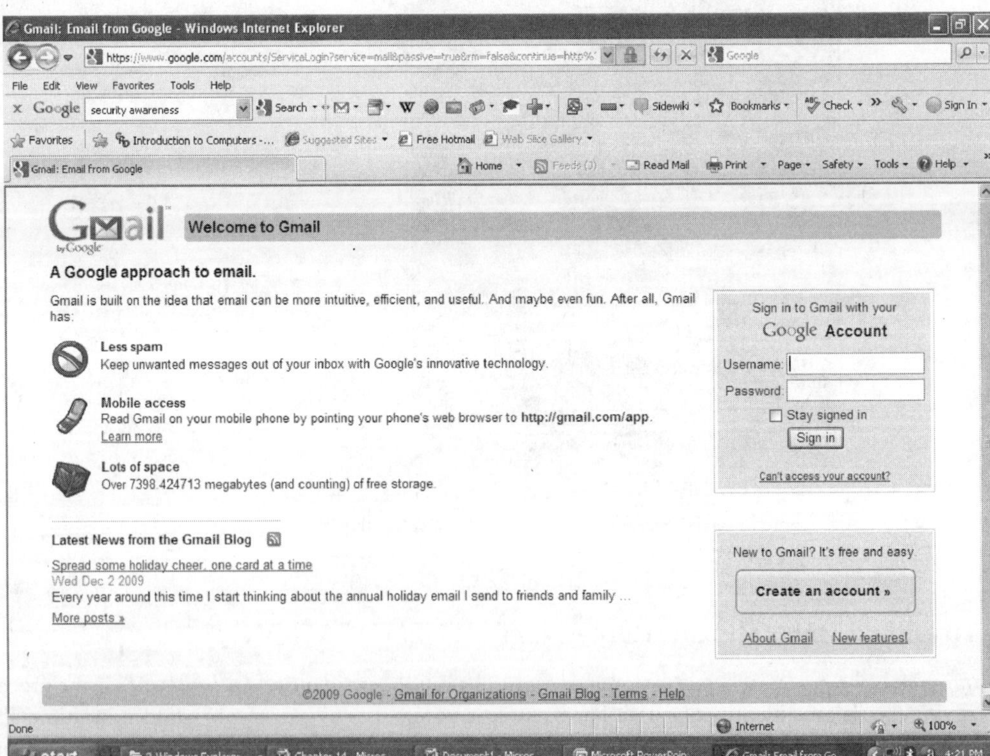

Figure 14.14 User authentication page

However, there are several security issues with the use of password, like, any invalid user if gets to know of a valid password can get access to the system, a simple password can be easily cracked etc. According to CERT, approximately 80% of all network security issues are caused by bad passwords. Some actions that can be taken to make the passwords safer are as follows:

- It is good to change passwords periodically. This decreases chances of cracking passwords.
- Make a password complex, like mix case, use numbers and special characters. This decreases ability of automated attacks by increasing possible character combinations.
- Use longer passwords so as to create exponentially higher number of permutations and combinations of characters used, making them difficult to break.
- Be cautious not to leave passwords lying around and don't share them with friends.
- Do not use your or your families' name, age, address, city etc., as part of the passwords.

Nearly all modern multiuser computer and network operating systems, at the very least, employ passwords to protect and authenticate users accessing computer and network resources. The passwords are not kept in plaintext, but are generally encrypted using some sort of hash scheme. For example, In Unix/Linux, all passwords are hashed and stored as a 13-byte string. In Windows NT, all passwords are hashed resulting in a 16-byte hash value.

14.10.2 Smart Card

A smart card is in a pocket-sized card with embedded integrated circuits which can process data. With an embedded microcontroller, smart cards have the unique ability to store large amounts of data, carry out their own on-card functions (e.g. encryption and mutual authentication) and interact intelligently with a smart card reader. A smart card inserted into a smart card reader makes a direct connection to a conductive contact plate on the surface of the card (typically gold plated). Transmission of commands, data, and card status takes place over these physical contact points.

The smart card is made of plastic, generally PVC. The card may embed a hologram. Using smart cards is a strong security authentication for single sign-on within large companies and organizations. Smart cards are used in secure identity applications like employee-ID badges, citizen-ID documents, electronic passports, driver license and online authentication devices.

14.10.3 Biometric Techniques

Biometrics is the science and technology of measuring and statistically analyzing biological data. In information technology, biometrics refers to technologies that measures and analyzes human traits for authentication. This can include fingerprints, eye retinas and irises, voice patterns, facial patterns and hand measurements, for authentication purposes. Figure 14.15 shows a fingerprint biometric device.

Biometrics is still not widely used, though it may play a critical role in future computers. For example, many PCs nowadays include a fingerprint scanner where you could place your index finger. The computer analyzes the fingerprint to determine your identity and authenticate you. Biometric systems are relatively costly and are used in environments requiring high-level security.

In the Hindi movie *Krissh*, the computer identified and authenticated the heartbeat (Biometric) of *Hrithik Roshan* to start working.

Figure 14.15 Biometric device (fingerprint)

14.11 OTHER SECURITY MEASURES

In addition to the above discussed security techniques, several other security techniques are used for security purposes. Some of these are listed below:

- **Intrusion Detection Systems**—They complement firewalls to detect if internal assets are being hacked or exploited. A Network-based Intrusion Detection monitors real-time network traffic for malicious activity and sends alarms for network traffic that meets certain attack patterns or signatures. A Host-based Intrusion Detection monitors computer or server files for anomalies and sends alarms for network traffic that meets a predetermined attack signature.
- **Virus Protection Software**—They should be installed on all network servers, as well as computers. They screen all software coming into your computer or network system (files, attachments, programs, etc.) preventing a virus from entering into the system.
- **Data and Information Backups**—It is required for disaster recovery and business continuity. Back-ups should be taken daily and periodically (weekly) and should be kept for at least 30 days while rotating stockpile.
- **Secure Socket Layer (SSL)** is an algorithm developed by Netscape Communications to provide application-independent security and privacy over the Internet. SSL is designed so that protocols such as HTTP, FTP, and Telnet can operate over it transparently. SSL allows both server authentication (mandatory) and client authentication (optional). It uses public-key cryptography (RSA algorithm). *HTTP Secure* (HTTPS) is an extension to HTTP to provide secure exchange of documents over the WWW.
- **IP Security (IPsec) Protocol**—The IPsec protocol suite is used to provide privacy and authentication services at the Internet layer. IPv4 is currently the dominant Internet Protocol version. IPv6 is the next-generation Internet Layer protocol for the Internet. IPv6 protocol stacks include IPsec, which allows authentication, encryption, and compression of IP traffic. IPsec can be used to protect any application traffic across the Internet. Applications need not be specifically designed to use IPsec, unlike SSL where the use of SSL must be incorporated into the design of application.

14.12 SECURITY AWARENESS

The aim of the security awareness is to enhance the security of the organization's resources by improving the awareness of the need to secure the system resources. Staff members play a critical role in protecting the integrity, confidentiality, and availability of IT systems and networks. It is necessary for an organization to train their staff for security awareness and accepted computer practices. Security of resources can be ensured when the people using it are aware of the need to secure their resources. Security awareness of staff includes the knowledge of practices that must be adhered to, for ensuring the security and the possible consequences of not using those security practices. For example, not disclosing your password to unauthorized users is a security practice, but if the users are not aware of the possible consequences of disclosing the password, they may disclose their password to other users, unintentionally, thus making their systems prone to security attack. In order to make the users and people in an organization aware of the security practices to be followed, regular training programs are conducted in organizations. Awareness is also promoted by regular security awareness sessions, videotapes, newsletters, posters, and flyers. Figure 14.16 shows a poster for security awareness.

Figure 14.16 Security awareness (A poster)

14.13 SECURITY POLICY

- A *security policy* is a formal statement that embodies the organization's overall security expectations, goals, and objectives with regard to the organization's technology, system and information.
- To be practical and implementable, policies must be defined by standards, guidelines, and procedures. Standards, guidelines, and procedures provide specific interpretation of policies and instruct users, customers, technicians, management, and others on how to implement the policies.
- The security policy states what is, and what is not allowed. A security policy must be comprehensive, up-to-date, complete, delivered effectively, and available to all staff. A security policy must also be enforceable. To accomplish this, the security policy can mention that strict action will be taken against employees who violate it, like disclosing a password.
- Generally, security policies are included within a *security plan.* A security plan details how the rules put forward by the security policy will be implemented. The statements within a security plan can ensure that each employee knows the boundaries and the penalties of overstepping those boundaries. For example, some rules could be included in the security policy of an organization, such as, to log off the system before leaving the workstation, or not to share the password with other users.
- The security policy also includes physical security of the computers. Some of the measures taken to ensure the physical security of a computer are—taking regular backups to prevent data loss from natural calamity, virus attack or theft, securing the backup media, keeping valuable hardware resources in locked room (like servers), to avoid theft of systems and storage media.

14.13.1 Formulating a Security Policy

Security policies are defined based on an organization's needs. A security policy includes approaches and techniques that an organization is going to apply or include in order to secure its resources. The steps followed while formulating the security policy are:

- *Analyzing Current Security Policies*—The vulnerabilities and the current security policies must be analyzed by the security administrators before defining an effective security policy. The security administrator is required to study the existing documents containing details of the physical security policies, network security policies, data security policies, disaster recovery plans, and contingency plans.
- *Identifying IT Assets that Need to be Secure*—The security administrator must identify the IT resources of an organization that need to be secure. It may include the following:
    - Physical resources like computers, servers like database servers and web servers, local networks that are used to share the local computer with the remote computer, private networks shared by two or more organizations, corporate network permanently connected to the Internet, laptop, manuals, backup media, communication equipment, network cables, and CDs.
    - Information resources like password, data, or applications. The data of an organization can be classified for security purposes based upon the sensitivity and the integrity of data. For example, public information, internal information, confidential information, and secret information
- *Identifying Security Threats and Likely Security Attacks*—After identifying the IT assets and classifying them, a security administrator must identify the various security threats to the assets. For example, in a bank the security threat to the database storing the account details of the customers may be—unauthorized access to information, attacks of viruses, worms and Trojan horses, natural disasters like earthquake, fire etc.

- *Defining the Proactive and Reactive Security Strategies*—A *proactive strategy* is a pre-attack strategy. It involves identifying possible damage from each type of attack, determining the vulnerabilities that each type of attack can exploit, minimizing those vulnerabilities and making a contingency plan. A contingency plan specifies the actions to be taken in case an attack penetrates into a system and damages the IT assets of the organization. A contingency plan aims at keeping the computer functional and ensuring the availability, integrity, and confidentiality of data. However, it is not possible for the security administrator to prepare a computer against all attacks. A *reactive strategy* is implemented on the failure of the proactive strategy. It defines the steps to be taken after the attack. It aims at identifying the cause of attack, vulnerabilities used to attack the system, damage caused by the attack, and repairing of the damage caused by the attack.

SUMMARY

- *Computer security* protects the data stored on the computing system and the data transmitted over a network. It focuses on security attacks, security mechanisms and security services.
- A *security threat* is a potential violation of security and causes harm.
- *Vulnerability* is a weakness of system that is left unprotected and is exposed to threats.
- *Security attacks* are the reasons for breach of security.
- *Malicious software or malware* is a software code intentionally included into a system with the intention to harm the system. Viruses, Trojan horses, Worms, and, Javascripts, Java applets, and activeX controls written with the purpose of attacking are malicious programs.
- *Hacking* is intruding into another computer or network to perform an illegal act.
- *DoS attack* makes the computer resource unusable or unavailable to its intended users thus preventing authorized users from accessing the resources on the computer.
- Packet sniffing, E-mail hacking and Password cracking are used to get the username and password of the system to gain *unauthorized access to the system.*
- *Security service* provides specific kind of protection to system resources. Security service ensures confidentiality, integrity, authentication, and non-repudiation of data. It provides assurance for access control and availability of the resources to its authorized users.
- *Security mechanisms* are tools that include algorithms, protocols or devices, that are designed to detect, prevent or recover from a security attack. They use cryptography, digital signature, firewall, user identification and authentication as countermeasures for security attack.
- *Cryptography* encrypts the data to protect the data in transit over a network. Cryptography schemes use a pair of algorithms for encryption and decryption, and a key. Secret key cryptography, Public-key cryptography, and hash functions are some cryptographic schemes.
- *Secret key cryptography* or *symmetric encryption* uses a single key for both encryption and decryption. It is difficult to distribute the key securely to the receiver if the receiver and the sender are at different physical locations.
- *Public-key cryptography* or *asymmetric encryption* uses a pair of keys—public key and private key, for encryption and decryption. The public key is shared freely, but private key is kept secret.
- *Digital signatures* are used to sign a computerized document. The digital signature scheme consists of key generation algorithm, signing algorithm and signature verifying algorithm.
- A *firewall* protects a local network from the threats it may face while interacting with other networks (Internet). Gateway, proxy server and screening routers are used as firewall.
- In *username and password authentication*, the system checks the username and password by comparing it to the stored password for that username.
- A *smart card* is a pocket-sized card with strong security authentication for single sign-on.
- *Biometrics* measures and analyzes human traits like fingerprints, eye retinas and irises, voice patterns, facial patterns and hand measurements, for authentication.
- Intrusion Detection Systems, Virus Protection software, Data and Information Backups, SSL, and IPsec protocol are *other security techniques* used for security purposes.

- The aim of *security awareness* is to enhance security of the organization's resources by improving the awareness of the need to secure system resources.
- *Security policy* states the management's overall security expectations, goals and objectives with regard to the organization's technology, system, and information.
- A *security plan* specifies how the rules put forward by security policy will be implemented.

KEYWORDS

Active attack *286*
ActiveX controls *288*
Application-level Gateway *297*
Asymmetric encryption *292*
Authentication *294*
Biometrics *298*
Block ciphers *291*
Certification Authorities (CA) *292*
Cipher *291*
Cipher text *291*
Circuit Filter Firewall *296*
Code *290*
Computer security *285*
Confidentiality *289*
Cryptography *291*
Decryption *290*
Denial of Service (DoS) *288*
Digital signature *294*
Digital Signature Algorithm (DSA) *292*
E-mail hacking *289*
Encryption *291*
Firewall *295*
Gateway *295*
Hacking *286*
Hash Function *291*
HTTP Secure (HTTPS) *300*
Integrity *289*
Intrusion Detection System *300*
IP Security (IPsec) Protocol *300*
Java applets *286*
Javascripts *286*
Key *293*
Malicious software *286*
Malware *286*
Network Address Translation (NAT) *294*
Non-Repudiation *290*
Packet filter Firewall *296*
Packet replay *289*
Packet sniffing *289*
Passive attack *285*
Password *289*
Password cracking *289*
Plaintext *291*
Private key *291*
Proxy Server *295*
Public key *291*
Public Key Cryptography (PKC) *291*
RSA *292*
Screening routers *295*
Secret Key Cryptography (SKC) *291*
Secure Socket Layer (SSL) *300*
Security attacks *285*
Security awareness *301*
Security mechanisms *285*
Security plan *302*
Security policy *302*
Security services *285*
Security threat *285*
Smart card *290*
Stream ciphers *291*
Symmetric encryption *291*
Trojan horse *286*
User identification *298*
User name *298*
Viruses *287*
Virus Protection software *300*
Vulnerability *285*
Worms *286*

QUESTIONS

Section 14.2

1. What do you understand by the term Computer security?
2. Define: (i) Security attack, (ii) Security mechanism, and (iii) Security service.
3. Define: (i) Security threat, (ii) Vulnerability, (iii) Passive attack, and (iv) Active attack.
4. A security attack may be a ______ attack or a ______ attack.
5. What are the targets of the security attack?
6. List some security attacks that can be made on the users of the computer.
7. List some security attacks that can be made on the computer hardware.
8. What kind of attacks can be made on the computer software?

Section 14.3

9. What is malicious software?
10. Give three examples of malicious programs.

11. List some properties of virus.
12. How can virus harm the computer?
13. Give an example of virus program.
14. Define a worm.
15. Give an example of a worm program.
16. What are Trojan horses?
17. Why is it advisable to keep the active control disabled on your computer?

Section 14.4

18. Define hacking.
19. What is a Denial of Service attack?
20. ________, ________ and ________ are the methods used to get the username and password of the system to gain unauthorized access to the system.
21. What do you mean by packet sniffing?
22. Name one packet sniffer software.
23. How does a password cracker work?
24. How is e-mail hacked?

Section 14.6

25. Security services ensure ______, ______, ______ and ______ of the data.
26. Define (i) Confidentiality, (ii) Integrity, (iii) Authentication, and (iv) Non-Repudiation.
27. ___________ is used for ensuring confidentiality.
28. Name any two methods that are used for authentication.
29. Non-repudiation deals with _________.
30. List three technologies used for implementing the security mechanisms.

Section 14.7

31. Define cryptography.
32. Define (i) Plain text, (ii) Cipher, (iii) Cipher text, (iv) Encryption, and (v) Decryption.
33. Define a key.
34. What is the significance of key in cryptography?
35. Name the three cryptographic schemes.
36. Why secret key cryptography is also called symmetric encryption?
37. Explain the working of Secret key cryptography.
38. What is the difference between a stream cipher and block cipher?
39. Name a secret key cryptography algorithm.
40. In public key cryptography, how is the public key different from the private key?
41. Why public key cryptography is also called asymmetric encryption?
42. Name a public key cryptography algorithm.
43. ________algorithm is used to provide digital signature.
44. What is the purpose of hash function?
45. Name a hash algorithm.
46. What is the function of Certification Authorities (CA)?

Section 14.8

47. What is the use of digital signature?
48. Is digital signature scheme a symmetric cryptography or asymmetric cryptography?
49. Name the three algorithms included in a digital signature scheme.
50. Explain the digital signature creation and verification using hash function.
51. Signer authentication, Message authentication, and Efficiency are three effects accomplished by digital signature. Explain.

Section 14.9

52. What is the purpose of firewall?
53. List the functions of firewall.
54. Explain the working of firewall.
55. Define: (i) Gateway, (ii) Proxy Server, and (iii) Screening Routers.
56. Name the three types of firewall.
57. How does the Packet filter Firewall work?
58. How does the Circuit Filter Firewall work?
59. How does the Application-level Gateway work?

Section 14.10–14.11

60. What is the difference between user identification and user authentication?
61. Name three authentication mechanisms.
62. Explain user identification and authentication.
63. What is the need of user authentication?
64. List some steps to make the password safe.
65. What is a smart card?
66. Name three areas where smart card is commonly used.
67. How does biometric technique help in user authentication?
68. What is the purpose of intrusion detection system?
69. What is the need of installing virus protection software on your computer?

70. What is the need of taking regular data and information backups?
71. How is HTTPS different from HTTP?
72. IPv6 protocol includes network security. Explain.

Section 14.12

73. What is the need of spreading security awareness?
74. What is a security policy?
75. What is the need of a security plan?
76. List the steps followed in formulating the security policy.
77. Explain in detail the formulation of security policy.
78. What IT resources need to be made secure in an organization?
79. What is the purpose of proactive security strategy?
80. What is the purpose of reactive security strategy?

Extra Questions

81. Give full form of the following abbreviations:

(i) DoS	(ii) SKC	(iii) PKC
(iv) DES	(v) AES	(vi) DSA
(vii) SHA	(viii) CA	(ix) NAT
(x) SSL	(xi) IPsec	

82. Write short notes on:
    (a) Security attack
    (b) Malicious software
    (c) Viruses
    (d) Trojan horse
    (e) Worms
    (f) Hacking
    (g) Security services
    (h) Cryptography
    (i) Secret key cryptography
    (j) Public-key cryptography
    (k) Digital signature
    (l) Firewall
    (m) Types of firewall
    (n) User identification and authentication
    (o) User authentication mechanisms
    (p) User name and Password
    (q) Security awareness
    (r) Security Policy
    (s) Formulating a security policy
83. Give differences between the following:
    (a) Passive security attack and Active security attack
    (b) Viruses and Worms
    (c) Malicious software and Hacking
    (d) Secret Key Cryptography and Public-Key Cryptography
    (e) Packet filter firewall and Circuit Filter firewall
    (f) Users identification and User authentication
    (g) Proactive Security Strategy and Reactive Security Strategy

15

WINDOWS XP

Contents

- Introduction
- Features of Windows XP
- The desktop—The task bar, the icons and shortcuts
- Structure of Windows—Title bar, menu bar, tool bar, scroll bar, status bar
- Windows XP explorer
  - The start
  - The window—Title bar, menu bar, standard bar, address bar, status bar
  - The view—Filmstrip, thumbnails, tiles, icons, list, details
  - Selecting files
  - Working with folders—Creating, deleting, copying, moving, changing
  - Files and folders properties—Showing, organizing, modifying
  - The search
  - The recycle bin—Open, restoring and deleting files or folders, emptying
  - Configuring screen—Desktop, screen saver, appearance, themes, settings
  - Configuring the mouse, adding or removing programs
  - Adding new hardware—Not plug & play, basic information about computer
  - System tools—Backup, character map, disk cleanup, system restore etc.
  - The scandisk
  - Windows XP media player, Windows XP help
  - Windows vista—Updated GUI, Windows instant search, Windows DVD maker, embedded start menu, the taskbar preview, Windows contacts
  - Windows 7—Desktop, Windows explorer, taskbar, devices, virtual hard disk, Windows action center, Windows biometric framework, wordpad

Why this chapter

Create, open, copy, hide, search, or delete a file or folder; view a folder's information, configure the appearance and theme of the screen, and, add new hardware and software are some of the tasks you perform quite often while working with the computer machine. For performing these tasks, you interact with the operating system. Windows XP is a most widely used and popular operating system. The purpose of this chapter is to introduce you to "Windows XP".

15.1 INTRODUCTION

There exist a number of operating systems, such as DOS, Windows 98, Windows NT, Windows XP, Windows Vista, Unix, Linux, DOS, Mac OS X Snow Leopard etc. Each Operating System (OS) has its own unique features. Windows XP belongs to the Windows family of OS. Windows XP represents an important change from the previous versions of Windows OS. Before Windows XP, Microsoft had two different operating systems, Windows 98 for personal use and Windows NT/2000 for business and professional environment. Windows XP is a convergence among both versions; the center of operating system Windows 2000 was divided to create Windows XP, and some adjustments were done to differentiate Windows XP Home Edition and Windows XP Professional.

The main benefits of Windows XP are:

- For domestic users, it has acquired the stability of Windows NT/2000. Thus, Windows XP is very stable and rarely crashes.
- For professional users, it provides greater compatibility with the hardware than Windows NT/2000.

In this chapter, the environment of Windows XP OS is discussed in detail. A brief description of Windows Vista and Windows 7 OS is also provided.

15.2 FEATURES OF WINDOWS XP

Windows XP has a new user system completely different from Windows 98. Some new features of Windows XP are:

- Multiple users with independent profiles can be defined. Each user can have different permissions that will allow the user to carry out certain tasks. Each user will have a different *Start* menu and *My Documents* folder that can be protected by password. Multiple users can also share folders. The system handles the different active users without interferences.
- It is better integrated to Internet Explorer.
- CDs can be burned by dragging and dropping to the recording unit. It is no longer necessary to install an additional program to record CDs.
- It has a useful way for showing pictures called Filmstrip.
- It's easier to configure a domestic network.
- It recovers better from errors. When a fatal error occurs Windows XP creates a register with all the information concerning the error and gives user the option of sending it to Microsoft, to be analyzed.
- Windows XP initializes faster than Windows 98.
- The Start menu and the Task bar have changed.
- Windows Movie Maker is a new component used for editing films.

15.3 THE DESKTOP

The entire screen on which all windows are displayed is termed as *Windows Desktop*. It is the first screen that appears when the operating system has initialized (Figure 15.1). All your work opens as individual windows on the Windows Desktop.

The Desktop has two parts—the portion where icons are displayed, and the Taskbar at the bottom of the Desktop window. The icons are small images located on the Desktop. For example, for Internet Explorer and for Recycle Bin. The Task Bar contains *Start button* and other parts.

In this chapter, we use the following terminology while working with the mouse:

- **Pointer**—a mouse pointer
- **Click**—press left button of mouse once
- **Double Click**—press left button of mouse twice
- **Right Click**—press right button of mouse once
- **Select**—move the pointer of mouse and keep the left button of the mouse pressed over the area that you want to select. The selected area will appear in a dark background.

We enclose the command in braces <Command> to represent the command to be clicked.

Figure 15.1 The desktop screen

15.3.1 The Task Bar

On the Desktop, Task Bar appears at the bottom of the screen. The task bar has four parts: (1) Start button, (2) Area for shortcuts, (3) The running programs, and, (4) The Notification Area.

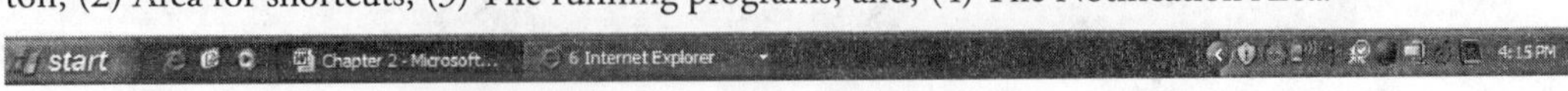

- **Start Button**: It  provides access to the entire range of options that Windows XP offers. If you click it, a menu as shown in Figure 15.2 is displayed.
  - It displays the list of programs that are permanently available and that are most frequently used. Like, Set Program Access and Defaults, Connect To, Printers and Faxes etc.
  - **All Programs** is used to view all the programs that are installed on the computer.
  - **Documents** provide access to the different parts of Windows XP that are most often used like—My documents, My Recent Documents, My Pictures.
  - **Control Panel** allows configuring and customizing of appearance of the computer.
  - **Search** is used to find files or folders.
  - **Help and Support** provides help and support to work on Windows.
  - **Run** allows directly executing certain commands, for example to execute a specific program, etc.
  - **Log Off** allows closing the current session.
  - **Turn Off Computer** allows restarting or turning off the computer.
- The area for shortcuts contains icons that are used to access a particular program quickly. To place an icon here, simply drag it from the Desktop. To execute, simply click on the icon. 

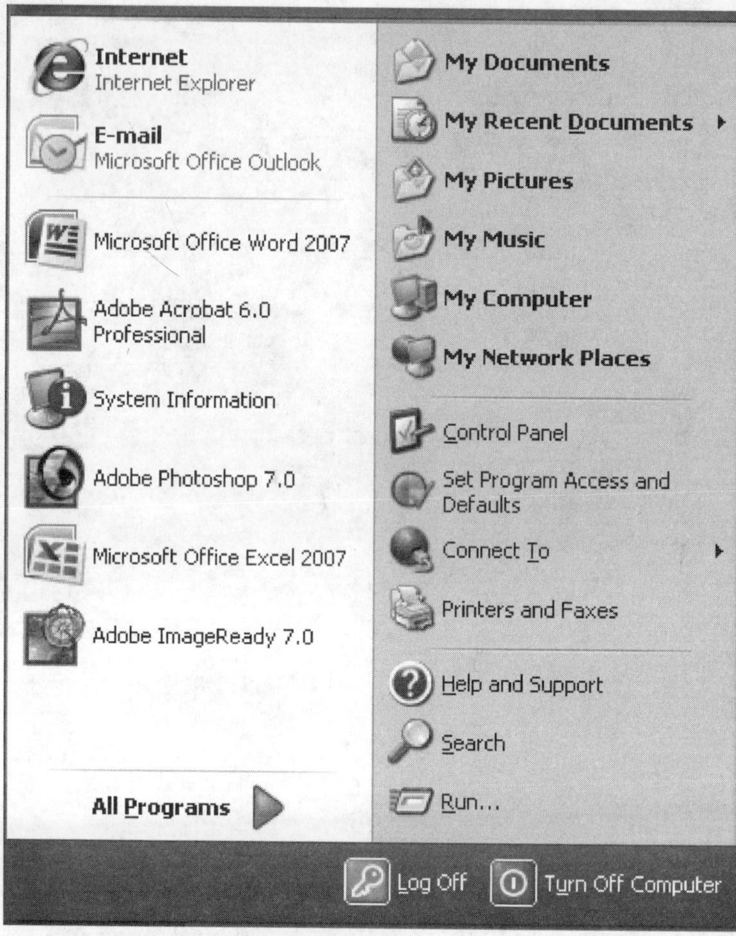

Figure 15.2 The start button

- **Running Programs** It shows the buttons of the application programs that are currently open. If the button is slightly darker, it is the button of the application program that you are currently working with. When there are several instances of the same program open at the same time they are grouped under a button. For example, if you have six windows of Internet Explorer opened at the same time, clicking on the button will display all windows of the Internet Explorer.

- **The Notification Area** contains icons that represent the programs that start up automatically when the computer is turned on. If a round button appears,  this allows you to expand or shrink the area that contains the icons of these programs. The time also appears here.

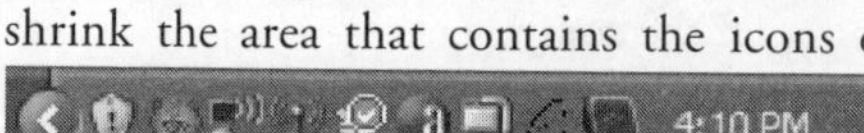

Double-click on an icon to open it.

15.3.2 The Icons and Shortcuts

The user can double-click the icon on the desktop to open it, for example, clicking on the icon will open up Internet Explorer.

- ⊙ **Organizing Icons on Desktop** using the following steps:
    - Right click on Desktop. <Arrange Icons By> (Figure 15.3)

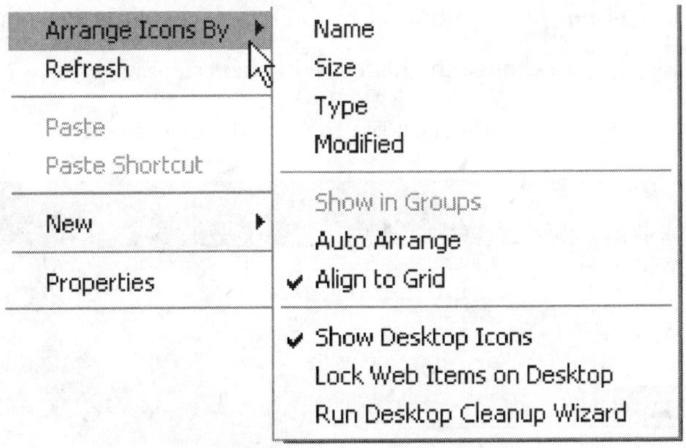

Figure 15.3 Arrange icons by

- Choose to organize by Name, Type, Size, or Modified (date).
- You can activate Auto Arrange, which arranges the icons one below the other.
- To customize the way the icons are organized, simply drag them with the mouse to where you want them. For this, Auto Arrange must be deactivated.

- ⊙ **Create Shortcuts** as follows:
    - Right click on Desktop. <New> <Shortcut> (Figure 15.4)

Figure 15.4 New shortcut

- A dialog box will appear. Indicate the program for which you want to create the shortcut. You can use Browse button, to find the program.
- Select the file or folder. <Ok> <Next>
- Type a name for the Shortcut. <Finish>
- Once you have the shortcut on the desktop, you can leave it there or drag it to the quick access bar on the task bar.

⊙ **Change Date and Time**—The computer has a clock located on the right side of the task bar.

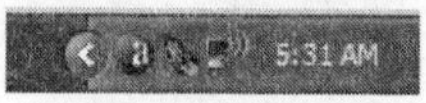

To change the Date follow these steps:

- Double-click on the clock on the Task bar to open the dialog box (Figure 15.5).

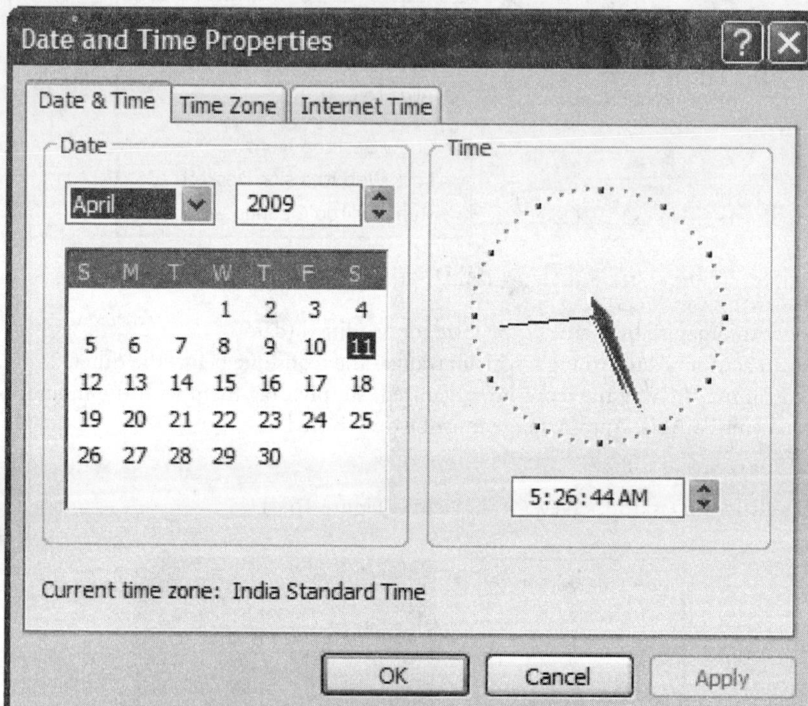

Figure 15.5 The clock

- Change the date by selecting the required month, year and day. Change the time by selecting the time digits.
- Click *Apply* if you want the change to take effect and remain in dialog box. Click OK if you want the changes to be permanent and the dialog box to close.
- Selecting <Time Zones> allows changing the meridian.

⊙ **Visualize the Tool Bars** as follows:

- Right Click on Task Bar. <Toolbars> (Figure 15.6)
- Select the toolbars that you wish to see. If next to the option a check mark appears it means that the tool is already visible.

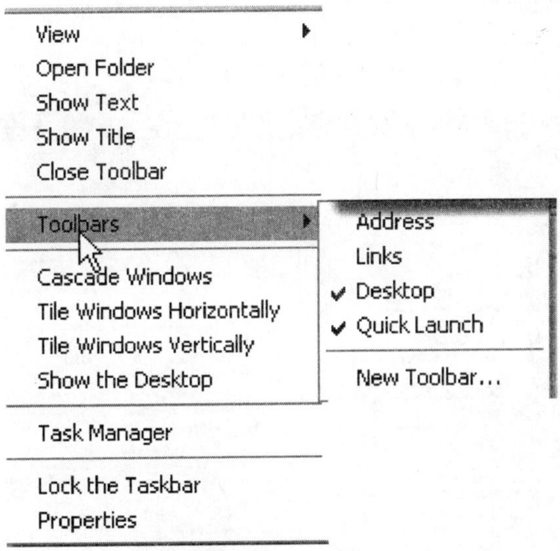

Figure 15.6 The toolbar

15.4 STRUCTURE OF WINDOWS

All the windows in Windows XP have the same structure. Figure 15.7 shows the contents of directory D:\ASHIMA GOEL. The structure of this window is very similar to the others.

- **Title Bar**—It contains name of the program you are working with and name of the opened document. The windows can be moved around the window desktop using this title bar. The top right corner has three buttons to minimize, maximize/restore, and close the window.
- **Menu Bar**—It is located under the Title bar and contains the related Pull-down menus for the currently active windows; for example—File, Edit, View, Favorites, Tools, and Help. Clicking on a menu name will activate a pull-down menu with various options to select. If you find an option that is grey or lighter colored, it means that it is not possible to select it at that moment.
- **Tool Bar** —It contains icons of the most often used commands that can be executed immediately. These commands can also be executed from the menu bar.
- **Scroll Bar**—The scroll bars allow us to move throughout the page in a quick and simple manner. Simply drag the bar with the mouse or click on the arrows. There are bars to move along the width of the page and bars to move along the height of the page. The little square with dots on the right is used to change the size of the window.
- **Status Bar**—It gives information to the user, depending on the window that is opened at the time. This bar is not shown by default in Windows XP. You can activate or de-activate it from the <View> <Status Bar>.
- **Borders for Resizing**—A thin border appears around the windows, which can be used to resize the current window. To resize the current windows, just place the pointer on the border of the windows

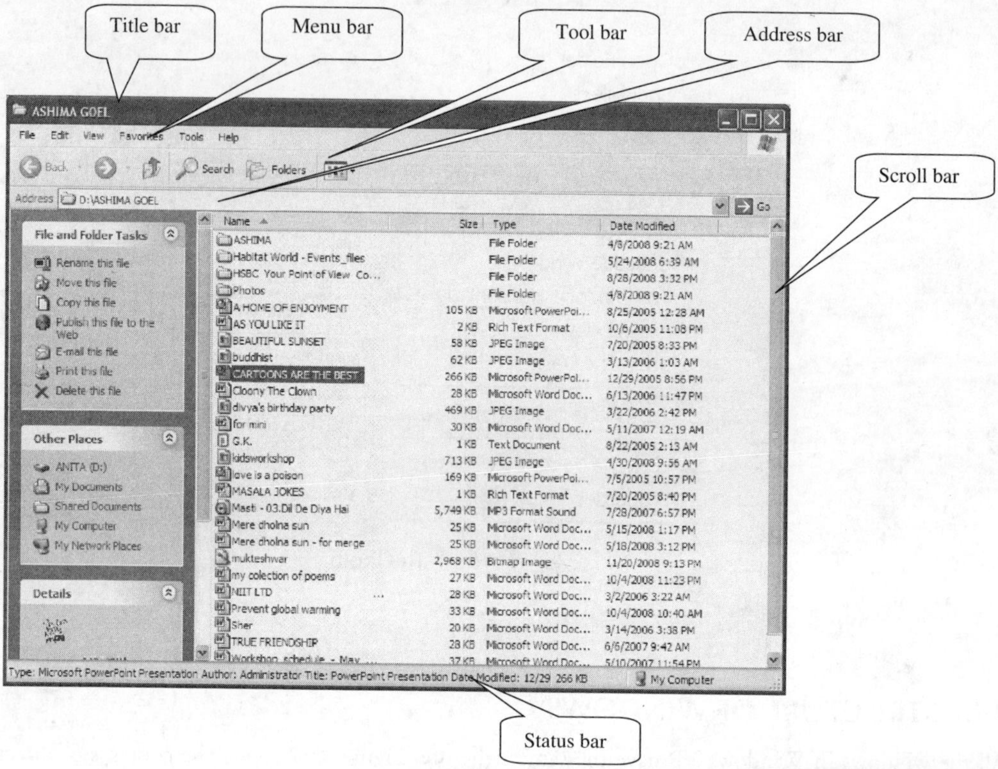

Figure 15.7 A window

(it will become two-headed arrow), click the mouse button, and then hold and drag to the desired location. The windows will change its size.

15.5 WINDOWS XP EXPLORER

Windows Explorer lets the user explore the contents of computer and do file management. It organizes and controls the files and folders of the different storage devices such as the hard drive, disk drive, etc. The Windows Explorer is also known as the File Manager. Windows Explorer is especially useful for copying and moving files. Windows Explorer allows to delete, see, copy, or move files and folders.

15.5.1 The Start

To start Windows Explorer

(1) Click on the icon 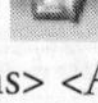 on the task bar or desktop, or,

(2) <Start> <Programs> <Accessories> <Windows Explorer> (Figure 15.8)

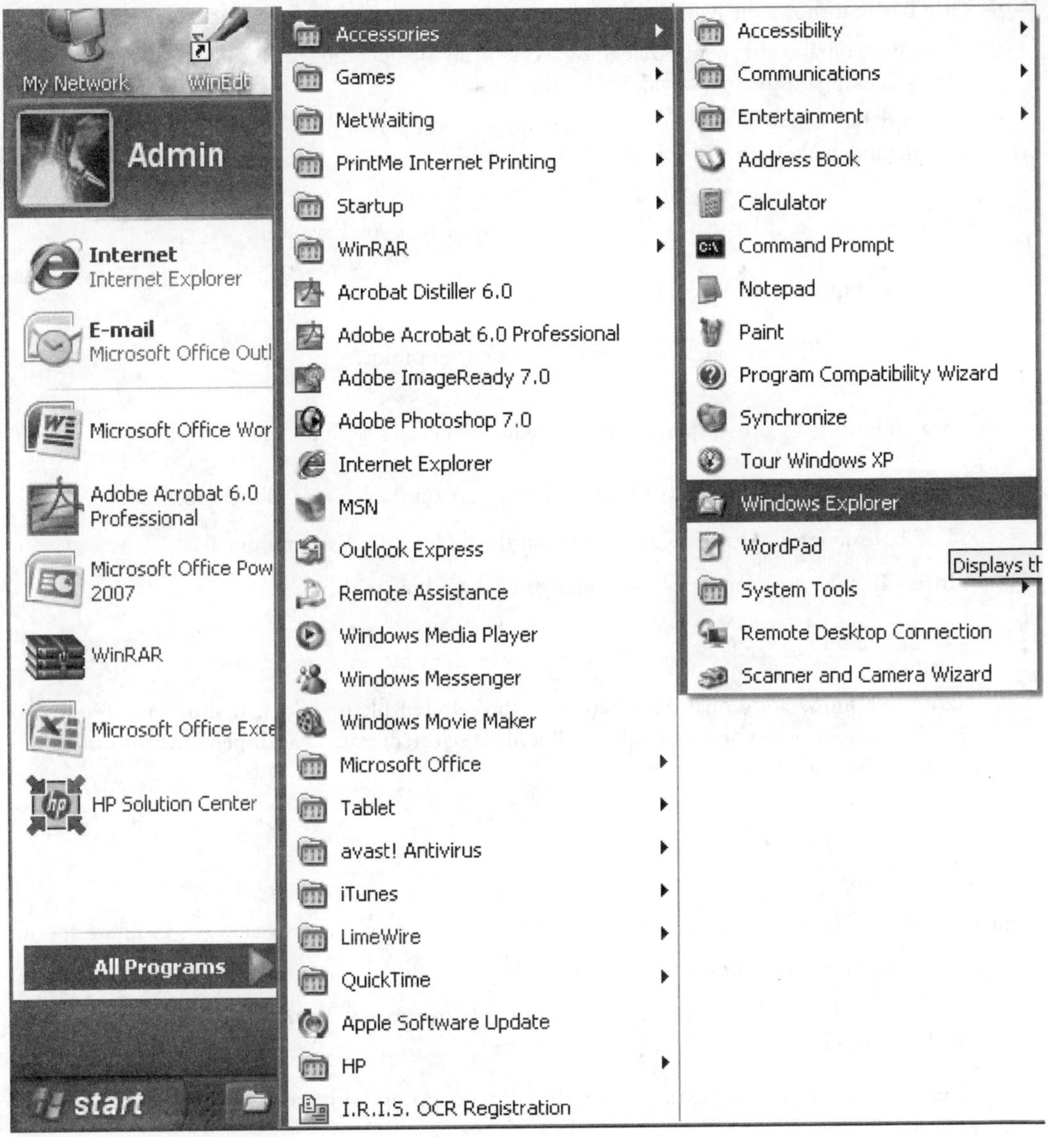

Figure 15.8 The start button

15.5.2 The Window

The window that opens when you start Windows Explorer has the same structure as discussed in the previous section. The explorer consists of two sections. On the left side there is the directory tree (in a hierarchical order) which shows the list of units and folders on the computer. On the right side there is a section, which shows all the files and folders that the user has selected on the left hand side. Windows Explorer has different bars that make up the window. These are as follows:

- **Title Bar** that shows the name of the folder you are in.
- **Menu Bar** contains the menus that allow access to all the operations that can be done with a file or folder. Clicking on the menu will display the options.
- **Standard Bar** contains the buttons for the most used operations. If this bar is not visible, select from the menu View, the option Toolbars, next select the option Standard buttons.
    - Back button 

 — to go to the last page that you have seen.
    - Forward button—to move one page forward.
    - Up button —to go up one level from the current folder.
    - Search button —displays a window where you can search for the file
    - Folders button —shows the folder's structure on the left side of the screen.
    - Last button —to change the views on the folders (details, Thumbnails)
- **Address Bar** shows the name of the folder you are working with.

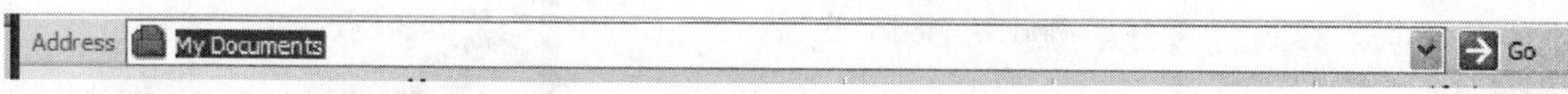

- **Status Bar** shows additional information of the selected file or folder. It shows the number of files the folder contains and its total size. If a file is selected, status bar displays the information of selected objects and their total size.

15.5.3 The View

Windows explorer allows the user to see the folder's information in different views to facilitate specific searching. On clicking of the button  a menu shows the different options (Figure 15.9) that can be selected to view a unit or a folder. The options are - (1) Filmstrip, (2) Thumbnails, (3) Tiles, (4) Icons, (5) List, and (6) Details.

- **Thumbnails**—A small representation of the content appears with the format of the image.
- **Filmstrip**—It is used to view the images only. On the bottom part a strip appears with the images in thumbnail format and on the top a larger representation of the image selected on the bottom is seen.
- **Tiles**—The files and folders are shown with large images with the name, file type, and size in KB
- **Icons**—The files are shown with an icon and the name of file.
- **List**—Shows small icons, one below the other, so it is easier to search by name. It shows only the name of file or folder.
- **Details**—Icons are shown one below the other, with some of their properties like size, file type, date of modification, etc.

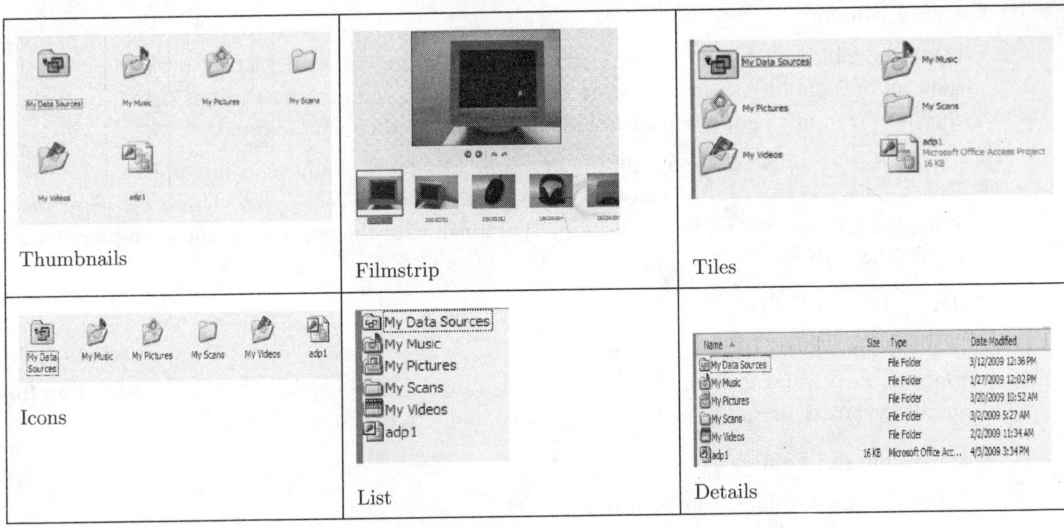

Figure 15.9 The view options

15.5.4 Selecting Files

The files on folders can be selected in three different ways depending on what files and folders you wish to select. Windows Explorer allows you to select a single file or folder, or several files or folders at the same time.

- To select a single file or folder—Click on the file or folder you want to select. Any operation you perform will only apply to the selected file or folder.
- To select several files and folders that are consecutive—
  - Click on the first element and then click on the last element while keeping <Shift> key on the keyboard pressed.
  - This can also be done with the mouse. Click on the left of the first file or folder (but not on it) and, without letting go, drag it. A frame appears that shows the area that the frame encompasses. Continue dragging until all the files and folders you wish to select are within the frame, then let go of the left mouse button
- To select several files and folders that are not consecutive—Click the first file or folder and while keeping the <Ctrl> key on the keyboard pressed, continue to click the other files and folders that you wish to select.

15.5.5 Working with Folders

Windows Explorer allows you to perform several operations on the files and folders stored in a directory. You can create a folder, delete a file or folder, copy a file or folder, move a file or folder, and change the name of a file or folder.

Creating Folders

- Open the folders that you have by clicking on the "+" located to the left of the folders. It will show all of the folders contained in it and the plus sign will become a minus sign "–" ; If you click on the minus sign, it will again hide the content of the folder selected.
- Open the folder in which you want to create a new folder by double clicking on it.
- <File> <New> <Folder>. A new folder appears with the name *New Folder*. This is the name that Windows gives to new folders by default. Type a name for the new folder, and then press *Enter* key on the keyboard.

Deleting Files or Folders

- Select the files or folders you want to delete.
- Once selected, you can delete the file or folder using—<File> <Delete>, or, Press delete button on the keyboard, or, Click on 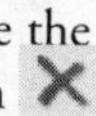. The deleted folder moves to the Recycle Bin.

Copying Files or Folders

- Select the files or folders you want to copy.
- Once selected, you can copy the file or folder using any one of the following ways:
  - <Edit> <Copy>. Open the folder or disk drive where you want to copy the file to. <Edit> <Paste>, or,
  - Click on Copy . A dialog box is displayed. Search for the folder where you want to copy the selected file or folder. If you click on the "+" that appears on the left, the contents of the folder will be displayed. Select and open the folder where you want to copy the file or folder. <Paste>.

Moving Files or Folders

- Select the files or folders you want to move.
- Once selected, you can move the file or folder using any one of the following ways:
  <Edit> <Move to Folder>. A dialog box is displayed. Search for the folder where you want to move the selected file or folder. If you click on the "+" that appears on the left, the contents of the folder will be displayed. Select and open the folder where you want to move the file or folder. <Move>.

Changing the Name of a File or Folder

- Select the file or folder whose name you want to change.
- Once selected, you can change the name of file or folder using any one of the following ways:
  - Right click. <Rename>. Write the new name, or,
  - <File> <Rename>. Write the new name.
- Click *Enter* key or click outside the file or folder so that the changes take place.

15.5.6 Files and Folders Properties

Both files and folders have their own characteristics, for example size, location, date of creation, attributes, etc. In Windows Explorer, to know the characteristics of a file or folder, do either of the following:

(1) <File> <Properties>, or,

(2) Right click on a file or folder. Select <Properties> from the displayed menu.

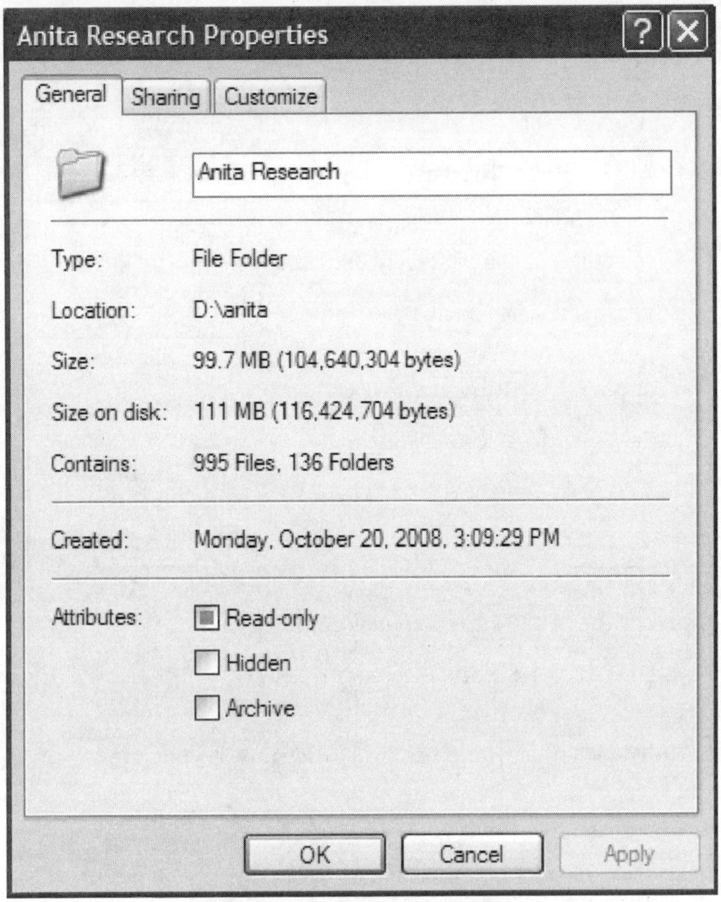

Figure 15.10 The file properties

A window with several tabs will appear (Figure 15.10). Depending on whether it is a folder or a particular file, the tabs that appear will vary. In case of a folder, the tabs that appear are *General, Sharing,* and *Customize*. *General* shows the Type of folder, Location, size, number of files it contains, and the date when the folder was created. *Sharing* contains information on the permission that is given to the other users of the network on our folders. *Customize* allows changing the properties of the folder.

In case of a file, the tabs that appear are *General, Custom, and Summary*. *General* (Figure 15.11) shows the characteristics of the files, modified saves the date the file was last modified and last accessed, the last time the file was opened regardless of whether changes were made or not, Attributes shows the attributes assigned to the file (read only, hidden, or archive).

⊙ Showing Hidden Files and Folders

- <Tools> <Folder options> <View> (Figure 15.12)
- In Hidden files and Folders—Check <Show hidden files and folders>. <OK>

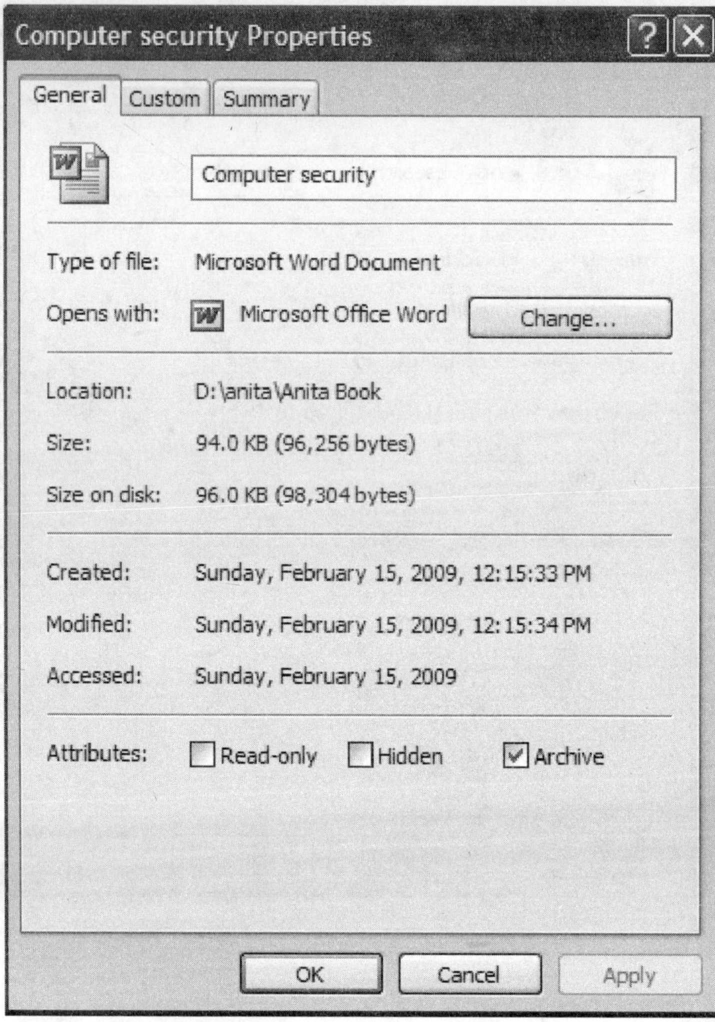

Figure 15.11 The file properties general tab

- **Knowing Types of Files**—To know the types of files registered in the computer and the program with which they open.
    - <Tools> <Folder Options…> <File Types>
    - On the window that appears, you can see all of the types of files that the computer can open. If you select any of them, the details of the program with which it opens will appear.
- **Organizing Folders**
    - Place cursor on the folder you wish to arrange.

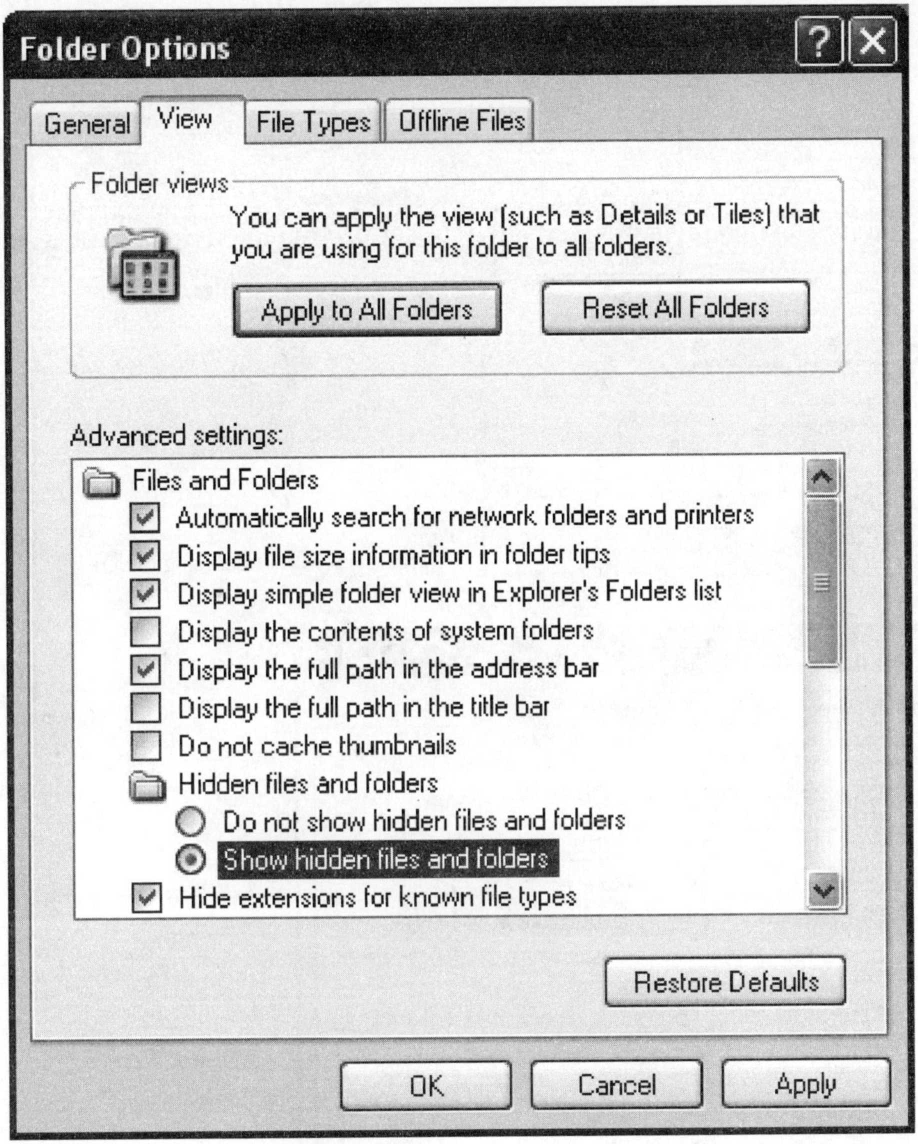

Figure 15.12 The folder options

- <View> <Arrange icons by> (Figure 15.13)
- Select the way (Name, Size, Type, Modified) you want to arrange the files in the folder.

⊙ **Modifying Windows Behavior**

- <Tools> <Folder Options> <General> (Figure 15.14)

You can modify the behavior, like—open a window in same window or new window, open using single click and double click, etc.

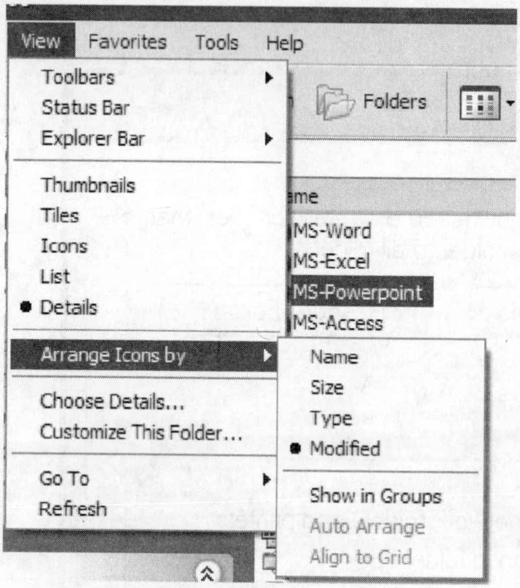

Figure 15.13 Organizing folders

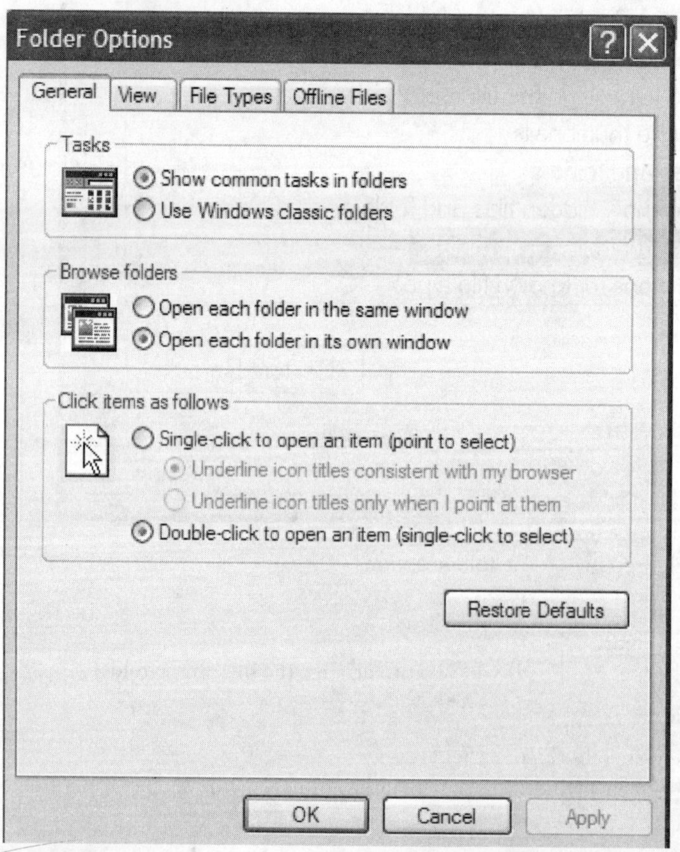

Figure 15.14 To modify window behaviour

15.6 THE SEARCH

With so many files and folders, sometimes it becomes difficult to locate a file or a folder in the directory. Windows XP provides Search option to search for hardware, a network, people in the directory, Internet pages, etc. To search click <Start> <Search>.

It allows you to search for files and folders, people, hardware, and on the Internet. The search pop-up screen will be displayed (Figure 15.15).

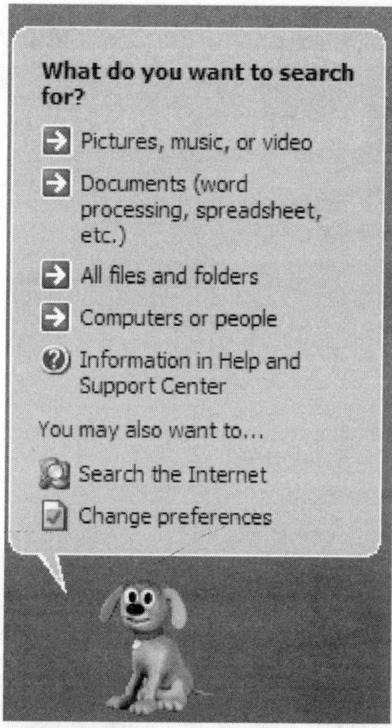

Figure 15.15 The search pop-up screen

15.7 THE RECYCLE BIN

The Recycle Bin is a space on the hard disk reserved to store information that is deleted. In the event of deleting a file or folder by mistake, it is possible to retrieve it from the Recycle Bin. If a deleted file needs to be restored, the Recycle Bin restores files or folders to the place from where they were deleted. For example, if a file is deleted from D:\My Documents, when it is restored, it will go back to this folder. Recycle Bin stores and maintains the deleted documents until the bin is emptied.

- **Open Recycle Bin**—To open the Recycle Bin, place the cursor on Desktop and double-click on the Recycle Bin icon. The Recycle Bin window (Figure 15.16) is similar to the Windows Explorer window, and has similar options. In the Recycle Bin shows the names of the deleted files and folders, their original location before it was deleted and the date and time when it was deleted.
- **Restoring Files or Folders**
  - Select the elements to be restored by clicking on them.
  - Click on the green arrow on the left side with <Restore the selected Items> or <Restore this Item> depending on whether you have selected more than one item or one item, or, Click on <File> <Restore>
  - The selected files will return to where they were located before deletion.
- **Deleting Files or Folders**—Once files and folders in the Recycle Bin are deleted, they are deleted permanently. To delete any file or folder from the Recycle Bin follow these steps:
  - Select the files to be deleted.
  - <File> <Delete>, or, press the *Delete* button on the keyboard.
  - A window appears asking if you are sure that you want to delete the selected file or folder. Click *Yes* if you are sure you want it deleted.
  - The selected files will disappear and cannot be restored.
- **Emptying the Recycle Bin**—There are three ways to empty the Recycle Bin as follows—
  - Open Recycle Bin Window. Click on <Empty the Recycle Bin>. A window will appear asking "Are you sure you want to delete these x items", where x is the number of elements currently in the Recycle Bin. Click *Yes* to empty it.

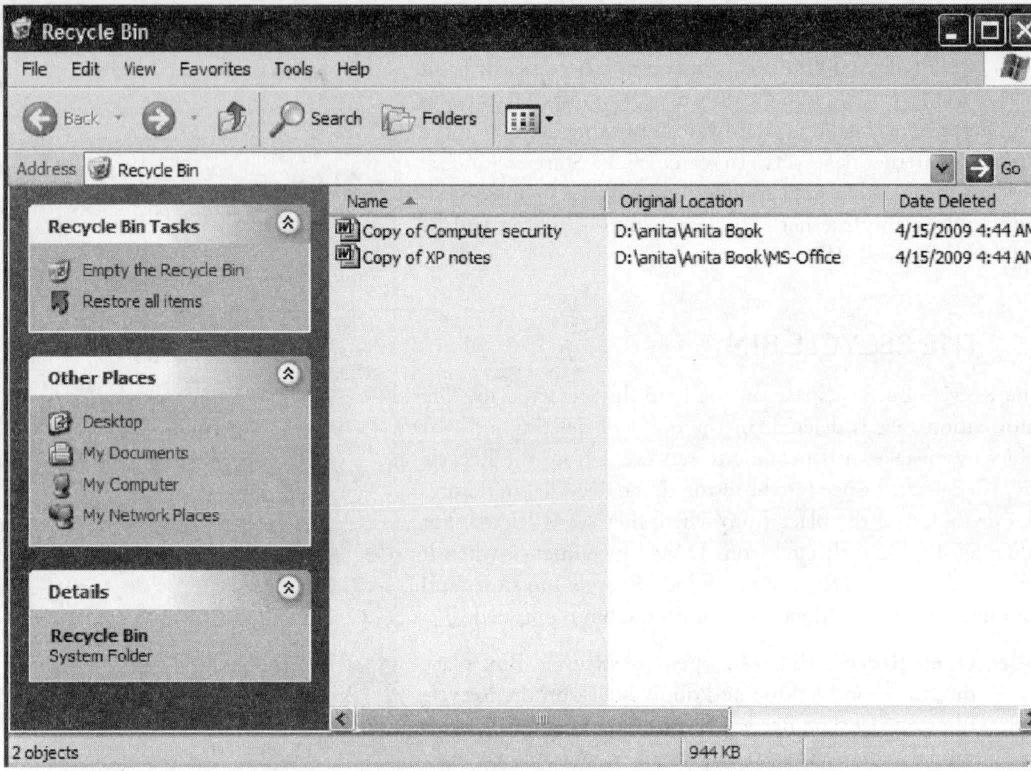

Figure 15.16 The recycle bin

- Open Recycle Bin window. <File> <Empty Recycle Bin>. A window will appear asking "Are you sure you want to delete these x items", where x is the number of elements currently in the Recycle Bin. Click *Yes* to empty it.
- Right click on the Recycle Bin icon on the desktop. <Empty Recycle Bin>

15.8 CONFIGURING THE SCREEN

A user spends long hours in front of the computer. Configuration of the screen is required to make the screen of the desktop comfortable for use. The user can configure the desktop screen as follows:

(1) On the Desktop, Right click on the screen where there are no icons on the screen.

(2) Select <Properties>. It will display the properties of the screen. It contains tabs like the Desktop, Screen saver, Appearance, Themes, and Settings.

(3) Configure the Desktop from here.

The different tabs are used to configure for different properties, as follows:

- **Desktop**—It is used to choose a new background or wallpaper from the list (Figure 15.17). The position of the wall paper on the screen can be centered, tiled or stretched. Centered displays the image in real size in the center of the screen, Tile displays the image with as many images as necessary to fill the screen, and Stretch displays the image once taking up the entire screen. The option Browse... allows the user to have another image that does not appear on the list as background. Once settings are made, click *OK*.

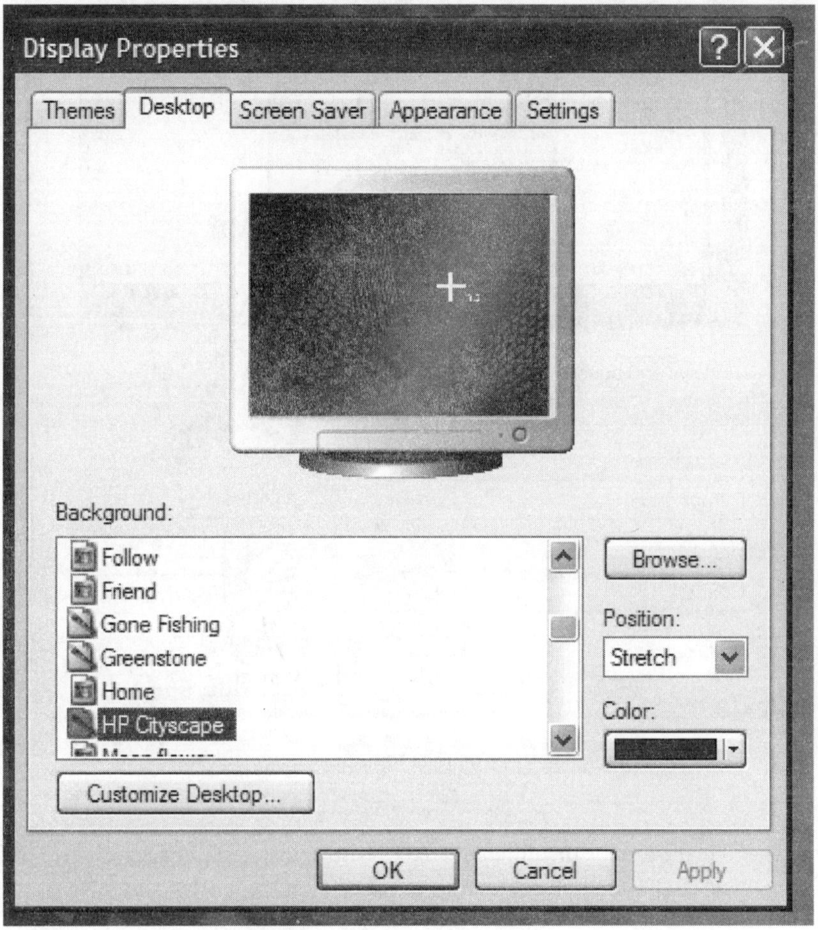

Figure 15.17 The desktop settings

- **Screen Saver**—Sometimes the computer remains inactive for a few minutes. A still image on the screen for too long and too often can damage the monitor. It is recommended to have a screen saver. Screen saver screen allows the user to make settings for the screen saver. Preview shows how the screen saver will look once it gets activated. Wait is the time it takes for the screensaver to appear. A setting is used to customize the image that is used as the screen saver. Password protect is a password protection to keep someone else from working on your account, on resume. It will allow you back to the normal screen only after you have entered the correct user password.
- **Appearance**—It is used to change the appearance of the Desktop screen like, the style you want, a color scheme and a font size (Figure 15.18). Once settings are made, click *OK*.

Figure 15.18 The desktop appearance settings

- **Themes**—A Theme groups the different characteristics that affect the appearance of Desktop by giving it a name. You can select a theme you prefer and on the bottom part you can see how it will look. If you wish to save the changes, click *Save as*, then name it and click *OK*.
- **Settings**—It allows you to select the monitor and graphics card, and choose the resolution and the color scheme (Figure 15.19). The resolution affects the size of the images. Selecting a color scheme decides the amount of colors with which the monitor will work with.

15.9 CONFIGURING THE MOUSE

The mouse is a tool that is used constantly and it is recommended to set it as per your convenience and needs. To configure the mouse, open the mouse properties window as follows:

<Start> <Settings> <Control Panel> <Printers and Other Hardware> <Mouse> (Figure 15.20)

You can do all settings for the mouse from here.

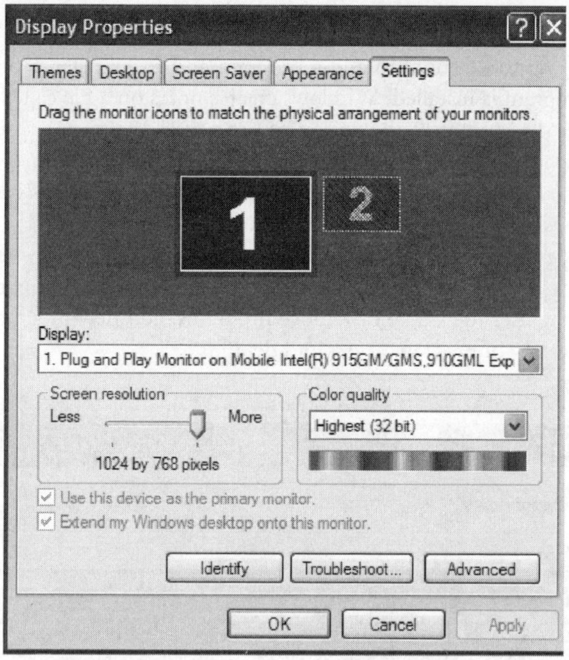

Figure 15.19 The desktop color settings

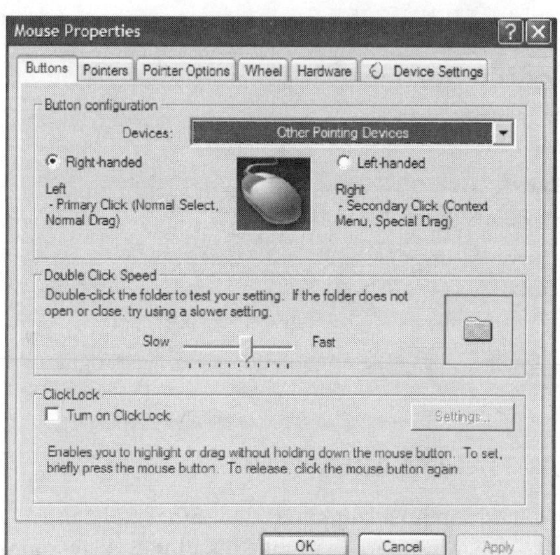

Figure 15.20 The mouse settings

15.10 ADDING OR REMOVING PROGRAMS

The Adding and Removing tool is used to add a program and to uninstall a program that is no longer needed. When a new program is installed, Windows creates notes on a file called Windows Register. The Windows Register stores the current configuration of the system, hardware, software, and different user configurations. A program that needs to be uninstalled cannot be done by simply deleting the files manually. If we delete, only the files linked to a program, the records that Windows created on the Register are not removed, so an inconsistency can occur.

To add or remove programs, open the Add or Remove Programs window as follows:

- <Start> <Settings> <Control Panel> <Add or Remove Programs> (Figure 15.21)

The window allows the user to change or remove programs, add new programs, add or remove Window components, and setting of program access and defaults.

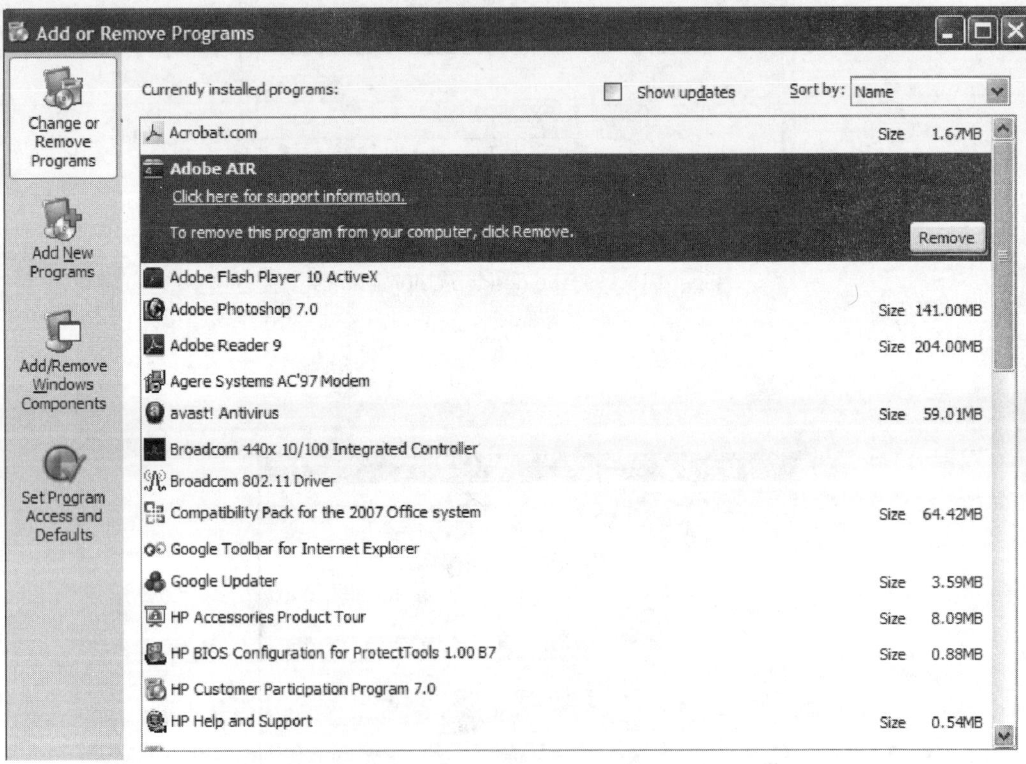

Figure 15.21 Setting to add or remove programs

15.11 ADDING NEW HARDWARE

When we want to add new hardware to a computer, two things can happen: either the component is Plug & Play or it is not. If the hardware to be installed is Plug & Play, simply connect the hardware and Windows will recognize and install it automatically. Conversely, if you connect the hardware and the Window recognizes it, then the hardware is Plug & Play. If the Windows does not recognize it, then the element is not Plug & Play and needs to be installed manually. For installing it, an Add new Hardware assistant is provided. When new hardware is installed, the computer needs driver for that hardware. The driver contains the files that describe the hardware and allows the computer to communicate with it.

⊙ To **add a hardware that is not plug & play**, open the window as follows—

- <Start> <Settings> <Control Panel> <Printers and Other Hardware> <Add hardware> (on the left of window) (Figure 15.22)
- The Add Window Hardware Wizard appears. Follow the instructions of the wizard for installation.

⊙ To see the **basic information about your computer** like the hardware of your system and their properties, do the following:

- <Start> <Control Panel> <Performance and maintenance> <See basic information about your computer>
- A window named *System Properties* will appear. It has various tabs. For example, the General tab shows generic information about your system, such as which processor is installed, etc. Select <Hardware> <Device manager>. It shows a list of all the hardware installed on your computer (Figure 15.23).

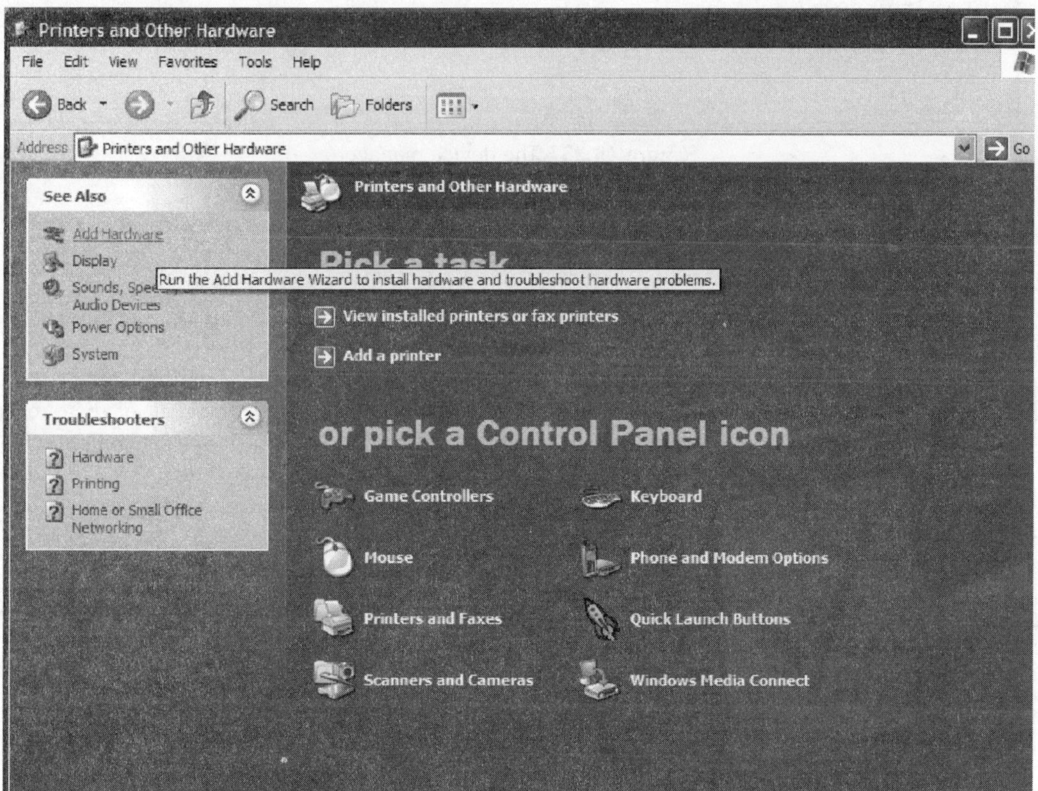

Figure 15.22 The window and other hardware screen

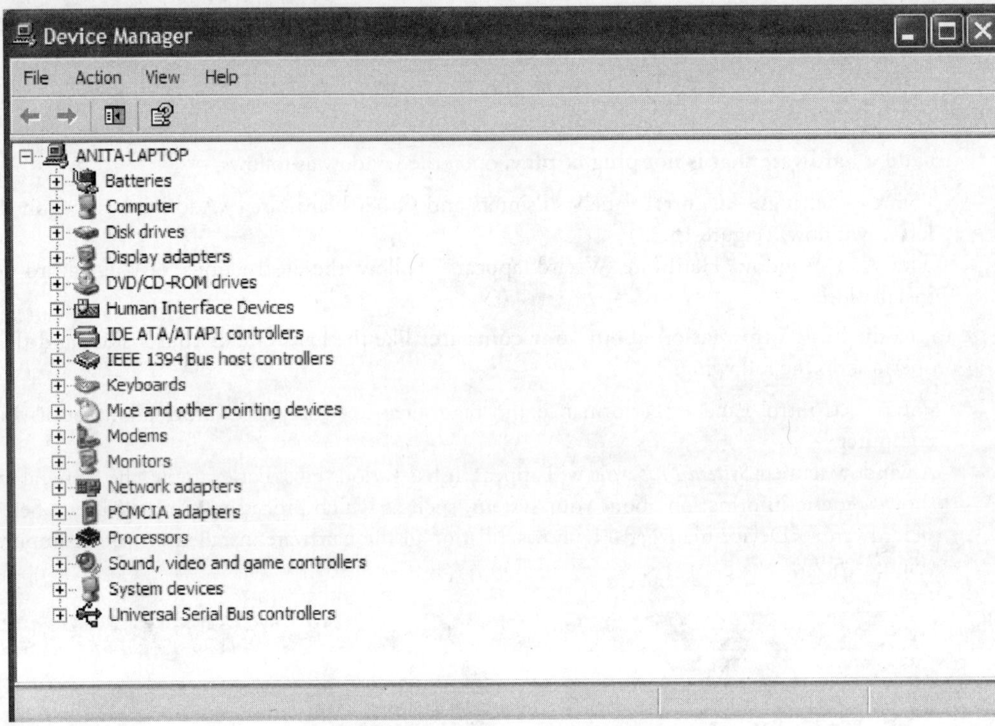

Figure 15.23 The device manager

15.12 SYSTEM TOOLS

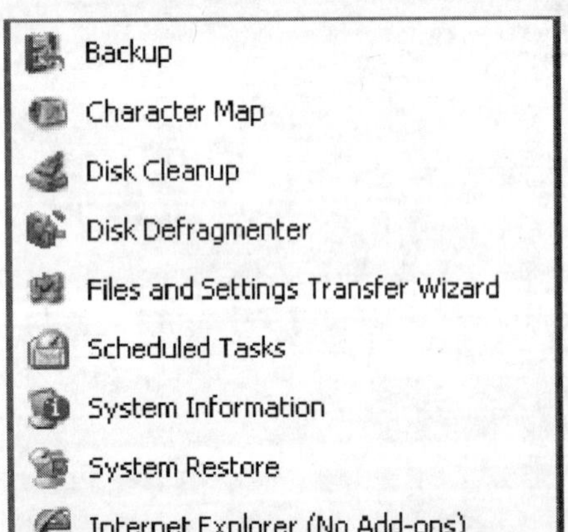

Figure 15.24 The system tools screen

Windows incorporates certain tools such as the Disk Defragmenter, the Disk Cleanup - the tool to free disk space, the Scheduled Tasks, etc. Almost all of these tools are designed to optimize the behavior of the computer. To select any of these tools, do the following:

<Start> <Programs> <Accessories> <System Tools> (Figure 15.24)

The window shows the different system tools like Backup, Character Map, Disk cleanup, Disk DeFragmenter, Files and Settings Transfer wizard, Scheduled Tasks, System Information, and System Restore.

- *Disk Defragmenter* reorganizes the information that is stored on the disk so that the free spaces between the information disappear, and the performance of the disk improves.

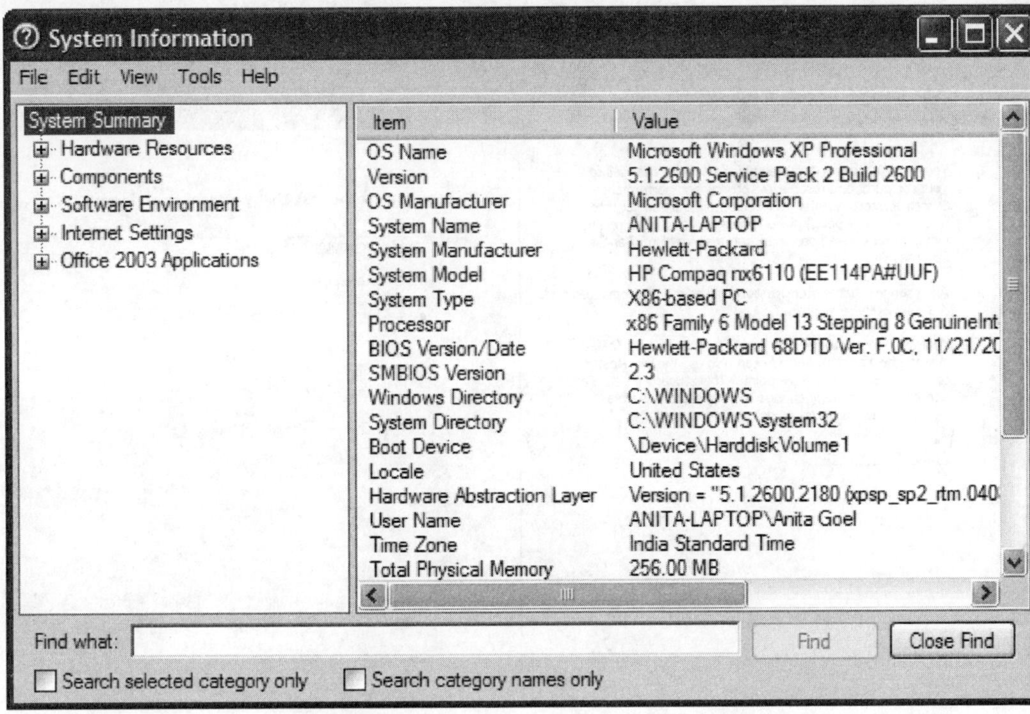

Figure 15.25 The system information screen

- *System Information* shows information regarding the system, such as the installed applications, the drivers, the processor, etc (Figure 15.25). It gives detailed information about the Hardware Resources, Components, Software environment, Internet Settings and MS-Office applications.
- *Disk Clean Up* allows you to empty the disk of information that you do not use, like temporary files, Internet files, or even files in the Recycle Bin.
- *Character Map* is useful to insert symbols that are not on the keyboard.
- *System Restore* restores the Windows registry, which is the place where all the information about changes to the configuration is kept (Figure 15.26). The system itself makes a copy of the registry every once in a while. With this tool, you can restore some of these copies or generate a new copy of the current registry when you are going to make important changes to the configuration of the system. If the new configuration does not work properly, you can go back and restore the system.
- *Scheduled Tasks* is used to schedule any program to run at specific times. For example, you can schedule the use of the Disk Cleanup for once a week, which will run automatically, once a week.

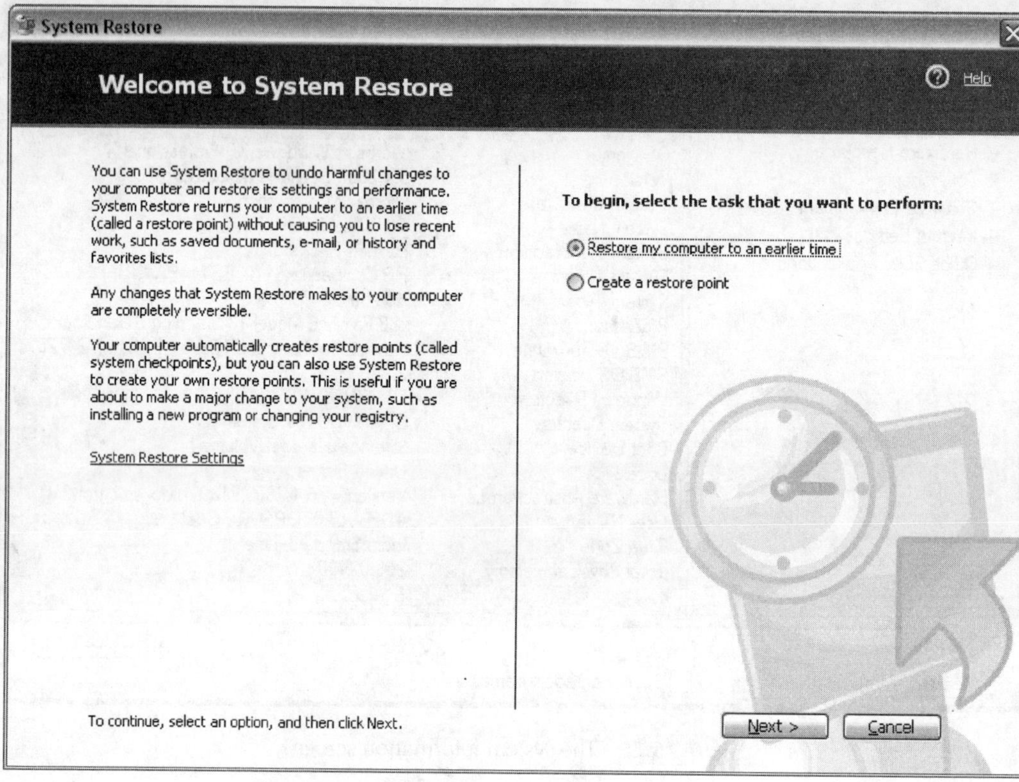

Figure 15.26 The system restore screen

15.13 THE SCANDISK

It is a tool used to search errors in the system's units and to repair those errors. When the computer is turned off in an abrupt manner it is possible that some files may get damaged. Normally when the computer is turned on, after being turned off abruptly (without using the option shut down from the Start menu), the Scandisk executes to check the system and repair any error that it may find. By using this tool we can fix the possible errors and therefore retrieve the information that it contains, although, it is not always possible to retrieve the information.

To use Scandisk, do as follows:

(1) Click on *My Computer* on desktop,

(2) Select the unit (drive) that you want to perform the scandisk on, for example unit (D:).

(3) Right click. <Properties> <Tools> <Check Now…> (Figure 15.27)

Once the scan has finalized a confirmation window will appear.

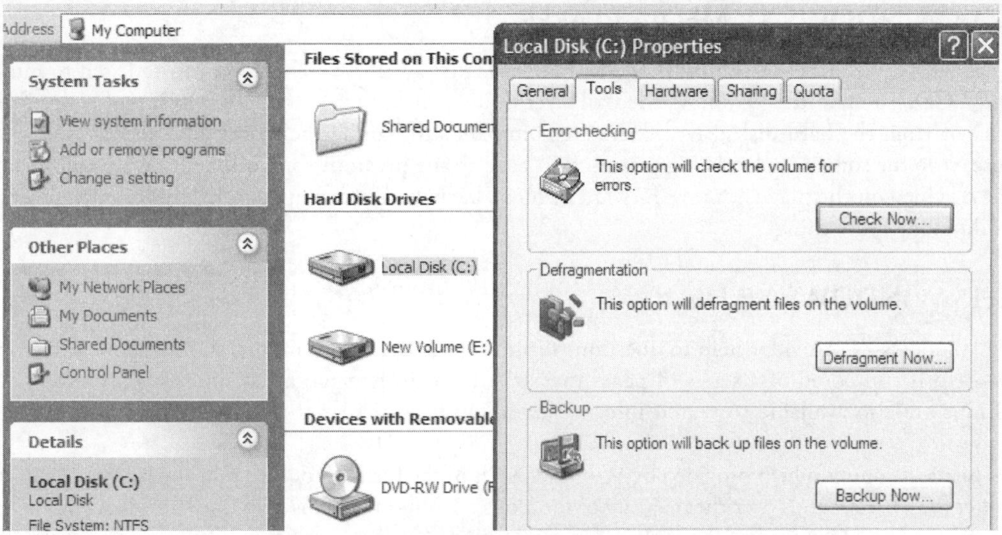

Figure 15.27 The scandisk

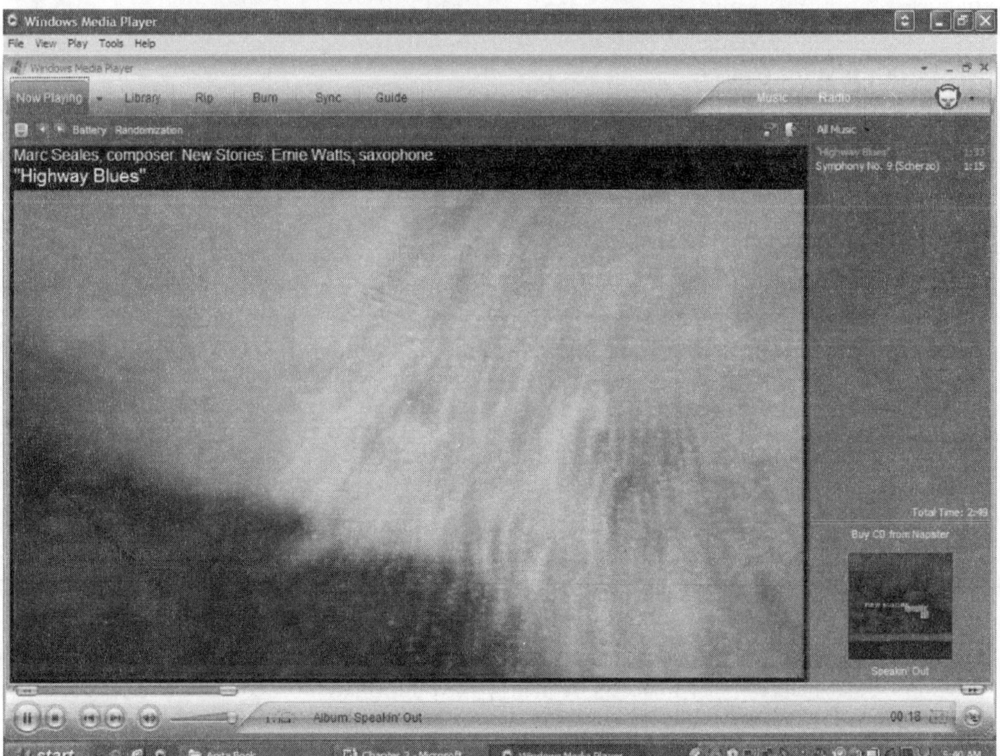

Figure 15.28 The windows media player

15.14 WINDOWS XP MEDIA PLAYER

Windows XP includes the Windows Media Player (Figure 15.28) which allows you to listen to music from a CD. To open the Windows Media Player double click on . It allows playing of songs from a CD or from the hard disk drive. There are commands to handle the player, like play as well as to pause, stop the song or video being played, skip back to the previous song on the list, skip to the next song or video on the playlist, move forward or move backward in a song, control the volume and you can do many more things.

15.15 WINDOWS XP HELP

The Windows XP provides help to questions regarding the use of a Windows XP component or tool. The help is composed of a series of pages that are similar in navigation, as the pages on a web site. Options are also available to search information about a particular theme from key words and key phrases.

The most common help provided by Windows XP is in the form of tooltips that appear by placing the pointer for a few seconds over the majority of the icons on Windows. This help is useful when you do not remember what an icon is for; the tooltip gives you a hint.

The main way to obtain help is facilitated by the help center and technical support. To open the Help and Support Center and use the help services click on Help and technical support from the <Start> <Settings> <Control Panel> menu.

15.16 WINDOWS VISTA

Windows Vista contains many changes and new features over its predecessor (Windows XP).

Microsoft's Windows Vista operating system is designed to give better results in less time. Its improved graphics look helps in multitasking, and its increased security system makes your data more secure but it needs very high systems specifications to run. The minimum specification of the computer on which Windows Vista can be installed is Pentium 4 or higher, 512 MB RAM, 32 MB video card and 40 GB hard disk. But, Windows Vista installed on the computer having the above specification makes the computer very slow. To have a reasonable speed of working with Windows Vista installed, you should have at least 2.0 GHz Pentium 4 or higher, 1 GB of RAM, 60 GB hard disk and 64 MB video RAM. The high system requirements are one of the key reasons for Windows Vista criticism.

Here, we highlight some of the key features of Windows Vista:

- **Updated GUI and Visual Style Dubbed Windows**—Aero is Microsoft's name for the GUI theme (Luna—Windows XP's interface). Aero allows for transparent windows edges, window fades and 3D task switcher. If your video card supports the Aero Glass interface, you get translucent title bars and animations. Aero interface enables you to quickly switch between windows and tasks.
- **Sidebar** (Figure 15.29) is the collection of items on the right side of the screen. It is a customizable window that makes it easy to access frequently used information. It contains a set of devices you can choose from. Some choices are:
  - Calculator, analog clock, notepad, recycle bin, games, puzzles, and currency converter.
  - CPU and memory meters to view the amount of system resources in use.

- Feed viewer for tracking items, news, sports etc. via RSS, and Feed watcher for monitoring the selected RSS feeds.
- Slide show that displays a continuous slide show of the photos in the Pictures folder.

⊙ The search facility in Windows Vista has been improved. You can use **Windows Instant Search** to search for anything on your computer.

Figure 15.29 The Windows vista sidebar

⊙ Multimedia tools like **Windows DVD Maker** have been included. It redesigns networking, audio, print, and displays sub-systems. It makes it easy to burn your movies to disc, and you can create chapters and menus that let you jump to specific scenes. You also have more control over the quality and size of your video files.

⊙ Windows Vista has improved the **Security of the User's Data**.

- New security systems like drive encryption, file system encryption and scheduled backups improve security of your data.
- The new IE7 browser keeps malicious software or Web sites from changing configuration settings.
- Windows Service Hardening keeps OS services from making changes to the registry, file system, etc., without your permission.
- Windows Firewall settings can be controlled both for the outbound traffic as well as inbound traffic.
- Network Access Protection agent prevents Vista clients from connecting to your network if they don't have the proper security updates.

⊙ **Embedded Start Menu** (Figure 15.30) includes Windows Mail (instead of Outlook Express), Windows Contacts (new address book), and Windows Calendar, in addition to the features of the Start menu of Windows XP.

⊙ **The Taskbar Preview** provides a preview of the open application icon. If there are multiple instances of that application, you will see all preview pages.

⊙ **Windows Contacts** replaces the Windows Address Book in XP. In addition to the features supported by Windows Address book, you can add photos to your contacts and import Windows Address Book files from another computer, and do much more.

⊙ Vista includes the **Windows Calendar** which provides good, basic appointment and event scheduling that you can view in a daily, weekly, or monthly layout. It includes a Task list and allows you to set reminders and recurring appointments. You can share your calendar with others on the local computer or the Internet. You can export your calendar to a website and allow others to subscribe to it, and you can subscribe to the calendars of others and view them side by side. You can also easily invite participants to meetings.

Figure 15.30 The Windows Vista start menu

- Vista includes the **Windows Photo Gallery** which replaces the Windows Picture and Fax Viewer in XP. The photo gallery helps you organize and view your digital photos and videos easily. You can do simple photo editing and print them.
- Vista includes several **New Games**, such as Ink ball and Chess Titans.

- **File Navigation** is easy in Windows Vista. For example, as you vertically scroll the folder tree, the window automatically scrolls horizontally to keep them in view. You can go directly to any folder in the hierarchy above the one you're in simply by clicking its name there.

Microsoft's Windows Vista operating system has a new look and incorporates lots of added functionality over its predecessor. Increased security system that makes your data more secure is one of its key features. However, running Windows Vista on a machine requires very high systems specifications.

15.17 WINDOWS 7

Windows 7 makes the most of powerful 64-bit PCs, the new desktop standard. It includes several feature advancements in touch, speech, handwriting recognition, support for virtual hard disk, and support for additional file formats, improved performance on multicore processors, improved boot performance, and kernel improvements. It includes performance improvements like sleep and resume quickly, and spot USB devices faster. It retains Windows Aero user interface and visual style introduced with Windows Vista.

Figure 15.31 Desktop in Windows 7

Here, we highlight some of the key features of Windows 7—

- Desktop (Figure 15.31) allows you to have new themes, slide shows, or gadgets on the desktop.
    - A desktop *Slideshow* changes the desktop background in a designated amount of time with a smooth fading transition.
    - *Themes* include desktop slideshow settings. A new control panel interface, accessible through *Personalize* context menu item on the desktop provides the ability to customize and switch between themes.
    - The sidebar of Windows Vista has been removed, but *Gadgets* can be placed on desktop. The Windows Media Center has been added to Windows 7, which adds playback of media in MP4, MOV, and many more multimedia containers with native codecs for H.264, MPEG4-SP etc.

⊙ Windows Explorer

- Libraries—Windows Explorer (Figure 15.32) in Windows 7 supports Libraries, virtual folders that aggregates content from various locations—including shared folders on networked systems if the shared folder has been indexed by the host system—and present them in a unified view. By default, a new user account in Windows 7 contains four libraries, for different file types: Documents, Music, Pictures, and Videos.
- Federated search—Windows Explorer also supports federating search to external data sources, such as custom databases or web services that are exposed over the web.

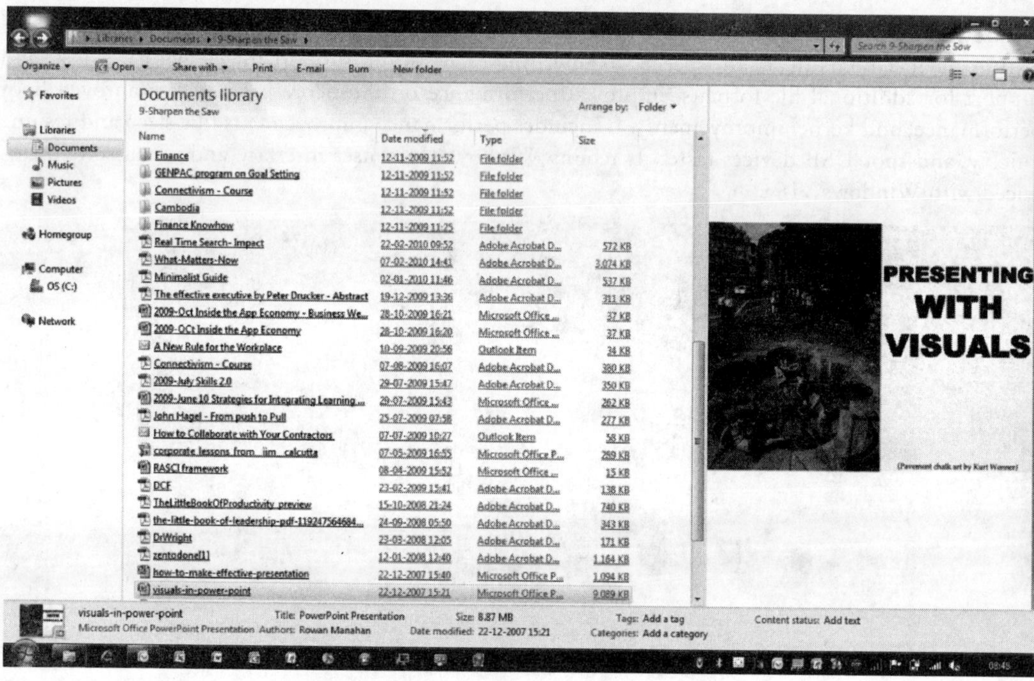

Figure 15.32 Windows explorer in Windows 7

⊙ Start menu—Windows 7's Start Menu has a fade-in highlight effect when the user moves the mouse over it.

- A *Devices and Printers* option has been added that displays a new device manager.
- *Taskbar Jump Lists* are presented in the Start Menu via a guillemet; when the user moves the mouse over the guillemet, or presses the right-arrow key, the right-hand side of the Start menu is widened and replaced with the application's Jump List. *Jump Lists* provide speedy access to your favorite pictures, songs, websites, and documents.

⊙ Windows 7 Taskbar provides better thumbnail previews, easier-to-see icons, and more ways to customize.

- It is 10 pixels taller than in Windows Vista to accommodate touch screen input and a new larger default icon size. The glass taskbar is more transparent.

- It is more application-oriented than window-oriented, and therefore doesn't show window titles. Applications can be *pinned* to the taskbar allowing the user instant access to the applications they commonly use.
- It shows a preview of the window. In a *thumbnail preview*, the name of the window is also shown. *Aero Peek* button when clicked or hovered over with the mouse, displays the desktop and gadgets by turning all windows transparent. *Aero Shake* allows users to clear up any clutter on their screen by shaking (dragging back and forth) a window of their choice with the mouse. *Snap* is a quick and new way to resize and compare windows on the desktop.

- Devices—There are two major new user interface components for device management in Windows 7, "Devices and Printers" and "Device Stage". Both of these are integrated with Windows Explorer, and together provide a simplified view of what devices are connected to the computer, and what capabilities they support. When a device such as a portable music player is connected to the system, the device appears as an icon on the task bar, as well as in Windows Explorer.
- The improvements and additions made to Windows 7 **Core Operating System** components include AVCHD camera support and Universal Video Class 1.1, fewer hardware locks and greater parallelism.
- The Enterprise, Ultimate, and Professional editions of Windows 7 incorporate support for the **Virtual Hard Disk** (VHD) file format. VHD files can be mounted as drives, created, and booted from.
- The Windows Security Center has been renamed to **Windows Action Center** which encompasses both security and maintenance of the computer.
- Windows 7 includes new **Windows Biometric Framework** which consists of a set of components that standardizes the use of fingerprint biometric devices. A new Biometric Device Control Panel is included which provides an interface for deleting stored biometrics information, troubleshooting, and enabling or disabling the types of logins that are allowed using biometrics.
- Windows 7 adds support for **Multiple Firewall** profiles. When your computer is connected to two or more networks at the same time Windows 7 applies a separate firewall profile to each network connection.

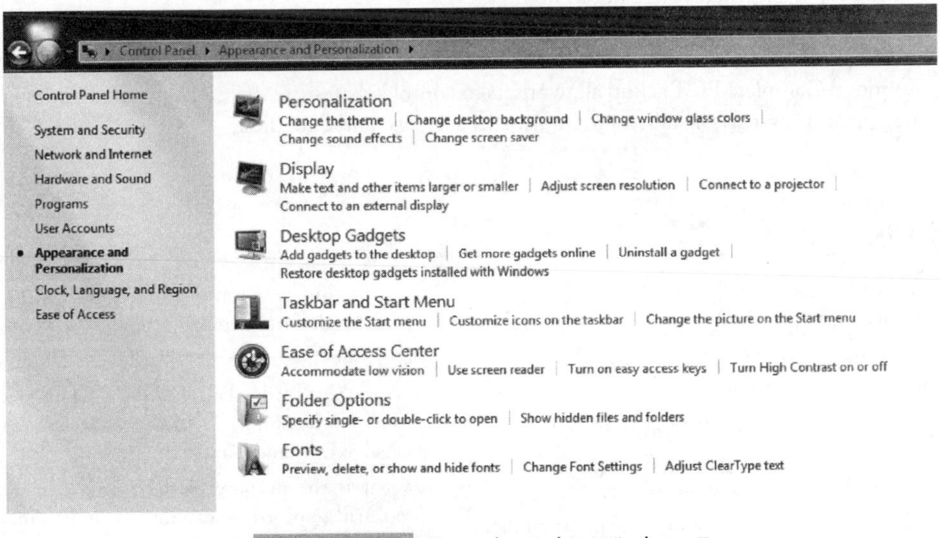

Figure 15.33 Control panel in Windows 7

- WordPad in Windows 7
  - Windows 7's start-up screen consists of an animation featuring four colored light balls (red, yellow, green, and blue).
  - Calculator has been rewritten, with multiline capabilities including Programmer and Statistics modes along with unit conversion and date calculation.
  - Many new items have been added to Control Panel (Figure 15.33) including: ClearType Text Tuner, Desktop Gadgets, Recovery, Troubleshooting, Location and Other Sensors, Credential Manager, Biometric Devices, System Icons, Action Center, and Display.
  - Paint and WordPad both have the new ribbon user interface.
  - Resource Monitor includes numerous new features, including an improved RAM usage display, display of TCP/IP ports being listened to, filtering processes using networking, filtering processes with disk activity etc.
  - For developers, Windows 7 includes a new networking API with support for building SOAP based web services in native code.
  - Windows 7 includes power-saving features, such as adaptive display brightness, which dims a laptop's display when the laptop has not been used for a while.
  - The windows borders and taskbar remain translucent when a window is maximized with Windows Aero applied.
- HomeGroup allows easy sharing of files and printers on a home network.
- Windows Live Essentials has programs like Mail, Movie Maker, Photo Gallery, and more.
- Windows Search allows you to search for virtually anything on your PC, instantly. It works like search folders i.e. allow pivoting views, and allow you to show content from various locations in one spot.
- Windows 7 supports remote media streaming which allows you to enjoy music and video on your home PC—even when you're not *at* home.
- It allows you to pair Windows 7 with a touchscreen, replacing a keyboard or mouse.
- Windows Complete PC Backup allows users to completely restore their PC environment including the operating system, installed programs, user settings, and data files.

QUESTIONS

1. What is the benefit of Windows XP over its predecessors?
2. List any five new features of Windows XP.
3. What is Windows Desktop?
4. Discuss about the different parts of Windows desktop screen.
5. Name the different parts of the Task Bar.
6. In which area does the date and time appear on the Windows screen.
7. List the different ways in which you can organize icons on desktop (Arrange icons by).
8. Describe the structure of Window in Windows XP.
9. Write steps to do the following —(1) Organizing icons on Desktop, (2) Create Shortcuts, and (3) Change Date and Time.
10. What is the purpose of the title bar, menu bar, tool bar, scroll bar and status bar in a Window of Windows XP.

11. What is the purpose of Windows XP Explorer?
12. List the different views in which you can see the folder information.
13. Explain in one or two lines, how the folder information is viewed in (1) Filmstrip, (2) Thumbnails, (3) Tiles, (4) Icons, (5) List, and (6) Details.
14. List the different ways of selecting a file or a folder.
15. Write steps to do the following—(1) Create a Folder, (2) Delete a File, (3) Copy a File, (4) Move a File, and (5) Change the name of a File.
16. What information is provided by the <Properties> of the folder.
17. Write steps to do the following—(1) Show Hidden Files and Folders, (2) Know the Types of Files, and (3) Organize Folders.
18. What is the purpose of Recycle Bin?
19. List the steps to restore a file from Recycle Bin.
20. List the steps to configure Desktop, Screen saver, and Screen appearance.
21. What is the purpose of Windows Register?
22. List the steps to add a non-plug & play hardware.
23. Name any three System tools.

Exercises

Instructions: For all the questions take the screen snapshots before you perform the exercise, and, after you perform the exercise.

To take a snapshot of the screen, do the following:

Step 1. <shift key> <function key (fn)> <print screen key (prt sc)>

Step 2. Open a new word document and <Paste> on it.

1. Create shortcuts for any two programs.
2. Change the date and time of your computer.
3. View the folder in Thumbnail format.
4. Create a new folder 'F'. Copy folder 'F' to a new directory. Move the folder from this new directory to another directory, and name it 'H'. Delete the original folder 'F'.
5. Search the location where a folder "X" is in your computer.
6. Empty the Recycle Bin.
7. Restore the deleted files in Recycle Bin.
8. Configure your screen. (Change its Appearance, Theme, Screen saver etc.)
9. Change the icon of your mouse, when it comes on a tooltip.
10. Use the Disk Defragmenter.
11. Use Disk Clean up.
12. Use the Character Map.
13. Find the system information.
14. Create a new System Restore point.
15. Schedule the disk cleanup task to run now, tomorrow, and day after at the same time.
16. While doing any of the above, enjoy the music. Play a song from the playlist using Windows Media Player.

MS-WORD 2007 16

Contents

Why this chapter

One of the applications for which the computer is quite often used is to create documents, like, an article, letter, brochure, web page, newsletter, project report and thesis. The documents may include images, graphics, sound elements and animation, in addition to the text. You use word processing software for creating the different kind of documents. MS-Word is commonly used word processing software. The purpose of this chapter is to introduce you to MS-Word.

16.1 INTRODUCTION

Word processing software is used for the creation of text-based documents. The word processing software provides tools for composing, editing, formatting, and printing of documents. In addition to text, documents can also contain images, pictures, graphics elements, sound clips and animations. The document can be a poster, report, letter, brochure, web page, newsletter, or, long document consisting of an index and links to various chapters.

There are many software packages available, to do the job of word processing. Some of the word processing software that works in DOS environment are WordStar, Easy Word, and Word Perfect. Examples of some more word processing software are—AppleWorks Word Processing for Windows and Mac, Applix Word for Linux, Microsoft Write for Mac, Notepad for Windows, and Star Office Writer. Some examples of online word processors are Google Docs, PDSText (a free online Unicode text editor for Indian Languages), Sun OpenOffice, and ZohoWriter.

MS-Word is a word processing software used in the Windows environment. It is one of the most popular word-processing software these days. MS-Word is a part of a bigger software package called MS-Office. In addition to MS-Word, MS-Office includes other software like MS-Excel (for spreadsheet), MS-PowerPoint (for presentations), and MS-Access (for database management).

MS-Word is a Graphical User Interface (GUI) based software, which makes it easy to use and understand. It has a wide range of tools and commands that are used for formatting the documents. Some of the important features of MS-Word are as follows:

- A document can be created and later edited, whenever required. Editing includes addition of text, modifying the existing text, or deleting a part of text. Editing can be done on a word, sentence, paragraph, page, or the complete document.
- The complete document or a part of the document can be reformatted.
- Some of the options available for the formatting of a document are—changing the font size, font color and font style, addition of page numbers, page header and footer, and headings.
- Various tools like spell check for checking spellings, mail merge for generating multiple copies of letters with different addresses, macros, and track changes for making corrections are available.
- MS-Word allows tables to be created and included in the text.

Graphical pictures can be included in a document using pictures from the Clip Art and the pictures imported from other files.

This chapter discusses the usage of MS-Word software in detail. There are many versions of the MS-Word software. Here, we will discuss MS-Word 2007.

In this chapter, the following terminologies are used, while working with the mouse:

- **Pointer**—a mouse pointer
- **Click**—press left button of mouse once
- **Double-Click**—press left button of mouse twice
- **Select**—move the pointer of mouse and keep the left button of the mouse pressed over the area that you want to select. The selected area will appear in a dark background.
- **Quick Menu**—Right click (press right button of mouse once) to get a quick menu

We enclose the command in braces <Command> to represent the command to be clicked.

16.2 STARTING MS-WORD

As already stated, MS-Word software is installed on the Windows operating system. MS-Word is menu-driven, GUI-based software. While working with MS-Word, using a mouse makes working on the MS-Word simpler although you can work to some extent using the keyboard also.

To start using the MS-Word software, *any one* of the following steps needs to be performed—

- If a shortcut key to MS-Word is available as an icon (a small picture that represents an object or program) on the Desktop, as shown in Figure 16.1, then **double-click** the icon, OR,
- **<Start> <Programs> <Microsoft Office> <Microsoft Office Word 2007>**. (Figure 16.2)

Figure 6.1 MS-Word 2007 icon

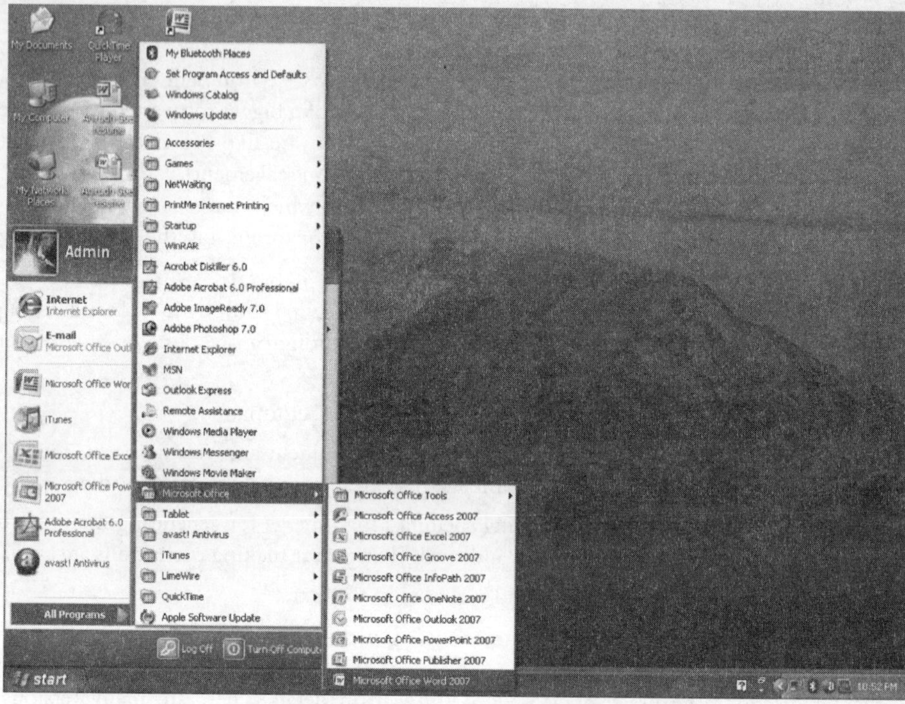

Figure 16.2 Start MS-Word 2007

16.3 MS-WORD SCREEN AND ITS COMPONENTS

The user interface of MS-Word 2007 is quite different from the previous versions of MS-Word. It has an improved navigation system which is easier to use. The main screen, as shown in Figure 16.3, consists of different components like the Ribbon, Ruler bar, Status bar, Scroll bar, and Work Area. The orientation of the Word 2007 layout and its general features are described as follows:

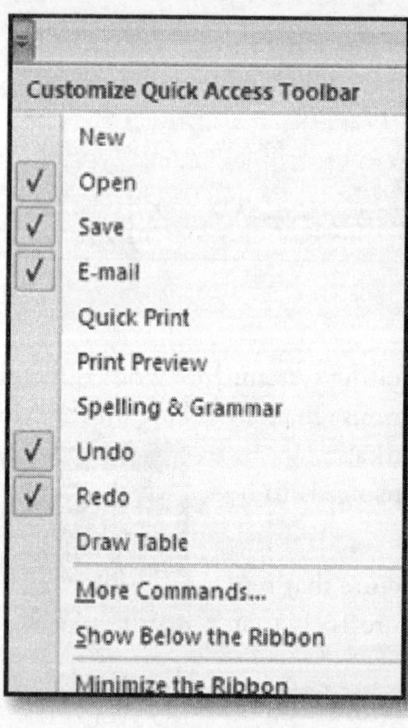

- The **Office Logo Button**  at the top left corner contains many task buttons for the document such as, *New, Open, Save, Save As, Print,* and *Close*. This button also has a list of the recent documents. Some of these commands include an expandable menu to provide additional options. (The Office Button replaces the File menu in earlier versions of Word).
- The **Quick Access Toolbar**  is to the right of the Office Logo button. It contains shortcuts for the commonly used tools, like, Save , Undo  (reverses the last change), and Repeat  (repeats the last action). The buttons that you wish to be displayed can be selected from the  *Customize Quick Access Toolbar*.

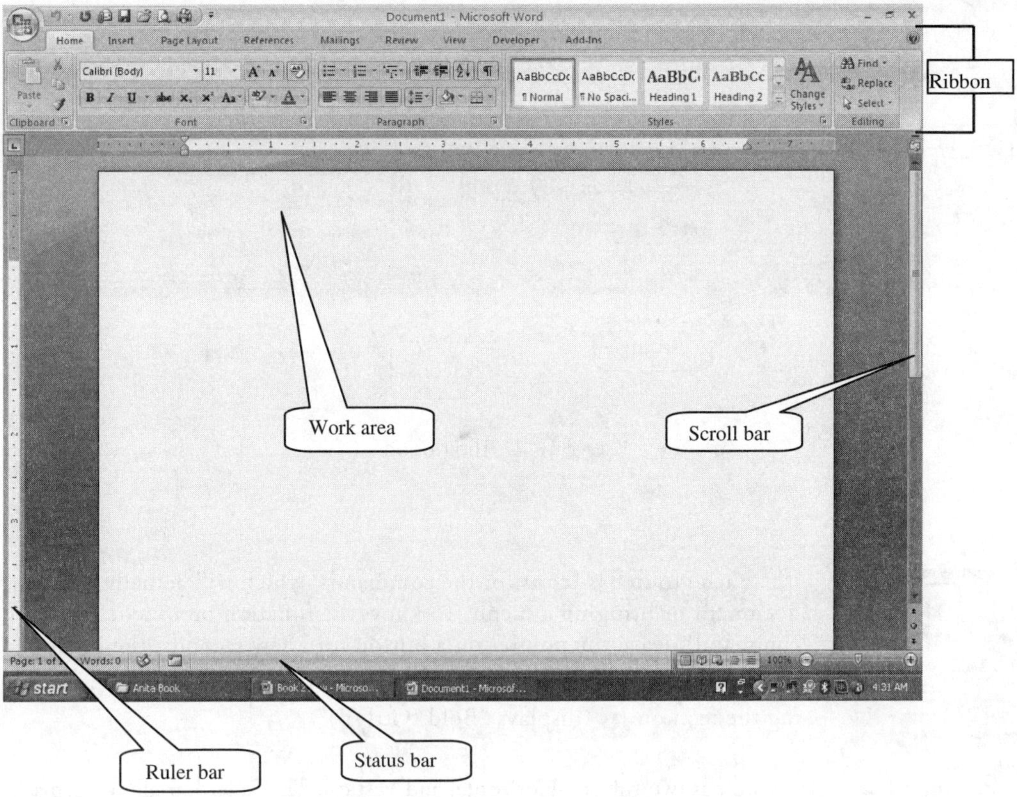

Figure 16.3 MS-Word 2007 screen

- **The Ribbon** is a set of tools and commands across the top of the screen (Figure 16.4). It consists of a panel of commands which are organized into a set of tabs (also known as the Tab Bar). Within Tabs, Groups are available, which are designated by the names located on the bottom of the Ribbon. Each group has icons for the associated command. The Ribbon (Tabs, Groups, and Icons) replaces traditional toolbars and menus of earlier versions of the MS-Word.
- The **Tabs** (Home, Insert, Page Layout, etc.) on the Ribbon contain the buttons needed to edit characters, text, and layout, as well as the additional tools that you may need.

- Each Tab consists of different **Groups**, like the Home tab has five groups namely, Clipboard, Font, Paragraph, Styles and Editing.

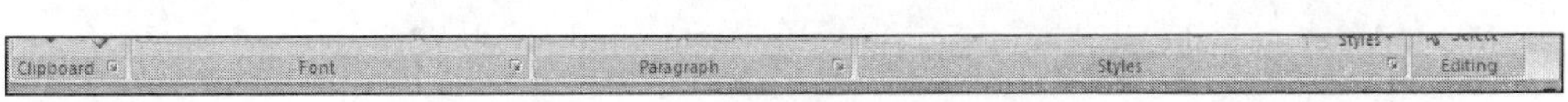

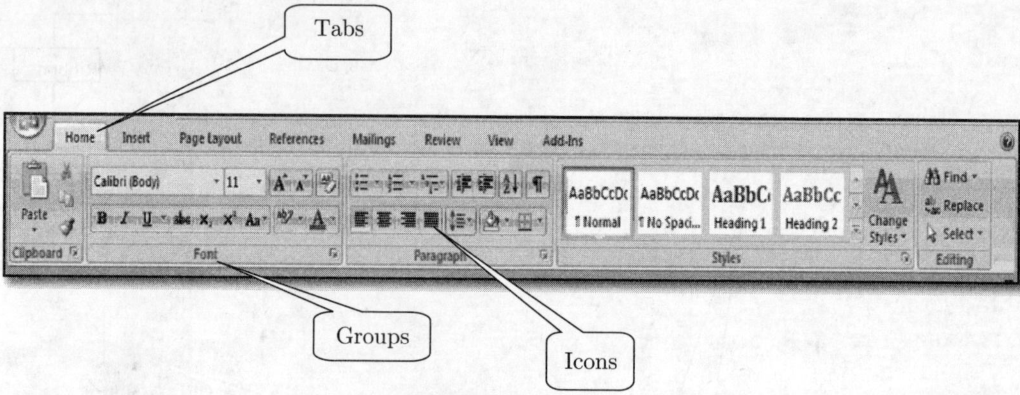

Figure 16.4 The ribbon

- Each group has **Icons** for the commands, which will actually format the document or bring up a menu. To know the function of an icon button (or command), leave the pointer on a button for a few seconds, the function of that button will appear in a small box below the pointer. For example, leaving the icon on **B** displays "Bold (Ctrl+B)".

- **Ruler Bar**—MS-Word has two rulers—Horizontal and Vertical. The Ruler Bar allows formatting of horizontal and vertical alignment of text in a document, by adjusting the tabs, indents and margins.

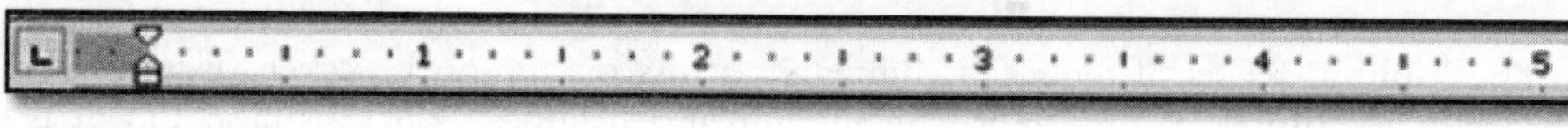

- **Status Bar**—It displays information about the currently active document. The information includes the current page number, total number of pages and the number of words in the document, zoom slider  etc. Right-click on the status bar will show you the Customize Status Bar (Figure 16.5) pop-up menu. You can select the options you want to view on the status bar.

- **Scroll Bar**—There are two scroll bars—horizontal and vertical. They help to scroll the content or the body of document. Scrolling is done by moving the elevator button along the scroll bar, or by clicking on the buttons with the arrow marked on them to move up and down, and left and right of a page.

- **Work Area**—It is the working area in the document window where the text of the document is typed.

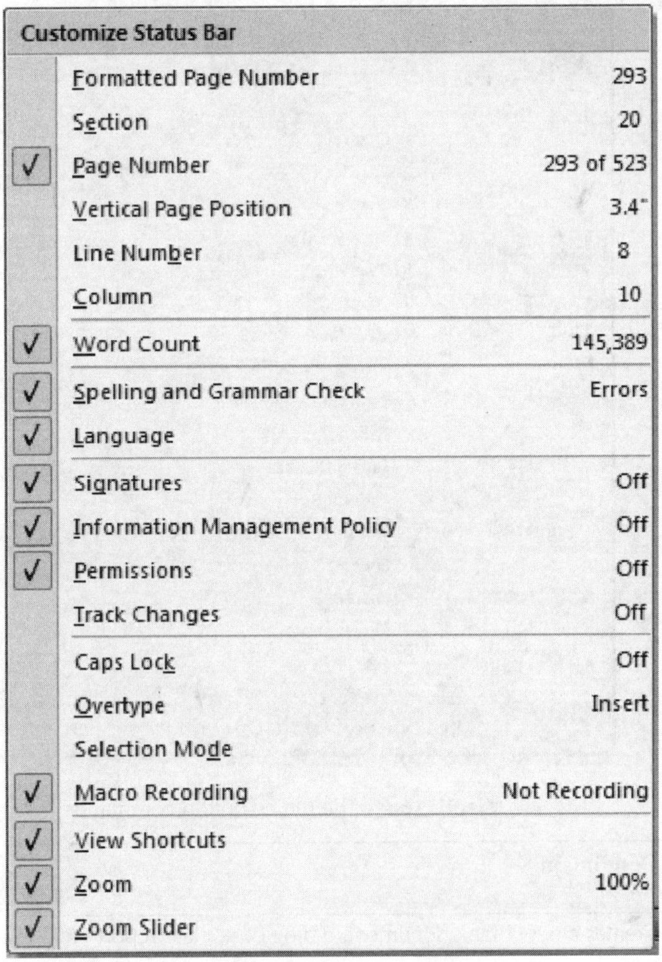

Figure 16.5 Customize status bar

16.4 THE OFFICE BUTTON

The Office Button is used to perform file management operations on the file (i.e. the document). It contains commands that allow the user to create a new document, open an existing document, save a document, print a document etc. The Office button contains nine commands, namely, New, Open, Save, Save As, Print, Prepare, Send, Publish, and Close. The Office button commands are shown in Figure 16.6.

Table 16.1 briefly describes the different commands available in the Office Button.

Some of the common operations that are performed using the commands of the Office Button are described as follows:

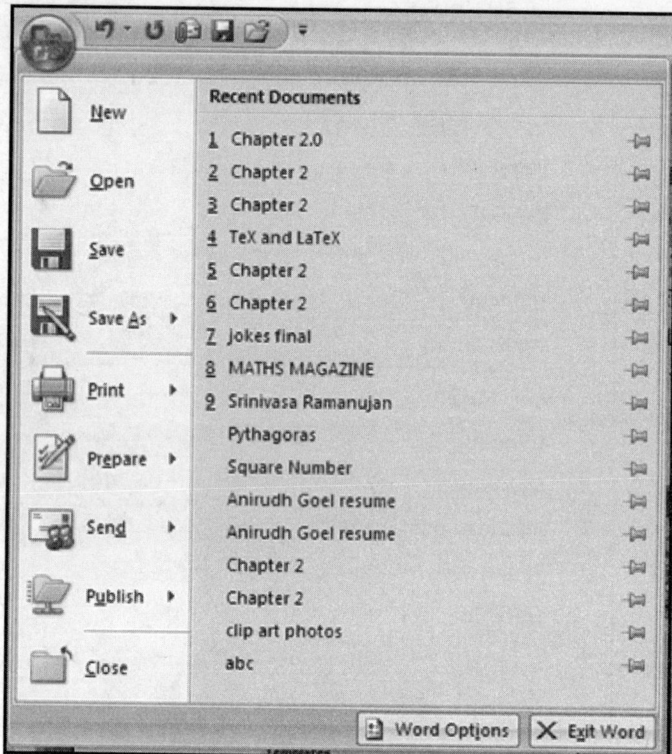

Figure 16.6 The Office button commands

Office Button Commands	Description
New	Creates a new blank document, a blog post, class report etc.
Open	Opens an already existing document
Save	Save a document for which a file name and location has already been specified
Save As	Use when you save a document for the first time or, to a different location, or at the same location with different name or with a new type of document. Here, you specify the filename for the document, the location where the document is to be stored, and the save type of the document. You can save the document as a Word document, Word 97-2003 document, Word Template etc.
Print	Print, Quick Print, or Print Preview the document. You can set properties like print quality, paper type, number of copies, color or grayscale, etc. Preview to see how the printed document will look after printing.
Prepare	Prepare the document for distribution. View document properties, encrypt document, grant permissions etc.
Send	Send a copy of the document to e-mail or to Internet Fax
Publish	Publish the document as a blog, create a new site for the document etc.
Close	Close an open document

Table 16.1 *Home tab commands description*

- **Saving a Document for the First Time:** < > **<Save As>**. You can save the document as a Word document, Word 97-2003 document, Word Template etc. (Figure 16.7). On selecting one of the Save As options, Word will display a dialog box. In the field next to File name, type a name with which you want to save the document. Navigate in the top portion of the dialog box to the folder where you want to save the document (choose the right directory where you want to save the file. You can use to go up in the directory, Use to create a new folder). You can also specify the save type of the document (Figure 16.8). Once you have saved your document for the first time, you can save further revisions by selecting the < > **<Save>**, or by clicking on the Save button in the Quick Access Toolbar.

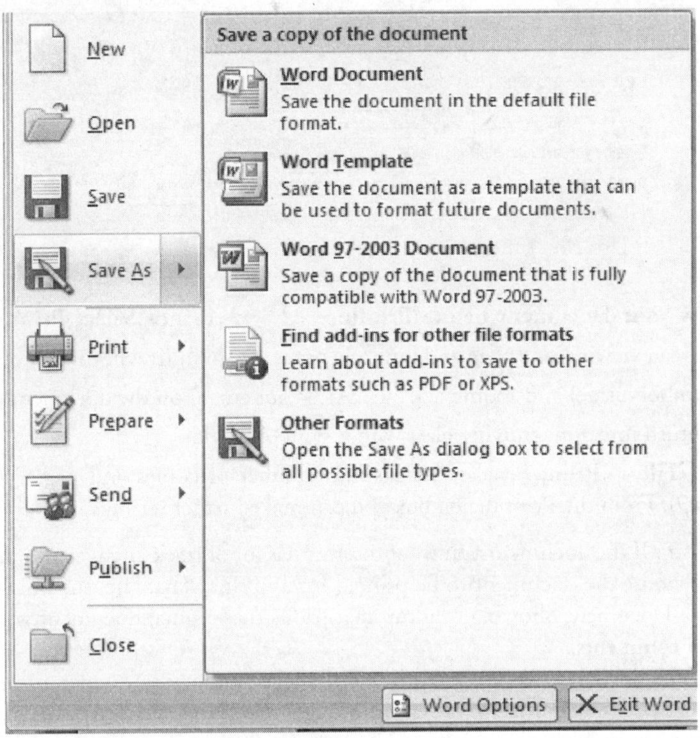

Figure 16.7 Save as option

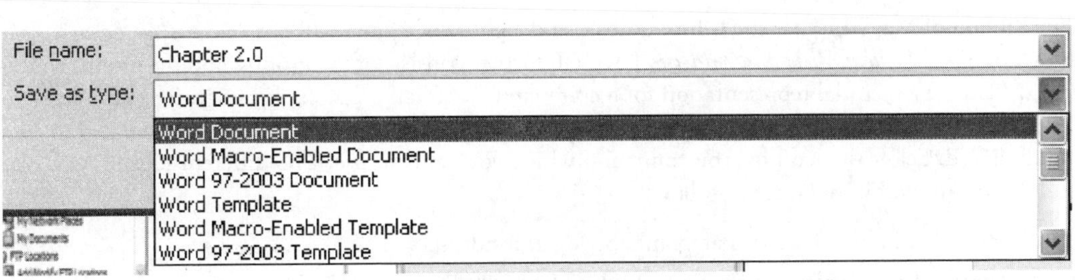

Figure 16.8 File save types

- **Saving a Document Under a Different Name:** Open the document by selecting the < > **<Open>**. Next, < > **<Save As>** A dialog box will appear. Navigate to the folder where you want to save the document and type in a new name for the document. Select the Save button. You now have two copies of the document, one with the original name, another with a new name.
- **Crash Protection:** < > **<Save As> <Tools><Save Options>.** Select the boxes for *Save Auto Recover* Information every <enter the minutes>. Reset the Minutes from 10 to 1. MS-Word would be able to recover a file one minute old.

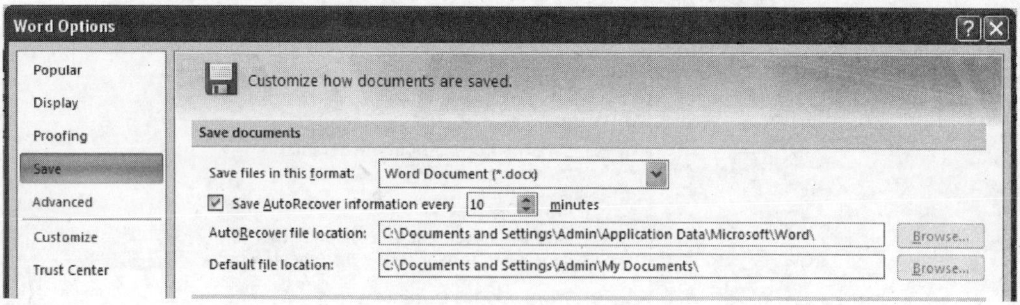

- **To Preview your Document before Printing:** < >**<Print> Select Print Preview**. You can switch between viewing one page and multiple pages, zoom in (it will turn into a magnifying glass with a + symbol inside) and zoom back out, place your cursor on the document and this time your cursor will turn into a magnifying glass with a-symbol inside.
- **To Print: <File> <Print>**. Make settings like number of copies and pages you want to print. (Figure 16.9). From the Print dialog box you can make further settings like:
  - *Print What* : If the document you want to print has lot of track changes and inserted comments, you can choose the document to be printed from "Print What" i.e. the final draft of the document, the Document Showing Markup that prints the original document with all of the visible edits and comments.
  - *Zoom*: If the document is formatted in a different size than your paper, use Zoom of the Print dialog box. Use the *Scale to Paper Size* drop-down menu to select the paper size. Zoom feature is also used to print multiple pages on a single sheet. Use the *Pages per Sheet* drop-down menu to print two, four, six, eight, or even sixteen pages onto one sheet of paper.

16.5 THE RIBBON

The Ribbon of MS-Word has the Office button, and eight tabs, namely, *Home, Insert, Page Layout, References, Mailings, Review, View and Add-Ins*. Each tab further consists of the groups, and the groups contain icons. *Icons* are a pictorial representation for a command. Each tab is self-explanatory; for example, if you want to insert any item into the document, click on the *Insert* tab. The groups and icons related to *Insert* are displayed. Select the icon for the command which you want to use. The different tabs in MS-Word and the groups within them are as follows:

- **Home**: Clipboard, Font, Paragraph, Styles, and Editing
- **Insert**: Pages, Tables, Illustrations, Links, Header & Footer, and Text

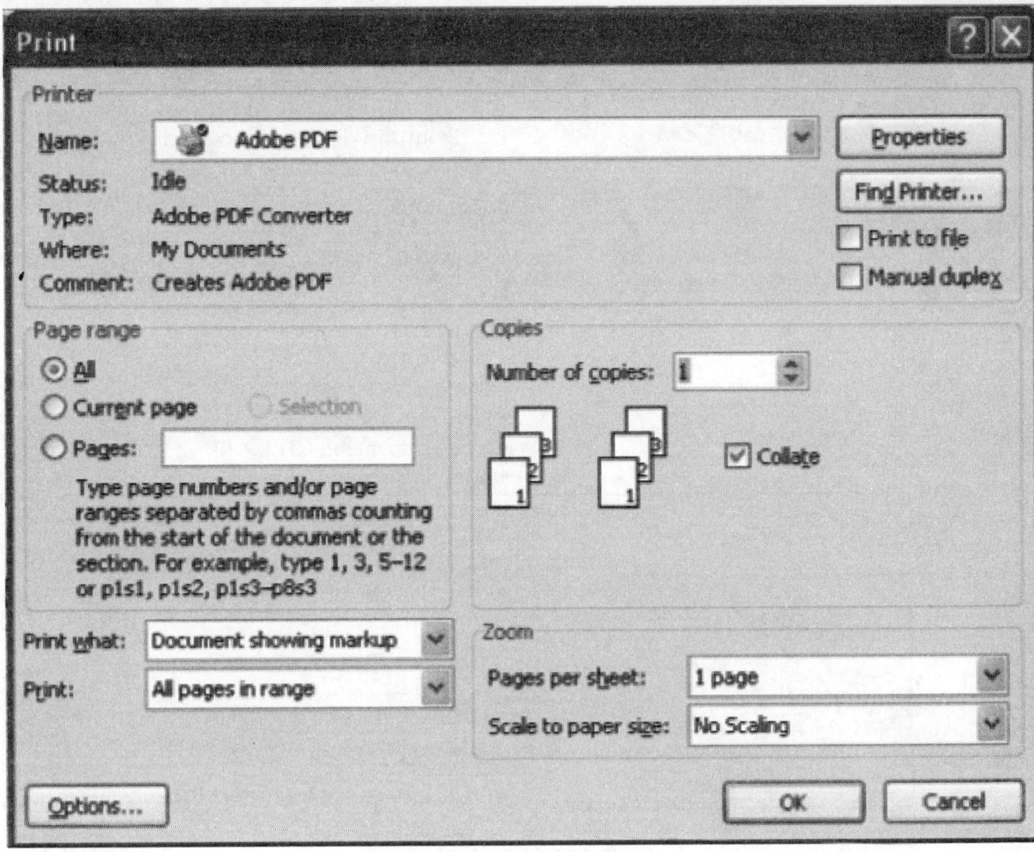

Figure 16.9 Print dialog box

- **Page Layout**: Themes, Page Setup, Page Background, Paragraph, and Arrange
- **References**: Table of Contents, Footnotes, Citations & Bibliography, Captions, Index, and Table of Authorities
- **Mailings**: Create, Start Mail Merge, Write & Insert Fields, Preview Results, and Finish
- **Review**: Proofing, Comments, Tracking, Changes, Compare, and Protect
- **View**: Document Views, Show/Hide, Zoom, Window, and Macros

The **Add-Ins Tab** can contain supplemental functionality that adds custom commands and specialized features to MS-Office products like MS-Word, MS-Excel, MS-PowerPoint. Automation add-ins, application add-ins, smart tags, and COM add-ins are some examples of add-ins. MindManager Pro 6, VisionArchive 2.0, and KwikTag 3.4 are some of the Microsoft approved add-ins for the Microsoft Office.

The commands in the Ribbon have various symbols associated with them, as shown in Figure 16.10. These symbols are interpreted as follows:

- **Simple Command**—The command starts executing when it is clicked.
- **Command Followed by Arrow**—Clicking on the arrow displays more options for the command.

Selecting a command	
Ways to select a command	**Using a command**
Click on a Tab + *Click on a Icon*	Click on any of the Tabs like Home, Insert etc. From the displayed icons, click on the icon you want to use.
Shortcut key *Ctrl + letter*	Some commands have shortcuts where you can press the **Ctrl** key and a **certain letter**. Some commonly used shortcuts are –
	• Paste: CTRL + V • Copy: CTRL + C • Undo: CTRL + Z • New document: CTRL + N • Open document: CTRL + O • print document: CTRL + P

Figure 16.10 Command symbols

- **Faded Command**—A faded command means that it is not available currently.
- **Group Dialog Box**—Clicking on this symbol displays the dialog box for the group.

The following sub-sections describe the different tabs in detail:

Working with MS-2007

- **Live Preview** applies temporary formatting on the selected text or object when the mouse moves over any of the formatting buttons. This allows you to preview how the text will appear with this formatting. The temporary formatting is removed if the mouse pointer is moved away from the button.
- **Mini Toolbar** pops up whenever text is selected. It provides easy access to the most commonly used formatting commands in Word. The Mini Toolbar also appears when you right-click on a selection of text.
- **File Format** for the documents created in Word 2007 is ***.docx*** (compared to *.doc* in previous versions). This format is based on XML. It uses the ZIP file container, which compresses the document up to 75% smaller than previous Office file formats. All previous versions of Word documents can be open in Word 2007.

16.5.1 The Home Tab

The Home Tab contains commands for the formatting of text. The Home Tab is also used for the editing of the document like find and replace, and to perform clipboard operations such as cut, copy and paste on the document. Figure 16.11 shows the Home Tab.

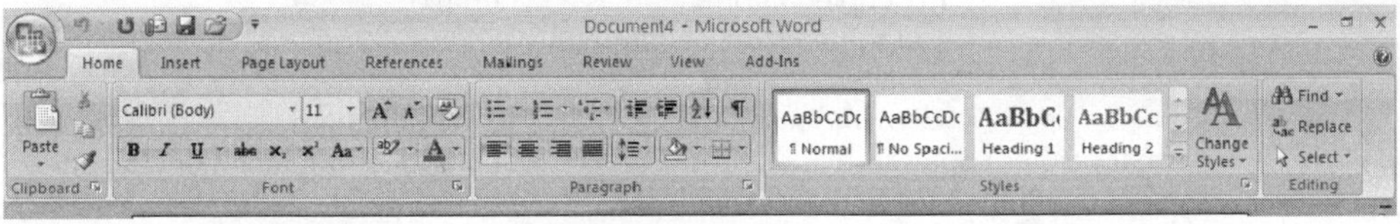

Figure 16.11 The home tab

There are five groups within this tab, namely, Clipboard, Font, Paragraph, Styles and Editing.

- The *Clipboard* group contains commands to cut, copy and paste text. The Format Painter is also present here.
- *Font* group commands allow change of the font - font face, style, size, effects (Superscript, Subscript, and Shadow etc.), color and character spacing. You can change these options before or after you type your text. In case of after, you need to select the text first.
- *Paragraph* group is used to change paragraph settings - alignment, indents, spacing, and pagination like spacing 1.5 lines, double spacing, indentation, and, spacing before and after a heading. Move your cursor to the line or paragraph you want to change.
- The *Styles* group allows quickly choosing a style and applying the style.
- *Editing* group contains commands to select, find and replace text.

Table 16.2 gives the commands in the different groups (*in left to right order*) of Home Tab along with a brief explanation.

> *To apply formatting to an already written text, first select the text and then apply the formatting*

Here, we describe briefly some of the operations that are performed using the commands of the Home Tab.

- **Move Text:** Select and highlight the section you want to move **<Home><Clipboard>**< <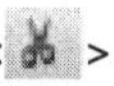>. Move the cursor to the place you would like the text to be inserted **<Home><Clipboard>** <>.
- **Copy Text:** Select and highlight the section you want to copy **<Home><Clipboard>**<>. Move the cursor to the place you want the copied text to be inserted **<Home><Clipboard>**<>
- **Find and Replace:** This is used to find a text, style or paragraph and then replace it with the new one. This option is useful if you want to find text strings at multiple places in the document, and replace all of them with the new one.

Home Tab Groups	Description
Clipboard	 • *Paste* the cut or copied information in clipboard at the location where cursor is pointing right now (*Paste Special* - To paste in a particular format. *Paste as Hyperlink* - Used with copy to paste the copied information as a hyperlink) • *Cut* the selected text from the document and put into clipboard for later retrieval. • *Copy* the selected item or text to the clipboard. • *Format painter* copies formatting from one place and applies it to another (To apply same formatting to many places, double-click the format painter button)
Font	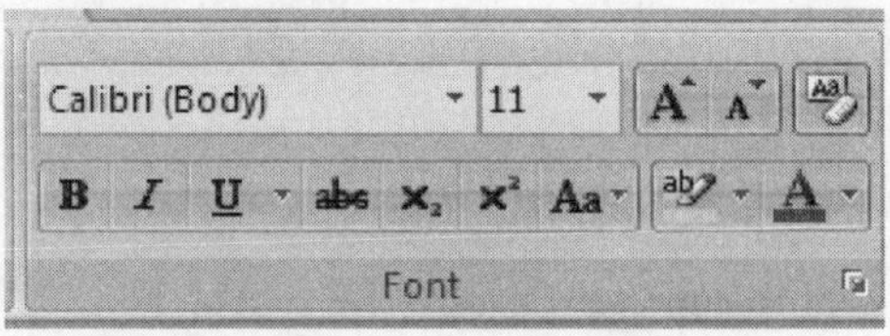 • Change Font face, change Font size • Grow Font, Shrink Font • Clear Formatting (Clear all formatting from selection, leave only plain text) • Bold, Italics, Underline • Strikethrough (draw a line through middle of selected text), Subscript, Superscript • Change case. You can change the case – sentence, lower, upper, title, or toggle. Select the text and click on an option • Text highlight color, Font color
Paragraph	 • Bullets (choose from different styles) • Numbered list (choose different formats) • Multilevel list (Choose from different styles) • Increase or decrease indent of the paragraph • Sort alphabetically or numerically • Show paragraph markups • Align text left, right, centre, and justify • Change spacing between lines • Color background behind selected text • Customize the borders of selected text. Add borders and shading. There are options to select for setting, style, color, width, fill color, and pattern. You will see a preview at the right. To remove a border or shading, select None.
Styles	 • Format titles using different styles like Caption, Emphasis etc. • Change style, color and font used in the document
Editing	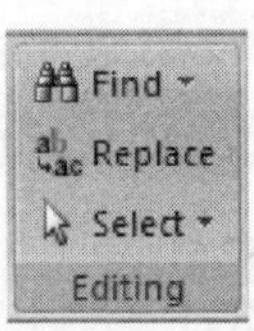 • Find text in the document • Replace text in the document (The user can go to a page, section etc. when using find and replace) • Select text or objects in the document

Table 16.2 *Home tab commands description*

To Select Multiple Text Entries that are scattered words, phrases, or paragraphs for the same action, select the first item with your mouse as you normally would. For subsequent items, press the CTRL key before you select them. Now you can perform any operation like italicize, boldface, or highlight on all the selected items.

16.5.2 The Insert Tab

The Insert Tab contains commands for inserting objects of many kinds in a document. The commands in this tab are used to add pages, tables, and images. It also includes commands to build an equation in the document, add symbols, special text, links, and, headers and footers. Figure 16.12 shows the Insert Tab.

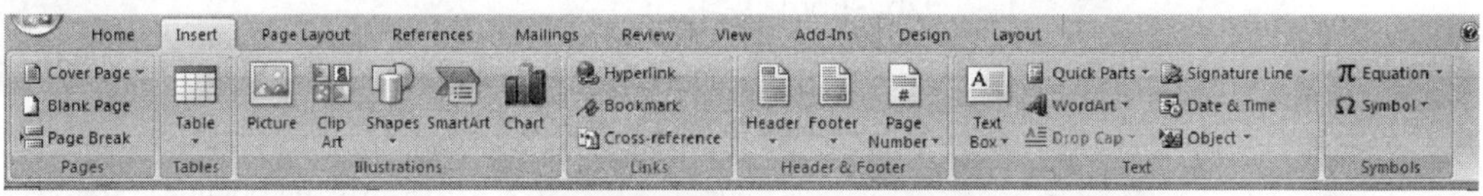

Figure 16.12 The insert tab

There are seven groups within this tab, namely, Pages, Tables, Illustrations, Links, Header and Footer, and, Text and Symbols.

- The *Pages* group contains commands to insert a cover page, blank page or a page break.
- *Tables* are used to draw and insert tables.
- *Illustrations* group allows insertion of pictures, clip art, shapes, smart art, and charts.
- The *Links* group is used to insert a hyperlink, bookmark, and cross reference.
- The *Header and Footer* group allows insertion of a header, footer, and page numbers.
- The *Text* group contains commands to insert a text box, word Art, date, and time.
- The *Symbols* group is used to insert symbols, and build mathematical equations.

Some of the Tabs appear only when you use them; like Picture Tools tab, Drawing Tools Tab, Table Tab and Chart Tools Tab

Table 16.3 gives the commands in the different groups of the Insert Tab along with a brief explanation.

The Insert tab is used to insert a page break, a diagram etc. When a command of the Insert tab is used, insertion takes place at the location where the cursor is present right now. So, before inserting the item, place the cursor at the location where the item is to be inserted. When you use the commands of the insert tab for insertion, you will see that most of the times, a dialog box will open which allows you to make specific settings, as per your requirement. Here, we will not discuss using the dialog boxes as they are self-explanatory, and are easy to use. Some of the operations using the Insert Tab commands are described below—

- **To Create Headers and Footers—<Insert> <Header & Footer>**. You will see a Header and Footer command. A Header and Footer tab is opened which allows creation of a Header and Footer, enter text or graphics into the Header or Footer area, insert page numbers, time or date, file name, author name, etc.

Insert Tab Groups	Description
Pages	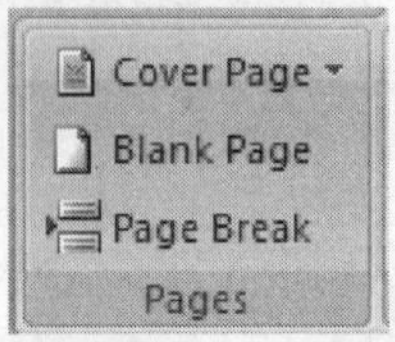 • Insert a fully formatted cover page (Different styles are available). • Insert a blank page at the current cursor position • Insert a page break. Start the content located at the current cursor position on the next page.
Tables	 • Insert or draw table in the document (convert text to table, insert an Excel spreadsheet, insert from one of the built-in tables). When a table is drawn, a Table Tool Design Tab (Figure 16.13) and Table Tools Layout Tab opens, which allows you to select Table Style options, Table Styles, and Table Borders.
Illustrations	 • Insert picture from a file. When a picture is inserted, a Picture Tool Format Tab opens (Figure 16.14) which contains commands to format the picture. • Insert clip art into the document (sounds, movies, and drawings) readymade shapes (lines, arrows, flowchart symbols etc.) • Insert a smart art graphics • Insert a chart (bar graph, pie chart, line area, surface etc.)
Links	 • Insert a hyperlink. Hyperlink to an existing file or web page, any place in the same document, to a new document, or to an email address. Target frame specifies the frame in which you want the hyper linked document to appear. To hyperlink to the same document, first create a bookmark at the location where you want to hyperlink, and select the bookmark to create hyperlink. A hyperlink is displayed in a blue color. • Insert a bookmark. Identifies a location or selection of text that you name and identify for future reference. For example, you might use a bookmark to identify text where you want a hyperlink to reach. • Insert cross reference
Header and Footer	 • To edit the contents of the header. The header will appear at the top of each page. You can choose the format of the header from the built-in ones. • To edit the contents of the footer. The contents of footer will appear at the bottom of each page. You can choose the format of the footer from the built-in ones. • Insert page number into the document at the top, bottom, or at the margins etc. You can select the position, alignment and format of the page numbers.

(Continued)

Insert Tab Groups	Description
Text	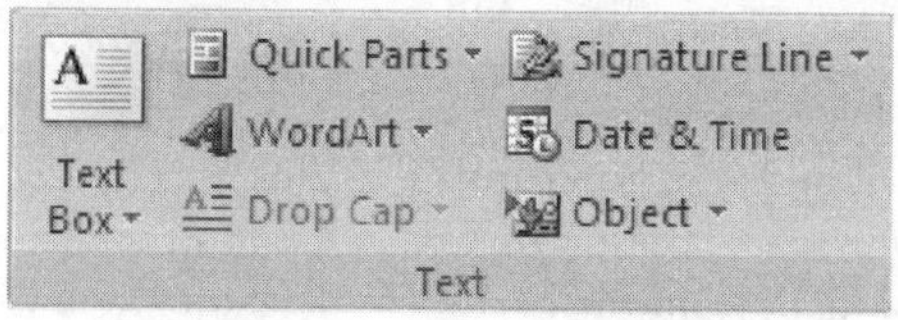 • Insert pre-formatted built-in text box or draw a text box. When a text box is inserted, a Text Box Tools Format Tab opens (Figure 16.15) which contains commands to format the text box. • Insert useful parts of content like fields • Insert a signature line that specifies the person's name who will sign it • Insert decorative text in the document, and, date and time into the document • A *Drop Cap* is an oversized capital at the beginning of a document or section. To make the first letter of a document large, select the letter and then use Drop Cap. • Insert an embedded object
Symbols	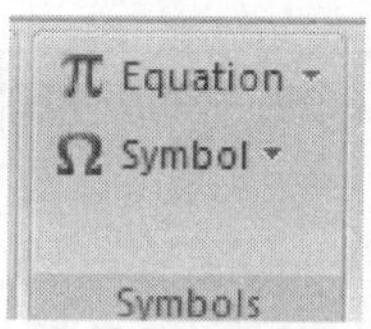 • Insert common mathematical equations or build your own equations (a new toolbar appears to insert an equation) • Insert symbols

Table 16.3 *Insert tab commands description*

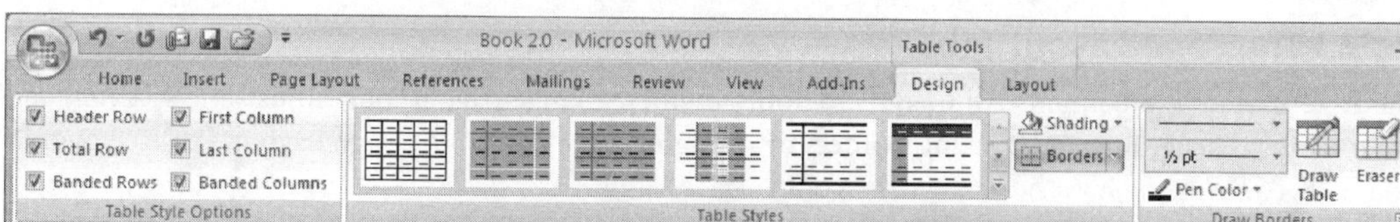

Figure 16.13 Table tools design tab

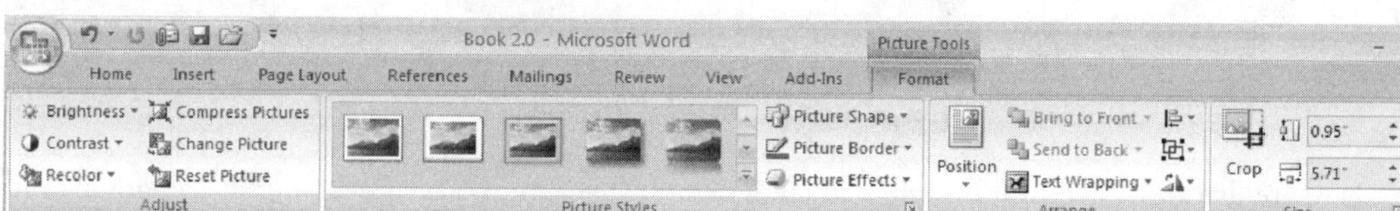

Figure 16.14 Picture tools format tab

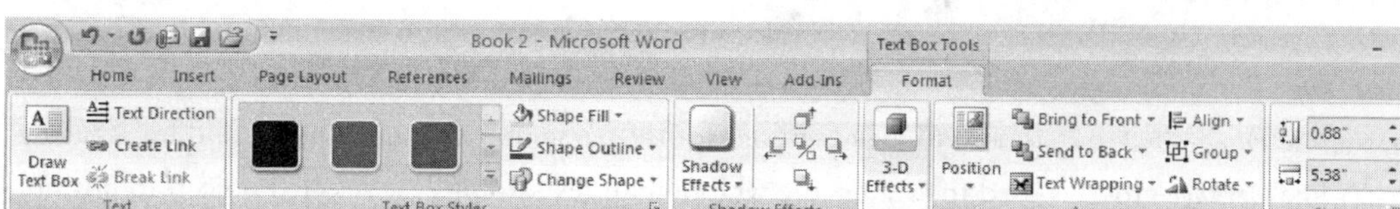

Figure 16.15 Text box tools format tab

- **Insert Bookmarks**—Position your cursor where you want to insert the bookmark in the document. **<Insert> <Links> <Bookmark>**. In the dialog box, give the bookmark a name, descriptive of the text or location. Click Add. To return to a bookmark, open the Bookmark dialog box, select one from the list, and click *Go To*.
- **Insert Hyperlink—<Insert> <Links> <Hyperlink>**. To link to another location in the same document, click *Place in This Document* option under *Link to*; In the dialog box's inner window, select a heading or existing bookmark from the document diagram. To link to another document, click the Existing File or Web Page option. Navigate to the proper folder and select the file's name.
- **To Insert Page Numbers—<Insert> <Header & Footer><Page Number>**. For more page number options, click on the Format button. To suppress page number on first page, uncheck the *Show Number on First Page* checkbox.
- **Insert File**—Insert the contents of file B into file A. Open file A and place your cursor at the location where you want to insert the contents of file B. Select **<Insert> <Text> <Object>** and use the dialog box to navigate to file B. Select it, and click on *Insert* button. The contents of file B will be included in file A at the position of the cursor in file A.

> To see a command in action; let's say you want to insert a picture in your document,
>
> - <Insert> <Picture>
> - Choose between stock pictures or navigate to your own folder of images.
>
> Click Insert, the selected image appears in your document

16.5.3 The Page Layout Tab

The Page Layout Tab contains commands to apply themes, change page layout, adjust line spacing, and also to adjust background by creating borders or changing page color. The Page Layout Tab is shown in Figure 16.16.

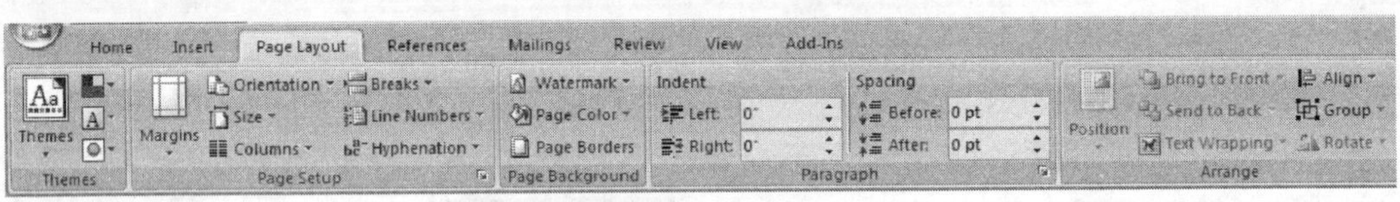

Figure 16.16 The page layout tab

There are five groups within this tab, namely, Themes, Page Setup, Page Background, Paragraph, and Arrange.

- The *Themes* group contains commands to change the overall design of the document including fonts and colors.
- *Page Setup* is used to set the margins, breaks, number of columns in a page, line numbers etc.
- *Page Background* group allows choosing a page background color, and page borders.
- The *Paragraph* group is used to make settings for the paragraph like indentation, and line spacing.
- The *Arrange* group is used to arrange the wrapping of text around the selected object, to position text in context of the selected object, and much more.

Table 16.4 gives the commands in the different groups of Page Layout Tab along with a brief explanation.

<table>
<tr><th>Page Layout Tab Group</th><th>Description</th></tr>
<tr><td>Themes</td><td>

- Themes are used to change the overall design of the document including theme font, theme color, and theme effect.
</td></tr>
<tr><td>Page Setup</td><td>
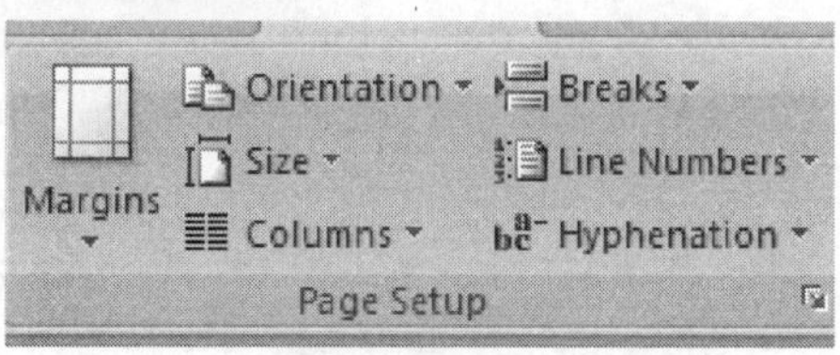

- Select margin for the whole document or the current selection
- Select orientation between portrait and landscape
- Insert Page or Section breaks
- Select a paper size like A3, A4, letter etc.
- Add line numbers on the margin alongside each line
- Split text into two, three, left or right columns. You can specify the number of columns, column width and spacing, equal column width, line between columns, and apply to whole document or this point forward.
- Turn on hyphenation, which allows the word to break line between the word syllables
</td></tr>
<tr><td>Page Background</td><td>
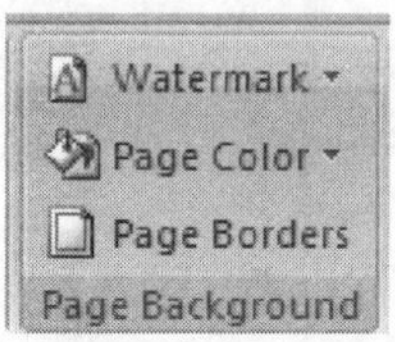

- Insert watermark behind the page like Confidential, original etc.
- Choose a color for the background of the page. You can choose from fill effects like gradient, texture, pattern, and picture
- Add or change the border around the page
</td></tr>
<tr><td>Paragraph</td><td>
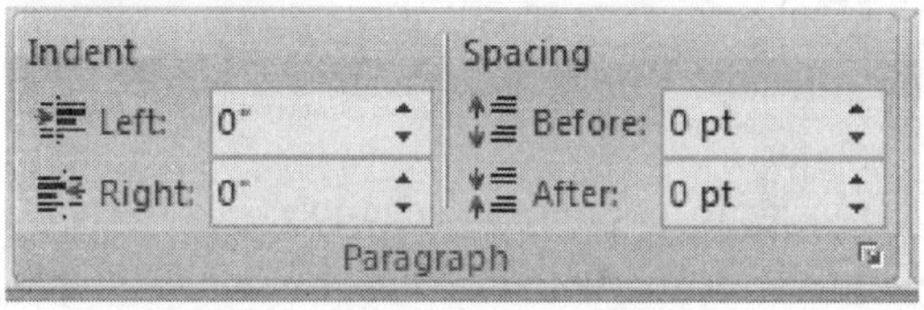

- Move in the left side or right side of the paragraph
- Change spacing between paragraphs by inserting space above and below the selected paragraph
</td></tr>
<tr><td>Arrange</td><td>
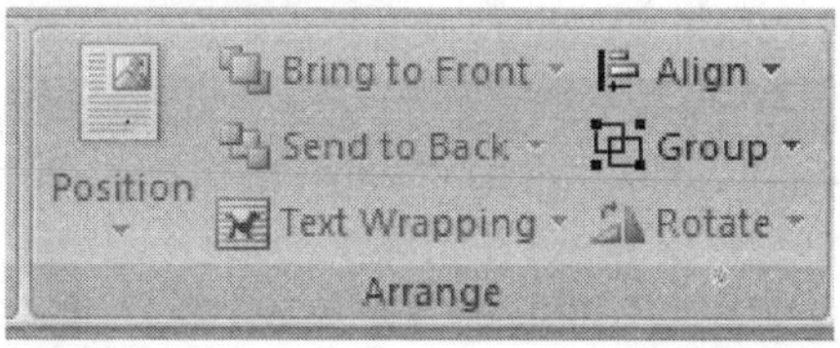

- Position the selected object on the page. The user can select from different positions.
- Bring the selected object in front of all other objects, or at the back of all other objects.
- Change the way the text wraps around the object
- Align the edges of multiple selected objects
- Group objects together so that they can be treated like a single group
- Rotate or flip the selected object horizontally, vertically, by 90° etc.
</td></tr>
</table>

Table 16.4 *Page layout commands description*

Some of the operations that are performed using the commands of the Page Layout tab are briefly described here.

- **To Change Page Margins:** For left or right page margins, point to a margin boundary on the horizontal ruler until it changes to a double arrow, and drag the margin boundary to the right or left. For top or bottom page margins, point to a margin boundary on the vertical ruler until it changes to a double arrow, and drag the margin boundary to the top or bottom.
- **To Specify Exact Page Margins: <Page Layout> <Page Setup><Margins>**. You can change either top, bottom, left, or right margins by clicking in the appropriate text boxes or on the arrows next to the numbers in Custom margins.

16.5.4 The References Tab

The References Tab contains commands for adding references of all kinds to a document. The commands in this tab are used to add Table of Contents, Bibliography, Index etc. The References Tab is shown in Figure 16.17.

Figure 16.17 The References tab

There are six groups within this tab, namely, Table of Contents, Footnotes, Citation & Bibliography, Captions, Index, and Table of Authorities.

- The *Table of Contents* group contains commands to create and update table of contents, and add text to it.
- *Footnotes* are used to insert or navigate footnotes and endnotes.
- *Citations & Bibliography* group allows insertion of citations and bibliography.
- The *Captions* group is used to insert captions in a Figure or Table, and to refer to them.
- The *Index* group is used to insert or update an index. An index is a list of keywords that are present in the document and also the page numbers on which they appear.
- The *Table of Authorities* group contains command to insert a table of authorities. A Table of Authorities lists the cases, statues, and other authorities cited in the document.

Table 16.5 gives the commands in the different groups of the References Tab along with a brief explanation.

16.5.5 The Mailings Tab

The Mailings Tab contains commands that are required to create envelopes and labels, do a mail merge or formatting of business letters. The Mailings Tab is shown in Figure 16.18.

<table>
<tr><th>References Tab Group</th><th colspan="2">Description</th></tr>
<tr><td>Table of Contents</td><td></td><td>• Add a Table of Content to the document. The user can select from the built-in styles
• Add the current paragraph as an entry in the Table
• Update the Table of Contents so that the entry refers to the correct page number</td></tr>
<tr><td>Footnotes</td><td></td><td>• Add footnotes to the document
• Add an endnote to the document. Endnotes are inserted at the end of the whole document
• Next Footnote is used to navigate between the footnotes
• Scroll the document to show where the footnotes and endnotes are located</td></tr>
<tr><td>Citations & Bibliography</td><td></td><td>• Insert citation for a book, periodical journal
• Manage sources – to list all the citations cited in the document
• Select the style of citation to use in the document
• Add a bibliography which lists all the sources cited in the document</td></tr>
<tr><td>Captions</td><td>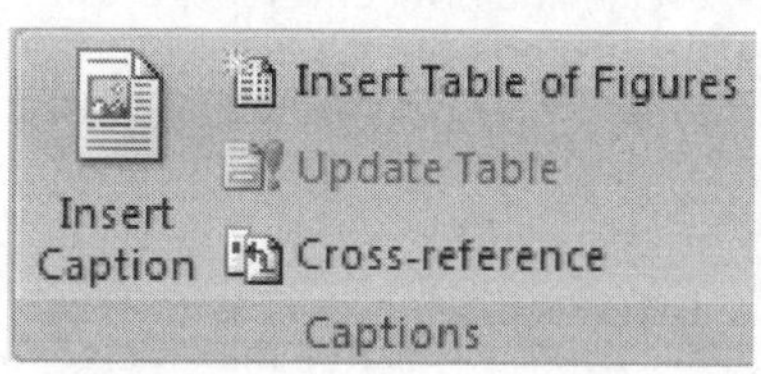</td><td>• Add a caption to a picture or an image. It inserts the caption below the image
• Insert Table of Figures into the document
• Update the Table of Figures
• Insert a cross-reference to a heading, figure or table</td></tr>
<tr><td>Index</td><td>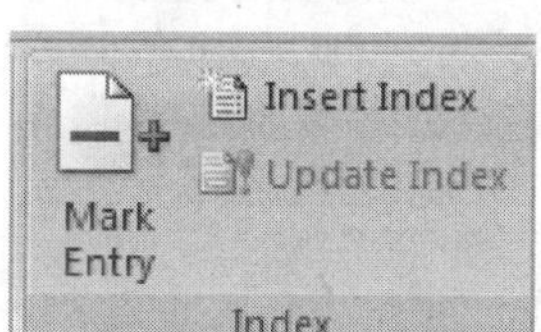</td><td>• Mark Entry includes the selected text in the index of document
• Insert an index into the document and the page numbers on which they appear
• Update the index</td></tr>
<tr><td>Table of Authorities</td><td></td><td>• Add the selected text as an entry in the Table of Authorities
• Insert a Table of Authorities into the document
• Update the Table of Authorities</td></tr>
</table>

Table 16.5 *References tab commands description*

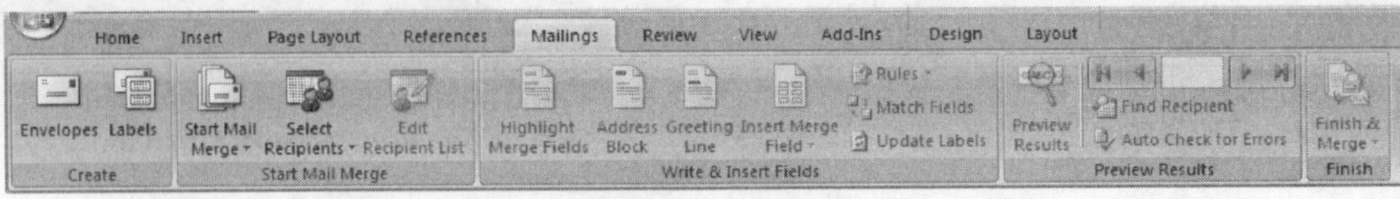

Figure 16.18 The mailings tab

There are five groups within this tab, namely Create, Start Mail Merge, Write & Insert Fields, Preview Results, and Finish.

- The *Create* group has commands to create envelopes and labels.
- The *Start Mail Merge* group contains commands to start the mail merge and select or edit the recipient list.
- *Write & Insert Fields* is used to write and insert the fields that are to be merged.
- *Preview Result* group shows how the merged documents will look like.
- The *Finish* group is used when you are satisfied with the preview and want to complete the mail merge.

The commands in the different groups of Mailings Tab along with a brief explanation are shown in Table 16.6.

Some of the operations using the Mailings Tab commands are described below:

Mailings Tab Group	**Description**	
Create		• Create and print envelopes • Create and print labels
Start Mail Merge	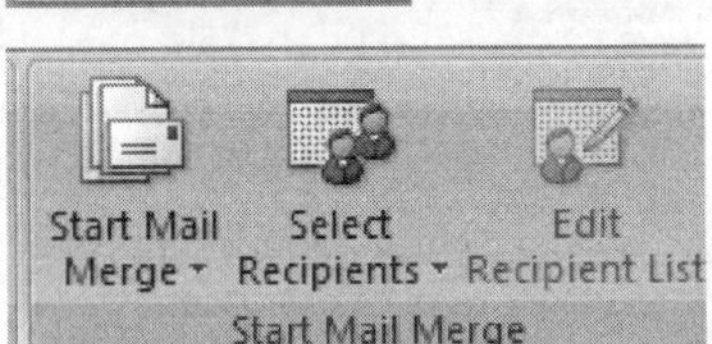	• Start a mail merge to create a letter that you want to send to different recipients • Select the recipients of your letter • Make changes to the list of recipients
Write &Insert Fields	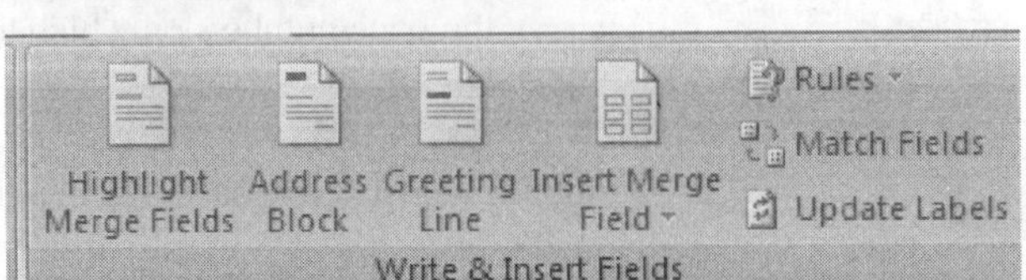	• Highlight the fields you have inserted into the document • Add an address to the letter • Add a greeting line to your letter (Dear Sir)
	• Add fields from the recipient list of your document (name, address etc.) • Specify rules to make decision-making ability in mail merge • Tells the meaning of different fields in the recipient list • Update information in the labels from the recipient list	

(Continued)

Mailings Tab Group	Description
Preview Results	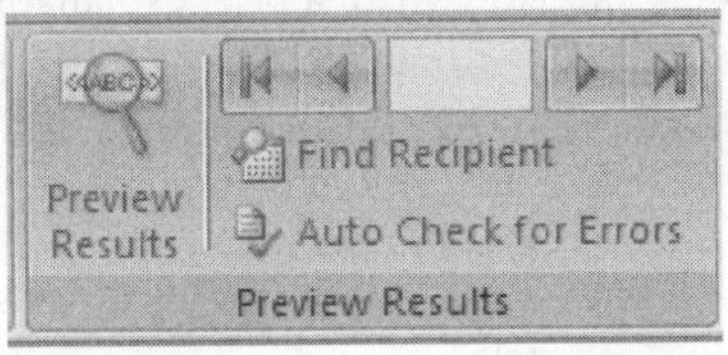 • To preview the merged data from the recipient field • To preview a specific record in the recipient list • Find by searching the text, and preview the specific record in the recipient list • Specify handling of errors when doing mail merge
Finish	 • Finish and complete the mail merge

Table 16.6 *Mailings tab commands description*

- **Make Envelopes:** If you've included the recipient's address at the top of a letter, you can prepare an envelope directly from the letter. **<Mailings> <Create> <Envelopes>.** MS-Word would have recognized the address and included it. If needed, input your *Return Address*. Click *Add to Document*, and the envelope will print as the first page of your letter.
- **Make Labels. <Mailings> <Create> <Labels>.** Type the text in this dialog box. Click *Options* to set the *manufacturer and product code number* of the label sheets you'll be printing on; this will format your Word document with the sheet's dimensions and layout. You can print a full page, or a single label, by targeting a row and column position on the sheet.

16.5.6 The Review Tab

The Review Tab contains commands for reviewing the document. The commands in this tab are used when there is a need to correct the contents of the document like tracking changes, checking spellings and grammar etc. The Review Tab is shown in Figure 16.19.

Figure 16.19 The Review tab

There are six groups within this tab, namely Proofing, Comments, Tracking, Changes, Compare, and Protect.

- The *Proofing* group has commands required for the proofing of document like the spelling and grammar checker, research etc.
- The *Comments* group contains commands to insert comments, and move back and forth among the comments.
- *Tracking* is used to track the changes made to the document. It contains commands to turn on the track changes, and to make settings for viewing the changes.
- *Changes* group contains commands to view the changes and accept or reject the changes.

⊙ The *Compare* group is used to compare or combine different versions of the document.

⊙ The *Protect* group contains command to protect the document by restricting its access.

The commands in the different groups of the Review Tab along with a brief explanation are shown in Table 16.7.

Review Tab Group	Description
Proofing	 • Check the spelling and grammar of text in the document • Open Research Task Pane and search through research material • Thesaurus suggests word similar in meaning to the selected word • Translate the selected text into a different language • Enable screen tip that translates the word you pause at, into another language • Set the language used to check the spelling and grammar of the selected text • Find the number of words, characters, paragraphs and lines in your document
Comments	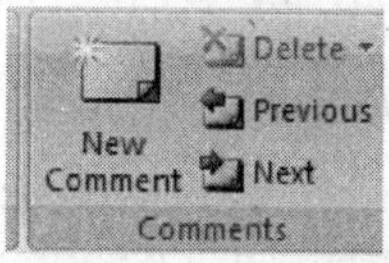 • Add a comment about the selection • Delete the selected comment • Navigate to the previous or the next comment
Tracking	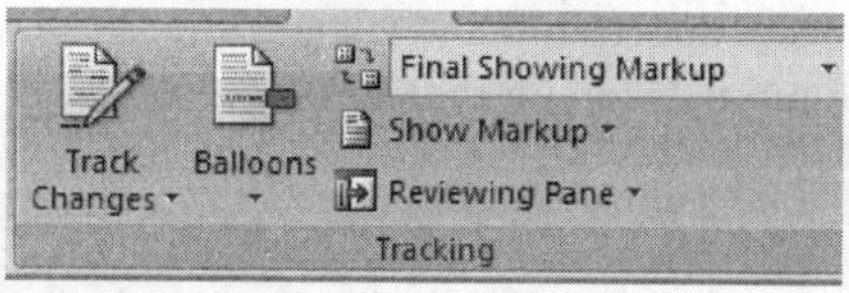 • Track all changes made to the document - insertion, deletion, and updates • Choose how to show the revision of the document • Choose how to show the proposed changes to the document • Choose the kind of markup to show in the document • Show revisions in a separate window
Changes	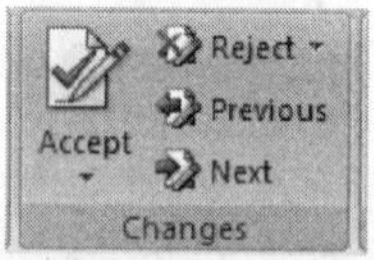 • Accept or reject the current change and move to the next proposed change • Navigate to the previous and next revision in the document so that you can accept or reject it
Compare	 • Compare or combine multiple versions of the document • Choose which source documents to show – the original document, the revised document or both
Protect	 • Restrict how people can access the document. You can restrict the formatting styles allowed, permit only comments to be added by others, or give permissions to different people to edit in specified sections.

Table 16.7 *Review tab commands description*

16.5.7 The View Tab

The View tab has commands that facilitate in viewing of document. The View Tab is shown in Figure 16.20.

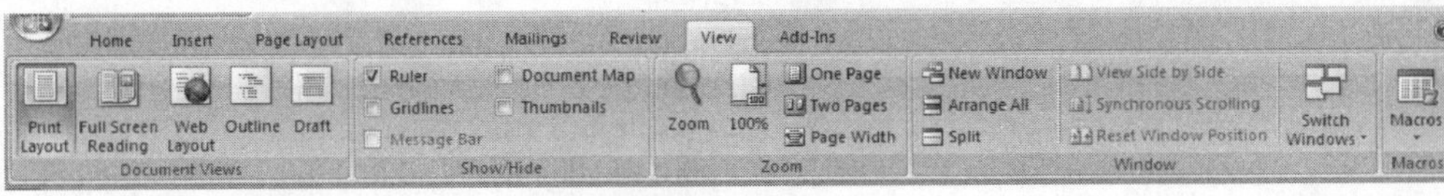

Figure 16.20 The View tab

There are five groups within this tab, namely Document Views, Show/Hide, Zoom, Window and Macros.

- The *Document Views* group has commands to view the document in different modes like the print layout, full screen reading etc.
- The *Show/Hide* group contains commands to show or hide the ruler, gridlines etc.
- *Zoom* is used to view the document in smaller or larger sizes. You can zoom with two pages on a single screen, increase the view to 200%, and so on.
- *Window* group contains commands to view the windows like, splitting the window, arranging all open windows etc.
- The *Macros* group is used to create or view a macro.

The commands in the different groups of View Tab along with a brief explanation are shown in Table 16.8.

View Tab Group	Description
Document Views	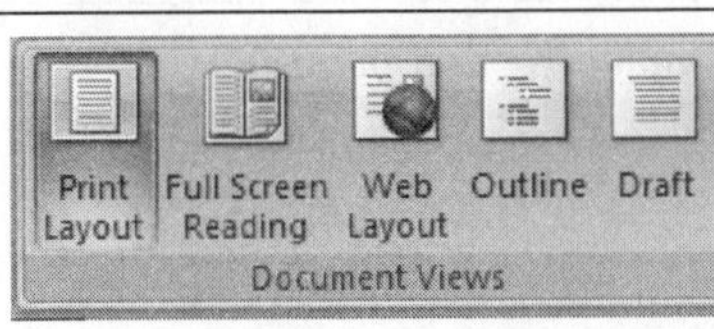 • View the document as it will appear on the printed page. It shows the entire page you are working on, including margins, header and footer information. • View the document in a full screen reading view. It maximizes the space available for reading and comments • View the document as it would look as a web page • View the document as an outline and show the outlining tools. Outline symbols and indentations show how the document is organized • View the document as a draft to quickly edit the text. Certain elements of the document like the header and footer will not be visible in this view.
Show/ Hide	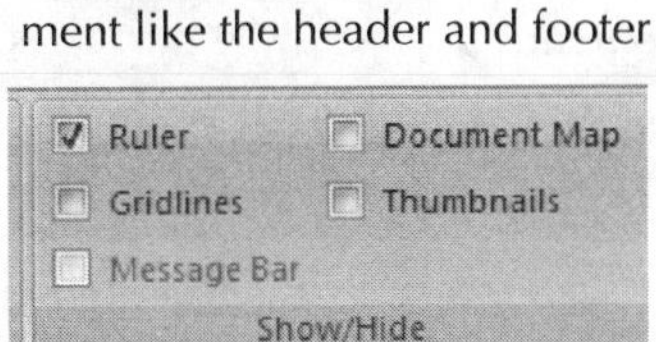 • Show or Hide the Ruler, Gridlines and the Message bar • Document map allows you to navigate the structural view of the document. It lists the headings of the current document. • Opens a Thumbnail pane which allows you to navigate a long document through small pictures of each page

(Continued)

View Tab Group	Description
Zoom	 • Opens Zoom dialog box to specify the zoom level • Zoom the document to 100% of normal size • Zoom the document so that one page or two pages fit into a single window • Zoom the document so that the width of the page matches the width of the window
Window	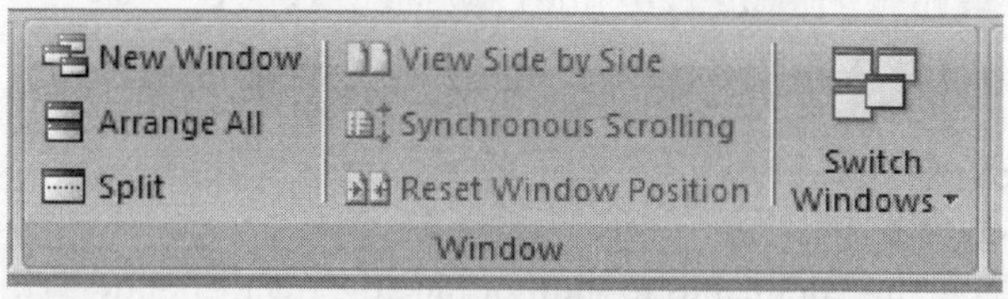 • Open a new window containing a view of the current document • Tile all open programs side-by-side on the screen • Split the current window two parts to see the different sections of the document at the same time • View two documents side-by-side, synchronize their scrolling so that they scroll together • Reset the window position so that the two documents can be viewed side-by-side and share the screen equally • Switch to a different currently open window
Macros	 • View the list of macros from which you can run, create or delete a macro

Table 16.8 *View tab commands description*

16.5.8 The Help

The Help button is located on the right most side of the Tabs in the Ribbon. Click on this button to get help for using any command of the MS-Word. On clicking on the help button, a screen as shown in Figure 16.21 appears. You can browse the Help for the command you want. You can also perform operations such as, search for a command and view Table of Contents.

16.6 SOLVED EXAMPLES

Here some examples are given, which show the generated output document.

Example 1: **Design a Magazine Cover. You must include the features mentioned below:**

(1) Page Border, (2) Select a background effect for the page, (3) Create a watermark, (4) Insert either a picture or clipart, and (5) Use WordArt.

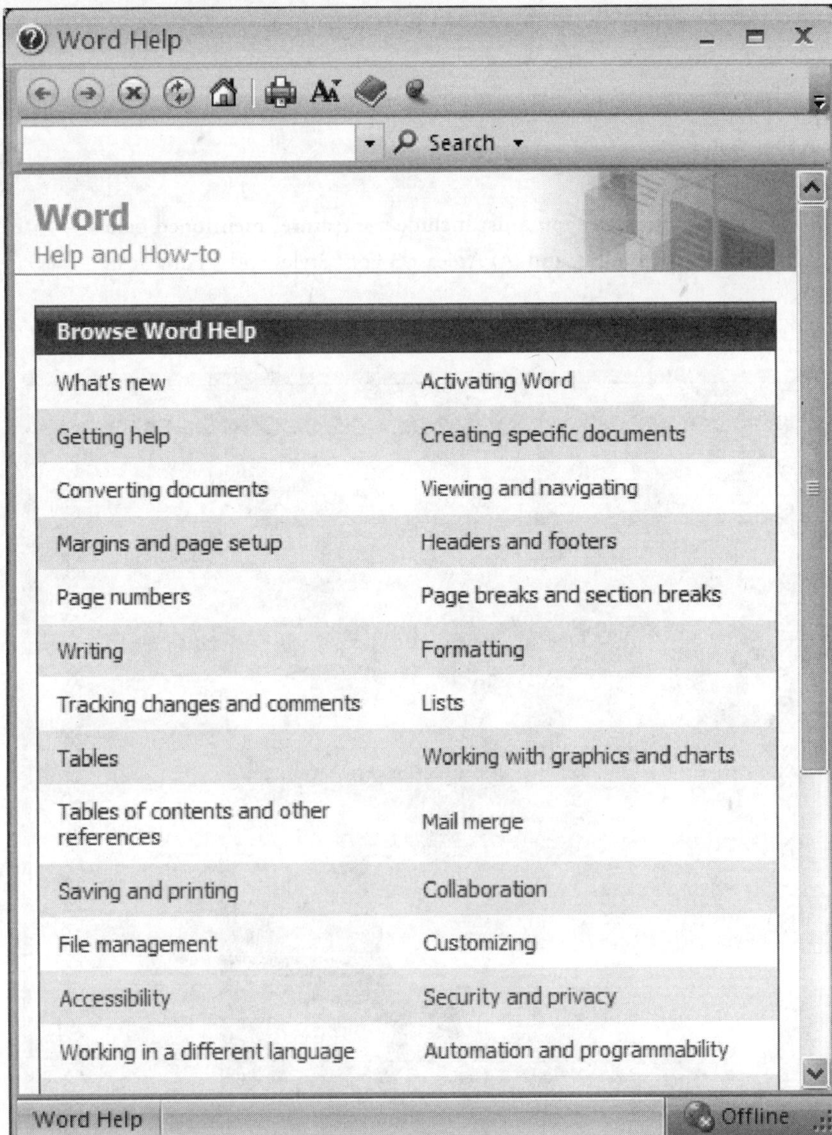

Figure 16.21 Word help

Solution 1:

- Open blank document. <> <New>
- Page Border. **<Page Layout> <Page Background> <Page Borders> <Art>**
- Background effect. **<Page Layout> <Page Background> <Page Color> <Fill Effects> <Texture>**
- Watermark. **<Page Layout> <Page Background> <Watermark>**

- Insert Picture. **<Insert> <Illustrations> <ClipArt>**
- Use WordArt. **<Insert> <Text> <WordArt>**
- You can also use more options like **Font Styles** etc.

A sample is shown in Figure 16.22.

Example 2: **Write your Resume. You must include the features mentioned below—** (1) Tables, (2) Alignment, (3) Bullets, and (4) At least 3 Font Styles and 3 Font Sizes.

Figure 16.22 A magazine cover

Solution 2:

- Open blank document. < > **<New>**
- To Print Title. Select a Font. **<Home> <Font> <Theme Font>** (You can select the Font Style, size, effects etc.).
- To align title at the centre. Select the title. <Home> <Paragraph> < >
- To insert Bullets. <Home> <Paragraph> < >
- To insert Table. **<Insert> <Tables>.** Select the number of columns and rows for the table. **<Insert Table>**

A sample is shown in Figure 16.23.

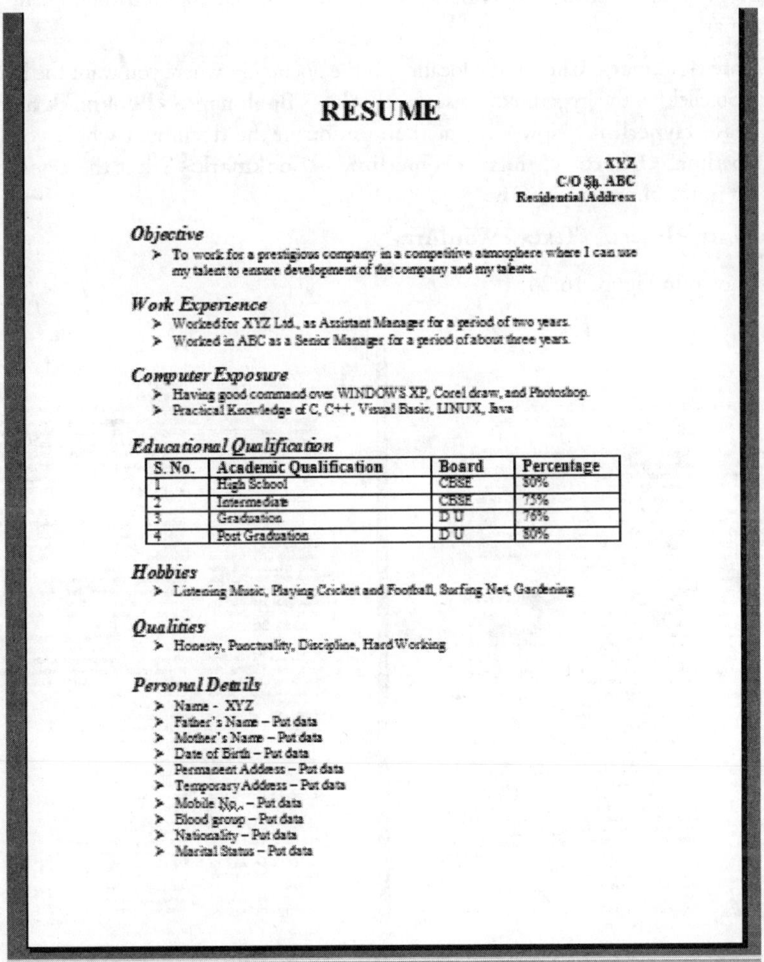

RESUME

XYZ
C/O Sh. ABC
Residential Address

Objective

- To work for a prestigious company in a competitive atmosphere where I can use my talent to ensure development of the company and my talents.

Work Experience

- Worked for XYZ Ltd., as Assistant Manager for a period of two years.
- Worked in ABC as a Senior Manager for a period of about three years.

Computer Exposure

- Having good command over WINDOWS XP, Corel draw, and Photoshop.
- Practical Knowledge of C, C++, Visual Basic, LINUX, Java

Educational Qualification

S. No.	Academic Qualification	Board	Percentage
1	High School	CBSE	80%
2	Intermediate	CBSE	75%
3	Graduation	D U	76%
4	Post Graduation	D U	80%

Hobbies

- Listening Music, Playing Cricket and Football, Surfing Net, Gardening

Qualities

- Honesty, Punctuality, Discipline, Hard Working

Personal Details

- Name - XYZ
- Father's Name – Put data
- Mother's Name – Put data
- Date of Birth – Put data
- Permanent Address – Put data
- Temporary Address – Put data
- Mobile No. – Put data
- Blood group – Put data
- Nationality – Put data
- Marital Status – Put data

Figure 16.23 A resume

Example 3: **Design an article of two pages for a magazine with three columns**

- Use at least 3 different Font styles, 3 Font sizes, 3 Font colors, 3 Font effects
- Use Hyperlink, Pictures, WordArt

Solution 3:

- Open blank document. < [Office Button] > <New>
- If you want the title to be in a single column, then first write the title. Select the font size, font style etc for the title. Press <Enter> key two times. Now select rest of the page and click **<Page Setup> <Columns>**. Select 3 columns.
- To get the first letter of the document big **<Insert> <Text> <Drop Cap> <Drop Cap Options> <Dropped>** <Lines to Drop> select 2.
- Insert Picture. **<Insert> <Illustrations> <ClipArt>**
- Create Hyperlink. To create a hyperlink, first create a bookmark, and then create a hyperlink to the bookmark.
    - **To Create Bookmark.** Click at the location in the document where you want the hyperlink to reach when you click on the hyperlink. **<Insert> <Links> <Bookmark> <Bookmark name> <Add>.**
    - **To Create Hyperlink.** Now click at the location in the document where you want to insert the hyperlink. **<Insert> <Links> <Hyperlink> <Bookmark>** Select the Bookmark name you inserted in the above step. **<OK>**
- Use WordArt. **<Insert> <Text> <WordArt>**

A sample is shown in Figure 16.24.

THE CASE OF THE BONSAI MANAGER- Lessons from Nature on Growing, R. Gopalakrishnan (2007)

Gopalakrishnan has gained a wealth of practical managerial experience during his tenure as the CEO of Arabia unit of Unilever, managing director of Brooke Bond Lipton India, vice chairman of Hindustan Level and, currently, as executive director of Tata Sons. In this book, he focuses on how to become a leader, and shares with the reader his personal anecdotes and stories on the subject. The author recognises that there is a shift in the leadership skill set from analytical, aggressive and directive to humane, participative and intuitive. During decision making, complete information is rarely available to the leader to arrive at a decision; successful managers or leaders complement knowledge with their intuition.

Bonsai

Bonsai is a Japanese art of creating beautiful ornamental plants. Bonsai are stunted plants grown in artificial conditions. In this book, the author refers 'Bonsai Manager' as one who has not run his course, so he has not been able to flourish by drawing sustenance from his natural environment. Just as no plant is created by Nature to be bonsai, no one sets out to become a bonsai manager. The growth of bonsai managers gets stunted through their own act of omission and commission. The absence of intuition results in constricting a manager.

Effective Leadership

Effective leadership is the result of integration of knowledge and intuition. Knowledge and intuition can be acquired and developed by aspiring manager or young leaders in contrasting ways. Knowledge can be taught and can be acquired from external resources. It is what the managers already know they possess. However, intuition cannot be taught, but, has to be learnt by your own. It is a set of understandings that the owner does not know about. When there is a lack of information, intuition plays a significant role in filling that gap. Successful and effective leaders use both - knowledge and intuition, in their decision-making process. Knowledge being pre-requisite, senior leaders are valued for their intuition. In this book, the author focuses on development of 'intuition' to become a successful manager. In the problems and solutions that are technical in nature, knowledge based on analysis works well. Intuition plays a key role where 'human' factors are involved.

The author emphasizes that there is no magic formula to develop intuition. However, intuitive leadership can be developed. In the practical world of the manager, human ambition, motivation and social relations play a very important role. The nature of human beings such as good conduct, character, honesty, sincerity and the complexity of employee behavior in an organisation are difficult-to-teach subjects. Anecdotes, parables and evocative stories can help managers learn about human nature and reflect on it. Such stories with Nature as a theme, appeal to most people. People are inspired by Nature - animals, insects, geology and plants around them. The author integrates 'management' and 'lessons from Nature on Growing' for development of intuition. The author refers intuition as 'gut feel' which is developed through keen listening, reflection, contemplation and mentoring. To familiarise the readers with the situations in which intuition plays a key role in decision making, the author narrates several personal anecdotes.

To First Page

CHAPTERS

The book is organized in five sections. The first and the second section are a discussion about analysis and intuition, and, a view about how the leader's intuition works, respectively. The last three sections focus on building intuition.

In the first section of the book, the author narrates an incident from his own experience to highlight the importance of intuition along with analysis. Section two is a discussion about the science underneath the working of intuition and the importance of storytelling to learn the untaught. Author explains that human brain has three inter-connected evolutionary levels that are wired together. The multiple wiring causes human responses to be instinctive or analytical. Strong intuition is developed when the Brain's Remote Implicit Memory (BRIM) is accessed and enhanced through practice and immersion. Practice means doing the same things so often that practice embeds processes into the implicit memory. Immersion means experiencing emotions and involvement so deeply that they stay in the memory forever. Storytelling is an important way of teaching and imparting knowledge on fuzzy subjects. Storytelling is related to management because an idea is united with emotion. Nature has caused emotions and wonderment in man's mind and leaves him with memorable impressions.

In the next section, author says that the 'space' in which the manager grows is extremely important for the development of intuition. He draws a comparison of a stunted manager with a stunted crocodile. Growth of crocodiles is stunted by restricting and constricting their space and the manager gets stunted when he operates and works at a level which is well below his potential. Growth of crocodile depends on diet and space available; manager's mental food (reading, training, people challenges) and his experience (new experiences, tough assignments) matter to him. Varied experiences with multiple challenges, multiple geographies spread over multiple domains and varied relationships help in building the intuition of manager. In Nature, threats cause adaptation, for example, fish stay fresh in a tank when threatened by sharks, African gazelle needs to run faster than next gazelle to survive from leopard, and, butterflies and moths have colors and textures that make them indistinguishable from a leaf or a tree bark. Similarly, threats provide a positive balance and are essential for healthy business because when threatened, the hidden resources get stirred.

Figure 16.24 A magazine article

Example 4: **Use mail-merge to submit your resume to three companies**

Solution 4:

⊙ Open blank document. < > <New>

⊙ **<Mailings> <Start Mail Merge> >Step by Step Mail Merge Wizard>.** A window opens on the right side of the screen. Now follow the six steps given below—

- **Select Document Type**—Select *Letters* (Figure 16.25)
- **Starting Document**—Select *use the current document.*
- **Select Recipients**—Select *Type a new list. Create.* (A window appears as in Figure 16.26. Enter the data).

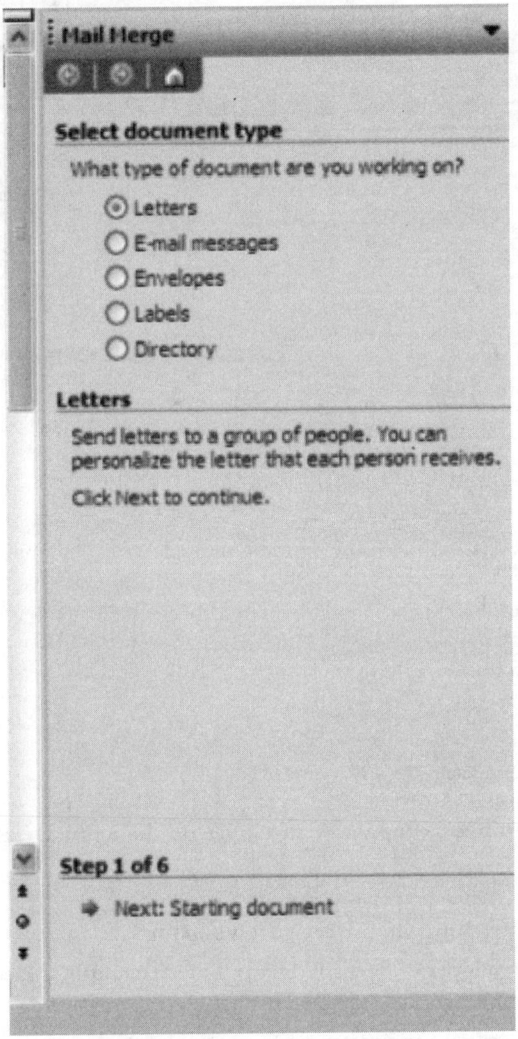

Figure 16.25 Starting mail merge

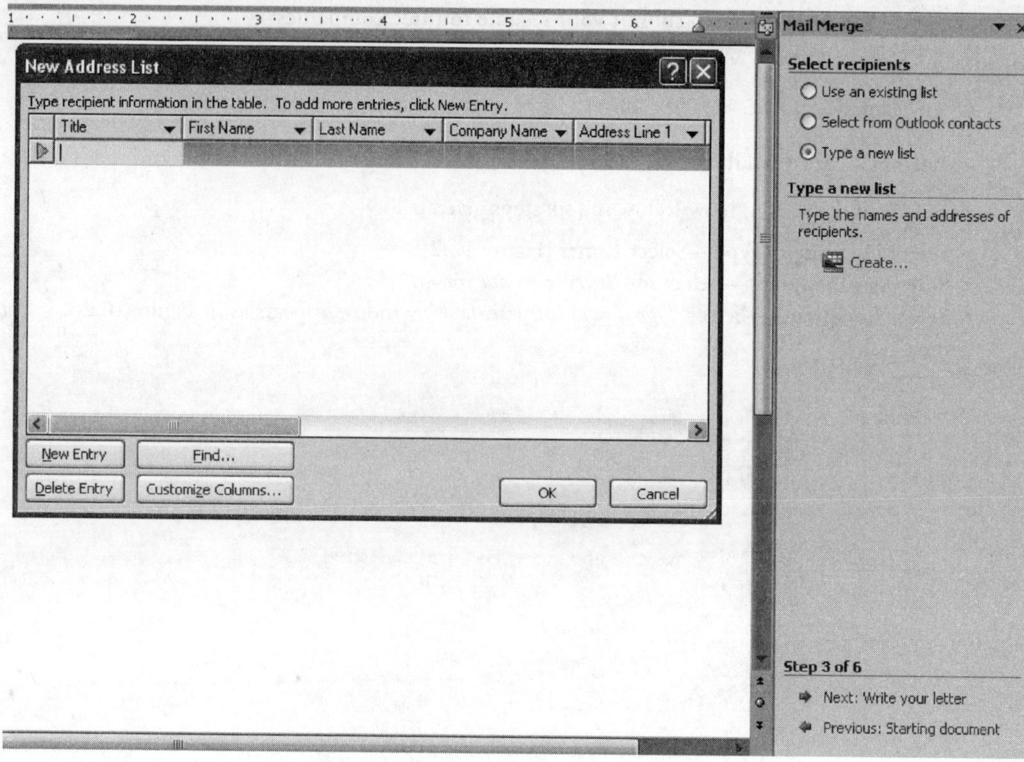

Figure 16.26 Creating new address list

- **Write Your letter**—Write your letter with address block, greetings etc, as shown in Figure 16.27.
- **Preview your letter**—Shows the letters merged with the mail addresses, as shown in Figure 16.28.
- **Complete the merge.** Will complete the merge.

Example 5: **Use macro to design letter head of your college**

Solution 5:

- Open blank document. <[Office button]> <New>
- <[Office button]> **<Word Options> <Popular> Check ☑ on the Show Developer tab in the Ribbon.**

  A Developer tab is displayed on the Ribbon

  ☑ Show Developer tab in the Ribbon ⓘ

- **Start recording. <Developer> <Record Macro>** Enter a name in **<Macro Name>**. Select the location to store in **<Store macro in>** <OK>. This will start the recording for the macro.
- Type the name of the college and insert the logo.

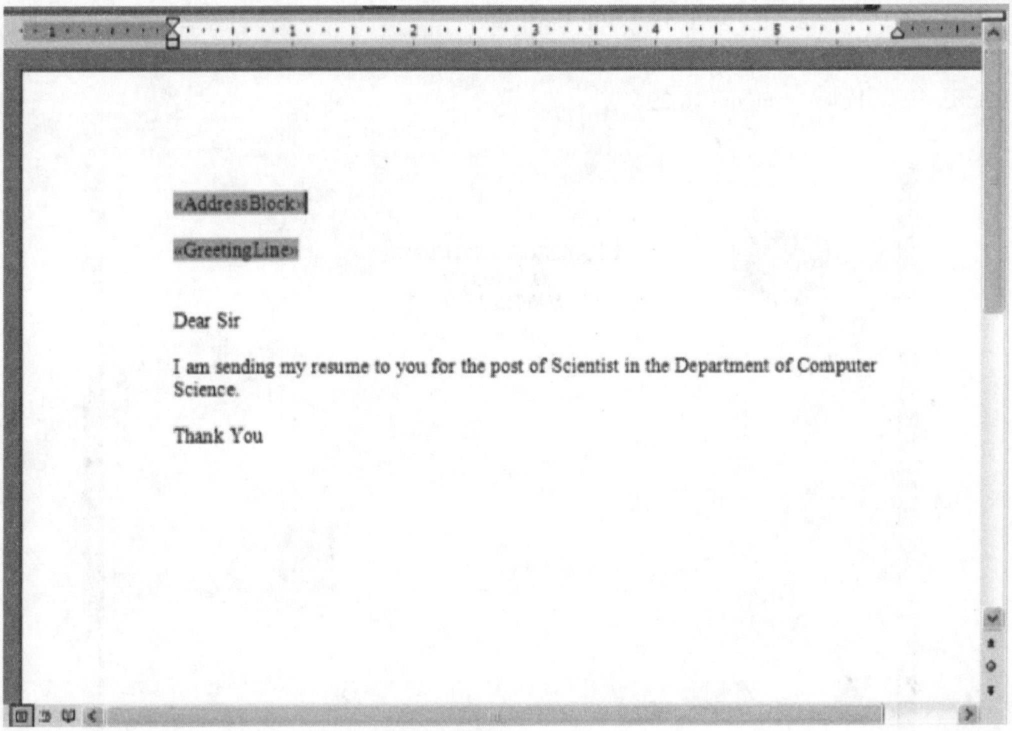

Figure 16.27 A mail letter

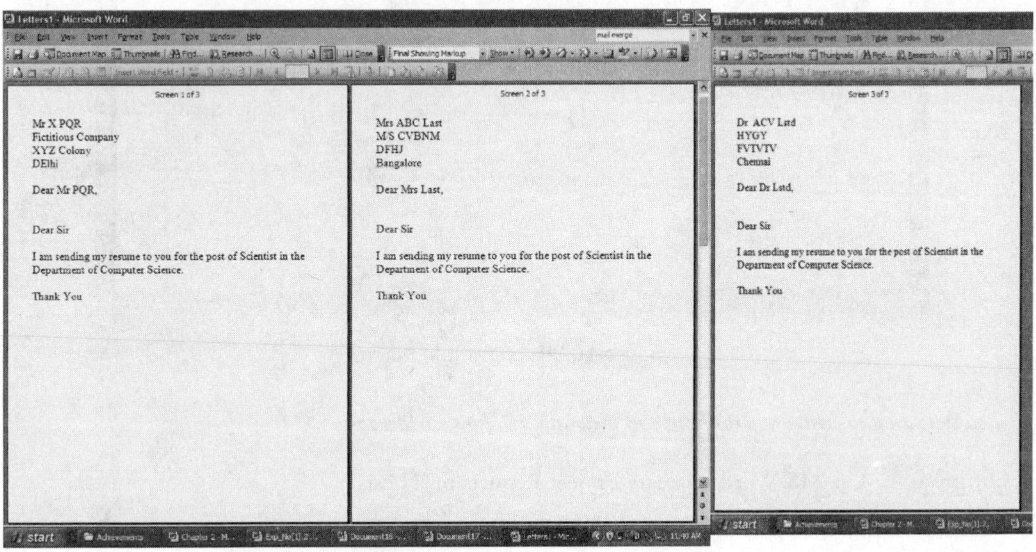

Figure 16.28 The merged mail

- ⊙ **Stop recording. <Developer> <Stop Recording>**
- ⊙ To run the macro. **<Developer> <Macros>**. Select your **<Macro name> <Run>**

A sample is shown in Figure 16.29.

Figure 16.29 A sample macro

PS: You can also create macros from the View tab <View> <Macro>

Example 6: **Use MS-Word to create Project Reports or Thesis**

Solution 6: A project Report or thesis has the following specific documentation requirements:

- Page settings (Size, No. of columns, Page numbers, header or footer etc.)
- Different styles for headings and sub-headings
- Table of Contents

- Figures and Tables
- Bibliography

While writing the report, care has to be taken about the following points:

- All figure headings are written using the same format.
- All table headings are written using the same format.
- The font style of the different headings and sub-headings should be consistent in the entire document.
- The table of contents should get updated with the update of the contents of the document
- References to the bibliography should get updated with the change in the bibliography.

The steps that must be followed while writing a project report or thesis are as follows:

- Open a blank document <File> <New>
- First create a *template* for the document; i.e. select the bullets and numbering and customize the various headings in terms of size, color, font style etc., the style to number the figures and tables etc. Then <Save As> <Word Template> to save the template.
- Use <References> <Insert Caption> to insert a bibliography. Use <References> <Cross-reference> to refer to the bibliography in the text. Updating the bibliography will automatically update the cross reference made to the bibliography. Similarly, to refer to a figure or table, use the cross-reference.
- After you have created the template, use the template and type-in your report or thesis.

EXERCISES

1. Design a "Thank You" card.
2. Design a "Seasons Greetings" card.
3. Design a "Birthday Invitation" card.
4. Design a "Get Well Soon" card.
5. Design a "Happy Birthday" card.
6. Design a poster inviting all students of your college to the Computer Festival.
7. Design a notice cum poster inviting all fresher for the fresher's party.
8. Design a notice cum poster inviting seniors for the farewell party.
9. Design a certificate that you receive at the end of the Semester for holding a position in the Computer Society.
10. Design your mark sheet.
11. Design the Time Table given to you at the start of the Semester without grid lines.
12. Prepare the list of practicals you shall do during the semester in an Index form.
13. Create a 5-page document. Use hyperlinks. Insert Bookmarks.
14. Prepare a notice giving you the schedule of your exams.
15. Use mail merge to print envelopes.
16. Convert Text to Table.
17. Create an organization chart of your Computer Society.
18. Create a web page having your own details using MS Word.
19. Open two documents in MS-Word and view them together.
20. Compare two documents using MS-Word.
21. Create thumbnails for your project.
22. Write 10 mathematics equations.
23. Use the Letter Wizard to write a letter to the principal asking for a two day leave.
24. Add addresses for five recipient of your letter in Q 23.
25. Use Macro to design the Computer Society Certificate.
26. Create a table to show the rate list of the Mother Diary Fruit and Vegetable Vendor. After you have created the table use the following - (1) Split the table to show the Vegetables and Fruits separately, (2) Split a Cell, and (3) Merge two cells.
27. Sort the Table created in Q 26 in decreasing order of rate list.
28. Insert a row in Table of Q 26, to write the Total of the "Rate" column. Find the total of all the rates.
29. Insert a column in the leftmost side of the table in Q 26 to include the S.No.

30. While printing the table in Q 26, hide the gridlines.
31. Convert the Table into a Text separating the Item name from the rate list by a hyphen "-" in Q 26.
32. Type name and addresses of 10 students separated by a comma. Now convert this text into a table. For example,

    Ashima, AkashDarshan Society
    Anirudh, Supreme Society
    Ajay, Ashiana Apartments

Some Extra Questions

1. Enter a list of 5 things you have to do this week. Number the list. Select the list again and turn on the bullet. Change the bullet symbol to any other character. Insert Date and time.
2. Check the spelling and grammar in an existing document. Use the "Replace All" option in Find and Replace to replace each instance of some word.
3. Create and print an envelope that includes your return address. Create a full page of return labels for yourself.
4. First type a one page document in double spacing. Apply the following to it:
   (a) Select the text and convert it into two columns. Make second column wider than the first and add a line between the columns.
   (b) Change the Page Orientation to Landscape.
5. Using Draw Table feature, insert a 7-column, 6-row table to create a calendar for the current month.
   (a) Enter the names of the days of the week in the first row of the table.
   (b) Centre the day names horizontally and vertically.
   (c) Change the font and font size as desired.
   (d) Insert a row at the top of the table.
   (e) Merge the cells in the row and enter the current month and year using a large font size.
   (f) Shade the row.
   (g) Enter and right-align the dates for the month in the appropriate cells of the table.
   (h) Change the outside border to a more decorative border. Identify two important dates in the calendar and shade them.
6. Create mailing labels to a select group of people from an existing data source file.
7. Create a form letter with fields to represent data in an existing data source file. Preview the merge to see that everything is correct. Merge to a new document. Save the data source file and your main document but discard the merge document.

The above questions can be made specific by including one or more of the following options:

- Font effects (Superscript, Subscript, Shadow etc.)
- Paragraph effects (Spacing 1.5 lines, Double Spacing, Indentation, Spacing Before and After a Heading)
- Enclose the Text in a Border
- Enclose the Page in a Border
- Select a Theme for a page
- Insert Bullets, Numbering, Outline numbering
- Display a page with two or three columns
- Add page Background effects (Color, Fill effects, Printed Watermark)
- Use built-in Styles and Formatting and show the formatting that has been applied
- Write the first letter of the document as big

  First letter. (Hint: Use Drop Cap)
- Insert Page Break, Date and Time, Symbols like £ Ω ½ © ™
- Include Salutation - Dear Madam: a comment
- Insert a Table of Content, Insert Cross-Reference (Used for creating referring to a location, Bibliography)
- Insert Caption (For Example "Table 1" on top side of a table
- Insert a Picture from File, ClipArt, and WordArt etc.
- Insert a diagram, a Text Box, a Bookmark, a comment, a hyperlink, a file
- Use Spelling and Grammar to check your document for spellings
- Convert your document into Arabic
- Find the number of pages, words, characters (with and without spaces), paragraphs and lines in your document (Hint: Use Word Count)
- Before typing your document, create a Template for your document headings and then start typing

Project: Create a document as follows:

- Open a New Blank document.
- Type the text of the document.
- Save the document in "Original.docx"
- The title should have the following Style
    - Font size—22
    - Font style—Arial Bold
    - Alignment—center
    - Font color—Dark Brown
- The text body should have the following Style
    - Font size—12
    - Font style—Times New Roman
    - Alignment—Justify
    - Font color—Black
- Insert an image from Clip Art. Wrap the text around the clip art as square tight
- Use bullets in the document with spacing 1.5 lines
- Set paper as size A4, Portrait. Set paper margin as Top - 1", Bottom - 1", Left - 1.5", Right - 1.05"
- Write the title of your document on the header of page. Write the page number and your name on the footer of page.
- Spell check the document.
- Save the document under a different filename - "revised.docx"
- Close the document

Exercise: First type the following lines. Then follow the instructions in each line and make changes to the text accordingly. For example,

Format this line as Bold, Italic, Underline, Times New Roman font face and 14pt font size.

<u>Format this line as Bold, Italic, Underline, Times New Roman font face and 14pt font size.</u>

1. Change the word 3rd so that it looks like 3rd.
2. Format this sentence so that the words, and not the spaces between the words, are underlined.
3. Change all of the text in this line to tOGGLE case.
4. Change the word C2H2SO4 so that it looks like $C_2H_2SO_4$.
5. Format this sentence to grow the font size and reduce the space between each letter by 1 point.
6. Format this line so that it is Bold, font size 28.
7. Enter this line of text. This wrd is miss spelt. Use spell check to correct spelling error.
8. Format this line to change it to a 24-point font of your choice. Copy this line three times. Underline two of the copies, using a different underline style for each.

Exercise: Follow the instructions in the following text to format the paragraphs. It also shows how the paragraphs will look after the formatting.

This is the start of a new paragraph.
Format this paragraph so that it is centre aligned. Change the line spacing to 1.5. Now add 12 points of blank space before the paragraph and 6 points of blank space after this paragraph. Adjust the paragraph so that the right side is indented by 0.3" and the left side is indented by 0.6". The first line should be indented by 0.5". This is the end of this paragraph.
It looks like the following example.

This is the start of a new paragraph.

Format this paragraph so that it is centre aligned. Change the line spacing to 1.5. Now add 12 points of blank space before the paragraph and 6 points of blank space after this paragraph. Adjust the paragraph so that the right side is indented by 0.3" and the left side is indented by 0.6". The first line should be indented by 0.5". This is the end of this paragraph.

It looks like the following example.

MS-EXCEL 2007

17

Contents

- Introduction
- Basics of spreadsheet
- Start MS-Excel
- MS-Excel screen and its components—Office logo button, quick access toolbar, ribbon, tabs, group, status bar, scroll bar, worksheet tab, row, column headings, active cell, formula bar, name box
- Office button—New, open, save, save As, print, prepare, send, publish, close
- Ribbon—Home, insert, page layout, formulas, data, review, view, add-ins
  - Home tab—Clipboard, font, alignment, number, styles, cells, editing
  - Insert tab—Tables, illustrations, charts, links, text
  - Page layout tab—Themes, page setup, scale to fit, sheet options, arrange
  - Formulas tab—Function library, defined names, formula auditing, calculation
  - Data tab—Get external data, connections, sort and filter, data tools, outline
  - Review tab—Proofing, comments, changes
  - View tab—Workbook views, show/hide, zoom, window, macros
  - Help
- Solved examples—Year-wise salesman sales, salary calculation, mark sheet calculation

Why this chapter

An electronic spreadsheet is used for analyzing, sharing and managing information for accounting purposes, performing mathematical calculations, budgeting, billing, report generation etc. Tools are included in the spreadsheet software to facilitate the creation of charts, graphs, data analysis etc. MS-Excel is commonly used electronic spreadsheet software. The purpose of this chapter is to introduce you to MS-Excel.

17.1 INTRODUCTION

A spreadsheet is a matrix of rows and columns, similar to an accounting notebook (ledger). A spreadsheet program is primarily used for mathematical calculations. A spreadsheet program is often used to prepare budgets, financial projections, billing, and other reports arranged in rows and columns. An electronic spreadsheet provides more flexibility, speed, and accuracy in comparison to a manually maintained spreadsheet. For example, if you change the numbers in a spreadsheet, you do not have to perform the calculations again. The spreadsheet does it for you. The spreadsheet program also provides tools for creating graphs, inserting pictures and chart, analyzing the data etc.

The spreadsheet software from different technology vendors are available for creation of spreadsheets. Apple Numbers, Microsoft Excel (MS-Excel), Corel Quattro Pro, and Lotus 1-2-3 are some of the spreadsheet software available in the market. Lotus 1-2-3 was the leading software when DOS was the predominant operating system. Several open-source spreadsheet software, like, Sun's OpenOffice.org Calc, Google Docs, KSpread, and Gnumeric are also available. IBM Lotus Symphony is freeware spreadsheet software.

MS-Excel is the most commonly known spreadsheet software. It is part of the MS-Office suite, and runs on Microsoft Windows, and Mac OS X operating systems. In addition to MS-Excel, MS-Office suite contains other software like MS-Word, MS-PowerPoint and MS-Access. MS-Excel is GUI-based software. MS-Excel includes tools for analyzing, managing, and sharing information, which helps during the decision making process. The spreadsheet in MS-Excel may contain charts, text, and other objects. Some of the important features of MS-Excel are as follows:

- It allows organization, tabulation, search, and exploration of data of large sizes.
- Based on the values entered in different cells in the spreadsheet, formulas can be defined, which automatically perform calculations.
- It allows the design of professionally looking charts with 3-D effects, shadowing, and transparency.
- The tables can be easily created, formatted, expanded, and referred to within formulas.
- The data can be filtered and sorted.
- PivotTable views enable you to quickly re-orient your data to help you answer multiple questions.
- Formatting of spreadsheet allows changing the font size, font color, and font style.
- A function library consists of various function groups like financial, logical, math & trignometry etc. from which you can apply long and complex formulas.
- Conditional formatting can be applied to discover patterns and to highlight trends in the data.

This chapter discusses the using of the MS-Excel software in detail. There are many versions of the MS-Excel software. Here, we will discuss the MS-Excel 2007.

> In this chapter, we use the following terminology while working with the mouse:
>
> - **Pointer** —a mouse pointer
> - **Click**—press left button of mouse once
> - **Double Click**—press left button of mouse twice
> - **Select** —move the pointer of mouse and keep the left button of the mouse pressed over the area that you want to select. The selected area will appear in a dark background.
> - **Quick Menu**—Right click (press right button of mouse once) to get a quick menu.
>
> *The commands are enclosed in braces <Command> to represent the command to be clicked.*

17.2 START MS-EXCEL

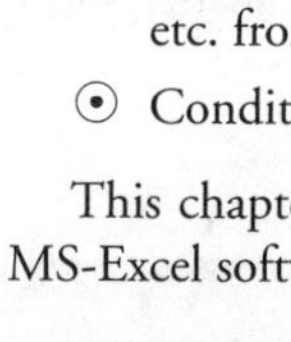

Figure 17.1 MS-Excel icon

The MS-Excel software for the Windows operating system should be installed on the computer. MS-Excel is a fully menu-driven software, and the commands are available as icons in various Tabs, and Groups. While working in MS-Excel, using a mouse makes working on MS-Excel simpler although one can work to some extent through the keyboard also.

To start using the MS-Excel software, *any one* of the following steps needs to be performed:

- If a shortcut key to MS-Excel is available as an icon on the Desktop, as shown in Figure 17.1, then **double-click** the icon, or

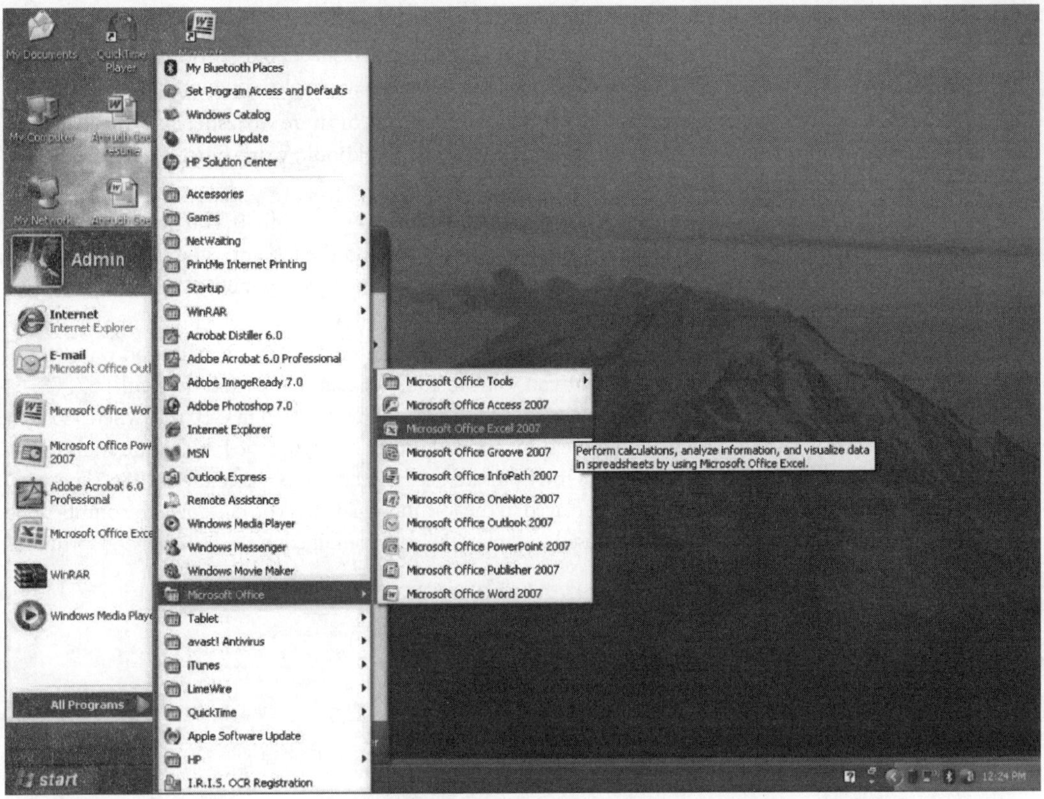

Figure 17.2 Start MS-Excel

- **<Start> <All Programs> <Microsoft Office> <Microsoft Office Excel 2007>**. (Figure 17.2)

17.3 BASICS OF SPREADSHEET

MS-Excel 2007 allows creation of spreadsheets. In this section, we will discuss the basics of spreadsheet (Figure 17.3).

- A *spreadsheet* is an electronic document that stores various types of data. There are vertical columns and horizontal rows.
- The intersection of each row and column is called a *cell*. A cell is named with the column letter first and then the row number. For example, cell A1, A2, B1, B3 etc. A cell is an individual container for data (like a box). A cell may hold data of the following types:
  - Numbers (constants),
  - Formulas (mathematical equations), and
  - Text (labels).

- A cell can be used in calculations of data within the spreadsheet.
- An array of cells is called a *sheet or worksheet.* A spreadsheet or worksheet holds information presented in tabular row and column format with text that labels the data. They can also contain graphics and charts.
- A *workbook* is a Microsoft Office document that contains one or more worksheets. A worksheet is a single document inside a workbook. However, the terms workbook, worksheet, sheet, and spreadsheet are often used interchangeably.
- Each new workbook created in Excel has three worksheets by default. If you want to rename a worksheet, right click on the tab <Rename>, or double click on the tab and type the new name for it. User can add more worksheets or delete some of them, as per requirements.
- A formula is an equation that calculates the value to be displayed. A formula when used in a worksheet, must begin with an equal to (=) sign. When using a formula, do not type the number you want to add, but the reference to the cells whose content you want to add. For example, to add the marks 67, 78, 66, 90, 85, and insert the result in C10 cell, you put the formula =SUM(C5:C9) in C10 cell, where C5 is the cell from where we want to start finding the sum, and C9 is the cell having the last data we want to add. After writing the formula, when you press the Enter key, cell C10 displays the result i.e. 386. The actual formula contained in the cell C10, gets displayed in the formula bar, when you click over the number 386. It is advisable to reference the cell as opposed to typing the data contained in the cell, into the formulas.

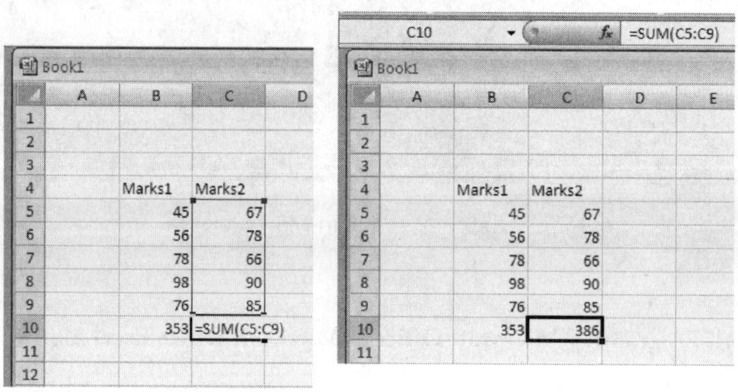

17.4 MS-EXCEL SCREEN AND ITS COMPONENTS

The user interface of the MS-Excel makes it easy to use Excel 2007. In contrast to the previous versions of MS-Excel, the new user-interface has an improved navigation system consisting of tabs which further consist of group of commands. The main screen is shown in Figure 17.3. At the top side of the screen is the Ribbon. Below the Ribbon are the Name box and the Formula box. There is a scroll bar, and at the lower side of the screen there are the Worksheet tabs and the Status Bar. The work area of the screen consists of rows and columns. The orientation of the Excel 2007 layout and its general features are described as follows:

- The **Office Logo button** at the top left corner contains many commands for the document such as, *New, Open, Save, Save As, Print,* and *Close*. This button also has a list of the recent documents. Some of these commands include an expandable menu to provide additional options. This Office Logo button replaces the File menu in the earlier versions of MS-Office.

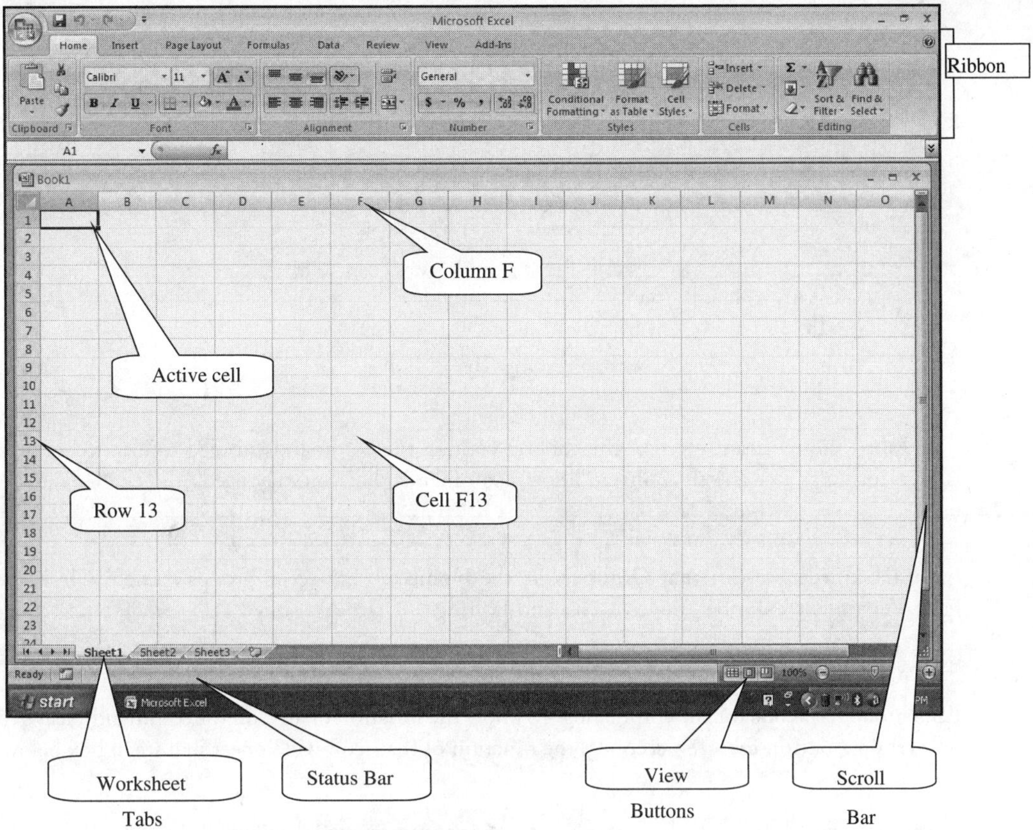

Figure 17.3 MS-Excel screen

- The **Quick Access Toolbar**  is to the right of the Office Logo button. It contains shortcuts for the commonly used commands, like, Save , Undo  (reverses the last change) and Repeat  (repeats the last action). The icons for the commands that the user want to get displayed on the toolbar can be selected from the 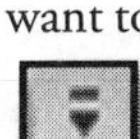 *Customize Quick Access Toolbar*

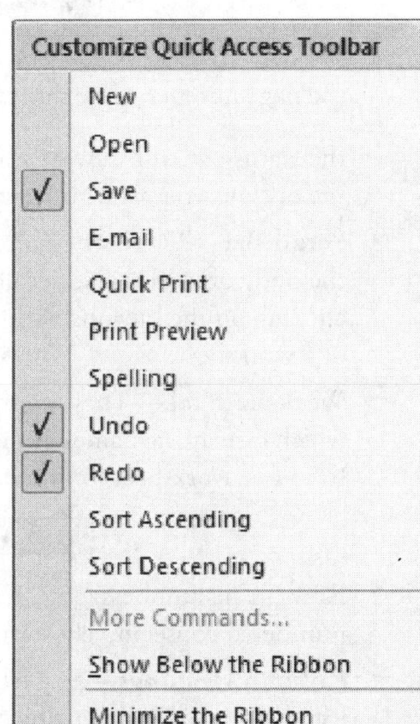

- The **Ribbon** consists of a panel of commands which are organized into a set of tabs (Figure 17.4). The layout of the Ribbon in MS-Excel is same as that of the Ribbon in MS-Word. Within Tabs are Groups, which are designated by the names located on the bottom of the Ribbon. Each group has icons for the associated command. The Ribbon (Tabs, Groups, and Icons) replaces the traditional toolbars and menus of earlier versions of MS-Excel.

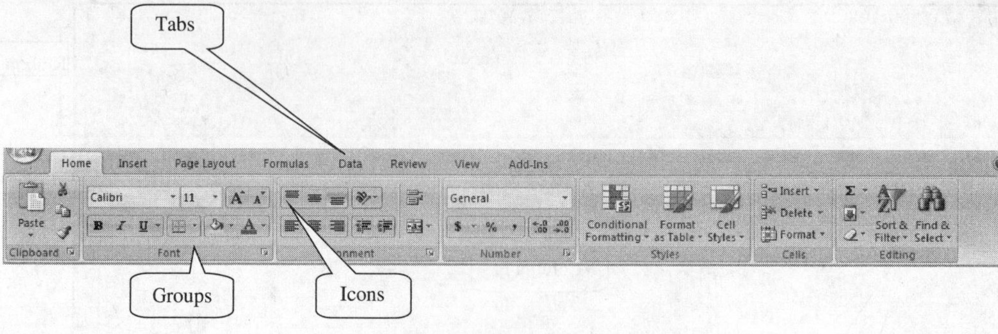

Figure 17.4 The ribbon

- The **Tabs** (Home, Insert etc.) on the Ribbon contain the commands needed to insert data, page layout, formulas etc. as well as any additional commands that you may need.

- Each Tab consists of different **Groups**, like the Home tab has seven groups namely, Clipboard, Font, Alignment, Number, Styles, Cells, and Editing.

- Each group has **icons** for the commands. To know the function of an icon (or command), leave the pointer on a button for a few seconds, the function of that icon will appear in a small box below the pointer. For  example, leaving the icon on  displays "Bold (Ctrl+B)".
- **Status Bar**—It displays information about the currently active worksheet. The information includes the page number, view shortcuts, zoom slider  etc. Right-click on the status bar will show you the Customize Status bar (Figure 17.5) pop-up menu. You can select the options you want to view on the status bar.
- **Scroll Bar**—There are two scroll bars—horizontal and vertical. They help to scroll the content or the body of worksheet. Scrolling is done by moving the elevator button along the scroll bar, or by clicking on the buttons with the arrow marked on them to move up and down, and left and right of a worksheet.
- **Worksheet Tab**—They are the tabs located at the bottom of  each worksheet in the workbook, which display the names of the sheets. A button is provided to insert a new worksheet. You can move from one worksheet to other using the arrow keys or by clicking on the appropriate worksheet tab.

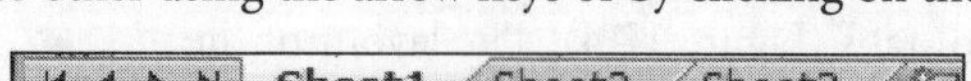

- **Row**—The numbers (1, 2, 3 ...) that appear on the left side of the worksheet window. The rows are numbered consecutively starting from 1 to 1,048,576 (approx. 1 million rows).
- **Column Headings**—The letters that appear along the top of the worksheet window. Columns are listed alphabetically starting from A to XFD i.e.16,384, (approx. 16,000 columns).

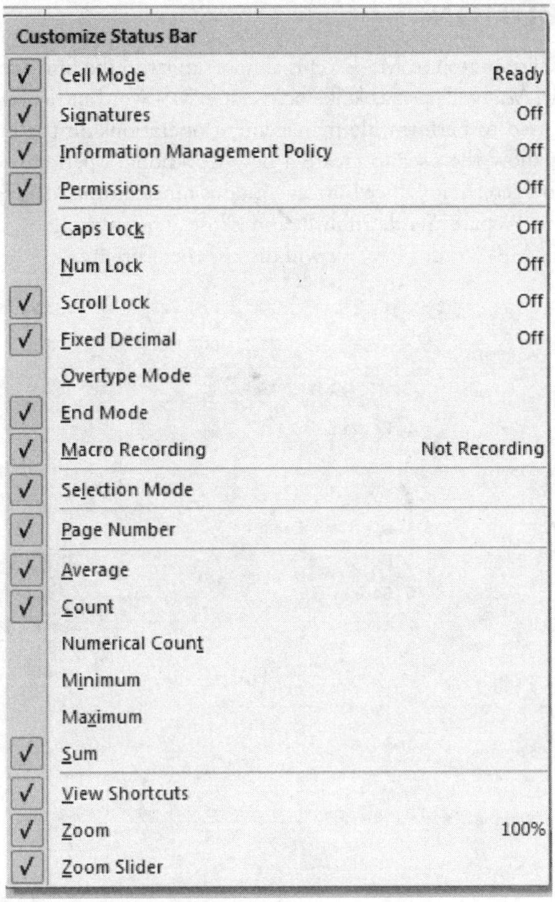

Figure 17.5 Customize status bar

- **Active Cell**—The intersection of a row and column is called a cell. The cell in which you are currently working is the active cell. A dark border outlining the cell identifies the active cell.
- **Formula Bar**—It is located beneath the Ribbon. Formula bar is used to enter and edit worksheet data. As you type or edit the data, the changes appear in the Formula Bar. When you click the mouse in the formula bar, an X and a check mark appear. You can click the check icon to confirm and complete editing, or the X to abandon editing.

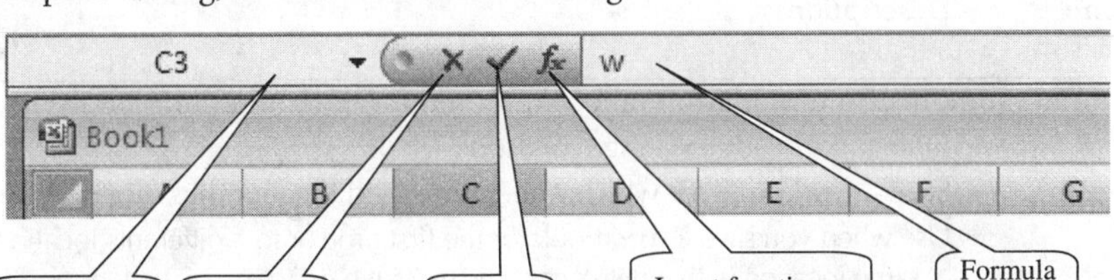

- **Name Box**—It displays the cell reference, or column and row location, of the active cell in the workbook window.

17.5 THE OFFICE BUTTON

The functionality of the Office button in MS-Excel is almost similar to the functionality provided in the MS-Word software. For example, *New* will open a blank document in MS-Word and a blank Workbook in MS-Excel.

The Office Button is used to perform file management operations on the file (i.e. the workbook). It contains commands that allow the user to create a new workbook, open an existing workbook, save a workbook, print a workbook etc. The Office button contains nine commands (Figure 17.6), namely, New, Open, Save, Save As, Print, Prepare, Send, Publish, and Close. The working of these commands is almost similar to their working in MS-Word. Here, we will discuss them briefly.

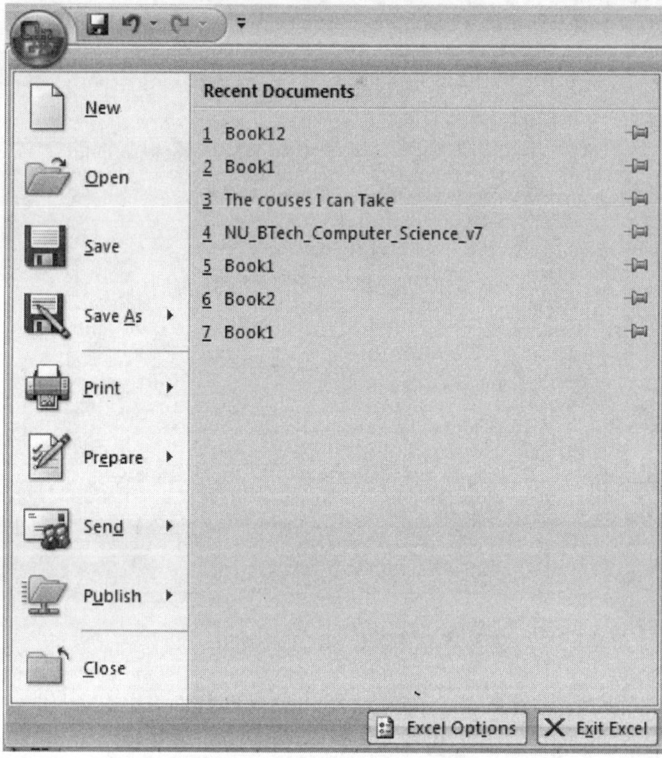

Figure 17.6 The office button commands

Table 17.1 briefly describes the different commands available in the Office Button.

Office Button Commands	**Description**
New	Create a new blank workbook.
Open	Open an already existing workbook.
Save	Save a workbook for which a file name and location has already been specified.
Save As	Use when you save a workbook for the first time or to a differents location, or at the same location with a different name or with a new type of work book. Here, you specify the filename for the workbook, the location where the workbook is to be stored, and the save type of the workbook. You can also save the workbook as a Excel Workbook, Excel Binary Workbook, Excel 97-2003 workbook etc. (Figure 17.7).

(Continued)

Office Button Commands	Description
Print	Print, Quick Print, and Print Preview the workbook. You can set properties like print quality, paper type etc. and print the active sheet or the entire workbook. Preview to see how the workbook will look after printing.
Prepare	Prepare the workbook for distribution. View workbook properties, encrypt document, restrict permissions etc.
Send	Send a copy of the workbook to e-mail or to Internet Fax.
Publish	Distribute the workbook to other people—Save for Excel services, share the workbook by saving it to a document management server, or create a new site for the workbook. (Figure 17.8).
Close	Close an open workbook.

Table 17.1 *Office button commands description*

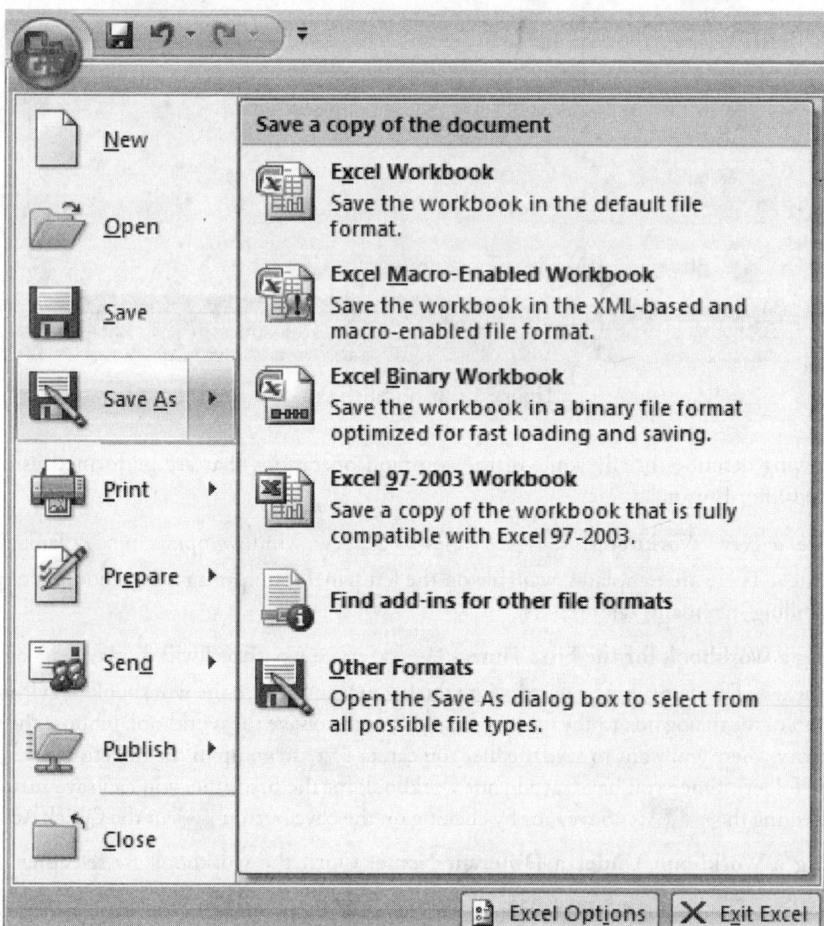

Figure 17.7 Save as option

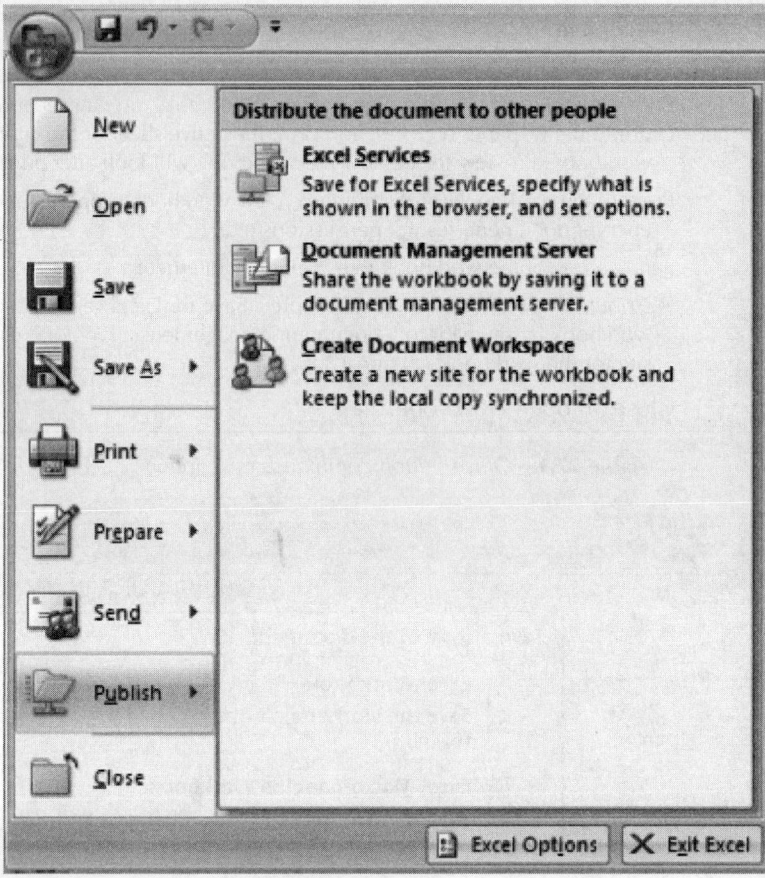

Figure 17.8 Publish option

The following describes briefly some of the common operations that are performed using the commands of the Office Button.

- **Create a New Workbook:** < > <**New**>. A new window opens up. <Blank Workbook> <Create>. There are templates available on the left panel for creating a workbook of a specific type (e.g. billing statement, sales report).
- **Saving a Workbook for the First Time:** < > <Save As>. Excel will display a dialog box. In the field next to File name, type a name with which you want to save the workbook. Navigate in the top portion of the dialog box to the folder where you want to save the workbook (choose the appropriate directory where you want to save the file. You can use to go up in the directory, Use to create a new folder). Once you have saved your workbook for the first time, you can save further revisions by selecting the < > <**Save**>, or by clicking on the Save button in the Quick Access Toolbar.
- **Saving a Workbook Under a Different Name:** Open the workbook by selecting the < > <**Open**>. Next, < > <**Save As**>. A dialog box will appear. Navigate to the folder where you want to save the workbook and type in a new name for the workbook. Select the Save button. You now have two copies of the workbook, one with the original name, another with a new name.

⊙ **Crash Protection:** < > **<Save As> <Tools><Save Options>**. Select the boxes for *Save Auto Recover* Information every <enter the number of minutes>. Reset the Minutes from 10 to 1. MS-Excel would be able to recover a file one minute old.

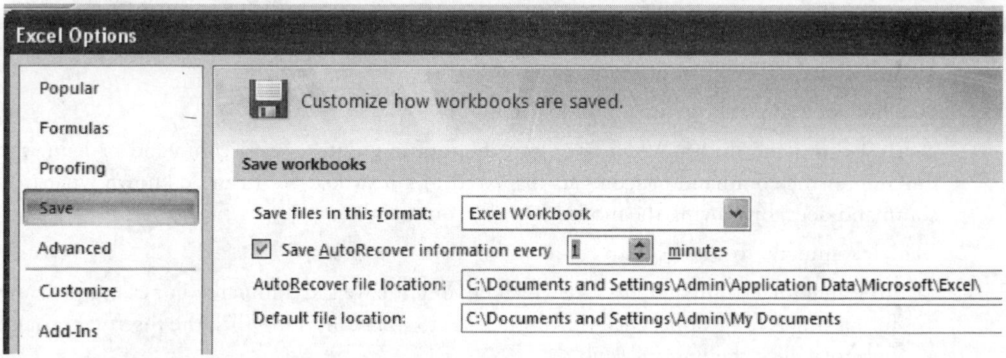

⊙ **To Print:** < > **<Print>**. Make settings like number of copies you want to print. (Figure 17.9). From the Print dialog box you can make further settings like—*Print What*, where you select what you want to print:

- Active worksheet
- Entire workbook; or
- The selection

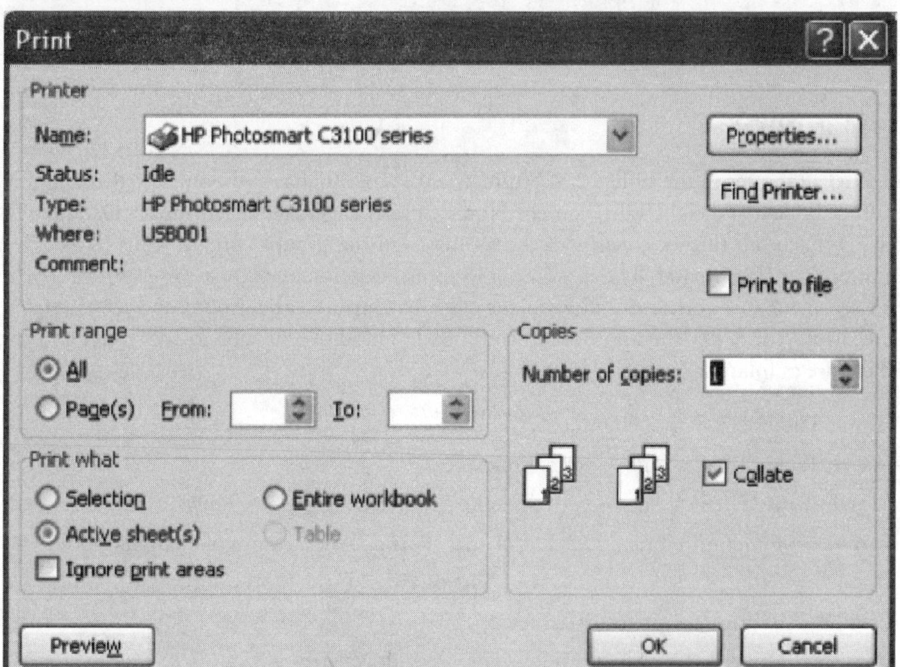

Figure 17.9 Print dialog box

Quick Tips—How to Learn MS-Excel

When working with MS-Excel, all you need to know is the following:

- **What a command does?**
- **When you want to perform a particular action, which command to use?**
- **How to use a command?**

Let's see how we can go about learning MS-Excel.

(1) What a command does—When you keep the mouse pointer over a command or icon, the function of the command or icon gets displayed in a text box. So it can be known what that command does, by moving the mouse over the command.

(2) Which command to use—

a. To search for a command, first see which tab might have the command. For example, if any formatting is to be done, click the Home Tab; to insert anything click the Insert tab; to use Formula, click the Formulas tab.

b. It is possible to find the required group and command, most of the time. The commands that have similar uses are grouped together in the same group in Excel 2007.

(3) Once the command is known, then we need to know how to use the command.

a. For most of the commands, first place the cursor in the worksheet at the position where the action is to happen, or, select the object on which you want the action to happen (for example formatting commands). Next, click on the command. The command gets executed.

b. In some commands, there are a set of steps to use the command.

17.6 THE RIBBON

Like the other programs in the Office 2007 suite, MS-Excel 2007 has a ribbon. The Ribbon of MS-Excel has the Office button and eight Tabs, namely, Home, Insert, Page Layout, Formulas, Data, Review, View, and Add-Ins. Each tab further consists of the groups, and the groups contain icons. Icons are pictorial representations for a command. The tabs in the Ribbon are self-explanatory; for example, if you want to do a page setup for the worksheet, click on the Page Layout tab. The groups and icons related to *Page Layout* are displayed. Select the appropriate command. The different tabs in MS-Excel and the groups within them are as follows:

- **Home**: Clipboard, Font, Alignment, Number, Styles, Cells, Editing
- **Insert:** Tables, Illustrations, Charts, Links, Text
- **Page Layout**: Themes, Page Setup, Scale to Fit, Sheet Options, Arrange
- **Formulas**: Function Library, Defined Names, Formula Auditing, Calculation
- **Data**: Get External Data, Connections, Sort & Filter, Data Tools, Outline
- **Review**: Proofing, Comments, Changes
- **View**: Workbook Views, Show/Hide, Zoom, Window, Macros

The **Add-Ins Tab** contains supplementary functionality that adds custom commands and specialized features to MS-Excel.

Selecting a command	
Ways to select a command	**Using a command**
Click on a Tab + *Click on a Icon*	Click on any of the Tabs like Home, Insert etc. From the displayed icons, click on the icon you want to use.
Shortcut key *Ctrl + letter*	Some commands have shortcuts where you can press the **Ctrl** key and a **certain letter**. Some commonly used shortcuts are—
	• Paste: CTRL + V •Copy: CTRL + C •Undo: CTRL + Z •New document: CTRL + N •Open document: CTRL + O •Print document: CTRL + P

The commands in the Ribbon have various symbols associated with them, as shown in Figure 17.10. These symbols are interpreted as follows:

Figure 17.10 Command symbols

- **Simple Command**—The command start executing when it is clicked.
- **Command Followed by Arrow**—Clicking on the arrow ▾ displays more options for the command.
- **Faded Command**—A faded command means that it is not available currently.
- **Group Dialog Box**—Clicking on this ⧉ symbol displays the dialog box for the group.

The following sub-sections describe the different tabs in detail.

Working with MS-Excel 2007

- **Live Preview** applies temporary formatting on the selected data or text when the mouse moves over any of the formatting buttons. This allows the preview of, how the text will appear with this formatting. The temporary formatting is removed if the mouse pointer is moved away from the button.
- **Mini Toolbar** is a floating toolbar that pops up whenever a text is selected or right-clicked. It provides easy access to the most commonly used formatting commands such as Bold, Italics, Font, Font size, Font color.
- **File Format** for the documents created in Excel 2007 is ***xlsx.*** (For earlier versions it was *.xls*)

17.6.1 The Home Tab

The Home Tab contains commands that are frequently used in an Excel worksheet. It contains commands for formatting of text and numbers, and text alignment. The Home Tab is also used for editing the content of sheet like sort and filter, find and select, and, to perform clipboard operations such as cut, copy, and paste on the sheet. Figure 17.11 shows the Home Tab.

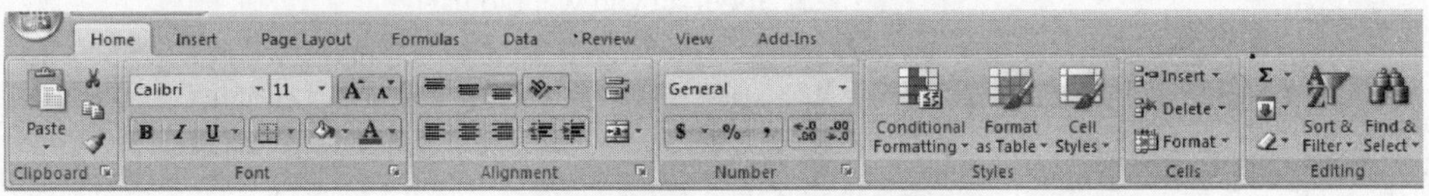

Figure 17.11 The home tab

There are seven groups within this tab, namely, Clipboard, Font, Alignment, Number, Styles, Cells, and Editing.

- The *Clipboard* group contains the cut, copy, and paste commands. The Format Painter is also present here. The Clipboard commands are used in the same manner as you use the MS-Word Clipboard commands.
- *Font* group commands allow change of the Font—font face, style, size, and color. These options can be changed before or after typing the text. The text whose font needs to be changed should be selected and then with the font commands in the Ribbon, or by menu obtained after right-click, the font can be changed.
- *Alignment* group is used to change alignment of the text in the cells—vertical and horizontal alignment, indentation, wrap the text, shrink it to fit within the cell, and merge multiple cells.
- *Number* group contains commands for number formatting e.g. Number, Date, accounting, decimals, comma style and percentage.
- The *Styles* group can be used to specify conditional formatting by defining formatting rules, convert a range of cells into a table by selecting a pre-defined Table Style, or, format a selected cell by selecting one of the built-in formatting styles.
- *Cells* allow the user to insert, delete or format the cells, and also whole columns, rows or sheets. Formatting includes renaming, hiding or protecting.
- *Editing* group contains commands to display the sum of selected cells, copy a pattern, clear the data, formats, and comments from a cell, sort and filter, or find and select specific contents within the workbook.

Table 17.2 gives the commands in the different groups (*in left to right order*) of the Home Tab along with a brief explanation.

Home Tab Groups		**Description**
Clipboard		• *Paste* the cut or copied items in Clipboard at the location where cursor is pointing right now (Paste Special—To paste in a particular format. Paste as Hyperlink—Used with copy to paste the copied items as a hyperlink.) • *Cut* removes the selected item from the sheet and pastes it onto a new place, where the cursor is pointing by using the *paste* command.

(Continued)

Home Tab Groups	Description
	• *Copy* copies the selected item and puts it on the Clipboard. • *Format painter* copies formatting from one place and applies it to another (To apply same formatting to many places, double-click the format painter button.)
Font	 • Change font face, change font size. • Increase font size, Decrease font size. • *Bold, Italics, Underline* • Apply *borders* to the currently selected cell. • *Color the background* of the selected cells. • Change the *font color.* • Click on the arrow in the bottom right corner of font to see the *Format Cells* dialog box.
Alignment	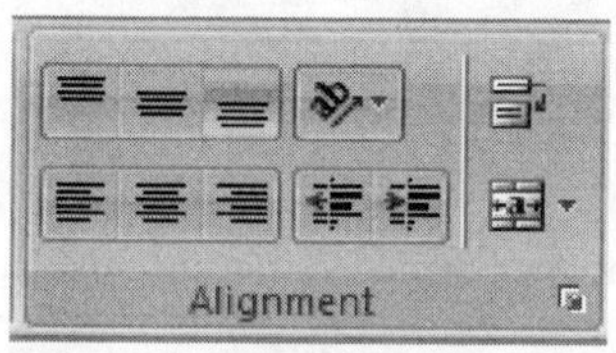 • Align text to the top, middle or bottom of the cell. • Change the text orientation within a cell for placing a label above a column. • Left align, center, or right align for horizontal alignment in a cell. • Increase, or decrease, the amount of indentation within a cell. • Wrap the text to make all content within a cell visible by displaying it on multiple lines. • Merge or unmerge the selected cells together and center the content of the cell. • Click on the arrow in the bottom right corner of Alignment to see the *Format Cells* dialog box.
Number	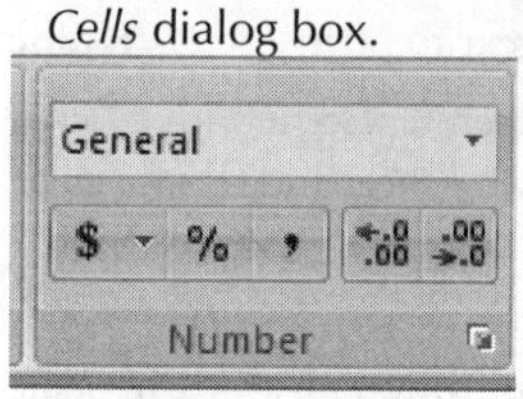 • Choose how a value in a cell is displayed—as currency, percentage, short date etc. It shows the most commonly used formats with a link to more formats. • Format the cell content to convert a number to a currency, percent, or decimal. Quick styles allows to choose a visual style for the shape or line • Increase or decrease the number of zeroes after the decimal (degree of precision) • Click on the arrow in the bottom right corner of Number to see the *Format Cells* dialog box
Styles	 • *Conditional formatting* highlights interesting cells, emphasize unusual values, and visualize data using data Bars, color scales, and icon sets • Format a range of cells and convert the range to a table by selecting a pre-defined table style • *Cell Styles* are pre-defined styles available to quickly format a cell

(*Continued*)

Home Tab Groups	Description
Cells	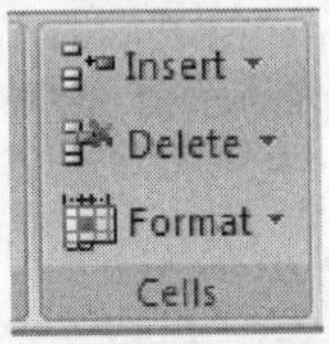 • *Insert* cells, rows, or columns into a worksheet, or insert additional worksheets into a workbook • *Delete* rows or columns • *Format* the cell—change row height or column width, change visibility, protect or hide cells
Editing	 • *Auto Sum* displays the sum of selected cells directly after the selected cells • Fills a pattern into one or more adjacent cells • *Clear* deletes everything from a cell, or remove formatting, contents, or comments • *Sort & Filter* arranges data for easy analysis (data can be sorted in ascending or descending order, or filter out specific values) • *Find & Select* (or replace) specific text, formatting or type of information within the workbook

Table 17.2 *Home tab commands description*

Here, we describe briefly some of the operations that are performed using the commands of the Home Tab.

- **Move Text:** Select and highlight the section you want to move <**Home**><**Clipboard**>< 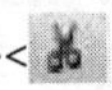 >. Move the cursor to the place you would like the text to be inserted <**Home**><**Clipboard**> <  >.
- **Copy Text:** Select and highlight the section you want to copy <**Home**><**Clipboard**><  >. Move the cursor to the place you want the copied text to be inserted <**Home**><**Clipboard**><  >
- **Find and Replace**: This is used to find a text and then replace it with a new one. This option is useful if you want to find a text at multiple places in the worksheet and replace all of them with a new one.

17.6.2 The Insert Tab

The Insert Tab contains commands for inserting objects of different kinds in a sheet. The commands in this tab are used to add illustrations, tables, links, text, and charts in a worksheet. Figure 17.12 shows the Insert Tab.

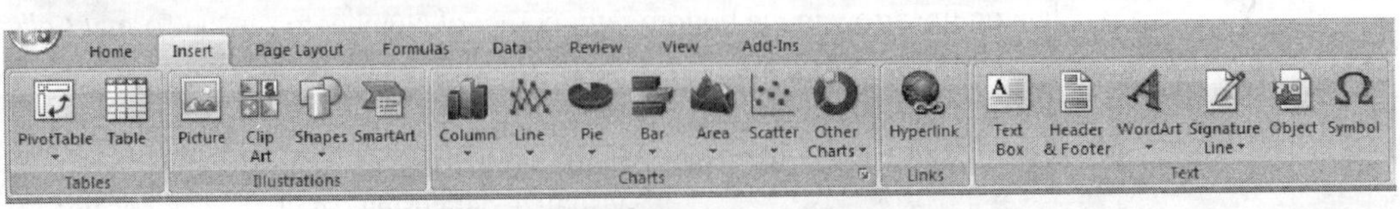

Figure 17.12 The insert tab

There are five groups within this tab, namely, Tables, Illustrations, Charts, Links, and Text.

- *Tables* are used to define a range of cells as a table for easy filtering and sorting, and create a pivot table or pivot chart to arrange and summarize data.

- *Illustrations* group allows insertion of pictures, clip art, shapes, and smart art.
- The *Charts* group helps to display data in a visual manner. It is used to insert different types of charts such as bar charts and pie charts.
- The *Links* group is used to insert a hyperlink to a place in the same workbook or an external one.
- The *Text* group contains commands to insert a Text Box, Word Art, Symbol, Digital Signature and Header And Footer.

> Some of the Tabs appear only when you use them; like Picture Tools tab, Drawing Tools Tab, Table Tools Tab, and Chart Tools Tab

Table 17.3 gives the commands in the different groups of the Insert Tab along with a brief explanation.

Insert Tab Groups	**Description**
Tables	 • Summarize data using a *pivot table* or pivot chart. *Pivot table* makes it easy to arrange and summarize complicated data and drill down on details. When a Pivot Table is inserted, a Pivot Table Tools Tab opens (Figure 17.13) • Create a *table* to manage and analyze related data. Tables make it easy to sort, filter and format data within a sheet. When a table is drawn, a Table Tool Design Tab (Figure 17.14) opens, which allows you to select Table Style options, Table Styles, external table data etc.
Illustrations	 • Insert picture from a file. When a picture is inserted, a Picture Tool Format Tab opens (Figure 17.15) which contains commands to format the picture. • Insert clipart into the document (sounds, movies, drawings) • Insert readymade shapes (lines, arrows, flowchart symbols etc.) into the document. A Drawing Tools Format Tab (Figure 17.16) opens. • Insert a smart art graphics. A Smart Art Tools Format tab opens.
Charts	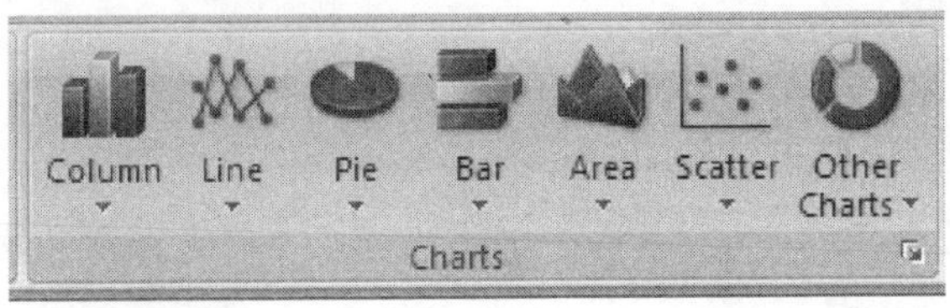 • Insert a column chart, line chart, pie chart, bar chart, area chart, scatter chart, or a chart of any other kind. A chart Tools design (Figure 17.17), layout and format tab opens for use.
Links	 • Insert a hyperlink to a web page, a picture, an email address or a program

(Continued)

Insert Tab Groups	Description
Text	 • Insert a text box that can be positioned anywhere on a page. • Edit the header and footer to the sheet. You can insert the page number, date and time, sheet name, picture etc. A Header & Footer Tools Design Tab (Figure 17.18) opens up. • Insert decorative text in the document • Insert signature line that specifies the individual who must sign • Insert an embedded object. • Insert symbols that are part of the keyboard into the document. When you click on *Symbol*, a symbol table pops up. You can select the symbol you want to insert.

Table 17.3 *Insert tab commands description*

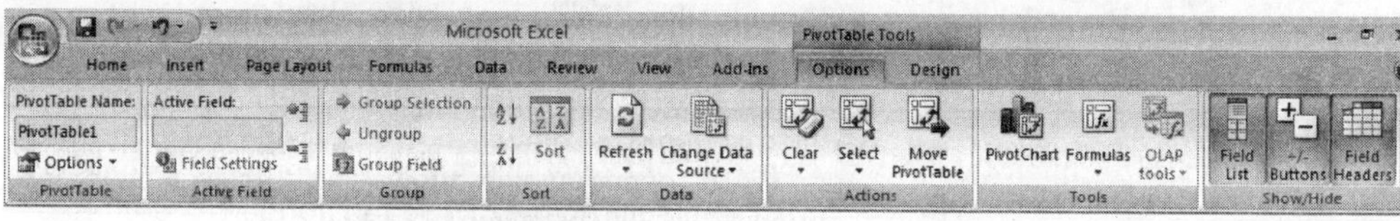

Figure 17.13 Pivot table tools options tab

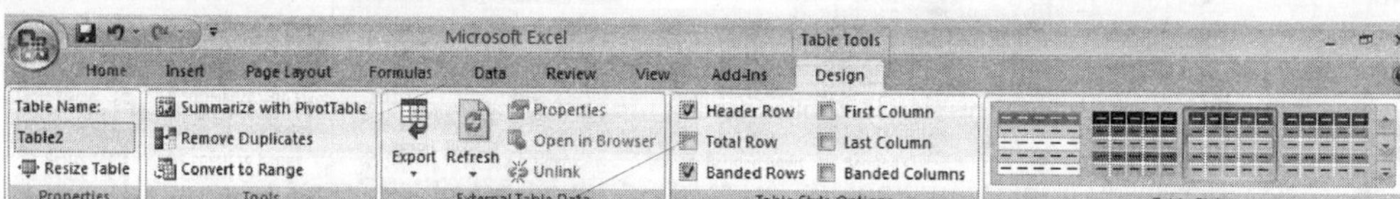

Figure 17.14 Table tools design tab

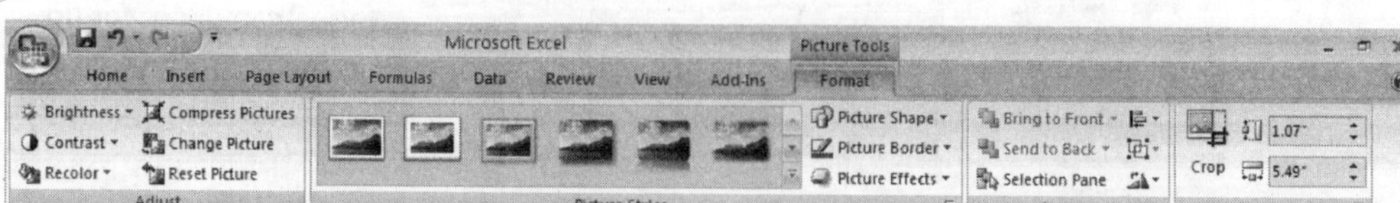

Figure 17.15 Picture tools format tab

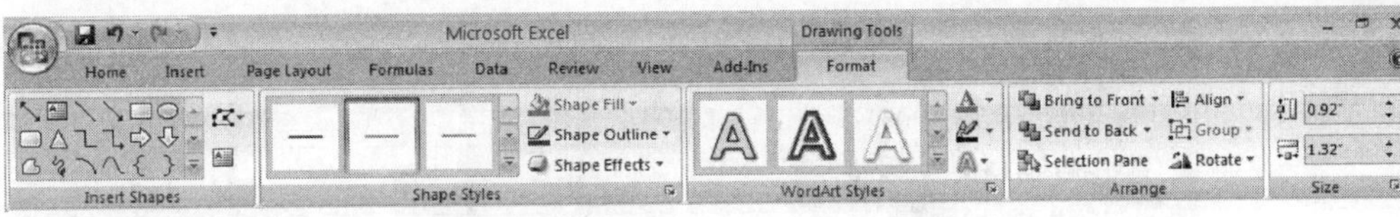

Figure 17.16 Drawing tools format tab

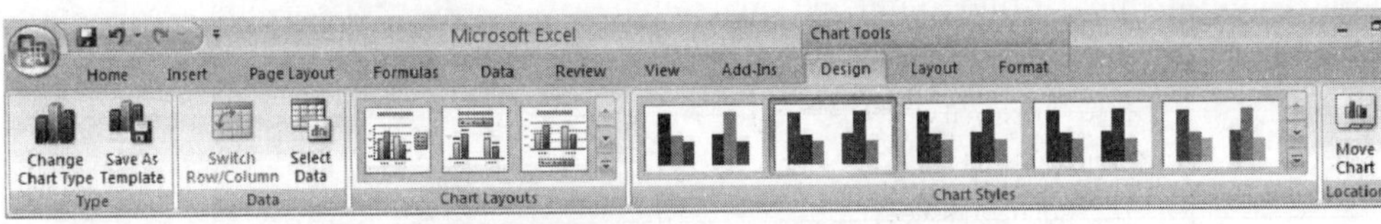

Figure 17.17 Chart tools design tab

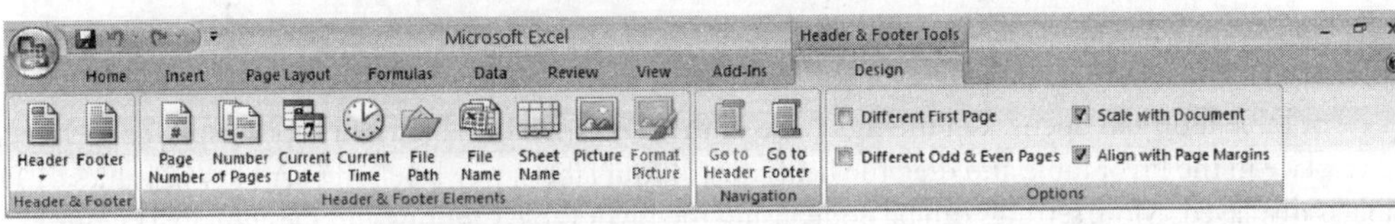

Figure 17.18 Header and footer tools design tab

When a command of the Insert tab is used, insertion takes place at the location where the cursor is present right now. So, before inserting the item, place the cursor at the location where the item is to be inserted. When you use the commands of the insert tab for insertion, you will see that most of the times, a dialog box will open which allows you to make specific settings, as per your requirement. Here, we do not discuss using the dialog boxes as they are self-explanatory, and are easy to use. Some of the operations using the Insert Tab commands are described below:

- **To Create Headers and Footers—<Insert> <Text><Header & Footer>**. Now you can edit the Header and Footer of your document. A Header and Footer tab is opened which allows you to add date and time, page number etc.
- **Insert Hyperlink—<Insert> <Links> <Hyperlink>**. To link to another location in the same document, click *Place in This Document* option under *Link to*; In the dialog box's inner window, select a cell reference. To link to another document, click the Existing File or Web Page option. Navigate to the proper folder and select the file's name. You can also add a link to a newly created document or an e-mail address.
- **Insert Text—<Insert> <Text> <Text Box>**. Click anywhere on the sheet where you want to insert the text box. Drag the corner points of the text box to change its size. Click within the box to type text. To format the text box, select the text box. <Drawing Tools> <Format>. Format the selected text box.
- **Insert PivotTable—<Insert><Tables><PivotTable>**. A Create Pivot Table dialog-box opens up. From the worksheet, select the table or range of cells to choose the data you want to analyze. (You must select the row headings). In the dialog box, select from whether you want to place the PivotTable in a new worksheet or an existing worksheet. Click <Ok>.

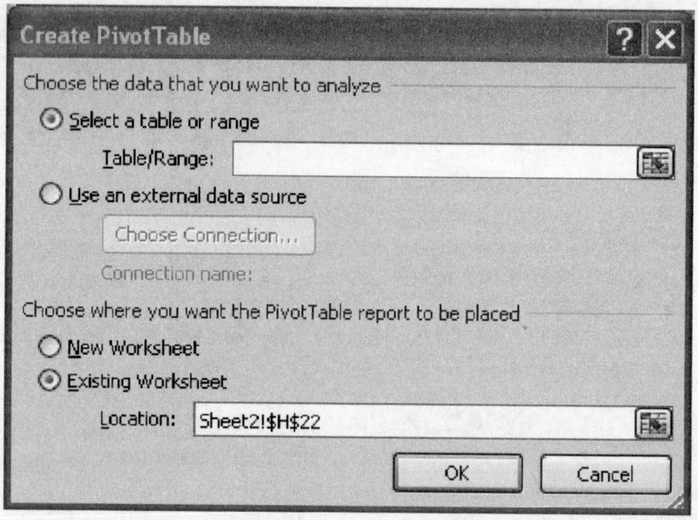

A PivotTable tools tab opens. On the right side of the sheet a PivotTable Field list is displayed. Select the fields to place in the PivotTable and drag the fields for column labels, row labels, report filter or values. A PivotTable is displayed. More settings can be done, using the PivotTable Options and Design tab. (Figure 17.19 shows the PivotTable created using the Names and Total marks of the students from a set of eight fields).

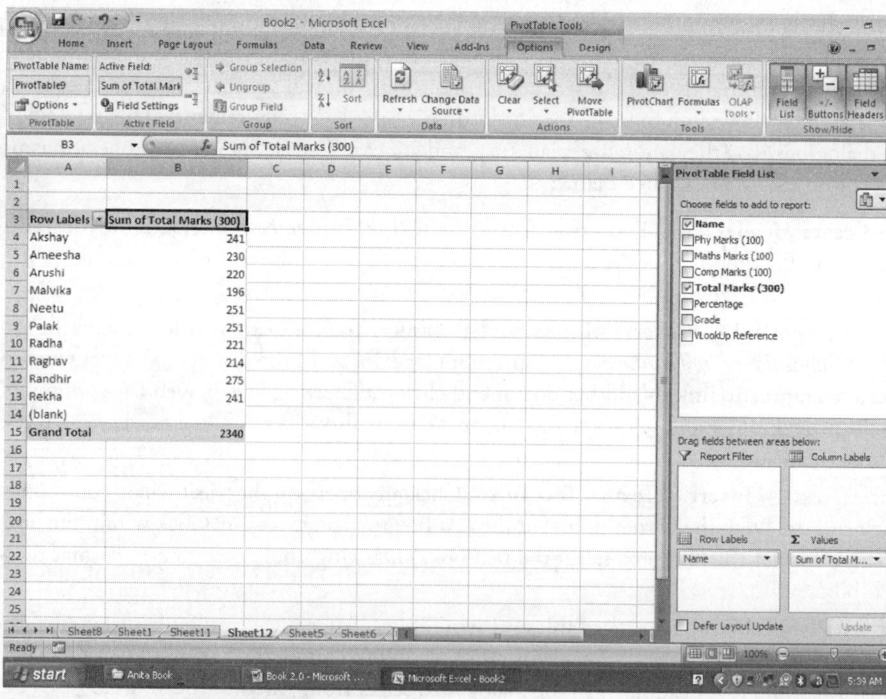

Figure 17.19 A pivot table example

17.6.3 The Page Layout Tab

The Page Layout Tab contains commands related to the layout and appearance of the pages in a document. It allows you to apply themes, change the page layout, and also provides options for viewing gridlines and headings. The Page Layout Tab is shown in Figure 17.20.

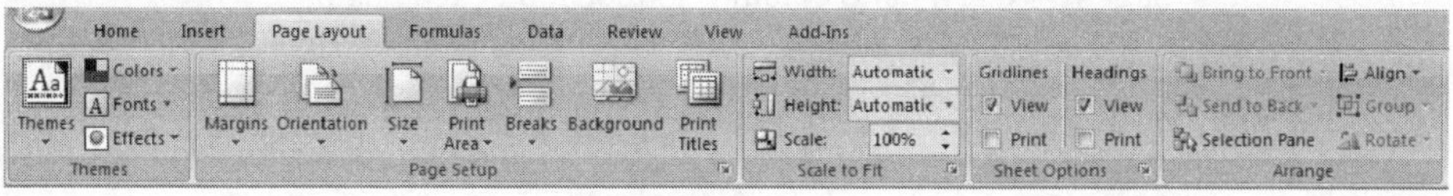

Figure 17.20 The page layout tab

There are five groups within this tab—Themes, Page Setup, Scale to Fit, Sheet Options, and Arrange.

- The *Themes* group contains commands to change the overall theme of current worksheet including fonts, colors, and fill effects.
- *Page Setup* is used to set the page margins, orientation, size, background, page breaks, print titles etc.
- *Scale to Fit* group allows specifying scaling of the page to force fit the document into a specific number of pages. It is possible to set the page width and height, stretch or shrink the printed output (scaling), and select the paper size and print quality.
- The *Sheet Options* group is used to switch sheet direction (right-to-left), view or print gridlines, and view or print worksheet headings (letters at the top of the sheet and numbers to the left of the sheet).
- The *Arrange* group is used to arrange, align or group the shapes and objects in the worksheet.

Table 17.4 gives the commands in the different groups of Page Layout Tab along with a brief explanation.

Page Layout Tab Group	Description
Themes	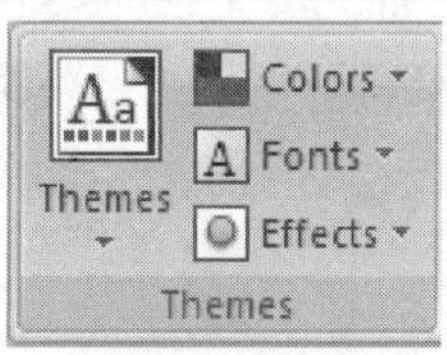 • Themes are used to change the overall design of the document including theme font, theme color, and theme effect.
Page Setup	 • Select margin for the whole document or the current section. • Select orientation between portrait and landscape. • Choose a paper size for the current section.

(*Continued*)

Page Layout Tab Group	Description
	• Mark a specific area of the sheet for printing. • Specify when a new page will begin in a printed copy. • Choose an image as a background of the sheet. • Specify the rows and columns to repeat on each page.
Scale to Fit	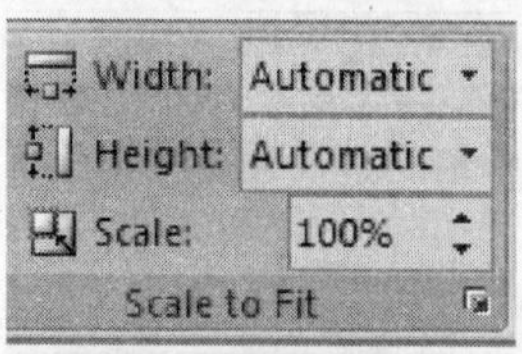 • Shrink the height and width of the printed output to fit in maximum number of pages. • Scale the printed output to a percentage of its actual size.
Sheet Options	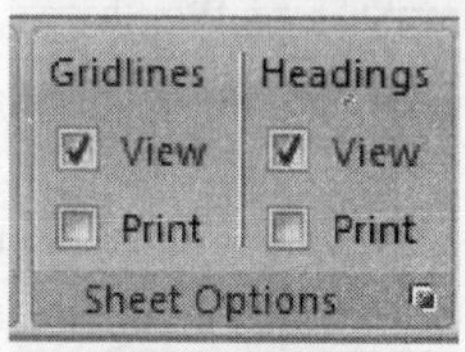 • Make settings to view and print the gridlines and the headings.
Arrange	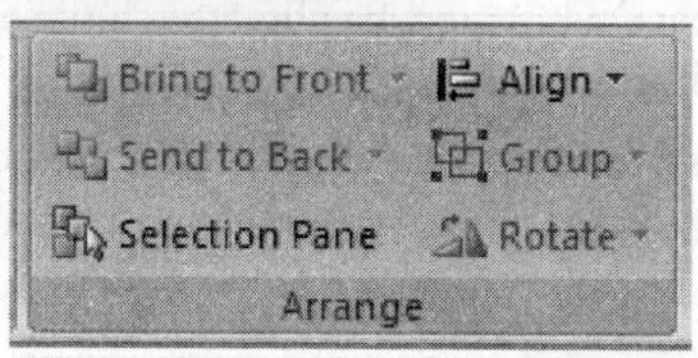 • Position the selected object on the page. The user can select from different positions. • Align the edges of multiple selected objects. • Group objects together so that they can be treated like a single group. • Rotate or flip the selected object horizontally, vertically, by 90^0 etc.

Table 17.4 *Page layout commands description*

⊙ Specify page margins—<Page Layout><Page Setup><Margins> Change either top, bottom, left, or right margins by clicking in the appropriate text boxes or on the arrows next to the numbers in Custom margins.

17.6.4 The Formulas Tab

The Formulas Tab allows the user to define equations in order to perform calculations on values in the worksheet. The Formulas Tab is shown in Figure 17.21.

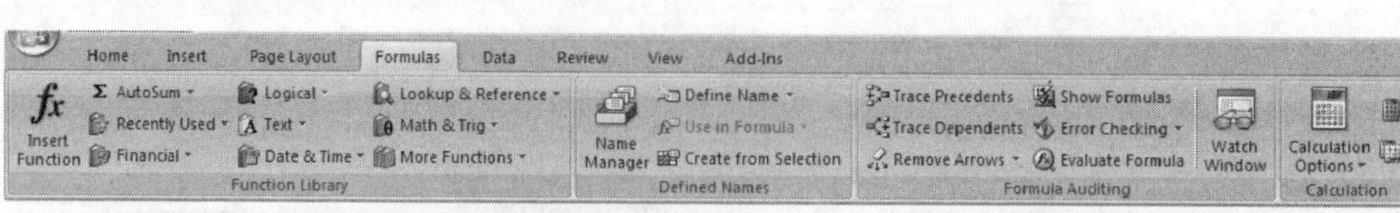

Figure 17.21 The formulas tab

There are four groups within this tab, namely, Function Library, Defined Names, Formula Auditing, and Calculation.

- The *Function Library* contains a library of functions (e.g. mathematical, logical, trigonometric, and math) that can be used to calculate or manipulate data.
- *Defined Names* allows the user to define names to be used to refer to specific formulas, and then allows searching for those names.
- *Formula Auditing* group includes commands to display formulas rather than results in a cell window, check for common formula errors, or trace precedents or dependents in cells that are referenced within a formula.
- *Calculation* allows user to specify calculation options for formulas—manual, automatic etc.

Table 17.5 gives the commands in the different groups of the Formulas Tab along with a brief explanation.

Formulas Tab Group	**Description**
Function Library	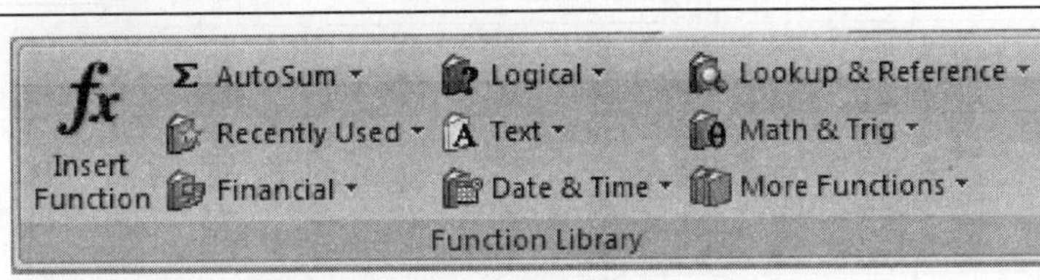 • Edit the formula in the current cell by choosing the function and editing the arguments in the selected cell. • Display the sum of the selected cells after the selected cells. • Browse and select from a list of logical functions like AND, IF. • Browse and select from a list of lookup and reference functions like ADDRESS, LOOKUP. • Browse and select from a list of recently used functions. • Browse and select from a list of text functions like LEN, Replace. • Browse and select from a list of math and trigonometric functions like ABS, FLOOR. • Browse and select from a list of financial functions like DISC, DB. • Browse and select from a list of date and time functions like DATE, HOUR. • Browse and select from a list of statistical, engineering and cube functions like AVERAGE, COMPLEX.
Defined Names	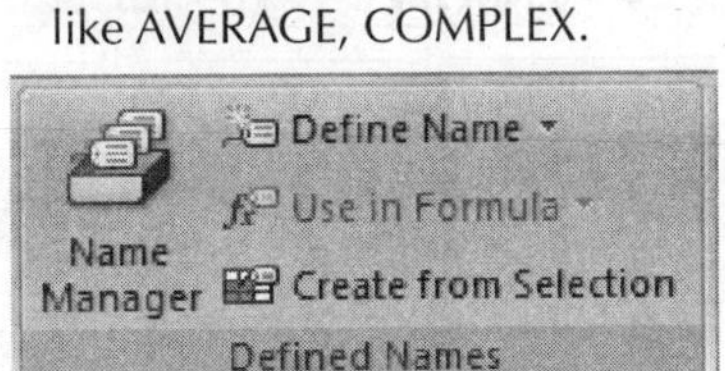 • Create, edit, delete and find all names used in the workbook. • Name cells so that can be referred in the formulas by that name. • Choose a name from this workbook and use it in the current formula. • Automatically generate names from the selected cells.

(Continued)

Formulas Tab Group	Description
Formula Auditing	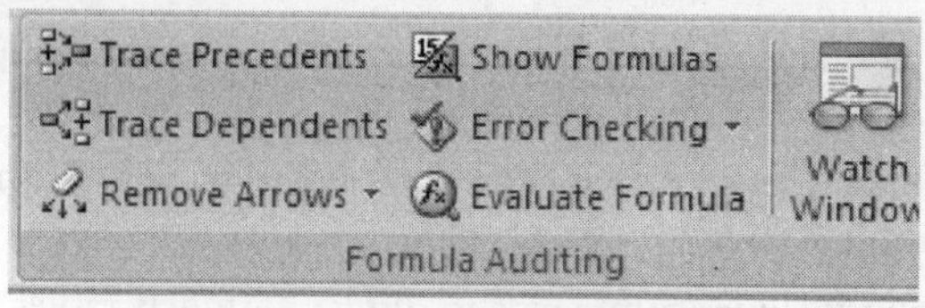 • *Trace Precedents*—Show arrows to indicate what cells affect the value of the currently selected cell. • Display the formula in the resulting cell instead of the resultant value. • *Trace Dependents*—Show arrows to indicate what cells are affected by the currently selected cell. • Check for common errors that occur in formulas. • Remove the arrows drawn by Trace Precedents and Trace Dependents. • Launch the Evaluate Formula dialog box to debug the formula. • Monitor the value of certain cells as changes are made to the sheet.
Calculation	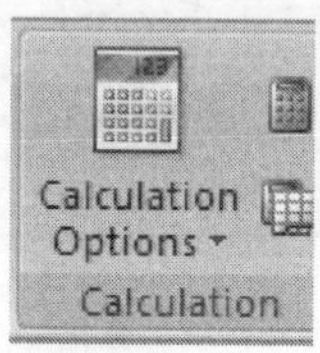 • Specify when formulas are calculated. • Calculate the entire workbook now. • Calculate the current sheet now.

Table 17.5 *Formulas tab commands description*

The formula addressing is briefly described below.

- Formula addressing—The formula can have relative addressing, absolute addressing, and mixed addressing.
  - *Relative address*—To repeat the same formula for many different cells, use the copy and paste command. The cell locations in the formula are pasted *relative* to the position we copy them from. In the original cell we wrote =SUM(B5:C5); when we copy this formula in the cell below, we see that the formula becomes =SUM(B6:C6), i.e. the function will look at the two cells to its left.

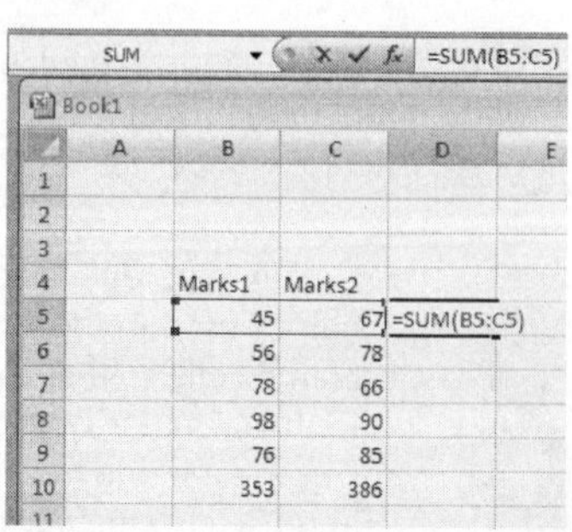

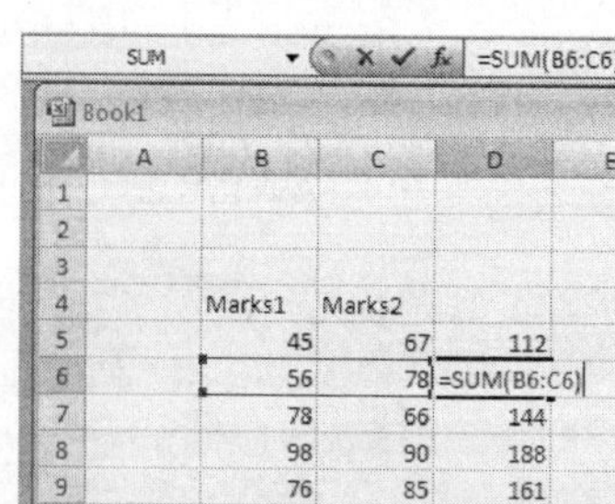

  - *Absolute address*—To keep a certain position that is not relative to the new cell location, use absolute positioning. For this, insert a $ before the column letter or a $ before the row number (or both). The $ sign locks the cell location to a fixed position. For example, =SUM($B$5:$C$5) will copy the same formula to every location we copy.

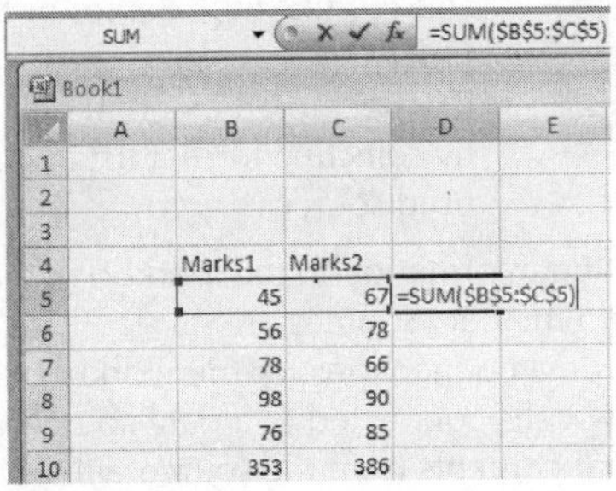

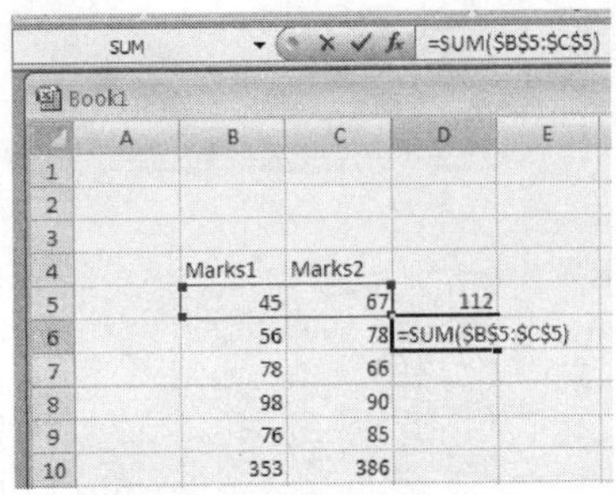

- *Mixed address*—A mix of relative and absolute addresses is used to keep some part relative and some absolute. For example, =SUM(B$5:C$5) has the column address relative and the row address absolute.

17.6.5 The Data Tab

The Data Tab contains the commands related to the retrieval and layout of data that is displayed on a worksheet. The Data Tab is shown in Figure 17.22.

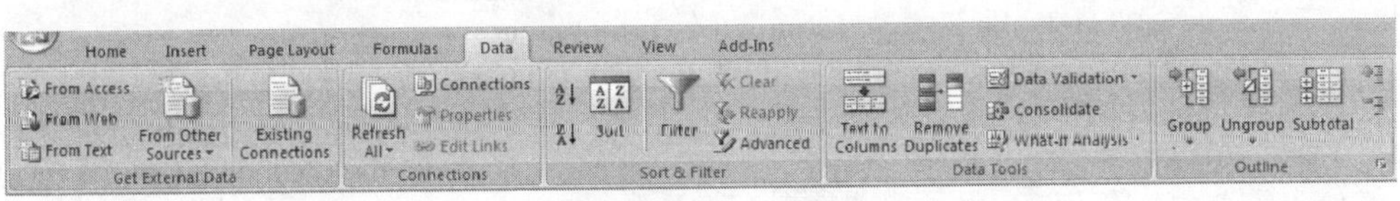

Figure 17.22 The data tab

There are five groups within this tab, namely, Get External Data, Connections, Sort & Filter, Data Tools, and Outline.

- The *Get External Data* group allows you to import data into Excel from external sources, such as an Access database, a Web page, a text file, etc.
- *Connections* include commands needed to create and edit links to external data or objects that are stored in a workbook or a connection file.
- The *Sort & Filter* group contains commands associated with sorting and filtering the data within a worksheet.
- *Data Tools* contains commands to remove duplicates, data validation, what if analysis, etc.
- *Outline* enables the user to group and ungroup a range of cells, and apply subtotals in a given column based on values of another column.

The commands in the different groups of the Data Tab along with a brief explanation are shown in Table 17.6.

Data Tab Group	Description
Get External Data	 • Import data from Access, a web page, a text file, and from other sources like SQL Server or Microsoft Query. • Connect to an external data source by selecting from a list of commonly used sources.
Connections	 • Update all the information in the workbook that is coming from the data sources. • Display all data connections for the workbook. • Specify how cells connected to a data source will update, what contents from the source will be displayed etc. • View all of the other files this spreadsheet is linked to, so that a link can be updated or removed.
Sort & Filter	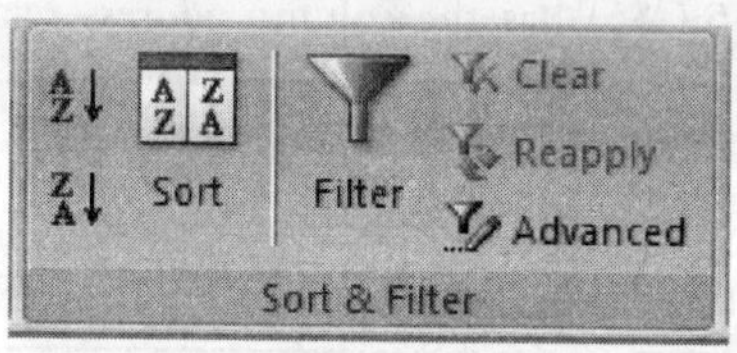 • Sort the selection from the lowest to the highest value or from the highest to the lowest value. • Launch the Sort dialog box to sort based on several criteria all at once. • Enable filtering of the selected cells. • Clear the filter and the sort state for the current range of data. • Reapply the filter and sort in the current range. • Specify complex criteria to limit which records are included in the result set of a query.
Data Tools	 • Separate the contents of one Excel sheet into a set of columns like Name into first name and last name. • Delete duplicate rows from the sheet. • Prevent invalid data from being entered into a cell. • Combine values from multiple ranges into one new range. • Try out various values for the formulas in the sheet.
Outline	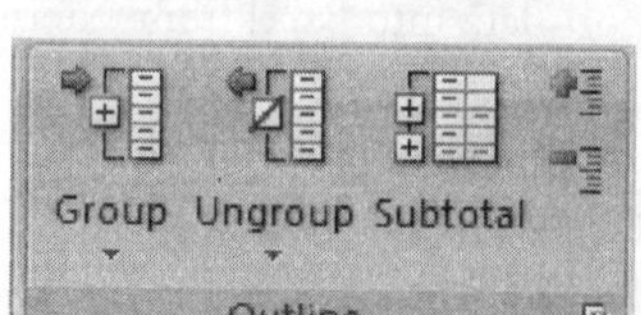 • Group a range of cells so that they can be together expanded or collapsed. • Ungroup the range of cells that were previously grouped. • Total several rows of related data together by automatically inserting subtotals and totals for the selected cells. • Show or hide a group of cells.

Table 17.6 *Data tab commands description*

17.6.6 The Review Tab

The Review Tab contains commands for review and revision of an existing document. The Review Tab is shown in Figure 17.23.

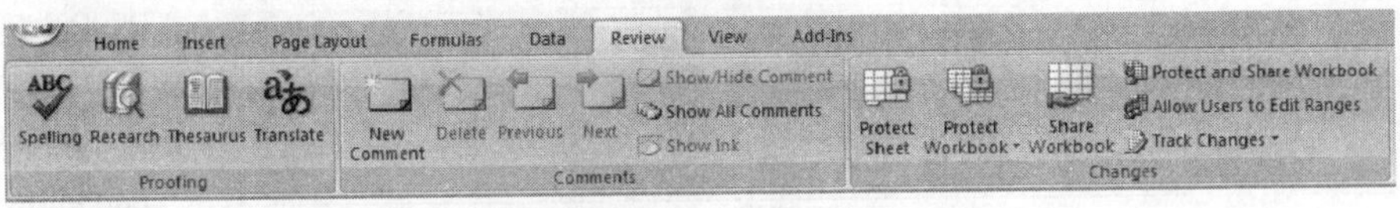

Figure 17.23 The review tab

There are three groups within this tab, namely Proofing, Comments, and changes.

- The *Proofing* group has commands required for the proofing of the document. It allows the spelling and grammar check, translate or check synonyms in the thesaurus, translate text into a different language, and search through reference materials such as dictionary or encyclopedia.
- *Comments* group contains commands to insert comments and move back and forth among the comments.
- The *Changes* group contains command to protect the workbook by restricting its access. It allows the user to specify how a workbook can be edited or shared with others, and allows the user to keep track of the changes made to it.

The commands in the different groups of the Review Tab along with a brief explanation are shown in Table 17.7.

Review Tab Group	Description
Proofing	 • Check the spelling and grammar of text. • Open Research Task Pane and search through research material. • Thesaurus suggests word similar in meaning to the selected word. • Translate the selected text into a different language.
Comments	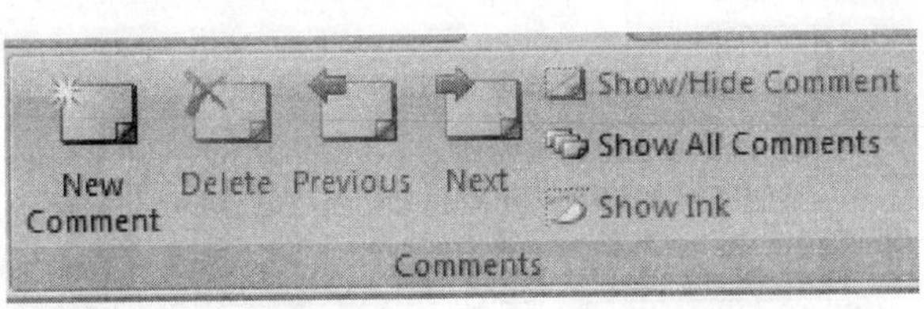 • Add a new comment about the selection. • Edit or Delete the selected comment. • Navigate to the previous or the next comment. • Show or hide comment attached to the selected cell. • Display all the comments in the sheet. • Show or hide any ink annotations on the sheet.

(*Continued*)

Review Tab Group	Description
Changes	 • Restrict how people can access the worksheet or the workbook. You can allow restricted access using passwords etc. • Allow multiple people to work in a workbook at the same time. • Share the workbook and protect it with a password at the same time. • Allow specific people to edit ranges of cells in a protected workbook or sheet. • Track all changes made to the document including insertions, deletions and formatting changes.

Table 17.7 *Review tab commands description*

17.6.7 The View Tab

The View tab has commands that affects how the document appears on the screen. The View Tab is shown in Figure 17.24.

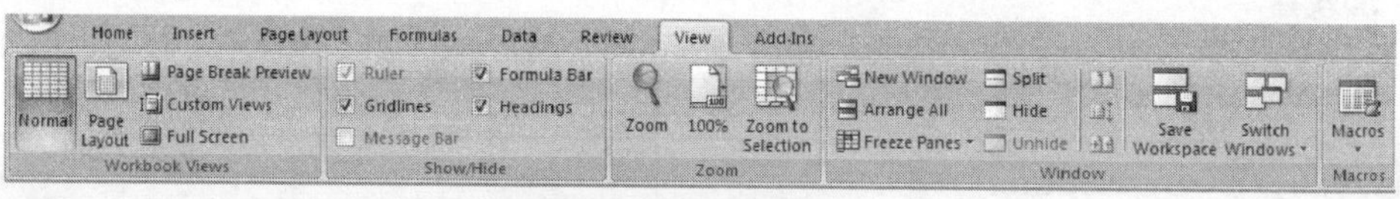

Figure 17.24 The view tab

There are five groups within this tab, namely, Workbook Views, Show/Hide, Zoom, Window, and Macros.

- The *Workbook Views* group has commands to view the document in different modes like normal, page break view etc. You can also create your own custom views or switch to full screen view.
- The *Show/Hide* group contains commands to show or hide the ruler, gridlines, message bar, formula bar, or worksheet headings.
- *Zoom* is used to view the document in smaller or larger sizes. You can zoom in and out with different options.
- *Window* group contains commands to create new windows, arrange all open windows and switch between them, freeze panes so that they continue to appear on the screen while scrolling, and save a workspace.
- The *Macros* group is used to create or view a macro. Macros allow you to define a sequence of actions to perform on a document or multiple documents that can be executed again and again simply by running the macro.

The commands in the different groups of View Tab along with a brief explanation are shown in Table 17.8.

View Tab Group	Description
Workbook Views	 • *Normal view* shows the document in the normal view. • *Page layout* allows viewing the document as it will appear in a printed page. You can see where the pages begin and end and also the header and footer. • View a preview of where the pages will break when printed. • Save a set of display and print settings as custom view. • View the document in the full screen mode.
Show/Hide	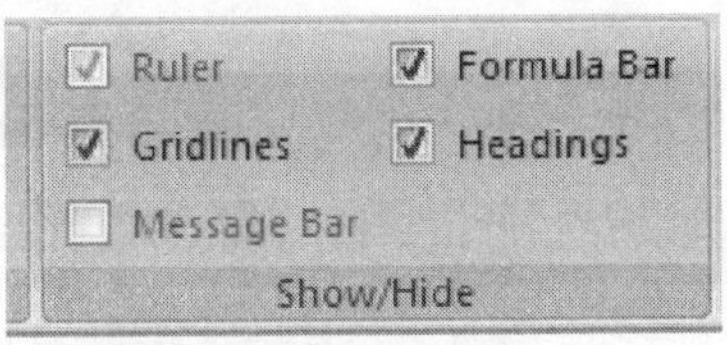 • Gridlines and rulers are used to measure and line up objects on a sheet. Show or Hide the Ruler, Gridlines, Message bar, Formula Bar, and the Headings.
Zoom	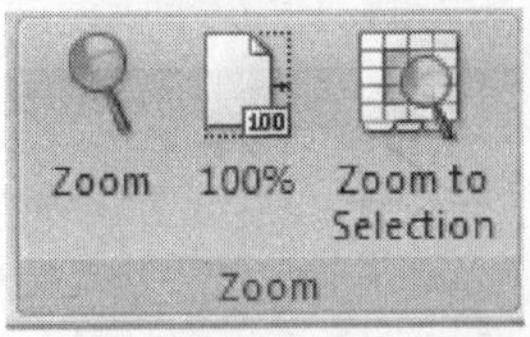 • Open Zoom dialog box to specify the zoom level such as 33%, 66%, 100%, or 200%. • Zoom the worksheet so that the currently selected range of cells fills the entire window.
Window	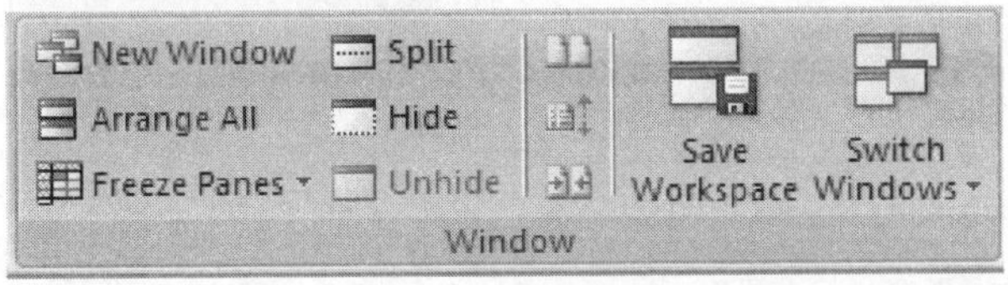 • Open a new window containing a view of the current workbook. • Arrange all open sheets side-by-side on the screen. • Keep a portion of the screen visible while rest of the sheet scrolls. • Split the window into multiple re-sizable panes containing views of your worksheet. • Hide or unhide the current window. • View two worksheets side-by-side so that their contents can be compared. • Synchronize the scrolling of two documents so that they scroll together. • Reset the window position so that the documents share the space equally. • Save the current layout of the window as workspace so that they can be restored later on. • Switch to a different currently open window.
Macros	 • View the list of macros from which you can run, create or delete a macro.

Table 17.8 *View tab commands description*

17.6.8 The Help

The Help button is located on the right most side of the Tabs in the Ribbon. Click on this button to get help for using any command of the Excel. On clicking on the help button, a screen as shown in Figure 17.25 appears. You can browse the Help for the command you want. You can also perform operations such as, search for a command and view the Table of Contents.

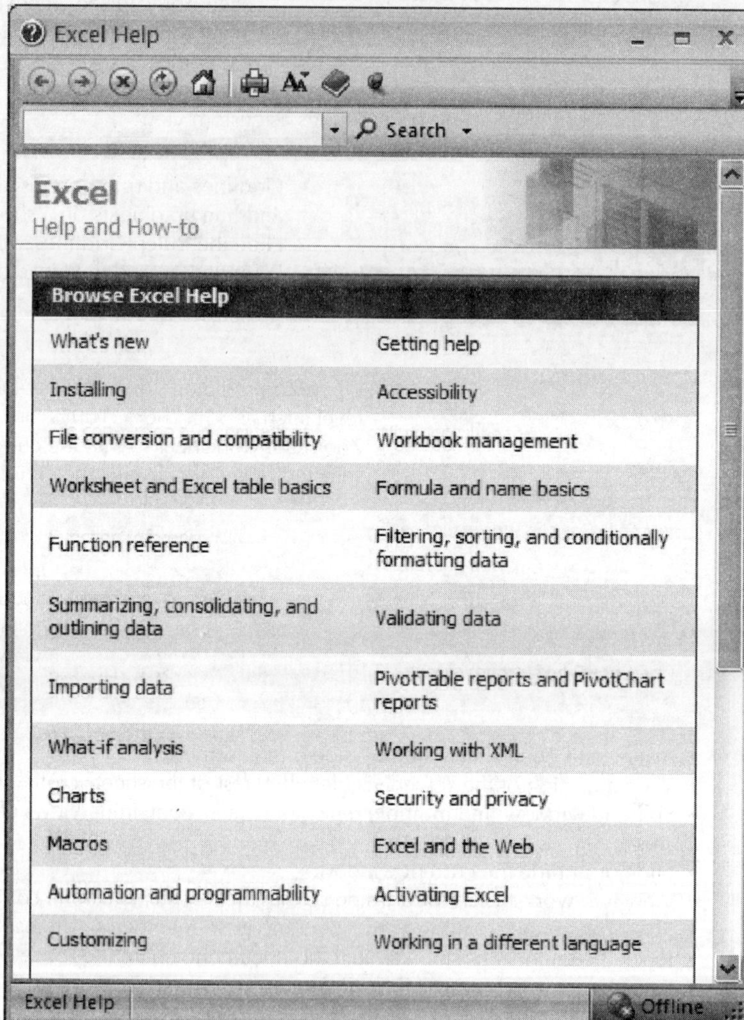

Figure 17.25 Excel help

Many of the concepts that you use while working with MS-Office suite are common for MS-Word, MS-PowerPoint and MS-Excel. For example, open, close, save, cutting and pasting are performed the same way in MS-Excel as they are in MS-Word and MS-PowerPoint. The menus are also arranged in a similar layout. If you are not sure how to do something in Excel, then try it as you would do in MS-Word or MS-PowerPoint, and it may work.

17.7 SOLVED EXAMPLES

Example 1: **The following table gives year-wise sale figures of five salesmen in Rs.**

Salesman	2004	2005	2006	2007
Sa1	10000	12000	20000	50000
Sa2	15000	18000	50000	60000
Sa3	20000	22000	70000	70000
Sa4	30000	30000	100000	80000
Sa5	40000	45000	125000	90000

- Calculate total sale year-wise.
- Calculate the net sales made by each salesman.
- Calculate the commission for each salesman - If total sales is greater than Rs.1,00,000/-, then commission is 5% of total sale made by the salesman, else it is 2% of total sale.
- Calculate the maximum sale made by each salesman.
- Calculate the maximum sale made in each year.
- Draw a bar graph representing the sale made by each salesman.
- Draw a pie graph representing the sales made by salesmen in year 2004.

Solution 1:

- Open blank workbook. **<New> <Create>**
- *Enter the headings of the table*
  - Double-click on the cell and type.
  - If name is too long, use Text Wrap : <Home><Alignment>< >
  - Use Text Orientation to change the direction of the text : <Home><Alignment>< >
- Double-click on the cells and enter the data.
- *Total Year-wise Sales:* Since you want to find the total, the function SUM is used.
  - If you already know that the SUM function is to be used, then type *=SUM(*. You will see that the format of the SUM function appears. Click on *number1* in the format and select the cells for which you want to find the total. It will write *=SUM(E10:E14*. Close the brackets *=SUM(E10:E14)*. This is the total sales of one year. Click on the cell in which you have found total and pull the plus sign to the other columns of the same row to get total year-wise sales of other years.
  - If you do not know that the SUM function is to be used, then use the options <Formulas> <Function Library>. Look for the appropriate function.
- *Net Sales for each Salesman:* Same method as for Total Year-wise Sales.
- *Commission:* Enter the IF formula.
  - Enter =IF(
  - Then select the cells whose value is to be checked. It will become =IF(I10

- Write the condition. >100000,0.05*(
- Again select the cells. It will become =IF(I10>100000,0.05*(I10), 0.02*(
- Again select the cells, and put brackets. The final formula will look like =IF(I10>100000,0.05*(I10), 0.02*(I10))

⊙ *Maximum sale made by each salesman*: Use MAX function: =MAX(E10:H10)

⊙ Maximum sale made in each year: Use MAX function: =MAX(E10:E14)

⊙ Select the cells and use <Home><Styles><Conditional Formatting> and <Home><Styles><Cell Styles> to give conditional formatting and style, respectively, to the cells.

⊙ *Bar graph:* <Insert><Charts><Bar> A Chart Tools Tab appears

- Select <Chart Tools> <Design> Select a Chart Style or change the style using <Chart Tools><Type> <Change Chart Type>

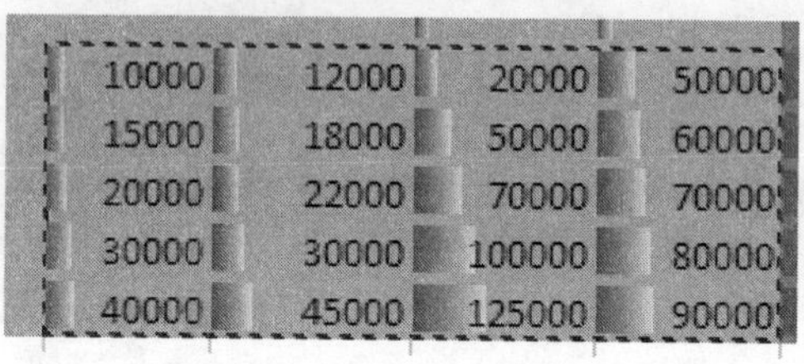

10000	12000	20000	50000
15000	18000	50000	60000
20000	22000	70000	70000
30000	30000	100000	80000
40000	45000	125000	90000

- <Chart Tools><Data><Select Data>. A dialog box appears. Either enter the cell numbers, or you can select the cells from the worksheet for which you want to make a chart. When you select, a dotted border appears around the selected cells. Next, click <OK> in the dialog box.
- A chart appears. Now use the <Chart Tools> <Layout> <Labels> to label and decide the placement of your chart axes, legend, title etc.
- Use <Chart Tools> <Layout> <Current Selection> <Format Selection> to format the chart area like fill texture, gradient etc.

⊙ *Pie graph:* <Insert><Charts><Pie>. A Chart Tools Tab appears. Follow the same steps as in Bar graph.

Figure 17.26 and Figure 17.27 show the sales table and the graphs.

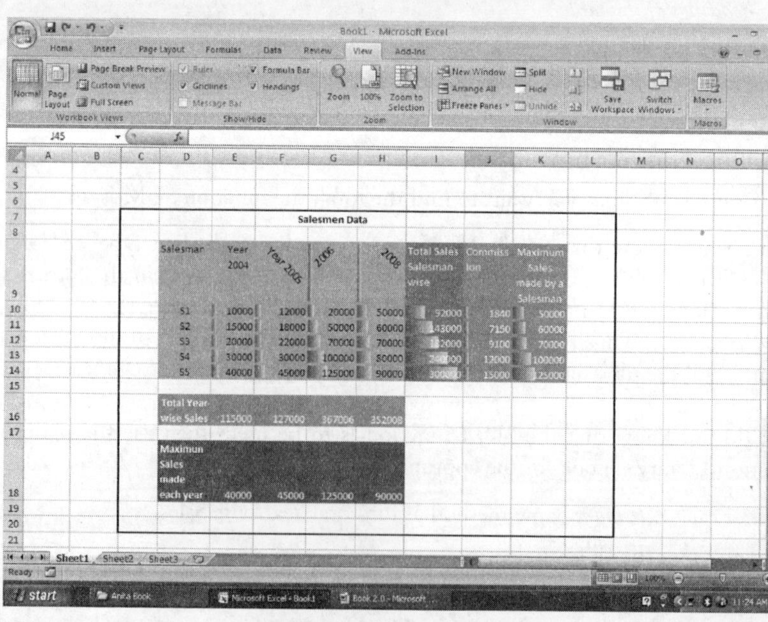

Figure 17.26 Sales table

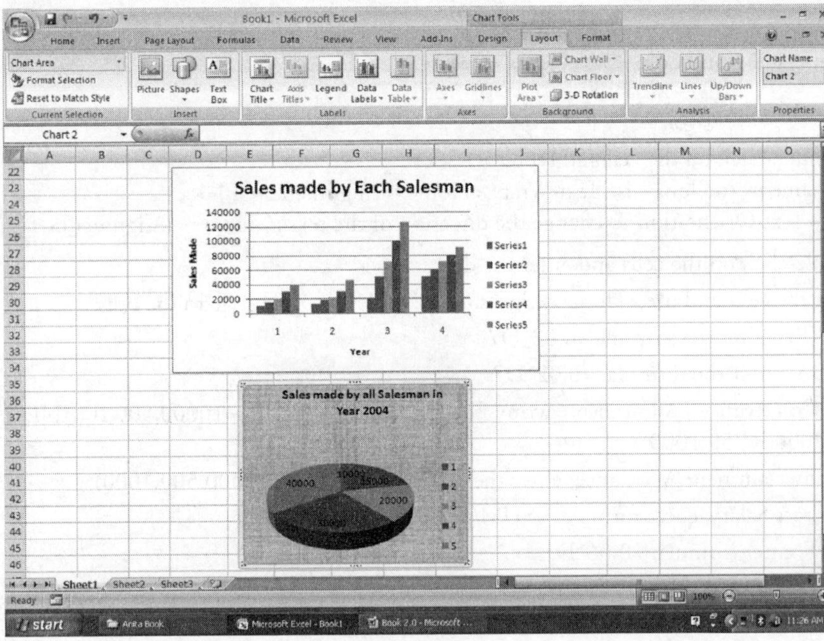

Figure 17.27 Bar graph and pie graph for the sales table example

Example 2: A school pays a monthly salary to its employees, which consists of basic salary, allowances, and deductions. The details of allowances and deductions are as follows:

- HRA is 30% of the Basic.
- DA is 20% of Basic.
- Conveyance Allowance is –
  - Rs. 500/-, if Basic is less than or equal to Rs.10000/-
  - Rs. 750/-, if Basic is greater than Rs.10000/- and less than Rs.20000/-
  - Rs. 1000/-, if Basic is greater than Rs.20000/-
- Entertainment Allowance is –
  - Rs 500/-, if Basic is less than or equal to Rs.10000/-
  - Rs.1000/-, if Basic is greater than Rs.10000/-
- PF deduction is 6% of Basic.
- IT deduction is 15% of the Basic.
- Calculate the following:
  - Gross Salary = Basic + HRA + DA + Conveyance + Entertainment
  - Deduction = PF + IT
  - Net Salary = Gross Salary - Deduction

Make a salary table and calculate the net salary of the employees.

Teacher Name   Basic Salary   HRA   DA   Conveyance Allowance   Entertainment-
Allowance   Gross Salary   PF   IT   Deduction   Net Salary

Solution 2:

- Open blank workbook. **<New> <Create>**
- *Enter the headings of the table*
    - Double-click on the cell and type.
    - If name is too long, use Text Wrap: <Home><Alignment>< >
    - Use Text Orientation to change the direction of the text : <Home><Alignment>< >
- Double-click on the cells and enter the data.
- Select the cells and use <Home><Styles><Cell Styles> to give style to the cells.
- For HRA enter the formula =0.03*D7
- For DA, enter the formula: =0.02*D7
- For Conveyance Allowance, write the formula: =IF(D7<=10000,500,IF(AND(D7>10000, D7<20000),750,1000))
- For Entertainment Allowance, enter the formula: =IF(D7<=10000,500,1000)
- For Gross Salary, enter formula: =SUM(D7:H7)
- For PF, enter formula: =0.06*D7
- For IT, enter formula: =0.15*D7
- For Net Deduction, enter formula: =SUM(J7:K7)
- For Net Salary, enter formula: =I7-L7
- Select the cells and use <Home><Styles><Conditional Formatting> and <Home><Styles><Cell Styles> to give different colors and style to the cells.

Figure 17.28 shows the salary table.

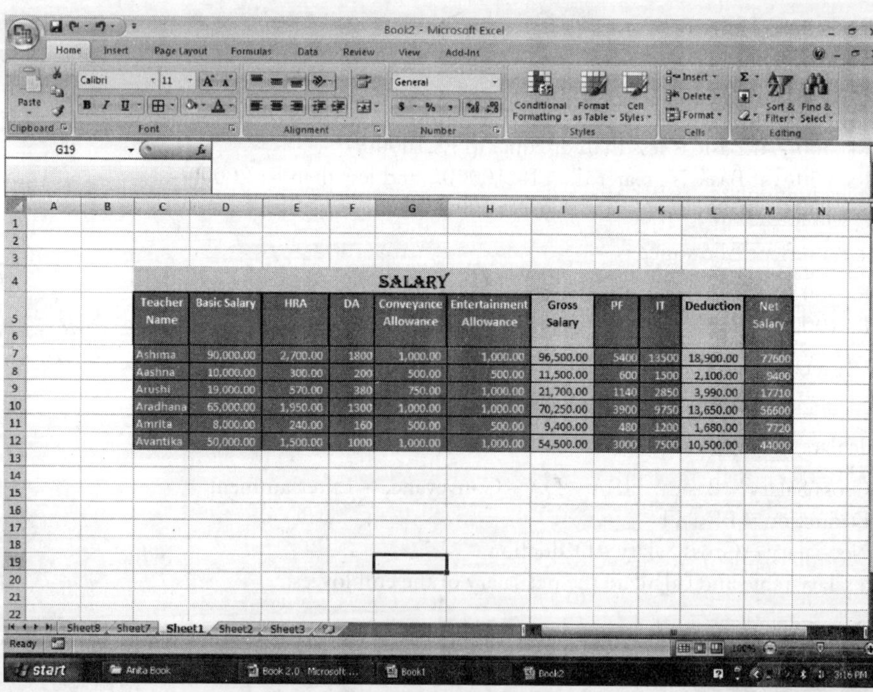

Figure 17.28 Salary example

Example 3: **Make a sheet having the fields—S. No., Name, Physics Marks, Math Marks, Computer Sc. Marks, Total Marks, Percentage, and Grade. Fill the data for the S. No., Name, Physics Marks, Math Marks, and Computer Sc. Marks.**

Calculate the following-

Find the Percentage of the student.

- Calculate Grade (A- > 90%, B- between 80%–90%, C- otherwise).
- Apply filter to display marks more than 80%.
- Enter the S. No. and get the Grade using VLOOKUP.
- Sort all records on Name.

Solution 3:

- Open blank workbook. **<New> <Create>**
- *Enter the headings of the table*
  - Double-click on the cell and type.
  - If name too long, use Text Wrap: <Home><Alignment>< >
  - Use Text Orientation to change direction of the text : <Home><Alignment>< >
- Double-click on the cells and enter the data.
- *To find the percentage*, use the formula =SUM(I8)/300.
- *To find Grade*, use the formula =IF(J8>0.9,"A",IF(J8>0.8,"B","C")). Figure 17.29 shows the Student Table with percentage and grade calculated.

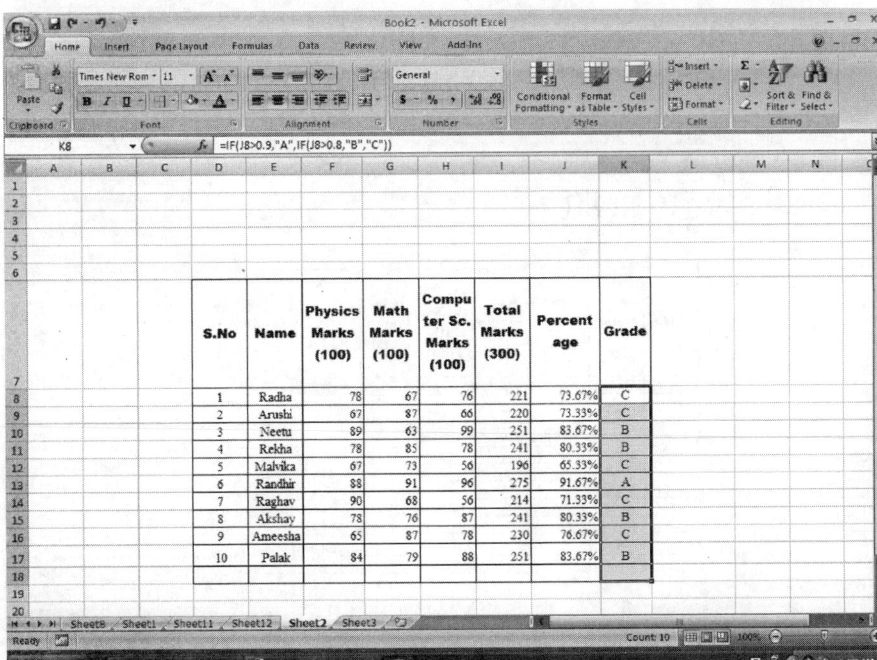

S.No	Name	Physics Marks (100)	Math Marks (100)	Computer Sc. Marks (100)	Total Marks (300)	Percentage	Grade
1	Radha	78	67	76	221	73.67%	C
2	Arushi	67	87	66	220	73.33%	C
3	Neetu	89	63	99	251	83.67%	B
4	Rekha	78	85	78	241	80.33%	B
5	Malvika	67	73	56	196	65.33%	C
6	Randhir	88	91	96	275	91.67%	A
7	Raghav	90	68	56	214	71.33%	C
8	Akshay	78	76	87	241	80.33%	B
9	Ameesha	65	87	78	230	76.67%	C
10	Palak	84	79	88	251	83.67%	B

Figure 17.29 Student marks example

⊙ *Apply Filter:*

- Select the column or columns on which you want to apply the filter. Here it is column Percentage.
- Click on <Data><Sort & Filter><Filter>. You will see that an arrow like ▾ appears in that column.
- Click on the arrow. A pop-up menu appears. Click on <Number Filters>. Select one of the displayed options. Here we select Greater Than….A Custom AutoFilter dialog box appears. Since we want all students having more than 80%, put .8 in the box on the right side. Click <OK>. Figure 17.30 shows filter applied to the Student Table.

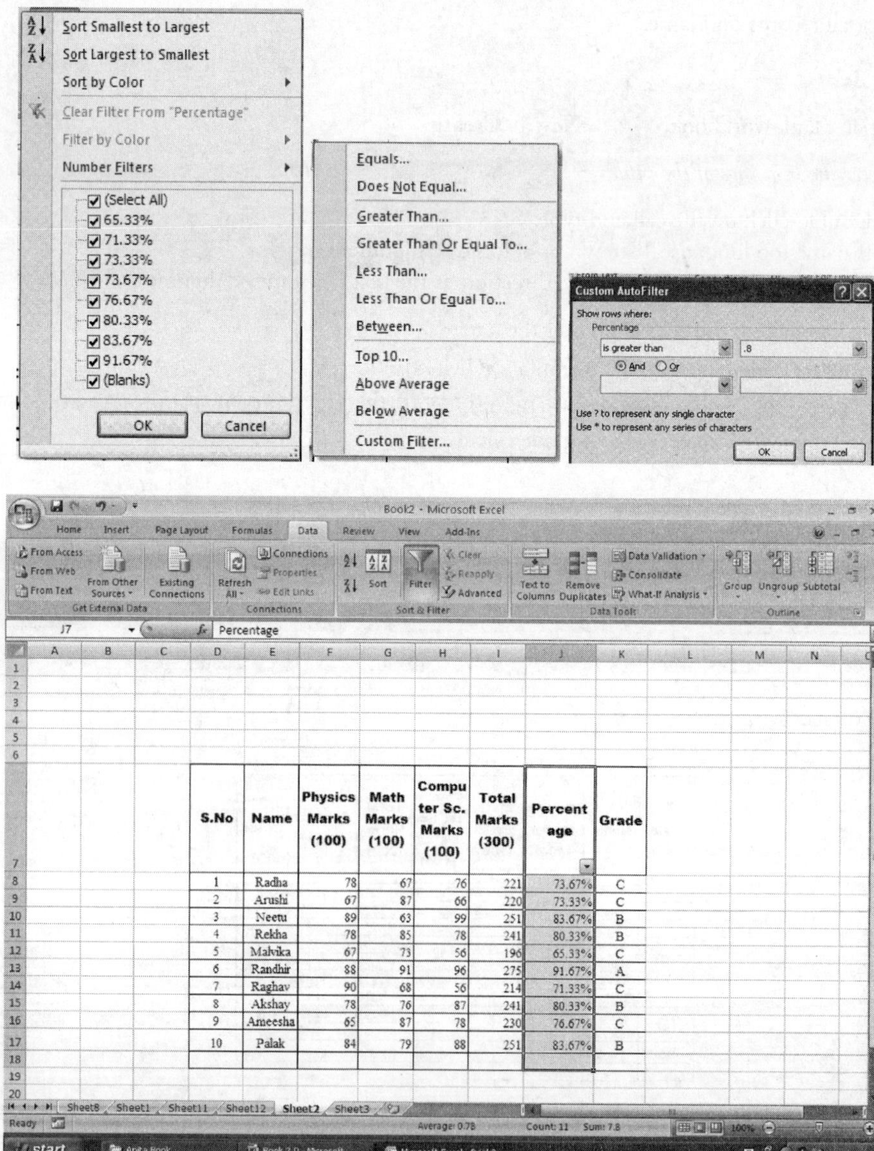

Figure 17.30 Student marks example with filter on percentage

- *Using VLOOKUP:* Use VLOOKUP formula, =VLOOKUP(D8,StudentTable,8)
  - D8 is the cell number of the S.No field. So, the first argument is the field for which we want to find the result.
  - StudentTable is the name given to the whole table. You can specify the cell range or define a name for the Table. To specify cell range, simply select the complete table. To define a name for the table- Select the table. <Formulas><Defined Names> <Define Name>. A New Name dialog box appears. Write the Name with which you want to refer to the Table. Here we write *StudentTable*. Click <OK>. In the VLOOKUP formula, the second argument is the table name.

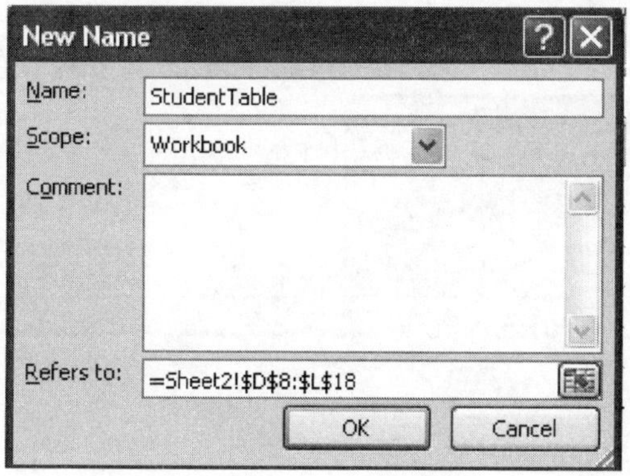

  - The third argument is the column number from where you want the result. Here we want the Grade, which is the 8th column in the Table.
  - So, use the formula =VLOOKUP(D8,StudentTable,8). Figure 17.31 shows VLOOKUP reference in the Student table.

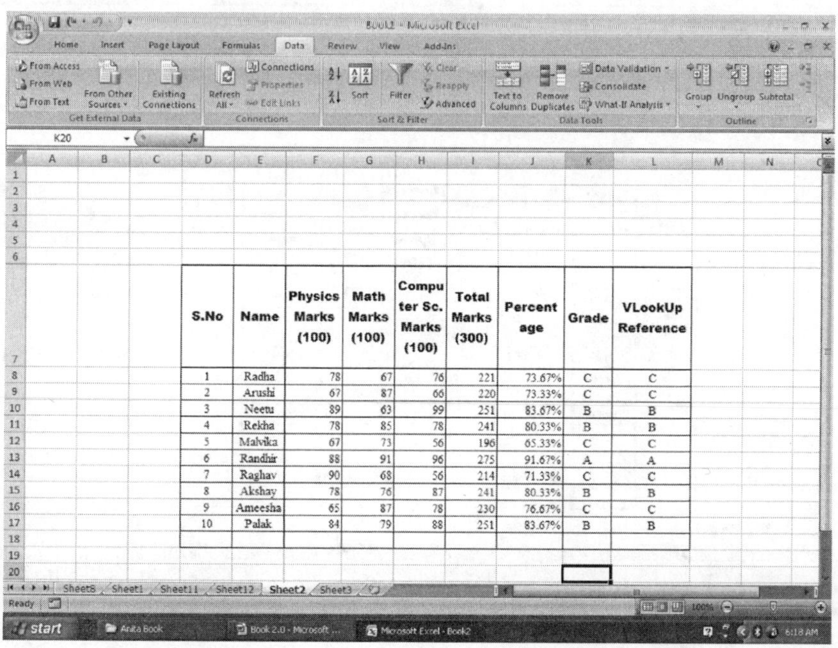

S.No	Name	Physics Marks (100)	Math Marks (100)	Computer Sc. Marks (100)	Total Marks (300)	Percentage	Grade	VLookUp Reference
1	Radha	78	67	76	221	73.67%	C	C
2	Arushi	67	87	66	220	73.33%	C	C
3	Neetu	89	63	99	251	83.67%	B	B
4	Rekha	78	85	78	241	80.33%	B	B
5	Malvika	67	73	56	196	65.33%	C	C
6	Randhir	88	91	96	275	91.67%	A	A
7	Raghav	90	68	56	214	71.33%	C	C
8	Akshay	78	76	87	241	80.33%	B	B
9	Ameesha	65	87	78	230	76.67%	C	C
10	Palak	84	79	88	251	83.67%	B	B

Figure 17.31 Student marks example with VLOOKUP reference

- *To sort the table on the field Name:* Select the column on the basis of which you want to sort. Click <Data><Sort & Filter> <Sort>.
    - If only one column of the table is selected, you get a Sort Warning. Click on <Expand the Selection> and <Sort>. You get the sorted table.
    - If you select multiple columns you get the Sort dialog box. Here you can specify the levels of sorting also (for example, level 1—sort on name, level 2—sort on total marks etc.). Click <OK>. You get the sorted table. Figure 17.32 shows the Student table after sorting.

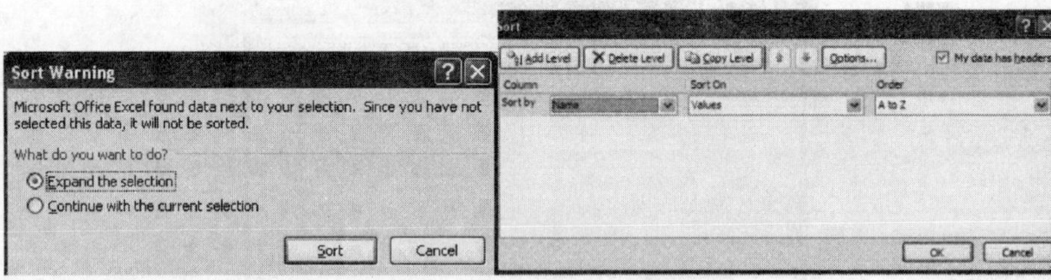

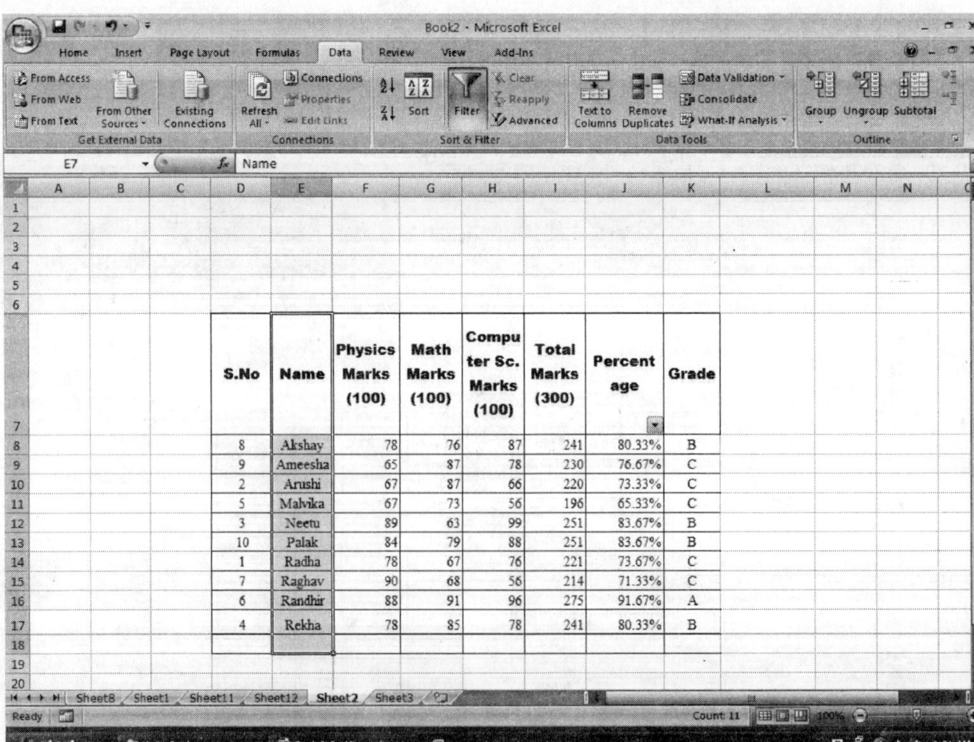

S.No	Name	Physics Marks (100)	Math Marks (100)	Computer Sc. Marks (100)	Total Marks (300)	Percentage	Grade
8	Akshay	78	76	87	241	80.33%	B
9	Ameesha	65	87	78	230	76.67%	C
2	Arushi	67	87	66	220	73.33%	C
5	Malvika	67	73	56	196	65.33%	C
3	Neetu	89	63	99	251	83.67%	B
10	Palak	84	79	88	251	83.67%	B
1	Radha	78	67	76	221	73.67%	C
7	Raghav	90	68	56	214	71.33%	C
6	Randhir	88	91	96	275	91.67%	A
4	Rekha	78	85	78	241	80.33%	B

Figure 17.32 Student marks example with sort on name

***Exercises*:**

1. Design a mark-sheet for a student as follows:

Mark Sheet				
Roll-No				
Name				
		Marks		
Subject	Practical	Theory	Total	Grade
Math				
English				
Physics				
Chemistry				
Computer Sc				
		Total Marks		
		Total Percentage		
		Remarks		

   (a) Calculate the total marks for each subject. Calculate the grade (A-90% or more, B - 80% -less than 90%, C-70% - less than 80%, D-60% - less than 70%, E—otherwise)

   (b) Calculate the total marks of all subjects and the total percentage. Depending on the total percentage write the following in remarks

      (i) Excellent—90% or more

      (ii) Very Good—80%-less than 90%,

      (iii) Good—70%—less than 80%,

      (iv) Fair—60%—less than 70%,

      (v) Poor—less than 60%

   (c) Use cell style to show colored cells

   (d) Use thick outline border

   (e) Use Font size, color and alignment for the text

2. Design the Time Table given to you at the start of the Semester, without grid lines.
3. Prepare a schedule of your exams.
4. Prepare the rate list of the Mother Dairy Fruit and Vegetable Vendor:

   (a) Sort the Table in decreasing order of rate list.

   (b) Find the total of all the rates.

   (c) While printing the table hide the gridlines.

   (d) Check the spelling and grammar in an existing document. Use the "Replace" option in Find and Replace to replace each instance of some word.

5. Create a 7-column, 6-row table to create a calendar for the current month.
   (a) Enter the names of the days of the week in the first row of the table.
   (b) Centre the day names horizontally and vertically.
   (c) Change the font and font size as desired.
   (d) Insert a row at the top of the table. Merge the cells in the row and enter the current month and year using a large font size. Shade the row.
   (e) Enter and right-align the dates for the month in the appropriate cells of the table.
   (f) Change the outside border to a more decorative border. Identify two important dates in the calendar, and shade them.
6. In a new workbook, create the worksheet. Name the worksheet as *Furniture Details*. Enter the data shown in the table below:

A	B	C
Item	**Quantity**	**Price/piece (Rs)**
Student Chairs	209	2005
Student Tables	101	5005
Stools	202	1005
Teacher Chairs	74	10009
Computer Tables	253	1100
Teacher Tables	77	3000

   (a) Calculate the total amount for each item (Quantity*Price/Piece) and also the total amount for all items.
   (b) Apply suitable formatting to currency entries (Rs.) and numbers.
   (c) Adjust the column widths where needed. Insert blank rows between column labels and data.
   (d) Use alignments, fonts, borders, and colors to format the "Furniture Details" worksheet. For example, put a border around the title, change the color of column headings to red, and center all the entries in Column B.
   (e) Create a header that includes your name, and a footer that includes current date. Change page orientation to Landscape.
   (f) Preview and print the worksheet.
7. Use the Furniture Table in Question 11 to do the following:
   (a) Prepare a bar chart for the data. Place the chart as an object in the worksheet.
   (b) Print the entire worksheet with the chart.
   (c) Print the entire worksheet without the chart.
   (d) Change the bar chart to an exploded pie chart. Add a title to the pie chart.
8. Create a worksheet as shown below:
   (a) Calculate the average, mode, and median.
   (b) Draw a bar graph.
   (c) Color all the responses more than 20% in a different color. Count these responses.

A	B
Question: Do you want the Class X board exam.	
The response shows the "Yes"	
Survey Number	Response (%)
1099112	300
1098114	250
1199045	340
1185432	150
1188765	400
1195666	100
1009999	40
1145566	270
1236598	503
Average	
Median	
Mode	

9. Create a worksheet as shown below:
   (a) Sort the data in the "Type" column. Filter the areas where "Rice" is supplied.
   (b) Use PivotTables in the this worksheet that uses the SUM function in the quantity. Change the SUM function to AVERAGE or COUNT.
   (c) Add/modify one or two new records to the data, and then reset the range for the PivotTable.

A	B	C	D
Distribution of Food Items within different areas			
Month	**Area**	**Type**	**Quantity(Kgs)**
Jan	Mayur Vihar	Rice	37000
Feb	Patparganj	Wheat	25500
Mar	Vivek Vihar	Sugar	15000
Apr	Vivek Vihar	Rice	13000
May	Vivek Vihar	Wheat	15500
June	Vivek Vihar	Maize	22000
July	Masjid Moth	Rice	17500
Aug	Masjid Moth	Wheat	21000
Sep	Masjid Moth	Sugar	29500
Oct	Masjid Moth	Maize	12900
Nov	Pitampura	Rice	25000
Dec	Pitampura	Wheat	21600

10. Open two documents and view them together.
11. Design a worksheet using the following functions—MODE, STDDEV, VARIANCE, MEDIAN, SIN, COS, TAN, COUNT, MAX, MIN, ABS, MOD, SUM, SUMIF, POWER
12. Design a worksheet as follows:

	A	B	C	D	E
			Club 15-A		
	Membership No.	Swimming Charges	Yoga Charges	Food Charges	Badminton Charges

(a) Enter data in the worksheet. (at least 15 records).

(b) Calculate the total charges for each member. If a member does not avail of a facility, the corresponding charge for that activity should be zero.

(c) Generate a separate report of the members who are not availing any of the facility.

(d) Draw a chart for each facility showing its percentage of use. (For example if 5 out of 15 people are not using swimming facility, the chart should show—swimming facility as 66.6% used, and the rest unused)

(e) Use the appropriate function to list the facility that is being most often used.

(f) Use appropriate function to find the members using the club facility the most. (Hint: maximum non-zero entries)

(g) Print the reports.

The above questions can be made specific by including one or more of the following options:

(a) Create and name range data to simplify use.

(b) Use Names and Labels in functions.

(c) Use Decision-Making functions such as SUMIF to calculate data based on the evaluation ?of criteria in another data range.

(d) Use Nested functions such as IF, AND, and OR to analyze data based on multiple conditions.

(e) Run and record a macro.

(f) Save macros in a Personal Workbook, the current workbook, or in a new workbook.

(g) Open multiple workbooks simultaneously.

(h) Copy and paste between workbooks.

(i) Use copy and Paste Special.

(j) Link data in multiple workbooks.

(k) Write linking formulas.

(l) Consolidate data based on its position in a worksheet.

(m) Consolidate data based on data categories.
(n) Outline worksheets to display or print various levels of worksheet detail.
(o) Use Pivot Tables to summarize and analyze large banks of data.
(p) Modify and expand a pivot table.
(q) Insert and rename sheet tabs.
(r) Change column width and row height.
(s) Use formula with Relative and Absolute cell addresses.
(t) Analyze formula syntax.
(u) Use Auto Sum, Auto Calculate, and AutoFill.
(v) Apply number formats to support worksheet data.
(w) Align cell entries, apply text formats, and apply cell borders for visual clarity.
(x) Clear cell contents, comments, and formatting.
(y) Undo and redo multiple actions.
(z) Spell check a worksheet.
(aa) Insert and delete rows.
(bb) Copy data to a predefined range.
(cc) Use comments in a worksheet.
(dd) Use Dates in functions.
(ee) Use Conditional Formatting.
(ff) Create Lists.
(gg) Sort on one column or multiple columns.
(hh) Filter list data to select specific date—Filter with custom criteria, Use Advanced Filters, Remove a filter, Use AutoFilter.
(ii) Use Subtotals.
(jj) Use the Chart Wizard to embed a chart on an Excel worksheet—bar, column, line, and pie charts.
(kk) Create a chart on a separate chart sheet.
(ll) Read series formulas that underlie charts.
(mm) Size or move a chart or a chart object.
(nn) Change chart types.
(oo) Format charts to improve their appearance.
(pp) Print charts with the corresponding worksheet data.
(qq) Protect a Worksheet.
(rr) Create a Template.
(ss) Use a Template to Create a Workbook (Hint: <Office button> <*New*>).
(tt) Import data into Excel.
(uu) Export data from Excel into a text file.

MS-POWERPOINT 2007 18

Contents

- Introduction
- Basics of PowerPoint—PowerPoint basics, PowerPoint terminology
- Start MS-PowerPoint
- MS-PowerPoint screen and its components—Office logo button, quick access toolbar, ribbon, tabs, groups, icons, notes pane, view buttons outline/slides tab, slide pane, ruler bar, status bar, scroll bar
- The office button—New, open, save, save as, print, prepare, send, publish, close
- The ribbon—Home, insert, design, animations, slide show, review, view, add-ins
- Home tab—Clipboard, slides, font, paragraph, drawing, editing
    - Insert tab—Tables, illustrations, links, text, media clip
    - Design tab—Page setup, themes, background
    - Animations tab—Preview, animations, transition to this slide
    - Slide show tab—Start slide show, set up, monitors
    - Review tab—Proofing, comments, protect
    - View tab—Presentation views, show/hide, zoom, color/grayscale, window, macros
- The help
- An example—Create a PowerPoint presentation

Why this chapter

An application of the computer is to use it for presenting our work to a large audience—as a speaker in a conference, as a manager in an organization, as an instructor in a class etc., using a presentation software. A presentation software facilitates creation of slides for presentation—inclusive of text, graphics, animation, movie clips, sound clips etc. MS-PowerPoint is commonly used presentation software. The purpose of this chapter is to introduce you to MS-PowerPoint.

18.1 INTRODUCTION

The Presentation software is used for creation of the slides, and to display the information in the form of presentation of slides. Presentation software are easy to use and provide an alternative to other older types of visual aids like hand-drawn slides, blackboards, whiteboards, posters, pamphlets, handouts, or overhead transparencies. A presentation software provide tools like editor that allow insertion and formatting of text, and, methods for inserting and manipulating graphic images along with sound and visual effects. The presenter and the participants, both benefit from the Presentation software. It provides an easier access to presenter's ideas and provides the participants with visual information in addition to the talk.

The presentations can be printed on paper or transparencies, displayed on a computer, or, projected using a video projector for large audiences. The presentations are of many different types like professional (work-related) presentations used by business people and corporate; education presentation used by educators, students, and trainers; entertainment presentation used for advertising; and presentations for general communication.

The presentation software from different vendors are available for the creation of presentation. Apple Keynote, Microsoft PowerPoint (MS-PowerPoint), Corel Presentations, and IBM Lotus Freelance Graphics are some of the presentation software available in the market. Several open-source presentation software, like, Sun OpenOffice, Impress, MagicPoint, and KPresenter are also available.

MS-PowerPoint is the most commonly known presentation software. It is a part of the MS-Office suite, and runs on Microsoft Windows and Mac OS X operating systems. MS-PowerPoint is a GUI-based software. MS-PowerPoint includes tools for word processing, outlining, drawing, graphing, and presentation management, which are all easy to use and learn. The slides in a MS-PowerPoint presentation may contain text, graphics, movies, and other objects, which may be arranged freely on the slide. Some of the important features of MS-PowerPoint are as follows:

- A consistent style in a presentation can be adopted by using a template or *Slide Master.*
- Interactive presentations can be made with a system of links and buttons to move to the next slide; and a full set of hyperlinks that function like a nested website, where the user chooses options.
- Background effects can be included in the slides.
- The entrance, emphasis, and exit of elements on a slide itself are controlled using Custom Animations.
- Transitions, or movements between slides can be animated in a variety of ways.

Figure 18.1 Shows a presenter making a presentation using PowerPoint

Figure 18.1 A presentation being made using PowerPoint

This chapter discusses the using of the MS-PowerPoint software in detail. There are many versions of the MS-PowerPoint software. This chapter discusses the MS-PowerPoint 2007.

In this chapter, we will use the following terminology while working with the mouse—

- **Pointer**—a mouse pointer
- **Click**—press left button of mouse once
- **Double Click**—press left button of mouse twice
- **Select**—move the pointer of mouse and keep the left button of the mouse pressed over the area that you want to select. The selected area will appear in a dark background.
- **Quick Menu**—Right click (press right button of mouse once) to get a quick menu

The commands used in this chapter are enclosed in braces <Command> to represent the command to be clicked.

18.2 BASICS OF POWERPOINT

MS-PowerPoint 2007 allows the creation of dynamic and high-impact presentations. In this section, we will discuss the basics of PowerPoint and introduce some PowerPoint terminology.

- **PowerPoint Basics**
  - A PowerPoint (PPT) presentation consists of a collection of slides.
  - A slide is a single screen that contains information that the presenter wants to show.
  - A presentation generally has a Title slide, a Presentation outline slide, several slides discussing the outlined topics, and the conclusion or summary slide.
  - The information can be in the form of text as bullet points, images or animation.
  - Bullet points are not complete explanations; rather they convey a basic thought that is expanded upon by the presenter, during the presentation.
  - The presenter can control the movement across the slides or the presentation can be pre-programmed to perform the navigation automatically.
- **PowerPoint Terminology**
  - *Master* contains formatting and design elements common to every slide in the presentation.
  - *Template* contains slide default settings for colors, fonts, bullet types, and graphics.
  - *Slide Show* is the PowerPoint Presentation given, using a projection device such as a video-data projector or an LCD overhead projector. Slideshows can be enhanced with clip art, Smart Art diagrams, tables, and charts. Custom animations can be used to enliven presentations. Themes and Quick styles allow you to apply styling quickly to a whole presentation of individual elements. In addition to the pre-prepared slide layouts, presenter can also create a customized slide layout, complete with placeholder text, using the Custom Slide Layouts. Smart Art graphics allows insertion of designer quality graphics into the presentations.
  - *Wizard* is a step-by-step guide for completing a task.
  - *Transitions* are the effect that takes place when you advance from one slide to the next. Transitions are available only with *Slide Shows.*
  - *Animations* are the sound and the movements that appear when a slide comes on the screen. For example, it can be used to have one line of text appear on the screen at a time.

- *Objects* can be the items that can be created with the drawing tools or the pictures that are imported from other sources (such as scanned images).
- *Clip Art* is the collection of pictures available in the PowerPoint *Clip Art* gallery.

18.3 START MS-POWERPOINT

The MS-PowerPoint software for the Windows operating system is installed on the computer. MS-PowerPoint is fully menu-driven software, and the commands are available in the form of Tabs, Groups and Icons. While working in MS-PowerPoint, using a mouse makes working on MS-PowerPoint simpler although one can work to some extent through the keyboard also.

To start using the MS-PowerPoint software, *any one* of the following steps needs to be performed—

Figure 18.2 MS-PowerPoint icon

- ⊙ If a shortcut key to MS-PowerPoint is available as an icon on the Desktop, as shown in Figure 18.2, then double-click the icon.
- ⊙ **<Start> <All Programs> <Microsoft Office> <Microsoft Office PowerPoint 2007>.** (Figure 18.3)

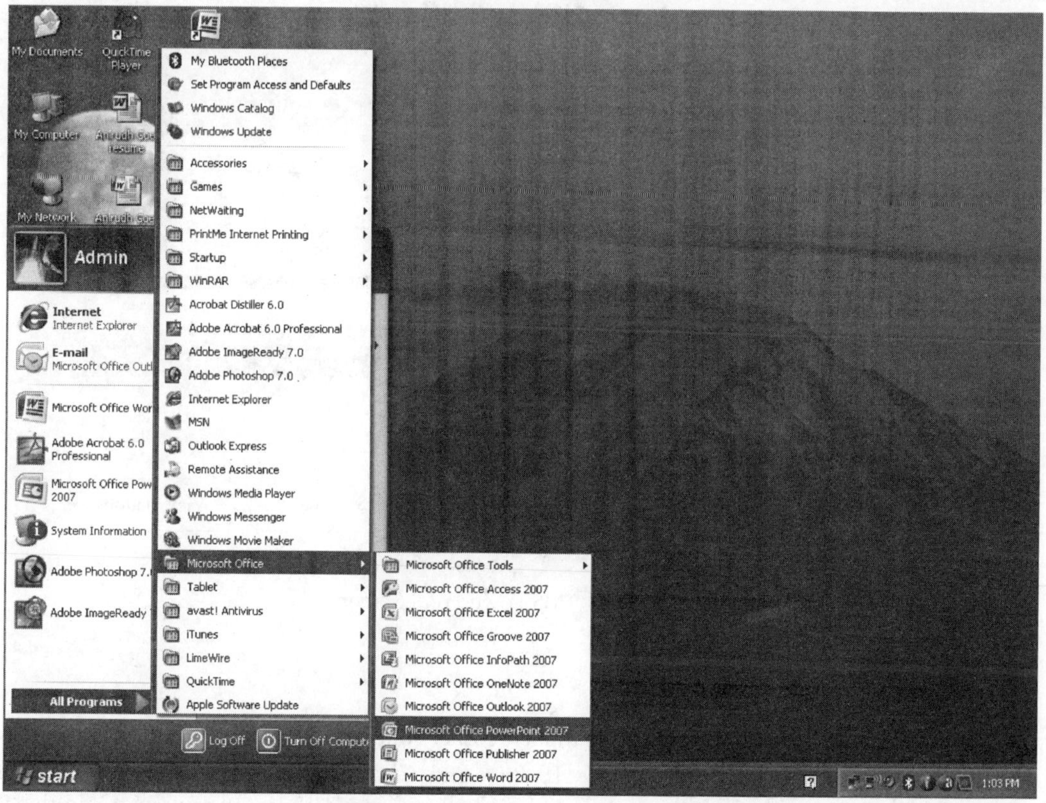

Figure 18.3 Start MS-PowerPoint

18.4 MS-POWERPOINT SCREEN AND ITS COMPONENTS

The main screen of the MS-PowerPoint that appears when the software gets started is shown in Figure 18.4. At the top side of the screen is the Ribbon. There is a ruler bar and a scroll bar, and at the lower side of the screen there is the Status Bar. The screen also consists of the view buttons, and the different panes like slide pane, notes pane, outline/slide pane. A brief description of the different components of the screen is given below:

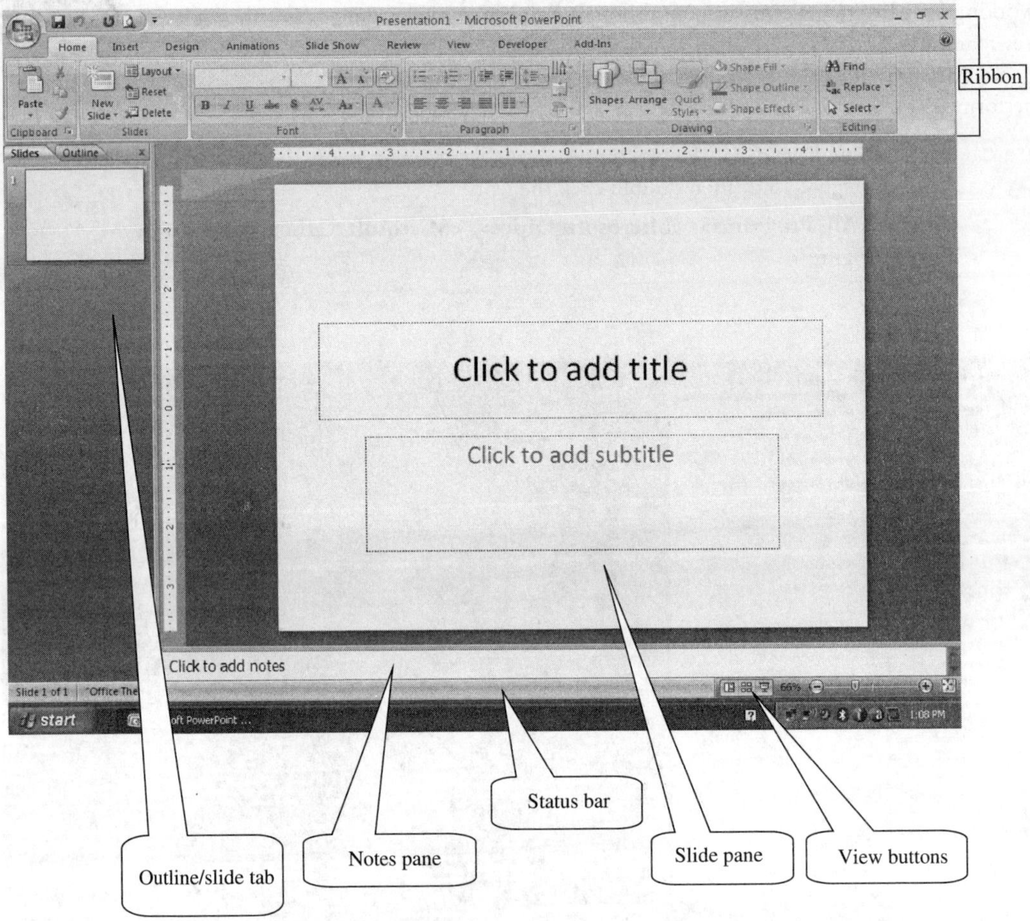

Figure 18.4 MS-PowerPoint Screen

- The **Office Logo Button** at the top left corner contains many task buttons for the document such as, *New, Open, Save, Save As, Print* and *Close.* This button also has a list of the recent documents. Some of these commands include an expandable menu to provide additional options.

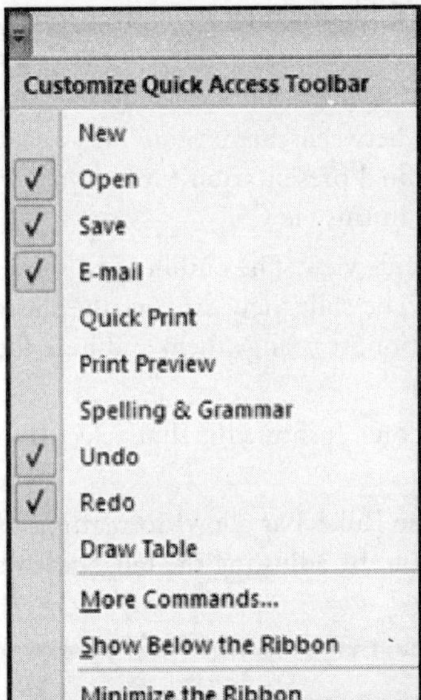

- **The Quick Access Toolbar**  is to the right of the Office Logo button. It contains shortcuts for the commonly used tools, like, Save, Undo (reverses the last change), and Repeat (repeats the last action). The buttons that the user wishes to be displayed can be selected from the *Customize Quick Access Toolbar.*

- **The Ribbon** is a set of tools and commands across the top of the screen (Figure 18.5). The layout of the Ribbon in MS-PowerPoint is same as that of the Ribbon in MS-Word and MS-Excel. It consists of a panel of commands which are organized into a set of tabs (also known as the Tab Bar). Within Tabs are Groups, which are designated by the names located on the bottom of the Ribbon. Each group has icons for the associated command. The Ribbon (Tabs, Groups and Icons) replaces the traditional toolbars and menus of earlier versions of MS-PowerPoint.

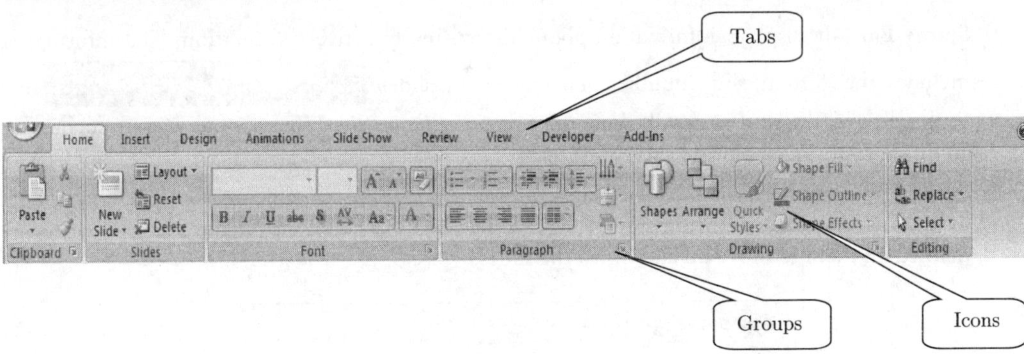

Figure 18.5 The ribbon

- The **Tabs** (Home, Insert etc.) on the Ribbon contain the buttons needed to edit characters, text, and layout, as well as the additional tools that you may need.

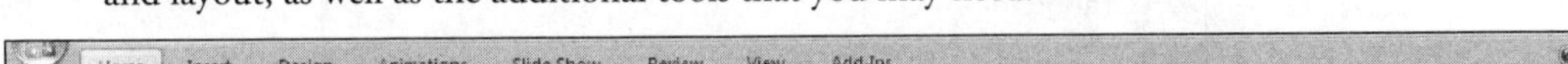

- Each Tab consists of different **Groups**, like the Home tab has six groups namely, Clipboard, Slides, Font, Paragraph, Drawing, and Editing.

- Each group has **Icons** for the commands, which will actually format the document or bring up a menu. To know the function of an icon button (or command), leave the pointer on a button for a few seconds, the function of that button will appear in a small box below the pointer. For example, leaving the icon on **B** displays "Bold (Ctrl+B)".

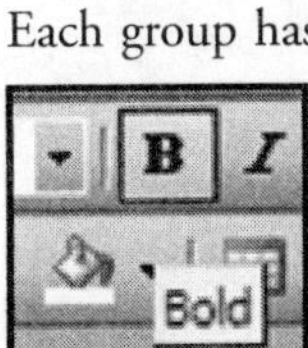

- **Notes Pane**—It is used by the presenter to makes the notes that are to be used while presenting.

- **View Buttons**—They enable user to look at the slides of PPT file on their computer in different ways. By default, PowerPoint opens the presentation in Normal View, which is the main view used to design and edit presentations. Slide Sorter presents slide miniatures, allowing the reorder of the slides, and pre-set the transitions between them. Slide Show shows the slides as if the presenter is actually presenting. The final presentation is presented in the Slide Show mode to the audience. Slides cannot be edited in this view.
- **Outline/Slides Tab**—It contains two views—outline view and slide view. The outline view shows the text of the slides in a larger format than the Normal view. The slide view displays the slides as thumbnails, where user can view all the slides in the presentation, rearrange them and hide the slides, as per requirements.
- **Slide Pane**—This is the work area where most of the editing is done. It shows the slide selected in the Outline/Slides tab as it will appear in the presentation.
- **Ruler Bar**—There are two rulers—Horizontal and Vertical. The Ruler Bar allows formatting of the horizontal and the vertical alignment of text in a presentation, by adjusting the tabs, indents and margins.

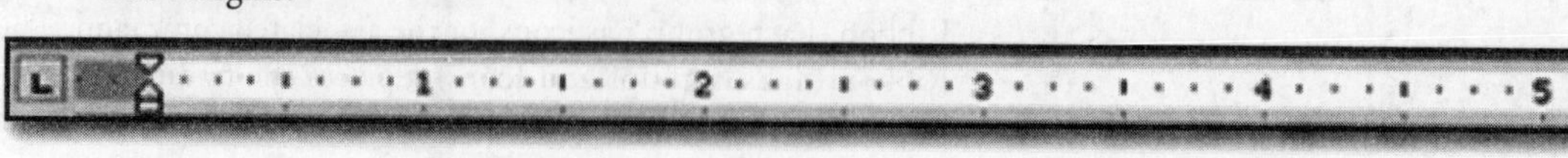

- **Status Bar**—It displays information about the currently active presentation. The information includes the current slide number, Theme, zoom slider  etc. Right-click on the status bar will show the *Customize Status Bar* (Figure 18.6) pop-up menu. The appropriate option can be selected on the status bar.
- **Scroll Bar**—The vertical scroll bar helps to scroll the slides of the presentation. Scrolling is done by moving the elevator button along the scroll bar, or by clicking on the buttons with the arrow marked on them to move up and down the slides.

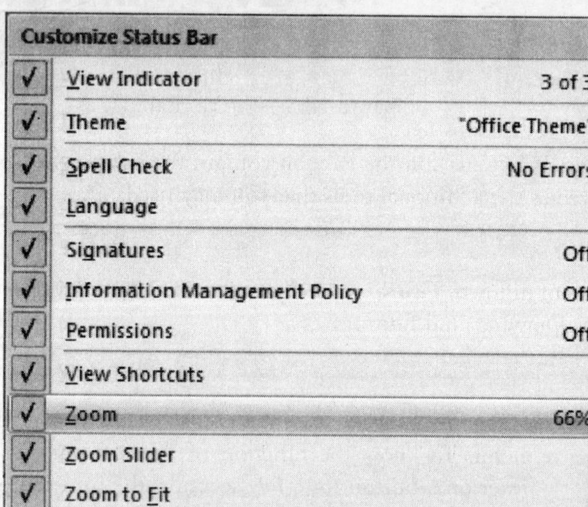

Figure 18.6 Customize status bar

18.5 THE OFFICE BUTTON

The functionality of the Office button in PowerPoint is almost similar to the functionality provided in the MS-Word or MS-Excel software. For example, New will open a blank document in MS-Word, a blank Workbook in MS-Excel, and a blank Presentation in MS-PowerPoint.

The Office Button is used to perform file management operations on the file (i.e. the presentation). It contains commands that allow the user to create a new presentation, open an existing presentation, save a presentation, print a presentation etc. The Office button contains nine commands (Figure 18.7), namely, New, Open, Save, Save As, Print, Prepare, Send, Publish, and Close. The working of these commands is almost similar to their working in MS-Word and MS-Excel, and are briefly discussed here.

Table 18.1 briefly describes the different commands available in the Office Button.

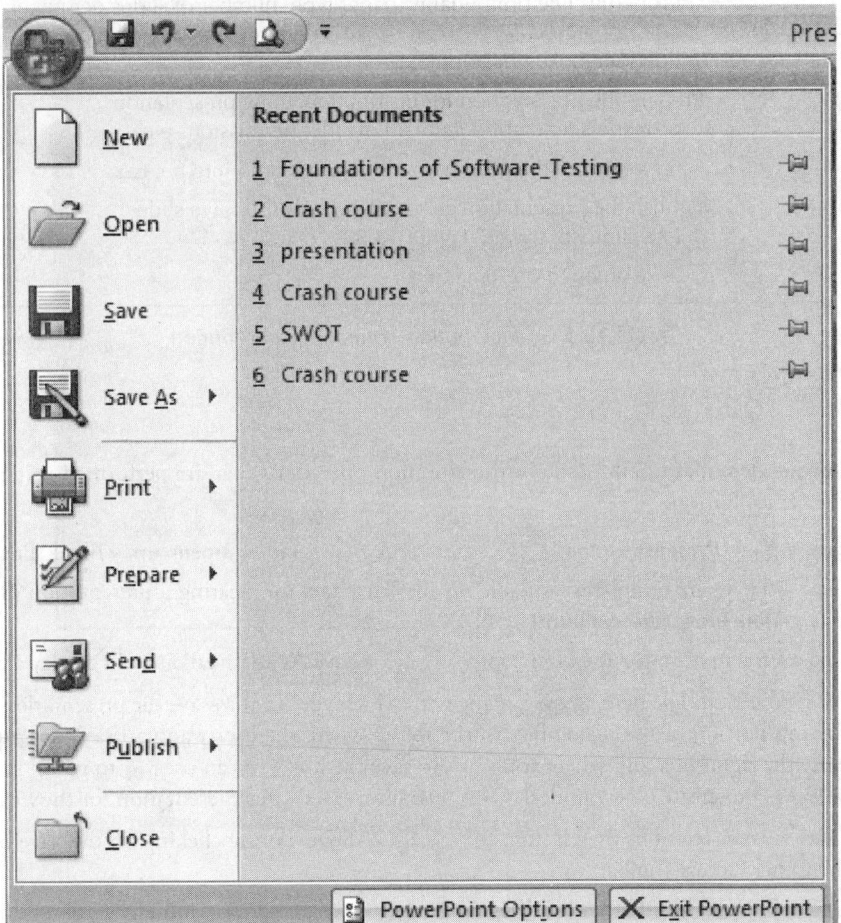

Figure 18.7 The office button commands

Office Button Commands	Description
New	Create a new blank presentation.
Open	Open an already existing presentation.
Save	Save a presentation for which a file name and location has already been specified.
Save As	Used when presentation is saved for the first time or to a different location, or at same location with different name or with a new type presentation. Specify the filename for the presentation, the location where the presentation is to be stored and the save type of the presentation. Presentation can also be saved as a PowerPoint presentation, PowerPoint show, PowerPoint 97-2003 presentation etc. (Figure 18.8).
Print	Print, Quick Print, Print Preview the presentation. Properties like print quality, paper type, number of slides per page, color or grayscale, etc. can be set. Preview to see how the presentation will look after printing.
Prepare	Prepare the presentation for distribution. View presentation properties, encrypt document, restrict permissions etc.
Send	Send a copy of the presentation to e-mail or to Internet Fax
Publish	Publish the presentation as handouts, to a CD, save slides to a slide library etc (Figure 18.9).
Close	Close an open presentation.

Table 18.1 *Office button commands description*

The following describes briefly some of the common operations that are performed using the commands of the Office Button:

- **Create a New Presentation:** < > **<New>**. A new window opens up. <Blank Presentation> <Create>. There are templates available on the left panel for creating a presentation of a specific type (e.g. quiz show, photo album).
- **Saving a Presentation for the First Time:** < > **<Save As>**. PowerPoint will display a dialog box. In the field next to File name, type a name with which you want to save the presentation. Navigate in the top portion of the dialog box to the folder where the user wants to save the presentation (choose the right directory where you want to save the file. You can use to go up in the directory, Use to create a new folder). Once you have saved your presentation for the first time you can save further revisions by selecting the < > **<Save>**, or by clicking on the Save button in the Quick Access Toolbar.
- **Saving a Presentation Under a Different Name:** Open the presentation by selecting the < > **<Open>**. Next, < > **<Save As>** A dialog box will appear. Navigate to the folder where you want to save the presentation and type in a new name for the presentation. Select the Save button. One now has two copies of the presentation, one with the original name, another with a new name.

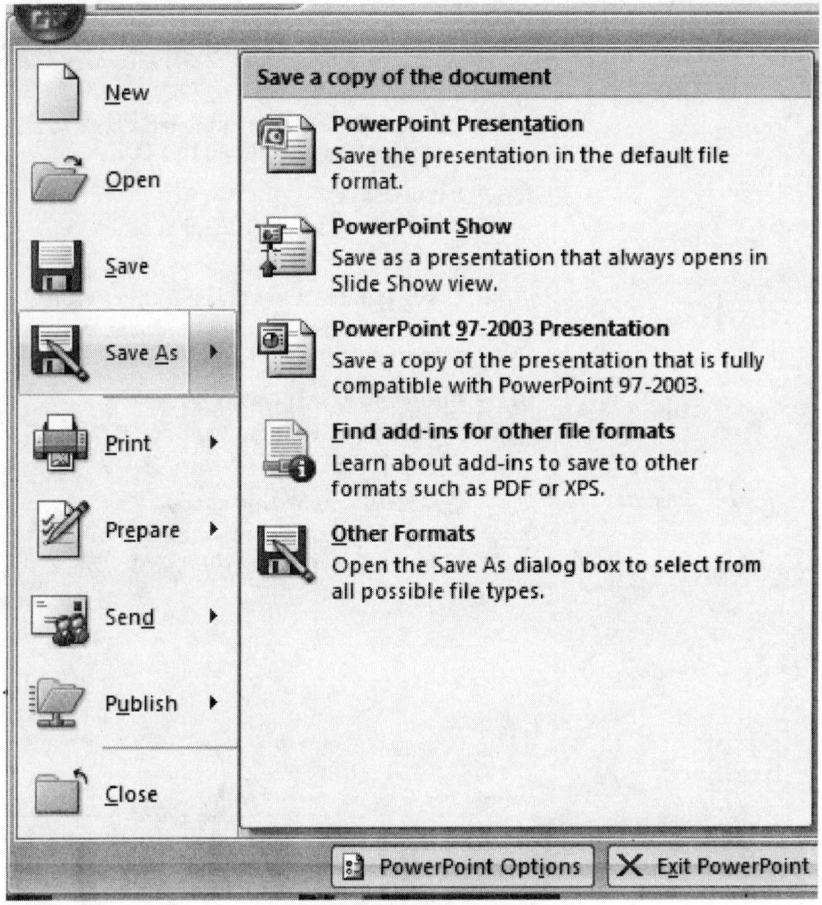

Figure 18.8 Save as option

- **Crash Protection:** < > **<Save As>** **<Tools><Save Options>**. Select the boxes for *Save Auto Recover* Information every <enter the number of minutes>. Reset the Minutes from 10 to 1. MS-PowerPoint would be able to recover a file one minute old.
- **To Preview your Presentation Before Printing:** < >**<Print> Select Print Preview**. User can switch between viewing one slide and multiple slides, zoom in, (it will turn into a magnifying glass

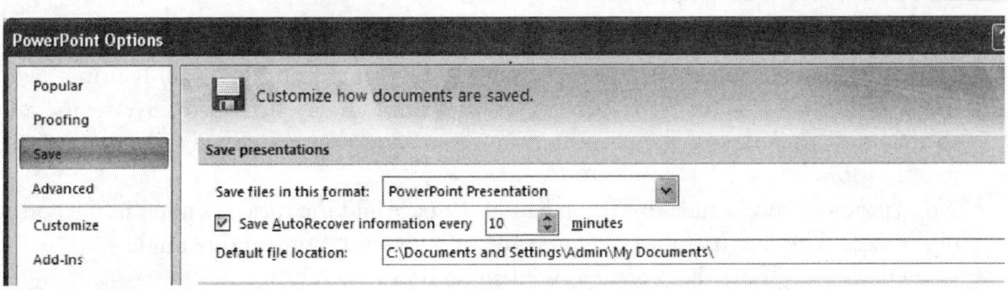

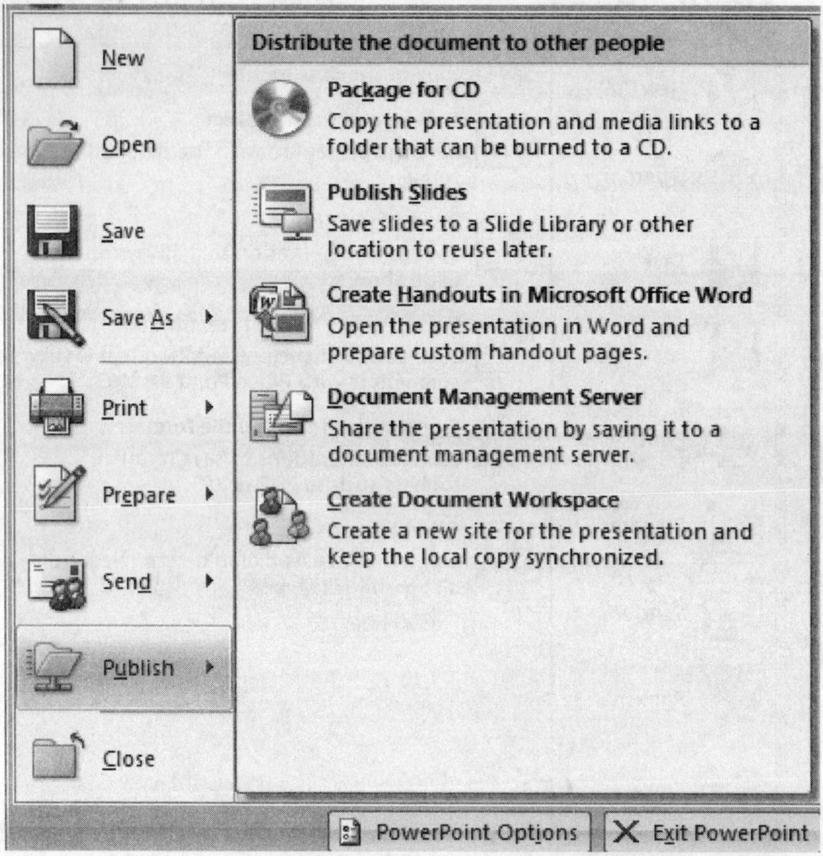

Figure 18.9 Publish option

with a + symbol inside) and zoom back out, place the cursor on the presentation and this time the cursor will turn into a magnifying glass with a – symbol inside.

- **To Print: <File> <Print>**. Make settings like number of copies and pages to be printed. (Figure 18.10). From the Print dialog box one can make further settings like—*Print What,* where one can select one of the following options:
  - A slide—Prints one slide per page in landscape orientation.
  - Handouts—it will ask the number of slides to be printed on one page. It prints two, three or six slides per page in portrait orientation. Handouts are useful to give to the audience so that they understand the presentation better, and they can handwrite notes during the presentation.
  - Notes pages—Prints a slide in the top half of the page and the speaker's notes in the bottom half of the page. They are useful for the presenter as it contains notes and reminders.
  - Outline views—Prints the presentation in an outline view

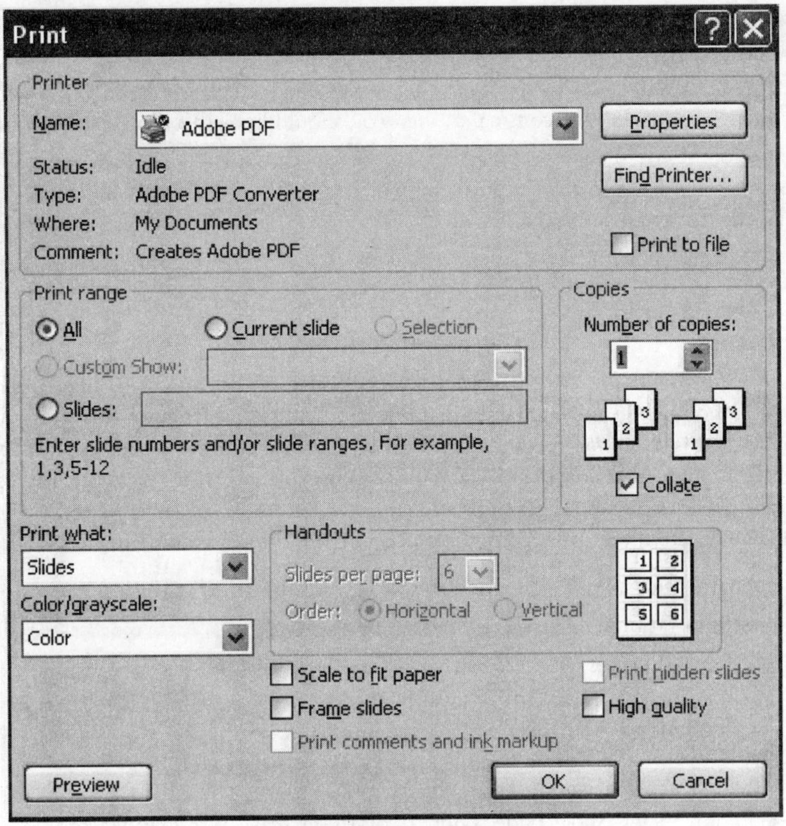

Figure 18.10 Print dialog box

Quick Tips—How to Learn MS-PowerPoint

When working with MS-PowerPoint, all one needs to know is the following:

- **What a command does?**
- **When you want to perform a particular action, which command to use?**
- **How to use a command?**

Here's a brief description for further enabling you to learn MS-PowerPoint:

(1) What a command does—When your keep your mouse pointer over a command or icon, the function of command or icon gets displayed in a text box. So you can know what a command does by moving the mouse over the command.

(2) Which command to use—

a. To search for a command, first see which tab might have the command. For example, if you want to do any formatting, click the Home Tab; to insert anything click the Insert tab; to design your slides click the Design tab.

b. You will be able to find the group and command you want, most of the time. The commands that have similar uses are grouped together in the same group in PowerPoint 2007.

(3) Once you are able to find the command, then you should know how to use the command.

a. For most of the commands, first place the cursor in the presentation at the position where the action is to happen, or, select the object on which you want the action to happen (for example formatting commands). Next, click on the command. The command gets executed.

b. In some commands, there is a set of steps to use the command. Simply follow the steps.

18.6 THE RIBBON

Like the other programs in the Office 2007 suite, PowerPoint 2007 has a ribbon. The Ribbon of MS-PowerPoint has the Office button and eight Tabs, namely, Home, Insert, Design, Animations, Slide Show, Review, View, and Add-Ins. Each tab further consists of the groups, and the groups contain icons. Icons are a pictorial representation for a command. Each Tab is self-explanatory; for example, for a page setup for the slide, click on the Design tab. The groups and icons related to *Design* are displayed. Select the Page Setup command. The different tabs in MS-PowerPoint and the groups within them are as follows:

- **Home**: Clipboard, Slides, Font, Paragraph, Drawing, Editing
- **Insert**: Tables, Illustrations, Links, Text, Media Clips
- **Design**: Page Setup, Themes, Background
- **Animations**: Preview, Animations, Transition to This Slide
- **Slide Show**: Start Slide Show, Set Up, Monitors
- **Review**: Proofing, Comments, Protect
- **View**: Presentation Views, Show/Hide, Zoom, Color/Grayscale, Window, Macros

The **Add-Ins tab** contains supplemental functionality that adds custom commands and specialized features to MS-PowerPoint.

The commands in the Ribbon have various symbols associated with them, as shown in Figure 18.11. These symbols are interpreted as follows:

Selecting a command	
Ways to select a command	**Using a command**
Click on a Tab + *Click on a Icon*	Click on any of the Tabs like Home, Insert etc. From the displayed icons, click on the icon you want to use.
Shortcut key *Ctrl + letter*	Some commands have shortcuts where you can press the **Ctrl** key and a **certain letter**. Some commonly used shortcuts are – • Paste: CTRL + V • Copy: CTRL + C • Undo: CTRL + Z • New document: CTRL + N • Open document: CTRL + O • Print document: CTRL + P

Figure 18.11 Command symbols

- **Simple Command**—The command start executing when it is clicked.
- **Command Followed by Arrow**—Clicking on the arrow ▾ displays more options for the command.
- **Faded Command**—A faded command means that it is not available currently.
- **Group Dialog Box**—Clicking on this ⧉ symbol displays the dialog box for the group.

The following sub-sections describe the different tabs in detail.

Working with MS-PowerPoint 2007

- **Live Preview** applies temporary formatting on the selected text or object when the mouse moves over any of the formatting buttons. This allows the preview of, how the text will appear with this formatting. The temporary formatting is removed if the mouse pointer is moved away from the button.
- **Mini Toolbar** pops up whenever text is selected. It provides easy access to the most commonly used formatting commands in Word. The Mini Toolbar also appears when you right-click on a selection of text.
- **File Format** for the documents created in PowerPoint 2007 version is ***.pptx***. (For earlier versions it is. *ppt*)

18.6.1 The Home Tab

The Home Tab contains commands for formatting of text, selecting a new slide and for drawing of objects. The Home Tab is also used for editing the content of presentation like find and replace, and to perform clipboard operations such as cut, copy, and paste on the presentation. Figure 18.12 shows the Home Tab.

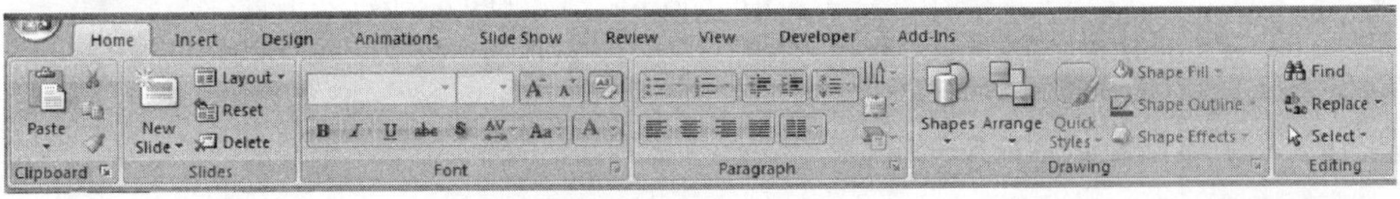

Figure 18.12 The home tab

There are six groups within this tab, namely, Clipboard, Slides, Font, Paragraph, Drawing, and Editing.

- The *Clipboard* group contains commands to cut, copy, and paste text. The Format Painter is also present here. The Clipboard commands are used in the same manner as one uses the MS-Word Clipboard commands.
- *Slides* group allows to select a theme and layout for a slide, reset a slide or delete a slide.
- *Font* group commands allows change of the Font—font face, style, size, effects (Strikethrough, Shadow etc.), color, and character spacing. These options can be changed, before or after typing the text. If case of after, select the text first.
- *Paragraph* group is used to change paragraph setting—alignment, indents, spacing, and pagination like Spacing 1.5, Double Spacing, Indentation, and, Spacing Before and After a Heading. Move the cursor to a line which needs to be changed.
- The *Drawing* group allows the quick selection from the in-built shapes, arranging the order and grouping the objects, filling, outlining, and adding effects to the shape.
- *Editing* group contains commands to select, and, find and replace text.

Table 18.2 gives the commands in the different groups (*in left to right order*) of the Home Tab along with a brief explanation.

> *To apply formatting to an already written text, first select the text and then apply the formatting.*

Home Tab Groups	Description
Clipboard	 • *Paste* the cut or copied information in Clipboard at the location where cursor is pointing right now (Paste Special—To paste in a particular format. Paste as Hyperlink—Used with copy to paste the copied information as a hyperlink. Duplicate—To duplicate a slide) • *Cut* removes the selected text from the presentation and puts into Clipboard for later retrieval. • *Copy* copies the selected item or text and puts it on the Clipboard. • *Format painter* copies formatting from one place and apply to another (To apply same formatting to many places, double-click the format painter button)
Slides	 • Add a *new slide* to the Presentation. • Change the *layout* of the selected slide. • Reset the position, size and setting of the slide to default values. • *Delete* the selected slide from the presentation.

(*continued*)

<table>
<tr><th>Home Tab Groups</th><th>Description</th></tr>
<tr><td>Font</td><td>

• Change Font face, change font size.
• Increase Font size, Decrease Font size.
• Clear formatting (Clear all formatting from selection, leave only plain text).
• Bold, Italics, Underline.
• Strikethrough (draw a line through middle of selected text).
• Shadow adds a shadow behind the selected text.
• Adjust the spacing between characters.
• Change case. Changes the case – sentence, lower, upper, title, or toggle.
• Select the text and click on an option.
• Change the Font color.</td></tr>
<tr><td>Paragraph</td><td>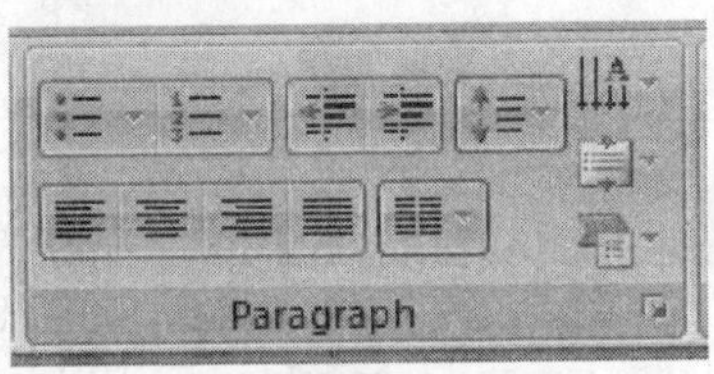

• Bullets (choose from different styles).
• Numbered list (choose different formats).
• Increase or decrease indent of the paragraph.
• Change spacing between lines.
• Change the direction of text to vertical, stacked or rotate the text.
• Align the text—change how the text is aligned within the text box.
• Align text left, right, centre, margins.
• Split text into two or more columns.
• Convert text into Smart Art graphics .</td></tr>
<tr><td>Drawing</td><td>

• Insert readymade shapes like circle, rectangles, arrow lines, flowchart etc.
• Arrange objects on the slide by changing their order, position, and rotation.
• Quick styles allows for choosing a visual style for the shape or line.
• Fill the selected shape with a solid color, gradient, picture or texture.
• Specify the color, width, and line style for the outline of the selected shape.
• Apply a visual effect to the selected shape like glow, shadow, reflection, and 3-D rotation.</td></tr>
<tr><td>Editing</td><td>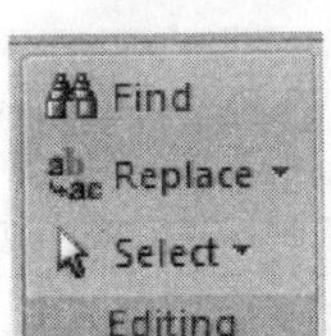

• Find text in the presentation.
• Replace text or objects in the presentation.
• Select text or objects in the presentation.</td></tr>
</table>

Table 18.2 *Home tab commands description*

Some of the operations that are performed using the commands of the Home Tab are briefly described here.

- **Move Text**: Select and highlight the section which needs to be moved **<Home><Clipboard>**< >. Move the cursor to the place where the text is to be inserted **<Home><Clipboard>** < >.
- **Copy Text**: Select and highlight the section to be copied **<Home><Clipboard>**< >. Move the cursor to the place where the copied text is to be inserted **<Home><Clipboard>**< >
- **Find and Replace**: This is used to find a text and then replace it with the new one. This option is useful for finding a text at multiple places in the presentation and replacing all of them with the new one.

> **To Select Multiple Text Entries** *that are scattered words, phrases, or paragraphs for the same action, select the first item with your mouse in a normal manner. For subsequent items, press the CTRL key before selecting them. Now perform any operation like italicize, boldface, or highlight on all the selected items*

18.6.2 The Insert Tab

The Insert Tab contains commands for inserting objects of all kinds in a presentation. The commands in this tab are used to add illustrations, tables, links, text, and media clips. It also includes commands to add symbols, slide number, a picture, clip art, shapes, and, headers and footers. Figure 18.13 shows the Insert Tab.

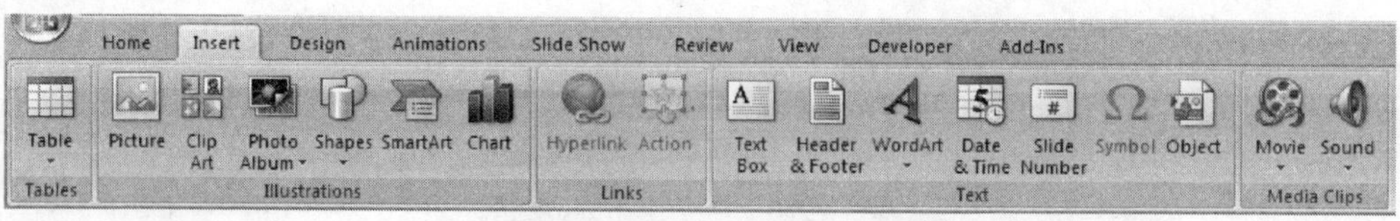

Figure 18.13 The insert tab

There are five groups within this tab, namely, Tables, Illustrations, Links, Text, and Media Clips.

- *Tables* are used to draw and insert tables.
- *Illustrations* group allows insertion of pictures, clip art, pictures from photo album, shapes, smart art, and charts.
- The *Links* group is used to insert a hyperlink, and to add action to an object.
- The *Text* group contains commands to insert a text box, word Art, date and time, slide number, and, header and footer.
- The *Media Clips* group is used to insert movie from a file, and sound from a CD or clipboard.

> Some of the Tabs appear only when you use them; like Picture Tools tab, Drawing Tools Tab, and Table Tools Tab

Table 18.3 gives the commands in the different groups of the Insert Tab along with a brief explanation.

Insert Tab Groups	Description

Tables

- Insert or draw table in the slide (insert an Excel spreadsheet, insert from one of the built-in tables). When a table is drawn, a Table Tool Design Tab (Figure 18.14) and Table Tools Layout Tab opens, which allows you to select Table Style options, Table Styles and The Table Borders.

Illustrations

- Insert picture from a file. When a picture is inserted, a Picture Tool Format Tab opens (Figure 18.15) which contains commands to format the picture.
- Insert clipart into the document (sounds, movies, drawings).
- Insert a photo album. Create a new presentation based on the set of pictures. Each picture is placed on a new slide.
- Insert readymade shapes (lines, arrows, flowchart symbols etc.) into the document.
- Insert a smart art graphics.
- Insert a chart (bar graph, pie chart, line Area, surface etc.).

Links

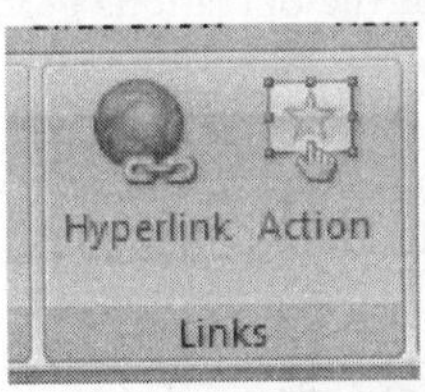

- Insert a hyperlink to a web page, a picture, an email address or a program.
- Add an action to the selected object to specify the action to be taken when the mouse hovers over it or when it is clicked.

Text

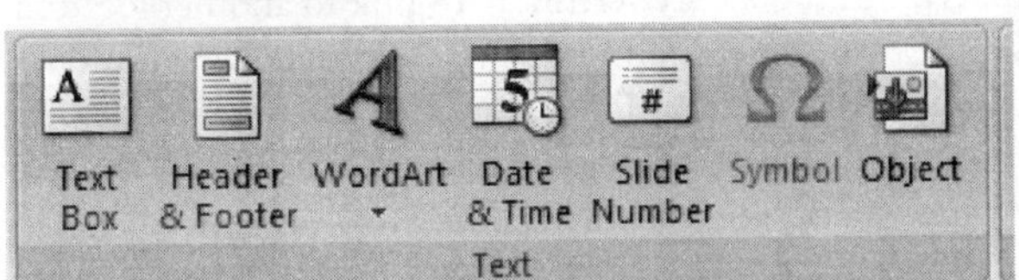

- Insert preformatted built-in text box or draw a text box. When a text box is inserted, a Text Box Tools Format Tab opens which contains commands to format the text box.
- Insert header and footer to the slide. Insert the slide number, date and time, both for the slides and the notes.
- Insert decorative text in the document.
- Insert date and time into the document.
- Insert slide number into the document.
- Insert symbols that are part of the keyboard into the document. When *Symbol* is clicked, a *symbol* table pops up. Select the symbol to be inserted.
- Insert an embedded object.

Media Clips

- Insert movie from a file or the clip organizer
- Insert sound from a file, clip organizer, a CD track or record the sound.

Table 18.3 *Insert tab commands description*

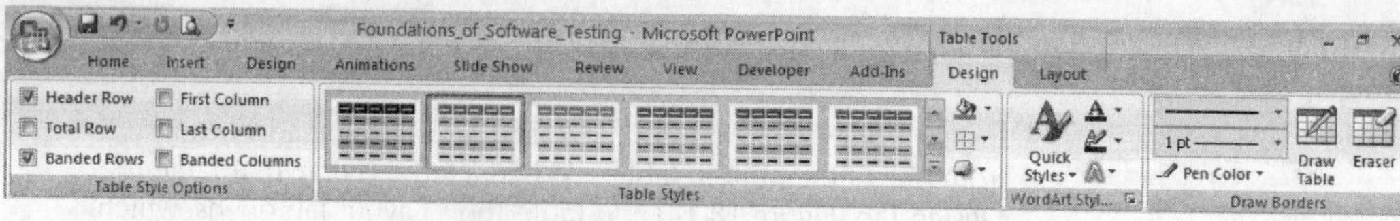

Figure 18.14 Table tools design tab

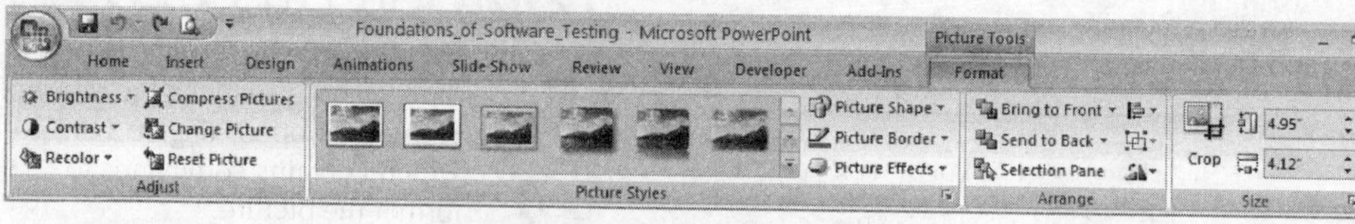

Figure 18.15 Picture tools format tab

When a command of the Insert tab is used, insertion takes place at the location where the cursor is present right now. So, before inserting the item, place the cursor at the location where the item is to be inserted. While using the commands of the insert tab for insertion, most of the times, a dialog box will open which allows making changes to specific settings, as per requirements. The dialog boxes are not discussed here, as they are self-explanatory and easy to use. Some of the operations performed using the Insert Tab commands are described below:

- **To create headers and footers—<Insert> <Text><Header** & **Footer>**. A Header and Footer command is seen. A Header and Footer tab is opened which allows the addition of date and time, slide number etc.
- **Insert Hyperlink—<Insert> <Links> <Hyperlink.>** To link to another location in the same document, click *Place in This Document* option under *Link to;* In the dialog box's inner window, select a heading from the document diagram. To link to another document, click the Existing File or Web Page option. Navigate to the proper folder and select the file's name. It is also possible to add a link to a newly created presentation or an e-mail address.
- **Insert Text**: **<Insert> <Text> <Text Box>**. In PowerPoint, all text is contained in Text Boxes. Click anywhere on the slide and drag corner points of the text box to change its size. Click within the box to type text. To format the text box, select the text box. <Drawing Tools> <Format>. Format the selected text box. To format the text in the text box; select the text. <Home> <Font> <Paragraph>. Format the Font, Size, color, and style of the selected text.

18.6.3 The Design Tab

The Design Tab contains commands to apply themes, change page set up, and to adjust the background style. The Design Tab is shown in Figure 18.16.

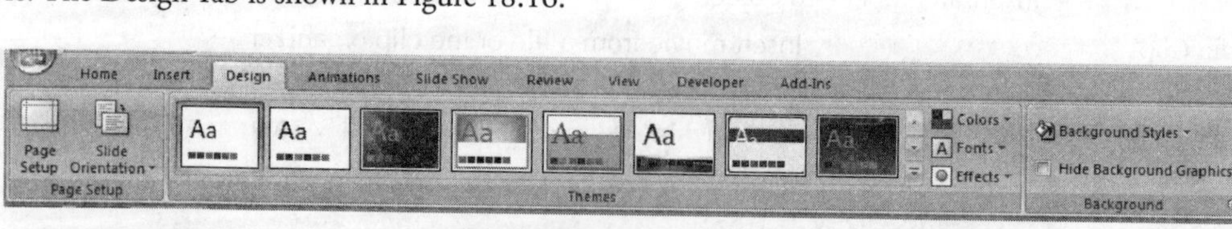

Figure 18.16 The design tab

There are three groups within this tab, namely, Page Setup, Themes, and Background.

- *Page Setup* opens a dialog box that sets up orientation of the slide, size of the slides and screen size on which the slide is to be shown.
- The *Themes* group contains commands to select a theme, font, color and effect, for the slides.
- *Background* group allows choosing a background style for the slide.

Table 18.4 gives the commands in the different groups of the Design Tab along with a brief explanation.

Design Tab Group	**Description**
Page Setup	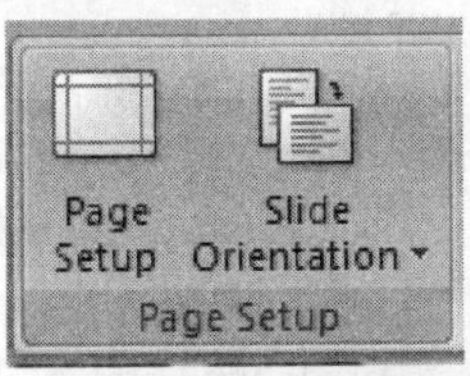 • A Page setup dialog box opens. • Select orientation between portrait and landscape of the slide and also of the notes and handouts. • Select a size for which the slide show is meant like A3, A4, banner, overhead etc. • Select the height and width of the slides.
Themes	 • Themes are used to change the overall design of the slide. You can also change the font, theme color, and theme effect.
Background	 • Choose a background style for this theme. Choose from fill effects like gradient, and picture. • Hide the background graphics of the theme.

Table 18.4 *Design commands description*

Some of the operations that are performed using the commands of the Design tab are briefly described below.

- **To Change the Background**: **<Design> <Background><Background styles> <Format Background>**. Format Background window appears. Set the color, solid or gradient, transparency, picture/texture fill etc.
  - <Close> to apply changes only to the current slide.
  - <Apply to All> to apply changes to all the slides.
- **To Change the Theme**: **<Design> <Themes>**. To preview the different themes for the slide, move the cursor over the theme buttons. Select a theme; the theme will apply to all the slides in the presentation.
  - <Colors> changes the color scheme of the current theme.
  - <Fonts> changes the font of the current theme.
  - <Effects> changes the effects of the current theme.

18.6.4 The Animations Tab

The Animations Tab contains commands for adding animations and transitions to the slide. Animation is the movement and sound that accompanies text or slides as they are introduced on the screen. Using animation in the slides by displaying text at crucial moments makes good impact on the audience. Transitions are the effects that a presenter can add to PPT and these effects get displayed during the Slide Show, as the presenter moves from one slide to the next. The Animations Tab is shown in Figure 18.17.

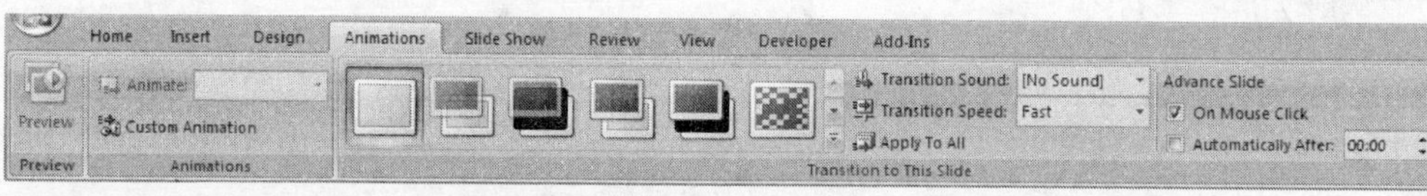

Figure 18.17 The animations tab

There are three groups within this tab, namely, Preview, Animations, and Transition to This Slide.

- The *Preview* group contains a preview button that displays a preview of the animation effects you selected for the slide.
- *Animations* allow creation of animation effects. To select a predefined effect, click on the *Animate* drop-down list, or click the Custom Animation button to specify a custom animation.
- *Transition to This slide* group allows setting the transition effect that is used when the slide is displayed in Slide Show mode.

Table 18.5 gives the commands in the different groups of Animations Tab along with a brief explanation.

Some of the operations that are performed using the commands of Animations tab are briefly described below:

- **To Create Custom Animation Effects**: **<Animations> <Animations> <Custom Animation>**. Custom Animation pane appears on the right side of the current slide. Select the object on the slide to which you wish to apply animation.
  - <Add Effect>. Select the animation style. "Entrance" styles have commonly used effects.
  - <Play>. Preview the animation.
  - <Modify Effect>. To modify the animation effects and order of the animated object. How to *Start* the animation, *Direction* of animation, *Speed* of animation. To change the order of animated objects - Select the object in the list under Modify. Hold on the mouse and bring up or down to change the order of object.
- **To Create Slide Transition**: **<Animations> <Animations> <Transition to This Slide>**. Select a transition effect which is needed. As the cursor moves over the transition buttons, the effects get previewed. Click on the transition effect to apply it.
  - <Transition Sound>. Apply sound effect for transition.
  - <Transition Speed>. Adjust the speed.
  - <Apply to All>. Apply the same transition effect to all the slides.
- **To Create Automatic Presentation**: **<Animations> <Transition to this Slide> <Advance Slide> <Automatically After>**. Set the time to automatically change to the next slide after certain time

Animations Tab Group	Description
Preview	 • Click on preview to see the animation effect of the selected slide.
Animations	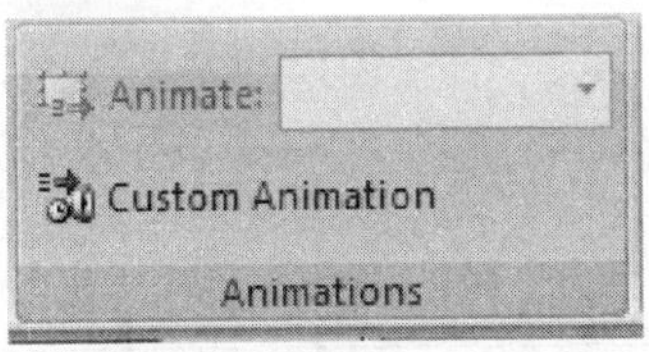 • *Animate* – Choose an animation effect to apply to objects in the slide. • *Custom animation* opens the custom anima tion task pane which lets the animation of the individual objects on the slide. Add effects like Entrance, Emphasis, Exit, Motion Paths etc, when to start the animated effect (on click etc.), and the speed of animation.
Transition to This Slide	 • Select the special effects that will apply during the transition between the previous slide and the current slide. • Choose the transition sound, transition speed and apply it to the current slide or to all the slides. • Select *On mouse click* if the slide is to be advanced on a mouse click during slide show. Select *Automatically after* and specify the time after which the slide should advance automatically during slide show.

Table 18.5 *Animations tab commands description*

duration. While making the PowerPoint presentation, the presenter need not forward to the next slide each time; it will automatically forward to the next slide after the specified time.

18.6.5 The Slide Show Tab

The Slide Show Tab contains commands that are required to setup and start the slide show. The Slide Show Tab is shown in Figure 18.18.

Figure 18.18 The slide show tab

There are three groups within this tab, namely Start Slide Show, Set Up, and Monitors.

- The *Start Slide Show* group contains commands to start the slide show from the start slide, current slide or to create custom shows. Custom shows allow the selection of slides from the current presentation and presents only the selected slides.
- *Set Up* is used to set up the slide show, record narration, rehearse timings etc.
- The *Monitors* group contains commands to make the monitor settings. The monitor can be chosen or its screen resolution can be set.

The commands in the different groups of Slide Show Tab along with a brief explanation are shown in Table 18.6.

An operation performed using the Slide Show Tab commands is described below:

<table>
<tr><th>Slide Show Tab Group</th><th>Description</th></tr>
<tr><td>Start Slide Show</td><td>

• Start the slide show from the beginning or the current slide.
• Create custom shows. A Define Custom Show window appears. Select the slides to be added to the custom show.</td></tr>
<tr><td>Set Up</td><td>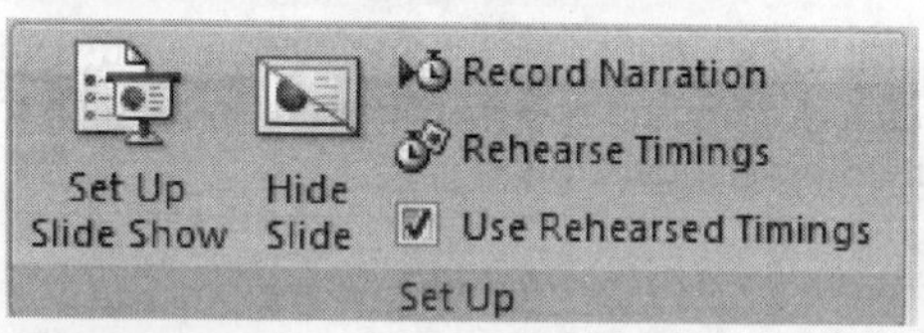

• Set up the slide show. Its window (Figure 18.19) allows to make settings for the show type, the slides to show, to advance the slides manually or using timings etc.
• It is possible to record the narration, rehearse the timing of presentation, hide a slide etc.</td></tr>
<tr><td>Monitors</td><td>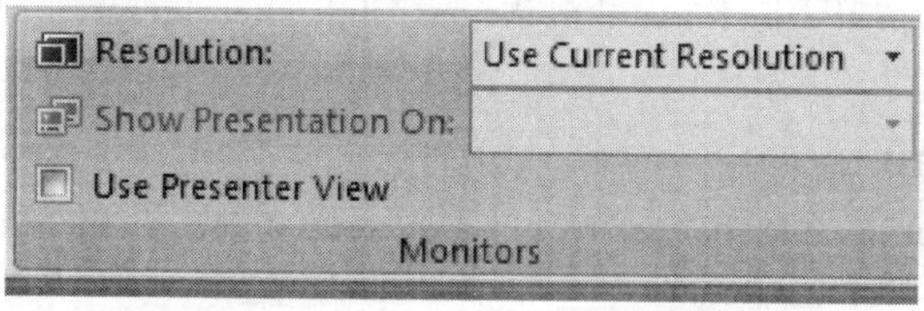

• Make monitor settings like the resolution of the monitor,
• Use presenter view to present the slide show and the speaker's view on two different monitors.</td></tr>
</table>

Table 18.6 *Slide show tab commands description*

- **Create Custom Show**: **<Slide Show> <Start Slide Show> <Custom Slide Show> <Custom Shows>**. A custom show window appears. To create a new custom show, click on *New*. A Define custom show window appears (Figure 18.20). Select the slide which you want to add to custom show. Click *Add* button (To select multiple slides, press the ctrl key on the keyboard and click on the slides you want to select. Click *Add* button).

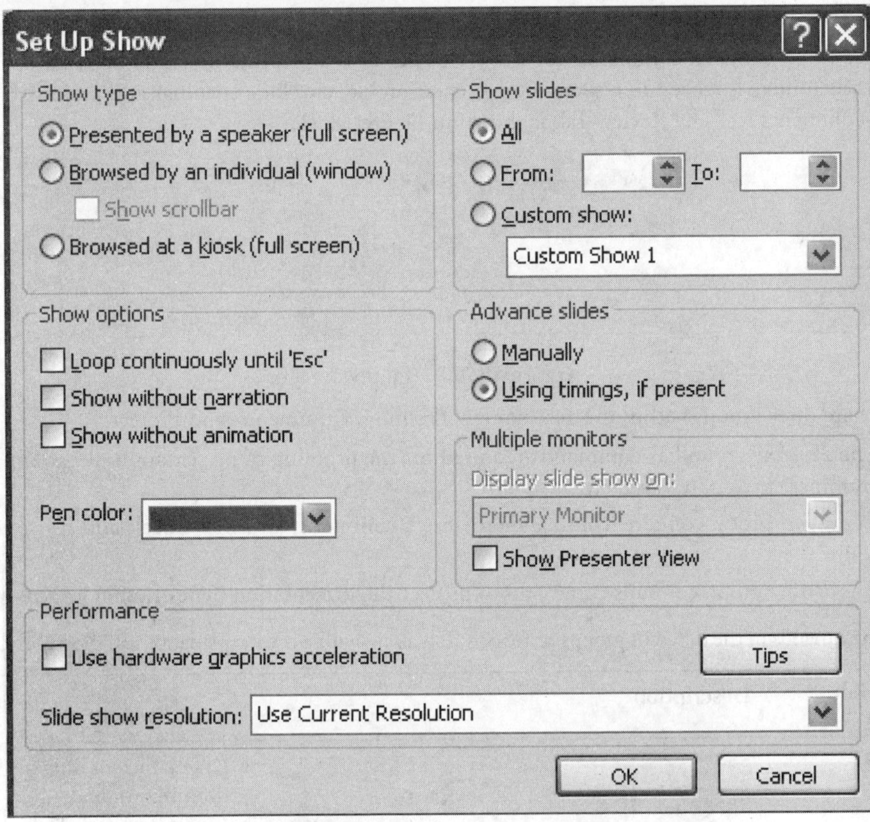

Figure 18.19 Set up show window

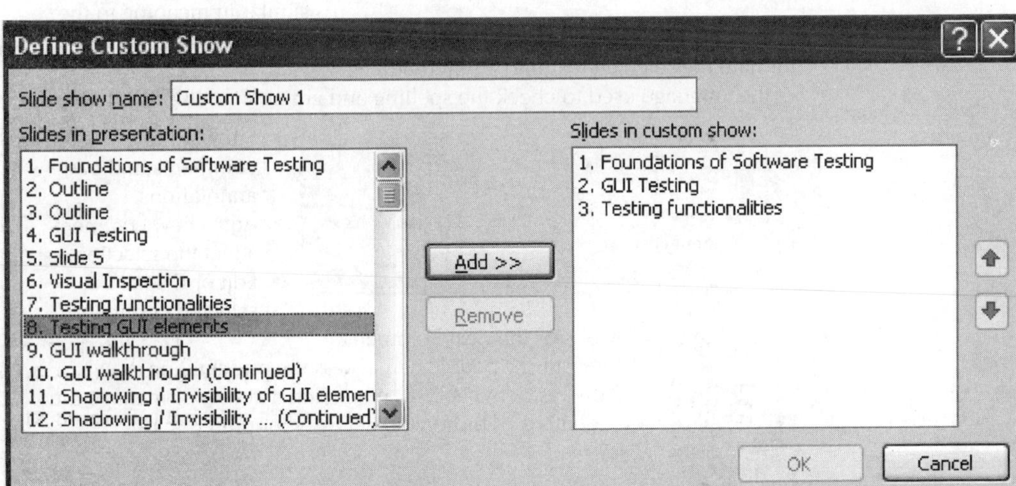

Figure 18.20 Define custom show window

18.6.6 The Review Tab

The Review Tab contains commands for the reviewing of the presentation. The commands in this tab are used when there is a need to correct the presentation like checking spellings and grammar, adding or viewing comments etc. The Review Tab is shown in Figure 18.21.

Figure 18.21 The review tab

There are three groups within this tab, namely Proofing, Comments, and Protect.

- The *Proofing* group has commands required for the proofing of presentation like the spelling and grammar checker, research etc.
- *Comments* group contains commands to insert comments and move back and forth among the comments.
- The *Protect* group contains command to protect the presentation by restricting its access.

The commands in the different groups of Review Tab along with a brief explanation are shown in Table 18.7.

Review Tab Group	Description
Proofing	 • Check the spelling and grammar of text. • Open Research Task Pane and search through research material. • Thesaurus suggests word similar in meaning to the selected word. • Translate the selected text into a different language. • Set the language used to check the spelling and grammar of the selected text.
Comments	 • Show all the comments and other annotations. • Add a new comment about the selection. • Edit or Delete the selected comment. • Navigate to the previous or the next comment.
Protect	 • Restrict how people can access the presentation. You can allow restricted access, unrestricted access or manage the credentials of those who access your presentation.

Table 18.7 *Review tab commands description*

18.6.7 The View Tab

The View tab has the commands that facilitate viewing the presentation. While working with the presentation, it is helpful to work with different views. For example, to edit the content of a slide, use the *Normal* view. The *Outline* and *Slides* view on the left side of the screen are not available in the View menu, but they are two additional significant view options. The *Outline* view displays a written outline of each slide of your presentation. The *Slides* tab displays the slides as thumbnails. The View Tab is shown in Figure 18.22.

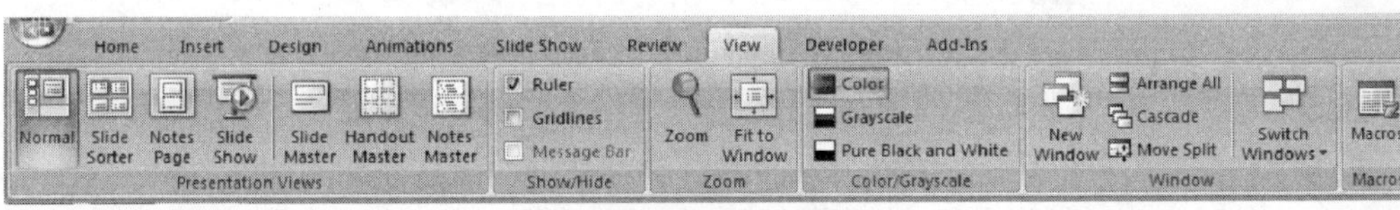

Figure 18.22 The view tab

There are six groups within this tab, namely Presentation Views, Show/Hide, Zoom, Color/Grayscale, Window, and Macros.

- The *Presentation Views* group has commands to view the presentation in different modes like normal, slide sorter, notes page, and slide show. It is also possible to view master slide, handout master, and notes master.
- The *Show/Hide* group contains commands to show or hide the ruler, gridlines etc.
- *Zoom* is used to view the presentation in smaller or larger sizes. Zoom to increase the view to 200% etc or decrease it below 100%.
- *Color/Grayscale* allows viewing the presentation in color, grayscale, and, black and white color.
- *Window* group contains commands to view the windows like, arranging all open windows side-by-side or in cascading style etc.
- The *Macros* group is used to create or view a macro.

The commands in the different groups of View Tab along with a brief explanation are shown in Table 18.8.

Some of the operations performed using the View Tab commands are described below:

- **Change the Order of the Slides:** Order of the slides can be changed in two ways:
  - **<View> <Presentation Views> <Slide Sorter>.** Simply drag the slide to the location where it is to be placed, or,
  - **<View> <Presentation Views> <Normal>.** Select *Slides* tab in the left frame. Thumbnails of the slides in the presentation can be seen. Click on a slide thumbnail and drag up and down to change the order.
- **Formatting Presentation in Slide Master:** The Slide Master acts as a template for the entire presentation. Altering anything on the Slide Master will change it for all the slides in the presentation. **<View> <Presentation Views> <Slide Master>.** *Slide Master Tab* appears on the left-hand side of Home Tab, which provides a set of Slide Master formatting groups - Edit Master, Master Layout, Edit Theme, Background, Page Setup, and Close to go back to Normal View.

<table>
<tr><th>View Tab Group</th><th>Description</th></tr>
<tr><td>Presentation Views</td><td>

• *Normal view* shows a window that splits into Slide, Notes, and the left pane where you can choose either Thumbnails or Outline. It shows the slide as it will appear during the presentation, and also allows editing of the slide from this view.

• *Slide Sorter* presents miniatures of each slide. It lets the wholesome picture of the presentation to be seen. Allows to easily sort, move, add, delete slides, reorder the slides and, add transitions between them.

• *Notes Page* displays a page layout of the notes and the slide. It allows rearranging the notes and comparing them to the content of your slide. Notes are not visible during the slide show.

• *Slide show* shows the slides as if they were actually being presented. Slides cannot be edited in this view.

• *Slide Master* opens a Slide Master tab (Figure 18.23), from where the layout and the design of the master slide, can be changed (Figure 18.26). It allows changing the properties of any text, bullet points, backgrounds, colors, etc. Changes on the Slide Master will be reflected on all the slides in the PPT file.

• *Handout Master* opens a Handout Master tab (Figure 18.24), from where the layout and the design of the handout slide can be changed (Figure 18.27). Edit the theme, page setup, background slides per page etc. Changes on the Handout Master will be reflected on the hand outs printed for the audience.

• *Notes Master* opens a notes master tab (Figure 18.25). It is possible to edit the theme, page setup, background slides per page etc. for the notes (Figure 18.28).

</td></tr>
<tr><td>Show/Hide</td><td>

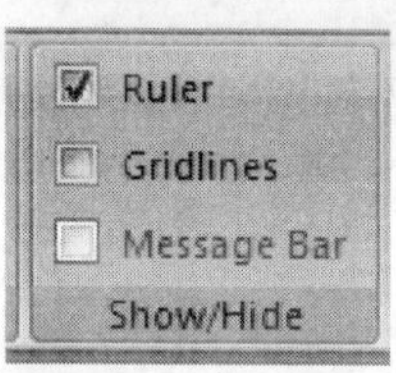

• Gridlines and rulers are used to measure and line up objects on a slide. Show or Hide the Ruler, Gridlines and the Message bar.

</td></tr>
<tr><td>Zoom</td><td>

• Open Zoom dialog box to specify the zoom level such as 33%, 66%, 100%, 200% etc.

• Zoom the presentation so that the slide fits the window.

</td></tr>
<tr><td>Color/Grayscale</td><td>

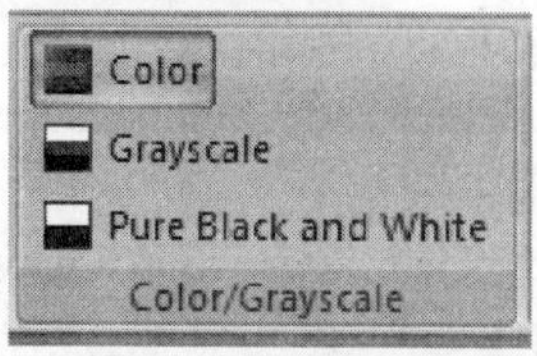

• View the presentation in full color, grayscale or black and white.

</td></tr>
</table>

(Continued)

View Tab Group	Description
Window	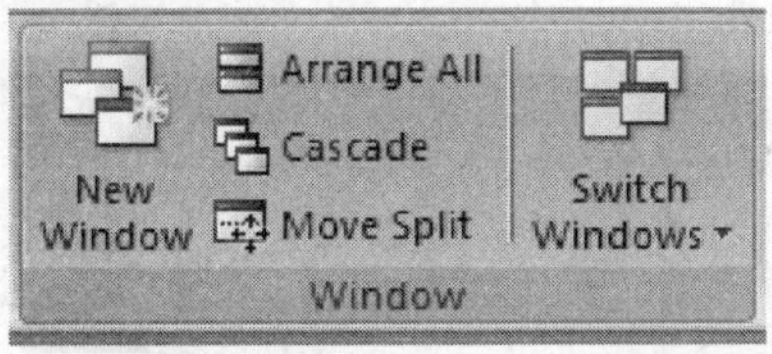 • Open a new window containing a view of the current presentation. • Arrange all open presentations side-by-side on the screen. • View all the open presentations in a cascading style. • Move the splitters which separate the different sections of the windows. • Switch to a different currently open window.
Macros	 • View the list of macros to run, create or delete a macro.

Table 18.8 *View tab commands description*

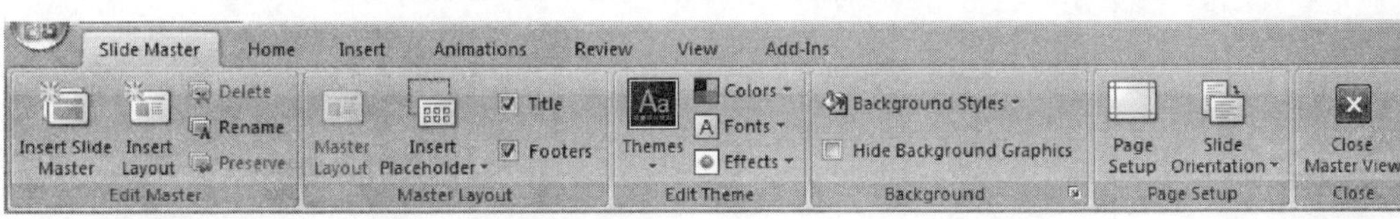

Figure 18.23 Slide master tab

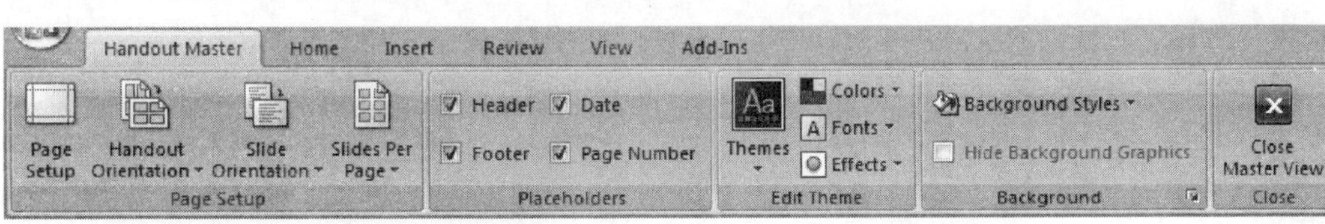

Figure 18.24 Handout master tab

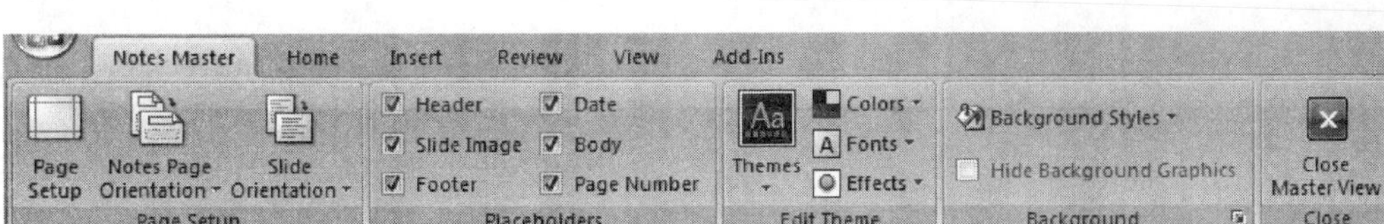

Figure 18.25 Notes master tab

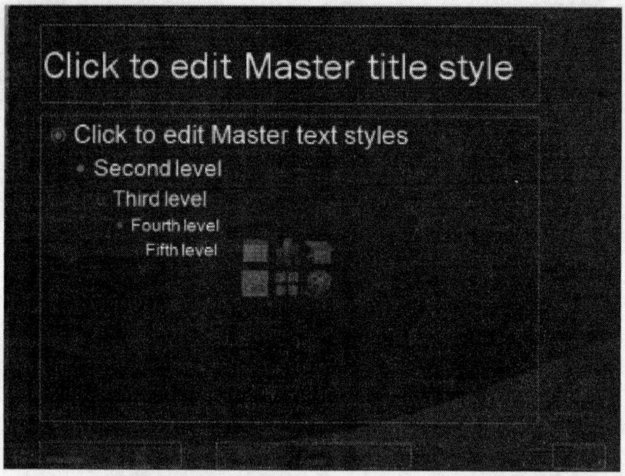

Figure 18.26 The master title style

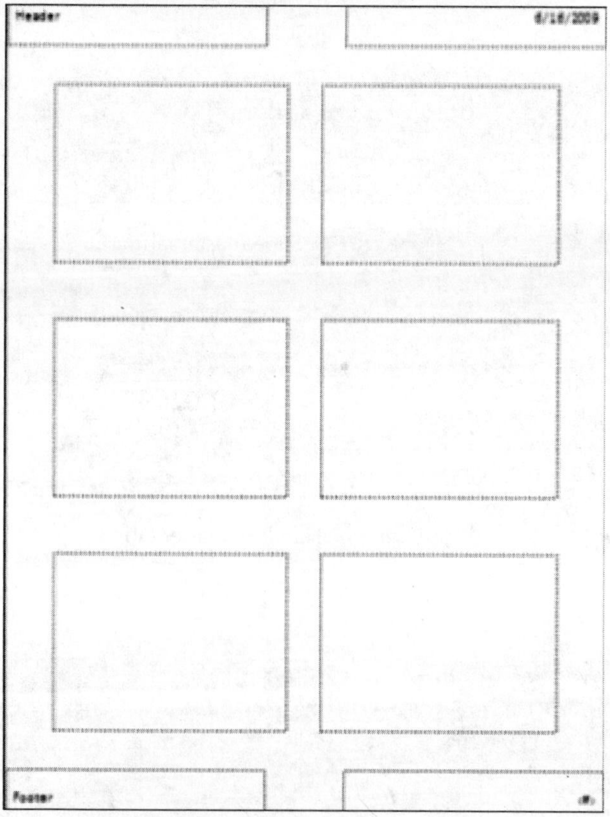

Figure 18.27 The handout master style

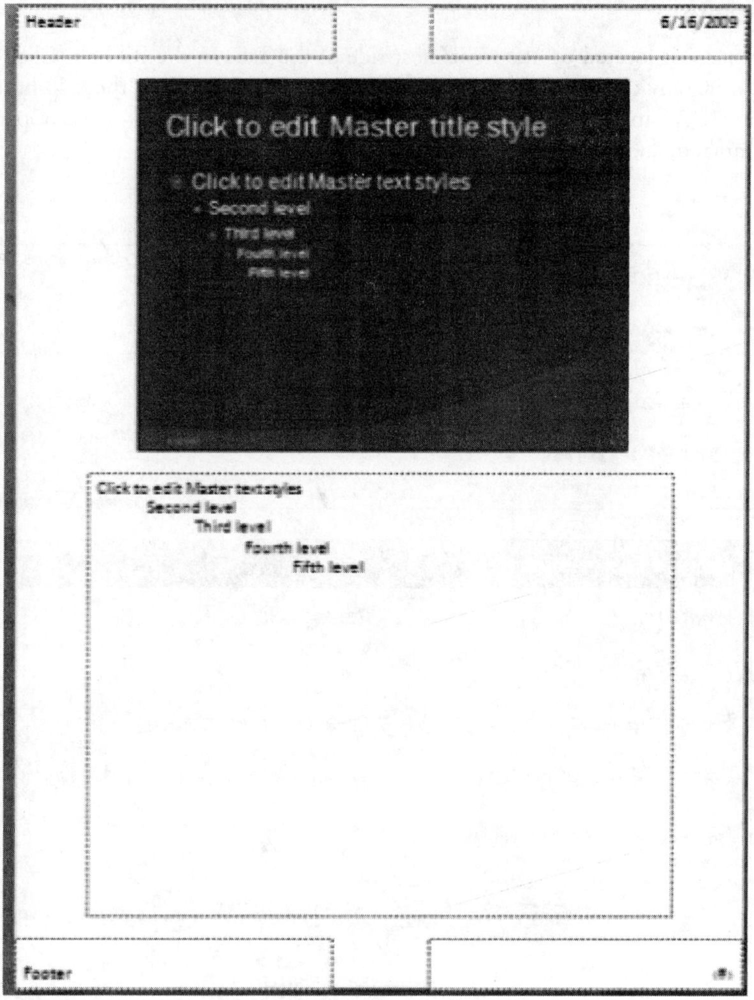

Figure 18.28 The notes master style

- **Present the Slide Show: <View> <Presentation Views> <Slide Show>.** You can move to the next slide, manually, using any of the following ways:
    - Click the left mouse button.
    - Hit the spacebar.
    - Use the arrow keys on the keyboard. Up and left to go back, right and down to go forward.
    - Click on the *Esc* key on keyboard to exit the Slide Show and go back to Normal view.

18.6.8 The Help

The Help button is located on the right most side of the Tabs in the Ribbon. Click on this button to get help for using any command of the MS-PowerPoint. On clicking on the help button, a screen as shown in Figure 18.29 appears, and the Help for any command can be browsed. Operations such as, search for a command, and view Table of Contents, can also be performed.

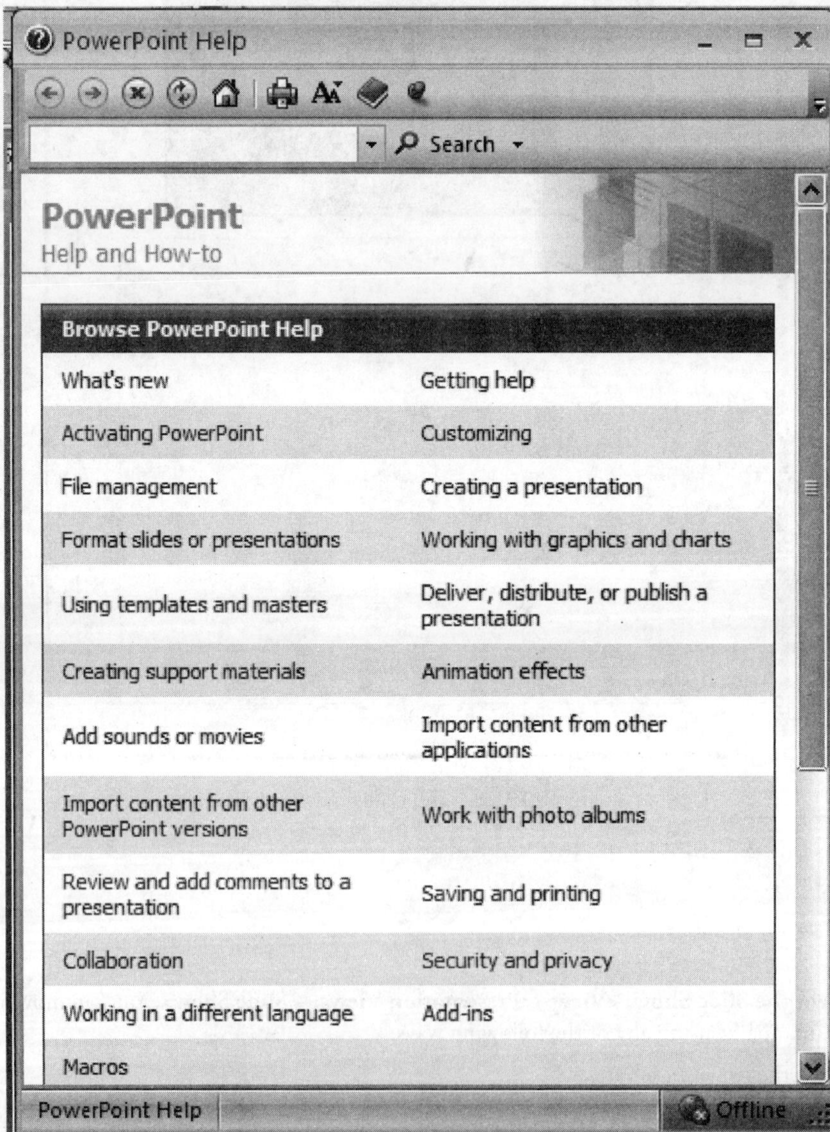

Figure 18.29 PowerPoint help

Many of the concepts that are used while working with MS-Office suite are common for MS-Word, MS-PowerPoint, and MS-Excel. For example, open, close, save, cutting and pasting are performed the same way in MS Word as they are in PowerPoint. The menus are also arranged in a similar layout. If you are not sure how to do something in PowerPoint, then try it as you would do in MS-Word, and it is likely to work.

18.7 AN EXAMPLE

Here we give an example to create a PowerPoint presentation.

Example 1: **Create a PowerPoint Presentation.**

Solution 1:

- Open blank presentation.  **<New> <Create>**
- Create a Master slide. **<View> <Presentation Views> <Slide Master>.** Select the theme, color, fonts, effects, background styles for your slide (Figure 18.30). Insert the title and footer in the slide (if required). A set of master slides (Figure 18.31) is created (Title slide, Title and layout slide, Blank slide etc.). It is also possible to create placeholders. *Insert placeholder* in the slide (Figure 18.32).

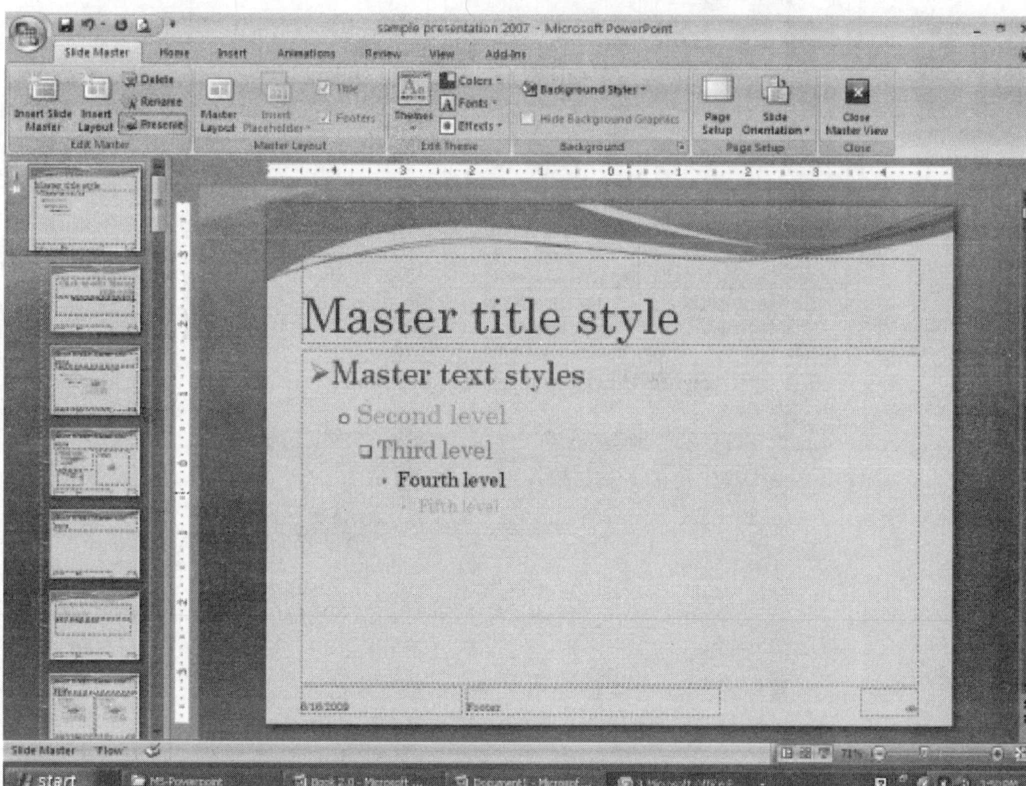

Figure 18.30 Master title slide

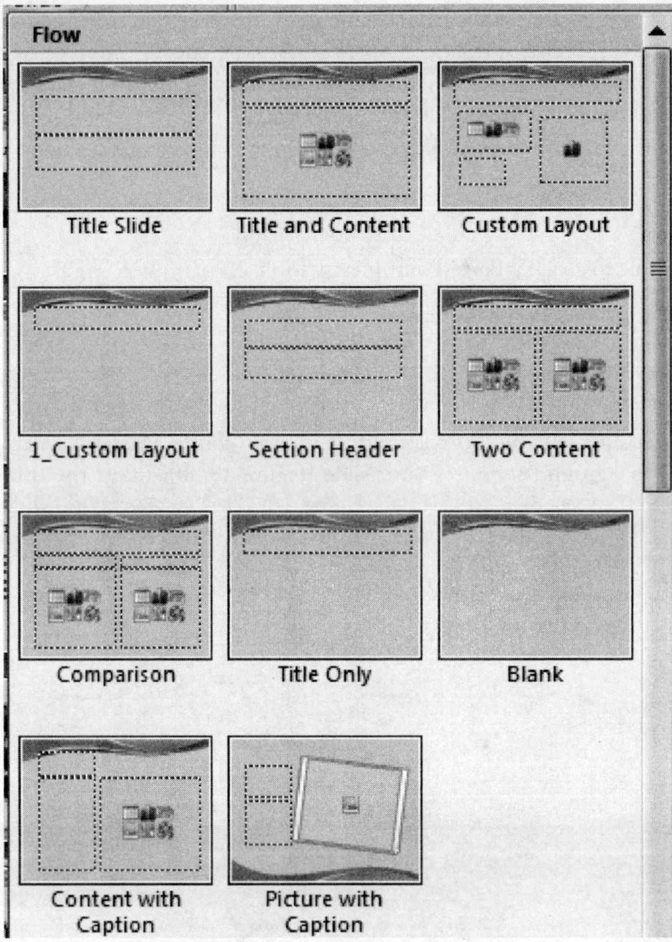

Figure 18.31 The set of master slides

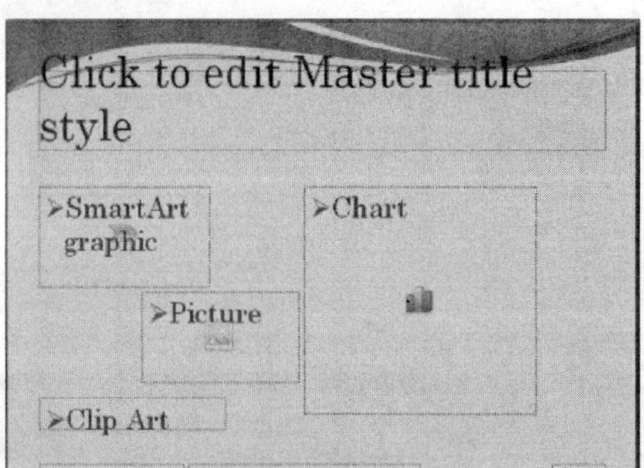

Figure 18.32 A master slide with your custom layout

- Now use the Master slides to create the presentation. **<Home> <Slides> <New Slide>.** Select the title slide. Write the content to it. The content can be text as bullet points, pictures, graphs, clip art etc. Then again add a new slide and write the content, and so on Figure 18.33, Figure 18.34 and Figure 18.35).

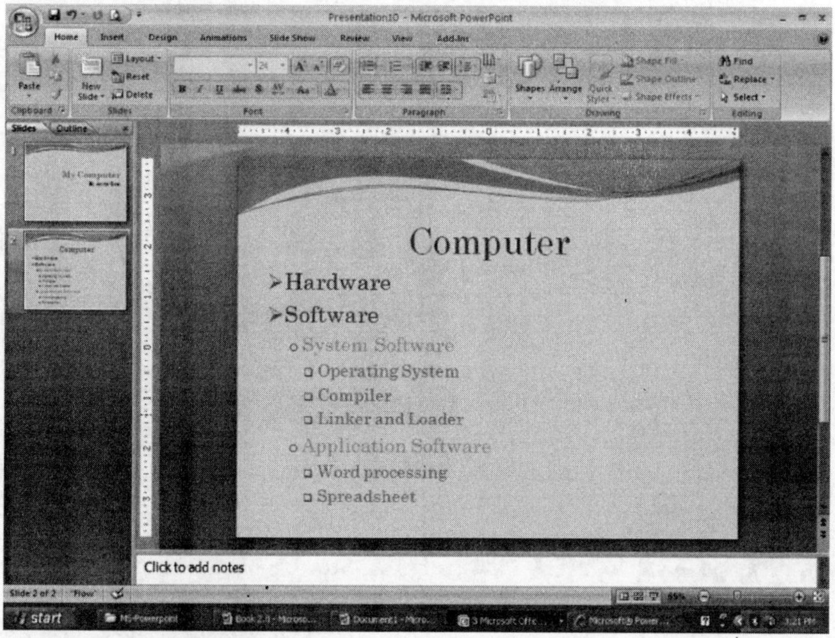

Figure 18.33 An example of slide using the master slide

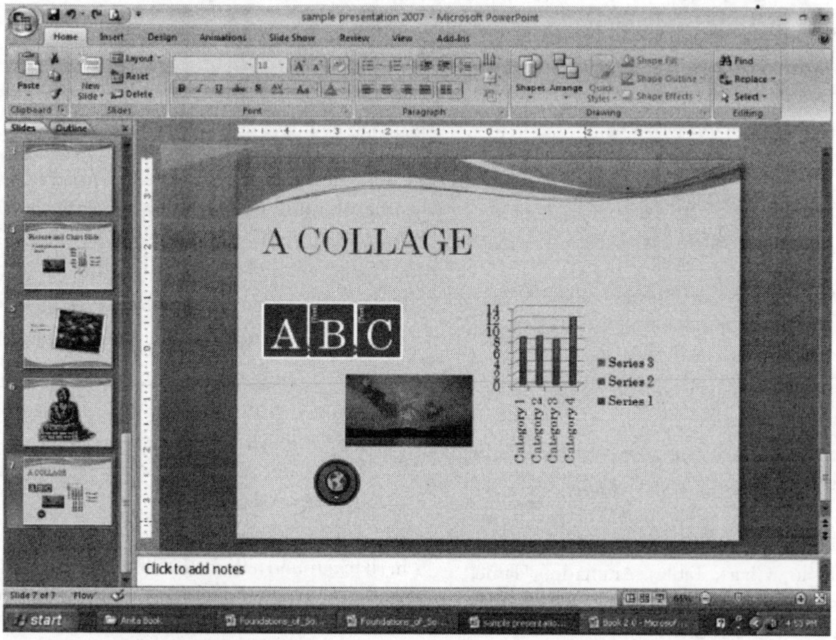

Figure 18.34 A slide made using the custom layout slide

Figure 18.35 An example of slide using master picture caption slide

EXERCISES

1. Design a birthday invitation card.
2. Design a "Thank You" card.
3. Design a "Seasons Greetings" card.
4. Design a "Get Well Soon" card.
5. Design a "Valentine Day" card.
6. Design a Magazine cover. Use the following: (1) Select a theme for the page, (2) Insert either a picture or clipart, and (3) Use WordArt.
7. Design a poster inviting all students of your college to the Computer Festival.
8. Design a certificate that you receive at the end of the Semester for holding a position in the Computer Society.
9. Create a 5-slide presentation on any topic. Use Images, Graphs, Chart, Tables, Animation, Time, Bullets, Transition, Sound, Hyperlink, Background template, Header and Footer.
10. View multiple presentations.

The above questions can be made specific by including one or more of the following options from the *Home Tab*

a. Text Font, Style (Bold, Italic), Size, Color
b. Font effects (Superscript, Subscript, Shadow etc.)
c. Alignment of text - left, right, center, justify
d. Bullets, Numbering
e. Paragraph effects - line spacing, spaces before and after a paragraph.
f. Change case - sentence, upper case, lower case, title case, toggle case.
g. Change slide design
h. Background effects - Fill gradient, texture, pattern, picture in the background of slides, or color of the background
i. Rotate the slide content. Change height and width.

j. Fill color and set transparency margin.

k. Change the design of arrows.

The above questions can be made specific by including one or more of the following options from the *Insert Tab:*

l. Insert Date and Time in slide.

m. Insert Slide number in slide.

n. Insert Footer in slide.

o. Insert Date and Time, Slide number and Footer on Notes and Handouts.

p. Insert a new slide.

q. Insert a Duplicate slide.

r. Insert Symbols like £ Ω 2/3 © ™.

s. Insert a Picture from File, ClipArt, WordArt, scanner or camera, auto shapes, organization chart etc.

t. Insert a diagram, a chart and an object.

u. Insert movies and sounds, sound from clip organizer file, play Audio CD track, record sound, movie from clip organizer, movie from file.

v. Insert a Table.

w. Insert a hyperlink.

x. Insert Lines, Curves, and Shapes - draw and format lines, draw a rectangle, ellipse, freeform lines.

The above questions can be made specific by including one or more of the following options from the *Review Tab:*

y. Use Spelling and Grammar to check the presentation for spellings.

z. Convert the slide into Arabic.

The above questions can be made specific by including one or more of the following options from the *Slide Show* Tab:

aa. View Show.

bb. Set up slide show - advance slide timings, show a few slides only, show without animation etc.

cc. Rehearse the timing of slide show.

dd. Record your narration.

ee. Insert Action buttons in slide show - buttons for home, help, information, backward, forward, beginning, end, return, document, sound, movie.

ff. Make action settings for the action buttons you have inserted. Action settings for mouse click and mouse over that button.

gg. Add Custom Animation.

hh. Add Slide Transition.

ii. Hide a Slide.

jj. Make Custom shows.

kk. Insert Sound, Transition Effects, Embed Video.

19

MS-ACCESS 2007

Contents

- Introduction
- Database terminology—Data, table, field, record, primary, relational database
- Start MS-Access
- MS-Access screen and its components—Office logo button, quick access toolbar, ribbon, tabs, groups, icons, navigation pane, navigation buttons, object tabs, view buttons
- The office button—New, open, save, save as, print, manage, e-mail, publish, close database
- The ribbon—Home, create, external data, database tools, add-Ins
  - Home tab—Views, clipboard, font, rich text, records, sort and filter, find
  - Create tab—Tables, forms, report, other
  - External data tab—Import, export, collect data, sharepoint lists
  - Database tools tab—Macro, show/hide, analyze, move data, database tools
- The help
- Solved example—Company relational database schema and queries

Why this chapter

Reservation of railway tickets, account details of customers of a bank, schedule of trains are some of the common applications that use computerized databases. A database management system is required to store, access, manipulate and manage data in the database. MS-Access is commonly used relational database management system. The purpose of this chapter is to introduce you to MS-Access.

19.1 INTRODUCTION

A database is a collection of logically-related and similar data. Database stores similar kind of data, for a specific purpose that is organized in such a manner that any information can be derived from it, when needed. The database is accessed for the retrieval, insertion, deletion, or updating of data. Database Management System (DBMS) is a software system for creating, organizing, and managing the database. DBMS provides an environment to the user to perform operations on the database for creation, insertion, deletion, updating, and retrieval of data.

Some of the common used DBMSs are—Oracle, IBM's DB2, Microsoft's SQL Server, and Informix. Some of the desktop based DBMSs are—Microsoft Access, Microsoft FoxPro, and Borland dBase. MySQL is a popular open source DBMS.

Microsoft Access is an application which allows the creation of databases for the Microsoft Windows family of operating systems. Microsoft Access is a Relational Database Management System (RDBMS).

It can also be used as a database server for a web-based application. It is supported by the ODBC and the .NET Framework.

Access is a tool for managing the databases. Database can store any kind of data—numbers, pages of text, and pictures. Databases can also handle wide range of data size—from a few hundreds to many millions. Access allows you to design and create complete databases with quick and easy data entry, maintain them, and search for information.

Within Access there are four major areas—Tables, Queries, Forms, and Reports.

- *Tables* store the data in your database.
- *Forms* make it easy to enter data in the tables. Data can be entered directly into a table or into a form (an interface for adding and editing data) which then places it into a table.
- *Queries* get information from the data stored in the tables. Filters and queries can be used to search a database.
- *Reports* allow printing of data, based on queries or tables created by the user. Reports enable the user to analyze the results of a search in a printed format.

Some of the important features of MS-Access are as follows:

- You can create tables and manage the tables.
- The data entry forms can be created easily.
- It allows building queries to analyze the data.
- Design reports to present the data.
- It allows filtering the data based on the text, numbers and date, and also sort the data.
- Attach files to the database.
- Access provides rich text support like bold etc. to the data stored in the tables.
- Access supports grouping of information in the reports like subtotals, count etc.

This chapter discusses the using of MS-Access software in detail. There are many versions of the MS-Access software. Here, we will discuss MS-Access 2007 version.

In this chapter, the following terminology is used while working with the mouse:

- **Pointer**—a mouse pointer
- **Click**—press left button of mouse once
- **Double Click**—press left button of mouse twice
- **Select**—move the pointer of mouse and keep the left button of the mouse pressed over the area that you want to select. The selected area will appear in a dark background.
- **Quick Menu**—Right click (press right button of mouse once) to get a quick menu

The command enclosed in braces <Command> represents the command to be clicked.

19.2 DATABASE TERMINOLOGY

The database terminology required for the use of MS-Access is described as follows:

- Data elements or data—a basic unit of information, e.g. "Ashima", 16, 100 etc.
- Table—a matrix of rows and columns.

- Field—a data category, e.g. name, age, marks. Fields make up the columns of a table.
- Record—information about a person or objects. Records make up the rows of a table
- Primary key—a field that uniquely identifies a record in the table. A student registration number is a primary key as it is unique to each student. A surname as primary key is impractical, as there may be many people with the same surname, and the primary key will not be unique.
- Relational database—The relational database may contain a single table stored as file, or, a collection of related tables stored together. The data elements are stored in different tables made up of rows and columns. The different tables are related through the use of common data elements. Storing of data in multiple tables allows you to store a wider range of data and offer greater flexibility in retrieving the information.

19.3 START MS-ACCESS

Figure 19.1 MS-Access icon

MS-Access software for the Windows operating system is installed on the computer. MS-Access is a fully menu-driven software, and the commands are available as icons in various Tabs and Groups. Using a mouse makes working on MS-Access simpler, although one can work to some extent through the keyboard also.

To start using the MS-Access software, *any one* of the following steps need to be performed:

- If a shortcut key to MS-Access is available as an icon on the Desktop, as shown in Figure 19.1, then **double-click** the icon.
- **<Start> <All Programs> <Microsoft Office> <Microsoft Office Access 2007>**. (Figure 19.2)

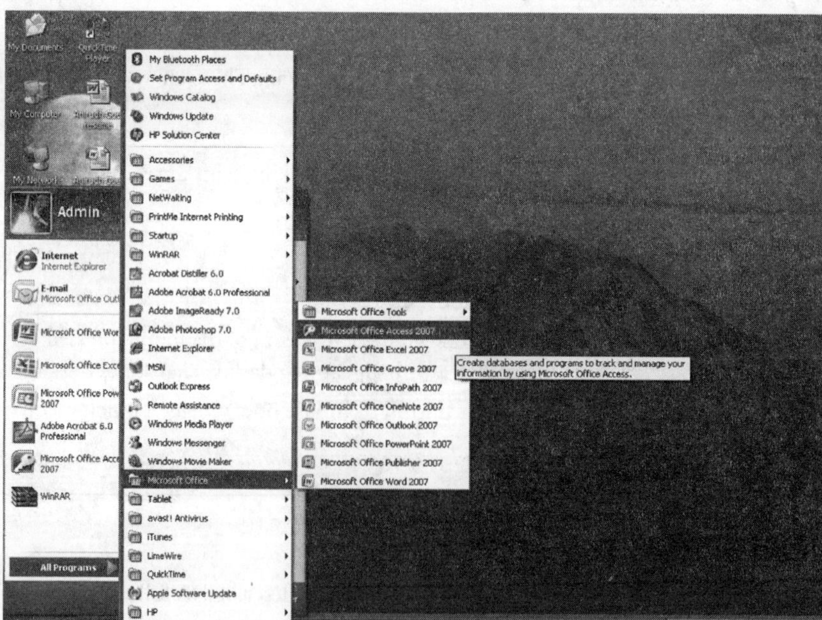

Figure 19.2 Start MS-Access

19.4 MS-ACCESS SCREEN AND ITS COMPONENTS

The user interface of MS-Access makes it easy for you to work in Access 2007. In contrast to the previous versions of MS-Access, the new user interface has an improved navigation system consisting of tabs which further consist of group of commands.

When Microsoft Access 2007 is started, the screen *Getting Started with Microsoft Office Access* screen (Figure 19.3) comes up.

Click <Blank database> <Create>

Enter the name of the database, and browse to the location where the database is to be stored on the disk.

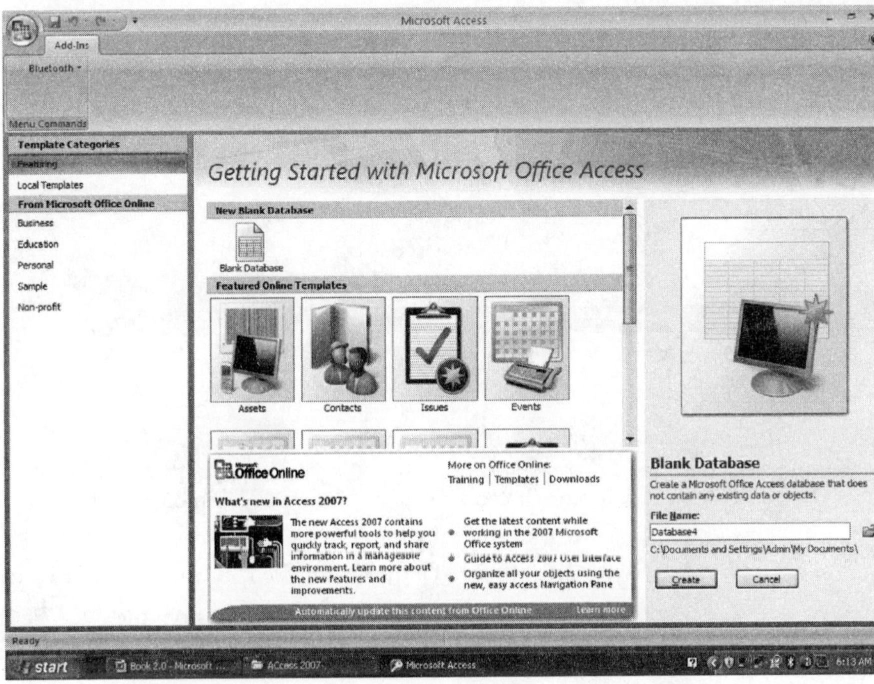

Figure 19.3 Getting started with Microsoft Office Access screen

Now, the MS-Access 2007 screen (Figure 19.4) comes up. This window consists of a number of components to make working in Access easier and more efficient. Some of the components are—Navigation Pane, Access work area, View Buttons, and Ribbon. On the MS-Access screen, some of the features like the Office Logo button, Quick Access Toolbar and Ribbon are common to all Microsoft Office programs like MS-Word, MS-Excel, and MS-PowerPoint. The orientation of the Access 2007 layout and its general features are described as follow:

- The **Office Logo Button**  at the top left corner contains commands for the document such as, *New, Open, Save, Save As, Print,* and *Close*. This button also has a list of the recent documents. Some of these commands include an expandable menu to provide additional options.
- The **Quick Access Toolbar**  is to the right of the Office Logo

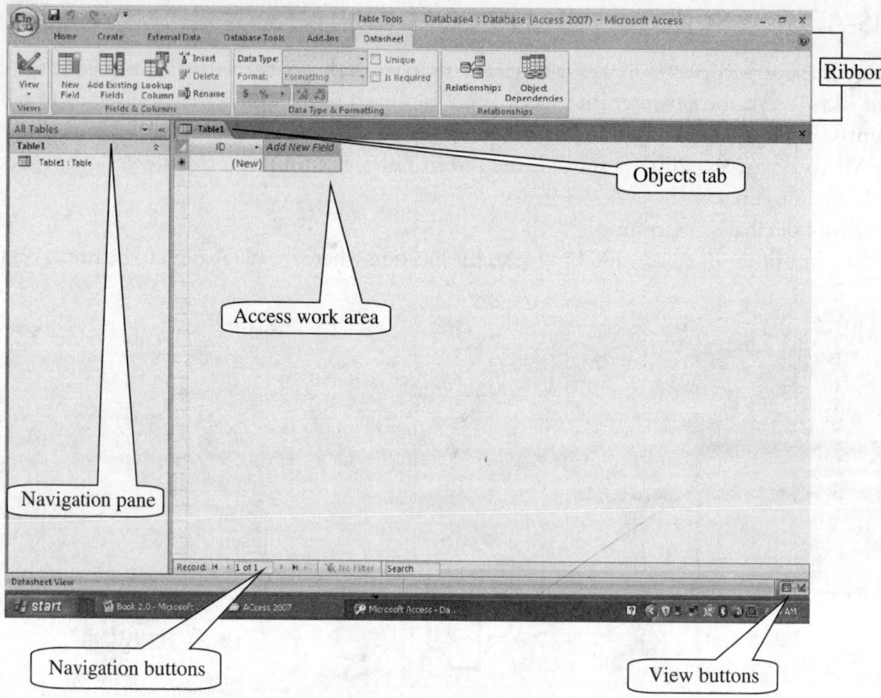

Figure 19.4 MS-Access 2007 screen

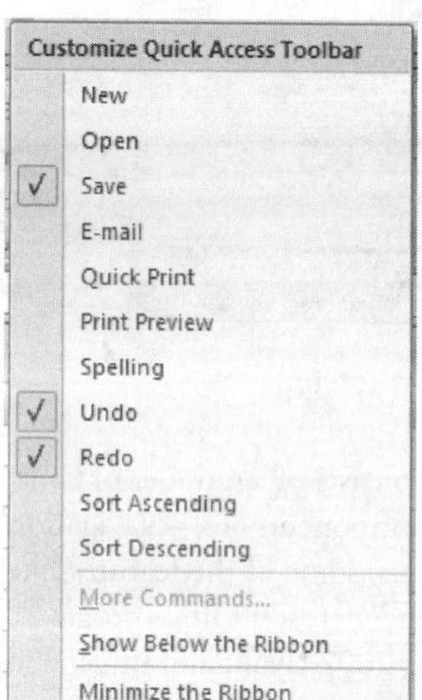

button. It contains shortcuts for the commonly used commands, like, Save , Undo (reverses the last change), and Repeat (repeats the last action). The icons for the commands that you want to get displayed on the toolbar can be selected from the *Customize Quick Access Toolbar.*

- The **Ribbon** consists of a panel of commands which are organized into a set of tabs (Figure 19.5). The layout of the Ribbon in MS-Access is the same as that of the Ribbon in MS-Word. Within Tabs are Groups, which are designated by the names located on the bottom of the Ribbon. Each group has icons for the associated command. The Ribbon (Tabs, Groups, and Icons) replaces the traditional toolbars and menus of the earlier versions of MS-Access.

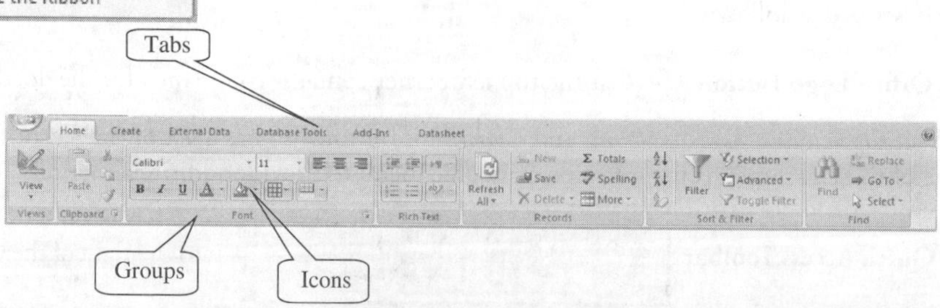

Figure 19.5 The ribbon

- The **Tabs** (Home, Create etc.) on the Ribbon contain the commands needed to insert data, create tables, forms, reports etc. as well as the additional commands that may be needed.

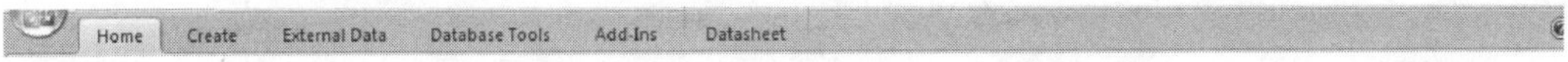

- Each Tab consists of different **Groups**, like the Home tab has seven groups namely, Views, Clipboard, Font, Rich Text, Records, Sort & Filter, and Find.

- Each group has **icons** for the commands. To know the function of an icon (or command), leave the pointer on a button for a few seconds, the function of that icon will appear in a small box below the pointer. For example, leaving the icon on **B** displays "Bold (Ctrl+B)".
- **Navigation Pane**—The Navigation Pane shows the entries for all the tables, forms, queries and reports that are created by the user. For opening database objects, click on one of these entry in the Navigation Pane, and the required object will open in Access work area window.
- **Navigation Buttons**—The navigation buttons display the record number on which you are currently working. It has buttons which allows you to move back and forth between the different records of the object. If data is entered in the search button, the cursor moves to the location of record where the search is true. Navigation buttons also allows the view of the filtered records.

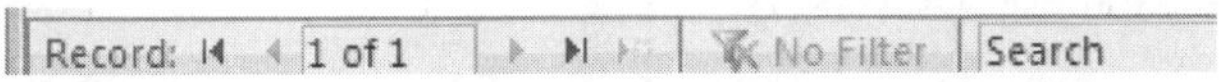

- **Object Tabs**—They display the tabs for the objects that you are working with, currently. On clicking on an object tab, the contents of the object are displayed in the Access work area.
- **View Buttons**—They contain buttons for the different views of the object, like Datasheet view, Design view, PivotTable view, and PivotChart. Clicking on a view displays the object view in the Access work area.

19.5 THE OFFICE BUTTON

The functionality of Office button in MS-Access is almost similar to the functionality provided in MS-Word, MS-Excel, and MS-PowerPoint software. For example, *New* will open a blank document in MS-Word, a blank workbook in MS-Excel, a blank presentation in MS-PowerPoint, and a blank database in MS-Access.

The Office Button is used to perform file management operations on the file (i.e. the database). It contains commands that allow the user to create a new database, open an existing database, save a database, print a database etc. The Office button contains nine commands (Figure 19.6), namely, New, Open, Save, Save As, Print, Manage, E-mail, Publish, and Close Database. The working of these commands is almost similar to their working in MS-Word. Here, we will discuss them briefly.

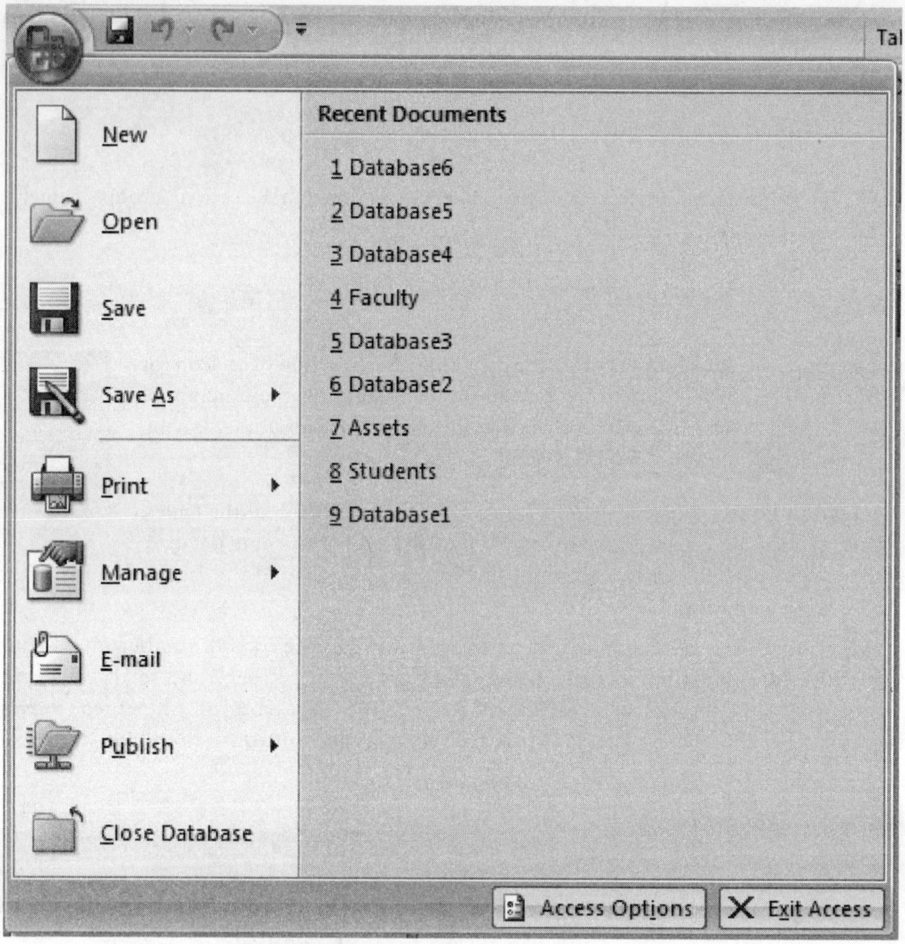

Figure 19.6 The Office button commands

Table 19.1 briefly describes the different commands available in the Office Button.

Office Button Commands	Description
New	Create a new blank database that does not contain any objects. You can also select from different templates like Assets, Faculty, Issues, and Tasks.
Open	Open an already existing database
Save	Save a database for which a file name and location has already been specified.
Save As	Use when you save the database at a different location or by a different name or with a different save type. Specify the filename for the database, the location where the database is to be stored, and the save type of the database (table, query, form or report). The database can also be saved as Access 2007 database, Access 2002–2003 database etc.

(Continued)

Office Button Commands	Description
Print	Print, Quick Print, Print Preview the database. Properties like print quality, paper type etc. and print the selected records or the entire database, can also be set. Preview to see how the database will look after printing.
Manage	View database properties, compact and repair the database and take back-up of the database (Figure 19.7)
E-mail	Send a copy of the database to e-mail
Publish	Share the database by saving it to a document management server, package the database, and apply a digital signature.
Close Database	Close an open database.

Table 19.1 *Office button commands description*

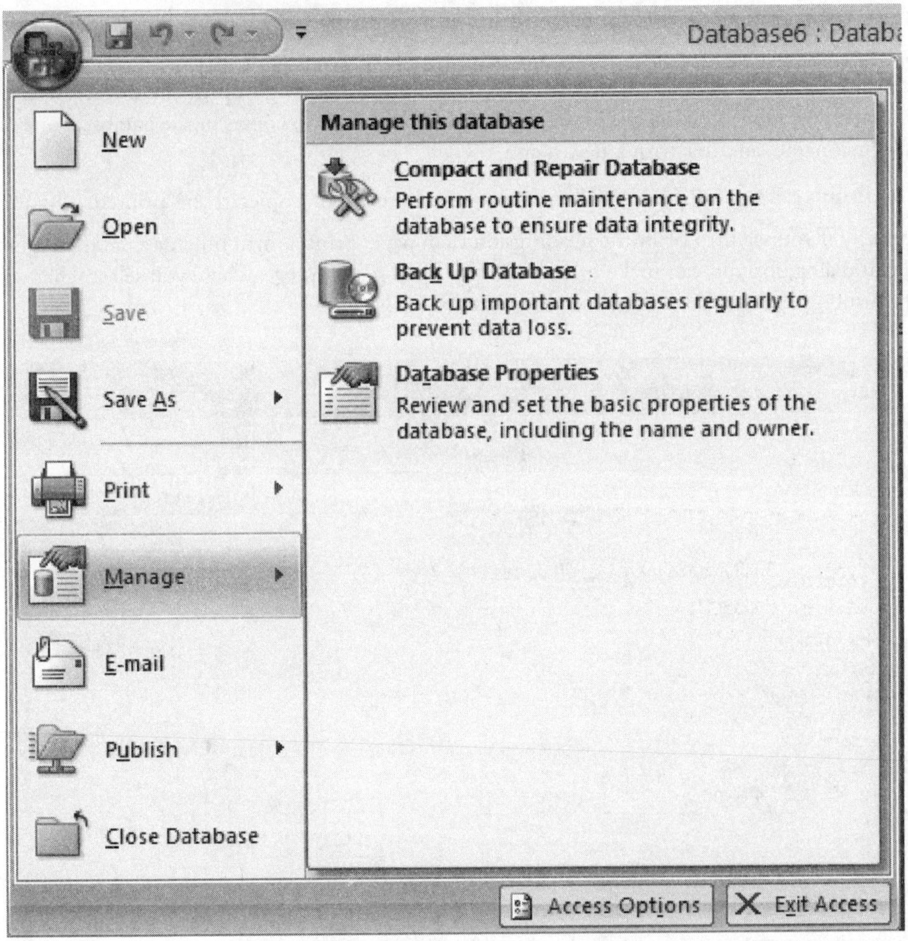

Figure 19.7 Publish option

The following describes briefly some of the common operations that are performed using the commands of the Office Button.

- **Create a New Database**: < > <**New**>. A new window opens up. <Blank Database> <Create>. There are templates available (Local Templates) for creating a database of a specific type (e.g. Faculty, Assets, Issues, Students). When you create a new database, it also asks you to name the database (unlike MS-Word, MS-Excel or MS-PowerPoint); browse for the folder where you want to save the database and give it a suitable name.
- **Saving a Database While Working**: < > <**Save**>, or, click on the Save button in the Quick Access Toolbar. Access will save the database with the name and at the location that you specified while creating this database.
- **Saving a Database Under a Different Name or at a Different Location**: Open the database by selecting the < > <**Open**>. Next, < > <**Save As**> A dialog box will appear. In the field next to File name, type a name with which you want to save the database. Navigate in the top portion of the dialog box to the folder where you want to save the database (choose the appropriate directory where you want to save the file. You can use to go up in the directory, Use to create a new folder). Select the Save button. You now have two copies of the database, one with the original name, another with a new name.
- **To Print**: < ><**Print**>. Make settings like number of copies to be printed. (Figure 19.8). Specify if you want to print the headings on each page, print a form only or a datasheet. From the Print dialog box you can make further settings like—*Print Range*, where you select what you want to print—page numbers, database, or selected records.

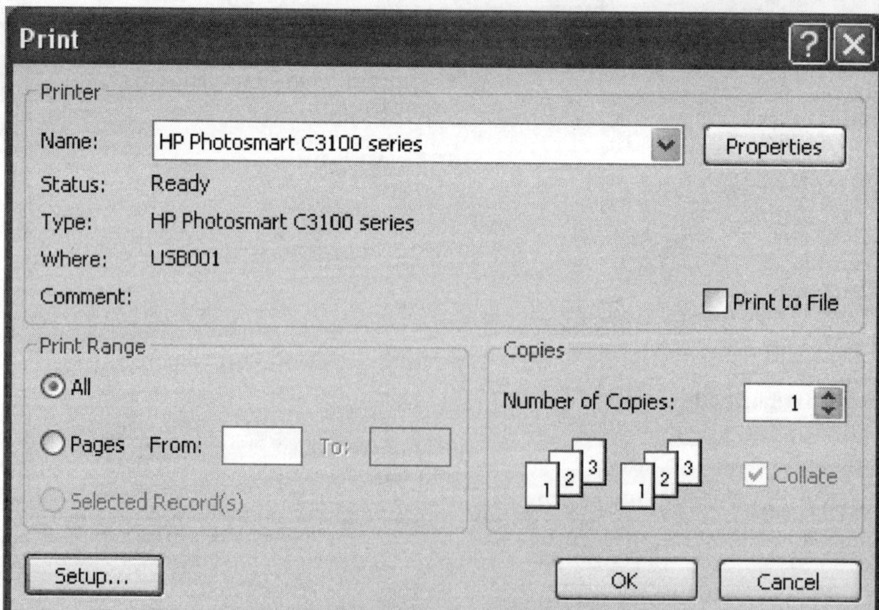

Figure 19.8 Print dialog box

Quick Tips - How to Learn MS-Access

When working with MS-Access, all you need to know is the following:

- What a command does
- When you want to perform a particular action, which command to use
- How to use a command

Here I describe how you can go about learning MS-Access.

(1) What a command does—When you keep your mouse pointer over a command or icon, the function of the command or icon is displayed in a text box. So you can know what a command does by moving the mouse over the command.

(2) Which command to use—

a. To search for a command, first see which tab might have the command. For example, if you want to do any formatting, click the Home Tab; to create a form, table or report click the Create tab; to import or export a data, click the External Tools tab.

b. You will be able to find the group and command you want, most of the time. The commands that have similar uses are grouped together in the same group in Access 2007.

(3) Once you are able to find the command, then you should know how to use the command.

a. For most of the commands, first you place the cursor in the database at the position where the action is to happen, or, you select the object on which you want the action to happen (for example formatting commands). Next, you click on the command. The command gets executed.

b. In some commands, there is a set of steps to use the command.

19.6 THE RIBBON

Like the other programs in the Office 2007 suite, MS-Access 2007 has a ribbon. The Ribbon of MS-Access has the Office button and five Tabs, namely, Home, Create, External Data, Database Tools and Add-Ins. Each tab further consists of the groups, and the groups contain icons. Icons are a pictorial representation for a command. The tabs in the Ribbon are self-explanatory; for example, if you want to create a form, click on the Create tab. The groups and icons related to *Create* are displayed on the screen. Select the appropriate command. The different tabs in MS-Access and the groups within them are as follows:

- **Home**: Views, Clipboard, Font, Rich Text, Records, Sort & Filter, Find
- **Create**: Tables, Forms, Reports, Other
- **External Data:** Import, Export, Collect Data, SharePoint Lists
- **Database Tools:** Macro, Show/Hide, Analyze, Move Data, Database Tools

The **Add-Ins tab** contains supplemental functionality that adds custom commands and specialized features to MS-Access.

The commands in the Ribbon have various symbols associated with them, as shown in Figure 19.9. These symbols are interpreted as follows—

- **Simple Command**—The command start executing when it is clicked.
- **Command Followed by Arrow**—Clicking on the arrow ▾ displays more options for the command.

Selecting a command	
Ways to select a command	**Using a command**
Click on a Tab + *Click on a Icon*	Click on any of the Tabs like Home, Create etc. From the displayed icons, click on the icon you want to use.
Shortcut key *Ctrl + letter*	Some commands have shortcuts where you can press the **Ctrl** key and a **certain letter.** Some commonly used shortcuts are– • Paste: CTRL + V • Copy: CTRL + C • Undo: CTRL + Z • New document: CTRL + N • Open document: CTRL + O • Print document: CTRL + P

Figure 19.9 Command symbols

- **Faded Command**—A faded command means that it is not available currently.
- **Group Dialog Box**—Clicking on this symbol displays the dialog box for the group.

The following sub-sections describe the different tabs in detail.

> **Working with MS-Access 2007**
>
> - **Mini Toolbar** is a floating toolbar that pops up whenever you right-click on a text. It provides easy access to the most commonly used commands such as Cut, Copy, Paste, Sort, and Filter.
> - **File Format** for the databases created in Access 2007 is *.accdb.* (For earlier versions it is *.mdb*)

19.6.1 The Home Tab

The Home Tab contains commands that are frequently used in an Access database. It contains commands for the formatting of text, text alignment, and performing operations on the records. The Home Tab is also used to change the views while working with tables. It is also possible to edit contents of the database like, sort and filter, find and select, and, to perform clipboard operations such as cut, copy, and paste, using the commands available in the Home tab. Figure 19.10 shows the Home Tab.

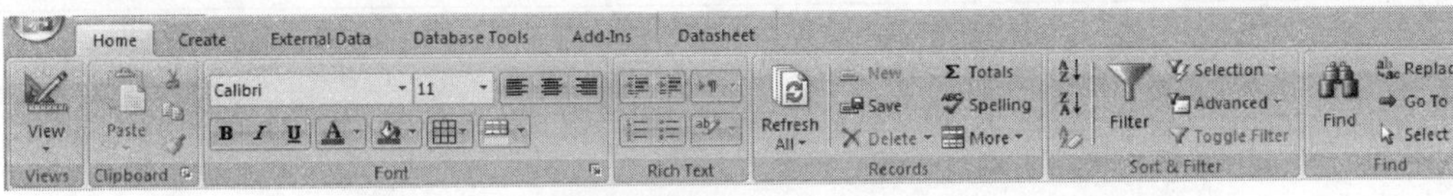

Figure 19.10 The home Tab

There are seven groups within this tab, namely, Views, Clipboard, Font, Rich Text, Records, Sort & Filter, and Find.

- *View* group allows you to select from the four views when working with the table.
- The *Clipboard* group contains the cut, copy and paste commands. The Format Painter is also present here. The Clipboard commands are used in the same manner as you use the MS-Word Clipboard commands.
- *Font* group commands allow change of the font face, style, size, and color. These options can be changed before or after you start typing of the text. If you use it after you have typed in the text, select the text first.
- *Rich Text group* is used to insert bullets or the numbered list, to increase or decrease the list level and to highlight the text color.
- *Records* group contains commands to perform operations on the records like add a new record, save a record, delete a record, perform spell check etc.
- The *Sort & Filter* group allows to sort the records in ascending or descending order, and to apply filters to the records.
- Find group contains commands to select, find and replace text in the document.

Table 19.2 gives the commands in the different groups (*in left to right order*) of the Home Tab along with a brief explanation.

Home Tab Groups	Description	
Views		• View as Datasheet view, Pivot Table view, Pivot Chart view and Design view. Datasheet view is the default view. It allows you to enter data into a table and lets you build the table as you insert new information. Design view lets you define all aspects of a table before you start using it.
Clipboard		• Paste the cut or copied items in Clipboard at the location where cursor is pointing right now (Paste Special – to paste in a particular format. Paste Append – to paste the copied items at the last of existing list). • Cut removes the selected item and puts into Clipboard for later retrieval. • Copy copies the selected item and puts it on the Clipboard. • Format painter copies formatting from one place and apply it to another (To apply same formatting to many places, double-click the format painter button).

(Continued)

Home Tab Groups	Description
Font	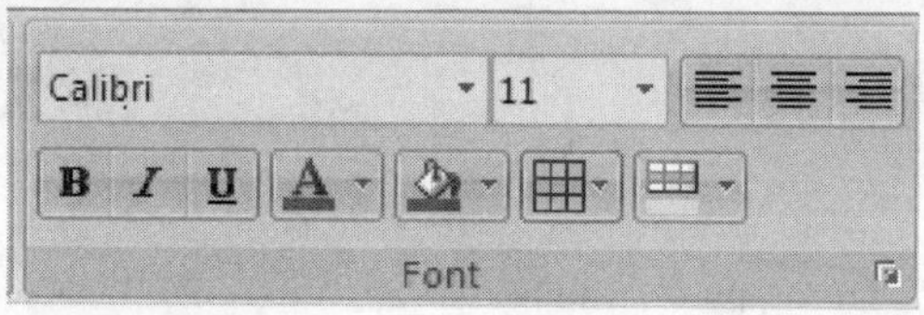 • Change Font face, change font size. • Align text left, centre or right. • Bold, Italics, Underline. • Change the Font color. • Color the background of the selected cells. • Show gridlines- horizontal, vertical, both or none. • Alternate fill the back color. In this, alternately the background is colored.
Rich Text	 • Increase or decrease the indentation level. • Set the direction of text to be displayed from left to right. • Start a numbered list or a bulleted list. • Make the text look like it is marked with highlighter pen.
Records	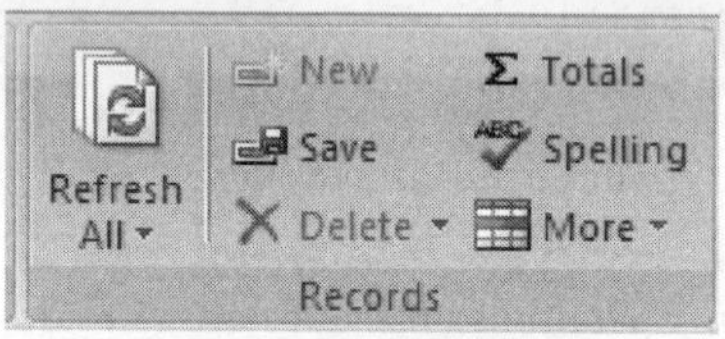 • Refresh all records when in datasheet view or in a form. • Create a new record in data sheet view or form. • Add the field Total Rows in the table to find the total number of records when in datasheet view. • Save the records when in datasheet view or in a form. • Perform spell check on the entries in a table. The Spelling dialog box will display when an error is located.. • Delete records from a table. • Adjust row height, column width, hide or unhide columns, freeze or unfreeze column. This button is only available in datasheet view.
Sort & Filter	 • Sort in ascending or descending order. • Clear the sort order that was applied to a table with the ascending and descending buttons. • Apply filter. A filter menu opens. Specify the criteria for displaying records in a table. • Selection – selects records that meet specified criteria in a table field. A list of entries in the field will display. Click the item in the list to display the records that match that criterion. • Advanced – opens the Advanced Filter menu; used to specify more advanced filtering options. • Toggle filter to display the filtered records and all the records in a table.
Find	 • Find a record meeting specified criterion. The Find and Replace dialog box will display where the criterion can be specified. • Replace – To locate data in a table and replace it with new data. The Find and Replace dialog box will display where the criterion can be specified. • Go to the First, Previous, Next, Last, or New record in a table. • Select the record where the insertion point is located or all records in a table.

Table 19.2 *Home tab commands description*

Here, some of the operations that are performed using the commands of the Home Tab are described briefly:

- **Move Text:** Select and highlight the section you want to move **<Home><Clipboard>< < >**. Move the cursor to the place you would like the text to be inserted. **<Home><Clipboard> < >**.
- **Copy Text:** Select and highlight the section you want to copy **<Home><Clipboard>< >**. Move the cursor to the place you want the copied text to be inserted. **<Home><Clipboard>< >**
- **Find and Replace**: This is used to find a text and then replace it with the new one. This option is useful for finding a text at multiple places in the database and replacing all of them with the new one.
- **Design and Datasheet view**: **<Home><View>.** Select from design view and datasheet view. In the design view (Figure 19.11), first design the structure of the table. Enter all the field names, their data types and field properties. In the datasheet view (Figure 19.12), enter the field names and also type-in the data.

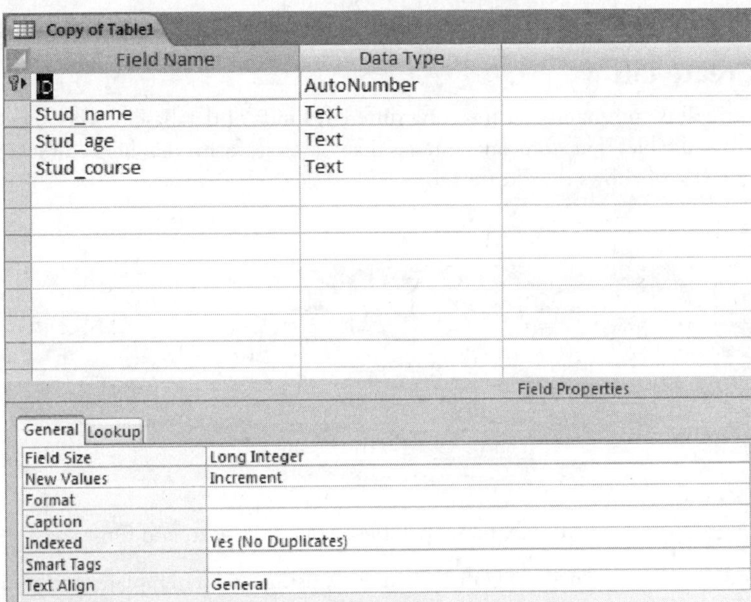

Figure 19.11 Design view

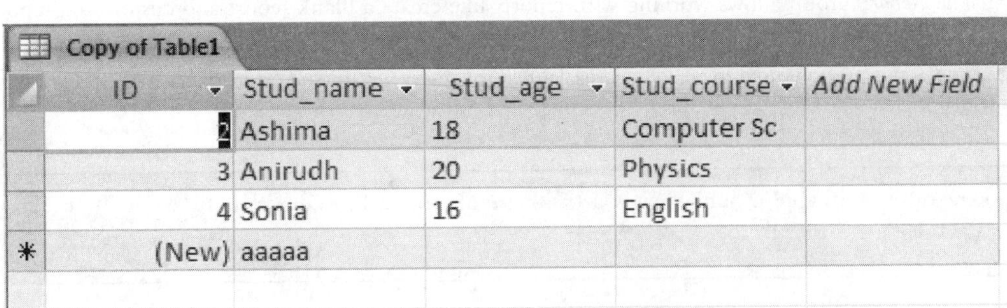

Figure 19.12 Datasheet view

- **Apply Filter: <Home><Sort & Filter> <Selection>.** Select from columns in the datasheet on which the filter needs to be applied. From the <Selection> select criteria for the filter. Figure 19.13, shows the select criteria "Equals Ashima". Filter symbol will be seen on the column on which the filter has been applied.

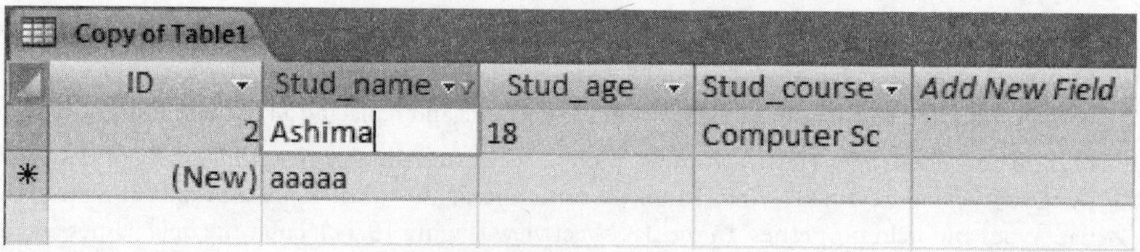

Figure 19.13 Apply filter

19.6.2 The Create Tab

The Create Tab contains commands for inserting different kinds of database objects. The commands in this tab are used to add tables that store data, queries that search it, forms that help edit it, and reports that help print it. Figure 19.14 shows the Create Tab.

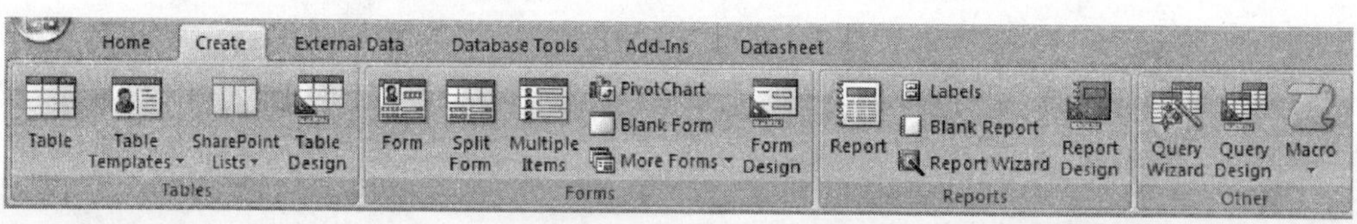

Figure 19.14 The create tab

There are four groups within this tab, namely, Tables, Forms, Report, and Other.

- *Tables* allow creation of a new table in Design view, using a table template, and creation of Share-Point lists.
- *Forms* group allows working with forms like create a form, split a form, and design a form.
- The *Reports* group allows working with reports like create a blank report and customized report, and to create a report in the design view.
- The *Other* group is used to create macros, launch the query wizard and create query in the design view.

> Some of the Tabs appear only when you use them; like Table Tools tab, Report Layout Tools Tab, and Form layout Tools Tab

Table 19.3 gives commands in the different groups of Create Tab along with a brief explanation. Some of the tool tabs that appear when a tool is used are shown from Figure 19.15 to Figure 19.18.

Create Tab Groups	Description
Tables	 • Table—create a new blank table. Specify the fields directly in the new table or open the table in Design view. • Table Templates—create a new table using a table template like contacts, issues, tasks etc. • SharePoint Lists—create a list on the SharePoint site and a table in the current database that links to the newly created list • Table Design—create a new blank table in Design view. Add fields, set indexing options and perform other advanced table-defined tasks
Forms	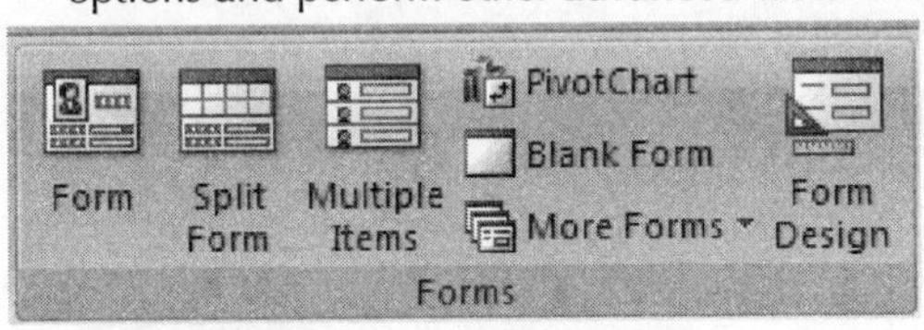 • Form—Create a form that lets you enter information one record at a time. • Split form—Create a split form that shows a datasheet in the upper section and a form in the lower section for entering information about the record selected in the datasheet. • Multiple items—Create a form that shows multiple records in a datasheet with one record per row. • Pivot Chart—to display data from a table in different types of relationships. • Blank form—to create a form that does not contain any fields or data. Move the fields into the form from the list of fields that appear on the right side of form. • More forms—to display a list of additional form creation options like Form Wizard, Datasheet, and Pivot Table. • Form design—to create a form in Design View.
Reports	 • Report—to create an instant report. • Labels—to launch the Label Wizard where standard or customized labels may be created. • Blank Report—to create a report without any fields specified. After the report has been created, fields can be inserted. • Report Wizard—to launch the Report Wizard to create customized reports. • Report Design—to create a report in Design View. Advanced design changes can be made to the report.
Other	 • Query Wizard—to create a simple query, crosstabs query, find duplicates query, or find unmatched query. • Query Design—to create a new blank query. The Show Table dialog box appears. Select a table for creating query. • Macro—to insert macros into the database.

Table 19.3 *Create tab commands description*

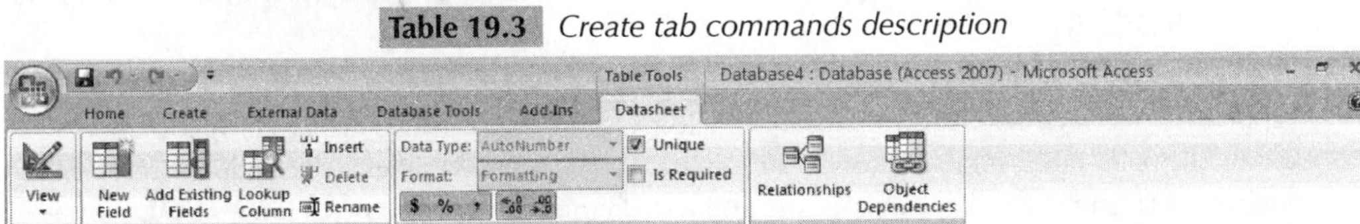

Figure 19.15 Table tools datasheet tab

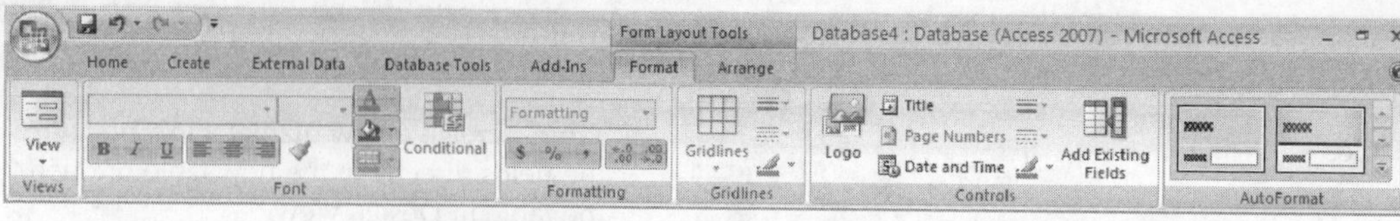

Figure 19.16 Form layout tools format tab

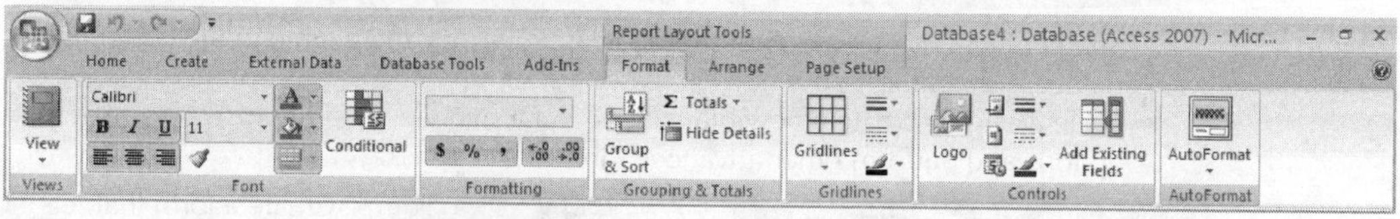

Figure 19.17 Report layout tools format tab

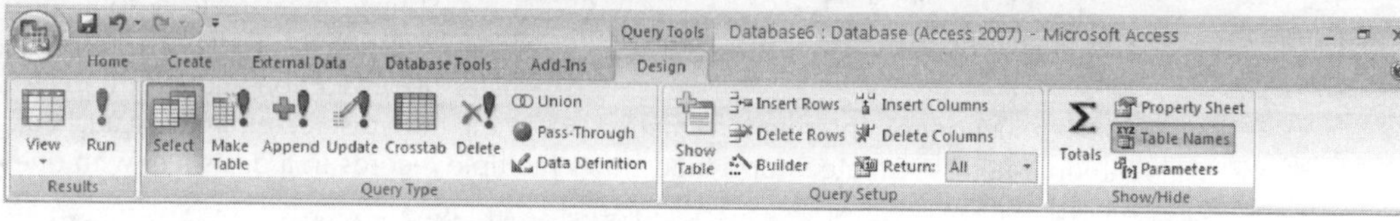

Figure 19.18 Query tools design tab

Some of the operations using the Create Tab commands are described below:

- **Create Table in Datasheet View: <Create><Tables><Table>.** A blank table is created. Add field names and their types. **<Table Tools datasheet>**. Click on a field in the table. <**Fields and Columns> <Rename>** to enter name of the field. Press Enter key. Add all field names. To change field types - **<Table Tools Datasheet> <Data Type and Formatting> <Data Type>.** A drop down menu shows the available data types. Select from it.
- **Create Form in Layout View: <Create><Forms><Blank Form>.** Drag the fields from the right side of the screen to the center, to be included in the form. Now, format the form. Insert title for the form - **<Form Layout Tools Format> <Controls Group> <Title>**. Insert Logo **<Logo>**. Select a format for the form **<Auto Format> <More>.** To view the form - Right click the form tab **<Form View>**. Save the form - Right click the form tab **<Save>.** This is a simple form. You can use other options also for further formatting of the form.
- **Create Report in Layout View: <Create><Report><Blank Report>.** Drag the fields from the right side of the screen to the center, to be included in the report. Now, format the report. Insert title for the report—**<Report Layout Tools Format> <Controls Group> <Title>**. Insert Logo **<Logo>**. Group and Sort - **<Group and Sort>.** Group, Sorts and Total windows will appear below the Report. Add a group, add a sort. To view the report - Right-click the report tab **<Report View>**. Save the report - Right-click the report tab **<Save>.**This is a simple report. It is possible to insert totals, sub-totals, conditional formatting and auto format, and other options, for further formatting the report.
- **Create a Query in Design View: <Create><Other><Query Design>.** A Show Table dialog box appears. Select a table. **<Add> <Close>.** A Select Query design grid is displayed. It contains several rows like field, table, total, sort, show or criteria. On clicking on a field, a selection arrow appears. Select a field from the list that appears. To view the query - **<Results> <View> <SQL view>.** To run the query - **<Results> <Run>**.

19.6.3 The External Data Tab

The External Data Tab contains commands for importing data into Access and exporting it to other programs. The External Data Tab is shown in Figure 19.19.

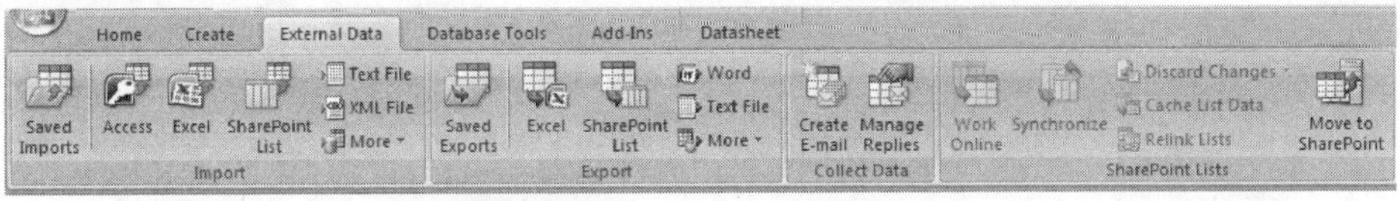

Figure 19.19 The external data tab

There are four groups within this tab, namely, Import, Export, Collect Data, and SharePoint Lists.

- The *Import* group allows import of data from different programs into the Access table.
- *Export* group is used to export database objects to other programs and formats.
- *Collect Data* group allows sending of forms through e-mail to different people, to collect data.
- The *SharePoint Lists* group are used when SharePoint services are available.

Table 19.4 gives the commands in the different groups of the External Data Tab along with a brief explanation.

External Data Tab Group	Description
Import	 • Saved imports—to view and run an import operation that was saved previously. • Access—to import data from or link to another Access database. • Excel—To import data from or link to an Excel file. • SharePoint list—to import data from or link to a SharePoint List. • Text file—to import a text file. • XML file—to import an XML file. • More—to display a list of additional formats from which data may be imported from.
Export	 • Saved Exports—to view and run an export operation that was saved previously. • Excel—to export the selected object in Access to an Excel worksheet. • SharePoint List—to export the selected object to a SharePoint list. • Word—to export the selected object to a Rich Text Format document. • Text File—to export a selected object to a text file. • More—to display a list of additional formats into which a selected object may be exported.
Collect Data	 • Create e-mail—to create an e-mail message that includes a form for collecting information from users. • Manage Replies—to view replies to data collected in email messages and use them to update databases.

(Continued)

External Data Tab Group	Description
SharePoint Lists	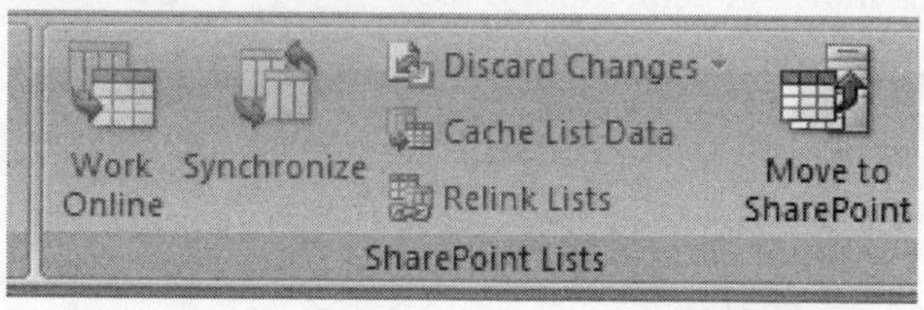 • Work Online—to take all data offline. The data is synchronized when the computer is reconnected to the network. • Synchronize the data between the database and the SharePoint server. • Discard changes made to the database on the SharePoint Server. • Cache List Data—to cache list data on the database server. • Relink Lists—to re-link the broken link between the database server and the SharePoint server. • Move to Share Point some or all parts of a database.

Table 19.4 *External Data commands description*

Some of the operations that are performed using the commands of the External Data tab are briefly described below:

- **To import data from Excel into a table: <Create> <Import> <External Data> <Excel>.** A Get External Data-Excel Spreadsheet window will appear. Browse to the location from where the worksheet is to be imported. Specify where to store the data in the current database. Select **<Import the source data into a new table in the current database>.** Click ok. An Import Spreadsheet Wizard appears. Follow the steps of the wizard. The spreadsheet will be imported to the table name you specify.

19.6.4 The Database Tools Tab

The Database Tools Tab has tools that help experts perform data analysis and add Visual Basic code (a scripting language). This tab is used for the linking of tables. The Database Tools Tab is shown in Figure 19.20.

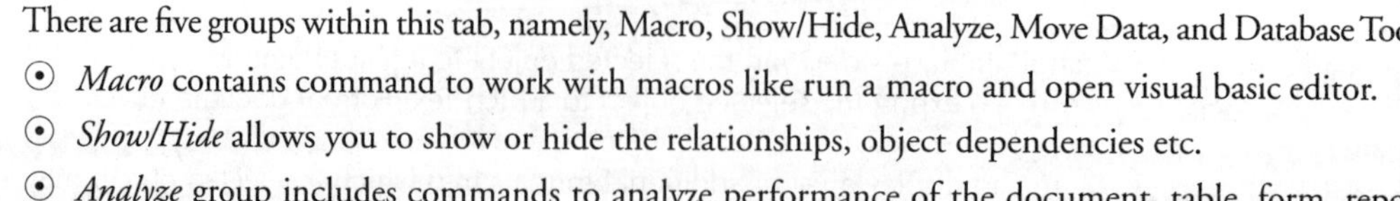

Figure 19.20 The database tools tab

There are five groups within this tab, namely, Macro, Show/Hide, Analyze, Move Data, and Database Tools.

- *Macro* contains command to work with macros like run a macro and open visual basic editor.
- *Show/Hide* allows you to show or hide the relationships, object dependencies etc.
- *Analyze* group includes commands to analyze performance of the document, table, form, report, and query.
- *Move Data* allows to move the data to a new server and to split the database into separate files.
- *Database Tools* contains tools to encrypt the database with password etc.

Table 19.5 gives the commands in the different groups of the Database Tools Tab along with a brief explanation.

Database Tools Tab Group	Description
Macro	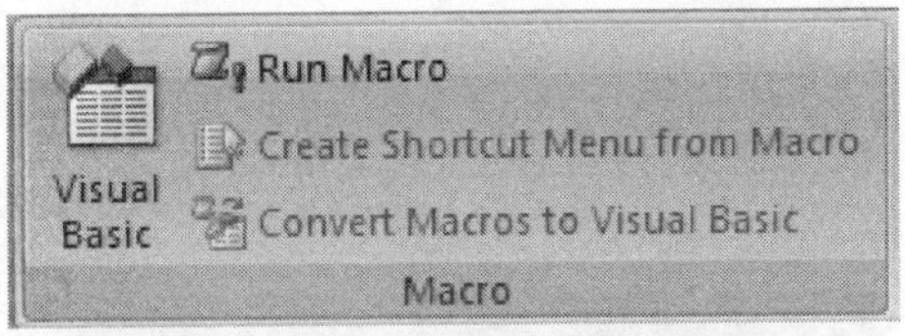 • Visual Basic – Launch the visual basic editor. • Run a macro, create shortcut menu from macro and convert macros to visual basic.
Show/Hide	 • Define how the data in the tables are related. • Open the object's property sheet to set its properties. • Show the database object like query and tables that rely on other objects. • Show or hide the message bar.
Analyze	 • Analyze the database documenter, analyze the performance of the table, form, query etc.
Move Data	 • Migrate some parts of the database to a new or an existing SQL server database. • Split the database into two files – one containing the table and the other containing the forms and queries.
Database Tools	 • Database tools for encrypting the database with password, switchboard manager etc.

Table 19.5 *Database tools tab commands description*

19.6.5 The Help

The Help button is located on the right most side of the Tabs in the Ribbon. Click on this button to get help for using any command of the Access. On clicking on the help button, a screen as shown in Figure 19.21 appears. Browse the Help for the specific command. It also allows for operations such as search for a command and view Table of Contents.

Many of the concepts that are used while working with MS-Office suite are common for MS-Word, MS-PowerPoint, MS-Access, and MS-Excel. For example, open, close, save, cutting, and pasting are performed the same way in MS-Access as they are in MS-Word, and MS-PowerPoint. The menus are also arranged in a similar layout. If you are not sure how to do something in Access, then try it as one would do in MS-Word or MS-PowerPoint, and it may work.

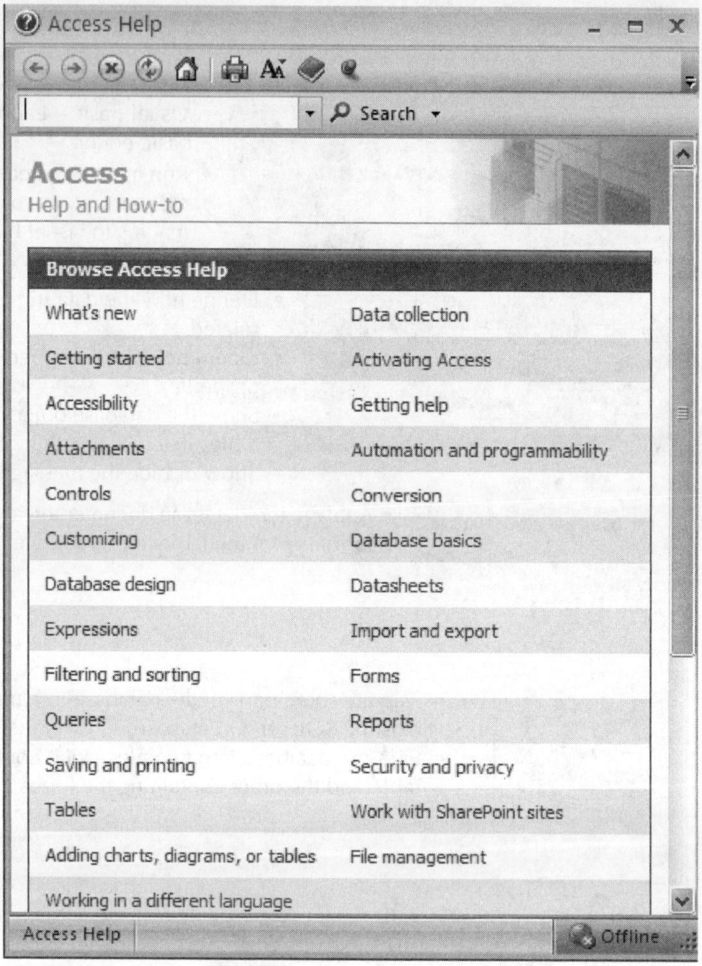

Figure 19.21 Access help

19.7 SOLVED EXAMPLE

This is an example to create a database and query it.

Example 1: **Create COMPANY relational database schema, as follows:**

COMPANY RELATIONAL DATABASE SCHEMA

RELATION NAME	ATTRIBUTES
EMPLOYEE	Fname, Minit, Lname, SSN, Bdate, Address, Sex, Salary, Superssn, Dno
DEPARTMENT	Dname, Dnumber, Mgrssn, Mgrstartdate
DEPT_DLOCATION	Dnumber, Dlocation
PROJECT	Pname, Pnumber, Plocation, Dnum
WORKS_ON	ESSN, Pno, Hours
DEPENDENT	ESSN, Dependent_name, Sex, Bdate, Relationship

The underlined fields are the primary key. Fill data into the table and perform the following Queries:

(1) Retrieve name of manager for each department and date on which they joined as manager.

(2) Retrieve the names of employees who work on all the projects that 'John Smith' works on.

(3) Retrieve for each female/male employee a list of the names of dependents.

(4) Retrieve department no., the no. of employees in the department and their average salary for each department managed by 'John Smith'.

(5) Retrieve for all employees their SSN and department name.

(6) Retrieve SSN, names, department no. of all employees whose salary is greater than the salary of all the employees supervised by him/her.

Solution 1.

- Open blank database. <New> <Create>.
- Create tables. <Create> <Tables> <Table>.
- Create six tables with given fields for the relation name Employee, Department, Dept_Dlocation, Project, Works_on, and Dependent.
- Fill the data into the tables. There is a relation between the table, which needs to be taken care when filling in the data. Employee (ssn) and Department (mgrssn); Department (dnumber) and Dept_Dlocation (dnumber); Project (dnum) and Department (dnumber); Project(pnumber) and Works_on (pno); Employee (ssn) and Works_on (essn); Dependent (essn) and Employee (ssn).
- Once all the tables with the data are created, design the query. <Create> <Other> <Query Design> <View> <SQL view>.
- The tables and the SQL queries are shown below.

EMPLOYEE TABLE

employee									
ssn	fname	minit	lname	bdate	address	sex	salary	superssn	dno
123456789	John	B	Smith	1/9/1965	731 Fondren, Huston,TX	M	30000	333445555	5
333445555	Franklin	T	wong	12/8/1955	638 Voss, Huston , TX	M	35000	888665555	5
453453453	Joyce	A	English	1/19/1968	3321 Castle, Spring, TX	F	25000	987654321	4
666884444	Ramesh	K	Narayan	6/20/1941	291 Berry, Bellaire, TX	F	43000	888665555	4
888665555	James	E	Borg	9/15/1962	975 Fire Oak , Humble,Tx	M	50000	333445555	5
987987987	Ahamed	V	Jabber	3/29/1969	980 Dallas, Huston, TX	M	25000	987654321	4
999887777	Alicia	J	Zelaya	11/10/1937	450 Stone, Huston,TX	M	55000	123456789	1

DEPARTMENT TABLE

department			
dnumber	dname	mgrssn	mgrstartdate
5	Research	123456789	5/22/1988
4	Administration	987654321	1/1/1995
1	Headquarters	888665555	6/19/1981

DEPT_DLOCATION TABLE

dept_dlocation	
dnumber	dlocation
1	Huston
4	Stafford
5	Bellaire
5	Huston
5	Sugarland

WORKS_ON TABLE

works_on		
essn	pno	hours
123456789	1	32
123456789	2	8
333445555	2	10
333445555	3	10
333445555	10	10
333445555	20	10
453453453	1	20
453453453	2	20
666884444	3	40
888665555	20	88
987654321	1	15
987654321	30	20
987987987	1	5
987987987	10	35
999887777	1	30
999887777	10	10

PROJECT TABLE

project			
pnumber	pname	plocation	dnum
1	ProductX	Bellaire	5
2	ProductY	Sugarland	5
3	ProductZ	Huston	5
10	Computerization	Stafford	4
20	Reorganisation	Huston	1
30	Newbenefits	Stafford	4

DEPENDENT TABLE

dependent				
essn	dependent_name	sex	bdate	relationship
123456789	Alice	F	12/30/1988	Daughter
123456789	Elizabeth	F	5/5/1967	Spouse
123456789	Michael	M	1/4/1988	Son
333445555	Alice	F	4/5/1986	Daughter
333445555	Joy	F	5/3/1958	Spouse
333445555	Theodore	M	10/25/1983	Son
987654321	Abner	M	2/28/1942	Spouse

QUERIES

1. Retrieve name of manager for each department and date on which they joined as manager.

Sql view

```
SELECT fname, lname, mgrstartdate
FROM department, employee
WHERE mgrssn=ssn;
```

Output

Query1		
fname	lname	mgrstartdate
John	Smith	5/22/1988
James	Borg	6/19/1981

2. Retrieve the names of employees who work on all the projects that 'john smith' works on.

Sql view

```
SELECT DISTINCT fname, lname
FROM employee, works_on
WHERE pno in (select pno
              from works_on,employee
              where fname='john' and lname='smith' and essn=ssn;)
              and essn=ssn;
```

Output

Query2	
Fname	lname
Franklin	wong
Ahamed	Jabber
Alicia	Zelaya
John	Smith
Joyce	English

3. Retrieve for each female/male employee a list of the names of dependents.

Sql view

```
SELECT fname, lname,employee.sex,ssn, dependent_name
FROM employee, dependent
WHERE employee.sex='m' and essn=ssn
UNION SELECT fname, lname,employee.sex,ssn, dependent_name
FROM employee, dependent
WHERE employee.sex='f' and essn=ssn;
```

Output

Query3				
Fname	lname	sex	ssn	dependent_name
Franklin	wong	M	333445555	Alice
Franklin	wong	M	333445555	Joy
Franklin	wong	M	333445555	Theodore
John	Smith	M	123456789	Alice
John	Smith	M	123456789	Elizabeth
John	Smith	M	123456789	Michael

4. Retrieve department no, the no of employees in the department and their average salary for each department managed by 'John Smith'.

<u>Sql view</u>

```
SELECT dno, count(dno) AS no_of_employees, avg(salary) AS avg_salary
FROM employee
WHERE dno in(select dno
        from department
        where mgrssn=ssn and fname='john' and lname='smith';)
GROUP BY dno;
```

Output

Query4		
dno	No_of_employees	avg_salary
5	1	30000

5. Retrieve for all employees their SSN and department name.

<u>Sql view</u>

```
SELECT ssn, dname
FROM employee, department
WHERE dno=dnumber;
```

Output

Query6	
Ssn	dname
888665555	Research
333445555	Research
123456789	Research
987987987	Administration
666884444	Administration
453453453	Administration
999887777	Headquarters

6. Retrieve SSN, names, department no. of all employees whose salary is greater than the salary of all the employees supervised by him/her.

Sql view

```
SELECT ssn, fname, lname, dno
FROM employee AS e1
WHERE e1.salary >
(
select max(salary)
from employee as e2
where e1.superssn=e2.ssn;
);
```

Output

Query8			
Ssn	fname	lname	dno
888665555	James	Borg	5
999887777	Alicia	Zelaya	1

Exercises:

1. Create Suppliers and Parts relational database schema as follows:

RELATION NAME	ATTRIBUTES
SUPPLIER	SNo, Sname, Status, City
PARTS	PNo, Pname, Color, Weight, city
PROJECT	Jno, Jname, City
SHIPMENT	Sno, Pno, Jno, Quantity

The underlined fields are the primary key. Fill in the appropriate data in the tables. Perform the following queries:-

a) Get full details of all the projects in London.

b) Get supplier no. for suppliers who supply project J1.

c) Get supplier details for suppliers who supply part P2.

d) Get supplier names for suppliers who do not supply part P2.

e) For each shipment get full shipment details, including total shipment weight.

f) Get all shipments where the quantity is in the range 300 to 750 inclusive.

g) Get all distinct part-color combinations.

h) Get supplier no. for suppliers in Paris with status > 20.

i) Get part nos. for parts that either weigh more than 16 pounds or are supplied by supplier S2, or both.

j) Get part cities that store more than five red parts.

2. Create Purchase order relational database schema, as follows:

PURCHASE ORDER RELATIONAL DATABASE SCHEMA

RELATION NAME	ATTRIBUTES
VENDOR	Vendorno, vname, street, city, region, zip, contact
PRICEINFO	Partno, vendorno, catno, price
POHEADER	Orderno, orddate, vendorno, invoiceno, status
PODETAIL	Orderno, partno, qty, unit-pr
PART	Partno, description
POHISTORY	Orderno, orddate, vendorno, invoiceno, pototal

The underlined fields are the primary key. Fill data into the table and perform the following Queries:

(a) Display all the rows in the part table, sorted by description.

(b) Display the part description for the part number 4.

(c) Select all columns of the PODETAIL table which a quantity greater than 500.

(d) Display all part numbers, descriptions, prices, catalogue numbers and vendor numbers and names.

(e) How many vendors are located in the city of NewYork?

(f) Find the unit price and quantity information for order number 1101.

(g) Which parts are priced at the lowest price?

3. Create the following tables:

RELATION NAME	ATTRIBUTES
BOOKS	Book_id, Book_name, Author_name, Publishers, Price, Type, Quantity
ISSUED	Book_id, qty_issued

The underlined fields are the primary key. Fill data into the table and perform the following Queries:

(a) Display book name, author name and price of books of Pearson publishers.

(b) Display book name, author name and price of books that have been issued.

(c) Give the output of the following queries

a. SELECT COUNT(DISTINCT Publishers) FROM Books;

b. SELECT COUNT(*) from Books;

c. SELECT SUM(Price) FROM Books WHERE Quantity > 5.

4. Create Library Management relational database schema, as follows:

LIBRARY MANAGEMENT RELATIONAL DATABASE SCHEMA

RELATION NAME	ATTRIBUTES
BOOK	Book id, title, pub_id
BOOK_AUTHORS	Book id, author name
BOOK_COPIES	Book id, branch id, noof_copies
BOOK_LOANS	Book id, branch id, card no, dateout, duedate
LIBRARY_BRANCH	Branch id, branch_name, address
BORROWER	Card no, name, address, phone
PUBLISHER	Pub id, Pub_name, address, phone_no

The underlined fields are the primary key. Fill data into the table and perform the following Queries:

(a) Retrieve the names of all borrowers who do not have any books checked out.

(b) For each library branch, retrieve the branch name and the total number of books loaned out from that branch.

(c) Retrieve the names, addresses, and number of books checked out for all borrowers who have more than five books checked out.

NETWORK AND INTERNET CONNECTIONS 20

Contents

- Introduction
- Start network connections
- Create a new connection—
  - Connect to dial-up modem, cable or DSL modem, LAN connection, private network, existing home or small office network, DCC between two computers
  - Select network connection type—Internet option, network at my workplace, home or small office network, advanced connection option
  - Getting ready—Choose ISP, set up connection manually, use the CD I got from an ISP
- Manage a network connection—Disable, enable and repair a network connection, configure IP settings
- Network setup
- Windows firewall
- Sharing of files
- Wireless network setup—Create wireless network, add a computer to an existing wireless network
- Connect using virtual private network
- Set up a wired network
- Automatic wireless network connections—Configure wireless network settings, available networks, automatically connect to non-preferred networks
- Set up Internet properties—Internet options
- Choose an Internet connection—Dial-up access, ISDN, DSL, cable modem, wireless Internet connections, T-1 lines, Internet over satellite

Why this chapter

Internet and networking is an important part of using the computer. To connect the computer to a network or the Internet, using wired or wireless connection, you need to set up a connection and also be able to manage it. In Windows XP, the *Network and Internet Connections* option allows you to do that. The purpose of this chapter is to introduce you to the Network and Internet connections of Windows XP.

20.1 INTRODUCTION

Windows XP provides many ways using which to network or link computers at home, at office or to the Internet. Windows XP provides easy-to-follow wizards to help create, manage, and secure your network. You can setup five types of network connections i.e., dial-up connections, local area connections, virtual private network connections, direct connections using serial or parallel cables, and, call in to a remote access server from your home or office. It is also possible to set up wired connections or wireless connections to connect to other computers or the Internet. Windows XP also allows setting up a *Firewall* that blocks access to the computer from the Internet or a network program and service that is not trusted.

In this chapter, we describe the *Network and Internet Connections* of Windows XP. The chapter describes creating and managing the network connections, setting up a wired and wireless connection, setting up the Firewall, and making Internet settings using the Internet options.

20.2 START NETWORK CONNECTIONS

The network connections setting in Windows XP specifies how to connect the computer to a network. It might also be needed to change the network settings if the Internet Service Provider (ISP) is changed.

The steps to start the network connections is as follows:

(1) <Start> <Control Panel> <Pick a Category> <Network and Internet Connections> <or pick a Control Panel icon> <Network Connections> (Figure 20.1)

(2) Windows XP displays the Network Connections window.

All the network connections (Figure 20.2) of the computer can be seen

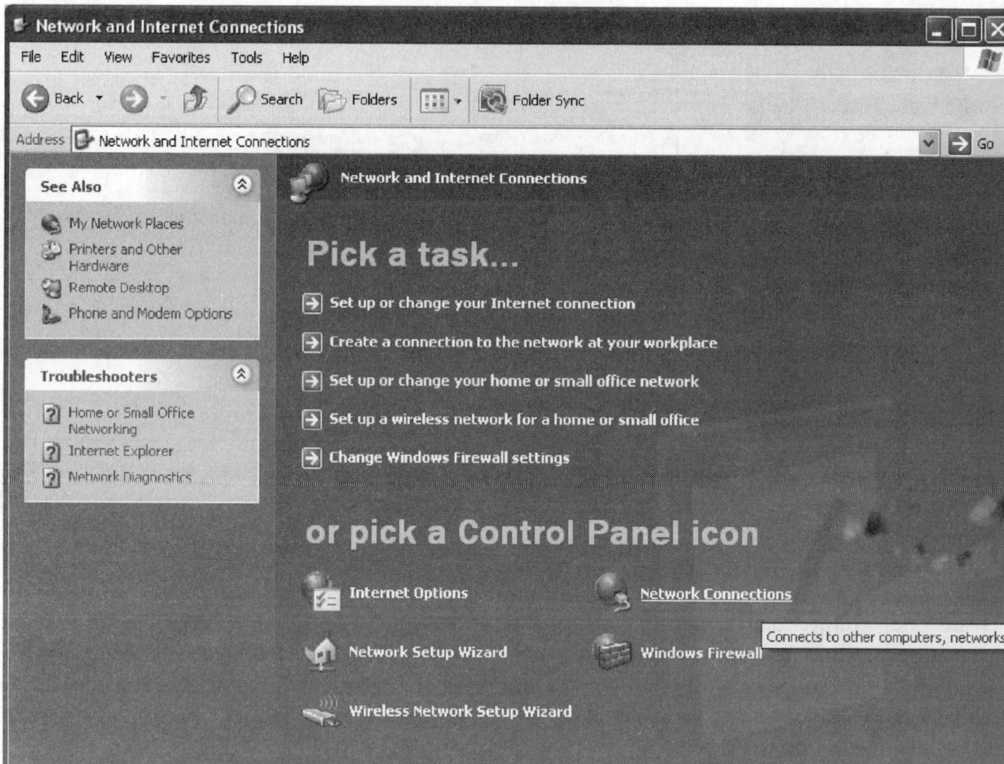

Figure 20.1 Network and internet connections

> In this chapter, the following terminology is used for working with the mouse
>
> - **Pointer**—a mouse pointer
> - **Click**—press left button of mouse once
> - **Right Click**—press right button of mouse once
> - **Double Click**—press left button of mouse twice
> - **Select**—move the pointer of mouse and keep the left button of the mouse pressed over the area that you want to select. The selected area will appear in a dark background.
>
> *The commands are enclosed in braces <Command> to represent the command to be clicked.*

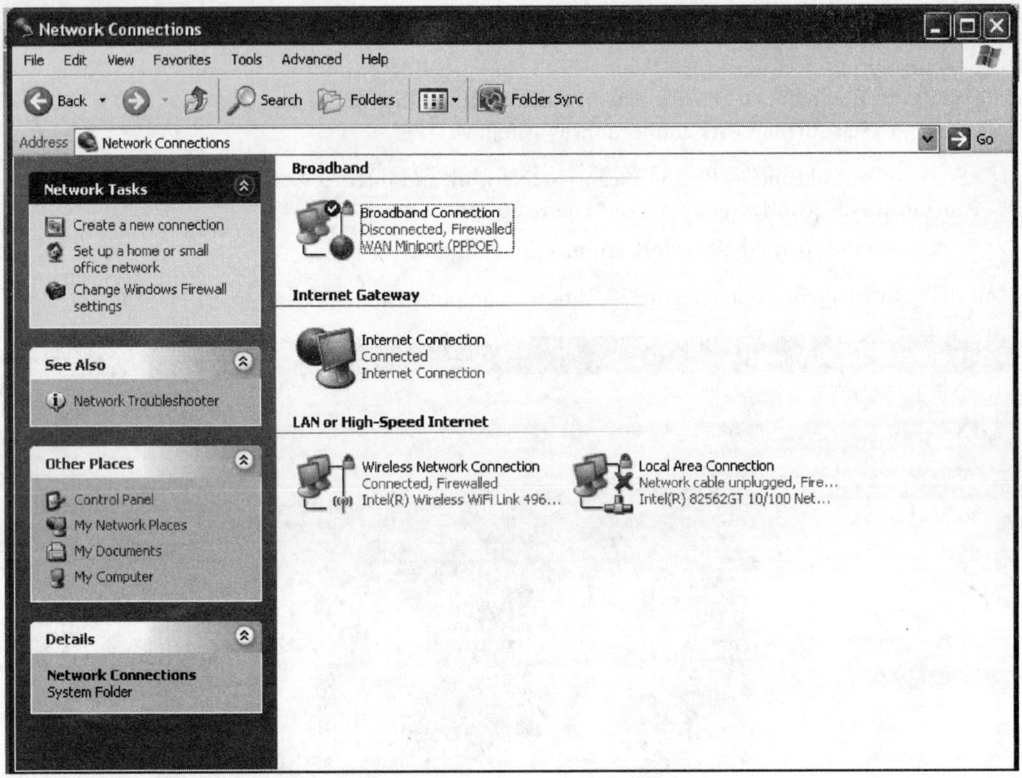

Figure 20.2 Network connections

20.3 CREATE A NEW CONNECTION

To create a new connection, the New Connection Wizard has to be started. The new connection wizard helps to create a connection to the Internet, to another computer, or to the workplace network. The New Connection Wizard supports setting up the different types of network connections like broadband, Virtual Private Network (VPN), modem dialup, serial port, parallel port and infrared. The New Connection Wizard allows the following:

- Set up a computer to connect to the Internet using a dial-up modem, a cable or DSL modem, or LAN connection. The Internet Service Provider (ISP) would have provided the settings to be included on the computer.
- Connect the computer to a private network, such as the company network, using dial-up or VPN connection to work from home or another location. Your company/organization must give the access right for the VPN.
- Connect the computer to an existing home or small office network or set up a new one. Assign a unique name for your computer and type in the workgroup name correctly.
- Set up a Direct Cable Connection (DCC) between two computers using serial, parallel, or infrared port.
- Set up your computer for incoming connection that allows other computers on the local network or on the Internet to connect to it.

To start the New Connection Wizard, do the following steps:

- <Start> <Control Panel> <Network and Internet Connections> <Network Connections>. A window opens.
- On the left side of window, on the tab *Network Tasks*, click <Create a new connection> (Figure 20.3)
- A New Connection Wizard opens. Click *Next* to continue.
- Select Network connection type. The Network Connection Type (Figure 20.4) presents three choices for Internet and private network setup:

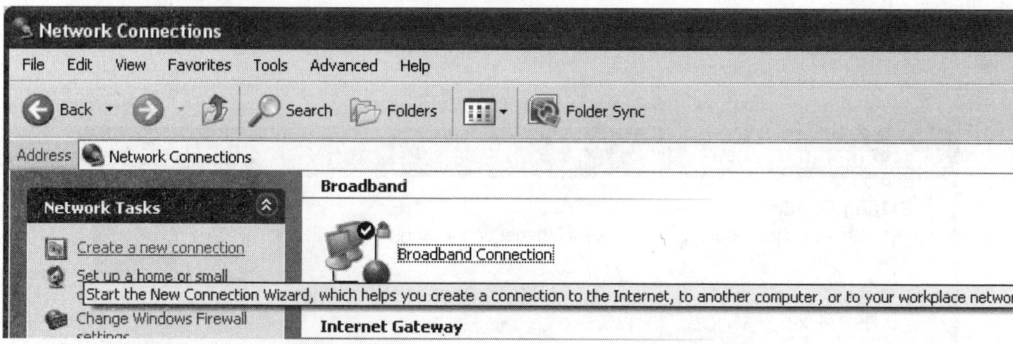

Figure 20.3 Create a new connection option

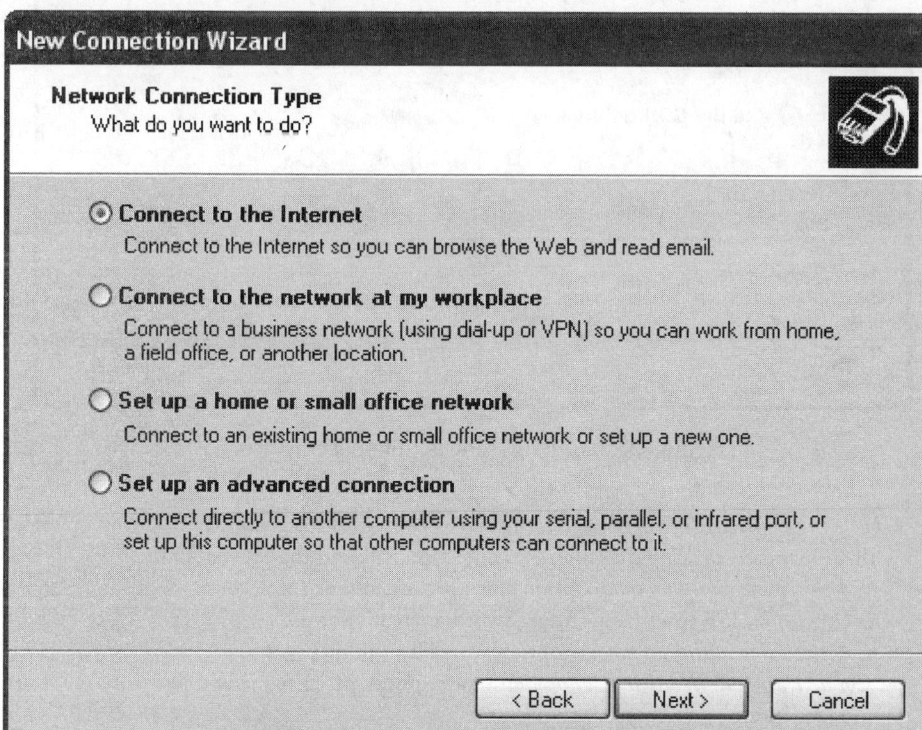

Figure 20.4 Network connection type

- *Connect to the Internet option* allows the user to choose from a list of ISPs, use a setup CD provided by the ISP, or set up a connection manually.
- *Connect to the network at my workplace* allows client-side setup of both dialup remote access and VPN services.
- *Set up a home or small office network* allows sharing an Internet connection, share files, folders and printers.
- *Set up an advanced connection option* supports serial, parallel and infrared port networking setups.

Select an option. To connect to the Internet, select the *Connect to the Internet* option. Click *Next* to continue.

⊙ The Getting Ready page (Figure 20.5) presents three choices as shown below:

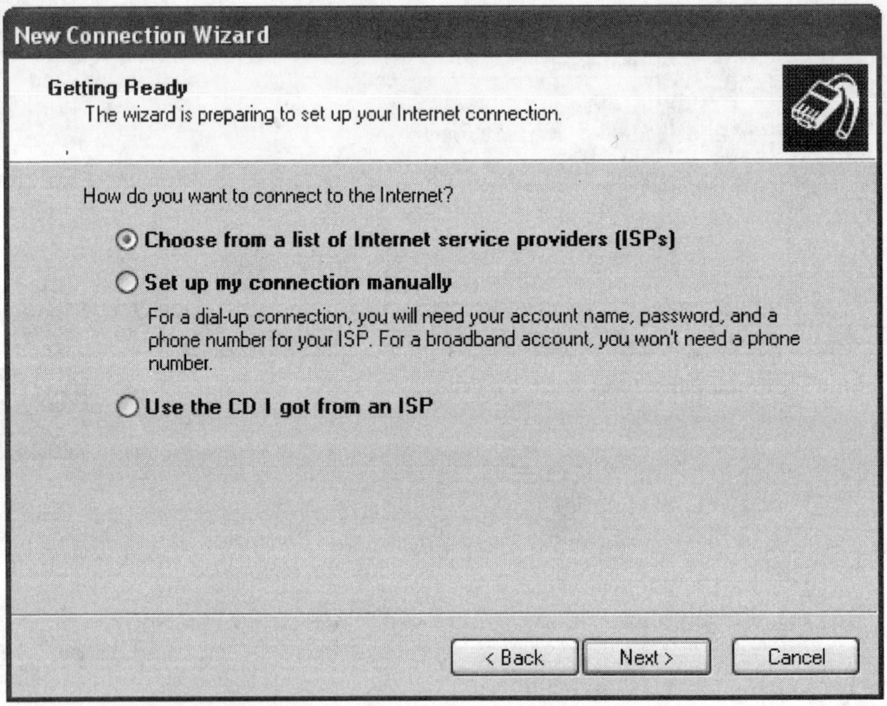

Figure 20.5 Getting ready for Internet connection

- *Choose from a list of Internet Service Providers* option gives instructions for setting up an account with an ISP, then making the Internet connection through that new account.
- *Set up my connection manually* option sets up connections for accounts that have already been opened with an ISP (username and password are ready for use).
  - *Connect using a dial-up modem* option works for phone line Internet services.
  - *Connect using a broadband connection* that requires a user name and password (DSL or cable modem Internet services).
  - *Connect using a broadband connection that is always on* (for "always on" DSL or cable modem services)

- *Use the CD I got from an ISP* option is used when an installation CD-ROM has been given to you by the ISP.
- Select *Choose from a list of Internet Service Providers*

⊙ Click *Finish.*

The Windows XP network connection wizard closes and a new window (Figure 20.6) opens.

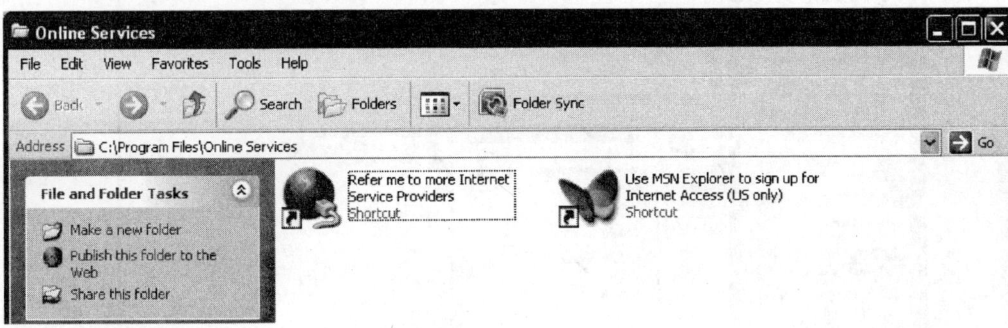

Figure 20.6 Online services

The *Refer me to more Internet Service Providers* launches a new Internet Connection Wizard. The *Use MSN Explorer to sign up for Internet Access (US only)* launches the MSN window.

20.4 MANAGE A NETWORK CONNECTION

Several network management tasks can be performed on a network connection. To manage a network connection, do as follows:

⊙ Click on the connection you want to manage. Network management task can be performed on this connection in two ways:

(1) On the left side, *Network Tasks* shows the list of possible tasks you can perform for this connection, or

(2) Right-click on the network connection you want to manage. A pop-up window appears (Figure 20.7). Select the task to be performed.

Some of the network management tasks you can perform on the selected network connection are as follows:

⊙ *Disable a network connection*—Right-click. <Disable>.

⊙ *Enable a network connection*—Right-click. <Enable>.

⊙ *Repair a network connection*—Right-click. <Repair>.

⊙ *Configure your Internet Protocol (IP) settings*—Use this option to specify the IP address and Domain Name System (DNS) servers. Right-click a network connection. <Properties>. *General* tab. In *This connection uses the following items* click <Internet Protocol (TCP/IP)>. Click <Properties>. In the Internet Protocol (TCP/IP) Properties dialog box (Figure 20.8), configure the network settings. Click OK. Click *close* to return to the Network Connections window.

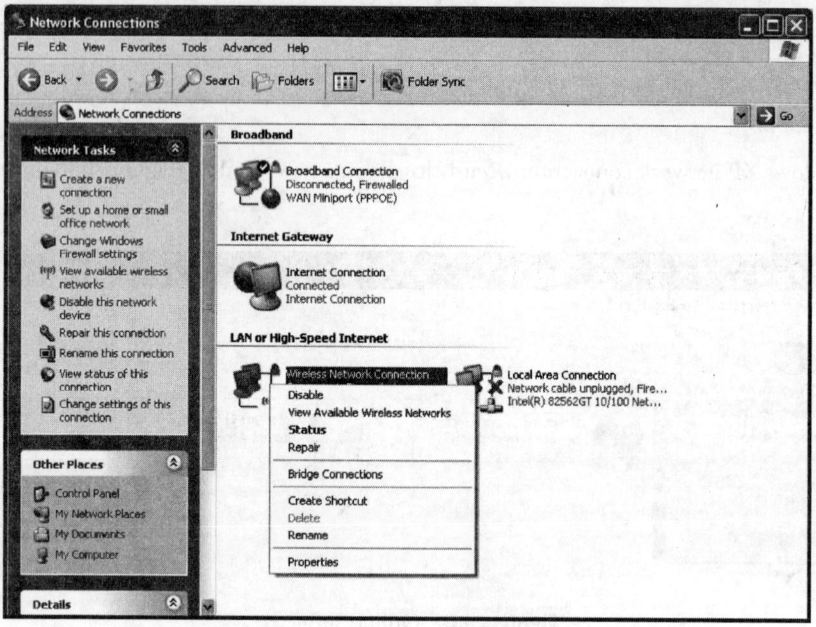

Figure 20.7 Network management tasks

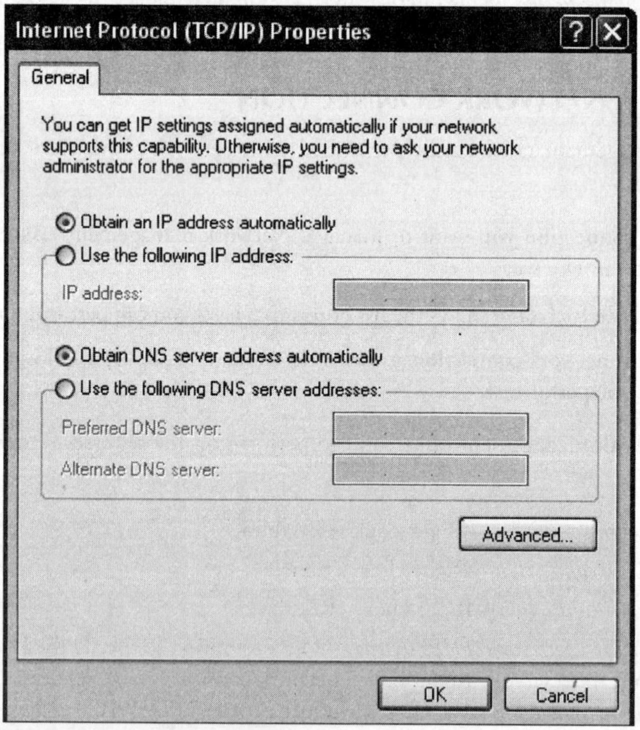

Figure 20.8 TCP/IP properties

20.5 NETWORK SETUP

The Network Setup wizard is used after physically connecting all computers in the network with the necessary hardware. The Network Setup Wizard helps do the following:

- Configure all computers in the network to share one Internet connection through a hub, gateway etc.
- Set up Windows Firewall to protect the computer or network when it is connected to the Internet.
- Enable file and printer sharing so that certain files, folders, or printers can be accessed by all computers in the network.

Network Setup Wizard can be used as follows:

- <Start> <Control Panel> <Network and Internet Connections> <Network Setup Wizard> (Figure 20.9).
- Click *Next*. On each window that opens follow the instructions and then click on *Next*. Finally you will reach the window showing *Finish*. Click on *Finish* to complete the setup.

Figure 20.9 Network setup wizard

20.6 WINDOWS FIREWALL

Windows firewall is a protective boundary that monitors the incoming traffic from the network and Internet. Using the firewall guards against the intruders and unauthorized persons over the network and the Internet. When connected to the Internet or a network, it blocks unauthorized access to the computer. However, the programs and services that you trust can access your computer. Windows Firewall does not provide the options to filter outgoing connections.

The Windows Firewall is turned on by default. In Windows XP, Windows Firewall is part of the Windows Security Center. Windows Security Center manages security setting of Internet Options, Windows Automatic Updates and Windows Firewall. It constantly checks whether Windows Firewall is on, and displays an alert message if it is turned off. Windows Security Center also monitors the antivirus software to ensure that it is updated.

The Windows Firewall  window can be opened in either of the following ways:

- <Start> <Control Panel> <Network and Internet Connections> <Windows Firewall>, or
- <Start> <Control Panel> <Network and Internet Connections> <Change Windows Firewall settings>, or
- <Start> <Control Panel> <Security Center> <Windows Firewall>, or
- <Start> <Control Panel> <Windows Firewall>, or
- <Start> <Connect To> <Show all connections> <Network Tasks> <Change Windows Firewall settings>, or
- <Start> <All Programs> <Accessories> <Communications> <Network Connections> <Network Tasks> <Change Windows Firewall settings>, or
- <My Network Places> <View network connections> <Network Tasks> <Change Windows Firewall settings>.

The Windows Firewall is opened as follows:

- <Start> <Control Panel> <Network and Internet Connections> <Windows Firewall>.
- Windows Firewall window opens (Figure 20.10). It has three tabs—General, Exceptions and Advanced. You can make the Firewall settings from here.

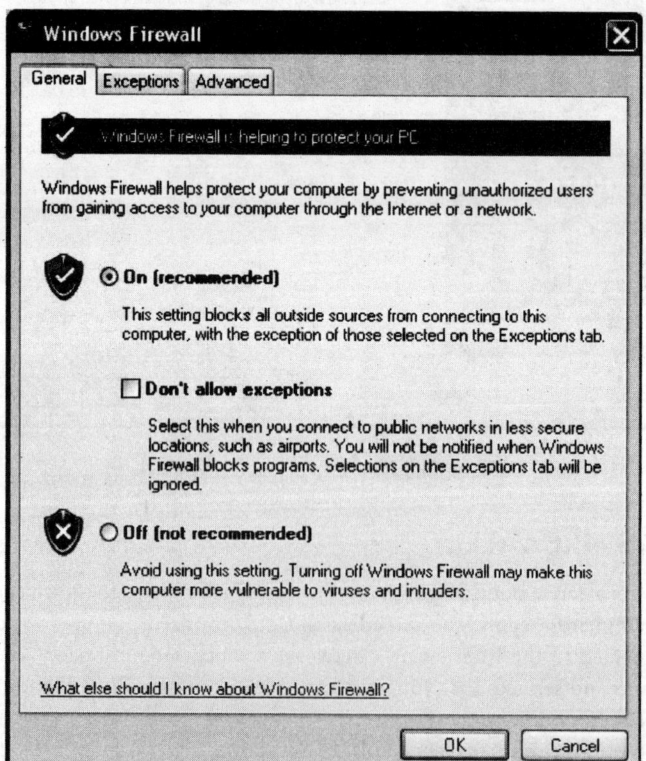

Figure 20.10 Windows firewall

20.7 SHARING OF FILES

Windows XP allows the local sharing and network sharing of the files and folders. To share a file or folder with other users, perform the following steps:

- Right-click on the folder name you want to share.
- Click <Properties>.
- Click <Sharing>.
- Click on *Shared Documents* for the local sharing (Figure 20.11). Click on *Network Setup Wizard* for the network sharing of the file or folder.

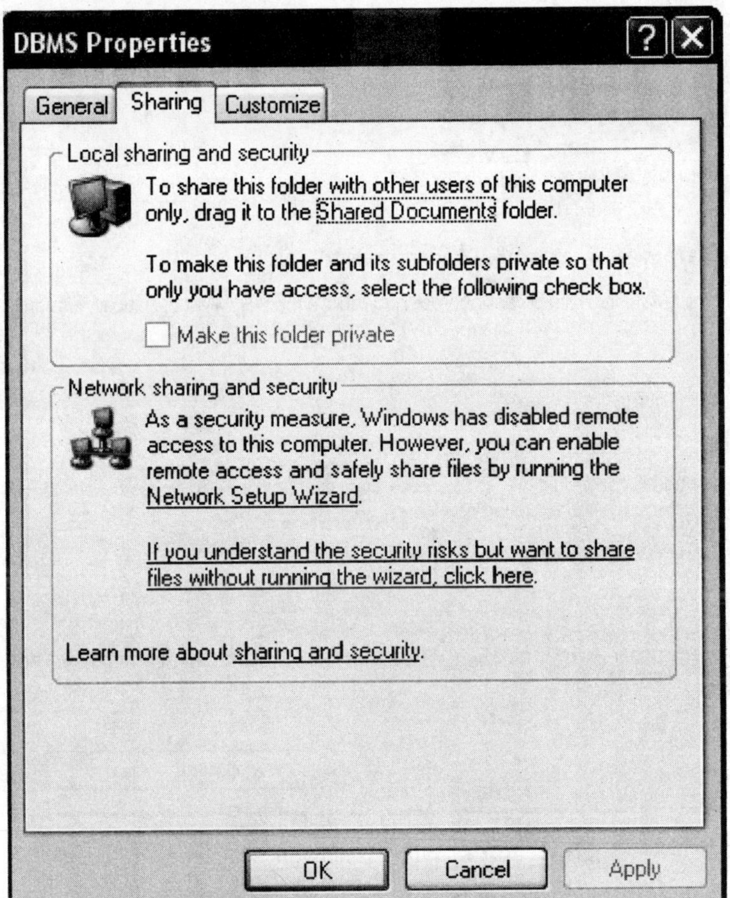

Figure 20.11 Sharing of files and folders

Sharing rights for the users can also be set. Permissions can be allowed or denied to specific users or groups for the sharing of the folder. To share the individual files, put the files in the same shared folder. All the files and folders in the parent shared folder will be automatically shared.

20.8 WIRELESS NETWORK SETUP

The Wireless Network Setup Wizard enables creation of a secure wireless network. Choose the security scheme to be Wired Equivalent Privacy (WEP) or Wi-Fi Protected Access (WPA). WPA gives stronger security to your network, but make sure that the hardware (network adapter and access point) supports WPA.

The Wireless Network Setup Wizard can be started as follows:

<Start> <Control Panel> <Network and Internet Connections> <Wireless Network Setup Wizard>

The Wireless Network Setup Wizard (Figure 20.12) helps to:

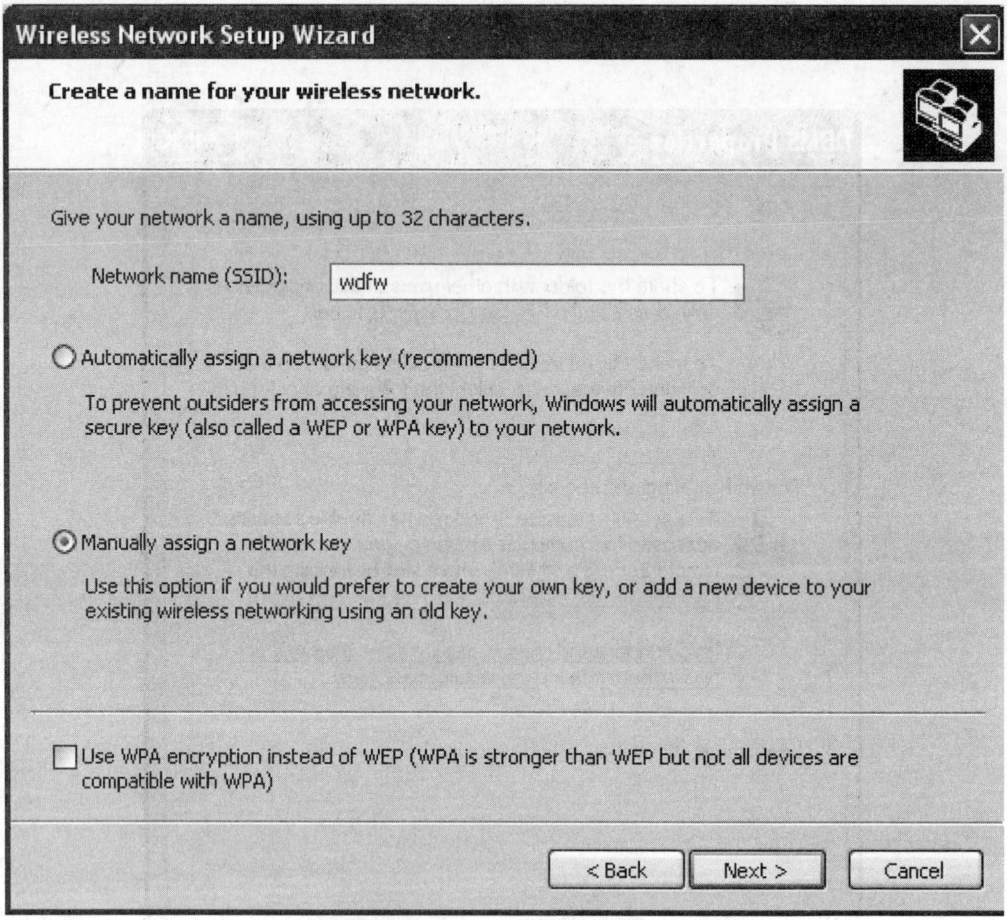

Figure 20.12 Wireless network setup wizard

- Create a wireless network in which a wireless access point connects all computers together. It is necessary to assign a network name—Service Set Identifier (SSID) and a secure key with either WEP or WPA encryption (Figure 20.13). *An SSID is the name of a wireless local area network (WLAN). All wireless devices on a WLAN must use the same SSID to communicate with each other. The SSID on wireless clients can be set either manually, by entering the SSID into the client network settings, or automatically by leaving the SSID blank.* You can save your network settings to a Universal Serial

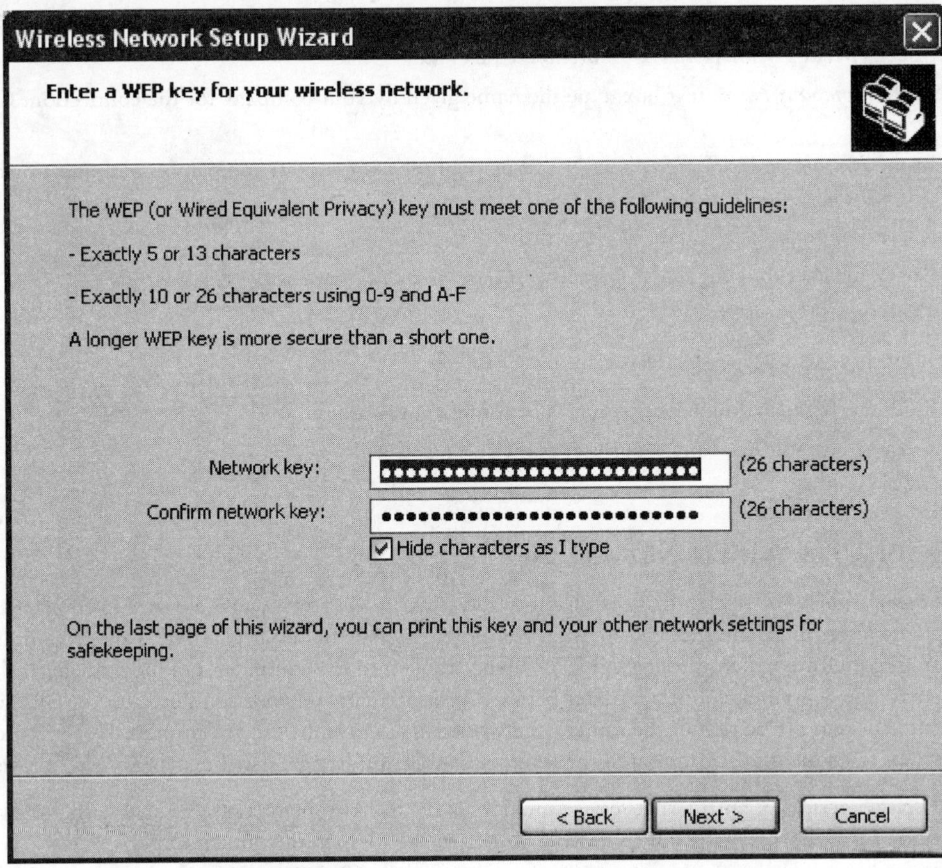

Figure 20.13 To enter a WEP key for wireless network

Bus (USB) flash drive and use it for configuring the wireless access point and other computers. The USB flash drive can only be used for setting up wireless LAN devices (e.g. access point, camera and phone) that support Windows Connect Now technology (WCN). There is an option to print the network settings and set up the network manually.

- Add a computer to an existing wireless network. You can use the USB flash drive to which settings were saved during your wireless network creation, or you can set up the network manually. To use the flash drive, just plug in the USB flash drive to each computer that you want to add to the existing wireless network and confirm that the computer will be added to the existing wireless network when prompted by the wizard. Then the computer will be configured automatically for joining the existing wireless network.

20.9 CONNECT USING VIRTUAL PRIVATE NETWORK (VPN)

A VPN provides remote users with secure access to the organization's network via public infrastructure such as Internet. To connect to the VPN, first make the settings required to make the connection, as follows:

- <Start> <Control Panel> <Network and Internet Connections> <Network connection> <Create a new connection>. The *New Connection Wizard* appears. Click *Next*.

- Select *Connect to the network at my workplace.* Click *Next.*
- Select *Virtual Private Network connection.* Click *Next.*
- In the *Company Name* text box, type the name given by your company for the connection. Click *Next.*
- In the *Host name or IP address* text box, type the host name of our company's computer to which you want to connect to. Click *Next.*
- Select *My use on.* Click *Next.*
- Check the checkbox for *Add a shortcut to this connection to my desktop.* Click Finish
- Click Cancel to exit.

To connect to the VPN, do as follows:

- From the *Desktop,* double click your VPN connection shortcut.
- A dialog box appears. Enter your user name and password.
- Click *Connect.*

20.10 SET UP A WIRED NETWORK

Wired networks offer good performance, reliability and security. Wired networks are used to connect your desktop computer to the Internet and to other computers in your home. If you have a single computer, connecting to the Internet requires plugging a network cable into the computer and the modem. If there is more than one computer, connect a router between your modem and your computers. If the computer is in a different room from that of the router, a network extender can be used to connect the computer.

The steps to connect the computer to the Internet connection using a wired network are as follows:

- Use the services of an Internet service provider (ISP) to have them configure an Internet connection to your home. Preferably, place the modem in the room with your computer.
- Your computer must have a Network adapter.
- Shut down your computer. <Start> <Turn off Computer> <Turn Off>.
- Connect the network cable given to you by your ISP to your network adapter. Connect the other end of the network cable to your modem.
- Start your computer and log on to Microsoft Windows.
- Windows automatically detects that you are connected to the Internet.

Your wired connection to the Internet is now ready for use.

20.11 AUTOMATIC WIRELESS NETWORK CONNECTIONS

Windows XP allows establishing a wireless network connection to Wi-Fi network routers and access points automatically. This feature helps to make wireless Internet or Wi-Fi network connections easily with laptop computers. The steps to be followed to establish a wireless network connection automatically are as follows:

- Check whether the Windows XP computer supports automatic wireless configuration. For this do as follows:
    - <Start> <Control Panel> <Network and Internet Connections> <Network Connections>
    - Right-click <Wireless Network Connection> <Properties>

In the Wireless Network Connection properties window, if you see a *Wireless Networks* tab, then you can automatically connect to wireless network connections. Click it.

- To enable automatic configuration, *Use Windows to configure my wireless network settings* checkbox must be checked on the Wireless Networks tab of the Wireless Network Connection properties window (Figure 20.14). Automatic wireless network configuration will be disabled if this checkbox is unchecked.

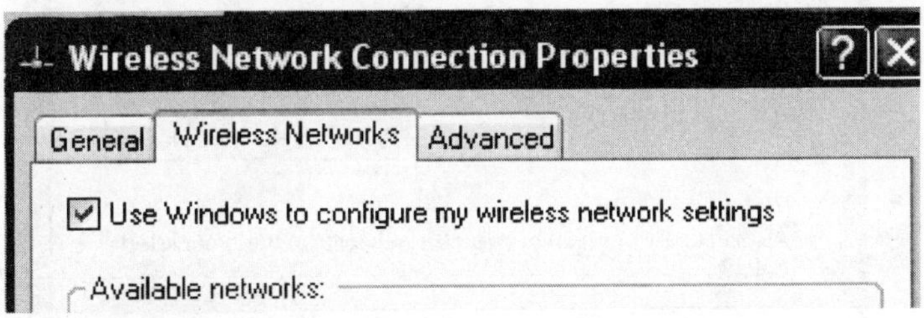

Figure 20.14 Use Windows to configure wireless network

- The Wireless Networks tab allows access to the set of *Available* networks (Figure 20.15). Available networks represent the active networks currently detected by Windows XP. To view the available networks, click the *View Wireless Networks* button on that page.

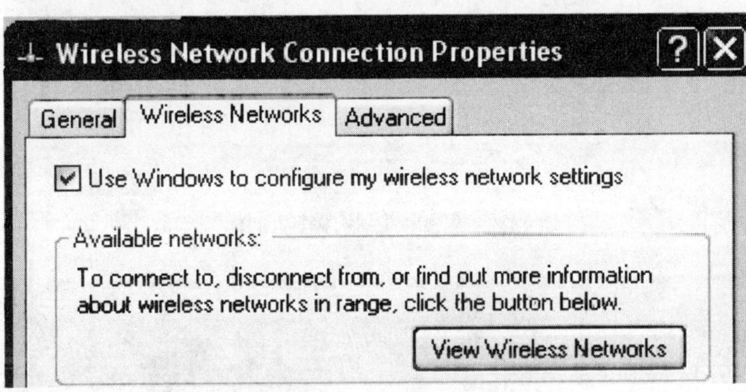

Figure 20.15 View wireless networks

- You can also build a set of "Preferred networks" (Figure 20.16) when automatic wireless configuration is active. This list represents a set of known Wi-Fi routers or access points you wish to automatically connect to in future. The order Preferred networks are listed here determines the order that Windows XP will automatically attempt when seeking to make a wireless connection. You can set this order to your preference.
- By default, Windows XP enables automatic wireless configuration support. Also, by default, Windows XP only auto-connects to Preferred networks.
- The *Advanced* button on the Wireless Networks tab of Wireless Network Connection properties controls the default behavior of Windows XP automatic connections. The *Automatically connect to non-preferred networks*, allows Windows XP to auto-connect to any network on the Available list, not just Preferred ones. This option is disabled by default.
- When the *View Wireless Networks button on the Wireless Network tab* is clicked, all the available wireless networks in range (Figure 20.17) are seen. Choose the network that you wish to connect to and click the *Connect* button.

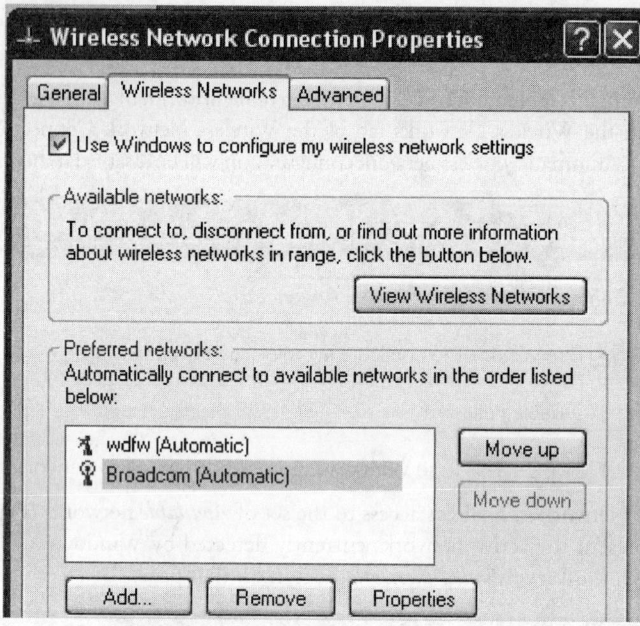

Figure 20.16 Preferred networks

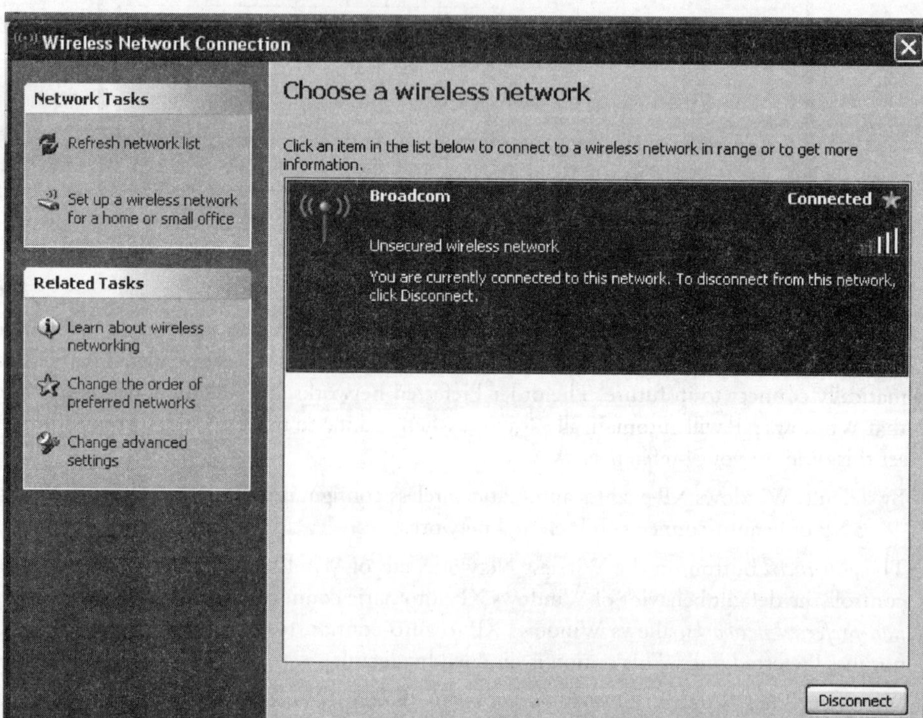

Figure 20.17 Choose a wireless network

- If the wireless network is protected, click Change advanced settings. A *Wireless Network Properties* window opens. Click on the *Wireless Networks* tab. In the Preferred network, select the network you want to connect to. Click <Properties>. A window opens. It has three tabs—Association, Authentication and Connection. Make the required entries in these tabs. Click <OK>.
- You should now be connected to the wireless network.

20.12 SET UP INTERNET PROPERTIES—INTERNET OPTIONS

Once you are connected to the Internet, you need to use the Web Browser to access the World Wide Web (WWW). The Internet Explorer is a Web browser software that comes bundled with the Windows software. Internet can be accessed by clicking on the Internet Explorer icon . The Internet Explorer settings can be modified using the Internet Options. Internet Options allows you to change the settings of Internet Explorer, but it cannot be used to change the settings of other Web browsers.

To Open Internet Options, do as follows:

- <Start> <Control Panel> <Network and Internet Connections> <Internet Options>.
- An Internet Properties window opens.

The Internet Properties window (Figure 20.18) has seven tabs—General, Security, Privacy, Content, Connections, Programs and Advanced. Specify the first Web page you see on starting the browser, delete

Figure 20.18 Internet properties

temporary Internet files stored on the computer, use Content Advisor to block access to objectionable material, and specify how colors and fonts are displayed on Web pages. You can also set the security level and specify which programs to use for e-mail. In short, you can make all the settings for the Internet browser from here.

20.13 CHOOSE AN INTERNET CONNECTION

With the growth of technology, the content on the Web has also changed. Now web applications include content like animations, online gaming, database-driven web sites and e-commerce. Thus, the need for speed as to how fast we can connect to the Internet has changed.

The overall connection speeds of the different types of Internet connections are given below. There can be variations amongst different Internet Service Providers (ISP).

- *Dial-up access* is economical but slow. Dial-up access uses normal telephone lines so the quality of the connection is not always good. Speed is 2400 bps to 56 Kbps.
- *Integrated Services Digital Network (ISDN)* is an international communications standard for sending voice, video, and data over telephone lines. Speed is 64 Kbps to 128 Kbps.
- *DSL* is an always on connection. ADSL is the most commonly deployed type of DSL. Speed is 128 Kbps to 8 Mbps.
- *Cable modem* gives you a broadband Internet connection that is designed to operate over cable TV lines. Speed 512 Kbps to 20 Mbps.
- *Wireless Internet Connections* uses radio frequency bands. Wireless Internet provides an always-on connection which can be accessed from anywhere geographically within a network coverage area. Their speed varies.
- *T-1 Lines* are a leased line option for businesses connecting. T-1 Lines support speeds of 1.544 Mbps.
- *Internet over Satellite (IoS)* allows a user to access the Internet via a satellite that orbits the earth. Speed: 492Kbps to 512 Kbps.

For home users, the ADSL connection is the best suited. It is a broadband connection, always on, not very expensive and can be used with the telephone line. It has a fairly good speed also. You can also connect your broadband connection to a wireless modem internally in the home, to access the Internet connection from any room of the house wirelessly.

21

USING LATEX

Contents

Why this chapter

Nowadays, the production of long articles and books uses a document preparation system that produces publication-quality typeset documents. The document preparation system includes programmable desktop publishing features and facilities for automating cross-referencing, tables, figures, page layout, bibliography etc. LaTeX is a family of programs designed to produce high quality typeset documents. The purpose of this chapter is to introduce you to LaTeX.

21.1 INTRODUCTION

TeX is a computer program for typesetting documents, created by D. E. Knuth. Typesetting involves formatting of the input text. TeX is a mathematical typesetting markup language. A file created using TeX may be printed on different kinds of printers and high-resolution typesetting machines. TeX is widely used by publishers to typeset books and mathematical journals.

LaTeX is a variant of TeX, written by Leslie Lamport. LaTeX is a document preparation system and document markup language for the TeX typesetting programs. LaTeX focuses on the structure of the document; TeX focuses on the visual typesetting details. LaTeX is a popular method of using TeX.

LaTeX is a family of programs designed to produce publication-quality typeset documents. It is particularly strong when working with mathematical symbols. It is suited for the production of long articles and books. It facilitates automatic numbering of chapters, sections, theorems, equations etc., and cross-referencing. LaTeX is widely used by academia and scientists because of its high-quality typesetting features achieved due to TeX. It offers programmable desktop publishing features.

LaTeX is free software, distributed under the LaTeX Project Public License. Here, we work in the Windows environment, while working with LaTeX.

21.2 CREATE LATEX DOCUMENT

To create a TeX document—

- Create a TeX file using a text editor. Some editors are specifically created for working with LaTeX like *WinEdt.*
- Save the TeX file with the .tex extension.
- Compile and run the TeX file. If you are using a LaTeX text editor, you can use the menu commands to run the file. For example, in *WinEdt*, Accessories>LaTeX, will execute the file and show the output.
- A program *Yap* previews and prints your LaTeX output.

21.3 COMPONENTS OF A LATEX DOCUMENT

- A LaTeX document must contain the following three components:
  (1) \documentclass{article}
  (2) \begin{document}
  (3) \end{document}
- \documentclass{article} tells LaTeX about the kind of document, as there are different style rules for different kinds of documents. We use the article document class. Other classes include report, book, and letter.
- The default font size for each class is 10 point.
- To use 11 point write, \documentclass [11pt]{article}. To use 12 point write \documentclass[12pt]{article}.
- The \documentclass command must appear at the start of the LaTeX document, before any other LaTeX commands.
- The space between \documentclass and \begin{document} is called the *preamble.* The commands for LaTeX that affect the whole document should be included in the preamble.
- The body of the document, where all text is included, must occur between the \begin{document} and \end{document} commands.

21.4 LATEX COMMANDS

Here, the common commands in LaTeX are described briefly.

- **Typing LaTeX Commands**
  - Surround any text that is to be printed as it is, with a \begin{verbatim} and a \end{verbatim} command.

⊙ **Page Numbering and Headings**—command \pagestyle

- It should always be between \documentclass{article} and \begin{document}. It can take the following forms:
  - \pagestyle{plain} is the default. It puts page number at the center of the bottom of the page and provides no headings.
  - \pagestyle{empty} provides neither page numbers nor headings.
  - \pagestyle{headings} provides page numbers and headings from any \section that you are using.
  - \pagestyle{myheadings} provides page numbers and custom headings.
- It can also be applied to a single page using \thispagestyle instead of \pagestyle.

⊙ **Creating a Title Page**

- Insert between the \documentclass command and \begin{document} command. The commands are:
  - \title{your title here}
  - \author{your name here}
  - \date{current date}
  - \maketitle
- After specifying the arguments of \title, \author, and \date, use \maketitle for this part to be typeset.
- \documentclass can take titlepage option—\documentclass[titlepage]{article}.
- By default, all entries produced by these commands are centered on the lines in which they appear.
- Choose the break points with the \\ command.
- To have author names side by side, use \and command.

⊙ **Sections**—

- \section{sectiontitle} numbers the sections
- \section*{sectiontitle} does not number the section.
- Both create separate sections with titles in a larger font size.

⊙ **Cross-References**—

- \label{name} to label the point in the document with some mnemonic
- Section \ref{name} to refer to that point. \ref{name} will be replaced by the number of the section containing the corresponding \label command. As with your bibliography citations, run LaTeX twice to generate these references.

⊙ **Abstracts**—Place text between \begin{abstract} and \end{abstract} commands. The abstract should come immediately after \maketitle.

⊙ **Double Spacing**— Put \renewcommand{\baselinestretch}{2} in the preamble.

⊙ **Hyphenation**—

- - (a single dash) is for hyphenating words.
- -- (two dashes) is for ranges of numbers.
- $-$ is a minus sign in math mode.

⊙ **Quotation Marks**— Beginning and ending quotation marks differ. In LaTeX, use "(on left side of the keyboard) to begin a quotation and " (on right side of the keyboard) to end a quotation.

⊙ **Changing the Appearance of Words**—

- \underline{phrase} to underline a phrase,

- \textbf{phrase} to print a phrase in boldface, and
- \emph{phrase} to italicize a phrase.

⊙ **Spacing Between Words**—

- One blank space is the same as thousand blank spaces.
- Tabs are treated like blank spaces.
- Blanks at the end of a line are ignored.
- A single "Enter" is treated like a blank space.
- More than one " Enter" marks the beginning of a new paragraph.

⊙ **Indenting**—By default LaTeX indents new paragraphs unless the paragraph follows a section heading. To change the indentation, use the \indent and \noindent commands, at the beginning of the paragraph in question.

- To choose the amount of indentation, use the command \setlength{\parindent}{size of indentation with unit}.
- This command affects the whole document, it should go in the preamble, between the \documentclass and \begin{document}.

⊙ **Centering Text**—By default, LaTeX will start all text at the left margin. To center a title, a table, etc., surround it with the commands \begin{center} and \end{center}.

⊙ **Line Breaks**—Use a ~ for a space that should not be used to break a line.

- LaTeX inserts more space at the end of a sentence than between its words. For an abbreviation like Dr. in the middle of a sentence, use a ~ (if the line should not be broken there) or a \ followed by a space (if the line could be broken there).
- To force a line to break at a given point, use \\.

⊙ **Mathematical Formulas**—There are two ways to insert mathematical formulas into the document – (1) Formula appears in a paragraph with text – the formula will be compressed vertically, and (2) To have formula appear in a separate paragraph, where there will be more space.

- For formulas that appear in a paragraph, surround them with $'s. For example, `$\alpha$` is a Greek alphabet, becomes, α is a Greek alphabet.
- To have formulas appear in their own paragraph, use matching $$ to surround them. For example,

```
$$
\frac{x+y}{x-y}
$$
```

Becomes $\frac{x+y}{x-y}$

⊙ **Greek Letters**—α is \alpha , β is \beta , γ is \gamma, δ is \delta, ε is \epsilon, θ is \theta, σ is \ sigma, Π is \Pi. There are many more.

⊙ **Exponents and Subscripts**—Use the ^ character (shift-6), to create exponents. For example, `$x^2$` produces x^2

⊙ **Fractions** can be written in two ways – with a diagonal fraction bar or a horizontal one. For example, `$(x+y)/(x−y)$` becomes (x+y)/(x−y), and

```
$$
\frac{x+y}{x-y}
$$
```

Becomes $\frac{x+y}{x-y}$

- **Functions**—Use a backslash in front of function names \cos, \max, \sin, \tan, \min
- **Relations**—$\leq$ as \le, $\geq$ as \ge, $\neq$ as \ne, $\parallel$ as \parallel, $\neq$ as \not=. There are many more.
- **Spacing in Math Mode**—Use the following to adjust the spacing that LaTeX uses in math mode.
  - \, produces a small space
  - \: produces a medium space
  - \; produces a large space
- **Constructing Tables**—Surround the entries with \begin{tabular}{justification} and \end{tabular} command. The justification should consist of l for left justification, c for centered justification, or r for right justification. Separate column entries by a &, and end each line with a \\. Use \hline to construct a horizontal line, and separate the l, c, and r's by a | wherever you want a vertical line. For example:

```
\begin{tabular}{|r|c|l|}
\hline
Right & Center & Left\\
\hline
alpha & beta & gamma\\
delta & epsilon & zeta\\
eta & theta & iota\\
\hline
\end{tabular}
```

- **Bulleted Lists**—Surround the information with \begin{itemize} and \end{itemize}, and begin each item with an \item. For example,

```
\begin{itemize}
\item A bulleted item.
\begin{itemize}
\item A nested bulleted item.
\end{itemize}
\item Another bulleted list.
\end{itemize}
```

- **Numbered Lists**—Surround the information with \begin{enumerate} and \end{enumerate}, and begin each item with a \item. For example,

```
\begin{enumerate}
\item A numbered item.
```

```
\begin{enumerate}
\item A nested numbered item.
\end{enumerate}
\item Another numbered item.
\end{enumerate}
```

- **Bibliographies**—LaTeX provides a mechanism for automatically linking citations with items in the bibliography. Surround the bibliography with \begin{thebibliography} and \end{thebibliography}. For each entry in the bibliography, start with \bibitem{label}, where label is some mnemonic for the reference.
  - A citation in the body of the document is made with \cite{label}, where label is the same as what occurs in the \bibitem{label}.
  - To keep track of new references that have been added, run LaTeX twice before previewing when using \cite.
- **Graphic File Formats**—There are a number of graphics formats out there, such as – bmp, eps, gif, jpg, pdf, ps. LaTeX works best with the postscript formats (eps, ps) which were around when the program was first created. For the other formats, LaTeX may or may not work. Using PDFLaTeX will produce a PDF document.
- **Graphics Package**—To include graphics in your document, use \usepackage{graphicx} in the preamble.
- **Including Graphics Within Your Document**—Use the \includegraphics{graphicfile} command to include the graphic file in the document. To control the size of the document, specify the height and width: \includegraphics[height=2in, width = 3in]{graphicfile}.

21.5 SOLVED EXAMPLES

Here some examples are given that use the various LaTeX commands.

Example 1: **Create a title for your article.**

Solution 1:

```
\documentclass [twocolumn, 11pt]{article}
\title{\HUGE\textbf{Preparation of Papers for IEEE TRANSACTIONS and JOURNALS (May 2007)}}
\author{First A. Author, Second B. Author, Jr., and Third C. Author, \textit{Member, IEEE}}
\begin{document}
\maketitle
\end{document}
```

Output

Preparation of Papers for IEEE TRANSACTIONS and JOURNALS (May 2007)

First A. Author, Second B. Author, Jr., and Third C. Author, *Member*, *IEEE*

August 19, 2009

Example 2: Create a section.

Solution 1:

```
\documentclass{article}
\begin{document}
\section{Introduction}
Hello how are you?
I am fine here.
\end{document}
```

1 Introduction

Hello how are you? I am fine here.

In the same exercise, if we use line break –

```
\documentclass{article}
\begin{document}
\section{Introduction}
Hello how are you?\\
```

```
I am fine here.
\end{document}
```

1 Introduction

Hello how are you?
I am fine here.

Example 3: Create a bulleted list.

Solution 1:

```
\documentclass [twocolumn, 11pt]{article}
\title{\HUGE\textbf{Preparation of Papers for IEEE TRANSACTIONS and JOURNALS(May 2007)}}
\author{First A. Author, Second B. Author, Jr., and Third C. Author, \textit{Member, IEEE}}
\begin{document}
\maketitle
\section{Introduction}
This is a display of bulled list
\begin{itemize}
\item Vegetables.
\begin{itemize}
\item Potato,
\item Tomato,
\item Brinjal,
\item Onion,
\item Spinach
\end{itemize}
\item Fruits.
\begin{itemize}
\item Apple,
\item Mango,
\item Banana,
\item Plum,
\item Peach
\end{itemize}
\end{itemize}
\end{document}
```

Output

Preparation of Papers for IEEE TRANSACTIONS and JOURNALS(May 2007)

First A. Author, Second B. Author, Jr., and Third C. Author, *Member, IEEE*

August 19, 2009

1 Introduction

This is a display of bulled list

- Vegetables.
  - Potato,
  - Tomato,
  - Brinjal,
  - Onion,
  - Spinach
- Fruits.
  - Apple,
  - Mango,
  - Banana,
  - Plum,
  - Peach

Example 4: **Create a numbered list.**

Solution 1:

```
\documentclass {article}
\begin{document}
\section{Introduction}
This is a display of numbered list
\begin{enumerate}
\item Abstract.
\item Introduction.
\item Section 1.
\begin{enumerate}
\item Section 1.1.
\item Section 1.2
\end{enumerate}
\item Section 2
\end{enumerate}
\end{document}
```

Output

1 Introduction

This is a display of numbered list

1. Abstract.
2. Introduction.
3. Section 1.
   (a) Section 1.1.
   (b) Section 1.2
4. Section 2

Example 5: **Write a paragraph, Use emphasize, bold, and bulleted list.**

Solution:

```
\documentclass {article}

\begin{document}

\section{Choose an Internet Connection}

With the growth of technology, the content on the Web has also changed. Now web applications include content like animations, online gaming, database-driven Web sites and e-commerce. Thus, the need for speed as to how fast we can connect to the Internet has changed.

Here, we give the overall connection speeds of the different types of Internet connections, though they can vary between \textbf{Internet Service Providers (ISP)}.

\begin{itemize}

\item \emph {Dial-up access} is economical but slow. Dial-up access uses normal telephone lines so the quality of the connection is not always good. Speed is 2400 bps to 56 Kbps.

\item \emph {Integrated services digital network (ISDN)} is an international communications standard for sending voice, video, and data over telephone lines. Speed is 64 Kbps to 128 Kbps.

\item \emph {DSL} is an always on connection. ADSL is the most commonly deployed type of DSL. Speed is 128 Kbps to 8 Mbps.

\item \emph {Cable modem} gives you a broadband Internet connection that is designed to operate over cable TV lines. Speed 512 Kbps to 20 Mbps.

\item \emph {Wireless Internet Connections} uses radio frequency bands. Wireless Internet provides an always-on connection which can be accessed from anywhere geographically within a network coverage area. Their speed varies.

\item \emph {T-1 Lines} are a leased line option for businesses connecting. T-1 Lines support speeds of 1.544 Mbps.

\item \emph {Internet over Satellite (IoS)} allows a user to access the Internet via a satellite that orbits the earth. Speed: 492Kbps to 512 Kbps.

\end {document}
```

Output

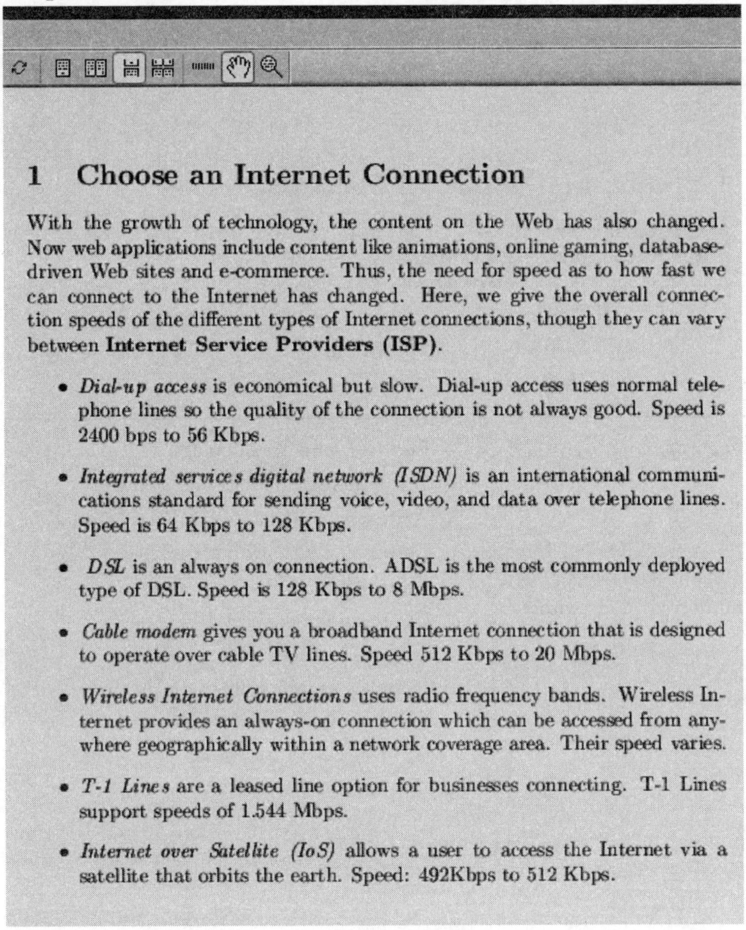

1 Choose an Internet Connection

With the growth of technology, the content on the Web has also changed. Now web applications include content like animations, online gaming, database-driven Web sites and e-commerce. Thus, the need for speed as to how fast we can connect to the Internet has changed. Here, we give the overall connection speeds of the different types of Internet connections, though they can vary between **Internet Service Providers (ISP)**.

- *Dial-up access* is economical but slow. Dial-up access uses normal telephone lines so the quality of the connection is not always good. Speed is 2400 bps to 56 Kbps.
- *Integrated services digital network (ISDN)* is an international communications standard for sending voice, video, and data over telephone lines. Speed is 64 Kbps to 128 Kbps.
- *DSL* is an always on connection. ADSL is the most commonly deployed type of DSL. Speed is 128 Kbps to 8 Mbps.
- *Cable modem* gives you a broadband Internet connection that is designed to operate over cable TV lines. Speed 512 Kbps to 20 Mbps.
- *Wireless Internet Connections* uses radio frequency bands. Wireless Internet provides an always-on connection which can be accessed from anywhere geographically within a network coverage area. Their speed varies.
- *T-1 Lines* are a leased line option for businesses connecting. T-1 Lines support speeds of 1.544 Mbps.
- *Internet over Satellite (IoS)* allows a user to access the Internet via a satellite that orbits the earth. Speed: 492Kbps to 512 Kbps.

Example 5: **Display some mathematical formulae.**

Solution:

```
\documentclass {article}
\begin{document}
\section{Some Mathematical Formulae}
Area of Circle is $ \pi * r^2$\\
Area of Rectangle is $ length * breadth$\\
Area of triangle is $1/2*base*height$\\
$sin(x) + cos(x) = 1$
$$
\frac{2}{10}
```

```
= \frac{4}{20}
= \frac{8}{40}
$$
\end {document}
```

Output

1 Some Mathematical Formulae

Area of Circle is $\pi * r^2$
Area of Rectangle is $length * breadth$
Area of triangle is $1/2 * base * height$
$sin(x) + cos(x) = 1$

$$\frac{2}{10} = \frac{4}{20} = \frac{8}{40}$$

EXERCISES

Type in a text and perform the following operations on it.

1. Put page numbering and headings
2. Create a Title Page – include title, author name and address (two authors side by side), and date.
3. Create sections both numbered and without numbers.
4. Include Abstract.
5. Double space the article.
6. Use Hyphenation in text. (Example sister-in-law)
7. Enclose a sentence in quotes.
8. Use underline, boldface and italics.
9. Write ten mathematical formulae.
10. Construct a table with entries.
11. Create a bulleted list.
12. Create a numbered list.
13. Add bibliography.
14. Include a graphics file in the document.
15. Print some part of text exactly as you have typed it.

APPENDIX A: ASCII CODING CHART

Dec	Hex	Char	Dec	Hex	Char	Dec	Hex	Char
0	00	Null	43	2B	+	86	56	V
1	01	Start of heading	44	2C	’	87	57	W
2	02	Start of text	45	2D	–	88	58	X
3	03	End of text	46	2E	.	89	59	Y
4	04	End of transmit	47	2F	/	90	5A	Z
5	05	Enquiry	48	30	0	91	5B	[
6	06	Acknowledge	49	31	1	92	5C	\
7	07	Audible bell	50	32	2	93	5D	]
8	08	Backspace	51	33	3	94	5E	^
9	09	Horizontal tab	52	34	4	95	5F	_
10	0A	Line feed	53	35	5	96	60	`
11	0B	Vertical tab	54	36	6	97	61	a
12	0C	Form feed	55	37	7	98	62	b
13	0D	Carriage return	56	38	8	99	63	c
14	0E	Shift out	57	39	9	100	64	d
15	0F	Shift in	58	3A	:	101	65	e
16	10	Data link escape	59	3B	;	102	66	f
17	11	Device control 1	60	3C	<	103	67	g
18	12	Device control 2	61	3D	=	104	68	h
19	13	Device control 3	62	3E	>	105	69	i
20	14	Device control 4	63	3F	?	106	6A	j
21	15	Neg. acknowledge	64	40	@	107	6B	k
22	16	Synchronous idle	65	41	A	108	6C	l
23	17	End trans. block	66	42	B	109	6D	m
24	18	Cancel	67	43	C	110	6E	n
25	19	End of medium	68	44	D	111	6F	o
26	1A	Substitution	69	45	E	112	70	p
27	1B	Escape	70	46	F	113	71	q
28	1C	File separator	71	47	G	114	72	r
29	1D	Group separator	72	48	H	115	73	s
30	1E	Record separator	73	49	I	116	74	t
31	1F	Unit separtator	74	4A	J	117	75	u
32	0	Space	75	4B	K	118	76	v
33	21	!	76	4C	L	119	77	w
34	22	"	77	4D	M	120	78	x
35	23	#	78	4E	N	121	79	y
36	24	$	79	4F	O	122	7A	z
37	25	%	80	50	P	123	7B	{
38	26	&	81	51	Q	124	7C	|
39	27	'	82	52	R	125	7D	}
40	28	(	83	53	S	126	7E	~
41	29	)	84	54	T	127	7F	□
42	2A	*	85	55	U	128	80	ç

(Continued)

Dec	Hex	Char	Dec	Hex	Char	Dec	Hex	Char
129	81	Ü	172	AC	¼	215	D7	╫
130	82	é	173	AD	¡	216	D8	╪
131	83	â	174	AE	«	217	D9	┘
132	84	ä	175	AF	»	218	DA	┌
133	85	à	176	B0	░	219	DB	█
134	86	å	177	B1	▒	220	DC	▄
135	87	ç	178	B2	▓	221	DD	▌
136	88	ê	179	B3	│	222	DE	▐
137	89	ë	180	B4	┤	223	DF	▀
138	8A	è	181	B5	╡	224	E0	α
139	8B	ï	182	B6	╢	225	E1	β
140	8C	î	183	B7	╖	226	E2	Γ
141	8D	ì	184	B8	╕	227	E3	π
142	8E	Ä	185	B9	╣	228	E4	Σ
143	8F	Å	186	BA	║	229	E5	σ
144	90	É	187	BB	╗	230	E6	µ
145	91	æ	188	BC	╝	231	E7	τ
146	92	Æ	189	BD	╜	232	E8	Φ
147	93	ô	190	BE	╛	233	E9	Θ
148	94	ö	191	BF	┐	234	EA	Ω
149	95	ò	192	C0	└	235	EB	σ
150	96	û	193	C1	┴	236	EC	∞
151	97	ù	194	C2	┬	237	ED	ø
152	98	ÿ	195	C3	├	238	EE	ε.
153	99	ö	196	C4	─	239	EF	∩
154	9A	Ü	197	C5	┼	240	F0	≡
155	9B	⇐	198	C6	╞	241	F1	±
156	9C	£	199	C7	╟	242	F2	≥
157	9D	¥	200	C8	╚	243	F3	≤
158	9E	Rs	201	C9	╔	244	F4	⌠
159	9F	ƒ	202	CA	╩	245	F5	⌡
160	A0	á	203	CB	╦	246	F6	÷
161	A1	í	204	CC	╠	247	F7	≈
162	A2	ó	205	CD	═	248	F8	·
163	A3	ú	206	CE	╬	249	F9	▪
164	A4	ñ	207	CF	╧	250	FA	·
165	A5	Ñ	208	D0	╨	251	FB	√
166	A6	ª	209	D1	╤	252	FC	n
167	A7	°	210	D2	╥	253	FD	f
168	A8	¿	211	D3	╙	254	FE	■
169	A9	⌐	212	D4	╘	255	FF	□
170	AA	¬	213	D5	╒			
171	AB	½	214	D6	╓			

Appendix B: EBCDIC Coding Chart

Dec	Hex	Char	Dec	Hex	Char	Dec	Hex	Char
0	00	NUL	43	2B		86	56	
1	01	SOH	44	2C		87	57	
2	02	STX	45	2D	ENQ	88	58	
3	03	ETX	46	2E	ACK	89	59	
4	04		47	2F	BEL	90	5A	!]
5	05	HT	48	30		91	5B	$
6	06		49	31		92	5C	*
7	07	DEL	50	32	SYN	93	5D	)
8	08		51	33		94	5E	;
9	09		52	34		95	5F	^
10	0A		53	35		96	60	-
11	0B	VT	54	36		97	61	/
12	0C	FF	55	37	EOT	98	62	
13	0D	CR	56	38		99	63	
14	0E	SO	57	39		100	64	
15	0F	SI	58	3A		101	65	
16	10	DLE	59	3B		102	66	
17	11		60	3C		103	67	
18	12		61	3D	NAK	104	68	
19	13		62	3E		105	69	
20	14		63	3F	SUB	106	6A	|
21	15		64	40	space	107	6B	,
22	16	BS	65	41		108	6C	%
23	17		66	42		109	6D	_
24	18	CAN	67	43		110	6E	>
25	19	EM	68	44		111	6F	?
26	1A		69	45		112	70	
27	1B		70	46		113	71	
28	1C	IFS	71	47		114	72	
29	1D	IGS	72	48		115	73	
30	1E	IRS	73	49		116	74	
31	1F	IUS	74	4A	[	117	75	
32	20		75	4B	.	118	76	
33	21		76	4C	<	119	77	
34	22		77	4D	(	120	78	
35	23		78	4E	+	121	79	‘
36	24		79	4F	| !	122	7A	:
37	25	LF	80	50	&	123	7B	#
38	26	ETB	81	51		124	7C	@
39	27	ESC	82	52		125	7D	'
40	28		83	53		126	7E	=
41	29		84	54		127	7F	"
42	2A		85	55		128	80	

(Continued)

Dec	Hex	Char	Dec	Hex	Char	Dec	Hex	Char
129	81	a	172	AC		215	D7	P
130	82	b	173	AD		216	D8	Q
131	83	c	174	AE		217	D9	R
132	84	d	175	AF		218	DA	
133	85	e	176	B0		219	DB	
134	86	f	177	B1		220	DC	
135	87	g	178	B2		221	DD	
136	88	h	179	B3		222	DE	
137	89	i	180	B4		223	DF	
138	8A		181	B5		224	E0	\
139	8B		182	B6		225	E1	
140	8C		183	B7		226	E2	S
141	8D		184	B8		227	E3	T
142	8E		185	B9		228	E4	U
143	8F		186	BA		229	E5	V
144	90		187	BB		230	E6	W
145	91	j	188	BC		231	E7	X
146	92	k	189	BD		232	E8	Y
147	93	l	190	BE		233	E9	Z
148	94	m	191	BF		234	EA	
149	95	n	192	C0	{	235	EB	
150	96	o	193	C1	A	236	EC	
151	97	p	194	C2	B	237	ED	
152	98	q	195	C3	C	238	EE	
153	99	r	196	C4	D	239	EF	
154	9A		197	C5	E	240	F0	0
155	9B		198	C6	F	241	F1	1
156	9C		199	C7	G	242	F2	2
157	9D		200	C8	H	243	F3	3
158	9E		201	C9	I	244	F4	4
159	9F		202	CA		245	F5	5
160	A0		203	CB		246	F6	6
161	A1	~	204	CC		247	F7	7
162	A2	s	205	CD		248	F8	8
163	A3	t	206	CE		249	F9	9
164	A4	u	207	CF		250	FA	
165	A5	v	208	D0	}	251	FB	
166	A6	w	209	D1	J	252	FC	
167	A7	x	210	D2	K	253	FD	
168	A8	y	211	D3	L	254	FE	
169	A9	z	212	D4	M	255	FF	
170	AA		213	D5	N			
171	AB		214	D6	O			

APPENDIX C: ABBREVIATIONS

ACC	Accumulator
ADC	Analog-to-Digital Converter
ADSL	Asymmetric Digital Subscriber Line
AES	Advanced Encryption Standard
AGP	Accelerated Graphics Port
AI	Artificial Intelligence
ALU	Arithmetic Logic Unit
AOP	Aspect-Oriented Programming
ASCII	American Standard Code for Information Interchange
ASP	Active Server Pages
ATM	Automated Teller Machine
ATX	Advanced Technology Extended
BIOS	Basic Input Output System
BIPS	Billion Instructions Per Second
BMP	BitMaP
bps	bits per second
CA	Certification Authority
CAD	Computer Aided Design
CAM	Computer Aided Manufacturing
CASE	Computer Aided Software Engineering
CBIS	Computer-Based Information System
CCITT	International Consultative Committee for Telephone and Telegraph
CD-R	Compact Disk-Recordable
CD-ROM	Compact Disk-Read Only Memory
CD-RW	Compact Disk-ReWritable
CGI	Common Gateway Interface
CIO	Chief Information Officer
CISC	Complex Instruction Set Computer
CLI	Command Line Interface
CMOS	Complementary Metal-Oxide Semiconductor
CODASYL	Conference on Data Systems Languages
COM	Computer Output on Microfilm
cps	Characters per second or cycles per second
CPU	Central Processing Unit
CRT	Cathode Ray Tube
CU	Control Unit
DAC	Digital-to-Analog Conversion
DARPA	Defense Advanced Research Projects Agency
DBA	DataBase Administrator
DBMS	DataBase Management System
DBTG	DataBase Task Group
DDL	Data Definition Language
DES	Data Encryption Standard
DHTML	Dynamic Hypertext Markup Language
DIMM	Dual In-line Memory Module

DML	Data Manipulation Language
DNS	Domain Name System
DOM	Document Object Model
DoS	Denial of Service
dpi	dots per inch
DR	Data Register
DRAM	Dynamic Random Access Memory
DSA	Digital Signature Algorithm
DSL	Digital Subscriber Line
DSS	Decision Support System
DVD-R	Digital Video Disk-Recordable
DVD-ROM	Digital Video Disk-Read Only Memory
EBCDIC	Extended Binary Coded Decimal Interchange Code
E-commerce	Electronic commerce
EDVAC	Electronic Discrete Variable Automatic Computer
EEPROM	Electrically Erasable Programmable Read Only Memory
EIS	Executive Information System
EISA	Extended Industry Standard Architecture
E-mail	Electronic-mail
ENIAC	Electronic Numerical Integrator And Calculator
EPROM	Erasable Programmable Read Only Memory
E-R Model	Entity-Relationship Model
ERP	Enterprise Resource Planning
ES	Expert System
FAT	File Allocation Table
FCFS	First Come First Served
FDD	Floppy Disk Drive
FDDI	Fiber Distributed Data Interface
FDM	Frequency Division Multiplexing
FLOPS	FLoating point Operations Per Second
FTP	File Transfer Protocol
GB	GigaByte
GHz	GigaHertz
GIF	Graphical Interchange Format
GNOME	GNU Object Model Environment
GUI	Graphical User Interface
HDD	Hard Disk Drive
HMD	Head-Mounted Display
HSL	Hue, Saturation and Lightness
HTML	Hypertext Markup Language
HTTP	Hypertext Transfer Protocol
HTTPS	Hypertext Transfer Protocol Secure
Hz	Hertz
I/O	Input/Output
IAB	Internet Architecture Board
IANA	Internet Assigned Number Authority
IC	Integrated Circuit
IESG	Internet Engineering Steering Group
IETF	Internet Engineering Task Force
IMAP	Internet Message Access Protocol
InterNIC	Internet Network Information Center

IPsec	IP Security
IR	Instruction Register
IRC	Internet Relay Chat
IRG	Inter-Record Gap
IRTF	Internet Research Task Force
IS	Information System
ISA	Industry Standard Architecture
ISDN	Integrated Services Digital Network
ISO	International Standards Organization
ISOC	Internet Society
ISP	Internet Service Provider
IT	Information Technology
JDBC	Java Data Base Connectivity
JPEG	Joint Photographic Experts Group
JSP	Java Server Pages
KB	KiloByte
KDE	K Desktop Environment
LAN	Local Area Network
LCD	Liquid Crystal Display
LED	Light Emitting Diode
LSI	Large Scale Integration
MAC	Media ACcess address
MAN	Metropolitan Area Network
MAR	Memory Address Register
MB	MegaByte
MBR	Memory Buffer Register
MHz	MegaHertz
MICR	Magnetic Ink Character Recognition
MIDI	Musical Instrument Digital Interface
MIPS	Million Instructions Per Second
MIS	Management Information System
MPEG	Motion Picture Experts Group
MSB	Most Significant Bit
MS-DOS	Microsoft Disk Operating System
NAP	Network Access Point
NAT	Network Address Translation
NIC	Network Interface Card
NLP	Natural Language Processing
NSF	National Science Foundation
NTFS	New Technology File System
OAS	Office Automation System
OCR	Optical Character Recognition
ODBC	Open Data Base Connectivity
OEM	Original Equipment Manufacturer
OMR	Optical Mark Recognition
OOP	Object-Oriented Programming
OS	Operating System
OSI	Open System Interconnection
PC	Personal Computer or Program Counter
PCB	Printed Circuit Board
PCI	Peripheral Component Interconnect

PDA	Personal Digital Assistant
PERL	Practical Extraction and Reporting Language
PHP	Hypertext Preprocessor
PKC	Public Key Cryptography
POP3	Post Office Protocol 3
POST	Power on Self Test
PROM	Programmable Read Only Memory
PS	PostScript
PSTN	Public Switched Telephone Network
RAM	Random Access Memory
RF	Radio Frequency
RGB	Red, Green and Blue
RIFF	Resource Interleave File Format
RISC	Reduced Instruction Set Computer
ROM	Read Only Memory
RR	Round Robin
RSA	Rivest, Shamir, Adleman
SAP	Systems, Applications and Products
SATA	Serial Advanced Technology Attachment
SHA	Secure Hash Algorithm
SIMM	Single In-line Memory Module
SJF	Shortest Job First
SKC	Secret Key Cryptography
SLSI	Super Large Scale Integrated
SMTP	Simple Mail Transfer Protocol
SO DIMM	Small Outline Dual In-line Memory Module
SPOOL	Simultaneous Peripheral Operation On-Line
SQL	Structured Query Language
SRAM	Static Random Access Memory
SSL	Secure Socket Layer
STP	Shielded Twisted Pair
TB	TeraByte
TCP/IP	Transmission Control Protocol/Internet Protocol
Telnet	Terminal Network
TIFF	Tagged Image File Format
TPS	Transaction Processing System
UNIVAC	UNIVersal Automatic Computer
URL	Uniform Resource Locator
USB	Universal Serial Bus
UTF	Unicode Transformation Format
UTP	Unshielded Twisted Pair
VDT	Visual Display Terminal
VLSI	Very Large Scale Integration
W3C	World Wide Web Consortium
WAN	Wide Area Network
WDM	Wavelength Division Multiplexing
WORM	Write Once-Read Many
WWW	World Wide Web
XML	eXtensible Markup Language
ZD	Zip Disk

APPENDIX D: ASSEMBLING A PC

1.1 INTRODUCTION

To own a Personal Computer (PC), either purchase a pre-built and pre-assembled computer, or, assemble a computer yourself. This chapter discusses the assembling of computer by the user. Assembling the computer by the user has several advantages. The user learns about the hardware components of computer and their interworking. The user can customize the computer according to their specific needs in addition to saving money and having fun.

1.2 COMPONENTS OF PC

A computer installed at your office or home generally has the following components externally—(1) System unit, (2) Keyboard, (3) Mouse, and (4) Monitor. In addition to this you may have other external components like printer, external drives etc., which can generally be attached to a port on the computer case.

- **System Unit** is the main component of computer. The system unit is a tower like unit which comprises of the *chassis* and the internal components of PC. The internal components of the PC include (1) Motherboard or system board, (2) Processor or CPU, (3) RAM, (4) Hard Disk Drive (HDD), (5) Power Supply Unit (PSU), (6) Optical drive, and (7) Video card or Graphics card. It also consists of fan and ports to connect components like keyboard, monitor etc.
- **Monitor** enables the user to view the text and the graphical output. The display devices may vary in shape, size and the technology used.
- **Keyboard and Mouse** enable the user to enter data into the computer.
- **Peripheral Devices** provide alternative methods for data input and output, or additional data storage. The external devices are connected to the system unit via a cable or a wireless connection.

1.3 PURCHASING PARTS OF PC

Several factors have to be kept in mind when deciding what parts to buy—

- **Compatibility**—All parts should be compatible with each other, particularly, CPU, motherboard and RAM.
- **Ergonomical Design**—Ergonomics deals with the designing of things so that they work with the human body. Ergonomics is important when you choose your keyboard, mouse and monitor. For example the size of monitor, monitor with adjustable height (tilt, angle), keyboard that does not strain the hand while typing, and mouse that is easy to hold. The ergonomically designed components are slightly costly, but they help prevent troublesome strain injuries to the neck, wrist and the fingers.
- **Price**—Nowadays, hardware components are available at prices that can fit different needs of the customer. While selecting certain components, think of upgradation in addition to the price. Look for components that support new standards and can be upgraded. For example, while you buy a motherboard, look for one that has room to add extra RAM chip when you require upgradation later.

1.4 SELECTING THE COMPONENTS

To build the PC, you will need to purchase the following components.

- Tower case or chassis
- Motherboard
- CPU/Processor
- DDR2 RAM
- Hard disk drive
- Optical drive
- Monitor
- Keyboard and Mouse

To decide the specification of the PC, look for the kind of applications that you wish to run on the PC. This will stop you from buying expensive components, which may not be required for the PC you assemble. The following sub-sections provide some guidance on deciding the configuration of the components required for building of the PC.

1.4.1 Tower Case or Chassis

- A tower case (Figure A.1) is required to hold the components together. Currently, tower cases come in standard ATX form factor, with common sizes- Mini, Midi and Full tower. Most budget tower cases come with the PSU.
- The number of bays for hard disk drives, optical drives you need to fit in the tower case makes you decide if you need a mini, midi, or a full tower case. The bigger the case, the more bays you have.
- It is generally advisable to purchase a midi or full tower case. It will ensure a good air flow.

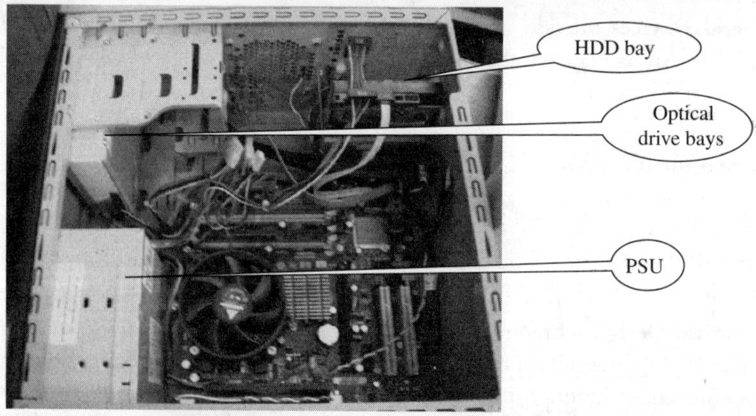

Figure A.1 Tower chassis

1.4.2 Motherboard or System Board

- A motherboard (Figure A.2) is a Printed Circuit Board (PCB) that connects the processor, memory and all expansion cards together to assemble a PC. It is the most important part of computer.

- The motherboard has chips and other components on it. The motherboard may come integrated with the various components like the modem, sound card, video card and other built-in features. Alternatively, motherboards are available with the standard built-in features, and slots are provided for the other components to be attached. For example, the user can choose a high-end video card with high speed for better graphics. It provides the user with the flexibility to upgrade one or more components on the motherboard. The built-in board is economical, but it becomes difficult to upgrade a component of the system board. To change a built-in feature on a board will require replacing the motherboard.

Figure A.2 Motherboard

- While choosing a motherboard consider the CPU interface, Chipset, IDE or SATA support, Expansion slot interfaces, and other connectors. Make sure that the motherboard is of a form factor compatible with the case.
    - **CPU Interface**—Is the plug into which the processor goes. The interface must be an exact match to the processor. Check with the motherboard manufacturer to ensure that the slot on the motherboard supports the CPU you want to use. If the motherboard, CPU, and heatsink/fan are not compatible and installed correctly, it can destroy the CPU and/or the motherboard.
    - **Chipset**—It determines the efficiency of RAM and Expansion Slots. Intel 915 supports up to 533MHz PC4200 DDRII RAM. Intel 925 supports up to 600MHz PC4800 DDRII RAM. The function of BIOS is important. Newer BIOS have temperature controls that shut down the computer if the temperature gets too high.
    - **IDE (ATA) or SATA Interface**—Currently, motherboards have SATA interface. The SATA interface has four separate slots that allow independent access and this increases the speed at which hard drives and optical drives work. The cables are also narrower, improving the flow of air inside the case. Additionally, two parallel, 44 pin IDE interface connectors are also provided on the motherboard.
    - **Expansion Slot Interfaces**—The motherboard comes with various expansion card slots and connectors. It generally comes with 4 different expansion slots—2 PCI and 2 PCI Express slot. The PCI slot is to connect sound card, modem etc. The PCI Express slot is used to connect a PCI-E graphics card.

- **USB**—In addition to USB 2.0 (Figure A.3) ports provided on the back panel, most motherboards have connectors for additional ports in the front of the case. USB 2.0 ports are used for connecting peripherals such as printers, external hard drives, MP3 players, cameras etc. The more USB ports the motherboard supports the better it is. The traditional 9-pin serial and parallel ports are much less used now, so, many motherboards have a single serial port and no parallel port.

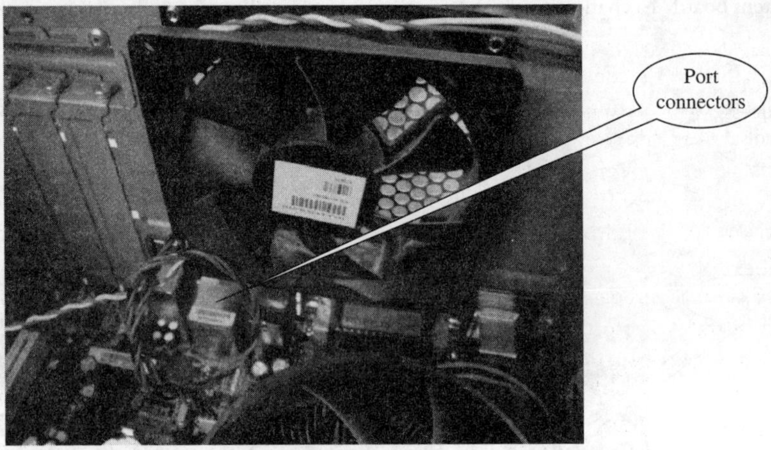

Figure A.3 Port connectors

- The *form factor* describes size and shape of the system board. It is the specification that provides the physical measurements for the size of components and where mounting devices for them are located. ATX is the most common form factor and is the de facto standard. An ATX motherboard has the standard I/O (Input/Output) connectors such as PS/2 ports, USB ports, parallel port, serial port, etc, built onto the motherboard. ATX motherboard fits into a standard ATX case. Other form factors are—microATX smaller than standard ATX at the cost of fewer expansion slots; WTX is for workstations and servers; BTX is designed for more efficient cooling; and Mini-ITX is smaller than BTX.
- *Number of Storage Drive Spaces*—Internal hard drives/floppy drives (which go in 3.5" bays) and internal CD/DVD drives (which go in 5.25" bays) take up space in the case. Make sure you consider how many drives you will need and what size slot they require. Optical drives and floppy drives need external slots, i.e. a hole in the case through which their face can be accessed. Hard drives go into an internal slot. Nowadays, floppy drives are not used.
- A *power supply* converts AC power from an electrical outlet to the DC power needed by system components. The power supply is a metal box in the rear of the system that is attached to the computer chassis and to the system board. The power supply contains the power cord plug and a fan for cooling, because it generates a lot of heat. A power supply with a rating of more than 300 watts is needed; any less will not reliably power modern components.
- Most cases mount one or more case *fans*, distinct from the fans that may be attached to the power supply, video card and CPU. The purpose of a case mounted fan is to move air through the system and carry excess heat out. Fans currently come in two basic sizes, 80mm and 120mm. Cases support either of them. The larger 120mm fans spin more slowly and are usually quieter fans, so they are generally preferred, though they cost a little more.

1.4.3 CPU/Processor

- CPU is the brain of computer. The faster the processor, the faster it will execute instructions and run the programs.
- CPU is a single microprocessor chip that is installed on the motherboard in a socket.
- The choice of CPU affects the speed of the computer more than any other single component. Some of the CPU properties you need to consider are—
  - Clock speed measured in GHz or MHz. It is the number of calculation cycles that the CPU can perform per second. A higher clock speed indicates a faster processor.
  - IPC or instructions per cycle, is the amount of work a CPU can do in a cycle. With modern processors this number is an average.
  - Front side bus speed (FSB) is the rate at which the CPU communicates with the northbridge chipset component on the motherboard, measured in MHz. A larger FSB value shows that your CPU is able to communicate with other components on the motherboard faster.
  - CPU plugs into a socket on the motherboard. It is important that the CPU is a complete match to the motherboard CPU socket.
  - Modern processors are either 32-bit or 64-bit. A processor can be called 64-bit if it will support running a 64-bit operating system. The newer chips from Intel and AMD support this for most 64-bit OSs.
  - Cache is memory implemented directly on the CPU. Generally, the larger the cache, the faster the system will run. Cache usually comes in three varieties, L1, L2, and L3. Usually only L2 cache size is shown. L3 is rarely used in processor design. L1 stays the same size throughout an entire processor product line.
  - Core of CPU is the heart of CPU. Dual-core processors (Intel Core Duo/Core 2 Duo and AMD Athlon 64 X2) have two processing centres (cores).
- Retail CPU's come in a package containing a HSF (Heat Sink Fan), instructions, and a warranty, often 3 years. OEM CPUs do not include these. The current CPU speeds and advantages change frequently.
- Intel and AMD are the leading processor manufacturers. Whichever manufacturer you decide to choose, purchase a compatible motherboard.
- Nowadays, dual core processors are common. The more cores a CPU has, the better it is. Intel Core 2 Duo and Athlon 64 X2 are both Dual Core, i.e., they have two CPU cores on one chip. Each core works separately hence the CPU can process two intensive tasks at the same time without slowing down the system. For example, you can run a virus checker in the background and use the word processor in the foreground without slowing the system down. Dual core processors are are 64 bit and support 64 bit OS.
- For video editing, CAD, or playing the latest 3D video games or other CPU intensive tasks use a quad-core or multi-core processor.

1.4.4 Memory—RAM

- Memory stores parts of the operating system and application data that is being run. More the memory of system, the more applications can be run simultaneously and also provides an overall better system performance.

- Currently, DDR2 or DDR3 SDRAM (Double Data Rate Synchronous Dynamic RAM) is being used. RAM has different bandwidths, ie 400, 533, 600, 733, 800. The DDR2-533 RAM is faster than DDR2-400 RAM.
- The RAM you need depends on the motherboard and chipset that has been selected. Chipsets that use dual-channel memory require use of two identical (size and speed) sticks of RAM. For example, an Intel Core 2 Duo CPU will support Dual-channel DDR2 800, 667 or 533. RAM should usually operate at the same clock speed as the CPU's Front Side Bus (FSB). DDR-2 memory must be run in pairs to run at double data rate. If you get 2GB of memory then buy 2 x 1GB modules.
- The amount of RAM to be used is a simple choice. 1 GB RAM is sufficient for most modern operating systems.
- Some common memory manufactures are Kingston, Corsair and Samsung.
- DDR RAM is identified by memory name or module name (Figure A.4). For example, 400MHz DDR2 RAM is known as DDR2-400, and its module name is PC2-3200 (3.2GB of bandwidth). 533MHz DDR2 RAM is called DDR2-533 and its module name is PC2-4200(4.2GB of bandwidth).

Figure A.4 RAM module

1.4.5 Video Card/Graphics Card

- Graphics card is used for displaying output to the monitor. The choice of graphics card depends on the need of the user.
- For computers which use 2D graphics for office applications and web surfing, an integrated graphic card is included on most motherboards. It also allows the user to run the monitor at various resolutions. An integrated graphics card with around 64MB or 128MB video memory is sufficient for your needs.
- For gaming, or 3D modelling, a 3D graphics card is needed with at least 256 MB or 512 MB of video memory. Companies like nVIDIA and ATI dominate the 3D graphics market.
- There are four different current graphics card interfaces: integrated, PCI, AGP and PCI-Express. Most motherboards that have integrated graphics also have one of the other three slot interfaces available to place a new card, if needed. Most current motherboards have PCI-Express slot as it offers much higher graphics bandwidth which results in higher performance. PCI-Express system supports up to 16x speeds. Older video cards use the standard PCI slots that are now growing obsolete due to limited speed and memory. It is recommended to buy a motherboard with a PCI-Express port so that you can use a PCI-Express graphics card.

1.4.6 Sound Card

- Sound card allows running of multimedia applications with sound, listening to music, or playing audio CD's. Most motherboards have built-in sound features. These are often adequate for most users.
- For gaming, sound card is a must. Sound cards made for gaming or professional music tend to do well for their particular purpose. In games, various effects are often times applied to the sound in real-time, and a gaming sound card is able to do this processing on-board, instead of using the CPU for the task. Professional music cards are built both for maximum sound quality and low transmission delay input and output. One of the popular sound cards is the Creative's soundblaster range.

1.4.7 Modem

- A modem is an essential if you intend to connect the PC to the Internet.
- Modem converts digital signals to analog so that it can travel via telephone line, and vice-versa. Analog modems are currently on the decline as they are being replaced by Digital modems which are used for high speed broadband Internet, also known as ADSL modem or ADSL routers.
- Modems can be attached via USB, a serial port, or an internal card slot. ADSL modems are mostly external. They connect to the serial port.
- Wireless ADSL routers are used if you wish to share Internet connection with multiple PCs.
- Some common ADSL Router suppliers are Netgear, Belkin and D-Link.
- Ethernet card—It is required to connect to a LAN, cable or DSL modem. It comes in speeds of 10 Mbps, 100 Mbps, or 1000 Mbps; which are designated as 10 Mbps, 10/100 Mbps or 10/100/1000 Mbps products. The 10/100 and 10/100/1000 are most commonly used. Generally, ethernet adapters are built into a motherboard. If it is not present, purchase one that can be inserted into a PCI slot. To get the full speed of ethernet card, a motherboard with built-in card is the best.

1.4.8 Hard Disk Drive

- Hard disk drive is a non-volatile storage media which stores the data including operating system, applications, user files and documents.
- Hard drives directly connect to the system board via atleast one cable for the data and one for the power. Most hard drives are internal, but some are external.
- When shopping for the hard drive, consider the following—
    - **Cache**—The cache of a hard drive increases the speeds of retrieving short bursts of information, and also allows prefetching of data. Cache of hard drive is normally 2MB, 8MB or 16MB large. Most hard drives have 8MB standard cache.
    - **Form Factor**—PCs usually use 3.5 inch hard drives. 2.5 inch drives are used in laptops.
    - **Capacity**—Hard disks are available that can store data from 160 GB to 1000 GB. For common user, hard disks of capacity 160GB to 500 GB are sufficient.
    - **Rotational Speed**—It is the speed at which the hard drive platters spin. The 2.5 inch laptop drives usually spin at 5400 RPM, and common desktop drives at 7200 RPM.
    - **Warranty**—Many manufactures offer warranty ranging from 30 days (OEM) up to five years. It is advisable to spend slightly more money to get the drive that carries a longer warranty.
    - **Interface of a Drive** is how the hard drive comunicates with the rest of the computer. PATA SATA, SCSI and USB are the hard drive interfaces that are available. Nowadays, the SATA drives are used. While purchasing the motherboard, check that it supports the SATA drive, or, purchase

a PCI card that will allow connecting the hard drive. PATA drives are losing popularity. SCSI drives are usually used on high performance workstations and servers. USB or IEEE1394 is used for connecting external drives.

- Some HDD manufacturers are IBM, Seagate, Samsung and Fujitsu.

1.4.9 Optical Drive

- Mostly all operating systems and applications software comes on CD. To watch DVD movies on your PC, a DVD-ROM is required which can perform all the tasks of a CD-ROM as well as play DVD movies.
- Optical disk drives are generally internal and generally have a 5.25 inch form factor.
- Optical disk and drives come in several types—CD-ROM, CD-R, CD-RW, DVD-ROM, DVD-R, DVD+R, DVD+R DL, DVD-RW, DVD+RW, DVD-RAM.
- The DVD dash drives are appoved by the DVD forum while DVD plus drives are not.
- New optical disk formats—Blu-ray disk (BD) and High density or high definition DVD (HD DVD) are two compatible optical disk standards intended for high density stotage of high definition video as well as data storage. Both use blue laser light to read and store data.The blue laser has a shorter wavelength than the existing CD and DVD laser technologies, which enables the system to store more data in the same amount of physical space. HD-DVD can hold 30 GB of data. BDs can hold upto 200 GB of data.
- Currently, DVD writers that are capable of burning 9GB of data to a disk can be purchased for an insignificant amount of money. When purchasing a DVD writer, check that it is capable of burning both the '+' and '-' standards, and is Dual Layer compatible. It is possible to burn almost all recordable DVDs currently on the market.
- Some CD/DVD-ROM manufacturers are Toshiba, Poineer, Hitachi, LG and Samsung.

1.4.10 Peripherals

Anything outside the computer case that connects to the computer is a peripheral. The keyboard, mouse and monitor are the minimum required peripherals. The choice in peripherals depends on personal preference and what you intend to do with your computer.

- **Mouse**—Optical mouse are commonly used nowadays. Purchase a decent-quality mouse made by companies such as Microsoft or Logitech. A low-end optical mouse may skip if moved too fast. Optical mouse generally have three buttons, which are sufficient for normal computer operation. However, if the computer is to be used heavily for gaming purposes, extra buttons in the mouse may be useful.
- **Keyboard**—Go for an ergonomically designed keyboard from a reputed company. If you have to key-in most of the time, the comfort of using the keyboard becomes a key factor in choosing an easy-to-use keyboard.
- **Monitor**—Currently, the most popular viewing device are TFT Flat panels, as they save desk space and are more comfortable to view. They are more affordable than before.
    - Monitors (Figure A.5) come is various sizes and refresh rate.
    - Monitors are measured diagonally. Nowadays, 17" monitor are becoming standard monitor, though you can also purchase 19" monitor.
    - Monitors consist of thousands of pixels. Smaller pixels produce high definition sharp display. Look for monitors with at least 0.25 mm dot pitch.

Figure A.5 Monitor

Figure A.6 Speakers

- If purchasing a 17" monitor, see that its refresh rate is at least 85 Hz at resolution of 1024*768. A 19" monitor should have resolution of at least 1280*1024 at 85 Hz.

⊙ **Printer and Scanner**—For home users, multi-function centres (Printer-Scanner-Copier) are often a cost-effective solution to purchasing printer and scanner separately. The printer-cum-scanner is connected to one port on the computer, and to one power point. A mid-range deskjet printer-scanner-copier works well for most people. If you plan to print photos, select a printer which can print at around 4800dpi. Also check the speed of the printer, and the cost of new cartridges, while selecting a printer. You can choose between a black and white, and, color printer.

⊙ **Speakers**—Computer speaker (Figure A.6) sets come in two general varieties; 2/2.1 sets (over a wide range of quality), and "surround", "theater", or "gaming" with four or more speakers, which are more expensive. Low-end speakers compromise sound quality. Powered speakers cost slightly more but sound much better. Headphones can offer good sound much more cheaply than speakers. If your have limited budget, and you prefer not to disturb others, then go for headphones which will give you good quality sound.

1.5 TYPICAL DESKTOP PC CONFIGURATION

⊙ When you purchase PC from the market or assemble it, your specifications may read as follows-

⊙ PC specs 1—

Intel® Pentium® 4 Processor 3.2GHz with Hyper-Threading Technology and 800MHz FSB
Intel® 865G chipset
1GB DDR2 dual-channel 400Mhz
80GB serial ATA150 7200rpm hard drive w/2MB cache
Integrated ultra ATA100 and serial ATA150 controllers
48x/24x/48x CD-RW/DVD combo drive
In 4-bay small form factor case: 1 PCI and 1 AGP
(8) USB 2.0 (2 in front and 6 in back) (1) Serial(1) Parallel(2) PS/2
(1) RJ-45 Integrated LAN(1) VGA(1) Microphone front audio ports
17" LCD Flat Panel Display
Integrated Intel® Extreme Graphics 2 with up to 64MB dynamic video memory
104+ Keyboard
USB Optical Wheel Mouse and mouse pad
Integrated Sound Blaster compatible audio
Integrated Intel® 10/100/1000 Ethernet (Gigabit) adapter

- PC specs 2—

  INTEL DUAL CORE-3.4 GHz
  17" SVGA MONITOR
  512MB DDR 2 RAM
  80 GB SATA HDD
  SPEAKERS
  MM KB
  MOUSE OPTICAL
  COMBO DRIVE
  CABINET WITH 400W SMPS
  10–100 MBPS LAN
  4x AGP FOR GAMING
  ONE PARALLEL PORT, 4 HIGH SPEED USB

1.6 ASSEMBLING THE PC

Before you start assembling the PC, make sure you have the following components—

- Metal casing with power supply and a set of screws, connectors and cables.
- Motherboard
- Processor
- RAM modules
- Storage devices—hard drive, DVD-ROM drives
- Expansion cards

Study the motherboard manual so that you are able to identify the different connectors. Also ensure that the PC power supply is unplugged from the mains.

Before unpacking the components from its original anti-static bags you must put on anti-static wrist strap, to discharge your self, otherwise you can damage the components by anti-static shock by touching the components. If you do not have an anti-static wrist strap, you can discharge your self by touching the metal case of the computer with one hand and touching the ground with the other, though this is not recommended.

Screws with a fine thread pitch are normally used for CD-ROM drives. The more coarsely-threaded screws are used for attaching hard drives.

1.6.1 Install Motherboard

- Unpack ATX case. Place the case on a desk with its open side facing you.
- Fix the back plate by placing it near the ATX back plate cut out and pushing the plate outwards, it will clip on (Figure A.7).
- The case comes with motherboard mounting screws. Place motherboard on top of the mounting screw holes. Put ATX devices on motherboard such as PS/2 and serial port facing towards ATX back plate cut out and push the motherboard. The devices will fit into their cut outs.

Figure A.7 Ports on backside of chassis

- Align screw holes on motherboard with screw holes on the case. Screw on using a screw driver. Now, the motherboard is mounted.
- Place ATX power connector (Figure A.8) to the motherboard. (ATX case comes with PSU and is already mounted to the case). Clip the ATX power connector on top of power socket on the motherboard. It will only fit one way; if it does not go in, try the other way round.
- The motherboard is then connected to the PC power supply. Inside the case a 12 or 24 pin female plug-in connector comes out of the power supply. This connector should be plugged into the matching socket connector on the motherboard, make sure that the 4 central wires are black (ground).
- Several other components must be connected to the mother board. The row of pins on the motherboard is used to wire the front panel on the case (pc speaker, power button, light indicators, etc.).

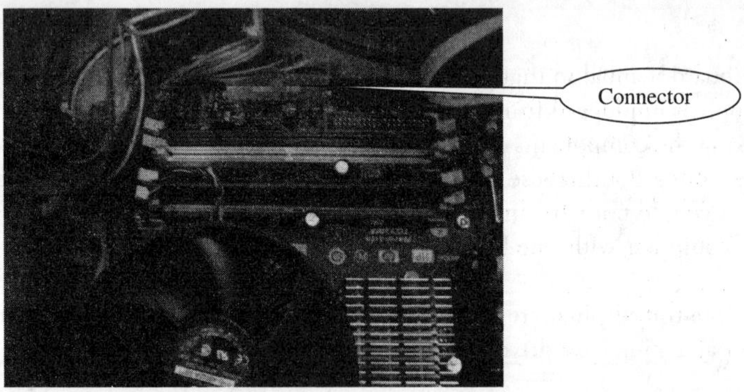

Figure A.8 Power connector on motherboard

1.6.2 Install Processor

- Locate the processor socket on the motherboard. For Intel Core 2 Duo, it is Socket 775.
- Raise the brown lever on socket and put the processor in place. The pin 1 of CPU should go into the pin 1 of socket. If you place it correctly, it will go in gently. Close the lever.

- A retail boxed CPU includes a heatsink + fan (Figure A.9). Both items usually come together in a single unit known as an "active heat sink". If you bought an OEM CPU make sure that the fan is correct for the speed of the CPU, otherwise CPU will overheat and may get damaged.
- Take off the plastic cover from the bottom of the CPU fan that covers the heat transfer pad. Now place the CPU fan on top of the CPU and push down the metal clips on the fan so that it clips onto the CPU socket. Observe the orientation of heat sink when installing—the step on the underside of heat sink should be level with the protruding edge of socket. Do not apply too much force as the central part of processor (silicon) is fragile and may get cracked.

Figure A.9 CPU heat sink

- CPU fan has a power connector which needs to be connected to CPU fan power socket on the motherboard.
- Nowadays, motherboards have automatic detection for the CPU frequency. Please refer to your motherboard manual for more details.

1.6.3 Install Memory

- Look for DDR2 banks (with white clip on each side) (Figure A.10).
- To insert DDR2 RAM module, release the clips so it bends to each side, place the memory module straight down into the slot. The notches on the bottom of the memory modules will help you align the module with the bank. Press down firmly without forcing. The two clips at each end should close by themselves.

1.6.4 Install Hard Drive

- The SATA cable connector is on the left hand side which consists of few pins. Next to the SATA connector on the right side is SATA power connector which consists of many pins.
- Place your hard drive into the HDD mounting slot of the case. The SATA connector should face outwards. Screw the HDD to the case using screws provided with the drive or ATX case.

Figure A.10 DDR2 RAM slots

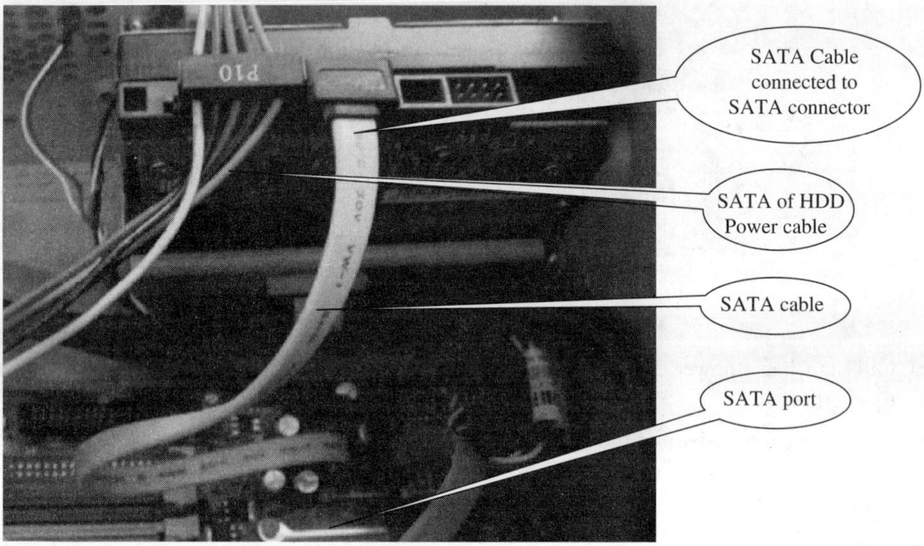

Figure A.11 SATA hard drive

- Connect one end of SATA data cable to SATA connector of the HDD. Fit the other end of SATA data cable to a SATA port on the motherboard (Figure A.11).
- Connect SATA power connector to the power socket of SATA hard drive.

1.6.5 Install Optical Drive

- On the SATA CD/DVD drive, you have the SATA cable connector and SATA power connector on the back side.
- Mount the CD/DVD drive into its mounting slot. Use the supplied screws to screw the drive into position.

- Connect one end of SATA data cable to SATA connector of the optical drive (Figure A.12). Fit the other end of SATA data cable to a SATA port on the motherboard.
- Connect SATA power connector to the power socket of SATA optical drive.
- Finally connect the power cable to power connector.

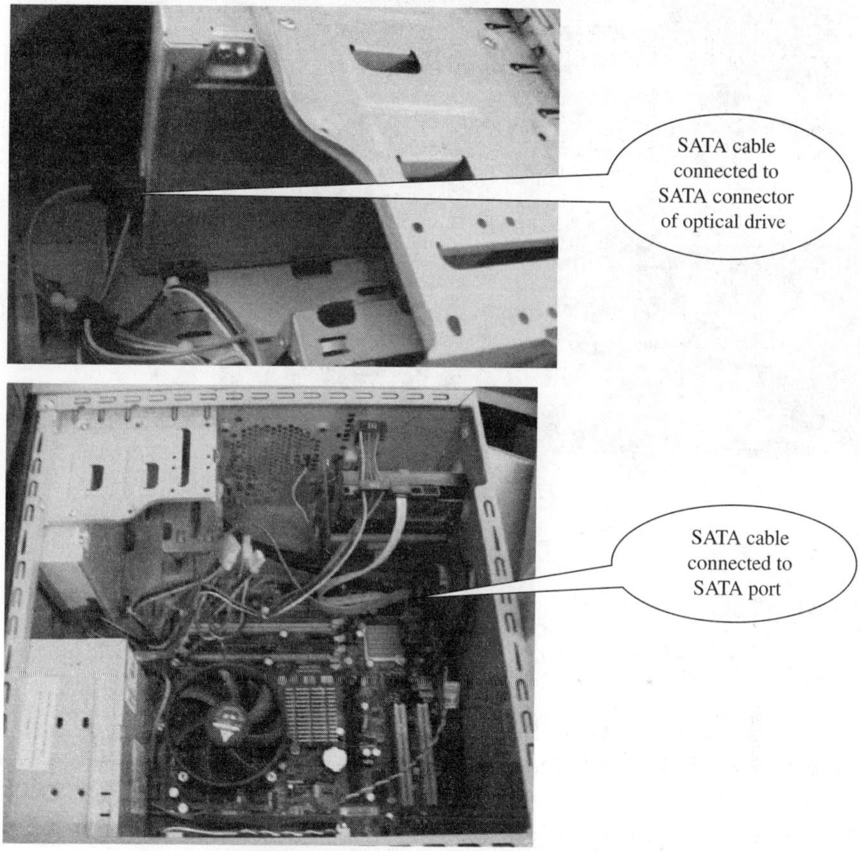

Figure A.12 Connecting optical drive

1.7 EXPANSION SLOTS

- Generally, the motherboard comes with the in-built sound card, modem, graphics card, LAN card etc. In case you wish to add your own card, expansion slots (Figure A.13) are provided in the motherboard.
    - PCI slots run at 32 bits. Most modern sound cards are designed with the PCI interface and connect to the PCI slot of the motherboard. Find a free PCI slot on your motherboard (assuming your modem is a PCI modem). Place your modem card on top of the slot and gently push it down into position.
    - PCI Express slots run at 64 bits. This is a very fast bus, used for graphic cards, and spotted by its brown colour.

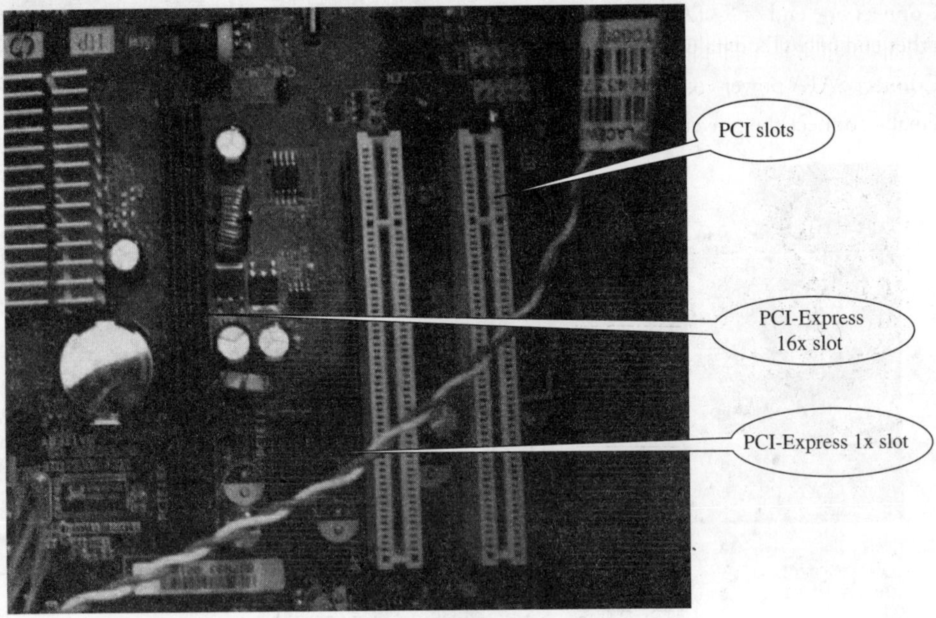

Figure A.13 Expansion slots

1.8 FINAL STAGE

After having installed all the necessary hardware, do the following things before switching on the PC for the first time.

- The ATX case (Figure A.14) has (1) a power switch which turns the PC on, (2) a reset switch for resetting the system, (3) a power LED which comes on when the PC is switched on, (4) a hard drive LED which flashes when data is being written or read from your hard drive, and (5) an internal speaker.
- Connect the switches and LED's to its corresponding connectors on the motherboard. To locate the connectors, refer to the motherboard manual. The connectors for the switches and LED's are normally grouped together.
- Every cable is normally labeled; they are normally named as follows, but could be slightly different on your system. (Power switch—PWR-SW; Reset switch—Reset; Power LED—PWR-LED; Hard drive LED—HDD LED; Speaker—SPK
- The connectors on the motherboard are also labeled. Refer to the motherboard manual which would provide details on which pins you should connect the cables to.
- After having connected all the cables to the correct pins on the motherboard close the cover of the ATX case but don't screw it. You might have possible problems that need rectifying. Connect all the cables to back of ATX case—main power cable that connects to the power supply, PS/2 mouse and keyboard that connects to the PS/2 ports. Monitor cable that connects to the graphics card port, etc.
- Switch on the monitor first. Now switch the PC on by pressing the power switch on the front of the ATX case. If you have performed all the tasks without any mistakes and providing that none of the main components are faulty, the PC should boot. When the PC boots you can see the name of BIOS

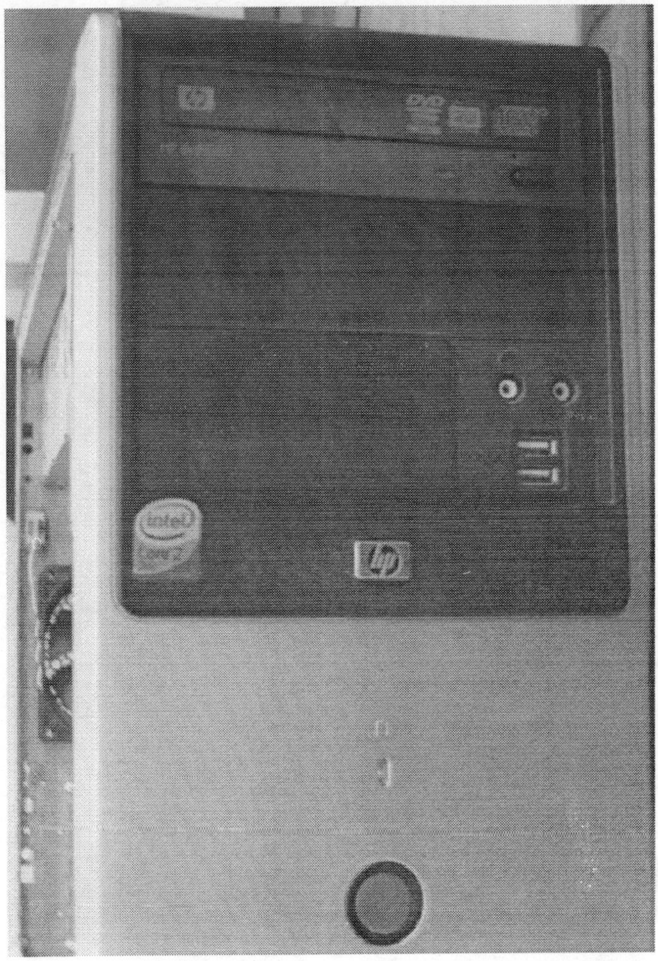

Figure A.14 Power and reset switch

manufacturer, displayed on the monitor. The CPU type, speed and the amount of memory is also displayed.

- Currently, plug and play BIOS are used which are set to automatic device detection by default. You can see the devices being detected followed by a prompt about missing operating system. Now, an operating system must be installed before actually using the computer.
- If things did not go smoothly and the PC does not switch on then do the troubleshooting.

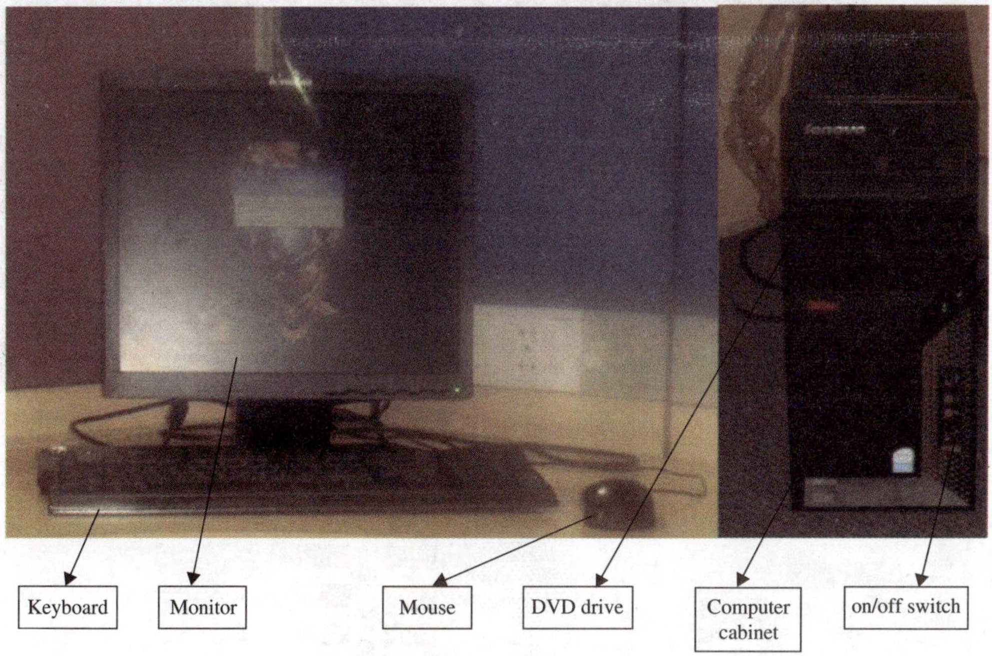

Figure 1.16 Personal Computer

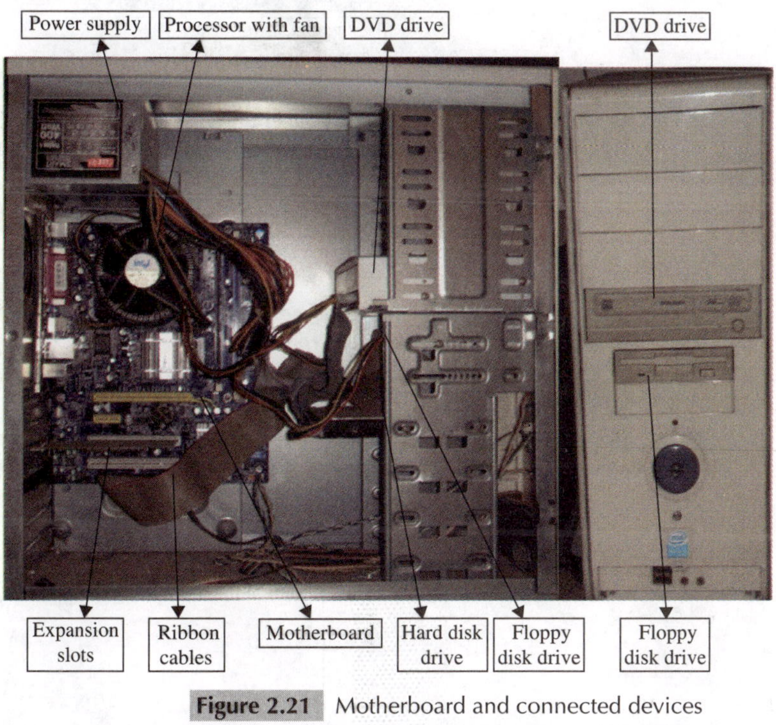

Figure 2.21 Motherboard and connected devices

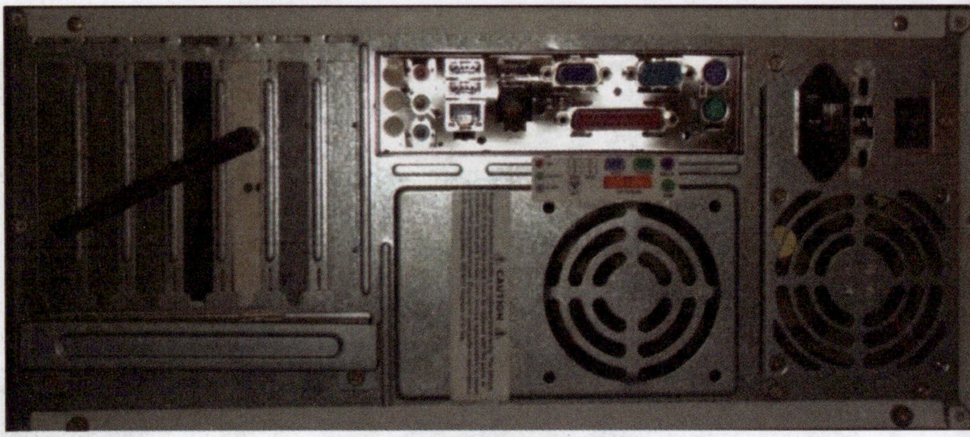

Figure 2.22 Rear view of a PC

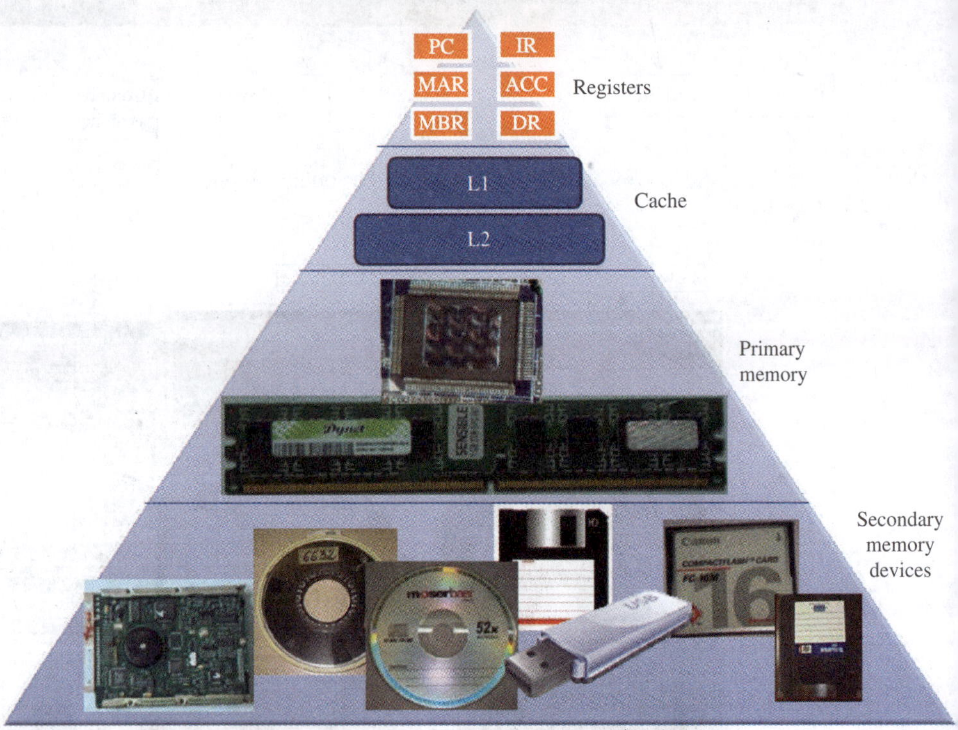

Figure 3.19 Computer memory hierarchy

Figure 4.28 Input-output devices

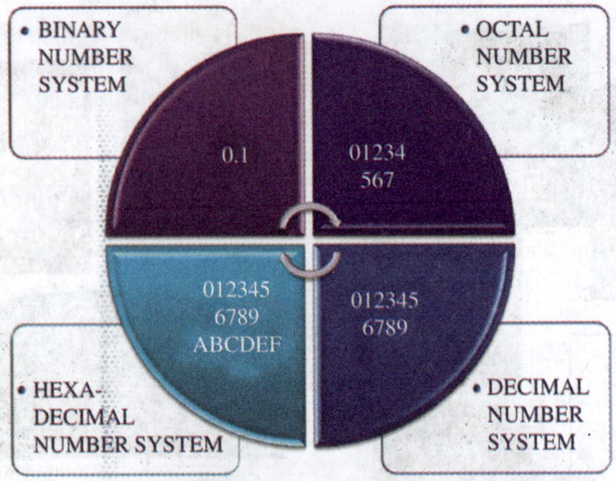

Figure 5.2 Number systems

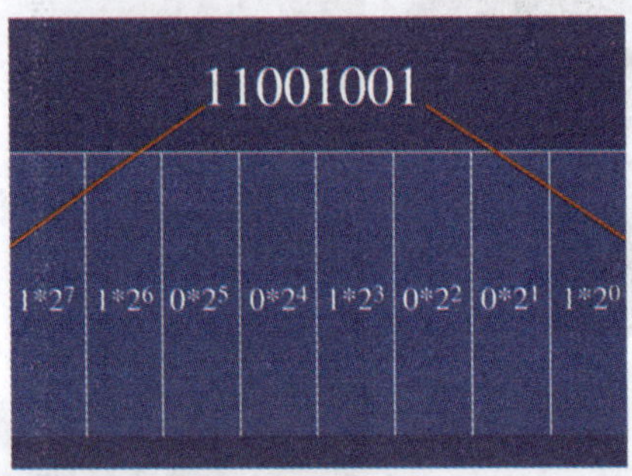

Figure 5.3 A binary number and its decimal conversion

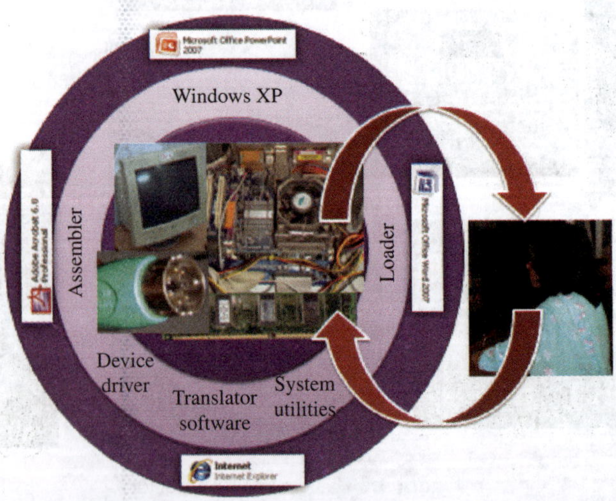

Figure 6.18 Interaction hierarchy of user with hardware

Figure 7.20 Different OS

Problem Statement

Write a program to find factorial of *n*

Algorithm

1. Read *n*
2. Multiply *n* with *n*–1 and store result in *fact*
3. Repeat step 2 until the value of *n* becomes 1
4. Print the value of *fact* which is the factorial of *n*

Pseudo code

```
READ n
INITIALIZE fact to one
INITIALIZE i to n
DO WHILE (i greater than 1)
{MULTIPLY i to fact and store in fact
DECREMENT i}
PRINT fact
STOP
```

Flowchart

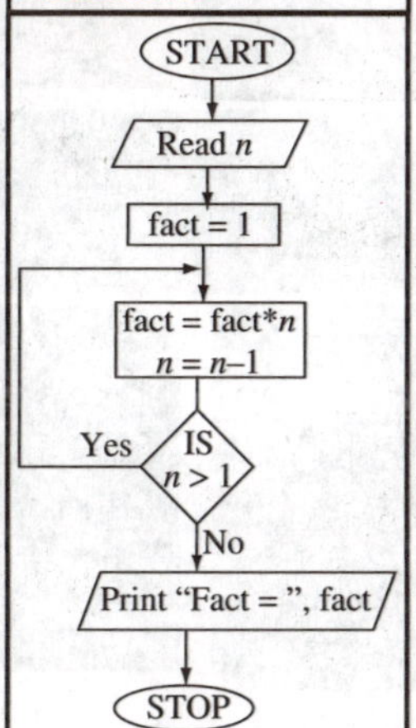

Program in C++

```
#include<iostream.h>
#include<conio.h>
class factorial
{     int n,i;
public:
void get_data ();
void facto();
} f;
void factorial:get_data ()
{ cout << "\n Enter the value of n: ";
  cin>> n; }
void factorial::facto()
{ int fact = 1;
    for(i=n;i>1;i--)
      fact = fact *i;
    cout << " Factorial of a number "
<< n << " is "<< fact;  }
void main()
{ clrscr();
    f.get_data ();
    f.facto();       }
```

Figure 8.7 Algorithm, pseudo code, flowchart, and program (in C++) for finding factorial on *n*

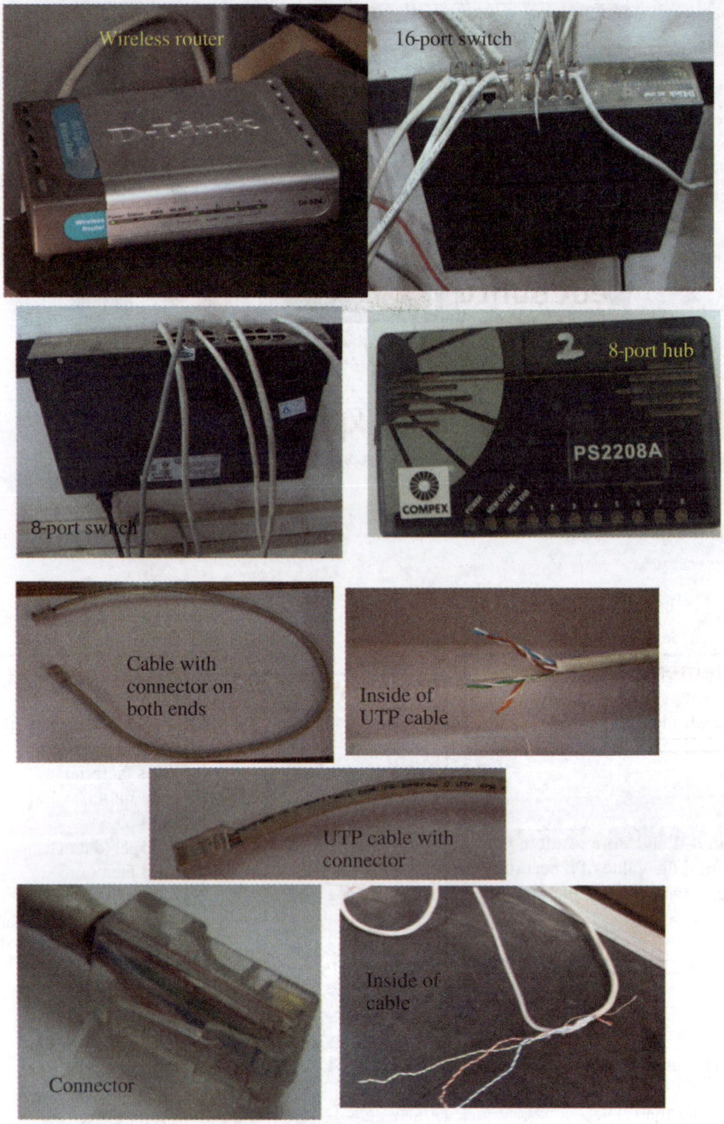

Figure 9.38 Network devices

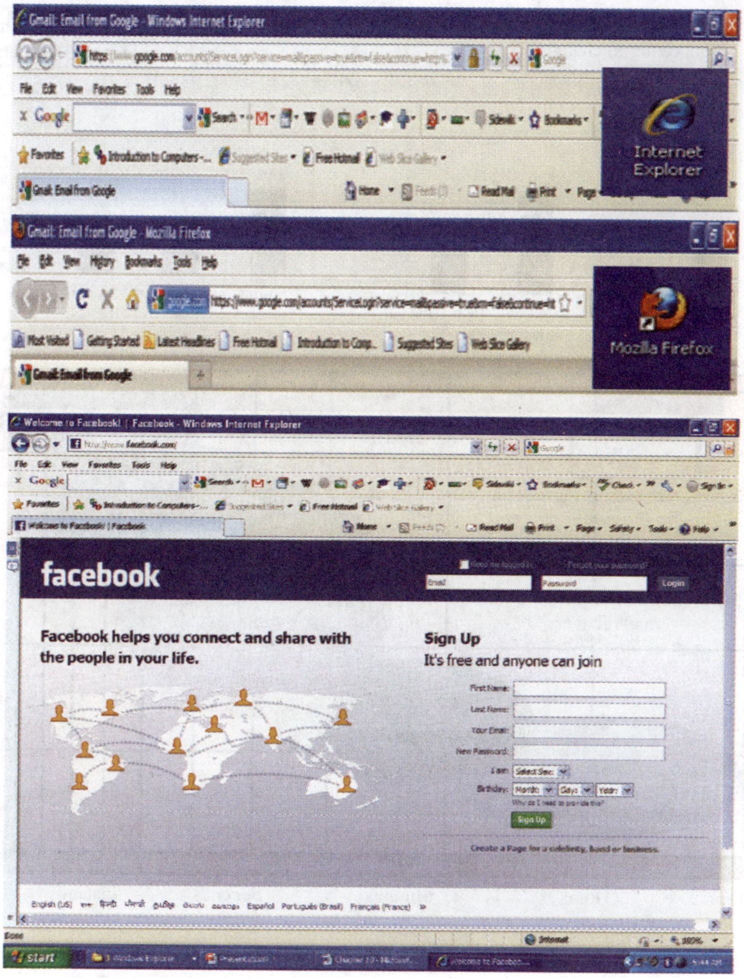

Figure 10.18 Web browser and social networking site

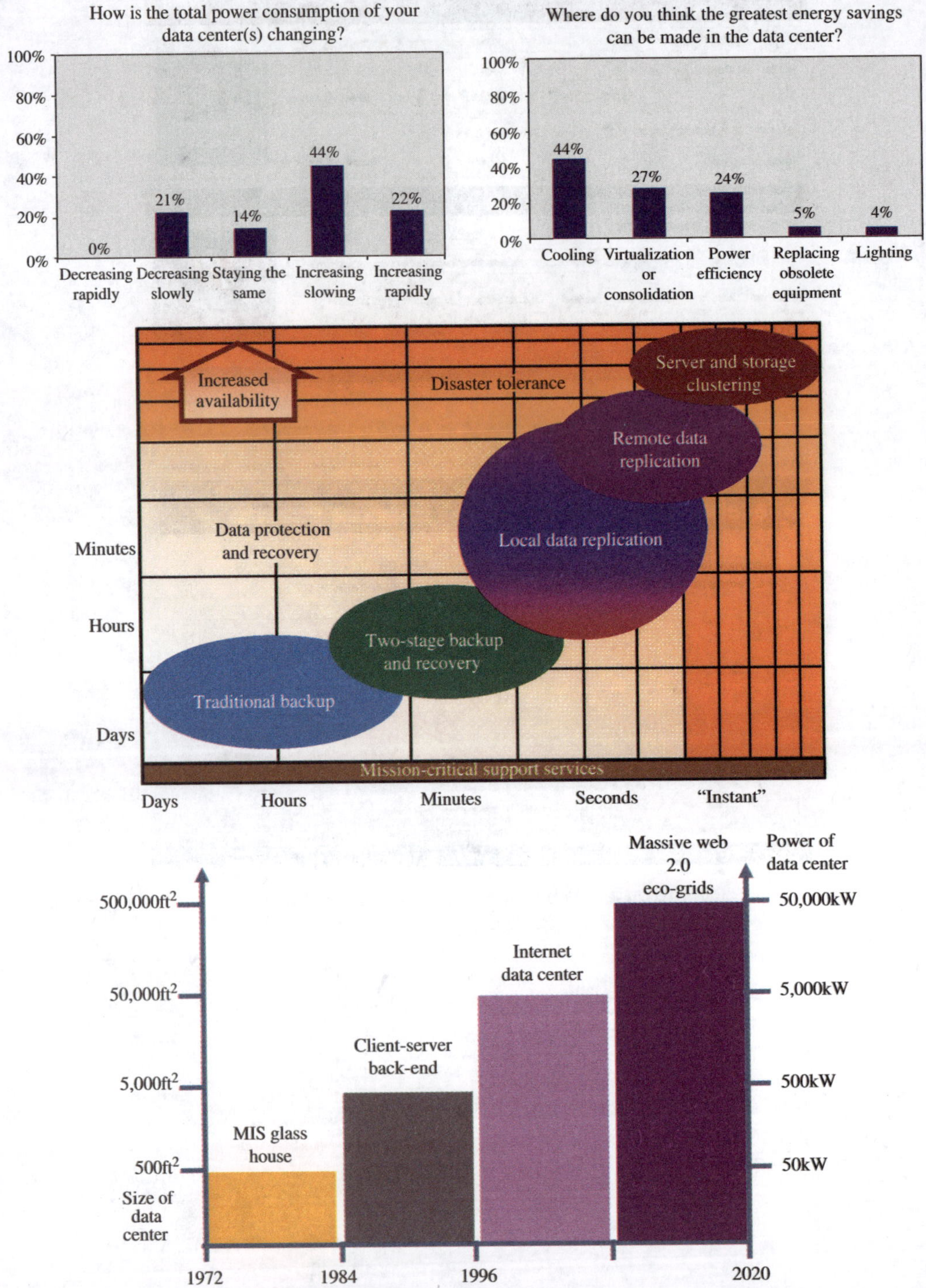

Figure 11.14 Information system reports

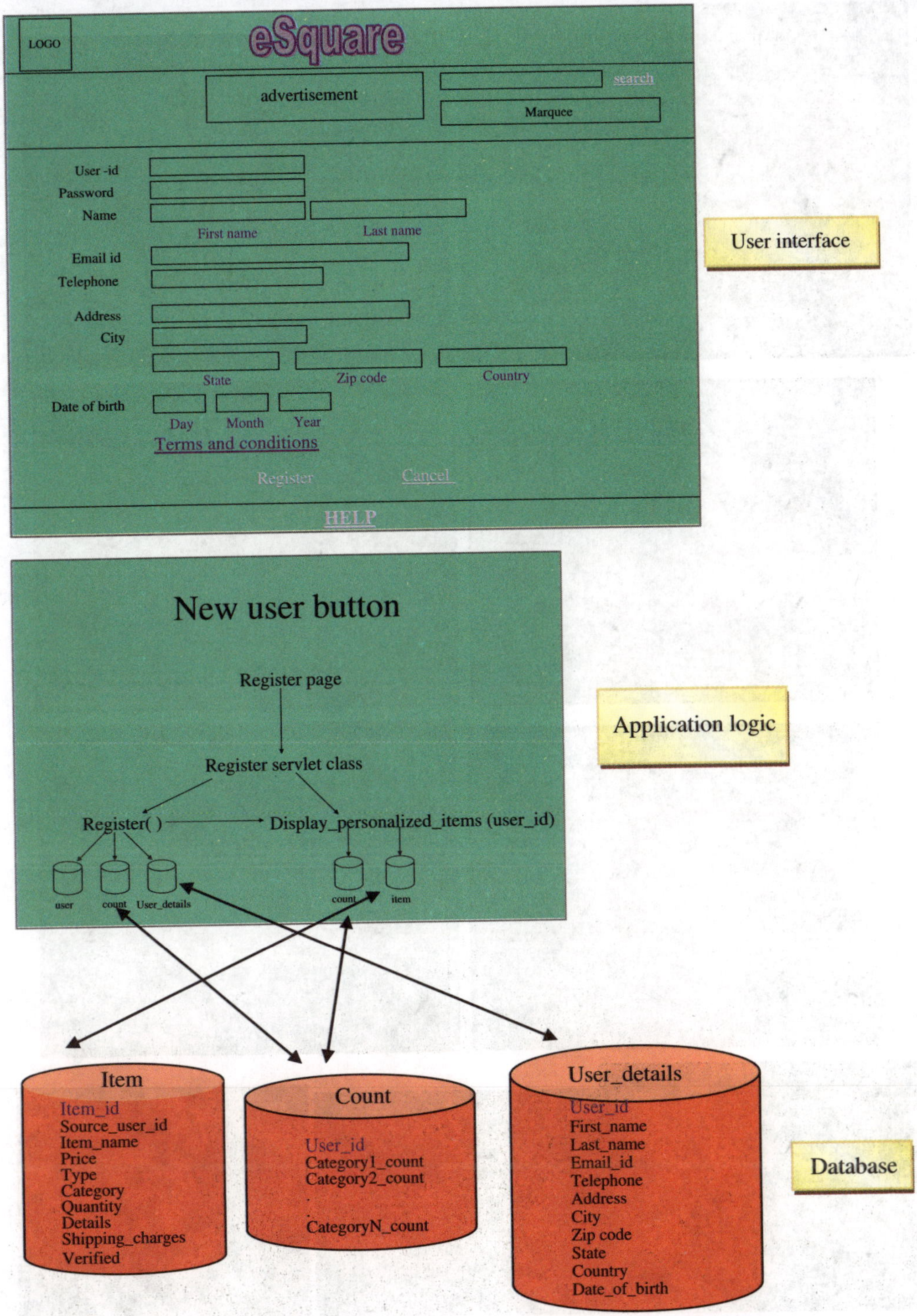

Figure 12.14 A 3-tier client-server application

Figure 13.29 Using animation

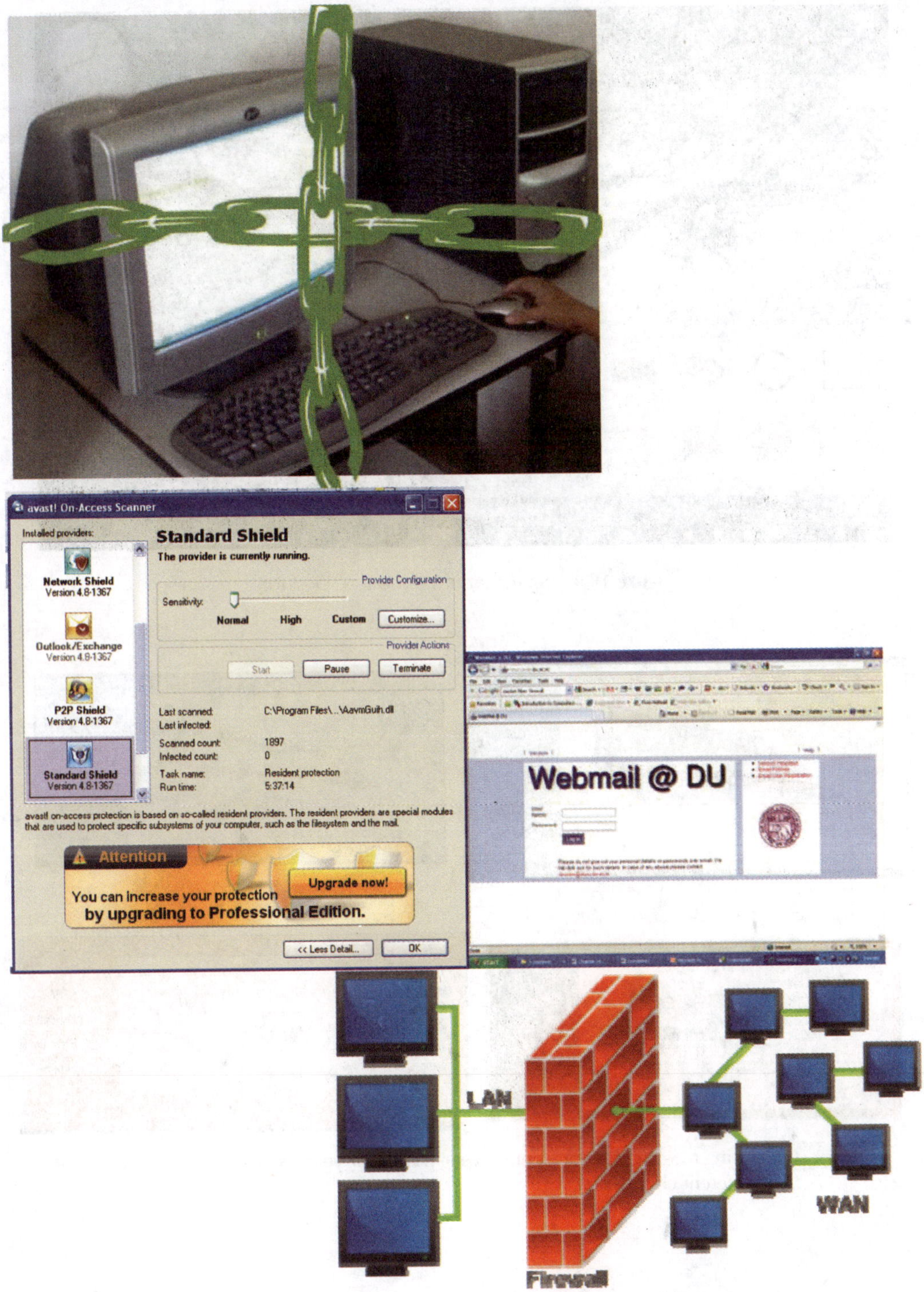

Figure 14.17 Security (hardware, software, users and data)

Figure 15.1 Snapshot of Windows 7 Desktop

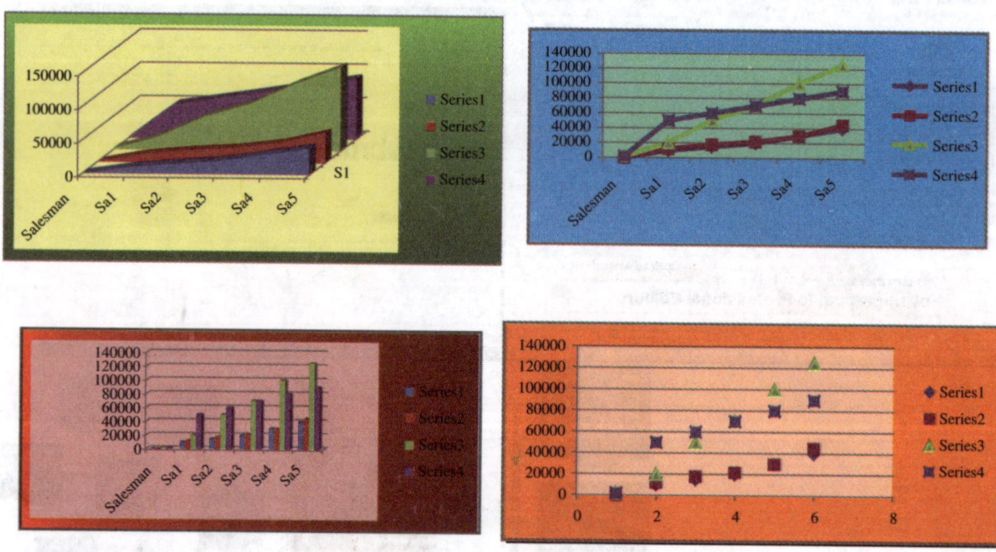

Figure 17(a) Using MS-Excel: Representing year-wise (four years) sales of five salesmen with different chart types

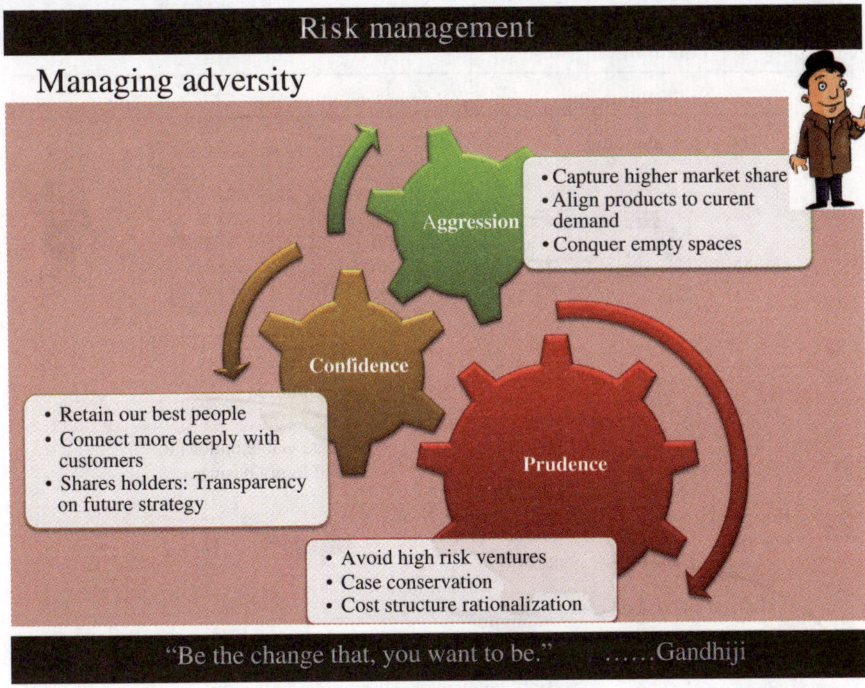

Figure 17(b)

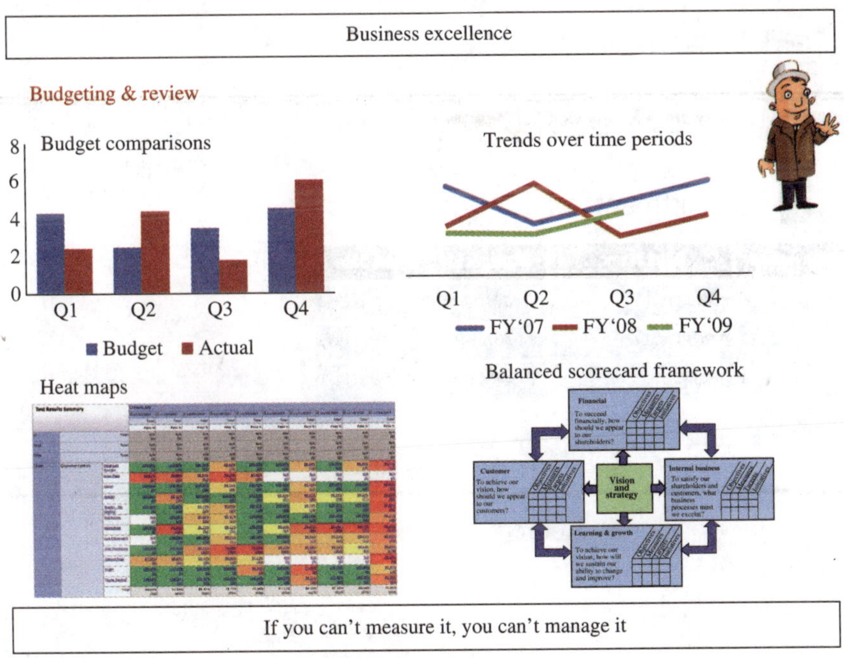

Figure 17(c)

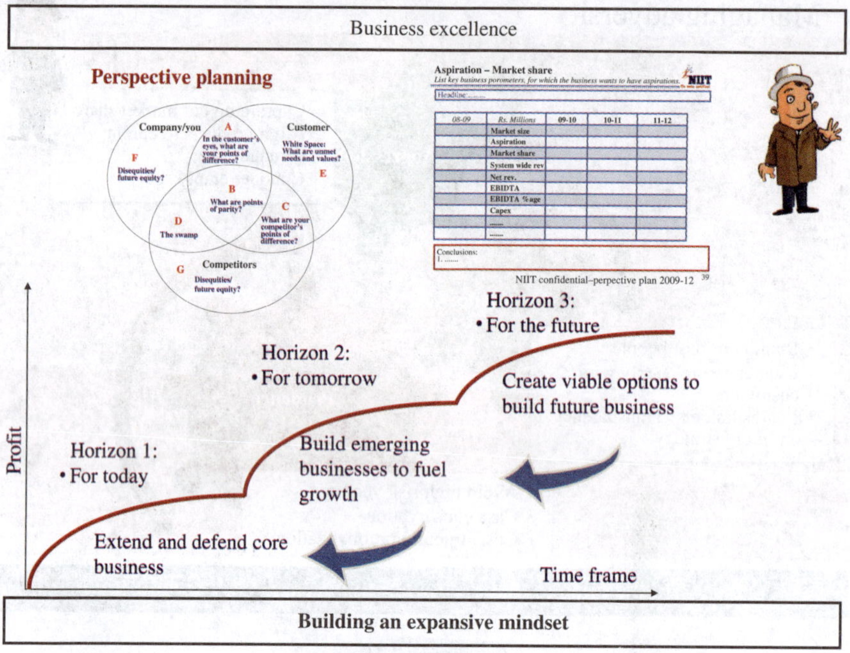

Figure 17(d)

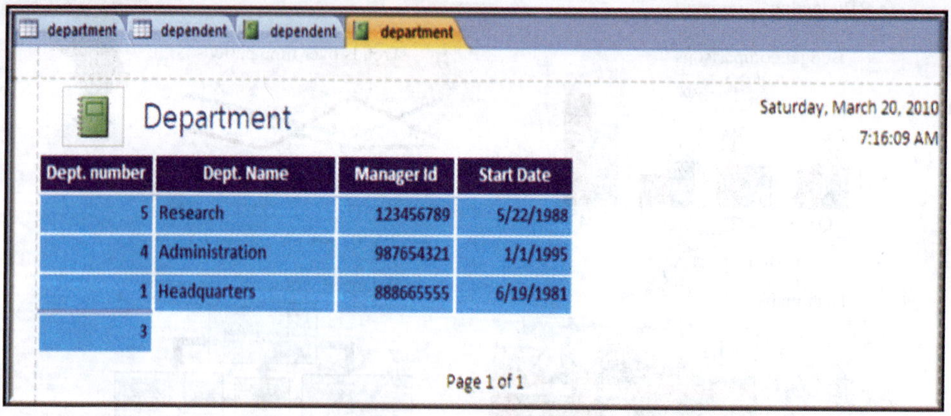

Dept. number	Dept. Name	Manager Id	Start Date
5	Research	123456789	5/22/1988
4	Administration	987654321	1/1/1995
1	Headquarters	888665555	6/19/1981
3			

Figure 17(e) Using MS-Access: A Report

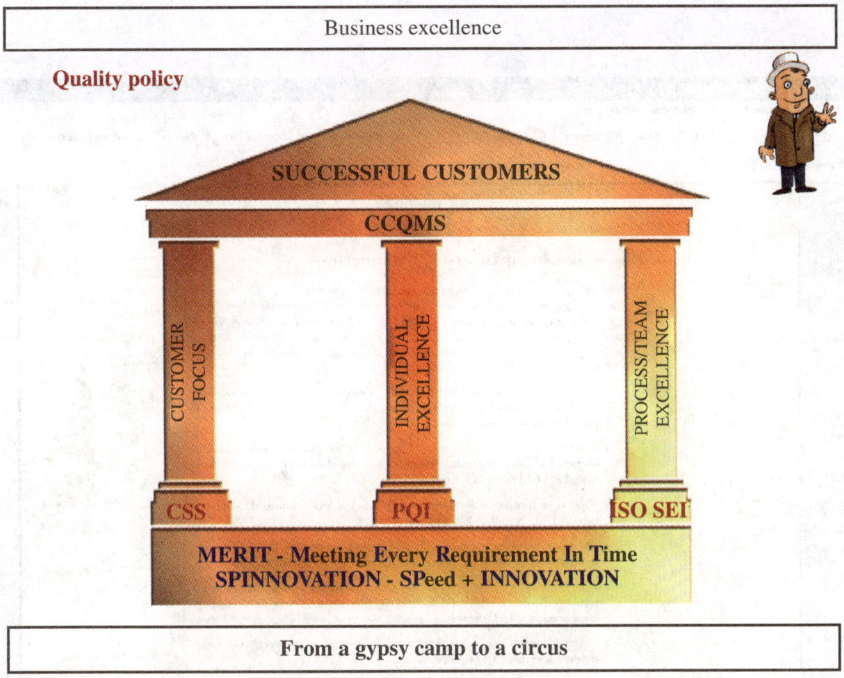

Figure 18.4 Using MS-PowerPoint

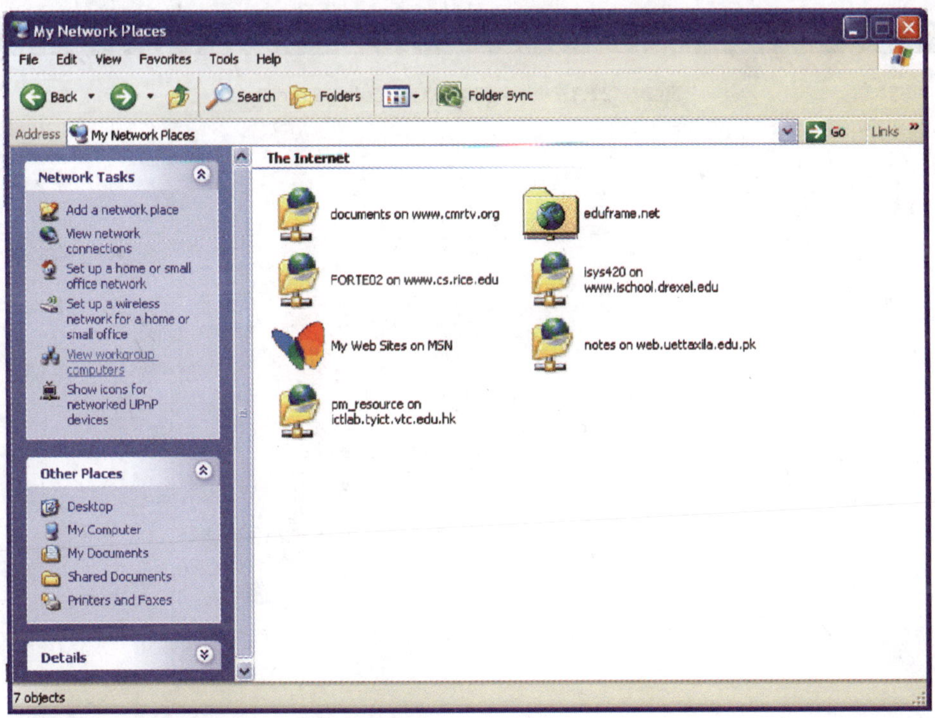

Figure 20.1 My network places

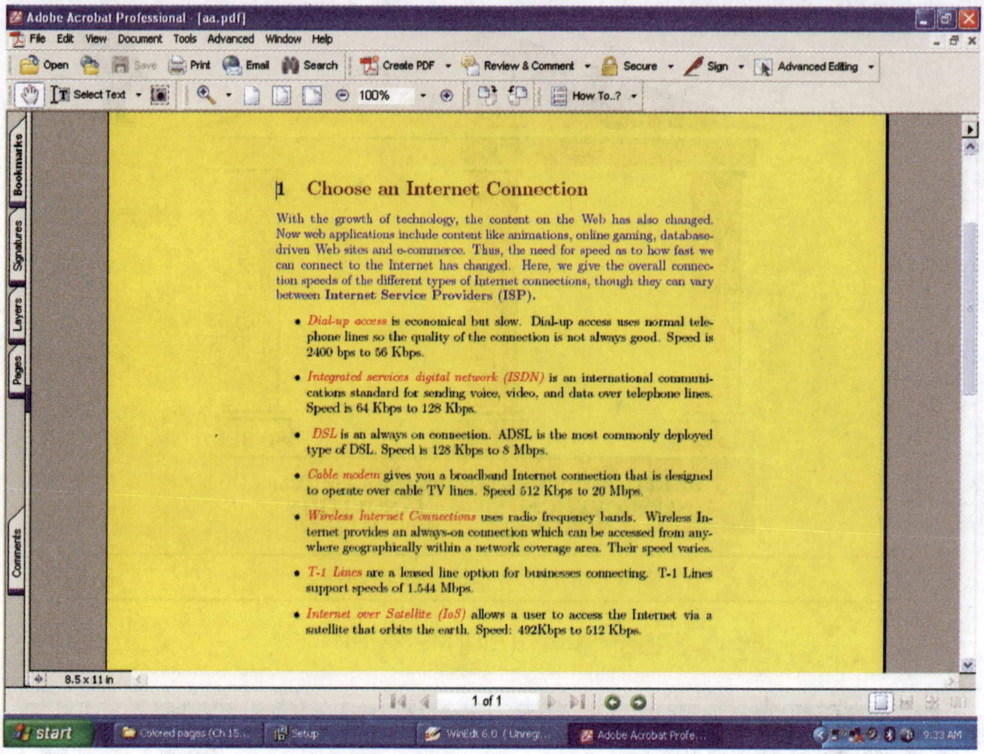

Figure 21.1 Using LaTeX: A coloured output

INDEX